International Handbook of Blockchain Law

International Handbook of Blockchain Law

A Guide to Navigating Legal and Regulatory Challenges of Blockchain Technology and Crypto Assets

Second Edition

Edited by

Matthias Artzt
Thomas Richter

Wolters Kluwer

Published by:
Kluwer Law International B.V.
PO Box 316
2400 AH Alphen aan den Rijn
The Netherlands
E-mail: lrs-sales@wolterskluwer.com
Website: www.wolterskluwer.com/en/solutions/kluwerlawinternational

Sold and distributed by:
Wolters Kluwer Legal & Regulatory U.S.
920 Links Avenue
Landisville, PA 17538
United States of America
E-mail: customer.service@wolterskluwer.com

ISBN 978-94-035-4157-0

e-Book: ISBN 978-94-035-4167-9
web-PDF: ISBN 978-94-035-4177-8

Editors

Dr Matthias Artzt is a certified lawyer and senior legal counsel at Deutsche Bank AG since 1999. Prior to joining Deutsche Bank, he worked as a lawyer at a law firm in Stuttgart, Germany. He has been practising data protection law for many years and was particularly involved in the implementation of the General Data Protection Regulation (GDPR) within Deutsche Bank AG. He advises internal clients globally regarding data protection issues as well as complex international outsourcing agreements involving data privacy-related matters and regulations. He is a graduate of the University of Tübingen, Germany, where he obtained his Doctor of Law. Moreover, he is a Certified Information Privacy Professional/Europe (CIPP/E) at the IAPP and has authored numerous articles on data protection law. Further, Matthias is a regular panel speaker at various national and international conferences, panels and webinars, e.g., at the Central Bank of Brazil and the Ecosystems 2030 in Spain. Further, he is a guest lecturer on European data protection law in postgraduate law courses at the University of Brunswick, Canada and the University of Brasilia, Brazil. He has an in-depth knowledge of the GDPR and its interfaces with other cutting-edge technologies, such as Cloud Computing, Artificial Intelligence, Blockchain, and Metaverse. Finally, Matthias is the editor-in-chief of the *International Journal of Blockchain Law* (IJBL) and the co-editor of the *International Handbook of AI Law*, published by Wolters Kluwer in 2024.

Thomas Richter is a technology and regulatory lawyer and an associate general counsel at Deutsche Bank AG. Prior to that, Thomas practised in the global law firm, White & Case, in their Frankfurt offices for several years. He is qualified to practise in Germany (Rechtsanwalt) and England & Wales (Solicitor). Thomas has more than ten years of experience in advising on complex multinational outsourcing and cloud transactions as well as artificial intelligence projects and innovation partnerships, including on the regulatory aspects. He has particular knowledge on the regulatory aspects of blockchain and is a frequent speaker and panellist on these questions. Thomas has extensive international experience and holds a law degree from the

University of Tübingen, Germany, and a Master of Laws in Commercial and Financial Law from King's College, London. He has also obtained a Certificate in Transnational Law from the University of Geneva, Switzerland. He had been seconded to Singapore for a period of three months in 2019. In his legal training, he worked, *inter alia*, for leading international law firms in Munich and Brussels.

Contributors

Prof Dr Lothar Determann practises and teaches International Data Privacy, Technology, Commercial and Intellectual Property Law. At Baker McKenzie in San Francisco and Palo Alto, he has been counselling companies since 1998 on data privacy law compliance and taking products and business models internationally. Admitted to practise in California and Germany, he has been recognized as one of the top ten Copyright Attorneys and top twenty-five Intellectual Property Attorneys in California by the *San Francisco & Los Angeles Daily Journal* and as a leading lawyer by *Chambers*, *Legal 500*, *IAM* and others. Prof Dr Determann has been a member of the Association of German Public Law Professors since 1999 and teaches Data Privacy Law, Computer Law and Internet Law at Freie Universität, Berlin (since 1994), University of California, Berkeley School of Law (since 2004), University of San Francisco College of the Law (fka Hastings, since 2010), Stanford Law School (2011) and University of San Francisco School of Law (2000–2005). He has authored more than 170 articles and treatise contributions as well as six books, including *Determann's Field Guide to Data Privacy Law* (5th ed. 2022, also available in Arabic, Chinese, French, German, Hungarian, Italian, Japanese, Korean, Portuguese, Russian, Spanish, Turkish and Vietnamese), *California Privacy Law – Practical Guide and Commentary* (5th ed. 2023), and *Determann*'s *Field Guide to Artificial Intelligence Law* (2024). His recent papers include Healthy Data Protection (http://ssrn.com/abstract=3357990); Electronic Form over Substance (http://ssrn.com/abstract=3436327); No One Owns Data (https://ssrn.com/abstract=3123957). For more information, *see* www.bakermckenzie.com. Contact: ldetermann@bakermckenzie.com.

Laura Douglas is a senior financial services lawyer, with over a decade of experience in the financial regulation group at Clifford Chance. Laura specializes in advising financial institutions and other market participants on financial markets and fintech regulation, with a particular focus on payments and crypto asset regulation. With a Master's in Physics and Philosophy, she is particularly interested in how technology is transforming financial services and the legal and regulatory response to these changes. Laura regularly speaks at industry conferences and events on payments and crypto asset regulation, has written numerous articles on these topics and notably co-led work on the 'regulation of crypto assets' section of the UK Law Society's legal and regulatory guidance report on blockchain in collaboration with Tech London Advocates and the Society for Computers and Law.

Chris Ewing is a senior legal counsel at Improbable, a London-based company providing technology, content, expertise and services to help companies and brands realize the full potential of virtual worlds and the metaverse. Improbable has also started a new venture called MSquared (M^2) which is building a network of interoperable metaverses, virtual worlds and experiences for users to socialize, play games, attend concerts, and, by leveraging blockchain technology, create and build value over time. As part of the legal team, Chris primarily advises Improbable and M^2 on commercial contracts, metaverse partnerships, open-source software, and data protection matters. Prior to working at Improbable, Chris was part of the commercial legal team at film and entertainment studio Warner Bros. UK and also spent four years working in the intellectual property & data protection practice group of international law firm White & Case.

Matthias Goetz, LLM (Cambridge), is partner at the law firm Nikol & Goetz, a boutique data protection law firm based in Germany. Admitted to practise law in Germany (Rechtsanwalt) and England & Wales (Solicitor), he advises national and international companies on German, English and European data (protection) law. Matthias regularly speaks at events and gives lectures on data protection law and publishes articles in leading data protection journals.

Andreas Holzwarth-Rochford holds a Diploma in Physics from the RTWH Aachen University, Germany. He is a German and European patent attorney as well as a European patent litigator (UPC) and has practised intellectual property law for more than twenty years. Further, he has prosecuted numerous IP applications and pled in numerous litigation hearings in the areas of physics and mechanical and electrical engineering, as well as software-implemented inventions. Andreas has significant technical experience in optics, laser technology, and new technologies, especially artificial intelligence, machine learning and blockchain applications, wireless data communications and network engineering. In addition to advising on the prosecution and enforcement of patent rights, Andreas supports M&A deals regarding IP due diligence, including freedom to operate (FTO) analysis. He also advises on the economic enhancement of R&D departments, especially regarding efficient patent document surveillance systems and service invention reporting systems, and supports clients in their efforts to find avoidance solutions for third-party rights. He provides counsel to start-up companies on the establishment of patent portfolios and strategies. Andreas has been elected as a delegate of the Federal Association of German Patent Attorneys (Bundesverband Deutscher Patentanwälte e.V) since January 2013. He is also a member of the European Practice Committee of the Intellectual Property Owners Association (IPO), the GRUR, the VPP, the LES, the Federal Association of German Patent Attorneys, the European Patent Litigators Association (EPLIT), the Institute of

Professional Representatives before the European Patent Office (epi), and the Interdisciplinary Center for IP of the University of Mannheim.

Dr Michael Jünemann is a co-head of the Global Finance and Financial Regulation Group and Head of the German Finance & Financial Regulation Group at Bird & Bird. With a deep understanding of the intricacies of legal frameworks surrounding fintech, he possesses the unique ability to effectively connect technology knowledge with capital markets law. Michael brings extensive experience in financial markets and payment services regulation, complemented by a dedicated focus on disruptive technologies and a strong commitment to fostering innovation in the fintech industry. He actively engages in professional development through participation in industry conferences and congresses, as well as providing interviews and expert opinions for various daily and trade press publications. Michael has been recognized by *Chambers and Partners Fintech*, *WWL*, and *Legal500* for his valuable insights and expertise in areas such as cryptocurrency, blockchain, and fintech.

William Long is a global co-leader of Sidley's highly ranked privacy and cybersecurity practice and also leads the EU Data Protection practice. William advises international clients on a wide variety of GDPR, data protection, privacy, information security, social media, e-commerce and other regulatory matters. William has been a member of the European Advisory Board of the International Association of Privacy Professionals (IAPP) and on the DataGuidance panel of data protection lawyers. He is also on the editorial board of e-Health Law & Policy and also assists with dplegal ('data privacy' legal), a networking group of in-house lawyers in life science companies examining international data protection issues. Representative matters have included: advising numerous international companies on the GDPR; advising companies on data privacy issues with Big Data, Internet of Things and profiling; advising a global e-commerce company in dealing with an international data security breach; and assisting a global manufacturing company with a global data protection project, including implementation of Binding Corporate Rules. William was previously in-house counsel to one of the world's largest international financial services groups. He has been a member of a number of working groups in London and Europe looking at the EU regulation of e-commerce and data protection and spent a year at the UK's Financial Law Panel (established by the Bank of England) as an assistant to the chief executive working on regulatory issues with online financial services. William is recognized in Chambers UK 2020 for Data Protection and Information Law, with sources telling the publication that he is 'extremely knowledgeable, not just about what the law requires but also about what the regulators think, and about the landscape of the market'. In the 2019 edition, he was described as bringing 'a broad depth of knowledge on the key areas of law', while in the 2017 edition, clients cite him as 'very knowledgeable, very practical and always solution-driven'. He is recognized in the *LMG Life Sciences Guide 2014* for Intellectual Property and Who's Who Legal 2017 for TMT. He has also been listed in Best Lawyers 2020 for Privacy & Data Protection Law and Who's Who Legal: Data 2020. William is recognized for both Data Protection, Privacy & Cybersecurity and Pharmaceuticals & Biotechnology in The Legal 500 UK 2017, with clients noting that his 'forward-thinking and proactive approach keeps him ahead of the curve' and describing his advice as 'thorough, timely and on the leading edge'. He is also included in the 2018 edition of *Best Lawyers for Privacy & Data Protection* and is listed in the Data chapter of *Who's Who Legal: Thought Leaders – Global Elite 2020*. William is also the author of a new book on the EU GDPR and a contributor to a number of books on data protection, including leading legal textbooks published by BNA in the area of privacy, cloud computing and the use of health data. William has been interviewed widely for his thought leadership, including in such leading publications as the *International New York Times*, *Financial Times* and *The Guardian* and writes for a number of publications, including *Data Protection Law & Policy*, *Computer Weekly*, *Cloud Pro* and *CIO Today*.

Jay Modrall is a senior counsel in the antitrust and competition practice of Norton Rose Fulbright LLP and head of its Brussels office. With over thirty years of experience, Jay is a leading advisor for EU and international competition and regulatory work. His competition law work includes the review and clearance of international mergers and acquisitions, advising on potentially restrictive agreements and abuses of dominant positions and the review and approval of State aid under EU law. Jay has written extensively on EU competition law and is a frequent speaker at EU law conferences, in particular, in relation to the policy and enforcement implications of digitization of the economy.

Kayvan B. Sadeghi is a partner and Co-Chair of the Fintech and Crypto Assets practice at Jenner & Block, LLP. A litigator for over twenty years and active in the blockchain industry since late 2016, he has been recognized by Chambers & Partners' Fintech Guide as a leading lawyer for Crypto Asset Disputes. Kayvan represents clients at the forefront of technology, finance, and media, helping them resolve litigation and enforcement matters that threaten their way of doing business. Based in New York, Kayvan serves as lead counsel for defendants and sophisticated plaintiffs in high-stakes litigation throughout the United States, often involving nine or ten-figure damages. He also defends clients in investigations before the US Department of Justice, the SEC, state attorneys general, and other regulators. In addition, Kayvan provides ongoing legal and regulatory advice to a broad array of clients globally. His clients include leading base layer protocols and their founders, CeFi and DeFi platforms, data oracles, crypto hedge funds and investors, NFT gaming projects, and others. Kayvan is a frequent author and speaker, has co-taught and guest-lectured courses on blockchain law at leading law schools, and serves as Co-Chair of the Legal Working Group of the Wall Street Blockchain Alliance.

Dr Philip Trillmich is a partner in the intellectual property practice group of global law firm White & Case. He is qualified to practise in England and Wales as well as in Germany. Philip advises on complex and often cross-border technology transactions, both on a stand-alone basis and in connection with joint ventures, strategic collaborations, mergers and acquisitions, restructurings, business separations and spin-offs. He has a special focus on the digital transformation of industries and the resulting innovative services and business models, in particular, in the areas of financial technology (fintech), digital health and smart technologies. For further details, *see*: https://www.linkedin.com/in/ptrillmich/.

Jake van der Laan is a Canadian lawyer and computer scientist. He has practised law for well over 30 years and during that time spent 12 years in private practice as a trial lawyer and 18 years working for a Canadian regulator as its Director of Enforcement and later its Chief Information Officer. He currently limits his practice to the legal issues arising from data use in technology, particularly in the context of cybersecurity and artificial intelligence. He is also a lecturer in the Faculty of Computer Science at the University of New Brunswick, Canada, where he teaches primarily Data Mining, Professional Practice, and Cybersecurity Risk Management courses. He has degrees in business administration and law and two degrees in computer science, and is currently working on his PhD, conducting research on how to make deep learning Artificial Intelligence models more explainable. Jake has been an ISACA Certified Information Security Manager (CISM) since 2018. He is a regular speaker and teacher with respect to emerging technology-related issues, particularly in the context of financial services and consumer protection regulation. *See* his LinkedIn page for more details at https://www.linkedin.com/in/jakevanderlaan/.

Summary of Contents

Table of Contents

List of Abbreviations

2WP	2-way Peg
ABGB	Austrian Civil Law Act
ABI	Application Binary Interface
ACID	Atomicity Consistency Isolation Durability
ADGM	Abu Dhabi Global Market
AI	Artificial Intelligence
AktG	German Stock Corporation Act (*Aktiengesetz*)
AML	Anti-Money-Laundering
AML Act	Act on Reporting and Using Specified Financial Transaction Information
AMM	Automated Market Maker
API	Application Programming Interface
ArbnErfG	German Act on Employee Inventions
ARIPO	African Regional Intellectual Property Organization
ARM	Advanced RISC Machines
ART	Asset-Referenced Token
ASCII	American Standard Code for Information Interchange
ASIC	Application-Specific Integrated Circuit
ATM	Automated Teller Machine
ATS	Alternative Trading System
B2C	Business-to-Consumer
BaaS	Blockchain-as-a-Service
BaFin	Germany Federal Financial Supervisory Authority
BCA	Business Companies Act (2020 Revision)

BCH	Bitcoin Cash
BFT	Byzantine Fault Tolerance
BGB	German Civil Code (*Bürgerliches Gesetzbuch*)
BGBl.	Bundesgesetzblatt
BIP	Bitcoin Improvement Proposal
BoE	Bank of England
bona fide	In Good Faith, Covenant of Good Faith and Fair Dealing
BSA	Bank Secrecy Act
BSC	Binance Smart Chain
BTC	Bitcoin
BVI	British Virgin Islands
Cal. Civ. Code	California Civil Code
CAP	Consistency, Availability, Partition (Tolerance)
CASP	Crypto Asset Service Provider
CBDC	Central Bank Digital Currency
CCPA	California Consumer Privacy Act
CD	Community Design
CDS	Central Securities Depositary
CEA	Commodity Exchange Act
CeFi	Centralized Finance
CESR	Committee of European Securities Regulators
CEX	Centralized Exchanges
CFAA	Computer Fraud and Abuse Act
CFT	Countering the Financing of Terrorism
CFTC	US Commodities Futures Trading Commission
CII	Computer-Implemented Inventions
CIRO	Canadian Industry Regulatory Organization
CIS	Collective Investment Schemes
CISG	United Nations Convention on Contracts for the International Sale of Goods
CJA	Criminal Justice (Money Laundering and Terrorist Financing) Act 2010
CJEU	Court of Justice of the European Union
CJN	EC Consolidated Jurisdictional Notice under the EUMR
CNIL	Commission Nationale Informatique & Libertes
CNMV	Spanish Stock Market Commission
CNMV	Comisión Nacional del Mercado de Valores
CO	Swiss Code of Obligations

COCP	Code of Organisation and Civil Procedure
Consob	Italian Supervisory Authority
CONSOB	Commissione Nazionale per le Società e la Borsa
CPO	Commodity Pool Operator
CPU	Central Processing Unit
CRD	Capital Requirements Directive
CRM	Customer Relationship Management
CRUD	Create Read Update Delete
CSA	Canadian Securities Administrators
CSD Regulation	Central Securities Depositories Regulation
CTA	Commodity Training Advisor
CVC	'Convertible' Virtual Currency
DAG	Directed Acyclic Graph
DAO	Decentralized Autonomous Organization
dApp	Distributed Application
DAR	Designated Activities Regime
DDoS	Distributed Denial-of-Service
DeFi	Decentralized Finance
DEX	Decentralized Exchange
DFAL	California Digital Financial Assets Law
DFSA	Dubai Financial Services Authority
DIFC	Dubai International Financial Centre
DLT	Distributed Ledger Technology
DLT Act	Federal Act on the Amendment of Federal Law to Developments in Distributed Ledger Technology (Switzerland)
DLT MTF	DLT multilateral trading facilities
DLT Pilot-Regime or DLTR	Regulation (EU) 2022/858 on the pilot-regime for market infrastructures based on distributed ledger technology
DLT SS	DLT securities settlement systems
DLT TSS	DLT trading and settlement systems
DPA	Data Protection Authority
DPF	Data Privacy Framework
DPFI	California Department of Financial Protection & Innovation
DPIA	Data Privacy Impact Assessment
DPO	Data Protection Officer
DPoS	Delegated Proof of Stake
DPT	Digital payment tokens

DSA	Digital Settlement Asset
DSF	Digital Settlement Facilities
DTO	Guide to Digital Token Offerings
DTO Guide	Guide to Digital Token Offerings on 14 November 2017 (Singapore)
e.g.	Lat. example gratia = for example
EAPO	Eurasian Patent Organization
EBA	European Banking Authority
EC	European Commission
ECB	European Central Bank
ECC	Elliptic Curve Cryptography
ECSPR	Regulation (EU) 2020/1503 on European crowdfunding service providers for business
EDPB	European Data Protection Board
EDPS	European Data Protection Supervisor
EEA	European Economic Area
EFD	Essential Facilities Doctrine
EFSA	Estonian Financial Supervisory Authority
EIP	Ethereum Improvement Proposal
EMD	Electronic Money Directive
EMR	Electronic Money Regulation 2011
EMT	Electronic Money Token
EOA	Externally Owned Account
EP	European Patent
EPC	European Patent Convention
EPO	European Patent Office
ERC	Ethereum Requests for Comments
erga omnes	Lat. towards all
ERTF	Electronically Recorded Transferable Rights
ESAs	European Supervisory Authorities
ESMA	European Securities and Markets Authority
ETC	Ethereum Classic
ETH	Ether
EU	European Union
EUIPO	European Union Intellectual Property Office
EUMR	EU Merger Regulation
EVM	Ethereum Virtual Machine

eWpG	German Electronic Securities Act (*Gesetz über elektronische Wertpapiere*)
FAQ	Frequently Asked Questions
FATF	Financial Action Task Force
FBA	Federated Byzantine Agreement
FCA	Financial Conduct Authority
FCM	Future Commission Merchant
FIEA	Financial Instruments and Exchange Act
FIL	Filecoin
FinCEN	US Financial Crimes Enforcement Network
FIN-FSA	Finnish Financial Supervisory Authority
FINMA	Swiss Financial Market Supervisory Authority
FINRA	US Financial Industry Regulatory Authority
FinSA	Swiss Financial Services Act
FinSO	Swiss Financial Services Ordinance
FINTRAC	Financial Transactions and Reports Analysis Centre of Canada
FISA	Federal Intermediated Securities Act
FISCMA	Financial Investment Services and Capital Markets Ac
FIT	Financial Instrument Test
FMA	Financial Market Authority
FMA	Italian Financial Markets Act
FM-GWG	Financial Markets Anti-Money Laundering Act
FPO	Financial Promotion Order 2005
FRAND	Fair, Reasonable and Non-discriminatory
FSC	Financial Services Commission
FSC Guidance	Guidance on Regulation of Virtual Assets in the Virgin Islands (BVI)
FSM Act	Financial Services and Markets Act 2022
FSMA	Financial Services and Markets Act 2000
FSMR	Financial Services and Markets Regulation 2015
FSRA	Financial Services Regulatory Authority
FTC	Federal Trade Commission
GAAP	Generally Accepted Accounting Principles
GB	Gigabyte
GbR	German civil law partnerships (*Gesellschaft bürgerlichen Rechts*)

GCCPO	Patent Office of the Cooperation Council for the Arab States of the Gulf
GDPR	General Data Protection Regulation
GmbHs	German limited liability companies (*Gesellschaften mit beschränkter Haftung*)
GPTO	German Patent and Trademark Office
GUI	Graphical User Interface
HMT	His Majesty's Treasury
HTLC	Hashed Time Lock Contract
i.e.	Lat. id est = that is
ICO	Initial Coin Offering
IDE	Integrated Development Environment
IDO	Initial DEX Offering
IEO	Initial Exchange Offering
IF	Investment Firm
IFMs	Investment Fund Managers
IFRS	International Financial Reporting Standard
IMEI	International Mobile Equipment Identity
inter alia	Lat. among other things
inter se	Lat. among or between themselves
IOSCO	International Organization of Securities Commissions
IoT	Internet of Things
IP	Internet Protocol
IP	Intellectual Property
IP Address	Internet Protocol Address
IPRG	Austrian International Private Law Act
IPRP	International Preliminary Report on Patentability
IPRs	Intellectual Property Rights
IRS	US Internal Revenue Service
ISA	Instruction Set Architecture
IT	Information Technology
ITAS Act	Innovative Technology Arrangements and Services Act
ITO	Initial Token Offering
ITS	Token Sale ITS
JMLSG	Joint Money Laundering Steering Group
J-REIT	Japan Real Estate Investment Trust
JSDA	Securities Dealers Association
JSTOA	Japan Security Token Offering Association

JVM	Java Virtual Machine
KAGB	German Kapitalanlagegesetzbuch
KDWP	Central Securities Repository of Poland (*Pol. Krajowy Depozyt Papierów Wartościowych*)
KMG	Capital Markets Act
KRX	Korea Exchange
KWG	German Banking Act (*Kreditwesengesetz*)
KYC	Know Your Customer
LCL	Last Closed Ledger
LD 25/2003	Italian Law Decree 25 of 17 March 2023
lege lata	Lat. the law as it exists
Liechtenstein FMA	Financial Market Authority of Liechtenstein
LMV	Spanish Securities Market Act (*Ley del Mercado de Valores*)
LN	Lightning Network
MAC	Media Access Control
MAR	Market Abuse Regulation
MAS	Monetary Authority of Singapore
MB	Megabyte
MDIA	Malta Digital Innovation Authority
MDIAA	Malta Digital Innovation Authority Act
MFN	Most Favored Nation
MFSA	Malta Financial Services Authority
MiCA(R)	Markets in Crypto Assets Regulation
MiFID II	Markets in Financial Instruments Directive II
MLR	Money Laundering, Counter-Terrorist Financing and Transfer of Funds (Information on the Payer) Regulations 2017
MPEP	Manual of Patent Examining Procedure
MSB	Money Services Business
MTF	Multilateral Trading Facility
NDA	Non-disclosure Agreements
nemo dat	Lat. nemo dat quod non habet = no one can give what they do not have
NFT	Non-Fungible Token
NIST	National Institute of Standards and Technology, U.S. Department of Commerce
OAPI	African Intellectual Property Organization
obiter	Lat. by the way

OFAC	Office of Foreign Assets Control
opt-in model	Closed-Loop Email Authentication
OSC	Ontario Securities Commission
OTF	Organized Trading Facility
P2P	Peer to Peer
P2PKH	Pay-to-Public-Key-Hash
P2WPKH	Pay-to-Witness-Public-Key-Hash
PACTE	Plan d'Action pour la Croissance et la Transformation de l'Entreprise
PCMLTFA	Proceeds of Crime (Money Laundering) and Terrorist Financing Act
PCT	Patent Cooperation Treaty
PFSA	Polish Financial Supervision Authority
PILA	Swiss Private International Law Act
PoET	Proof of Elapsed Time
PoH	Proof of History
PoS	Proof of Stake
PPC	Peercoin Cryptocurrency
PRIIP	Packaged Retail and Insurance-Based Investment Products
PRU	Pre-registration undertaking
PS Act	Payment Services Act 2019
PS Amendment Act	Payment Services (Amendment) Act 2021
PS Regulations	Payment Services Regulations 2019
PSA	Payment Services Act
PSD II or PSD2	Second Payment Services Directive
PTAB	Patent Trial and Appeal Board
PTS	Proprietary Trading System
Q&A	Questions and Answers
Quid	Lat. one or another
RAM	Random Access Memory
RCD	Registered Community Design
RCH	Recognized Clearing House
REACT	California Regional Enforcement Allied Computer Team
RIE	Recognized Investment Exchange
RISC	Reduced Instruction Set Computer
Rome I	Regulation (EC) no 593/2008 of the European Parliament and of the Council of 17 June 2008 on the law applicable to contractual obligations

Rome II	Regulation (EC) no 864/2007 of the European Parliament and of the Council of 11 July 2007 on the law applicable to non-contractual obligations
RPCA	Ripple Protocol Consensus Algorithm
RPM	Resale Price Maintenance
SAFT	Simple Agreement for Future Tokens
SARs	Suspicious Activity Reports
SCA	Emirates Securities and Commodities Authority
SCC	Standard Contractual Clauses
SDN	Specially Designated Nationals
SEC	Securities and Exchange Commission
SEF	Swap Execution Facilities
SFA	Securities & Futures Act of Singapore
SGX	Software Guard Extensions
SHA (256)	Secure Hash Algorithm (Generating a 256-bit Hash Digest)
SIBA	Securities and Investment Business Act (2020 Revision)
SIM	Mobile Phone Identity, Which Is Stored on a SIM Card
SMA	Finnish Securities Markets Act
SQL	Structured Query Language
SRO	Self-Regulatory Organization
SSS	Securities Settlement System
STO	Security Token Offering
STO Guideline	Guideline for the Issuance and Distribution System for Securities Tokens
TCP	Transmission Control Protocol
TEE	Trusted Execution Environment
TFEU	Treaty on the Functioning of the European Union
TFR	Transfer of Funds Regulation
TGE	Token Generation Event
TIA	Transfer Impact Assessment
TOR	The Onion Router Network
TPS	Transactions Per Second
TRIPS	Trade-Related Aspects of Intellectual Property Rights
TVL	Total Value Locked
TVTG	Tokens and TT Service Provider Act
TXID	Transaction ID
UAE	United Arab Emirates
UK	United Kingdom

UK ICO	United Kingdom Information Commissioner's Office
UKJT	United Kingdom Jurisdiction Taskforce
UKJT	UK Jurisdiction Taskforce
UNICODE	Computing Industry Standard for the Encoding, Representation, and Handling of Text
UNIDROIT	International Institute for the Unification of Private Law
UNL	Unique Node List
UP	Unitary Patent
UPC	Unified Patent Court
US	United States
USD	United States Dollar
USPTO	US Patent and Trademark Office
UTXO	Unspent Transaction Output
VASP	Virtual asset service providers
VASP Act	Virtual Assets Service Providers Act, 2022
VBER	EU Vertical Block Exemption Regulation
VCP Act	Finnish Act on Virtual Currency Providers
VDF	Verifiable Delay Function
VFAA	Malta Virtual Financial Assets Act
VFAs	Virtual Financial Assets
vice versa	Lat. by the other way around
WAG	Austrian Securities Supervision Act
WIPO	World Intellectual Property Organization
WpHG	German Securities Trading Act (*Gesetz über den Wertpapierhandel*)
WpIG	German Investment Firm Act (*Gesetz zur Beaufsichtigung von Wertpapierinstituten*)
WpPG	German Securities Prospectus Act (*Wertpapierprospektgesetz*)
WSE	Warsaw Stock Exchange
WTO	World Trade Organization
XCMP	Cross-Chain Message Passing
XML	Extensible Markup Language
XRP	Ripple Cryptocurrency
ZuFinG	German Future Financing Act (Zukunftsfinanzierungsgesetz)

Preface

The first edition of the Handbook of Blockchain Law was released in July 2020. When we were approached to consider a second edition, we did not need to be convinced. The second edition was overdue because blockchain technology has significantly developed since 2020 and many more blockchain use cases have been created to date. There was also a need to update the first chapter (Understanding Blockchain) which provided an accessible explanation of how a blockchain and the various related technologies work. This chapter has been expanded to include an expanded discussion of the proof of stake consent mechanism, as well as new content addressing, for example, the ERC-721 Token Standard for NFTs, decentralized exchanges, staking, stablecoins, and CBDCs, among others.

In addition, many of the chapters touching on legal issues associated with blockchain technology have been revised, in particular Capital Markets, Data Privacy and Regulation. The authors have also spent considerable time and effort to update their chapters with released court rulings, policies and guidance issued since the first edition (for example, the revised Market Definition Notice for competition cases recently adopted by the European Commission). With that in mind, we would like to not only welcome and thank some new authors but also renew our thanks to all authors who have continued their chapter. Without their commitment, the second edition of the Handbook would not have been possible. This second edition again comprises chapters written by highly esteemed experts and lawyers: Jake van der Laan, Prof. Dr Lothar Determann, Dr Philip Trillmich, Andreas Holzwarth-Rochford, Dr Michael Jünemann, William Long, Jay Modrall, Laura Douglas and Kayvan B. Sadeghi. It is also worth noting that there are additional authors who have contributed to the Capital Markets Chapter under the direction of Dr Michael Jünemann. This chapter is essentially a merger of multiple country reports contributed by renowned lawyers from around the globe. We acknowledge their highly valuable work and wish to explicitly thank Johannes Frank, Philipp Kinsky, Klim Stashevsky, Mikhail Khodosevich, Kirsti Pent, Mika Puurunen, Bertrand Levy, Dr Michael Jünemann, Niall Esler, Giuseppe d'Agostino, Stefano Febbi, Johannes Dür, Nicole Debrincat & Omar Zerafa, Aleksandra Widziewicz, Piotr Lesinski, Jose Luis Lorente Howell, Olivier Favre, Fabio Elsener,

Sara Hall, Daniel Fuke, Mike Stephens, James Gatto, Kim Kit Ow, Gerard Ng, Jongbaek Park, Gregory Man, Jessica White and Takashi Itokawa.

The Information Security chapter could not be continued. However, crypto crimes, scams and any sort of industry disruption in the crypto space are subject to many litigations and various publications. Thus, we decided to leave this chapter out and focus on another area closely linked with blockchain: crypto asset regulations in the European Union, United Kingdom and the United States. Digital asset regulation has gained significant traction in the last few years and is now one of the pre-eminent topics in the blockchain space. We have underpinned its importance by changing the subtitle of this book. With the numerous updates and added chapters on crypto asset regulation, which boil down to a comparative analysis of crypto asset regulation in the European Union (MiCA) against the regulatory developments in the United States and United Kingdom, this larger second edition provides broader legal guidance on the current state of blockchain law. We are confident that this updated approach will create added value for our readers.

Blockchain law has continued to grow as a specialized legal domain over the past number of years. This Handbook underscores this idea. Some universities have already set up courses aimed at helping to understand the characteristics of blockchain technology and obtaining skills in applying the law to factual scenarios to enable legal counsel to more effectively navigate the blockchain legal landscape, solve legal problems, and counsel clients effectively and professionally. This updated Handbook is a valuable resource towards that end.

Dr Matthias Artzt
Thomas Richter
Frankfurt, 15 March 2024

CHAPTER 1

Understanding Blockchain

Jake van der Laan

§1.01 INTRODUCTION

Blockchain and distributed ledger technology (DLT),[1] including functionality such as smart contracts, have been identified as potential solutions for a variety of business problems. Many of its proponents point to the benefits of removing centralized trusted intermediaries, the immutability[2] of the data stored on a blockchain, and/or potential improvements in the efficiency of existing business processes as reasons for implementing these technologies.[3] There are others who remain quite sceptical of the efficacy of blockchain-based solutions,[4] particularly given the large number of past and current blockchain- and cryptocurrency-related schemes and scams.[5] This chapter is not intended to support either camp or to otherwise pass any sort of judgment on the merits of blockchain and its related technologies. It simply seeks to explain how it all works. A good understanding of these technologies is important to anyone considering implementing blockchain-based solutions or anyone rendering advice with respect to them.

This chapter sets out a pathway to understanding blockchain and its related technologies in an iterative manner suitable for non-technical professionals with little or no background in math or computer science. Necessary core concepts and some key

1. These are not the same thing. A blockchain is a *type* of distributed ledger technology.
2. The inability to change data after it has been committed to the blockchain.
3. Amazon lists over thirty thousand titles after a search for 'blockchain book'. *See* https://www.amazon.ca/s?k=blockchain+book (accessed 10 Jan. 2024).
4. *See*, for instance, Robinson, J., 'BitCoin: The Naked Truth about Bitcoin' Amazon Digital Services 26 (2014): 149; Gerard, D., 'Attack of the 50 Foot Blockchain: Bitcoin, Blockchain, Ethereum & Smart Contracts' (2017); Popper, N., 'Digital Gold: The Untold Story of Bitcoin' (2015), and Faux, Zeke, 'Number Go Up: Inside Crypto's Wild Rise and Staggering Fall' (2023).
5. Stanford, E., Crypto Wars: Faked Deaths, Missing Billions and Industry Disruption. Kogan Page Publishers (2021).

components are explained first. With that foundation, the functionality of a blockchain is explained. This then enables the exploration of subsequent innovations such as smart contracts, other distributed data structures, and additional consensus mechanisms.

This approach to explaining blockchain is rooted in observations made after having sought to explain blockchain and DLTs to hundreds of non-technical people over the past decade. That experience revealed the critical importance of explaining the various underlying technical building blocks in detail first. It also made it clear that for many, certain aspects of the blockchain – particularly hashing functions and Proof of Work difficulty – are more difficult to grasp than others. Additional time is therefore spent on setting out detailed explanations of these concepts by breaking them down into understandable pieces.

Most of the core concepts in this chapter are explained in the context of the Bitcoin and Ethereum blockchains, as they are the most used blockchains at the time of writing. A solid understanding of the core components of how the Bitcoin blockchain is implemented is a good foundation for delving into more intricate topics, such as the Ethereum blockchain, smart contracts, other consensus mechanisms, and the more recent Decentralized Finance (DeFi) set of functionalities.

It must also be pointed out that this chapter does not profess to be a comprehensive technical manual for all variants of blockchain implementations. It would take many more pages to do so. This explanation is written for legal professionals, and in pursuing an effective introductory explanation, a balance between page-length explanatory detail has been pursued and hopefully achieved.

For those readers seeking more detailed explanations or specifics, a resource list for further reading is provided at the end of the chapter.

§1.02 CORE CONCEPTS

[A] Record-Keeping

Blockchains are a method of record-keeping and documenting details. Humans have been record-keepers for thousands of years,[6] usually as a way to 'crystalize' human memory so as to ensure that commitments, obligations, entitlements, tallies, etc., were tracked in a provable manner.

Throughout history, record-keeping methodologies have been adopted to enable tax assessment and collection and have also become a backbone of the banking system. Over time, more sophisticated record-keeping mechanisms and accounting systems were developed for these and other purposes, which today are embodied in standards such as GAAP and IFRS (*see* https://en.wikipedia.org/wiki/Accounting_standard).[7]

6. *See*, for instance, https://www.metmuseum.org/art/collection/search/329081 (accessed 10 Jan. 2024).
7. https://www.ifrs.org/ (accessed 10 Jan. 2024).

Records have been traditionally kept by the individuals or parties seeking to benefit from the recorded state of something which such records provide. In this vein, businesses have for centuries used financial records to track their various revenues and expenses, inventory, goods sold, etc. Banks have used them to maintain records of the various entitlements and obligations of their customers. Governments have used them to track tax obligations and many other bits of data about the citizenry, to track budgets and to inform public policy, among many other things.

Today, much of our record-keeping is entrusted to professionals who use computers running sophisticated database systems and is centralized[8] within the organizations maintaining them.

The accuracy and reliability of records maintained in this manner are traditionally accepted based on *trust in the record-keeper* itself. To bolster such trust, and as weaknesses in a particular record-keeping mechanism revealed itself,[9] ethical obligations have over time been imposed on these record-keepers through legal duties and standards, as well as explicit regulation.[10]

Blockchain offers a novel way of record-keeping which seeks to shift this traditional trust away from the record-keeper *to the record-keeping systems themselves*. This is achieved by way of what are essentially 'data storage tricks' which ensure that what is stored can be relied upon to not have been altered once it has been committed to the blockchain.[11]

The building blocks of these 'storage tricks' have been well known for some time. It is the combination of them by Satoshi Nakamoto[12] in the famous 2008 paper 'Bitcoin: A Peer-to-Peer Electronic Cash System'[13] that spawned the interest in blockchain as a potential alternative record-keeping solution for businesses and governments.

Let us now review some of blockchain's technical building blocks as well as some basic computational concepts to lay the foundation for understanding how blockchain and its related technologies work.

---

8. It must be noted that within such organizations there usually exist robust backup and redundancy systems to safeguard these records.
9. For a recent example *see* the accounting practice changes arising from the Enron scandal, commonly known as Sarbanes-Oxley: https://www.bccpa.ca/news-events/cpabc-newsroom/2022/march/twenty-years-later-lessons-from-enron/ (accessed 18 Dec. 2023).
10. *See*, for instance, the extensive record-keeping standards with which Canadian Chartered Public Accountants must comply, available at: https://www.cpacanada.ca/en/business-and-accounting-resources/cpa-canada-handbook-the-standards-and-guidance-collection (accessed 10 Jan. 2024).
11. Some will argue that the blockchain eliminates the need for trust, but it is submitted that is not the case. Trust is actually *shifted* to the various methodologies employed in the blockchain, including its various human-controlled aspects, such as programming of the applicable blockchain software and software applications used to access the blockchain.
12. It must be pointed out that 'Sathoshi Nakamoto' appears to be a pseudonym for one or more persons. It is not currently known who these persons are (or perhaps were).
13. https://bitcoin.org/bitcoin.pdf (accessed 10 Jan. 2024).

[B] How Computers Encode Data

Many of blockchain's underlying concepts, ideas and operational components include the use of things like digital keys, digital signatures and numerical addresses. In seeking to understand these, it is helpful to have a basic idea of how computers handle data and information.

At its most basic level, a computer uses electronic switches, or transistors, to store data. A switch is a small electronic device which can be used to store two settings, or states, off and on, which are traditionally used to represent the number 0 or 1.[14]

Two switches (or 'bits' as they are known to computer scientists) can, for example, be used to represent – through their various combinations of either off or on – the numbers, or values, from 0 to 3 (Figure 1.1).

Figure 1.1 Binary Form of the Numbers 0 to 3

	Bit A	Bit B
0	0	0
1	0	1
2	1	0
3	1	1

With three switches, or bits, one can increase the storage capacity to any of the numbers from 0 through 7. With 4 bits, it is possible to capture 16 numbers, and so on.

As one adds another bit, the number of combinations increases by a power of 2 each time. A set of 8 bits (referred to as an *octet* or a *byte*[15]) can thus represent 2^8, or 256 different things, such as the numbers 0 to 255.

These various combinations of sets of bits can be used to encode complete sets of characters like the alphabet. This then makes the digitization of text possible. To that end, and very early on in the development of computers, it was agreed among computer scientists that certain characters would be represented by certain combinations of bits in an octet or byte. These agreements are known as *encoding standards*. Two very popular and often used encoding standards are ASCII[16] and UNICODE. The latter has several different standards for representing all the different characters used by the languages of the world.[17]

Encoding standards, together with the ability to place many billions of very small transistors on silicon storage devices, or magnetically representing zeroes and ones on magnetic tapes or drives, enabled the storage of very large volumes of text and data in digital form.

---

14. A switch can also be used to represent other binary type states, such as yes/no and true/false.
15. It is likely better to use octet as there is no ambiguity that it references 8 items. Some implementations of a byte have used 7 bits.
16. The American Standard Code for Information Interchange was initially based on using only 7 bits.
17. https://home.unicode.org (accessed 10 Jan. 2024).

[C] How Computers Store Large Numbers

In our day-to-day interaction, the base-10 system is used for counting and representing mathematical values. A base-10 counting system is a methodology to represent a specific quantity by way of a sequence of digits between 0 and 9. The set of digits in a base-10 number represents different powers of 10 in sequence, with the smallest power always on the right. For example, the number 123 is really a short way of saying $3 \times (10^0) + 2 \times (10^1) + 1 \times (10^2) = 3 + 20 + 100 = 123$. (Note that any number raised to the power 0 (zero) is always 1.)

A computer is limited to only using zeroes and ones to represent a number, given that it is built on switches which can only represent two states. The number system which uses only two states (0 and 1) is called base-2 or the *binary* system of counting.

Like the base-10 system, each location in the base-2 number represents a power of the base and thus allows one to count incrementally by adding up the sequence of the number of times the various powers of 2 occur in the number. For example, in the case of the binary number 1011, this works as follows: (again, counting from right to left): $1 \times (2^0) + 1 \times (2^1) + 0 \times (2^2) + 1 \times (2^3) = 1 + 2 + 0 + 8 = 11$.

Compare the numbers 0 through 9 in both base-10 and base-2 (Figure 1.2).

Figure 1.2 The Numbers 0 Through 9 in Base-10 and Base-2 (Binary)

0	00000000
1	00000001
2	00000010
3	00000011
4	00000100
5	00000101
6	00000110
7	00000111
8	00001000
9	00001001

Many computer programs use base-16 (commonly referred to as *hexadecimal*, or 'hex') to represent numbers in half-byte (4-bit) segments.[18] When representing these numbers in writing, it was agreed to add the letters *a* through *f* to the above table to denote the base-2 values of 1010 through 1111 (which are the base-10 values of 10 through 15) (Figure 1.3).

18. Because one can create sixteen different combinations of zeroes and ones with 4 bits. Note that the first four bits in the above example are all zeroes for the first sixteen hex numbers.

Figure 1.3 The Numbers 10 Through 15 in Hexadecimal and Binary

a	00001010
b	00001011
c	00001100
d	00001101
e	00001110
f	00001111

As an example, here is the number 123,456,789 in binary and base-16:

Binary: 111010110111100110100010101
Hex: 75BCD15

To indicate that a particular number is in hexadecimal, it is customary to place 0x in front of it. The above hex number 75BCD15 can thus also be written as 0x75BCD15. Likewise, a binary number may be preceded by '0b' for the same purpose.

As will be seen later, many of the components of a blockchain use the hex format to represent various important numbers.

Some other components (such as some public key addresses) may use yet another form of numeric encoding called *base-58* which was designed to avoid confusion between digits which look the same.[19] Bitcoin addresses are sometimes represented in this format.

[D] Computer Programming

A computer, at the most basic level, performs two core functions: data storage and data manipulation. A computer is really nothing more than a very fast data manipulator.

The storage function involves the placing of programming code, and data contemplated for manipulation by that programming code, on one or more storage devices such as a hard drive, and moving it to random-access memory (RAM) if some manner of computation involving that data is required.

The manipulation function involves the retrieval of data from RAM and doing something with, or to, that data based on rules set out in programming code before re-storing it back into a memory location or a storage device.

Modern programming languages permit the manipulation of data using several logical building blocks which can be combined in an unlimited manner to create very detailed logical processing sequences. These logical sequences, also known as *programs*, can perform complex operations and automate many processes and workflows which involve the manipulation of data or information.

19. Base-58 uses the numbers 1–9 as well as both upper- and lower-case letters but skips characters prone to confusion, such as the letter Oh and the number Zero, as well as the letters I, L and the number One.

It is helpful to gain a basic understanding of some of the building blocks of a computer program, particularly in anticipation of the later explanation of smart contracts.

[1] Variables

A variable is a certain amount of storage space (a quantity of bytes) reserved in the computer's RAM which can be accessed (for retrieval or modification) by referencing the name of the variable.[20]

A variable is sometimes further described by the kind of data that should be put in the reserved memory location. For example, a variable may be 'typed' as an integer, which means that the memory space's content will be interpreted as being an integer.[21] Most program languages have many different types of variables available for use,[22] and most allow the creation of custom variable types as well.[23]

[2] Control Structures

A control structure examines and compares variables retrieved from memory and directs program flow based on that comparison. The most often used control structure is the *if … then … else* statement which allows branching based on the value of certain input variables supplied to the *if … then … else* statement. For example, the following code uses such a statement to display different messages based on the provided value of the variable age (of a person)[24] (Figure 1.4).

20. The programming language looks after translating the variable name to the actual memory location in order to make it easier for the programmer.
21. Which will also mean that if one tries to put something into the memory location which cannot be an integer, such as the letter 'D', the computer will let us know that an error has occurred. This type of error is very common in programming and is called a 'type mismatch'.
22. Usually referred to as *primitive* data types. *See*, for example, the taxonomy for such built-in primitive variable data types in the Java programming language, available at: https://docs.oracle.com/javase/tutorial/java/nutsandbolts/datatypes.html (accessed 10 Jan. 2024).
23. Particularly so in the case of programming languages which follow the object-oriented paradigm to programming, where very complex objects with many different attributes can be created as effectively 'super variables'.
24. Note that in many programming languages, the code which is executed together as part of a branch from a control structure is placed between two 'squirrely' brackets ({ and }).

Figure 1.4 An Example of an If … Else Statement

```
if (age < 20 and age > 12)
{
        print "this person is a teenager"
}
else
{
        print "this person is not a teenager"
}
```

Another often used control structure is the *while loop* which allows the repeated execution of a section of logic for as long as a condition is *true*. Here is a *while loop* example which displays an integer variable as long as it is not 11, as it is being incremented by one, starting from 1 (Figure 1.5).

Figure 1.5 An Example of a While Statement

```
variable = 1
while (variable < 11)
{
        print variable
        variable = variable + 1
}
```

Control structures can be used to build ever more complex functionality from very basic building blocks,[25] which can then be stored as *functions* or routines and re-used in other computer programs. For example, it is very easy to build a multiplication function (seeking to multiply x and y) given an existing simple addition function by simply adding y to y, x number of times. Once such a multiplication function is created and can be accessed as a function (or as a *callable* set of code), it can then be used to create another yet more intricate function to calculate the *power* of a number, and so on.

All programming languages have developed extensive sets of such complex functions, procedures and reusable code called *libraries*. Libraries can be accessed, or called, by any computer program written in the applicable programming language without having to re-invent a large set of functions and procedures. This is one of the

25. Which build on the very basic capacities of the core circuitry of a computer's Central Processing Unit or CPU. A CPU has only a limited set of core functionalities, including addition and multiplication. The power of a CPU is in being able to do billions of these basic operations per second.

most important features of modern programming – the ability to re-use and build on existing code.

In many cases, sets of libraries for a particular program also include functionality known as an *Application Program Interface* or API, which allows other programming languages, and in some cases devices with programmatic functionality, to interact with programs written in the language for which the API is available.[26]

[3] Data Structures

Data structures are methods of storing data in computer memory in a particular way to enable certain capabilities for manipulating that data, which would be (much) more difficult or not possible without that data structure.

In many instances, data structures incorporate or enable certain relationships between data elements which then facilitate indexing, sorting, editing, or other functionality, including certain kinds of calculations. Data structures in many cases also help with the efficient access and manipulation of data stored in memory.

[a] The Array

An *array* is an example of a simple data structure, which is simply a list of items in order. Here is an example of an array containing the months of the year (Figure 1.6).

Figure 1.6 An Array of the Months of the Year

Jan.	Feb.	Mar.	Apr.	May	Jun.	Jul.	Aug.	Sep.	Oct.	Nov.	Dec.
0	1	2	3	4	5	6	7	8	9	10	11

The location of an element in an array is referred to as its *index*, displayed above below each month.[27]

An array is useful if one wants to relate a specific location in that array with the ranked order of the data items stored. In the above example, the months of the year are thus listed in the order in which they occur.

Another example is the list of ingredients in packaged food, usually found on its label. This array is usually required to be listed in the order of prevalence of the ingredients listed. The ingredient with the highest percentage of content goes first, the ingredient with the next highest goes next, and so on. The structure of the array thus embodies a sorted list without needing to do anything further.

26. *See*, for instance, the API for the Java programming language at: https://docs.oracle.com/en/java/javase/21/index.html (accessed 10 Jan. 2024).
27. Note that many programming languages start the index at 0, which is perhaps a bit counterintuitive but makes it easier for the computer, which deems 0 to be just as good a number as 1.

[b] *The Linked List*

The *linked list* is another example of a data structure. A linked list is a set of data objects where each data object, in addition to storing some data value, keeps track of the location of the next item in the list by way of a pointer (usually pointing to the memory address of the next item in the list) (Figure 1.7).

Figure 1.7 A Linked List

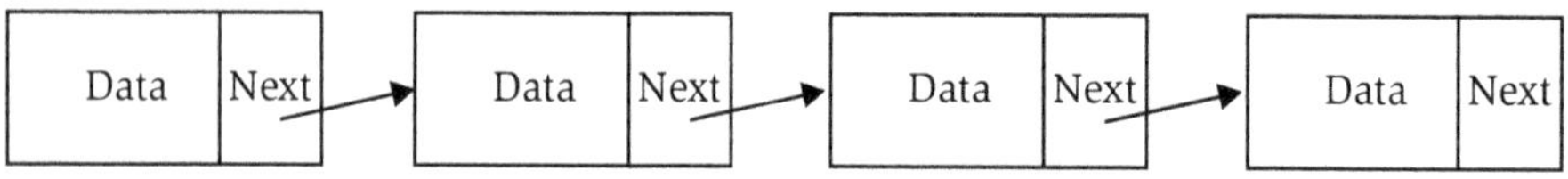

Linked lists are very useful for maintaining an ordered list because it is very easy to insert or remove elements from the list. For example, to insert a new element in an ordered list, one only needs to update the pointer of the previously ordered item in the list. Compare this to an array where one would need to shift all subsequent list members over one location to the right.

The core idea behind the linked list (tying data elements together with a pointer) is also used in a slightly different way in a blockchain.

[4] Syntax

The syntax of a programming language is the set of rules for translating a logical process or workflow into a sequence of instructions which the computer can understand and execute.

When writing a program in a specific language, it is very important to fully understand that language's syntax. Any misunderstanding of the syntax can lead to errors in the instructions which may go unnoticed in the final implementation of a program until a set of conditions arises which causes the execution of the program to go awry. These types of errors are often referred to as 'bugs', and no computer program is without them.[28]

It should be noted at this point that bugs or errors in how computer programs run can occur not only from syntax errors in the code but also from such things as:

- errors in the operating system software of the computer, for instance, how the operating manages its memory;
- errors in the hardware configuration of the computer, for instance, how data traffic is managed on the motherboard of the computer;

28. With the exception perhaps of the code written to power the lunar missions in the late 1960s and early 1970s.

- logical errors in the code which fail to contemplate the full range of possible values for input variables to programmatic control structures and may thus cause unintended program flow and/or memory overflows[29] as a result.

No computer program of any complexity is without some bugs.

[5] From Program Code to Machine Code

A computer language, such as Java, Python or Visual Basic, is actually a large computer program written to make programming of computers easier for humans. These higher-level languages use simple English words to represent their syntax, and many have complex integrated editing tools with a great deal of features.[30]

The product of these high-level programming languages is a relatively easy-to-read text file, compliant with the structural formatting and syntax requirements of the specific programming language used. This file is not directly usable by the computer for execution, however, and must first be converted to *machine code* interpretable by the Central Processing Unit (CPU)[31] of the computer on which the code is to be executed.

The type of machine code required depends on the architecture of the CPU in question. Machine code for an Intel processor[32] is different from that for an ARM processor,[33] for example. The required machine code is determined by the *instruction set* for the CPU, which can be thought of as the complete list of available instructions which can be issued to the CPU by a computer program.

The program which translates the program language specific text file into machine code is called a *compiler*.[34] The product of a compiler is a long string of zeroes and ones called a *bitstream*, which in the case of a computer program is usually referred to as a *binary*.

In some cases, an intermediary code interpreter called a *virtual machine*, *process virtual machine*, or *runtime environment* sits between the programming language and the CPU.

Such a virtual machine is used to create the ability to execute a particular program on any CPU for which a virtual machine exists.[35] The Java programming language uses the *Java Virtual Machine*, or JVM, exactly for this purpose, and it is one of the reasons why this language is so popular: it can run on many different types of hardware.

---

29. For instance, by placing a value in a memory location which is too large for the reserved space, which can then result in overwriting the next memory location.
30. Referred to as Integrated Development Environments, or IDEs.
31. The 'brains' of the computer, which contain hardwired circuitry which can execute basic computer instructions at a very high rate.
32. Found in most desktop computers.
33. Advanced RISC Machines, which is used in many mobile and embedded devices.
34. This is a dramatic oversimplification of what a compiler does, but it is sufficient for our limited purposes.
35. A virtual machine thus allows a programming language to become *multi-platform*.

In the case of the JVM, the compiler does not generate binary code but rather a *bytecode* file, which the JVM then converts to machine code usable by the specific hardware being used.

In many cases, the binary or bytecode is transmitted to a computer or virtual machine for execution using hex encoding. As we will see, this is also how smart contracts are encoded and transmitted to the blockchain.

[E] Computer Architecture

Given all the above functionalities, a computer is physically organized with the following key components and associated functionalities:

(1) The Central Processing Unit (CPU), which executes instructions stored in memory.
(2) Memory, primarily of two types: Random-Access Memory (RAM), which is volatile[36] memory used for temporary storage of data and program instructions that the CPU is currently using, and secondary memory, which is non-volatile memory used for long-term storage, such as a hard drive.
(3) Registers, which are small, high-speed storage locations within the CPU used for temporarily holding data during processing.
(4) The Instruction Set Architecture (ISA), which is the set of commands or instructions that a CPU understands and can execute. These are pre-programmed into the CPU.
(5) Cache Memory, which is high-speed memory located between the CPU and RAM and which is used to store frequently accessed data and instructions for faster retrieval.
(6) The Bus System, which is a set of communication pathways that transfer data between components. They include the address bus (identifying memory locations), data bus (transferring actual data), and control bus (managing the operation of components).
(7) The Motherboard, which is the main circuit board that connects and facilitates communication between the CPU, memory, storage, and peripheral devices.
(8) A System Clock, which synchronizes the operations of the CPU and other components, ensuring that computational work is properly coordinated and sequenced.

In addition to these, a computer will also have a set of input devices, such as a keyboard, mouse, touch screen, of scanner, which allow users to interact with the computer by providing data or commands, as well as output devices, such as a monitor, printer, and speakers.

36. 'Volatile' in this context means that the storage is not persistent if the storage medium loses power.

[1] *Optimizing Computer Architecture*

Over the last number of decades, there has been a great deal of innovation in making computer architectures perform at ever faster rates. Among these, the most effective improvements have resulted from technologies which enable simultaneous processing of multiple instructions by the computer. These include:

- Pipelining or Parallel Processing, which usually involves breaking down the execution of instructions into multiple stages, allowing the CPU to work on different instructions at the same time.
- Multi-Core Processors, which is the installation of multiple integrated processor cores on a single computer chip. Such chips are designed to optimize parallel processing.

These parallel processing features are integral to the capabilities of today's computing hardware.

§1.03 THE MATHEMATICS OF BLOCKCHAIN

[A] The Hash Function

A function is a mathematical recipe for turning an input into a desired output based on a clearly articulated formula or algorithm. For example, the addition function 'C = A + B' takes the variables A and B as inputs and generates the desired output C by adding A and B together.

One group of functions relevant to understanding blockchain is the set of *hash functions*. Hash functions are used to convert a usually large input of data into a much smaller, fixed-length output to create a unique 'signature' of the larger input.

A hash function thus maps the input data to a numerical key. This key is usually referred to as the *hash value* or *hash digest,* or just the *hash* (Figure 1.8).

Figure 1.8 A Hash Function

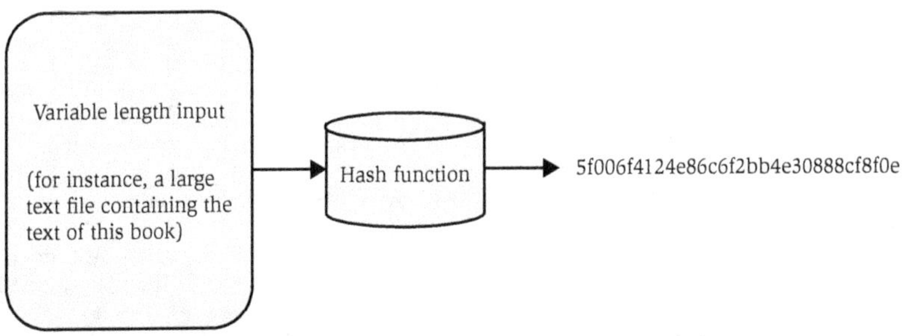

Most hash functions work by taking the input data, chopping it up into smaller sections and then applying certain functions to those smaller chunks. The division and remainder – or *modulo* – function is often used in this process, which gives a hash function a 'one-way' property: it is not possible to recreate the original input from the eventual hash generated by the function.[37]

These hash functions then shuffle and/or combine the outputs from these smaller chunks in a predefined manner and reapply the modulo, or some variant, again. This process is continued until a single output of the desired length is achieved.

The output of a hash function is often written in hex. For example, the very popular hashing algorithm SHA256[38] (which is used in the Bitcoin blockchain) will output a 64-bit hash digest which might look like this:[39]

5e884898da28047151d0e56f8dc6292773603d0d6aabbdd62a11ef721d1542d8

Note that this hex value is the following very large number in base-10:

42,758,200,014,260,304,871,795,218,010,112,217,441,437,394,933,425,264, 440,882,844,866,153,524,052,696[40]

Hash functions are used in many applications, including storing passwords, digital certificates to support encryption, and indexing of large data sets. More refined hashing functions are used to assist in ensuring that data is not corrupted or has not been changed.

[B] The Cryptographic Hash Function

One specific type of hash function is particularly relevant to our understanding of blockchain: the *cryptographic hash function*. Like a regular hash function, the cryptographic hash function takes a data input of variable length and generates a fixed-length hash digest as its output.

A cryptographic hash function has some specific and very useful properties which the blockchain takes advantage of.

[1] The 'Always the Same' Property

A cryptographic hash function will always generate the same hash value for the same input. This is usually described by computer scientists and mathematicians as the

---

37. Further discussed *infra*. Appreciate that the remainder function is very helpful in creating a 'one-way' function, given that the same remainder can arise for many different divisions. For example, 10 divided by 3 leaves remainder 1. 16 divided by 5 also leaves remainder 1. A specialized implementation building on this property, which is often used in public key encryption, is the *elliptic curve* function, available at: https://blog.cloudflare.com/a-relatively-easy-to-understand-primer-on-elliptic-curve-cryptography/ (accessed 10 Jan. 2024).
38. *See* https://csrc.nist.gov/csrc/media/publications/fips/180/4/archive/2012-03-06/documents/fips180-4.pdf (accessed 10 Jan. 2024) for the standard description of this algorithm. It is a complicated process.
39. Available at: https://www.fileformat.info/tool/hash.htm (accessed 10 Jan. 2024).
40. This is a 78-digit number and one of the 2^{256} possible outputs from the SHA256 hashing algorithm. Note that the number of digits of that number can be determined by calculating n log 2, in this case 256 log 2 which equals 78.

'deterministic' property. A function which is non-deterministic will generate different outputs because a certain amount of randomness exists in how the function works. An example of a non-deterministic function is the rolling of a set of dice.

[2] The 'Digital Signature' Property

A cryptographic hash function also uses a formula which ensures (with an extremely high level of confidence[41]) that the hash digest will be *unique*. A hash digest thus becomes a *digital signature* of the input data and can be used to determine whether an input has been modified or not.

In the use of a cryptographic hash function, the smallest possible change (i.e., one bit or character) in the input data will generate a completely different output digest (Figure 1.9).

Figure 1.9 An Example of How a Minimal Change in Input Generates a Completely Different Hash Digest

Input text	SHA256 hash digest
This is sample text submitted to the SHA256 hashing algorithm. We will change it just a little bit by adding a period to the end of this sentence below	bbadbf8c5138b8c9ced5c5197082ff5b3 6c9128f009bbb4cb450389c626c0214
This is sample text submitted to the SHA256 hashing algorithm. We will change it just a little bit by adding a period to the end of this sentence below	9d2f5d3b509a0334e752a0aaa0fe468f3 4affdddcclc1912aeeee75321117514

This is a very valuable feature which enables a cryptographic hash function to serve several useful purposes. For example, this property is exploited when transmitting digital files over the internet to ensure they arrive on the receiver's computer in identical form to that sent by the sender. That process works as follows:

- The sender feeds the digital file (of any size) to one of a number of available cryptographic hashing functions[42] and generates a hash digest, usually somewhere between 32 and 128 bits in length.

41. Particularly in the case of *structured data*, i.e., data which follows a pattern, such as the grammar of a language. This property is sometimes also referred to as the function having 'strong collision resistance'.
42. For further review and testing with a number of these hashing algorithms: https://www.tools4noobs.com/online_tools/hash/ (accessed 10 Jan. 2024).

- The sender transmits the digital file to the recipient over the internet and also sends particulars of the cryptographic hash function used, together with the generated hash digest.
- The receiver feeds the received digital file to the cryptographic hash function, generating a hash digest.
- If the receiver's hash digest matches the hash digest sent by the sender, then we must conclude that the received file is identical to the one transmitted by the sender.
- If the hash digests do not match, then there was an error in transmission, and the file needs to be resent.

[3] The 'No Reverse Engineering' Property

A cryptographic hash function is also a 'one-way function' which means it is not possible to recreate or 'reverse engineer' the original file from the hash digest.

One might think that calculating all possible permutations of the input data and then looking for the digest in that list to find the original input data is an option. This is, however, computationally prohibitive – it would require computational power, and time, well beyond the capability of current computer technology – particularly with large input data sets of different sizes.[43]

One-way functions are very useful in many applications, including public-private key encryption.[44]

[C] The Hash List

One application of a cryptographic hash function is the *hash list*. The hash list is used a lot in peer-to-peer (P2P) file sharing systems (*see* the P2P Networks section *infra*) to ensure that the various distributed pieces of a file come together to reconstitute the original file without errors. In that context, a hash list (Figure 1.10) functions as follows:

- The file being shared is broken up into several smaller pieces, called data blocks, which are sufficiently small to enable easy transmission over the internet as packets[45] or groups of packets.
- Each block is hashed, and the hash value is added to a separate hash list.
- Once all block hashes have been added, the hash list file is itself hashed and a *top hash* is generated.
- The top hash file is kept by a trusted authority.

43. These types of problems are called *intractable* which means they cannot be solved within the bounds of our foreseeable computational capacity, *see* https://en.wikipedia.org/wiki/Computational_complexity_theory#Intractability (accessed 10 Jan. 2024).
44. *See* the discussion *infra*.
45. A packet is a small block of data, easily transmissible between computers.

- Anyone wishing to obtain the file from the P2P network will first obtain the top hash file from the trusted source.[46]
- With that file in hand, the hash list can then be obtained from any other source (i.e., any other sharing user on the P2P network) for comparison with the top hash.
- If the hash of the hash list file matches the top hash, the user can proceed to download the various data blocks from any of the other users on the network who have those blocks available.
- Every block's hash is compared with the hash value for that block in the confirmed hash list file, and if it matches, it is accepted as genuine.

Figure 1.10 A Hash List

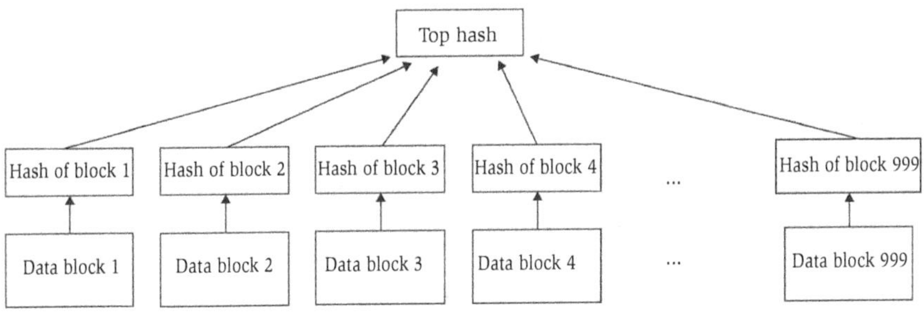

Given the properties of the cryptographic hash function, one is assured that if the hash of a received data block is not the same as the hash found in the hash list, a change or corruption is present in that block of data, necessitating a retransmission or obtaining the block from another source.

Using a hash list to verify the integrity of a file in blocks has another advantage in that it is much easier to determine where data errors exist than if one simply hashed the whole file. Fixing 'bad data' is thus much easier and faster.

[D] The Merkle Tree

A Merkle tree (also sometimes referred to as a *binary hash tree* or just *hash tree*) takes the ideas behind the hash list a step further for even better data integrity.

Rather than creating a simple list of hashes of data blocks, a Merkle tree incorporates data hashes into an upside-down tree-type structure, much like one might organize a family tree for a genealogy project. The individual elements in the tree are referred to as *nodes*, and every node has two children and one parent.

46. In the case of BitTorrent, this file actually contains both the top hash and the hash values for all the data blocks for the file being shared.

At the bottom of the tree are the various data block nodes (sometimes referred to as *leaves*[47]), which are hashed individually, and their hash digests are then combined in pairs and hashed together again to create a parent hash. These parent hashes are, in turn, paired together and hashed again to create 'grandparent' hashes, and so on.

The Bitcoin blockchain uses a Merkle tree to organize and verify the integrity of every individual transaction contained in a block of transactions. To that end, the content of a leaf is limited to only one transaction. Hashes are combined using the above approach until there is only one hash at the top of the tree.

This top hash is called the *Merkle root* (Figure 1.11).

Figure 1.11 A Simple Merkle Tree

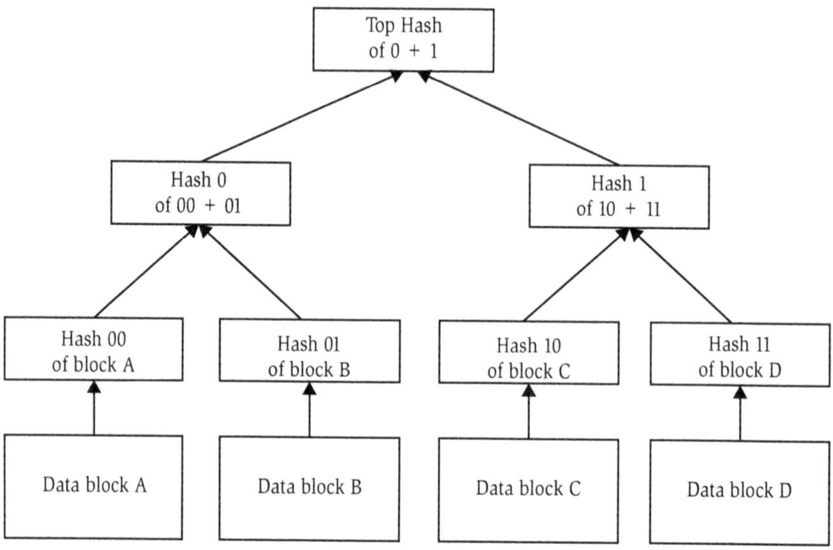

The Merkle trees used in the Bitcoin blocks use the double-SHA256 hashing algorithm.[48]

[E] Public-Private Key Encryption

The ability to successfully encode, or encrypt, a message into a form which can only be read by the intended recipient, and no one else, has been something which mankind has pursued for centuries.[49]

47. Leaves are not stored in the Merkle tree.
48. Applying SHA256 twice.
49. For a short overview of the history of cryptography, *see* https://pdfs.semanticscholar.org/938a/24139dbf089d4d8a4318445c471e1e7f0aee.pdf (accessed 10 Jan. 2024).

Until the 1970s or so, the only solution was any of a number of different variants of *symmetric key* approaches (Figure 1.12), where the key for encryption was the same as the key used to decrypt the message.

In every encryption scheme, an encryption key converts the original message into gibberish using some sort of predefined algorithm.[50]

Figure 1.12 Symmetric Key Encryption

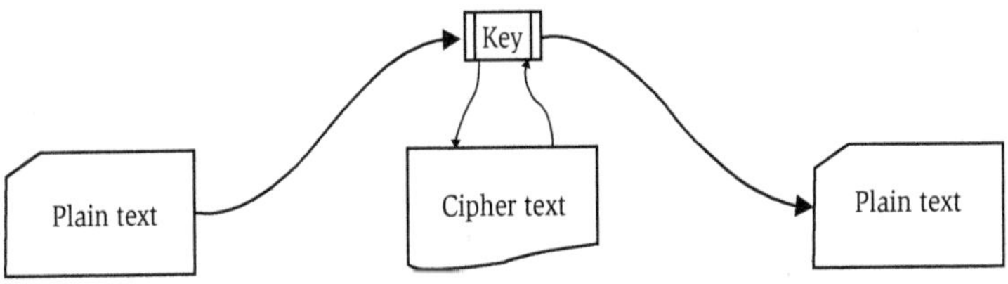

A very simple encryption key is the *substitution cypher* for which a key might look like this (Figure 1.13).

Figure 1.13 A Simple Substitution Cypher

A	B	C	D	E	F	G	H	I	J	K	L	M	N	O	P	Q	R	S	T	U	V	W	X	Y	Z
Q	W	Z	A	R	K	B	J	C	L	S	D	X	E	Y	U	H	T	P	G	V	N	F	M	O	I

Using this cypher, the phrase 'blockchain is simple' encrypts as 'wdyzsxjqe cp pcxudr'.

With symmetric key encryption, both the sender and the receiver use the same key, which they must also *both* keep secret. In addition, a cypher must be resistant to any of a number of potential decryption attacks.[51] Achieving both of these conditions is not always easy.

Over the centuries, many intricate systems were developed with the intent of recreating and safeguarding this common key and making it resistant to decryption attacks, sometimes changing it daily via a predetermined formula or mechanical aid.

The most famous example of creating and managing the common key in a very complex manner is the Enigma machine used by the Germans in World War II. Enigma used an elaborate system of changing codes and rotary dial settings to generate the

50. An encryption key is used to convert the original message into gibberish using some sort of predefined usually complex algorithm. An example of such an algorithm is AES, the Advanced Encryption Standard, available at: https://en.wikipedia.org/wiki/Advanced_Encryption_Standard (accessed 10 Jan. 2024).
51. There are many different methodologies for this, starting with simple frequency and message structure analysis. For example, in the example given, the presence of a two-character word is an opportunity to explore the limited set of two-character words which might work, to give some insight into what the replacement key values might be.

same key for both the sender and the receiver of a message based on the time the message was sent.[52]

The need for these types of elaborate strategies in the context of protecting confidential communications largely disappeared with the invention of *public-private key encryption* (or public key cryptography) in the 1970s.[53]

Public-private key encryption does not require that the sender and the receiver both keep a single (encryption and decryption) key secret.

Instead, every participant in a secret communication channel now has two keys: a *private* key which that person keeps secret and a *public* key (Figure 1.14) which is published to the world. The beauty of this approach is that no elaborate mechanism needs to be designed to share a common key. Implementation is thus much easier.

The manner in which these keys are used to encrypt messages involves the use of 'one-way functions' which make it easy to generate an encrypted output but impossible[54] to reverse engineer the input from that output if only the public key is known.[55] If one knows the private key, however, decrypting the message is trivial.

Figure 1.14 Basic Public Key Encryption

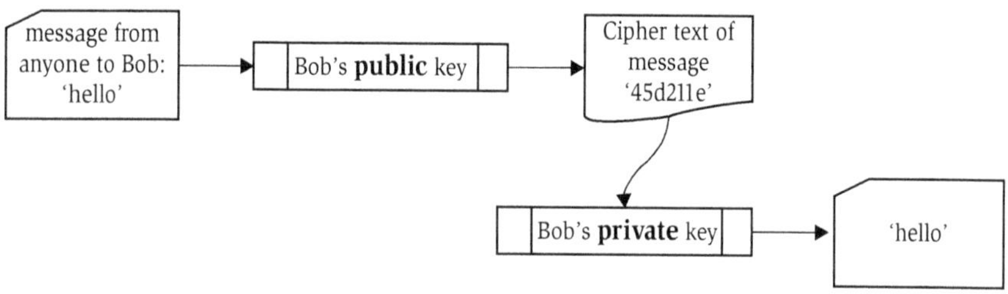

Public-private key encryption thus makes it very easy to create encrypted messages (using the public key) that only the holder of the private key can read.

Likewise, a message signed with a sender's private key can be authenticated by decrypting it with the public key. The ability to so decrypt it confirms that the message was in fact sent by the sender, assuming the sender has been able to keep the private key completely secret.

52. An online version is available at: https://cryptii.com/pipes/enigma-machine (accessed 10 Jan. 2024).
53. That is not to say that symmetric key encryption disappeared. It too has evolved and continues to be used in many different forms today, for other situations where encryption is required.
54. This impossibility relies in many cases on the fact that factoring sufficiently large integers is not possible with our current or foreseeable computational capabilities. Determining whether two factors combine to produce a large integer (the one-way aspect of factorization), however, is a trivial exercise.
55. The 'one-way' function used in most encryption methodologies exploits the fact that it is quite easy to multiply very large prime numbers together but very difficult (i.e., computationally infeasible) to find the originating prime factors from the resulting product.

This type of a public-private key encryption application is usually referred to as a 'digital signature' process and is used in a number of authentication processes online (Figure 1.15).

Figure 1.15 Digital Signatures: Using Public Key Encryption to Authenticate a Message

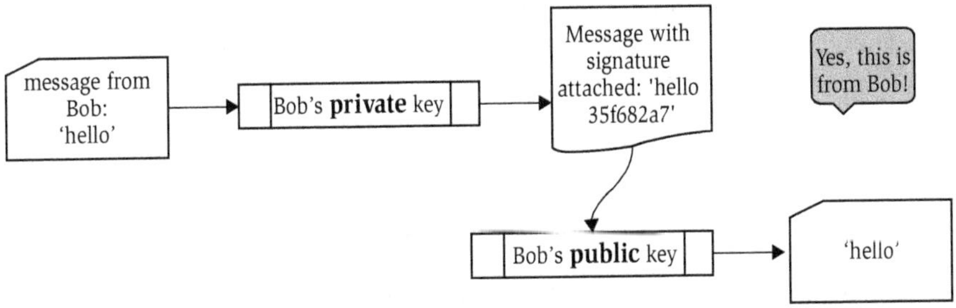

Public-private key encryption can thus also be used to confirm that a particular message originated with the holder of the private key. In this manner, public-private key encryption is used in the Bitcoin blockchain to validate the authenticity of transactions submitted to the blockchain.[56]

Anyone wishing to participate in the Bitcoin network must create a private key (which is just a random number between 0 and 2^{256}) and then derive a public key from that number using the (one-way) ECC (elliptic curve multiplication) function,[57] which can be easily done with most programming languages.[58]

Once a public key has been created, it can be given to someone who wants to send Bitcoin to that person for inclusion in the intended transaction.[59]

Typing in private and public keys can be difficult and is prone to errors. For this reason, some public-private key encryption systems will include a *checksum* in their addresses, which can then be used to validate that a particular key is properly constituted. For example, Bitcoin addresses include a 4-bit checksum which can be used to programmatically confirm that a specific address does not have a typo.[60]

---

56. Some participants in the blockchain space will suggest that the blockchain itself is encrypted. In the case of Bitcoin, this is not the case.
57. This is a function often used to create public-private key pairs. In simple terms, the function works by multiplying a 'starting point' along an elliptic function to reach another point (the 'resulting point') on the function curve. The resulting point becomes the public key, and the multiplier becomes the private key. It works because it is very difficult to find the multiplier, given the starting and resulting point.
58. Or online at a site like https://www.bitaddress.org (accessed 10 Jan. 2024).
59. *See* below for what all goes into a Bitcoin transaction. Also note that in some cases, a *hash* of the public key may be included instead.
60. A similar approach is used to provide a rudimentary check on the constitution of such things as credit card and social security or social insurance numbers.

The Ethereum blockchain addresses do not contain a checksum, which has resulted in many a misconfigured, but confirmed, transaction, resulting in inaccessible and thus lost cryptocurrency.

§1.04 DATABASE CONCEPTS

A database is a large set of data digitally organized in a manner consistent with a database standard. A database standard is a specific design approach to make the storage and retrieval of usually large volumes of data and information convenient and efficient. Numerous different database standards and design approaches have been created to meet the specific data analysis needs of data owners.

A database standard will embody the concepts and techniques for the management of the data in the database, as well as the *data model* used, that is, how the various types of data within the database relate to each other.

A popular database data model is the *Relational Model* which seeks to articulate data as tables with relationships inside and among them.[61] For example, in the case of a school, one might store information about a student in a student table, with the various attributes, or properties, of that student stored as elements of that table (Figure 1.16).

Figure 1.16 An Example of Student Database Table

Student ID	Name	Date of Birth
1434	John Smith	2 August 1998
1675	Peter Jones	5 July 2001
3221	Mary Hynes	6 April 1999

One could then also store courses taught in a separate table (Figure 1.17).

Figure 1.17 An Example of Course Database Table

Course ID	Course Name	Semester Offered	Instructor
225	Math 1103	Fall 2018	K. Friedman
674	Physics 2106	Fall 2018	J. Fung
609	Computer Science 4407	Winter 2019	P. Kirby

And one could list grades for courses taken by students in yet another table, simply referencing the IDs from the other two tables (Figure 1.18).[62]

61. Traditionally, these relationships are of three kinds: one to one, one to many, or many to many.
62. This type of table is usually referred to as a *junction table.*

Figure 1.18 An Example of Grades Database Junction Table

Student ID	Course ID	Grade
1434	225	65
1675	225	77
1675	674	76
3221	609	88
3221	225	90

A Relational Model is often used where the data being stored is structured; i.e., it is known in advance what the various bits of data (attributes or properties) are. An example of a Relational Model-based database standard is the *Structured Query Language* or SQL.[63]

Another popular data model is the *Extensible Markup Language* or XML, which is used extensively to represent semi-structured data (i.e., data entities which may have attributes or properties that are different or perhaps not fully known at the time of the database design).

An example of data suitable for modelling with XML is a text message (Figure 1.19). It is likely that one might want to add additional attributes or properties to a text message in the future (such as audio or video files, perhaps).

Figure 1.19 An Example of XML Representation of a Text Message

```
< text message >
        < to > Peter < /to >
        < from > Jake < /from >
        < heading > Hi! < /heading >
        < body > How are you? < /body >
        < emoji > smiley < /emoji >
< /text message >
```

[A] Database Operations

All commercial databases enable the manipulation of data with four key operations (usually referred to as CRUD):

(i) CREATE a new record (based on the implementation of a data model).
(ii) READ a stored record.
(iii) UPDATE a stored record (i.e., change a value associated with a particular entity or attribute of an entity).
(iv) DELETE a stored record.

63. https://en.wikipedia.org/wiki/SQL (accessed 10 Jan. 2024).

Many software programs which deal with large amounts of data will use a separate database to store this data in order to exploit the far superior abilities of a database to index and search, particularly where large data volumes are concerned. To facilitate this, many databases provide interface functionality through which programs can connect to them. Many online databases also provide such interfaces, usually referred to as *web services*, to enable the making of search requests and the obtaining of the results over the internet.

[B] A Transaction Log Distinguished from a Database

It is worthwhile pointing out the difference between a transaction log and a database.

A transaction log, of which the blockchain is an example, is a chronological record to which new records are added by appending them to the end of the log.

An 'append-only' transaction log does not meet the definition of a traditional database because it is not possible to perform all four of the CRUD operations. It is only able to perform two operations: CREATE (and then only by adding data to the end of the file) and READ.

The absence of the capacity to UPDATE and DELETE has several impacts on the ability to efficiently deal with information kept solely in a transactional log. These include the following:

- The transaction log continuously gets larger. It is not possible to 'clean up' the data by eliminating updated entries. As a result, transaction logs – if not managed in some other manner – can get very large. As an example, the Bitcoin blockchain continues to grow at the rate of about 1 Gigabyte roughly every four days.[64]
- The efficiency of finding information stored becomes more difficult as the log grows larger. This requires the use of separate databases (which do have CRUD functionality) to quickly find the right data, such as that required to determine a particular address' entitlement reflected in a blockchain.

[C] Database Transactions: The ACID Properties

A database is changed through one or more of the CRUD transactions. To maintain database integrity, these transactions must comply with what are commonly referred to as the *ACID principles* or properties:

- *A – Atomicity*. The entire database transaction either takes place or does not take place at all.[65] Partial completion of a transaction, such as only the debit of one account without a credit to another, is not permitted.
- *C – Consistency*. The database must be consistent both before and after the transaction. In other words, the data contained in the database is persistently

64. As of 27 Dec. 2023, the Bitcoin blockchain is 537 GB in size.
65. This principle is sometimes also referred to as the 'all or nothing' rule.

correct. For example, a transaction which transfers a balance from one account to another, once completed, maintains the correct total balance of funds in both accounts.

- *I – Isolation.* Transactions do not interfere with each other and are completed independently. Intermediate states are not visible to the rest of the database. For example, in the case of a transfer between two accounts, the database only sees the before and after states of the transaction.
- *D – Durability.* Changes to the database because of a successful transaction persist in the event of a system or power failure. This usually requires that they have been successfully written to a non-volatile storage state.

There is an active academic discussion on the extent to which these principles are achievable in and/or applicable to a blockchain.[66] In general terms, the functionality of a properly constructed blockchain should be able to achieve the aims of the ACID, albeit in a different way.

§1.05 NETWORKING FUNDAMENTALS

The ability of two computers to connect and exchange data is the backbone of the internet. It is helpful to have a basic understanding of how this works, on our path towards understanding the blockchain.

Computers communicate by sending long strings of zeroes and ones to each other over high-speed wires connecting them together. To enable these zeroes and ones to take on meaning, certain standards – known as *protocols* – have been developed which allow a sending computer to put together a string of zeroes and ones on one end, which are interpretable and make sense to the computer on the other end.

A well-known protocol for sending data over the internet in this way is the Internet Protocol (or IP).[67] The IP protocol transmits data between computers in packets, which are just long strings of zeroes and ones with a predefined structure.

The IP protocol also includes standards for identifying every computer uniquely on the network, with what is known as an *IP address*. The IP address is used much in the same way as an address for a residence – to send something to the right destination.[68]

66. *See*, for instance, Tai, S., Eberhardt, J. and Klems, M., *Not ACID, Not BASE, but SALT*, Proceedings of the 7th International Conference on Cloud Computing and Services Science. SCITEPRESS-Science and Technology Publications, Lda, 2017, available at: https://pdfs.semanticscholar.org/0d43/aee2f9d95d6487c61526696e51bb4385b8c8.pdf (accessed 10 Jan. 2024).
67. Successful data transmission over the internet requires the use of another protocol as well, the Transmission Control Protocol or TCP, but for the purpose of explaining network communications, it is not necessary to delve too far. The IP and TCP protocols are often referred to together as the 'TCP/IP Suite'.
68. At the local network level an IP address is tied to the physical hardware identifier of a computer known as the MAC, or Media Access Control, address.

IP addresses are denoted as sets of numbers separated by dots, such as 144.101.65.131[69] or FE80:0000:0000:0000:0202:B3FF:FE1E:8329.[70]

Under the IP protocol, a sending computer will put together a long string of zeroes and ones in a manner consistent with the standard template set out in the IP protocol specification.

A receiving computer will look for a specific pattern of zeroes and ones to denote the start of a packet and then start parsing out the various components of the packet after that based on the rules of the applicable protocol specification.

The two main components of an IP packet are the *header* and the *payload*. The header contains various administrative type information such as the version of the protocol used, the IP address of the sending computer, and the length of the packet. The payload is usually raw data to be used by an application program on the destination computer.

The way in which data is packed for transmission over the internet is not dissimilar to how it is stored in blocks in a blockchain.

[A] P2P Networks

A P2P network is a network of computers which can aggregate, distribute, and share resources, like the storage of files, processing capacity or bandwidth. These shared resources are available to each of the peers (members) of the network via a protocol specific to the P2P network.

Unlike a traditional client-server model of networking, a P2P network does not have a centralized host or authority which controls the network's activity – every peer acts as both a server and a client.

Any necessary controls to enable the network to function without a centralized server-type authority are embedded in the P2P software being run on each of peers (or nodes) on the network.

One of the earliest P2P networks was Napster – created in 1999 – which was used to (illegally) share music files over the internet.[71]

P2P networks are prevalent today and are used in a wide array of applications,[72] including blockchain.

A P2P network is a form of *distributed* computing, which effectively is a group of computers connected together to achieve a common goal.

---

69. This format is known as IP4.
70. This format is known as IP6. Note the use of hexadecimal again!
71. Napster still exists, although it has now transformed into a legitimate music streaming service, available at: https://napster.com (accessed 10 Jan. 2024).
72. For example, BitTorrent, a very popular file sharing application, is used for much of the illegal file sharing of media around the world. An example for a more legitimate use, Microsoft uses peer-to-peer functionality to distribute software updates to the vast number of computers running the Windows 10 operating system.

[1] The Consensus Problem

A common problem in many distributed computing applications is ensuring that they have a common set of identical data elements, for example, a ledger or a price list, to reference. This challenge of ensuring data consistency in a distributed system containing data which is regularly changed or updated is known as the *consensus* problem.

In the case of a ledger of entitlements or obligations, keeping a copy of the same ledger up to date on many computers connected over the internet creates a significant consensus challenge. How does one keep them all consistent?

The Bitcoin blockchain has an ingenious[73] way of achieving this.

§1.06 CORE BLOCKCHAIN FUNCTIONALITY

With a good grasp of some of the key underlying concepts and ideas, it is now possible to move on to exploring the actual functionality of a blockchain.

First, it is important to appreciate that a blockchain is nothing more than a large file comprised of blocks, containing sets of transactions, arranged in chronological order. It is, at its root, and as noted previously, *a sequential 'append-only' transaction log* with some special features.

These special features relate to how blocks of transactions are linked together to prevent them from being altered or tampered with. Let us dig a bit deeper into how this works by examining the Bitcoin blockchain as an example.

To help understand the Bitcoin blockchain, think of the blockchain file as a long train - locomotive and wagons - with the wagons individually sealed and also connected together in a particular way so that the wagons cannot be separated or the contents in the individual wagons changed (Figure 1.20).

Figure 1.20 The Blockchain Train

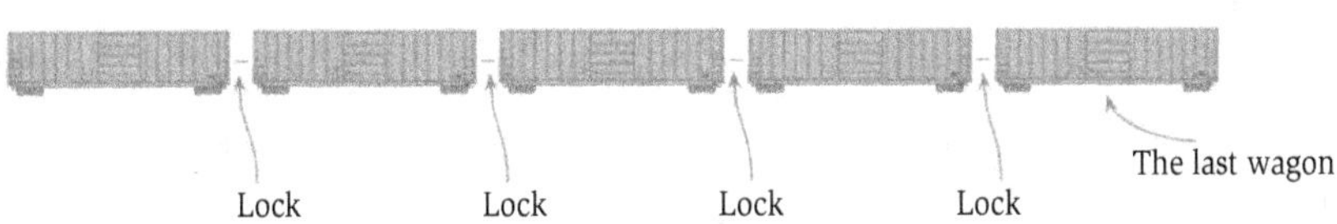

In this train analogy, the locomotive wagon contains the first transactions in the blockchain (sometimes referred to as the *genesis* block), and the wagons that follow contain bundles of transactions which have each been subsequently added in chronological order. The last wagon of the train contains the most recently added set of transactions.

Every wagon in the train is like a *block* in the blockchain, where each block contains a series of transactions which have been added.

73. This is not to suggest that the Bitcoin blockchain approach to reaching consensus is perfect. It is not. As we will see, it has a high cost and has significant scaling issues.

In the case of the Bitcoin blockchain, this block is around 1 MB in size, which represents around 2,000–2,500 transactions per block, on average.[74]

[A] Tying Blocks Together to Prevent Tampering

As explained above, a cryptographic hash function can be used to confirm that an input data set has not been altered, since it was hashed: if a reapplication of the cryptographic hash function to a (copy of the) data set generates the same hash digest, then it is certain that the data set has not been altered and/or that the copy of the data is the same as the original.

We can apply this functionality to a *series* of separate files or data sets by including the hash of one dataset/file (block) *into the content* of the next dataset/file (block). This approach then protects the integrity of this series of datasets.

Applying this to the train example, we can continuously protect the integrity of all data in a sequential transaction log, such as a blockchain, by applying this process as follows to each block, or wagon, of the train, starting with the first block (the locomotive) (Figure 1.21):

- The data (sets of new transaction information) to be added is placed in a block, to which the cryptographic hash function is applied, generating a unique hash digest for that block.
- This unique hash digest is next placed *inside* the data set for the following block (together with whatever transactions will be part of the following block), and this data set (i.e., the hash digest from the previous block together with the transaction data) is subjected to the same cryptographic hash function again, generating another unique hash digest for this second block.
- This second unique hash digest is, in turn, placed inside the data to be hashed for the third block, and so on.

Figure 1.21 Forward-Embedding Hash Digests

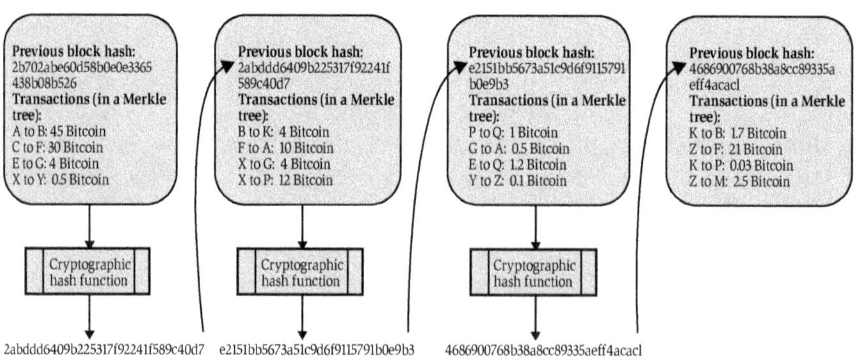

74. At the time of the writing of this chapter. This amount does fluctuate. *See* https://www.blockchain.com/en/charts/n-transactions-per-block?timespan=all (accessed 10 Jan. 2024).

With this approach of embedding the hash digest from one block *inside the data* to be hashed for the next block, a couple of important outcomes are achieved:

(i) The integrity of *all the data* contained in all the sequential blocks is now tied together in an immutable chain of forward-embedded hash digests. In other words, any alteration of any data in a block will immediately change the hash digest for that block, which will then no longer match the embedded hash digest at the beginning of the next block, signalling a loss of integrity of the data.

(ii) It is easy to verify the integrity of the data in any block (wagon) at any time by recalculating the hash digest of every block in the chain and comparing it with the hash digest embedded in the data for the next block.[75] If anywhere along the line a mismatch is encountered, then the data in that block (wagon) has been altered. To identify which specific transaction was altered, one simply examines the Merkle tree hash consistency within the block data itself.

[B] Adding a Time Cost

The above approach of tying together blocks with forward-embedded hash digests has a weakness. If one can control the storage of the whole blockchain, it is possible to make an alteration and then simply recalculate all the hashes for all the blocks. Such a successful alteration and recalculation would still present in a manner consistent with the above tamper-proof strategy.

To eliminate this weakness, Satoshi Nakamoto added a *time cost* to the process of adding a block to the blockchain in order to make any such recalculation process very difficult. This invention is known as *Proof of Work.*[76]

A key aspect of Proof of Work relies on the imposition of a *maximum value* for the hash digest generated by the hashing of a particular block. In order to appreciate how that process works, it is necessary to gain an understanding of two additional concepts: the *nonce* and the *probabilities* of generating particular hash digest values.

[1] The Nonce

A *nonce* is a *number used once.* Think of it as a number which is changed without repeating a value, for example, by incrementing it like a counter.

75. Note that changing the hash digest in the second block to match the hash digest generated from the altered first block, so as to hide the alteration, will not work, as this change of the second block will change the forward-embedded hash digest in the third block, and so on.

76. Sometimes also referred to as Nakamoto Consensus.

[2] *The Probabilities of Generating a Particular Hash Value*

[a] *Randomness*

The first idea to understand is that of *randomness*, which is the quality of an event lacking any sort of pattern of occurring. Rolling a dice[77] is a random event because any of the six outcomes is equally likely to occur.

Rolling a weighted dice is not a random event. One of the potential outcomes is more likely to occur than the other five.

An event outcome which has the property of randomness is called a *random variable.*

[b] *Sample Space*

A *sample space* is the range of all possible values for a random variable. It can be thought of as a complete list of all the possible ways that the random variable event could happen. For example, if a particular random variable generates a number between 0 and 101, then the sample space is all the numbers from 1 to 100.

The sample space also has a size. Mathematicians call it a *cardinality*, which in the case of the above example of 100 possible outcomes is 100.

Knowledge of the sample space cardinality allows the determination of certain probabilities about that random variable. The roll of dice is a good example to illustrate this point.

A dice has six sides, and there are therefore six ways that the event of the roll of a dice can happen (its sample space is six). The chance, or probability, of getting any one of those sides is the prevalence of that event within the size of the sample space. In the case of the dice, that is one divided by six – one-sixth – or 0.166666666666.

Likewise, pulling a *specific* card from a well-shuffled deck of cards (which has a sample space of 52) is 1/52 or 0.01923076923.

[3] *Not Replacing Generated Events*

Something interesting happens to the probability of an event if an event is removed from the sample space after it has been generated. In the case of a shuffled deck of cards from which one seeks to select a specific predetermined card, this is achieved by not replacing a card drawn from a deck after drawing it.

Note how the probability of drawing the desired card changes as the sample space gets smaller (Figure 1.22).

77. Some might argue one should use 'die' as a singular, but some Googling suggests it is now acceptable to use 'dice' as the singular instance as well.

Figure 1.22 Change in Probability in a Shrinking Sample Space

# of cards drawn	Remaining sample space	Probability of drawing the desired card
1	51	1/51 = 0.0196
10	42	1/42 = 0.0238
20	32	1/32 = 0.0312
30	22	1/22 = 0.0454
45	7	1/7 = 0.1428
50	2	1/2 = 0.5000

The critical nuance to appreciate is what happens to the probability of the desired event if generated (or drawn) events are not replaced *and* the desired event is not a specific item in the sample space (such as a card) but is satisfied if one selects (or draws) an event *within a particular range* within the sample space (such as if the desired event is a black card below 5).

Let us explore that question with the example of generating a random number less than or equal to 10 in a sample space of all numbers from 1 to 1,000. It should be obvious that the first attempt at generating a number less than or equal to 10 from a sample space of the first 1,000 numbers is 10/1000 or 0.01.

Note what happens to this probability as more numbers are drawn from the sample space without finding one less than or equal to 10 (Figure 1.23).

Figure 1.23 Probability of Generating a Number in a Subset

Numbers drawn	Remaining sample space	Probability of generating a number less than or equal to 10
1	999	10/999 = 0.01001
10	990	10/990 = 0.0101
100	900	10/900 = 0.0111
300	700	10/700 = 0.0142
500	500	10/500 = 0.0200

As more events are drawn from the sample space, the probability of getting a number less than or equal to 10 steadily increases. There comes a point, usually after a significant number of selections from the sample space, where the probability of finding a number within the desired range becomes close to 1 or a certainty.

[4] A Cryptographic Hash Function Behaves Like a Random Variable

Recall from the discussion of the SHA256 hash function that it generates a 64-bit hash digest (which is a large number in hex format).

It turns out that the hash digest generated by a particular input file behaves very much like a random variable. In other words, the likelihood of generating a particular hash digest number within the SHA256 sample space is for all intents and purposes *equal* for all numbers within that space.

The input to the hashing function can be changed by adding a nonce to the input data and changing it (for instance, by incrementing it) after each hash. This will generate a new unique – and random – hash digest each time (Figure 1.24).

Figure 1.24 Different Nonces Generate Different Hash Digests

Data	**Nonce**	**SHA256 hash digest**
This is some text we are hashing		a2d973f3bf58343a27a3d3f95704b9567d7e534af876c575db5d450ea5e277d3
This is some text we are hashing	1	30c6f072dd5dc63871ee254f994a3ed52f2c1e4a2545910aa288ccca03831b2d
This is some text we are hashing	2	dc275df4716b2c207cb06cb4a2e7809bfdfc6c9ad4cedf45f3482327b3e40f3e
This is some text we are hashing	3	c3da9d7ceab0d66a20b1e290db1af09115f63e7370a1924e8e9d63837506b38a
This is some text we are hashing	4	7425946654639d5c6719620e64e46ba0221875ddfb198878627b1de9bdb25bd8
This is some text we are hashing	5	c3e6f7c957240b39750653863a53b38908b0f730fd4184671f0d858b0914c53f
This is some text we are hashing	6	427e922f9af5b0586268e867323ac6d71e087881b53e2c2b9b957a7197a8a76c

The sample space for the SHA256 hash digest is *very* large: it comprises all numbers between 0 and 2^{256}, a number with seventy-eight digits.[78]

The current hash rate of the Bitcoin network is around 100 million trillion[79] hashes per second. Even if that network was committed solely to generating all possible hashes for SHA256, it would still take *trillions* of years to do so. The likelihood of generating a *specific number* as a hash digest for a particular input file with a changing nonce is very unlikely.

Recall that with a random variable, as the sample space gets smaller, the probability of generating a specific event increases consistently. It goes without saying that at some point – as the sample space gets smaller – the desired event will be generated (assuming it is possible to generate all possible events within a reasonable amount of time).

As noted, with SHA256, this is not feasible if one is looking for a single number. However, if instead the task is to find a hash digest *below a certain value*, in other words, within a small subset of the sample space, then the time required to find a valid hash digest decreases to reasonable levels.

It is this correlation between computational capacity and the size of the subset of the sample space which Proof of Work exploits.

The core idea is to force the commitment of significant computational resources to the finding of a particular hash value (and its associated nonce), which is predictable to take a certain amount of time, so as to impose a *time cost* on adding a new wagon to the train or block to the blockchain.

78. 2^{256} is 115,792,089,237,316,195,423,570,985,008,687,907,853,269,984,665,640,564,039,457, 584,007,913,129,639,936.
79. 100,000,000 x 10^{12} or 100,000,000,000,000,000,000.

[5] Requiring a Hash Value Below a Certain Value

It turns out that it is possible to estimate – with a great deal of certainty – how long a computational resource (in terms of trillions of hashes per second in the case of the Bitcoin network) will take to find a hash value below a certain threshold value using the above 'change the nonce' process repeatedly.

It is also then quite easy to adjust that threshold to keep that time requirement reasonably constant should the computational capacity to hash (the hash rate) change.[80]

Satoshi Nakamoto decided that this time constant should be around 10 minutes and developed a formula for calculating this difficulty threshold (the number below which the hash digest must be, also known as the *target hash*) every 2,016 blocks (or every two weeks) based on the hash rate of the Bitcoin network.

In the Bitcoin blockchain, the hashing difficulty has steadily grown, although it has seen some dips, particularly when the price of Bitcoin falls significantly. At the time of writing of the first edition of this book, its value (on 3 October 2019) was 12,759,819,404,409.[81] By December 2023, it had risen to 72,006,146,478,567.

This number can also be understood as how many times more difficult it is to find a number below the threshold than to generate any hash value in SHA256's sample space.

As of October 2019, the target hash for Bitcoin required a successful hash digest to have at least 18 leading zeroes, like this one for block 597707:

000000000000000000110 bbc354868a8849aa01ff271877500e0e2aa869c69f

By December 2023, a successful hash digest required at least 20 leading zeroes, like this one for block 823285:

00000000000000000000 da8bacc152a5c084809de66bed20f60fa55d7e947c96

[C] The Proof of Work Process

Taking advantage of the predictable time within which one is highly certain to find a hash digest below the target hash, it is now possible to proceed as follows:

(1) Set the target hash consistent with ten minutes of computation to find a valid hash digest below the target hash.
(2) Take a data set (in our case, a series of transactions and the hash digest from the previous block) and combine it with a nonce value.
(3) Submit this to the SHA256 algorithm and examine the hash digest:

80. Given that these two variables are correlated.
81. The current difficulty level is available at: https://www.coinwarz.com/difficulty-charts/bitcoin-difficulty-chart (accessed 10 Jan. 2024).

(a) If the hash digest is above the target hash, change the nonce and repeat step 2 (remember that after about ten minutes of this, one is highly likely to have found a winning hash).

(b) If the hash digest is below the target hash, then eureka! – the Proof of Work is considered complete (what happens after that will be discussed further below).

Note what this process does for the immutability of the blockchain.

First, the ability to verify the various hashes of the data to confirm the integrity of the blockchain is not affected. Recalculating a few hashes and comparing them is a trivial exercise, and it is easy to recalculate all hashes in all blocks in the blockchain within a reasonable amount of time.

Second, falsifying and recalculating the whole blockchain has now become prohibitively difficult. If one wanted to change a transaction in a block, a recalculation would now take ten minutes *per block*. The further back a block is in the blockchain, the more time it will take to recalculate it and thus the more secure it becomes. Note that if one wanted to change the blockchain from a very early block in the blockchain onwards, it would take about as much time as the age of that block.[82]

[1] A Note on Nonces

On the Bitcoin blockchain, the nonce field, maintained in the block header, is 32 bits long. A variable of that length has about 4 billion permutations. The block timestamp changes every second. This means that if a node can perform more than 4 billion hashes per second, which is very likely with some of the dedicated hashing hardware now available, the nonce runs out of steam in being able to generate unique hash values for the block in question. This is known as 'nonce exhaustion'.

In order to address this problem, a second nonce, known as the *extranonce*, is added when required by exploiting some extra space in the coinbase field[83] usually reserved for notes or other arbitrary data.

It should now be clear how a blockchain creates and maintains immutability of the blocks of transactions it contains. The next step towards a complete understanding of the blockchain is an appreciation of how it maintains the internal consistency of the transactional data itself. This is of course critically important if a blockchain is used for tracking such things as cryptocurrency balances for their owners.

82. Admittedly recalculating the earlier blocks would take less time today than it took when these were initially created, as the target hash was much larger then, given the much lower hashing rate of the network.

83. The coinbase field is the first transaction in a blockchain block, and it includes the block reward (discussed *infra*).

§1.07 TRANSACTIONS ON THE BITCOIN BLOCKCHAIN

Ownership of a Bitcoin on the Bitcoin blockchain is stored as a confirmed entitlement entry somewhere in the blockchain. This entitlement entry is called a *transaction*, and it has several components:

- A link to a previous transaction or transactions in the blockchain which hold certain entitlement amounts which are the source for the entitlement created in the particular transaction at hand. These are referred to as the *inputs* to the new transaction (and as *outputs* from the old transaction).
- An encryption mechanism to validate that the person entitled to the output(s) has authorized the transaction.[84] This mechanism is referred to as the Script-PubKey or the *locking script*. Think of the transaction having been digitally signed by the person sending the Bitcoin to someone else.
- The value that the transaction holds, to be spent/claimed by the new holder in a future transaction. As noted, this value is referred to as the *output* of the transaction.
- A unique identifier called a TXID (Transaction ID), which is created by hashing the transaction data (above) twice with the SHA256 cryptographic hash function.[85] It is this TXID by which a subsequent transaction will identify this transaction as an input.

Note that the blockchain transaction does not store any information about the person who holds the entitlement. Also, the transaction data in the Bitcoin blockchain is not encrypted and is easily viewable by anyone.[86]

[A] Bitcoin Scripting

It is possible to impose some limited decision-making logic upon transactions on the Bitcoin blockchain, for instance, to require the authorization of a transaction by a third party. These are referred to as 'scripted transactions'. A control which assigns spending authority to multiple persons in that manner is referred to as a *multi-signature* transaction.[87]

---

84. These are configurable in any of a number of different ways, incorporating quite complex logic if desired.
85. Recall that this will generate a unique ID, given the highly reliable collision resistance of SHA256. A quirky bug of the Bitcoin blockchain places this ID on the blockchain in reverse order, which necessitates that one search for the reverse of the TXID to find it. Most transaction search tools make this requirement opaque to the user.
86. The suggestion by some that the Bitcoin blockchain is encrypted is thus incorrect, and it is usually a clear indication that the person suggesting the same does not have a full understanding of how the Bitcoin blockchain works.
87. This functionality becomes very useful in the use of sidechains, as will be discussed in section §1.18[B], *infra*.

[B] Entitlement Tracking

All bitcoin entitlement arises because of one or more transactions which have been previously committed to the blockchain. Entitlement entries can thus be traced back - through time - to some point when new entitlement was created for the first time. On the Bitcoin blockchain, such new entitlement, i.e. new Bitcoin, is created as a result of the *mining reward*, discussed *infra*.

In order to make this sequential entitlement tracking process work properly, it is necessary to explicitly track any residual entitlement if an amount *less than the output* entitlement from a specific transaction existing in the blockchain is being transmitted to another person. To illustrate this nuance, assume Jim has an output transaction on the blockchain with a value of 0.5 BTC, and he wishes to transmit 0.1 BTC of that to Larry. To properly record this activity, *two* output transactions need to be created: one to transmit 0.1 BTC to Larry and another to transmit 0.4 BTC *back* to Jim (this can be thought of as the 'change' one might receive in a store when paying for a small item with a bill larger than the cost).[88]

Once a transaction's outputs have been claimed as inputs for future transactions, that transaction is deemed to have been 'spent' to guard against double spending.

Any transaction which has an unclaimed output is known as an *Unspent Transaction Output* or UTXO.

[C] The UTXO Database

The UTXO database is maintained alongside the Bitcoin blockchain to keep track of all currently available unspent outputs on the Bitcoin blockchain. This separate database is necessary to maintain an appropriate level of efficiency in processing transactions. Having to retrieve outputs from the blockchain every time one wants to verify an output entitlement would require a full read-through of the ever-growing blockchain file (which at the time of writing of the second edition was well in excess of 500 GB) which is prohibitively difficult and time-consuming to do.[89]

[D] Wallets

As noted, every transaction stored on the blockchain is tracked according to the public keys of the parties sending and receiving a Bitcoin entitlement. The key to effecting and securing transactions on a blockchain is the use and safeguarding of the corresponding private key.

88. On the Bitcoin network if this second transaction is not created, any change is claimed as a transaction fee, and thus effectively lost to its holder.
89. The UTXO database stores this data and indexes it for easy access in a file of about 3 to 4 GB.

Safeguarding the private key is important. Several options are available:

- Memorize 'seed phrases' which can be used to generate the key.[90]
- Write the private key on a piece of paper and store it in a secure place.
- Store the private key on a USB-based 'hardware wallet'.
- Store the private key in wallet software, which runs on a computer, mobile device or in a browser online.
- Provide the key to a custodian for safekeeping (many exchanges provide this service as part of their account creation and maintenance services).

When using a third-party wallet application, be it standalone or as part of the offering of an exchange account, the process generally works as follows, from a user's perspective:

- Download and instal any required wallet software. This usually involves securing it with a strong password and generating a backup of the wallet's recovery seed.
- 'Fund' the wallet by adding entitlement on a blockchain. This can usually be done by adding the public key of an existing entitlement, or purchasing new entitlement through the wallet, usually with fiat currency.
- Once funded, a wallet can be used to conduct transactions. Transactions will require the provision of details, including the recipient's address, an amount, and the setting of a cap on the transaction fee. Most wallets will have features to permit the user to review and confirm a transaction before submitting it.
- Once submitted, the wallet application will broadcast the transaction to the applicable blockchain network for addition to the memory pool (discussed in more detail *infra*).
- The wallet software will then usually monitor the blockchain for confirmation that the transaction has been processed and added to the blockchain, at which point the transaction is deemed confirmed, and will be so reflected in the wallet application.

Given a basic understanding of how the Bitcoin blockchain protects against tampering as well as how it ensures internal integrity of the various balances recorded, the next step is to explore how this all works in a distributed P2P network. This raises some new issues which require some additional ingenuity to resolve.

90. *See*, for example, https://iancoleman.io/bip39/ (accessed 15 Dec. 2023).

§1.08 THE DISTRIBUTED BLOCKCHAIN

[A] The Bitcoin Network

The Bitcoin network is made up of thousands of computers connected together over the internet. As in many other P2P networks, each of these computers is referred to as a *node*.[91]

Every node runs a copy of the Bitcoin blockchain software[92] which allows it to do a couple of things (among other administrative stuff) in relation to the Bitcoin blockchain:

- Maintain a copy of the Bitcoin blockchain file[93] and verify and add new blocks to that copy.
- Maintain a copy of the UTXO database to verify that transactions have the required inputs to be added to the blockchain.
- Grab transactions from the *memory pool* (explained below) to create a candidate block.
- Repeatedly hash a candidate block (with an included nonce) to try, and find a hash digest below the target hash.

The general 'workflow' within the Bitcoin network is as follows:

(1) A person holding some amount of Bitcoin submits a transaction to (a node of) the Bitcoin network for confirmation to the blockchain.
(2) The transaction is verified as valid (i.e., the outputs have valid inputs, and it complies with the various formatting requirements and a bunch of other constraints).
(3) The transaction is added to a 'transaction holding area' called the *memory pool*.
(4) The various computers (nodes) in the Bitcoin P2P network each select a group of (different) transactions from the memory pool to fill a new block, called a *candidate block*, which that node is going to try to add to the blockchain.

---

91. On the Bitcoin network, there are different kinds of nodes which perform different aspects of the workflow of the network. A node which can do all the different processes is referred to as a full node. To keep things simple, a reference to a node here means a full node.
92. Which is available as open source, *see* https://bitcoin.org/en/download (accessed 10 Jan. 2024).
    The open-source availability of the Bitcoin code has given rise to many 'copycat' cryptocurrencies which function largely the same way as Bitcoin with minor adjustments to certain parameters. The best example of this is likely Litecoin, *see* https://litecoin.org/ (accessed 10 Jan. 2024).
93. Which as of the writing of the second edition of this chapter was approaching 540 GB in size. It grows by approximately 150 MB per day or around 1 GB each week.

(5) Nodes then compete to be the first to find a hash digest below the target hash for their candidate block.[94] This hash digest finding exercise is commonly referred to as *mining*.
(6) The first node to find a valid hash digest broadcasts that fact, as well as a copy of the candidate block used to find it (including the nonce), to all other nodes on the network.
(7) The other nodes very quickly verify[95] that the block transactions and the hash digest are valid, and if so add this block to their copy of the blockchain.
(8) Once 51 % of all active nodes on the network have confirmed the validity of the block in this manner, the block is considered to be officially confirmed on the blockchain, and the official ledger embodied in the blockchain is expanded to now include the transactions in this latest block.[96] This critical step, together with the initial transaction validation (which prevents selecting an input which has already been spent), avoids running into the *double spending problem* (covered in more detail *infra*). Sometimes a winning hash is found by two nodes at almost the same time, which leads to groups of nodes accepting different new blocks into their version of the blockchain (there are rules for resolving this, discussed *infra*).
(9) The winning node gets a reward for finding the winning hash value. This value was 'pre-recorded' at the beginning of the winning block (at the time of its composition before the mining process was started) in what is known as the *coinbase transaction*.[97]
(10) As soon as a node accepts a new block on its blockchain, it will discard any block it was working on and select a new set of transactions from the memory pool and start the process at step 3 above anew. (This can lead to some issues if a node quickly finds a subsequent valid block connected to a prior valid block which it has added to its blockchain, but which has not (yet) been accepted by 51 % of the network and may by then conflict with another blockchain version on the network. How this is resolved is discussed in the Adding a Mined Block section *infra*.)
(11) When all nodes on the network have converged to a common longest blockchain, there is then deemed consensus about the confirmation of the included transactions.

A closer examination of some of these components is helpful.

94. To be clear, every node's candidate block contains a unique set of different transactions obtained from that node's memory pool.
95. Remember, it only takes one execution of the hash algorithm to confirm.
96. This is a bit of an oversimplification of this process. *See* the heading called 'Adding a Mined Block' for more detail.
97. Or generation transaction. Transaction fees, discussed below, are also tracked here. There is a specific place in the block for this transaction.

[B] The Memory Pool

The memory pool is a database which contains transactions received by a node from Bitcoin holders who are looking to have these transactions confirmed on the blockchain. The memory pool is like a 'waiting room' for transactions.

There are rules about which transactions should be selected first. Transactions which refer to older outputs on the blockchain or which transfer larger amounts are prioritized.

This waiting room also has a priority queue, in that bitcoin holders who want to have their transactions chosen for inclusion in a candidate block can incentivize the node to pick their transaction by including a transaction fee (more on that below).

[C] Adding a Mined Block

The primary rule by which the main blockchain is maintained is that it must be the chain of blocks of transactions which has the *highest amount of cumulative difficulty*[98] associated with it. This usually matches the chain with the highest number of blocks, but not always. Things can get a bit challenging if several blocks are successfully mined by different nodes at almost the same time.

In order to handle this effectively, a node may, in addition to a block recently added to its copy of the blockchain, maintain additional blocks which have been successfully mined in that they also validly extend the local copy of the blockchain but have not (yet) been confirmed by a majority of the nodes. These blocks may have been received from other nodes.

These different paths for growing the blockchain are referred to as *secondary chains*. If a block mined after a block in a secondary chain causes the cumulative difficulty to be the highest, then that will result in a change in the official blockchain – as maintained by that node – within the two latest blocks of the official blockchain. The node will then start selecting new candidate blocks to proceed from this new longest blockchain onwards.

It may also happen that mined blocks are received out of order, in that an intermediate block is missing. This is usually the case if the previous block hash digest reference in the received block is non-existent in the blockchain. A node will hold on to these 'orphan' blocks for a few block mining cycles to see if the missing block shows up. If it does, it will assess whether its inclusion changes its 'greatest difficulty' version of the blockchain.

The creation of such alternate potential longest chains within the Bitcoin network is known as 'forking' of the blockchain.[99] In the Bitcoin network, forks of the length of one block occur somewhat regularly, but to date, they have all resolved with the receipt

98. Think of this in terms of total computational cost for all the blocks so far, which is essentially the sum of the difficulties of each of the blocks.

99. There are blockchain forks which are more consequential as a result of software upgrades to the blockchain software. *See* the discussion under Blockchain Forks, section §1.09, *infra*.

of the following block, which then causes the blockchain to converge to a common stable version.

There is a relationship between the incidence of forks and the length of the confirmation time dictated by the Proof of Work for a particular blockchain: the shorter (in terms of time) that the required Proof of Work time cost is, the higher the likelihood of forks occurring. This has been one of the considerations weighing against the desire by some to shorten the Proof of Work time requirement of Bitcoin in order to speed up the confirmation time of transactions.

[D] The Double Spending Problem

The double spending problem is a potential issue in distributed digital record-keeping systems. One can foresee the possibility of double spending where a distributed ledger, without an effective method for achieving consistency among all the versions of the ledger, may permit the spending of an entitlement multiple times by repeating a transaction on an older (non-updated) version of the ledger.

In a traditional physical cash system, double spending is not an issue because once one hands over a physical coin, one no longer possesses it, making it impossible to spend it twice.

A fundamental challenge in creating a distributed ledger without a centralized authority is solving the double spending problem. It should be evident by now that three core aspects of the distributed Bitcoin blockchain process effectively eliminate[100] any chance of double spending:

(1) The validation of unspent entitlement (an unspent output on the blockchain) before any transaction is even considered for addition to the ledger.
(2) The forward-embedded cryptographic hash digest tracking system which ensures that the ledger data is verifiably immutable.
(3) The Proof of Work barrier to prevent someone from going back and redoing number 2.

[E] The Mining Reward

As noted, every successfully mined block accepted by 51% of the nodes creates a new entitlement to bitcoin, usually claimed by the owner of the successful node.

This reward is recorded in a special section of the winning block called the *generation* or *coinbase transaction*. Because this entitlement is created out of nothing, it does not have a pointer to a previous output transaction on the blockchain.

100. But not absolutely. *See* the section on the 51% attack, §1.08[G], *infra*.

The coinbase transaction has some features of note:

- It has a place for the mining node to insert notes. As previously noted, mining nodes now use this area to store an additional nonce for the purpose of pursuing a Proof of Work hash digest.
- This space is also sometimes used to identify that a block was mined by a group of miners. Other miners have used it for all kinds of (sometimes bizarre) messages.[101]
- A block reward cannot be spent for 100 blocks (or around sixteen hours). This is to ensure that a potential blockchain fork does not invalidate the entitlement.

The Bitcoin reward halves every 210,000 blocks or about every four years. In 2009, when the Bitcoin blockchain was started, this reward was 50 bitcoin. This was halved to 25 bitcoin in November 2012 and halved again in July 2016 and May 2020.[102] At the time of writing of this second edition, the reward stands at 6.25 bitcoin, with the next halving anticipated to take place in April 2024.

[F] Mining Pools

As the price of bitcoin started to increase in 2011, more and more individuals and organizations became interested in mining bitcoin for profit. This, in turn, grew the pool of nodes as well as the global hashing power of the Bitcoin network.

This hashing race was fuelled even more in 2013 with the development of hardware specifically designed to perform very high rates of block hashing.[103]

In order to yet further improve their chances of finding the winning hash first, many node operators joined forces by establishing mining pools, through which they coordinated the mining of new blocks at ever increasing hashing speeds. Mining pools distribute mining rewards to their various participants using a methodology usually specified in the mining pool membership agreement.

Many of these mining pools are made up of hundreds of thousands of participants all over the world. Commercial mining pools, or hashing farms, started to enter the network after 2013 as well. By 2013, it had become quite unrealistic for an individual miner to expect to be able to compete against these mining pools and find a winning hash with any probability.

A further effect of the creation of mining pools is a degree of re-centralization of the Bitcoin nodes within the network, particularly in the case of larger mining pools with centralized decision-making.

101. Explore: http://www.bitcoinstrings.com/ (accessed 10 Jan. 2024), to see these messages.
102. This halving will continue until 2140 at which time no more bitcoin will be created, at least according to the current rules.
103. The processors used by these 'mining rigs' are called *Application Specific Integrated Circuits* or ASICs.

[G] The 51 % Attack

Given that it takes a 51 % majority of miners to confirm the longest Bitcoin blockchain, this also means – in theory – that this same majority can compromise that blockchain. Such a group could exploit the rule that the longest/most difficult chain is the valid one by creating intentional forks of longer length than – say – the last 4 or 5 blocks of the blockchain, thereby undoing what would otherwise be an irreversible set of transactions. This longer chain would then be adopted as the correct blockchain by virtue of this foundational Bitcoin blockchain principle.

A theoretical malicious actor, who had access to 51 % of the hash capacity of the Bitcoin blockchain, could thus cause his or her previously confirmed payment to another person to be redirected or reversed or introduce double spend transactions into the blockchain going forward.

A 51 % attack's likelihood of succeeding diminishes significantly as the transactions being sought to be manipulated are further back in the blockchain.

It is not actually necessary to have 51 % of the hashing power to be able to successfully execute this type of attack (although at 51 % such an attempt is *guaranteed* to succeed). Some suggest as little as 30 % will do the trick.[104]

The chance of a 51 % attack succeeding on the Bitcoin blockchain, given the size of the network and volume of miners, is highly unlikely but cannot be ruled out. The fact that much of the hashing power is now increasingly centralized with a small group of hashing farms/pools does not abate this risk.

In the case of a smaller or differently constructed blockchain, this risk may be much higher, as has been evident from several such attacks on smaller cryptocurrencies.[105] Most notably, the Ethereum Classic blockchain appears to have been the victim of a 51 % type of attack in January 2019.[106]

Much like any complex computer-based system, a blockchain has a number of other potential vulnerabilities at the various stages of its workflow life cycle, which are beyond the scope of this chapter.[107]

§1.09 BLOCKCHAIN FORKS

The software which runs on the nodes of a blockchain network is updated from time to time to add new features or to make changes in how the blockchain functions.

---

104. Available at: https://www.oreilly.com/library/view/mastering-bitcoin/9781491902639/ch08.html (accessed 10 Jan. 2024).
105. Saad M., et al., *Exploring the Attack Surface of Blockchain: A Systematic Overview* (arXiv preprint arXiv:1904.03487, 2019), available at: https://arxiv.org/pdf/1904.03487.pdf (accessed 10 Jan. 2024).
106. https://bravenewcoin.com/insights/etc-51-attack-what-happened-and-how-it-was-stopped (accessed 10 Jan. 2024).
107. *See* Saad et al., *supra* n. 97, at note 64; Chen, H., et al., *A Survey on Ethereum Systems Security: Vulnerabilities, Attacks and Defenses* (arXiv preprint arXiv:1908.04507, 2019), available at: https://arxiv.org/pdf/1908.04507.pdf (accessed 10 Jan. 2024); Alkhalifah, A., et al., *A Taxonomy of Blockchain Threats and Vulnerabilities*, available at: https://www.preprints.org/manuscript/201909.0117/v1/download (accessed 10 Jan. 2024).

These code changes are considered adopted when a majority of nodes on the network instal and start using an updated version of the blockchain software. These code updates or changes to the blockchain code are referred to as *forks* (Figure 1.25).

Figure 1.25 A Blockchain Fork

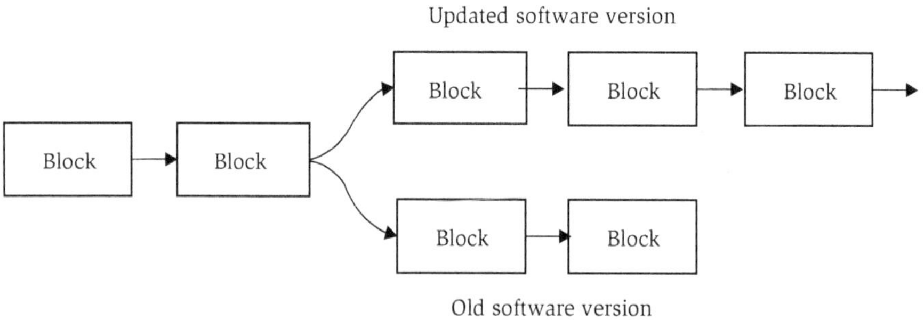

There are two types of forks with different impacts on the blockchain.

[A] The Soft Fork

Updates which are backwards compatible with prior versions of the blockchain software are known as *soft forks*. A node running an old version of the software will still be able to submit transactions and participate in the blockchain but may not benefit from some of the new features offered by the newer blockchain software version. Nodes on a blockchain usually seek to instal updated software for that reason.

[B] The Hard Fork

Blockchain software updates which are *not* backwards compatible with older versions of the blockchain software are called *hard forks*.

Hard fork changes are usually significant and change fundamental aspects of how a blockchain functions, such as the block size, hashing algorithm used, or how consensus is reached.

In some cases, the blockchain running on the older version of the software, or rather, the persons behind the nodes who may disagree with the rationale for the hard fork or the effects of it, may break off and continue as a separate blockchain. This event is referred to as a *contentious hard fork*. The 2016 DAO hack[108] of the Ethereum network resulted in a contentious hard fork after a large number of node owners disagreed with a rollback of the blockchain in order to reclaim a large amount of

108. The SEC report on its investigation of the DAO gives a good overview of this event, available at: https://www.sec.gov/litigation/investreport/34-81207.pdf (accessed 10 Jan. 2024).

ether[109] lost due to the hack. As a result, Ethereum split into two blockchains: Ethereum and Ethereum Classic.

The Bitcoin network has also experienced four hard forks so far, largely as a result of a fundamental agreement over how Bitcoin should function or evolve:

- Bitcoin Cash, which hard forked from Bitcoin at block 478558 on 1 August 2017.
- Bitcoin Gold, which hard forked from Bitcoin at block 491407 on 24 October 2017.
- Bitcoin SV, which hard forked from Bitcoin Cash at block 556766 on 15 November 2018.
- eCash, which hard forked from Bitcoin Cash at block 661648 on 15 November 2020.

A quirk of a contentious hard fork is that anyone having an entitlement in the blockchain before the hard fork will end up with entitlement in *both* blockchains after the hard fork.

A hard fork may also be initiated because of the planned evolution of the blockchain network itself. The Ethereum blockchain software has proceeded, and continues to proceed, along a planned path of soft and hard forks which makes incremental planned changes to the fundamental functionality of that blockchain.[110]

§1.10 BLOCKCHAIN AS A PLATFORM

[A] Ethereum

Ethereum is a blockchain-based platform which launched in 2015 following Vitalik Buterin's 2013 publication of a white paper laying out its intended functionality.[111]

Ethereum, in addition to being able to track transactions on a blockchain, adds computing functionality to the blockchain by creating the ability to also store program code on the blockchain and then being able to run that code within the Ethereum network to manipulate the state of variables stored on the blockchain. Ethereum thus seeks to implement the blockchain as a distributed computer.

The cryptocurrency used on the Ethereum platform is called *ether*.[112] The Ethereum platform also uses another cryptocurrency called *gas*[113] for the purpose of providing 'fuel' to contract accounts on Ethereum.

109. The Ethereum cryptocurrency, *see* section §1.10.
110. https://ethereum.org/en/history/ (accessed 15 Dec. 2023).
111. https://www.weusecoins.com/assets/pdf/library/Ethereum_white_paper-a_next_generation_smart_contract_and_decentralized_application_platform-vitalik-buterin.pdf (accessed 10 Jan. 2024).
112. There is a whole hierarchy of terms for various quantities of ether: https://www.wallstreetmojo.com/gwei/ (accessed 10 Jan. 2024).
113. The exchange rate from ether to gas can be viewed at: https://coincodex.com/convert/gas/ethereum/ (accessed 10 Jan. 2024).

In general terms, the Ethereum blockchain worked very much like the Bitcoin blockchain up until 15 September 2022 (when it moved to a Proof-of-Stake consensus approach[114]), with a few notable differences:

- The Ethereum block confirmation time was around 15 seconds, compared to 10 minutes for Bitcoin.
- Ethereum did not use a UTXO approach to tracking transactions and entitlement but rather uses something called *state transitions*. State transitions are discussed further below.
- The Ethereum mining reward was relatively constant and did not halve on a schedule like Bitcoin. The block reward hovered around two ether per block.
- The Ethereum Proof of Work used a different hashing function called *Ethash*. The Ethash function has evolved since 2015 and incorporated a Proof-of-Stake scheme every fifty blocks, designed to thwart the effect of ASIC-based mining rigs gaining too strong a foothold in the Ethereum mining ecosystem.
- The Ethereum blockchain has no block size limit. Instead, it has a 'gas' limit.

[1] Gas: Limiting How Long a Program Can Run

A poorly written piece of code running forever on a blockchain-based distributed computer has to be avoided, as it would grind the whole system to a halt.[115] This is a significant problem, as it is not possible to determine generally, based on a program's code and the input to that code, whether a program will execute and stop or whether it may run on forever.[116]

The simple solution to this problem is to automatically terminate any code or program which runs out of a predefined resource associated with that particular code or program. On the Ethereum platform, this solution is implemented by requiring every computational transaction to have a certain amount of computational fuel, or *gas*, associated with it, which terminates execution if it runs out before the program has finished running.[117] The downside of this approach is that a program which has run out of gas will end execution and will not result in any state change to the blockchain.

Every Ethereum transaction must be accompanied by gas for this purpose. The benefit of the use of gas goes to the mining nodes as payment for their work in confirming the transaction.

---

114. *See* the section on Proof of Stake, *infra*.
115. This is particularly so in the case of Ethereum, which cannot execute code in parallel but only in series, one program, or smart contract, after another.
116. This is known as the Halting Problem, which was conclusively proven (using a contradiction proof) by Alan Turing in 1936.
117. A program's gas cost depends on how the logic inside it executes. Some code sections or components may be more expensive to run than others.

[2] An Ethereum Transaction

An Ethereum transaction has the following components:

- An *Ethereum address* to which the transaction is being sent.
- A *digital signature* confirming that the transaction emanates from a valid Ethereum account.
- A sequence number called a *nonce* but with a different purpose than the Proof of Work process used by the Bitcoin blockchain. On the Ethereum blockchain, a nonce is a running sequential number reflecting the series of transactions confirmed for the digitally signed destination, i.e., Ethereum address. This number helps ensure that transactions sent are processed (executed) in the order intended by the sender and that every transaction is unique.[118]
- A *gas price*, which is the exchange rate the sender is willing to pay to get gas for the transaction, expressed in an amount of ether per gas unit.
- A *gas limit*, which is the maximum gas the sender is prepared to buy to have the transaction processed. The sender of the transaction must have a credit balance in excess of the amount of ether this represents in order for the transaction to be processed.
- A *value*, which is the amount of ether being sent.
- *Data*, or the variable references and values to be used by any contract to which the transaction has been sent.

Given the very short block confirmation time of Ethereum, it is almost impossible to cancel an Ethereum transaction once it has been submitted to the memory pool. One strategy which may be successful in a rare case is the very fast resubmission of a transaction with more gas using the same nonce.[119]

Multi-signature transactions are implemented with a smart contract (explained *infra*) which contains code requiring incoming transactions from all authorizing signatories before completing a particular transaction.

[3] Ethereum Transaction Account Types

Activity on the Ethereum blockchain is tracked through two types of accounts:

(1) Externally Owned Accounts (EOA).
(2) Contract accounts.

118. The Ethereum network code checks that any new transaction arriving and about to be processed is the next in line from the Ethereum address referenced in that transaction, by comparing its nonce to the last nonce associated with that address on the blockchain.
119. Similar strategies for cancelling a memory pool submitted bitcoin transaction exist, which involve submitting another transaction to the memory pool with a higher fee.

[a] The EOA

An EOA is similar to a Bitcoin 'user account'[120] in that it is comprised of a public-private key pair which provides a means to access ether entitlement, as well as manage and run code stored on the Ethereum blockchain.

Ethereum tracks entitlements in a different way from Bitcoin. Instead of the Bitcoin UTXO model, Ethereum uses an *account state* model, which is essentially a running balance associated with a particular public key address that is updated as transactions are processed and confirmed on the Ethereum blockchain.[121]

[b] The Contract Account

A contract account is an account, referenced by its public address, which contains executable program code. It is created as a special type of transaction sent to the Ethereum blockchain *zero address*. This address can only be used as a destination in a transaction which seeks to add a new contract account to the Ethereum blockchain.

Programs stored on the Ethereum blockchain in this manner are usually referred to as 'smart contracts'. These programs are then accessed by sending a transaction containing data to the new contract account's public address. The contract is then executed via the Ethereum Virtual Machine or EVM.

[4] The Ethereum Virtual Machine

As noted previously, a virtual machine is a 'runtime environment' which acts as a bridge between a specific programming language and the hardware and architecture on which code in that programming language is sought to be executed.

The EVM works in the same way, except that there is no underlying hardware or operating system where code and data are stored and manipulated. With Ethereum, all of that is done using the computational capacity of the nodes on the network and the code and data stored on the blockchain.

The EVM does require that the program code be in a particular form of bytecode which it can interpret. It is this bytecode that is stored on the blockchain inside the smart contract.

---

120. As previously discussed, Bitcoin does not really have 'user accounts' in the traditional sense, given that it only requires a public-private key pair to participate.
121. It should be noted that in the event a transaction references a public key address not previously referenced on the blockchain, a new EOA account is 'opened' and the incoming balance recorded and added to the public key address identified in the transaction. If this happens as a result of having entered the public key address in error, any ether contained in the transaction is lost, once confirmed, as there exists no corresponding private key with which to update the account.

[B] Other Platforms

Since the launch and success of Ethereum, a number of other smart contract-capable platforms have emerged. Of these, Solana, Cardano, and Binance Smart Chain are the current primary players. These platforms generally work in a similar manner as Ethereum with certain differences in the choice in consensus mechanism (the various types of these are discussed in more detail *infra*) and other adjustments to improve the number of transactions capable of being processed.

A brief summary of the approaches taken by each of these platforms follows.

Solana uses a unique Proof-of-History (PoH) (further discussed below) combined with Proof-of-Stake (PoS) consensus mechanism, which aims to enable a high transaction processing rate as well as low transaction costs. Solana supports smart contracts through its Solana Program Library (SPL) and is compatible with the Ethereum EVM.

Cardano uses a Proof-of-Stake (PoS) consensus mechanism[122] called *Ouroboros*, which is touted as being energy efficient. Cardano is built in layers, separating the ledger (the Cardano Settlement Layer) from the computation layer (the Cardano Computation Layer). Cardano also supports smart contracts written for the Ethereum blockchain by way of its 'Ethereum Virtual Machine – Cardano Compatible' (EVM-CC) functionality. This compatibility is achieved through a sidechain that actually runs the Ethereum Virtual Machine but settles contracts on the Cardano blockchain.

Binance Smart Chain (BSC) uses a delegated Proof-of-Stake (DPoS) consensus mechanism,[123] where a limited number of nodes are chosen to validate transactions. BSC touts high transaction throughput and low fees as its distinguishing features. BSC has native compatibility for smart contracts written for the Ethereum blockchain.

§1.11 SMART CONTRACTS

Smart contracts on the Ethereum blockchain, or any of the similar implementations referenced above,[124] are simply bits of computer code committed to (i.e., stored on) the Ethereum or other smart contract-capable blockchain.[125] Notwithstanding their name, they are neither smart nor legal contracts.[126]

122. Discussed in more detail below.
123. Again, discussed in more detail below.
124. There is not a great deal of difference in the core structure of what a smart contract is and how it is generally implemented in a particular blockchain. Some use different programming languages and have some additional features, but a good understanding of how smart contracts work in Ethereum readily translates to an understanding of an implementation in another blockchain platform, as it may relate to its legal implications.
125. Which cannot be changed, other than by replacing it with a new 'smart contract'.
126. But the term has stuck, nonetheless. This is regrettable as it continues to fuel the perception that smart contracts have certain magical properties when in fact, they are no different than any other computer code. *See also Smart Contracts and 'Code is Law' – Some Additional Considerations*, International Journal of Blockchain Law, Volume 4, December 2022, https://gbbcouncil.org/wp-content/uploads/2022/12/Volume-IV-International-Journal-of-Blockchain-Law.pdf (accessed 10 Jan. 2024).

Smart contracts are a series of programmed steps, like any other computer program, and are not imbued with any specific properties just because they are called 'smart'. The perception by many that these program code snippets have some sort of artificial intelligence capability, particularly now that artificial intelligence applications are increasingly used, is unfortunate.

A smart contract can use a number of programmatic components found in programming languages, such as control structures, data types and certain data structures, discussed previously. A smart contract can also call other smart contracts and pass data to them.

As with any program, a smart contract will execute exactly as it is coded, which does not mean it will necessarily perform the intended functionality of its designer and coder. Smart contracts on the blockchain have bugs, and many have execution errors. If a smart contract is committed to the blockchain with code errors which cause execution to fail or halt, then any desired state changes will not be committed to the blockchain. Any committed gas will, however, be spent.

An Ethereum smart contract can programmatically hold a balance of ether and can also transfer out ether in the same manner.

If the programmer includes certain self-destruction functionality in a smart contract when adding it to the blockchain, then that smart contract can be subsequently deleted, i.e., rendered inoperable. If self-destruction code is not included, an Ethereum smart contract cannot be deleted. Nothing will happen if a transaction is sent to the address of a deleted smart contract.

The available sophistication of smart contracts is significantly limited by the distributed nature of the EVM. Smart contract code simply cannot run as efficiently as it would on a single computer where data is stored in very fast RAM.[127] This severely limits the complexity of smart contracts.

Smart contracts only run when they are 'called' by a particular incoming transaction and always execute sequentially, in the order in which the transactions calling them are added to the blockchain. On all but one platform, two smart contracts cannot be executed in parallel, i.e., run at the same time.

The Solana network has developed a limited capacity to parallelize smart contract execution which it calls SeaLevel. SeaLevel generally functions as follows:[128]

- A mining node determines which accounts are being accessed by each transaction.
- It then builds parallel queues for processing as separate processor threads,[129] ensuring all accounts accessed multiple times are listed sequentially in the same queue.

127. The Ethereum Virtual Machine, currently the most popular platform for smart contracts, has roughly 1/5,000th of the compute power of a Raspberry Pi 4, a $45 utility computer. *See* https://www.usenix.org/publications/loginonline/web3-fraud (accessed 10 Jan. 2024).

128. *See* https://medium.com/solana-labs/sealevel-parallel-processing-thousands-of-smart-contracts-d814b378192 for a more detailed summary of the Solana network features (accessed 12 Dec. 2023).

129. A processor 'thread' is a single sequence of instructions processed together. A computer capable of parallel processing can process multiple threads at the same time.

- Non-overlapping transactions are enabled for separate parallel processing, as is.
- Once so organized, threads are processed by the individual node. All parallelization thus happens on the processor threads in that individual node.

[A] Programming Smart Contracts

Smart contracts can be written in any of several languages before being compiled into bytecode. The most popular language for programming Ethereum contracts is Solidity.[130]

An Ethereum contract program, once compiled, will store information with respect to how a user can interact with the smart contract in a file called the *Application Binary Interface*. This file provides details on the available functionality and required input data for such functionality. In the case of Solidity, this file is generated by the compiler for use by anyone wishing to use a particular smart contract. This file is not stored on the blockchain.

[B] Oracles

In order to maintain the integrity of a distributed blockchain, every piece of code contained in a smart contract stored on the blockchain *must* execute the same exact way each time – in other words, it must give the same result for every node which runs it.

This is not a problem if the variables which are inputs to the code are constant and set out in the transaction. It becomes a problem, however, when:

- the contract code requires some form of randomness, for instance, if the contract codifies a game of chance like a lottery or a card game;
- inputs to the contract vary depending on the time of execution, for instance, as a result of varying prices of a commodity with respect to the sale of which the contract is programmed to perform some function.

Ethereum solves this problem by allowing the creation of trust relationships upon which a smart contract can rely in receiving data from certain external (i.e., off-chain) sources covered by such a trusted relationship. These trusted sources are hard coded, or embedded, in a smart contract. Such hard coding allows the smart contract to retrieve trusted data when required and use it.

Smart contracts which embed trust in external sources are called *oracles*. An oracle ensures that all other executions of the same contract (by other nodes) will use the same inputs for whatever data the oracle is trusted to provide.

130. A derivative of JavaScript. An overview of the language, as well as its code, may be found at: https://github.com/ethereum/solidity (accessed 10 Jan. 2024).

An oracle can update the value it is trusted to provide, for instance, in the case of the price of the commodity, by maintaining a historical list of data values within the contract. If the data being tracked is large, a hash may be stored instead to verify the correctness of any large data set retrieved from a separate 'off-chain' resource.

Oracles may also be used to perform computationally intensive calculations off-chain, for instance, where the gas cost of such computations exceeds the block gas limit.[131]

Oracles are often centralized and therefore a single source of data. It is important that 'trust-ability' be confirmed before incorporating an oracle into a smart contract.

[C] Decentralized Applications

Decentralized applications, or dApps, are smart contracts, or a set of smart contracts, which interact with an off-chain interface to enable applications which users can access, usually through a browser-based interface.

In the case of Ethereum, this can be achieved by installing a browser extension called Metamask.[132] A dApp combines 'on-chain' core functionality of an application (the 'back end') with 'off-chain' interface functionality ('the front end'). The front-end portion of a dApp can, in turn, be maintained on one of several separate distributed networks created for that purpose.[133] Any required dApp messaging can also be off-loaded to yet another distributed network like Whisper.[134]

DApps have been developed to enable blockchain-based application functionality for gaming,[135] token marketplaces[136] and gambling.[137] One of the first popular dApps was Cryptokitties,[138] a game application which allowed users to create and breed digital pet cats. This game went viral for a period of time in late 2017, severely impacting the ability of the Ethereum network to function due to the volume of transactions being submitted to the network. This event exposed a number of Ethereum's functional complexity and scalability limitations.[139]

There now exist numerous Ethereum-like platforms which offer smart contract and dApp functionality, including the previously referenced Binance Smart Chain,[140]

---

131. Which is a number that changes based on the combined input from Ethereum mining nodes, which can change this limit within a certain range. To see the current gas limit, go to: https://etherscan.io/blocks (accessed 10 Jan. 2024) and look for the 'Gas Limit' column.
132. https://metamask.io/ (accessed 10 Jan. 2024). Metamask also functions as a digital wallet.
133. https://ethersphere.github.io/swarm-home/ (accessed 10 Jan. 2024).
134. https://github.com/ethereum/wiki/wiki/Whisper (accessed 10 Jan. 2024).
135. *See*, for example, https://www.mycryptoheroes.net (accessed 10 Jan. 2024).
136. Usually referred to as 'exchanges', which is somewhat problematic as that term is attributed to regulated exchanges in many jurisdictions. *See* the discussion under Initial Coin Offerings, *infra*. An example of an exchange DApp is available at: https://idex.market/eth/idex (accessed 10 Jan. 2024).
137. *See*, for example, https://www.cloudbet.com/ (accessed 11 Jan. 2024).
138. https://www.cryptokitties.co (accessed 10 Jan. 2024).
139. https://spectrum.ieee.org/cryptokitties (accessed 10 Jan. 2024).
140. https://www.bnbchain.org/en/bnb-smart-chain (accessed 10 Jan. 2024).

Solana,[141] and Cardano,[142] as well as EOSIO,[143] NEO,[144] Waves,[145] TRON,[146] and Stratis,[147] among others.

A list of popular dApps is maintained on the DappRadar website.[148]

§1.12 TOKENS ON THE BLOCKCHAIN

The most prevalent use of Ethereum and similar platforms has to date been the creation of *tokens*. Tokens are 'smart contract'-based encapsulated 'entitlement tracking' functionality for a particular purpose.

Contract-based tokens allow the use of a distributed ledger for record-keeping without the necessity to create a new and separate blockchain. Some proposed[149] uses of tokens include the following:

- Tracking entitlement of a virtual medium of exchange (cryptocurrencies).
- Tracking game credits or cloud-storage entitlement.
- Maintaining a digital registry for land titles.
- Keeping an index of birth certificates or marriage data.
- Tracking voting or collecting census data.

Token balances are separate and distinct from ether and gas balances on the Ethereum platform. Token balances are created and stored *within smart contracts* and not explicitly on the Ethereum blockchain, as is the case with ether.

Standards have been developed for the creation of Ethereum tokens at the smart contract level. The most often used standards are ERC-20[150] and ERC-721, discussed in more detail below. Some other standards relating to token smart contracts are:

- ERC-223: Intended to protect against accidental smart contract transfers.
- ERC-809: Used to 'rent' non-fungible tokens.
- ERC-1238: A standard for non-transferable tokens ('badges').

141. https://solana.com/ (accessed 10 Jan 2024).
142. https://cardano.org/ (accessed 10 Jan. 2024).
143. https://eos.io (accessed 11 Jan. 2024).
144. https://neo.org (accessed 11 Jan. 2024).
145. https://wavesplatform.com (accessed 11 Jan. 2024).
146. https://tron.network (accessed 11 Jan. 2024).
147. https://stratisplatform.com (accessed 11 Jan. 2024).
148. https://dappradar.com/rankings (accessed 29 Dec. 2023).
149. Although there is a great deal of enthusiasm about these use cases, actual commercially successful implementations remain elusive.
150. ERC stands for Ethereum Request for Comments. A full list of ERC standards is available at: https://eips.ethereum.org/all (accessed 11 Jan. 2024). An ERC is a step in the process for Ethereum platform improvements. *See* the discussion on Ethereum governance, section §1.13[B] *infra*.

[A] The ERC-20 Token Standard

This standard sets out a minimum set of functionalities which every compliant Ethereum-based token smart contract must have.[151] Every ERC-20 compliant token smart contract must have (among others):[152]

- A *totalSupply* function which returns the total number of tokens in existence.
- A *balanceOf* function which returns the token balance for a particular address.
- A *transfer* function which allows a sender to transfer tokens to a designated address.

An ERC-20-compliant token smart contract will also have the functionality to track information of tokens issued and their ownership through two lists:

(1) Token entitlement by owner.
(2) Delegation of spending authority (an 'allowance') by an owner.

These two lists inform and support two default types of token transactions within the token contract:

(1) Transfers by a person who is a holder of a quantity of tokens within the contract to another person.
(2) Delegated transfers on behalf of a person who is a holder of tokens, to another person.

The second type of transaction enables the exercise of control over token distribution by a centralized entity (such as an Initial Coin Offering (ICO) issuer) or a third-party intermediary (such as a token marketplace[153]).

These functionalities enable a certain level of interoperability between token smart contracts which comply with the standard.

[B] The ERC-721 Token Standard (NFTs)

ERC-721 is the *non-fungible* token (NFT) standard on the Ethereum blockchain.[154] It defines a set of rules and interfaces that enable the creation and management of *unique* digital tokens.

Unlike fungible ERC-20-based tokens, each ERC-721 token is distinct and cannot be exchanged on a one-to-one basis with another token.

---

151. A number of other blockchain platforms have also adopted the ERC-20 token standard for their blockchains.
152. The full specification is available at: https://theethereum.wiki/w/index.php/ERC20_Token_Standard (accessed 11 Jan. 2024).
153. Sometimes referred to as an 'exchange' as noted previously. *See* the discussion with respect to Initial Exchange Offerings, section §1.12[B][3] *infra*.
154. Available at https://eips.ethereum.org/EIPS/eip-721 (accessed 10 Dec 2023).

Key features of the ERC-721 token standard are as follows:

- Each token is unique and can thus represent a distinct digital or physical asset.
- An ERC-721 token cannot be divided into smaller units. Each token represents 'a whole'.
- ERC-721 tokens are transferable (through the *transfer* function specified in the ERC-721 standard).
- ERC-721 tokens can have associated metadata, which provides additional information about the token, such as its name, description, and properties. This metadata is stored off-chain.
- ERC-721 tokens implement a set of standardized functions like *balanceOf*, *ownerOf*, *approve*, *transferFrom*, and others.

ERC-721 tokens have been used to create digital collectibles on a number of different platforms. Some of the more popular implementations include Bored Ape Yacht Club, a collection of images of cartoon apes, which have been algorithmically generated,[155] the similarly constituted Crypto Punks,[156] and the more mainstream NBA Top Shots, a collection of short NBA game video 'moments'.[157]

There also exist several marketplaces for NFTs, with OpenSea[158] currently being the largest.

NFTs that represent digital works, such as art, music, or other media, usually do not, or cannot, store the associated file on the blockchain, given the usually larger size of such a file. NFTs thus function more like a 'certificate of ownership'[159] which points to a web address where the associated file is stored. There is nothing preventing that destination web address from discontinuing the storage of the file, or replacing it with another file, a vulnerability known as 'link rot'.

[C] Crowdfunding on the Blockchain

The most prevalent use of ERC-20-compliant blockchain tokens to date has been as a means of crowdfunding for novel technology-related projects (many of them seeking to leverage blockchain in some new way).

Unlike traditional crowdfunding, tokenized crowdfunding offers the added feature that crowdfunding tokens can – in many cases – be traded on a secondary market almost immediately.[160]

155. https://boredapayechtclub.com/ (accessed 10 Dec. 2023)
156. https://cryptopunks.app/ (accessed 10 Dec. 2023).
157. https://nbatopshot.com/ (accessed 10 Dec. 2023). It must be noted that the 'owner' of an NBA Top Shot 'moment' accrues no intellectual property rights with respect to the video referenced by the NFT. Owning the NFT effectively amounts to 'bragging rights' in the ownership of the NFT, without any actual rights in the underlying media.
158. https://opensea.io/ (accessed 10 Dec. 2023).
159. Although what is actually 'owned' may be little more than the link itself, as opposed to the file, resource or item it points to.
160. Which raises a host of consumer-protection concerns.

This blockchain-based crowdfunding and subsequent secondary trading are done in several slightly different ways. It is helpful to briefly describe each. Their legal implications will be discussed in later chapters.

[1] Initial Coin Offerings

An Initial Coin Offering (ICO) (or Initial Token Offering or ITO) is the process by which a new, usually ERC-20 compliant, token is released for purchase and subsequent trading on a blockchain-based platform like Ethereum.

The ICO process generally[161] works as follows:

- A 'white paper' is prepared detailing the venture with respect to which a token is to be issued for fundraising purposes.
- A smart contract for a token sale is written and added to a tokenization platform like Ethereum.[162]
- A website is created describing the venture and listing the individuals behind the venture. The white paper is also made available for download from this website. The website will also list the period of time during which the ICO will be active, i.e., when tokens may be purchased by sending transactions to the token smart contract.
- The venture may seek the listing of its token on any of several marketplaces or 'exchanges',[163] so as to enable secondary trading after the ICO is completed.
- A promotional campaign is undertaken by advertising the ICO on social media platforms and forums.
- Once the ICO launches, tokens are purchased by sending transactions to the token smart contract.
- After the ICO is completed, tokens may become tradeable if they have been accepted for listing on an exchange. At this point in time, the underlying venture will also take the proceeds from the ICO and use them to fund the venture.[164]

ICOs were very popular between 2017 and 2020, with in excess of 5,000 ICOs being launched. Since that time, and with the emergence of NFT-based projects, the

161. It must be noted that there is no defined ICO process methodology. The enumerated steps are not always followed and then not always in the order set out here.
162. It is possible to launch an ICO completely on its own blockchain and network as well, but this is rarely done given the significantly increased resources required.
163. The use of the term 'exchange' in the context of the trading of tokens is somewhat problematic, given that this term is – in many jurisdictions – a term of art meant to identify a securities marketplace, which after meeting a large set of regulatory requirements is recognized by a regulatory authority as a regulated 'exchange'. In the financial markets, an organization recognized as an exchange carries with it a certain level of professional *gravitas*, which in many cases is not justified in the cryptocurrency and token markets. Nonetheless, the term has stuck, and marketplaces will thus be referred to herein as 'exchanges' for the sake of consistency with the practice in the cryptocurrency space.
164. Which in many cases requires conversion of the proceeds from a cryptocurrency into some sort of fiat currency.

popularity of ICOs has abated, but they are still being launched, albeit at a much lower rate.[165]

A sizable ecosystem continues to exist around the creation of, trading in, and speculation with ICO tokens. This includes hundreds of exchanges,[166] ICO consulting and promotion companies, token rating agencies, token custodians, etc.

[2] Token Generation Events

A Token Generation Event, or TGE, is the same as an ICO from a functional perspective.

Some differentiate a TGE on the basis that the underlying functionality is more in the nature of a 'utility' or that the token is affiliated with a dApp.

[3] Initial Exchange Offerings

An Initial Exchange Offering, or IEO, is effectively an ICO underwritten by an exchange. A venture seeking to raise funds approaches an exchange offering this option[167] and seeks to comply with its requirements to complete an IEO. Once accepted, the token issuance for the venture is managed through the exchange.

In order to buy into an IEO, a purchaser will first need to create an account with the exchange which is offering or underwriting the IEO.[168] Once an account has been set up,[169] the user can proceed to purchase the IEO tokens through the exchange's trading platform.

Note that in the case of an IEO, token ownership may not be tracked on a blockchain but rather in the accounting system of the exchange.

There is a general expectation that an exchange which is offering an IEO has conducted a certain level of due diligence with respect to the IEO before offering it.[170]

Secondary trading in purchased tokens is straightforward, given the fact that they are already tradeable on the exchange underwriting the IEO.

[4] Security Token Offerings

A Security Token Offering, or STO, is very similar to an ICO from a functional perspective but differs in one material (legal) aspect: an STO token tracks ownership of some real-world underlying asset, such as shares in a company.

STOs are therefore presumed by their issuers to be securities offerings.

165. *See*, for example: https://icobench.com/ for a current list of ICO projects (accessed 29 Dec. 2023).
166. *See* https://coinmarketcap.com/rankings/exchanges/ (accessed 11 Jan. 2024).
167. *See*, for example, https://launchpad.binance.com/ (accessed 11 Jan. 2024).
168. The exchange may pre-purchase a large number of tokens for distribution on its platform and may also charge fees to the token issuer for the services it provides.
169. Which on a proper exchange should include Know Your Client (KYC) and Anti Money Laundering (AML) compliance procedures.
170. This due diligence may be more focused on ensuring that the IEO will be successful rather than on protecting investors.

[5] A Note on Token Fungibility

As noted above, 'fungibility' is the property of *interchangeability* of a commodity or good. For example, one barrel of crude oil is as good as another. Fungibility is usually thought of as one of the fundamentally useful properties of paper money.

Fungibility of a particular entitlement to a cryptocurrency or token stored on a blockchain might become *tainted* by the history of ownership of that particular token if any prior transactions were connected to illegal or otherwise suspect conduct.

Given the use of Bitcoin as the primary medium of exchange on the Dark Net, this poses a particular problem for that cryptocurrency.[171] Law-enforcement agencies as well as a number of private firms have assembled databases tying bitcoin addresses to a variety of illegal activities.[172]

Several 'privacy coins' attempt to prevent these types of connections from being made.[173]

§1.13 BITCOIN AND ETHEREUM GOVERNANCE

Bitcoin and Ethereum blockchain functionality are wholly controlled by the blockchain code running on each of the nodes of these networks. No component of its operation is controlled by the exercise of human discretion. There is, thus, at least in theory, no need for governance like one might find in other types of P2P networks, such as Wikipedia.[174]

However, in the absence of an operational governance structure, it is still necessary to make changes to the blockchain network code from time to time to address security issues or add enhancements, for instance. Processes have been developed for this purpose.

[A] The Bitcoin Governance Process

The primary groups which influence the code base of the Bitcoin network are the Bitcoin Core development group and the group of miners operating Bitcoin nodes.

The Bitcoin Core development group is a small group of software developers who have the rights to update the core Bitcoin software. This group was led by Wladimir

171. One investigation suggested that almost half of all Bitcoin addresses are associated with some form of illegal activity, available at: https://www.independent.co.uk/life-style/gadgets-and-tech/news/bitcoin-price-fall-criminals-blockchain-anonymous-cryptocurrency-zcash-monero-dash-a8174716.html (accessed 11 Jan. 2024).
172. *See*, for example: https://www.elliptic.co/ and https://www.chainalysis.com (both accessed 11 Jan. 2024).
173. *See* Berg, A., *The Identity, Fungibility, and Anonymity of Money* (10 Jul. 2018), available at: https://ssrn.com/abstract=3211011 or http://dx.doi.org/10.2139/ssrn.3211011 (both accessed 11 Jan. 2024).
174. *See* https://wiki.p2pfoundation.net/Peer_Governance (accessed 11 Jan. 2024).

van der Laan[175] until his apparent resignation in mid-2022. There are reports that van der Laan delegated his code update rights at that time.[176]

The core code, or *code base*, for Bitcoin is maintained in a Github[177] software repository available online.[178] Github is a company which provides online hosting of code repositories using the Git open-source version control software. Git uses a Merkle tree structure to ensure the integrity of a particular code repository or 'repo' and to track all changes made.

Anyone can interact with a Github-hosted repository in several ways:

- 'Forking a repo'. This process allows anyone to build on top of an existing set of programming code. Forking involves copying an existing repo, making changes and then publishing this updated code.
- 'Pull requests'. Anyone who has forked a repo and thinks that the added code would be great to incorporate into the original project repo can ask the owners of the original project to consider incorporating the forked repo into the original project.
- Networking. One of Github's ecosystem's primary benefit is the communication and collaboration among software developers that it enables.[179]

[1] Bitcoin Improvement Proposals

A change to the Bitcoin protocol is mediated through a Bitcoin Improvement Proposal or a 'BIP'. The BIP process was created in 2011 and took a page from the Python Enhancement Proposal process for improving the Python programming language.[180]

A Github repository tracking the status of all BIPs is maintained online.[181] There are three general categories of BIPs:

(i) A *Standard Track BIP*, which proposes a structural or functional change to the Bitcoin protocol as embodied in the code base.
(ii) An *Informational BIP*, which provides clarity or information to the community but does not propose any new feature or change.
(iii) A *Process BIP*, which proposes a change which does not directly impact the code base, but may suggest new procedures, changes to decision-making in development, or changes to tools used in developing Bitcoin.

175. No relation to the author.
176. https://en.bitcoin.it/wiki/Wladimir_van_der_Laan, https://protos.com/bitcoins-longest-serving-lead-maintainer-calls-it-quits-names-no-successor/ (accessed. 15 Dec. 2023).
177. https://github.com (accessed 23 Dec. 2023).
178. https://github.com/bitcoin/bitcoin (accessed 23 Dec. 2023).
179. It is possible to also use Git and Github to manage version control for any types of files, not just software code, as well as conduct project management: https://github.com/features/project-management/ (accessed 23 Dec. 2023).
180. https://www.python.org/dev/peps/pep-0001/ (accessed 23 Dec. 2023).
181. https://github.com/bitcoin/bips (accessed 23 Dec. 2023).

A BIP generally proceeds as follows:[182]

- Anyone seeking a change in the Bitcoin protocol first raises the issue on the Bitcoin protocol discussion mailing list[183] to gauge interest and receive preliminary input.
- If there is interest, the BIP is submitted to the BIP Git repository as a pull request and assigned a number.
- An assessment is made as to whether the change requires a soft fork or a hard fork.
- The proponent of the BIP or someone else who supports it (sometimes referred to as the 'champion') writes the code to implement the proposed change.
- The code is examined, tested and discussed in a 'peer-review' type process.
- Once there appears to be sufficient support, a date for the roll out of the software is proposed.

The adoption of the change then depends on how many of the nodes on the network actually instal the updated version. A soft fork BIP requires 'clear miner majority' which means that 95 % of miner nodes must upgrade their software to include the BIP. A hard fork BIP requires that the 'entire community' adopt it by installing an update that includes the BIP. This is a difficult and uncertain threshold. As a result, there have been no hard fork BIPs to date.

The most discussed and controversial BIP was likely BIP141 dealing with the 'Segregated Witness' soft fork proposal. It deserves a bit of further discussion.

[2] Segwit

As noted previously, the Bitcoin block size was limited to 1 MB at the time the Bitcoin network was launched. This 1 MB block size limitation is a significant scalability barrier for Bitcoin as it permits only a limited number of transactions to be processed every ten minutes.

The combination of the small block size and the ten-minute Proof of Work requirement limits the number of transactions which can be processed on the Bitcoin network to somewhere between four and five transactions per second (TPS). Compare this to the capacity of the VISA network to process up to 56,000 TPS.[184]

Prior to Segwit, the Bitcoin network was vulnerable to a potential weakness in the Bitcoin transaction process, known as *transaction malleability,* which could be exploited to change transaction ownership information before transactions were confirmed within a particular block.

In order to attempt to cram more transactions into a block as well as eliminate the transaction malleability problem, a proposal was made to store the transaction

182. This a high-level summary. *See* BIP002 for a full description, available at: https://github.com/bitcoin/bips/blob/master/bip-0002.mediawiki (accessed 23 Dec. 2023).
183. https://lists.linuxfoundation.org/mailman/listinfo/bitcoin-dev (accessed 23 Dec. 2023).
184. The VISA network takes about twelve seconds to process the total *daily* volume of transactions processed by Bitcoin.

signature data[185] for a particular block *outside* the main Bitcoin blockchain, but still on the same network, using a *sidechain*.[186]

This proposed process of 'segregating the witness' to block transactions became known as Segwit and was first proposed in BIP141. Segwit was activated by way of a soft fork in August 2017. Some members of the Bitcoin community did not agree with this change and hard forked a new blockchain which they named Bitcoin Cash (BCH).[187]

Another Segwit proposal, known as Segwit2X,[188] was subsequently made with a view to doubling the Bitcoin block size to 2 MB. This (hard fork-based) proposal was controversial and was not adopted.

These Segwit proposals illustrate the difficulties often encountered in governing a distributed blockchain protocol without any central authority.[189] It is a slow, arduous and frustrating process.

[3] Taproot

Another important, and more recent, set of changes to the Bitcoin codebase, known as Taproot, made several privacy- and smart contract-related changes.

Taproot is comprised of several BIPs, including BIP 340 (Schnorr signatures), BIP 341 (Taproot), BIP 342 (Tapscript), and BIP 114 (MAST).

These BIPs add the following improvements:

- Schnorr signatures, a type of digital signature that allows for more compact multi-signature schemes, leading to further space savings in the blockchain and improved scalability.
- A new scripting system called Tapscript, which allows for more complex smart contracts to be implemented with greater efficiency.
- Enhanced privacy by enabling the ability to combine multiple signature types, such as Pay-to-Public-Key-Hash (P2PKH) and Pay-to-Witness-Public-Key-Hash (P2WPKH), and making them indistinguishable.
- The addition of the MAST data structure which allows for the efficient encoding of multiple potential spending conditions in a single Merkle root, which permits more complex conditions to be encoded in the limited space available for this in a Bitcoin transaction. This aids in enabling more complex smart contracts.

The Taproot BIPs were designed to be backward compatible to ensure a smooth transition and widespread acceptance of the upgrade across the Bitcoin network.

185. Which usually takes up about 65% of the storage space for an average transaction.
186. Sidechains are covered in more detail under section §1.18[B] *infra*.
187. https://www.bitcoincash.org/ (accessed 11 Jan. 2024).
188. https://en.bitcoin.it/wiki/SegWit2x (accessed 11 Jan. 2024).
189. For a more detailed description of Segwit and all the consensus challenges encountered, *see* https://bitcoinmagazine.com/articles/long-road-segwit-how-bitcoins-biggest-protocol-upgrade-became-reality (accessed 11 Jan. 2024).

Bitcoin miners signalled support for the upgrade on 12 June 2021, with a 90% consensus. The upgrade was fully activated as a soft fork at block 709,632 on 14 November 2021.

[B] Ethereum Governance

Ethereum is currently governed through a consensus-based code update process called the Ethereum Improvement Proposal, or EIP.[190] It functions largely in the same manner as a BIP but does have a more extensive proposal documentation requirement. Ethereum also has a more formalized issue discussion protocol known as the Ethereum Request for Comment, or ERC, as discussed previously. An ERC can turn into an EIP.

[C] Off-Chain and On-Chain Governance

Both the BIP and EIP processes are referred to as 'off-chain governance' in that the approval process for changes is not tracked or executed on the blockchain.

Another approach to managing proposed changes to a blockchain's protocol is through 'on-chain' governance, where the rules and processes for change are encoded in the blockchain protocol itself.

On-chain governance usually uses a (node-based) voting mechanism process of some sort to achieve consensus regarding proposed changes. EOS[191] and TEZOS[192] are blockchains seeking to follow this model. Both have been fraught with discontent.[193]

There is the possibility that Ethereum may adopt some form of on-chain governance with a future hard fork.[194]

§1.14 MOVING BEYOND ETHEREUM

By 2015, and with the relative success[195] of Bitcoin and Ethereum, additional blockchain-based projects were being created.

These projects generally followed two approaches to blockchain implementation described as *public* and *private* blockchains.[196] In addition, with the advent of a number of other distributed ledger and shared database-related technologies, the term *DLTs* emerged. Before exploring the details of some of these projects in more detail, it is helpful to have a general understanding of what these three terms mean.

190. A list of EIPs is available at: https://github.com/ethereum/EIPs (accessed 11 Jan. 2024).
191. *See* the EOS white paper: https://github.com/EOSIO/Documentation/blob/master/TechnicalWhitePaper.md#governance (accessed 11 Jan. 2024).
192. *See* the TEZOS white paper: https://tezos.com/whitepaper.pdf (accessed 11 Jan. 2024).
193. https://www.coindesk.com/soon-chain-governance (accessed 11 Jan. 2024).
194. https://ethereum.org/en/governance/ (accessed 29 Dec. 2023).
195. In the sense that the value of a bitcoin had increased dramatically.
196. There are others who parse the different types of blockchains using additional criteria, such as whether the blockchain is permissioned or not. Given that a public blockchain is usually permissionless and a private blockchain usually permissioned, this additional distinction is not significant from a functional perspective.

[A] Public (Permissionless) Blockchains

This type of blockchain allows anyone to participate *without a specific identity*. Like Bitcoin and Ethereum, many of these blockchains require the use of a native cryptocurrency combined with a Proof of Work or similar consensus mechanism to stand in the place of a centralized trusted authority.

Trust in public blockchains is usually created and enforced with mathematical/algorithmic structures.

Due to these requirements, public permissionless blockchains are in many cases slow and energy intensive.[197]

[B] Private (Permissioned) Blockchains

This type of blockchain is used among a set of *identified participants*, usually in the context of a commercial relationship of some sort where a common record among the participants is beneficial or desirable. Permissioned private blockchains are also sometimes referred to as 'consortium' blockchains.

Many of these types of blockchains do not use a Proof of Work and/or cryptocurrency approach to consensus but rely instead on simpler and less-resource-intensive mechanisms.

Given the fewer participants (and therewith nodes), a private blockchain is likely to be more centralized than a public blockchain. Corda[198] and Tendermint[199] are examples of private blockchain platforms. Most enterprise blockchains (discussed below) are private blockchains.

Trust in private blockchains is usually enforced by contract or reputation.

[C] Distributed Ledger Technologies

This term emerged to describe a broader group of technologies which pursue some form of distributed ledger solution on the basis of a wide variety of storage modalities, P2P network topologies and consensus mechanisms.

As is often said, 'every blockchain is a DLT, but not every DLT is a blockchain'. Some of the more novel DLTs do in fact not use a blockchain to store the ledger data, but instead rely on other data structures, such as directed graphs or even traditionally secured distributed databases.

Before examining some examples of DLTs and other consensus mechanisms, it is helpful to gain a bit of insight into some theoretical aspects of distributed consensus-seeking networks, which inform an understanding of some of the challenges and limitations of distributed ledger systems.

197. For example, the Bitcoin blockchain's energy consumption exceeds that of many countries, https://digiconomist.net/bitcoin-energy-consumption (both accessed 11 Jan. 2024).
198. https://corda.net/ (accessed 11 Jan. 2024).
199. https://tendermint.com/ (accessed 11 Jan. 2024).

§1.15 DISTRIBUTED SYSTEM CONSENSUS THEORY

Establishing consensus among a distributed network of computers is not a new problem and has been studied from a theoretical perspective for decades.

Given that in today's world there is often the need to synchronize the same data among computers in many different locations, research and development of consensus algorithms is fundamental to many areas of applied computing.

Research in this area has generated many helpful insights into some key attributes and limitations of a distributed consensus-seeking network which should inform the design of these systems. A brief overview of some core concepts and theory follows.

[A] Synchronous Versus Asynchronous Processes

A *synchronous* process involves sequential steps in a process that are connected and completed in order. No step is started until the previous step is finished. An example of a synchronous process is a queue at a theatre's ticket window – every customer must be served in order.

Synchronous processes require clear messaging with respect to when a specific step is completed to avoid the process halting indefinitely.

Asynchronous processes have steps which are not connected and may be completed out of order. An example of an asynchronous process is servicing a set of tables at a restaurant. People sitting at these tables can place orders and receive food independently from each other and without any sequencing requirement.

Most consensus processes will only work if they are *asynchronous* as any synchronous process will stop if a particular step fails to complete (for instance, because of an unresponsive, uncooperative or malicious[200] node).

An asynchronous consensus system introduces additional challenges.

[B] The FLP Impossibility Result

In 1983, three computer scientists proved mathematically that consensus is not guaranteed in any distributed asynchronous system where even one host, or node, may fail.[201] This is commonly known as the *FLP Impossibility Result.*[202]

To solve this problem, consensus mechanisms must have methodologies for dealing with bad nodes (whether malicious or not) and/or slow networks.

200. For example, a node seeking to change the value with respect to which consensus is sought.
201. Primarily because it is not possible to distinguish between a currently unavailable (slow) node and a crashed (failed) node.
202. FLP stands for Fischer, Lynch and Patterson, the last names of the three authors of the seminal paper: Michael J. Fischer, Nancy A. Lynch, and Michael S. Paterson, *Impossibility of Distributed Consensus with One Faulty Process*, 32 J. ACM 2 (April 1985), 374–382. http://dx.doi.org/10.1145/3149.214121 (accessed 11 Jan. 2024). *See also* https://groups.csail.mit.edu/tds/papers/Lynch/jacm85.pdf (accessed 11 Jan. 2024).

This is usually achieved by imposing some sort of time limit on the consensus-reaching process.

[C] Consensus Mechanism Properties

Any process for achieving fault-tolerant[203] consensus among a distributed set of computers with respect to the state of a certain database or other record-keeping system must have mechanisms to achieve *termination*, *agreement* and *validity*:

- *Termination* (or *liveness*) means that all nodes on the network follow a (multi-stage) process which is certain to end, i.e., eventually decides on a value of something with respect to which consensus is sought.[204]
- *Agreement* (sometimes also called *consistency* or *safety*) means that some majority of valid nodes can reach an agreement on the same value.
- *Validity* means that the value proposed for consensus is introduced by a process agreed upon within the network.

This is not always easy to do.

[1] The CAP Theorem

Another important aspect of a distributed consensus network is the practical interplay between three physical aspects of such a network: its *consistency*, *availability* and *partition tolerance*, or CAP for short:

- *Consistency* is the extent to which all nodes on a network have the same data.
- *Availability* is the extent to which the nodes on the network are accessible by users of the network.
- *Partition tolerance* is the extent to which the connections between the nodes in the network persist, i.e., are active and working.

The CAP Theorem[205] states that in the event of partition within a distributed network, the users of the network must choose to have either consistency *or* availability but cannot have both. An example will make this clear.[206]

Assume a network of five automatic teller machines (ATMs) for a bank. Each ATM maintains and stores a copy of a ledger containing the bank balances of the bank's customers.

203. Meaning it will still function if a number of nodes fail or are unreachable.
204. In a database, liveness requires that a transaction either abort or commit, usually within the bounds of some time constraint.
205. This is a bit of an oversimplification, which is appropriate for our purposes. *See* https://www.analyticsvidhya.com/blog/2020/08/a-beginners-guide-to-cap-theorem-for-data-engineering/ for a more detailed description (accessed 11 Jan. 2024).
206. An additional and more detailed, but somewhat technical, example is available at: https://mwhittaker.github.io/blog/an_illustrated_proof_of_the_cap_theorem/ (accessed 11 Jan. 2024).

The five ATMs are connected on a network, and the network operates some sort of consensus process to ensure each ATM's copy of the ledger is identical to those maintained by the other ATMs.

As long as the network functions correctly and all five ATMs are connected – i.e., there are no *partitions* (some ATMs or ATMs whose version of the ledger is not up to date due to a network connectivity problem), then the ATMs can all be consistent and available.

However, if for some reason the network fails or is unavailable for two of the ATMs, then the balances at those ATMs may not be up to date; that is, they are at risk of being *inconsistent*, which means that making them *available* to consumers may result in inconsistent ledgers within the network (new transactions on the disconnected ATMs not being present on those which maintain connectivity).

A choice needs to be made to either:

- keep the ledgers consistent while the partition exists by making the two ATMs unavailable to consumers (risking the consumers' discontent); or
- risk the inconsistency of the ledger by keeping the ATMs available for the users, risking potential double spending or other transactional inconsistencies (to the chagrin of the bank).

In today's complex distributed systems, the three CAP attributes are not binary – yes or no – type states. They should be thought of as *levels* within a particular system. In other words, a desired increased level of consistency in a system with a certain level of partitioning will result in a decreased level of availability.

The CAP Theorem is a material barrier to the usability of any distributed consensus network.

§1.16 OTHER DLT AND CONSENSUS APPROACHES

[A] Byzantine Fault Tolerance (BFT)-Based Networks

There are now many blockchains or DLTs which explore the use of consensus mechanisms quite different from the Proof of Work approach used by Bitcoin and Ethereum.

Many of these are evolutions of more traditional consensus algorithms used in distributed databases, which find their root in a family of algorithms commonly referred to as the *Paxos protocols*.[207] These protocols generally follow an iterative multi-phase, *voting-based* methodology to confirm transactions rather than some manner of random delegation of confirmation to a particular node (as is the case with Proof of Work).

In the context of DLTs, these types of approaches are usually referred to as 'Byzantine Fault Tolerance' consensus mechanisms. Byzantine refers to the 'Byzantine

207. *See* https://en.wikipedia.org/wiki/Paxos_(computer_science) (accessed 11 Jan. 2024).

Generals Problem', a famous consensus theory problem involving (potentially) untrustworthy members of a group reaching consensus on a common decision.[208]

Many blockchain purists do not consider BFT-based ledger systems to be true blockchains, given that many of these ledger networks require a degree of centralization of certain aspects or components of the consensus process.

Two often-referenced examples of the BFT approach to consensus are Ripple[209] and Stellar.[210]

[1] Ripple

At the use case level, Ripple aims to be a global currency exchange network with (close to) real-time settlement. It operates much like *Hawala*, a delegated and distributed money transfer system used in the Middle East and Asia.[211]

Ripple employs *Ripple Gateways* to create the ability for any user to send money to another Ripple user on the network. A Gateway is usually some banking or financial services entity which acts as a credit intermediary on the network by sending and receiving currency entitlements to addresses on the Ripple ledger.[212]

The Ripple cryptocurrency, XRP, is used as a liquidity mechanism within the network. Every Ripple transaction also involves the charging of a small amount of XRP as a transaction fee which is then 'burned' with the completion of that transaction.[213]

XRP tokens are 'pre-mined' and are not used as part of any token-incentivized consensus mechanism.[214] Instead, Ripple consensus uses the *Ripple Protocol Consensus Algorithm* (RPCA).[215]

The RPCA uses a 'Byzantine fault tolerant agreement protocol' over collectively trusted subnetworks[216] to guard against double spending and achieve consensus.

The Ripple consensus protocol generally works as follows:

(1) Every node maintains a copy of the shared ledger of XRP transactions, known as the *last-closed ledger* or LCL.
(2) Every node maintains a *unique node list* (UNL) of other (trusted) nodes from which it will receive messages (called proposals) regarding transactions

208. For a good paper explaining and exploring the problem, *see* https://lamport.azurewebsites.net/pubs/byz.pdf: (accessed 11 Jan. 2024).
209. https://www.ripple.com/ (accessed 11 Jan. 2024).
210. https://www.stellar.org/ (accessed 11 Jan. 2024). Stellar was created by Jed McCaleb, a co-founder of Ripple.
211. https://en.wikipedia.org/wiki/Hawala (accessed 11 Jan. 2024).
212. For a more detailed explanation, *see* Ripple's excellent documentation webpage at https://xrpl.org/introduction.html (accessed 11 Jan. 2024).
213. With the idea being that this destruction enhances the value of an individual XRP token by virtue of a decreasing total supply.
214. There are currently approximately 100 billion XRP tokens in existence.
215. *See* https://xrpl.org/consensus.html#introduction for a detailed explanation of the RPCA (accessed 11 Jan. 2024).
216. https://arxiv.org/pdf/1802.07242.pdf (accessed 11 Jan. 2024).

proposed to be added to the ledger. Every node will have a different UNL established by whoever controls the node.

(3) In addition to the proposals received from its UNL, every node is also able to accept new transactions proposed to be added to the LCL, like the memory pool in Bitcoin.

(4) The RPCA proceeds in *rounds* as follows:
- Each node assembles valid transactions submitted to that node and which have not been previously included in the LCL, into a list known as the 'candidate set'.
- Each node collects the proposals from all the nodes on whose UNL it appears and votes to confirm the transactions in them where a proposal transaction matches a candidate transaction.
- Once a transaction achieves 50% of the votes from nodes on the UNL, it is transmitted to the network as a proposal to other servers.
- Another round takes place, and this time the vote requirement is upped to 60%, and then 70% and finally 80%.
- Rounds continue to be repeated until the consensus timer runs out.[217]
- All transactions in the candidate set which have votes of 80%[218] of the UNL or more are now added to the LCL. Any transactions with insufficient votes are discarded.

Much like Bitcoin and Ethereum, Ripple ties together LCL versions (similar to blocks in Bitcoin and Ethereum) by incorporating a hash digest of the previous version in the header information of the next.[219]

Given the very rapid LCL commitment time, Ripple can process many more transactions than Bitcoin or Ethereum. Its current capacity is about 1,500 TPS.

[2] Stellar

Stellar uses a consensus model called *Federated Byzantine Agreement* (FBA), which is similar to the RPCA used by Ripple with one important difference. Unlike Ripple, the Stellar model does not have a centralized recommended validator node list maintained by a centralized authority. Instead, each node individually decides which other nodes it trusts. As a result, the Stellar approach finds more favour with blockchain purists seeking a highly, if not completely, decentralized ledger system.

217. Which is about 3.5–4 seconds.
218. This threshold is usually referred to as the *quorum* parameter.
219. *See* https://xrpl.org/img/ledger-changes.png for a graphical representation of this component of the Ripple consensus process (accessed 11 Jan. 2024).

This node-specific list of trusted nodes is called a *quorum slice*. Quorum slices on the network overlap and via that overlap engage in the process of a voting round like that used by Ripple.[220]

[B] Proof-of-Stake-Based Networks

Proof of Stake is yet another consensus mechanism sometimes used in cryptocurrency-based blockchains. It is notable that the Ethereum project transitioned to Proof of Stake with a hard fork on 15 September 2022.[221]

Peercoin[222] is a good example of a blockchain which has implemented a Proof-of-Stake consensus mechanism.[223]

[1] Peercoin

In 2012, Peercoin became the first blockchain to use Proof of Stake.[224]

In Peercoin's model, owners of Peercoin's token (PPCoin or PPC) pursue a 'minting' process to confirm transactions to be added to the Peercoin blockchain.[225]

This minting process is based on the idea of 'coin age', which is simply a number generated by multiplying the number of coins held by a particular user by the number of days since they were last transacted. Committing tokens to the consensus process is referred to as 'staking coinage'.

A small reward is paid to anyone who stakes their coinage to confirm a new block to the blockchain. Minting generates a reward equal to approximately a 1% annual return for anyone who participates in this process.

Minting works largely like the Bitcoin mining process, with the following important differences:

- The intended node user ('validator') instals a wallet client program which has a unique address and permits connection to the Peercoin network. The validator adds PPC to the wallet by sending transactions to this unique address.[226]

220. For a more detailed explanation of quorum slices and how they work, *see* https://towardsdatascience.com/federated-byzantine-agreement-24ec57bf36e0 (accessed 11 Jan. 2024).
221. Which reduced power consumption of the network dramatically. *See* https://www.mdpi.com/2813-2432/2/2/6#:~:text=On%2015%20September%202022%2C%20the,reduced%20energy%20consumption%20by%2099.98%25 (accessed 11 Jan. 2024).
222. https://www.peercoin.net/ (accessed 11 Jan. 2024).
223. *See also* Tendermint by Cosmos, Dfinity, Nxt, BlackCoin, NuShares/NuBits and Qora for similar implementations.
224. The Peercoin white paper is available at: https://www.peercoin.net/whitepapers/peercoin-paper.pdf (accessed 11 Jan. 2024).
225. The general functionality of the Peercoin blockchain has a great deal of similarity to the Bitcoin blockchain as it is based on the Bitcoin open-source code.
226. Note that Peercoin also initially had a Proof of Work-based mining process which enabled the creation of users who held PPC, which they could then use in the minting process.

- Once PPC coins are added to the wallet, they 'age' as long as no transactions are conducted with those coins. Once coins have aged thirty days, they can be used as a stake in the block confirmation process.
- The block confirmation process uses a hashing process like Bitcoin but with a much smaller sample space. In addition, the difficulty of finding the target hash is reduced in proportion to the size of the coin age of a particular node. As a result, the likelihood of a particular node finding the winning hash is greatly increased if it has a large coin age. Nodes with the largest coin age thus have the highest probability of 'winning' a block.
- A winning node includes its stake in the confirmed block and retransmits its stake back to its wallet (thus reducing the coin age to zero and starting the ageing process for those tokens all over again).
- The validating node is incentivized to confirm only valid transactions, as any fraudulent transaction inside a confirmed block will result in the node forfeiting its stake.[227]
- The official blockchain is identified by participating nodes accepting the blockchain with the highest cumulative coin age as the official version.[228]

The Ethereum Proof-of-Stake process works in a slightly different way. Somewhat simplified, the Ethereum implementation is as follows:[229]

- A validator stakes 32 ETH in a Proof-of-Stake smart contract on the Ethereum blockchain.
- The validator then joins an 'activation queue'. This queue limits the number of validators and allows them to participate in order, as validators are selected from the queue.
- New validators are chosen every 12 seconds in what are called 'slots'. Each slot has at least 128 validators, referred to as a 'committee'.
- Slots are organized into 32 slot 'epochs'. Every slot in an epoch has a different committee.
- In each slot, one validator is randomly selected from the committee to be the 'block proposer'. This validator creates a new proposed block from the memory pool and sends it out to other nodes on the network.
- Activated validators receive this proposed new block and check it for validity. If valid, the validator sends a vote (called an attestation) in favour of that block across the network. A validator can only attest to one block per epoch for the slot its committee was assigned to.
- Once a two-thirds majority of validators vote for a block, it becomes 'justified'.

227. The integrity of the blockchain is separately verified to this end by validation software running on the nodes of the network.
228. Recall that in the Bitcoin blockchain this is done by seeking the longest blockchain, i.e., the one with the highest cumulative difficulty.
229. For a more detailed technical explanation, *see* https://www.preethikasireddy.com/post/how-does-the-new-ethereum-work (accessed 11 Jan. 2024).

- When a subsequent block also becomes justified, the block becomes 'finalized'.
- It is then added to the blockchain using the established forward hashing approach.
- As blocks are added in this manner, the fork with the greatest accumulated amount of votes becomes the valid new blockchain.
- The block proposer receives an amount of ETH as a reward determined by a formula.

If a validator votes for an invalid block, it runs the risk of being penalized by having a portion of its staked ETH taken away.

It must be noted that since Ethereum's implementation of Proof of Stake, a number of researchers have identified potential security issues with Ethereum's implementation.[230] The severity and/or significance of these issues, and whether they can be resolved with updates to the Ethereum implementation, remains to be determined.

[C] Delegated Proof-of-Stake-Based Networks

Delegated Proof of Stake (DPoS) is a variant of Proof of Stake, developed in 2013, where token holders do not seek to individually compete to validate blocks but rather delegate their stake or vote to delegates to do the validation on their behalf.

DPoS can be thought of as a way to introduce the Bitcoin mining pool concept into a Proof-of-Stake network.

A purported advantage of DPoS is faster confirmation time due to a smaller set of delegated validators participating in the validation process.

A disadvantage is that the system is more decentralized (given the limited number of confirming nodes) and that delegated nodes must maintain a high level of availability on the network.

DPoS was first implemented on the BitShares network.[231]

[1] BitShares

In the BitShares network, delegated validators are called *witnesses*.[232]

230. *See*, for example, Schwarz-Schilling, Caspar, et al., *Three attacks on proof-of-stake Ethereum*, International Conference on Financial Cryptography and Data Security, Springer International Publishing, 2022; Neu, Joachim, Ertem Nusret Tas, and David Tse. *Two attacks on proof-of-stake GHOST/Ethereum*, arXiv preprint arXiv:2203.01315 (2022); Pavloff, Ulysse, Yackolley Amoussou-Guenou, and Sara Tucci-Piergiovanni. *Ethereum Proof-of-Stake under Scrutiny*, Proceedings of the 38th ACM/SIGAPP Symposium on Applied Computing. 2023; and Derouiche, Emir. *The Relationship Between Voting Power Distribution and the Bug Resilience of an Ethereum Proof-of-Stake Blockchain*. MS thesis. NTNU, 2023.
231. Other examples are Lisk, Steem, EOS and Tezos.
232. Or block producers.

BitShares token holders hold votes in proportion to the number of tokens they hold. In turn, witnesses hold votes in proportion to the size of the stake they represent (which includes their own stake as well as any stakes held by nodes who delegated to, or voted for, that particular witness). In the case of BitShares, the number of witnesses must be between 20 and 101 nodes.[233]

The BitShares DPoS algorithm generally works as follows:

- A schedule of block confirmation processes is maintained, with one confirmation slated every three seconds.
- Every witness is assigned a future time slot for which it will complete the confirmation process.
- A voting process among the witnesses is followed (in the same manner as that of a regular Proof-of-Stake process) until two-third plus one of the witnesses have voted to confirm.

  DPoS-based systems appear to have the potential to process transactions at a very high rate, approaching those achieved by centralized systems, such as Visa or Mastercard, although an actual working implementation at those rates remains elusive at the time of writing.

[D] Proof-of-History-Based Networks

As mentioned above, the Solana network uses a mechanism called 'Proof of History' (PoH) in its general Proof-of-Stake-driven consensus-reaching approach.

PoH is not a consensus algorithm on its own but rather a mechanism that assists in achieving a more efficient and scalable consensus protocol by providing a historical record of the order of transactions. It generally works by adding timestamps to transactions before they are added to a block. These timestamps are created using a cryptographic function called the Verifiable Delay Function (VDF). The VDF is computationally intensive and makes it difficult to retroactively manipulate the timestamps. These timestamps are used to order the blocks in the blockchain and ensure their immutability. Embedding timestamps, in this matter, decreases communication overhead in the network and can assist in greater efficiency.

Because of this approach as well as a number of other innovations, the Solana blockchain is (currently) capable of processing transactions at very high rates.[234]

[E] Directed Acyclic Graph-Based Networks

A directed acyclic graph, or DAG, is yet another proposed approach to a decentralized ledger.

233. Other DPoS networks may use different ranges. For instance, EOS and Steemit use 21 as the upper bound.
234. With block confirmation times well below one second. For a more detailed explanation of the Solana consensus approach, *see* the Solana white paper at https://solana.com/solana-whitepaper.pdf (accessed 11 Jan. 2024).

The DAG-based mechanism is quite different from the approaches covered so far. To understand how it works, a quick review of graph theory basics is in order.

[1] Graph Theory Basics

In mathematics, a graph is a data structure which maps certain relationships, usually in the context of some sort of network (e.g., friend relationships on Facebook or computers on a network which have direct connections).

A graph is made up of *vertices* or *nodes* which are connected with *edges* or *links* (Figure 1.26).

Figure 1.26 A Simple Graph

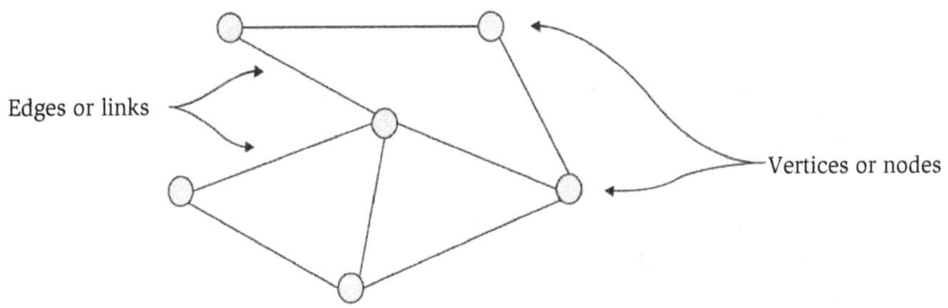

Edges may have directions and thus represent the nature of the relationship between two vertices or nodes.

If a graph is structured in such a way that the relationships in the graph can only flow in one way, that is without any loops allowing a circling back, then the graph is referred to as a *directed acyclic graph* (Figure 1.27).[235]

Figure 1.27 A Sample Directed Acyclic Graph

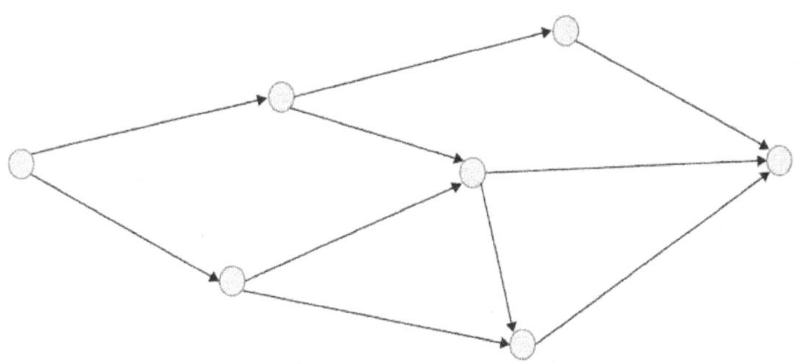

235. Sometimes also called a *digraph*.

An example of a directed acyclic graph is a river system which only flows in one direction and merges with tributaries as one proceeds along its flow from source to sea.

[2] Using a DAG as a Ledger

A DAG can also point backwards and thus create an authorization system for sequential transactions, where a particular node or vertex represents a transaction, and later vertices approve the state of previous transactions by creating a link to those vertices. Such links then represent approval.

A potential key advantage of this approach is the possibility of allowing multiple transactions to be validated simultaneously.

IOTA[236] is an example of a DAG-based consensus algorithm.

[3] IOTA

The IOTA DAG-based consensus algorithm is called Tangle[237] and was first proposed in 2018 (Figure 1.28). Tangle is open source, feeless and permissionless.

It generally functions as follows:[238]

- All tokens for the system are created and instantiated in the first (*genesis*) vertex/node of the DAG.[239]
- Unapproved transactions are called *tips*, given that they are ends without approving nodes on the graph. Approved transactions are called *sites*.
- In order to become a candidate for confirmation, each new tip needs to identify, and link to, two previously approved transactions in the graph. This can be done directly (i.e., node A is approved by nodes B and C) or indirectly (i.e., node A is approved by B, which in turn is approved by C).

236. https://www.iota.org/ (accessed 11 Jan. 2024).
237. Some also refer to the IOTA DAG generally as 'the Tangle'.
238. This is a simplified overview. For a detailed description, *see* the Tangle white paper, available at: https://assets.ctfassets.net/r1dr6vzfxhev/2t4uxvsIqk0EUau6g2sw0g/45eae33637ca92f85dd9f4a3a218e1ec/iota1_4_3.pdf (accessed 11 Jan. 2024).
239. Note that therefore there is no mining in a DAG-based ledger.

Figure 1.28 IOTA Tangle Detail

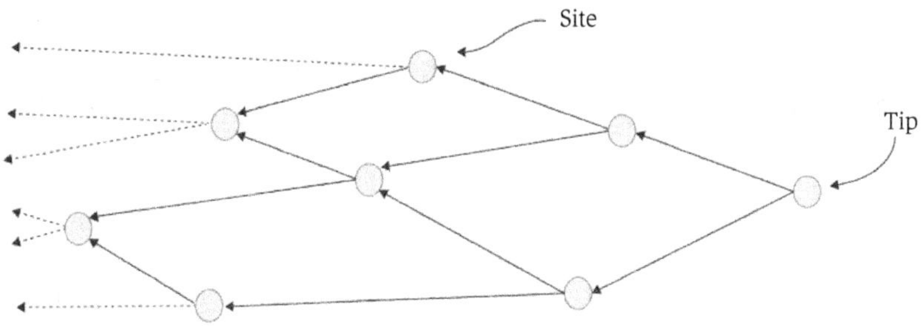

- Each transaction tracks the number of subsequent tips that have approved it. This value is called its *weight* or *cumulative weight*. As the weight increases, the confidence in the transaction increases.
- A candidate tip will select two existing tips in the network to confirm. This is done randomly.
- In order to approve these two current tip transactions (behind it in the DAG), the node seeking to add its tip will first confirm that the transactions to which it intends to link (and thereby confirm) are non-conflicting in the DAG, i.e., that they do not constitute a double spend.
- Once that is confirmed, a hash algorithm is applied to the linking transactions and the hash stored in the tip so as to connect these transactions together and make them immutable (this is similar to the forward embedding of hash values used in the Bitcoin blockchain).
- The cumulative weight of the confirmed tips (which are now no longer tips but sites) is adjusted upwards.
- The process carries on in this manner, and more tips are continually added to the Tangle.
- The cumulative weight of confirmed transactions continues to increase as more tips are added, and once the cumulative weight of a particular transaction (site) reaches a certain level as a percentage of all subsequent tips which have approved the transaction, the transaction can be accepted as confirmed.[240]

IOTA and other DAG-based distributed ledgers have struggled with wider adoption of this approach despite efforts to add smart contract functionality more recently.[241]

240. *See* https://blog.iota.org/the-tangle-an-illustrated-introduction-79f537b0a455 for a detailed description of this step (accessed 11 Jan. 2024).
241. https://wiki.iota.org/get-started/introduction/shimmer/introduction/ (accessed 11 Jan 2024).

§1.17 ENTERPRISE BLOCKCHAIN PLATFORMS

[A] Hyperledger

In 2015, the Linux Foundation started the development of an open-source blockchain incubator with a view to creating blockchain platform technologies for enterprise use. This project was christened 'Hyperledger'.[242] Hyperledger seeks to be a reference architecture for enterprise blockchain implementations.

The Hyperledger project includes several different initiatives, which are currently progressing through defined development states – proposal, incubation and active – set out by the project. An overview of the Hyperledger DLT 'Landscape' is maintained dynamically online.[243]

The most substantive initiatives pursued by Hyperledger to date are Fabric and Sawtooth.[244]

[1] Fabric

Fabric is a permissioned blockchain framework[245] initiated by IBM with the goal of creating modular blockchain functionality which can be combined to create (or generate) solutions to enterprise problems. Fabric includes functionality to encrypt transactions and partition data on a blockchain for the purpose of enabling compliance with various privacy and data protection obligations of enterprise uses.

Fabric also supports smart contracts, which it calls *chaincode*.[246]

[2] Sawtooth

Sawtooth is a blockchain project[247] started by Intel which seeks to provide a flexible and modular architecture for enterprise DLT solutions. Sawtooth can be implemented in both permissioned and permissionless states and can implement a variety of consensus algorithms.

Two innovations pursued by the Sawtooth project deserve mention: The Proof of Elapsed Time (or PoET) consensus algorithm and the idea of *transaction families*.

242. https://www.hyperledger.org/ (accessed 11 Jan. 2024).
243. https://dltlandscape.hyperledger.org/ (accessed 23 Dec. 2023).
244. A complete list of projects is available at https://dltlandscape.hyperledger.org/projects (accessed 23 Dec. 2023).
245. https://www.hyperledger.org/projects/fabric (accessed 11 Jan. 2024).
246. *See* https://hyperledger-fabric.readthedocs.io/en/release-1.4/chaincode.html for a technical reference (accessed 11 Jan. 2024).
247. https://www.hyperledger.org/projects/sawtooth (accessed 11 Jan. 2024).

[3] Proof of Elapsed Time Consensus

Both the Proof-of-Work and Proof-of-Stake consensus mechanisms select one node in the network to complete the validation of the next block on a blockchain in a manner not dissimilar to a lottery. In the case of Proof of Work, it is the first node which finds the (largely random) target hash. In the case of Proof of Stake, it is the node with the largest coin age (which also follows a random pattern).

PoET is yet another approach to selecting a node to be responsible for validating the next block of transactions on a blockchain on the basis of randomness.

PoET was invented by Intel and is novel in that it is the first consensus mechanism which uses specialized computer CPU functionality to enable it. This functionality is a new instruction set for the execution of code called Intel Software Guard Extensions, or SGX. SGX is incorporated in most Intel CPUs manufactured after 2015.

SGX adds a new set of security-focused capabilities to any CPU on which it is enabled, including the ability to encrypt a portion of a computer's memory (called an *enclave*) and completely segregate the code and data placed in that enclave from view and access by the rest of the computer.[248] Intel calls this a Trusted Execution Environment, or TEE.

The instruction set for the TEE permits it to provide an *attestation* confirming that the code loaded into the TEE has been correctly initiated and has not been altered or otherwise compromised and can therefore be reliably executed.

This functionality is used in the PoET consensus approach as follows:

- A new node seeking to join the consensus network downloads the network's specific PoET consensus code and loads it into its TEE. The consensus code contains a timer object which can generate a timer instance of random duration.
- The TEE provides a signed attestation confirming that the consensus code is properly installed and loaded. The attestation enables the node to initiate a 'join' request to the other nodes on the network.
- If a majority of nodes accept the attestation, the node is added to the network as a consensus participant.

The consensus process then proceeds, in rounds, as follows:

- At the start of the round, each node receives a timer instance of random duration from its TEE, and the timer starts running.
- The node whose timer expires first is the 'winner', and it transmits a signed certificate to the network, proving and confirming its timer time, together with the block it seeks to confirm.

248. Some recent reports suggest that SGX may not be as secure as suggested, available at: https://www.theregister.co.uk/2019/02/12/intel_sgx_hacked/ and https://en.wikipedia.org/wiki/Foreshadow (both accessed 11 Jan. 2024).

- Other nodes confirm the winning timer time, accept the winner and add the winner's confirmed block to their local copy of the blockchain.

PoET is a very efficient consensus mechanism and scales easily. It is an easy method to create and enforce a desirable time cost for every block without the need for a cryptocurrency or the large resource cost of the mining process in a Proof of Work-based blockchain. PoET also does not tie up the network nodes' entitlements, as is required in a Proof-of-Stake implementation.

On the downside, it is dependent on a proprietary technology which runs afoul of the precept of placing trust only in the distributed network. If the desire for a completely distributed blockchain is less pressing (i.e., if the focus is on ensuring a common immutable ledger among a private group of parties), PoET would appear to be a more usable consensus solution for such a permissioned (private) blockchain.

[4] Transaction Families

The transaction family concept takes smart contract infrastructure one step further by creating the ability to use *purpose-specific* instruction sets and runtime functionalities in the implementation of a blockchain for a defined purpose.[249]

A blockchain designer can select only those functionalities it deems necessary to run the blockchain. This reduces the footprint of the blockchain code and further reduces the attack surface for a potential attack on the blockchain.

§1.18 SCALING THE BLOCKCHAIN

Blockchains, particularly those which rely on Proof of Work, have significant scalability issues, primarily with respect to increasing the speed of processing transactions and the ability to store a large amount of data about the state of the ledger embodied in the blockchain.

Increasing the block size and reducing the hash time go some way to improving these. Some of the alternative consensus mechanisms discussed above also help improve scalability further, but no combination of these options has yet been revealed as a *panacea* to blockchain's scalability challenges.

As a result, the search for other solutions to this problem continues. A couple of approaches to making blockchain more scalable are explained below.

[A] Sharding

One approach to dealing with the scalability problem is to adopt the *sharding* process used in traditional distributed database systems. The Ethereum foundation is pursuing

249. *See* https://sawtooth.hyperledger.org/docs/1.2/app_developers_guide/intro_xo_transaction_family.html for an example (accessed 11 Jan. 2024).

this option, under the name 'Danksharding', as a scaling solution for the Ethereum network, with a current delivery date planned for some time in 2024.[250]

Sharding involves separating a database into distinct partitions or *shards*, usually consistent with some logical way of splitting the dataset itself. For example, in a database of customers, one might shard the database based on the customers' geographic location and place data from different geographic areas on separate servers.

Applying this idea to a blockchain involves breaking up a blockchain into segments, for instance, based on the numerical value of the addresses with entitlements in the ledger. Each of these segments is then assigned a set of nodes responsible for confirming transactions for that segment only.[251] Such a set of nodes is called a *committee*. Committees confirm blocks for their shard, which once confirmed are added to a separate master chain, which is usually called the *beacon chain*.

A sharded blockchain can theoretically process transactions in parallel (to the degree of the number of shards) and thereby improve the transaction speed of the whole blockchain.

Implementing a sharded blockchain is not easy, however, as it brings additional challenges with respect to security and resolving cross-shard communications.

With respect to security, a small set of 60–80 networked nodes is clearly more susceptible to attack than a large, distributed network of thousands of nodes, like the Bitcoin and Ethereum networks.[252] It thus becomes much easier to corrupt a shard, which in turn can corrupt a beacon chain. Ongoing research has suggested some possible solutions to this problem, including rotating the membership of the committee for a shard confirmation cycle each round (which is referred to as an *epoch*), as well as having certain trusted nodes act as quality control samplers of transactions.

As it relates to cross-shard communication, a mechanism is needed to resolve transactions which have effects in distinct shards (such as an account entitlement tracked in Shard 1 being transferred to an account tracked in Shard 2). This is proposed to be achieved with a *receipts exchange* process which at a high level works as follows:

- Person A in Shard 1 wants to send an amount to Person B in Shard 2.
- Shard 1 creates a receipt for the transaction, in essence setting the money aside subject to confirmation from Shard 2.
- The receipt is sent to Shard 2, which verifies the receipt and credits Person B and then sends a confirmation back to Shard 1 to confirm the reduction in the balance of Person A.

250. https://ethereum.org/en/roadmap/danksharding/ (accessed 23 Dec. 2023).

251. Wang, G., et al., *SoK: Sharding on Blockchain* Article 4, 21, 1st ACM Conference on Advances in Financial Technologies, AFT 2019, 21–23 Oct. 2019, Zurich, Switzerland. ACM, New York, NY, USA, available at: https://doi.org/10.1145/3318041.3355457 (accessed 11 Jan. 2024). In 2019, a number of universities expressed an intention to collaborate in this area, *see* https://www.computerworld.com/article/3334542/mit-stanford-and-others-to-build-blockchain-payments-network-to-rival-visanet.html (accessed 11. Jan. 2024), but there does not appear to have been a great deal of activity since then.

252. Given that much less hash power is required to dominate a committee than the whole network.

Test implementations of this asynchronous approach demonstrate that there is a risk of an in-atomic transaction[253] occurring if there is a high volume of cross-shard transactions taking place and there are dishonest nodes participating in the validation process.

The problem of solving cross-shard communications continues to be an active area of research,[254] and the reader is encouraged to conduct additional online research to identify new developments in this area.

The first blockchain to seek to implement a form of sharding was Zilliqa in 2017.[255] Zilliqa shards only the transaction processing component of the blockchain and not its state storage, and for that purpose creates a new shard every 600 nodes. Its test network demonstrated the ability to process 2,500 TPS.[256] As noted, the Ethereum foundation is pursuing the implementation of sharding for that network.

[B] Sidechains

Another approach to improving the scalability challenge is the use of a *sidechain*.

A sidechain is simply another, usually differently structured blockchain or DLT, to which transaction processing is off-loaded. Sidechains are thought to be a feasible solution to enable consumer payment functionality with respect to cryptocurrency blockchains, such as Bitcoin, where small transactions are not practical, due to either the length of the confirmation time or the fees involved.

A sidechain generally works as follows:

- A quantity of entitlement is locked on the main blockchain.
- The same quantity of entitlement is created and unlocked on the sidechain.
- Transactions are performed with the entitlement on the sidechain.
- Once the sidechain transactions are completed or the owner wishes to update the main blockchain, the sidechain entitlement is locked (or in some cases made unusable or *burned*), and the main blockchain entitlement is updated and unlocked again.

This paired locking and unlocking between a blockchain and a sidechain is referred to as a *2-way peg* or 2WP. The reliability of 2WP is key, as any weakness in its implementation impacts the reliability and integrity of both the blockchain *and* the sidechain. Specifically, the 2-way peg must ensure *settlement finality*[257] on *both* blockchains is reliable.

253. For example, only one of the two required steps in the transaction completing.
254. *See* Kudzin, Alexander, et al. 'Scaling Ethereum 2.0 s Cross-Shard Transactions with Refined Data Structures'. Cryptography 6.4 (2022): 57, for a good overview of the current state. The paper is available online at https://www.mdpi.com/2410-387X/6/4/57 (accessed 11 Jan. 2024).
255. https://zilliqa.com/ (accessed 11 Jan. 2024).
256. https://cointelegraph.com/tags/zilliqa (accessed 11 Jan. 2024).
257. That is, not subject to being reversed.

There is also a *one-way peg*, in which the lock and transfer only happens in one direction. Once this one transfer is completed, the entitlement on the transferring blockchain is rendered useless or burned.

Sidechains can employ different consensus mechanisms than the main blockchain.

[1] The Lightning Network

The best-known example of a sidechain implementation is the Lightning Network or LN.[258] The LN was first proposed in 2016 as a potential solution to the Bitcoin scaling problem discussed previously and has been implemented with some success at the time of writing of the second edition of this book. Since mid-2022 it has maintained around 17,000 active nodes and around 50,000 channels.[259]

The idea behind the LN is to temporarily move a certain amount of bitcoin entitlement off-chain into a 'payment channel' on the LN, where day-to-day transactions can then be completed.

After a particular period of time, or at the option of the payment channel owners, the payment channel is closed, and the blockchain is updated to reflect any entitlement adjustments as a result of the transactions completed in the payment channel.

The LN is made up of nodes, much like a blockchain network. Each node can communicate with other nodes, hold a balance of entitlement transferred from the blockchain, and establish payment channels with other nodes to facilitate the exchange of entitlement between or via node owners.

In order to engage in a payment transaction, two nodes must either have established a direct payment channel or have existing payment channels through other nodes which create a path between the two nodes wishing to transact.

Creating and using a payment channel between two nodes on the LN generally works as follows:

- The two nodes create a multi-signature address on the blockchain (in essence, functionality which requires both their (digital) approvals to complete a transaction), and each makes a deposit of entitlement to the address.
- The multi-signature address also has functionality (using scripting or a smart contract) which creates an approved but unsubmitted 'commitment transaction'. This commitment transaction returns the initial deposits back to the respective nodes.
- As the two nodes engage in transactions in their payment channel, they create updated commitment transactions signed by both nodes and which they both store (but not on the main blockchain). As long as there is entitlement in the

258. The Lightning Network white paper is available at: https://lightning.network/lightning-network-paper.pdf (accessed 11 Jan. 2024).
259. To put this in context, the VISA credit card network currently has 44 million participating merchants.

payment channel to fund a transaction, unlimited transactions can be completed there.
- Either node can close the payment channel at any time by broadcasting its latest commitment transaction to the blockchain, as a result of which the respective entitlements of the nodes are then updated on the blockchain.

Nodes with open payment channels are connected to enable transactions between parties which do not have a (direct) payment channel open between them. The communications between nodes are encrypted in layers to prevent a paying node from seeing the payment channels through which the receiving node is reached.[260] The network seeks to find the shortest path between two nodes in order to optimize the time to complete a transaction.

A specific individual transaction inside a payment channel with multiple hops proceeds as follows:

- The intended beneficiary A of the transaction issues an invoice to the intended payor C through intermediary node B, which includes a hash value of a random number (called the *pre-image*) generated by A.
- C sends back a signed transaction to B, together with the hash value sent by A. The logic in the transaction will not transmit any funds from B to C, unless B is provided with the original random number generated by A (from which the hash value was derived).
- B submits a transaction to C with the hash value received from A.
- C provides the original number to B, which authorizes the transaction from C to B.
- B can now unlock the transaction from B to A, and the transaction is complete.

In some cases, a period of time is specified within which this process must be completed. This is called a *Hashed Time Lock Contract*, or HTLC.

The LN model has been active for a number of years but is not without its problems.[261] It remains to be seen whether this approach will become usable for the average consumer.

[C] Multilayer Blockchains

Another approach to addressing the scalability issues of public blockchains is to use a 'multilayer' blockchain, where various layers of the transactional workflow, each with

260. This is done in a manner similar to the Tor network and is beyond the scope of this chapter. For a good explanation of how this works, *see* https://2019.www.torproject.org/about/overview.html.en (accessed 11 Jan. 2024).
261. For example, nodes need to be online at all times in order to transact, there are difficulties in finding the shortest path between nodes if the network gets large, and there is the 'inbound capacity problem': https://blog.muun.com/the-inbound-capacity-problem-in-the-lightning-network/ (accessed 11 Jan. 2024).

their own blockchain, are optimized to provide scalability or other benefits (such as enhanced privacy) to a specific operational component.

For example, one might layer together three blockchains as follows:

- Layer 1: A public blockchain to track a currency entitlement.
- Layer 2: A private blockchain to store smart contracts based on business logic.
- Layer 3: A public blockchain to enable communications between users.

Each of the various blockchains within such a system is connected together with a 2WP or a similar type of locking logic in order to maintain immutability and transaction finality between the various layers within the system.

There are several projects seeking to explore the use of multilayer blockchains in the Internet of Things (IoT) where instead of users, devices are connected in a separate layer.[262]

[D] Rollups

Another approach to addressing the scaling challenge is the 'rollup', which is another way of 'side processing' entitlement-based blockchain transactions. Unlike sidechains, however, rollups do not use a separate blockchain. Instead, they simply bundle a set of transactions into an as small as possible set of update balances and then submit these back to the main blockchain for confirmation.

There are two main types of rollups, which differ primarily in their approach to security – dealing with invalid transactions:

(i) Optimistic Rollups rely on what is referred to as a 'fraud-proof' system, which initially assumes all transactions to be valid, with the ability of users to challenge incorrect transactions for a certain period of time (the 'challenge period') after confirmation on the main Ethereum chain.
(ii) ZK-Rollups use what is known as a 'zero-knowledge proof'[263] for succinctly proving the validity of transactions without revealing the details.

Rollups are also used quite extensively within the Decentralized Finance (DeFi) ecosystem, discussed further below.

262. *See*, for example, Badr, S., Gomaa, I. and Abd-Elrahman, E., '*Multi-tier Blockchain Framework for IoT-EHRs Systems*' Procedia Computer Science 141 (2018): 159–166 available at: https://www.sciencedirect.com/science/article/pii/S187705091831812X/pdf?md5 = a019303c3f8b4d28728c53bbbe80807f&pid = 1-s2.0-S187705091831812X-main.pdf (accessed 11 Jan. 2024).

263. A zero-knowledge proof is a cryptographic concept that allows one party (the prover) to demonstrate to another party (the verifier) that they know a specific piece of information (such as the sender, receiver, and transaction amount) without revealing what that information is. In essence, it proves the transaction validity without disclosing the actual details. There are various types of zero-knowledge proofs, such as zk-SNARKs (zero-knowledge succinct non-interactive arguments of knowledge) and zk-STARKs (zero-knowledge scalable transparent arguments of knowledge), each with its own use cases and applications in cryptography.

[E] Cross-Chain Bridges

With the use of multiple blockchains, an ability to transfer information between them is needed. To that end, a number of platforms provide this functionality, including Thorchain, Polkadot and Cosmos.

By way of example, the Polkadot platform works as follows:

- Polkadot has a *relay chain*, which acts as the main chain in the network. It connects and secures different blockchains, which it calls *parachains*.
- Communication between parachains is achieved through a mechanism called *Cross-Chain Message Passing* (XCMP).
- When assets need to move from one blockchain to another, the Polkadot platform ensures their secure transfer effectively by locking the assets on one chain and minting equivalent assets on the other.
- Validators on the Polkadot network play a crucial role in ensuring the security and consensus of cross-chain transactions. They validate the correctness of the messages passed between chains.

§1.19 BLOCKCHAIN AS A SERVICE

With the current level of maturity of cloud platforms, many companies have started to provide Blockchain as a Service (BaaS) solutions for enterprise customers. A simple online search for 'BaaS' will reveal the various vendors in this space.

§1.20 DECENTRALIZED FINANCE

[A] Introduction

In our traditional centralized finance ecosystem (CeFi), intermediaries like banks and financial institutions facilitate transactions, manage assets, and provide various financial and other consumer services. Users place trust in these intermediaries, generally due to past experience, and the generally effective regulatory framework within which they operate.

Decentralized Finance, or 'DeFi', is an attempt to replace this traditional financial ecosystem with one where this regulation-mediated trust is sought to be replaced by trust in blockchain-based automation, primarily via smart contracts and decentralized applications (DApps) (Figure 1.29).

Figure 1.29 Trust in the Context of Traditional and Decentralized Finance

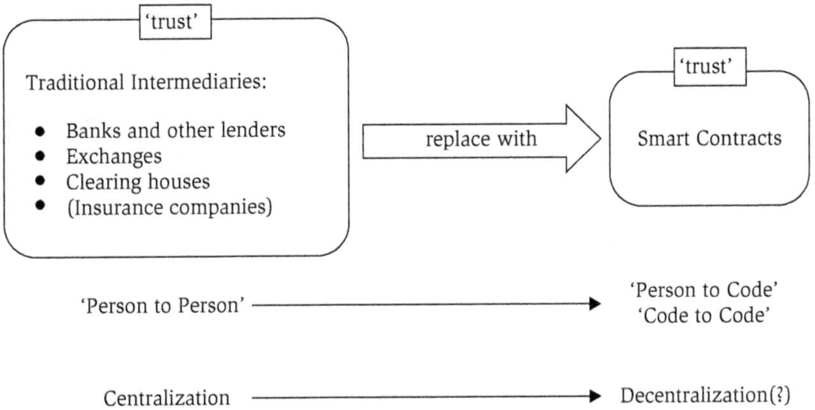

Two key touted features of DeFi are *interoperability* and *permissionless access*.

Interoperability is intended to enable a user to access a variety of services with a digital wallet containing entitlements on one or more blockchains, i.e., use different applications and functionalities enabled by open blockchain platforms.

Permissionless access purports to create access to these services for anyone, without the constraints of any entry barriers, such as the need to create accounts, or provide Know Your Client (KYC) particulars to a provider.

Within the DeFi ecosystem, reference is sometimes made to Layer 1 and 2 solutions. In this context, Layer 1 refers to the base blockchain layer where the main transactions and smart contracts are stored and executed. It is the foundational layer for DeFi and includes blockchains like Ethereum and Binance Smart Chain.

Layer 2 solutions are built on top of Layer 1 blockchains and are designed to address scalability and transaction cost challenges posed by Layer 1.[264]

The key idea is to move certain blockchain-based entitlement to a Layer 2 encapsulated system, securely conduct a set of transactions within Layer 2, and periodically update the main chain with revised entitlement balances. The Lightning Network is an example of a Layer 2 solution.

Access to (and from) the DeFi system[265] is currently primarily achieved through the conversion of CeFi-based assets (usually fiat currency) to digital assets tracked in wallets (Figure 1.30).

264. Given the transaction limits inherent in blockchains, as discussed previously.
265. Sometimes referred to as the 'on and off ramp'.

Figure 1.30 Interplay Between the Centralized Finance and Decentralized Finance Ecosystems

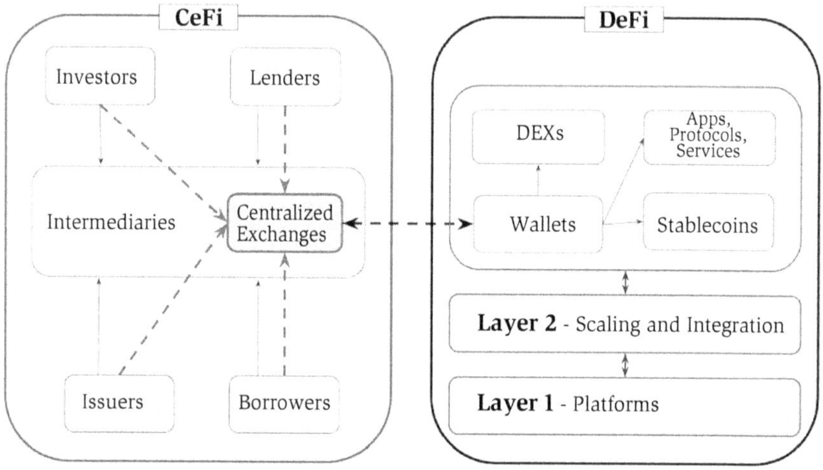

Once within the DeFi ecosystem, a number of services, protocols and products are available, which implement and use many of the technologies discussed in this chapter.[266] Some of the more popular and prominent offerings are briefly explained below.[267]

[B] Decentralized Exchanges (DEXs)

Within the DeFi ecosystem, it is possible to trade cryptocurrencies and tokens, not unlike how currencies and stocks are traded in the traditional financial markets.

Unlike the traditional markets, DeFi enables such trading without the need for a centralized authority. In the DeFi space, decentralized 'exchanges'[268] (or DEXs) facilitate fully automated peer-to-peer trading using established blockchains, smart contracts, and various decentralized protocols. Popular DEXs include UniSwap, SushiSwap, and PancakeSwap.

In order to trade using a DEX, a user usually connects their cryptocurrency wallet to the DEX. This connection allows the DEX to then access the user's funds in response to trading orders authorized by the user.

266. There exist numerous services, protocols and products within the DeFi ecosystem, some more successful than others. This section does not aim to be comprehensive, but identifies the more mature projects, as assessed by the author at the time of writing.
267. Many of the core functionalities used in the below examples are re-used, usually with some modification, to enable a number of other DeFi services and products, including derivatives and insurance.
268. As previously noted, this is arguably an improper use of the term 'exchange', given its specific meaning in securities law as a regulated entity. Nonetheless, I will use this term, given its prevalence and adopted use, with that caveat.

A user seeking to trade selects the desired trading pair and submits their order to the DEX trading smart contract, which then seeks to fill it using one of several models.

The traditional trade model is the order-book approach, and some DEXs use this methodology to effect trades and determine price. An order book is a digital list of buy and sell orders for a particular asset at price levels set by parties wishing to trade.[269] Order books can either be on-chain or off-chain, although the latency and fee implications of storing orders on-chain have prevented the effective practical implementation of the former on slower confirmation/high fee blockchains such as Ethereum. To address this, a faster sidechain or a high-speed blockchain can be used. If a low degree of latency is required, then an off-chain order book is the only option, but this introduces a degree of centralization into the trading process, which some may find undesirable.

Given these issues with order-book-based models, the creators of most DEXs have chosen to do away with the order book and operate on the automated market maker (AMM) model, which utilizes *liquidity pools* to fill orders.

Liquidity pools are reserves of tokens locked in a smart contract maintained by the DEX (*see* 'Staking' below). The DEX charges a fee for a trade, which is used in part to fund rewards for staking token holders.

On an AMM-based DEX, the trading price is determined by a mathematical formula. The most widely used formula is the *constant product formula*. A constant **k** (determined by the DEX creator) is set and used to determine the price for a token pair by maintaining product equivalence between the quantities of two tokens, using the formula **k = A * B**, where **A** and **B** are the quantities of tokens A and B in the pool. This approach to price determination seeks to embody a (perhaps somewhat crude) form of supply and demand dynamics. If a token is bought, its quantity in the pool decreases, leading to a higher price for that token. Conversely, if a token is sold, its quantity in the pool increases, resulting in a lower price. A number of other formulas are also used in a similar manner.[270]

A weakness of this approach is that it has no sensitivity for the price of a particular token pair outside the AMM liquidity pool and is susceptible to manipulation strategies such as front running and wash trading. As a result, AMMs are not without criticism.[271]

In both approaches, trades are settled on the blockchain through the execution of a smart contract.

[1] Initial DEX Offerings (IDOs)

On some exchanges, new tokens can be launched with very little administrative friction simply by adding the required smart contract functionality to the AMM for the DEX.[272]

269. Including the usual parameters for price limits, market price trading, etc.
270. For instance, Constant Sum and Constant Mean.
271. *See*, for example, https://kenaninstitute.unc.edu/rethinc/wp-content/uploads/2022/03/Park_-Andreas-Automated-Market-Makers.pdf (accessed 11 Jan. 2024).
272. *See* https://cointelegraph.com/learn/initial-dex-offering-ido for a detailed guide (accessed 11 Jan. 2024).

[C] Staking

The DeFi ecosystem offers opportunities for the holders of tokens to earn a return by 'staking' such assets with various protocols. Staking involves a form of deposit of tokens, by way of sending them to a smart contract, not unlike a fiat currency deposit to a traditional bank. The depositor assumes a certain amount of risk in doing so and in return is provided with a reward of some kind. The receiving protocol can use staked tokens for various purposes, including maintaining a liquidity pool, lending, and speculation. From the proceeds of these activities, a portion is returned to the staked token holders, usually by way of a proprietary token (i.e., not the token which was staked).

The DeFi ecosystem maintains a metric called *Total Value Locked* (TVL) as an indicator of the total quantity of assets that are staked, locked or deposited in its various protocols and platforms.[273]

[D] Stablecoins

A stablecoin is a token, the price of which is pegged to some underlying fiat currency such as the US dollar or the Euro. For example, the stablecoin Tether (USDT) is pegged to the US Dollar 1:1.

Stablecoins are used for several purposes, including the following:

- As part of a trading pair, to facilitate trading and hold assets during price volatility.
- Making payments.
- Funding smart contract execution (like 'gas' on the Ethereum blockchain).

There are two categories of stablecoins.

[1] Centralized Stablecoins

A centralized stablecoin is issued and maintained by way of an issuer-controlled smart contract on one or more blockchains. Centralized stablecoins are typically directly backed by reserves held by the issuer. The issuer has full control over the stablecoin's monetary policy, including the issuance and redemption of tokens.

Examples of centralized stablecoins include Tether (USDT), USD Coin (USDC), and TrueUSD (TUSD).

[2] Decentralized Stablecoins

A decentralized stablecoin is not managed by a centralized entity but by encoded logic in a smart contract. A decentralized stablecoin is not necessarily backed by its

273. *See* the Defi Llama website at https://defillama.com/ (accessed 11 Jan. 2024).

underlying asset. In the absence of that, there are several methods by which this type of stablecoin seeks to maintain price stability:

- Algorithms which respond to changes in demand and usually adjust the number of stablecoins in circulation to influence the price to remain close to the peg. When the stablecoin's price is above its peg, new tokens are minted, and when it is below the peg, tokens are burned or removed from circulation.
- Collateralization by other assets, such as cryptocurrencies or tokens. If the stablecoin deviates from its target value, the smart contract may trigger actions, such as liquidating collateral or minting new stablecoins.

Many decentralized stablecoins have a token-based governance mechanism where specific 'governance token' holders can participate in the decision-making process for the specific stablecoin. This may include voting on changes to the protocol, adjustments to parameters, or upgrades to the algorithm.

Examples of decentralized stablecoins are DAI (part of the MakerDAO protocol), sUSD (part of the Synthetix protocol), and the Terra stablecoin UST.

Algorithmic stablecoins backed by other tokens, and not verifiably stable assets, can be very volatile in maintaining their peg, as was demonstrated by the Terra/Luna debacle.[274]

[3] Central Bank Digital Currency

Stablecoins need to be distinguished from a *Central Bank Digital Currency* (CBDC) which is a completely different kind of digital asset. A CBDC is a digital version of an established fiat currency and has all the trappings of such a currency:

- Issued and regulated by the country's central bank (not a private entity).
- Backed by the full faith and credit of the government of the country.
- Considered legal tender within the applicable country.
- They are centralized and do not use DLT technology.

An online CBDC status tracker is available.[275]

[E] Borrowing

The DeFi ecosystem has numerous protocols for the borrowing of digital currency (tokens). In many cases, loans are extended in the form of a stablecoin, proprietary to the lending platform. The process used by MakerDAO,[276] the oldest borrowing platform, illustrates the usual steps:

274. *See* https://www.nber.org/system/files/working_papers/w31160/w31160.pdf for a good overview (accessed 11 Jan. 2024).
275. https://cbdctracker.org/ (accessed 11 Jan. 2024).
276. https://makerdao.com/en/ (accessed 11 Jan. 2024).

- The putative borrower must have a wallet that supports Ethereum transactions as well as a balance of ETH or another accepted (ERC-20 based) cryptocurrency to use as collateral.
- The user connects the wallet to the MakerDAO platform by creating an account.
- The user accepts the *collateralization ratio* for the platform. A collateralization ratio is often used to ensure stability of the particular lending system by guarding against significant fluctuations in the price of the staked collateral. The ratio depicts the amount of collateral that the borrower must maintain with respect to the number of borrowed tokens. For example, if the required ratio is 150%, the borrower needs to provide collateral worth 150% of the amount of DAI to be borrowed.
- The user locks (stakes) the chosen collateral in a smart contract by way of a wallet-intermediated transaction.
- Once the collateral is locked, the borrower can generate DAI, the MakerDAO stablecoin, against it. Fees are usually also charged for this process.
- The transaction is confirmed on the applicable blockchain and once complete will result in a DAI entitlement in the borrower's wallet.
- The borrower can now use the DAI balance like any other stablecoin.
- Repayment is achieved by transferring the borrowed DAI, together with applicable interest and fees, back to the smart contract.

It is very important for borrowers to carefully monitor the applicable collateralization ratio. If the value of the collateral decreases significantly, and absent a 'top up', (part of) the collateral may be automatically liquidated by the smart contract.

FURTHER READING

Andreas M. Antonopoulos. 2017, Mastering Bitcoin: Programming the Open Blockchain (2nd ed.) O'Reilly Media, Inc.

Andreas M. Antonopoulos. 2018, Mastering Ethereum, available at: https://github.com/ethereumbook/ethereumbook/blob/develop/book.asciidoc (accessed 11 Jan. 2024).

Imran Bashir. 2023, Mastering Blockchain (4th ed.) Packt Publishing.

Nick Furneaux. Investigating cryptocurrencies: understanding, extracting, and analyzing blockchain evidence. John Wiley & Sons, 2018.

Siraj Raval. 2016, Decentralized Applications, O'Reilly Media, Inc.

CHAPTER 2
Regulatory Aspects of Blockchains

Thomas Richter

§2.01 BLOCKCHAIN AS A REGULATORY SUBJECT

Technology regulation is ever increasing, and blockchain is right in the middle of it. When the first blockchain uses cases appeared several years ago, there was no regulation that would have specifically addressed this technology with its unique characteristics. This did, obviously, not mean that blockchains were operating 'above the law' or in a legal vacuum but were subject to all 'applicable' laws, while the question has been raised whether blockchain is even 'alegal' and resistant to regulation.[1] Determining the applicability of laws that were issued when blockchains were still unknown or at least not a topic which would have particularly been reflected in such regulation, or which even would have been taken into account in the legislative process, was not always very easy. Over time, the picture has changed though, based on three major reasons.

First, blockchain has factually been 'clustered' into various major use cases, which are, for example, digital assets, digital money, tokenization, the metaverse and decentralized applications, non-fungible tokens (NFTs) and smart contracts. Pertinent regulatory topics are mainly determined by the very use case nowadays, which is exemplarily shown by specific crypto asset regulations that are emerging.[2] Second, the increasing convergence of blockchain with other technologies, notably its integration with Artificial Intelligence (AI), creates an additional layer of complexity when it comes to the regulatory aspects, as this potentially triggers the multiplication of regulatory

1. *See* Primavera De Filippi, Morshed Mannan and Wessel Reijers, *The alegality of blockchain technology*, Policy and Society, Volume 41, Issue 3, September 2022 (16 Feb. 2022), pp. 358-372; available at https://doi.org/10.1093/polsoc/puac006 (accessed 10 Mar. 2024).
2. *See* Chapters 6 and 7 of this book, *infra*, with an overview on crypto asset regulation in the EU, the UK and the US.

regimes for a given use case. And third, regulatory discussions for use cases are often cutting across blockchain and non-blockchain subjects, as shown by the Digital Euro project of the European Central Bank[3] which includes an element of 'decentralization' but is not as such a 'blockchain project', and which stands exemplarily for a more technology-neutral approach to challenges that would have been formerly attributed to the blockchain as well.[4]

All of the above may suggest that it might be sufficient to approach blockchain regulation from a pure use case-specific background. However, blockchain was, is and will remain a technology that has certain special and inherent features and characteristics, which are of important relevance for any regulatory assessment more generally. This chapter aims to provide an overview of certain key regulatory questions which are raised by such features of the blockchain technology. It does not refer to any specific law or use case but aims to serve as a general guide to assessing such fundamental regulatory questions against the specific features in an effort to avoid the appearance of what has been described as a 'law lag'[5] in which the law lags behind the developments of a new technology and its impact. Therefore, it does also not foster any specific use case but tries to examine blockchain as a generic technology open to many applications in the first place. The chapter is not intended to cover any specific kind of blockchain regulation, for which a comprehensive case-specific review remains indispensable, but to provide initial guidance on the potential legal and regulatory implications and pitfalls when dealing with blockchains. More specific guidance on particular legal and regulatory aspects can be found in the following chapters of this handbook.

[A] The 'Legal Factor'

Addressing blockchain issues has been a challenge for lawmakers and regulators due to its unique characteristics, in particular decentralization, questions over jurisdiction and anonymity. At the same time, legal certainty is key for every individual or organization, and it is a prerequisite for the deployment of blockchain technology to have sufficient clarity on the legal questions that are associated with it, and specifically the legality of the very use case. While it could be observed in the 'early days' that not

3. *See* https://www.ecb.europa.eu/paym/digital_euro/html/index.en.html (accessed 10 Mar. 2024).
4. And described by the ECB as follows: '*Third, the principle of technological neutrality[12] suggests that the proposed regulations should take no stance on how the digital euro would fulfil user needs and as to the evolution of its functional and technical design features. The inclusion of provisions requiring or prohibiting specific designs or technical features might constrain any or all of the following aspects: the smooth functioning, evolution and demand for the digital euro, and the Eurosystem's ability to define and implement monetary policy independently. Legislation containing provisions on these issues might risk being unable to withstand technological developments in the fast-changing field of digitalisation of money and payment services*', Opinion of the European Central Bank of 31 October 2023 on the digital euro (CON/2023/34), para. 3.5 (p. 4); available at https://www.ecb.europa.eu/pub/pdf/legal/ecb.leg_con_2023_34.en.pdf?495c419f19a78fd8d5f40e7cffffb331 (accessed 10 Mar. 2024).
5. Carla L. Reyes, *Moving Beyond Bitcoin to an Endogenous Theory of Decentralized Ledger Technology Regulation: An Initial Proposal*, 61 Vill. L. Rev. 202-203 (2016).

all market participants were fully aware of any and all legal and regulatory implications of their usage of blockchains in certain use cases, there is now increasing sensitivity to clear legal questions first and act then. This may be called the 'legal factor', a factor that should take into account not only 'by design' the legal and regulatory implications in the process of developing blockchain models and their legal structuring but also the actual and ongoing deployment in a specific way to ensure the latter is and remains legally compliant. For this, a thorough understanding of the interaction between the blockchain features and legal concepts is indispensable.

[B] The Meaning of 'Blockchain' in the Context of Regulation

[1] The Relevance of a Legal Definition

The first chapter of this handbook provides a technical understanding of blockchain and has described the various forms of blockchains and their technical characteristics and has also delineated blockchains from the distributed ledger technology in a broader sense.[6] But what does blockchain mean in a legal context and how is it defined? It is probably not unsurprising that there is no generally agreed legal definition of blockchain, given that it is still a relatively new technology without a comprehensive legal history. There is only limited definitional precedence, in particular compared to the attention that blockchain has attracted over the past few years also in the legal community. One of the reasons for this may be that for legal purposes blockchain has rarely been looked at from the perspective of a generic technology but has mostly been reviewed in a specific use case scenario like crypto assets/tokens or initial coin offerings. Further to that, the blockchain technology is not very easily accessible as such and comes in various different types and forms. Also, given the new and complex nature of blockchain technology, most legal publications start with an introduction that is rather a technical explanation than a legal definition to provide the reader and legal professional with a basic *technical* understanding in the first place.

However, establishing a legal definition of blockchain goes beyond the question of obtaining an understanding of how that technology works and what its characteristics are. It is about putting blockchain in a legal and regulatory context and finding the right subject matter definition to use it in law. A clear definition is a prerequisite to legally addressing blockchain, for example, in statutes or in contracts. For example, the EU Blockchain Observatory and Forum has postulated the need for policymakers 'to clearly define what blockchains and Smart Contracts are under the law'[7] as one of the

6. *See* Chapter 1, §1.14[C], *supra*. Most of the issues discussed in this chapter are common to other distributed ledger technology solutions as well and hence can be applied accordingly.
7. Thematic Report of the European Blockchain Observatory and Forum, *Legal and Regulatory Framework of Blockchains and Smart Contracts* 7 (27 Sep. 2019), available at: https://www.eublockchainforum.eu/sites/default/files/reports/report_legal_v1.0.pdf (accessed 10 Mar. 2024).

eight guiding principles.[8] The Government of Liechtenstein, in justification of the first-of-its kinds 'Blockchain Act' at the time,[9] had highlighted the importance of a technology-neutral definition of the term 'blockchain' to avoid that the scope of the act may become outdated and too narrow in a few years,[10] a problem that is common in technology regulation, given the speed of tech cycles.

For these purposes, this section starts with a description of the various forms of blockchains as such distinction is relevant for the legal assessment, as well as a description of the relevance of the underlying technological standard. It outlines the specific characteristics that are inherent to the blockchain technology and as such have a shaping influence on the legal assessment.

[2] Various Organizational Forms of Blockchains

'The' blockchain does not exist. The blockchain technology comes in various different forms and may be best described as a 'class of technology'.[11] While there is no generally agreed typology of the organizational forms of blockchains, they may be mainly distinguished by their organizational set-up and the underlying protocol that is used.

In terms of organizational forms, blockchains are mostly distinguished by the criterion of who can read a blockchain and who can transact on it (i.e., execute and/or validate individual transactions).[12] The following classification takes these factors into account but draws specific attention to the legal implications that the categorization may have and therefore looks at the participants, the admission process and the initiators.

The first distinction is between so-called public and private blockchains. This relates to the potential participants that such blockchains target (*who can join a blockchain*). Public blockchains are open to anyone, and the group of addressees is not

8. The other seven are: 'Communicate legal interpretations as broadly as possible', 'Choose the right regulatory approaches for the question at hand', 'Harmonise the law and interpretations of it', 'Help policy makers develop an understanding of the technology', 'Work on high-impact use cases first', 'Closely monitor developments in less mature use cases and encourage self-regulation', and 'Make use of blockchain as a regulatory tool', Thematic Report of the European Blockchain Observatory and Forum, *supra* n. 7, at 7-8.
9. Liechtenstein Token and Trusted Technology Service Provider Act (*Gesetz über Token und VT-Dienstleister*) (3 Oct. 2019), text of the Act available at: https://www.gesetze.li/konso/pdf/2019.301 (accessed 10 Mar. 2024) – in German language only.
10. *Bericht und Antrag der Regierung an den Landtag des Fürstentums Liechtenstein betreffend die Schaffung eines Gesetzes über Token und VT-Dienstleister (Token- und VT-Dienstleister-Gesetz; TVTG) und die Abänderung weiterer Gesetze, Nr. 54/2019*, 55. In German language only.
11. Roman Beck & Christoph Müller-Bloch & John Leslie King, *Governance in the Blockchain Economy: A Framework and Research Agenda*, 19(10) J. Assoc. Inform. Sys., Article 1 1021, available at: https://aisel.aisnet.org/cgi/viewcontent.cgi?article=1835&context=jais (accessed 10 Mar. 2024).
12. Amanda Anderberg, et al., *Blockchain Now and Tomorrow: Assessing Multidimensional Impacts of Distributed Ledger Technologies*, Susana Figueiredo Do Nascimento & Alexandre Roque Mendes Polvora (eds), EUR 29813 EN, Publications Office of the European Union 14, available at http://publications.jrc.ec.europa.eu/repository/bitstream/JRC117255/blockchain_online.pdf (accessed 10 Mar. 2024).

limited or specified. No specific admission process is applied. It would anyway be impossible to apply any form of discretionary admission requirements, as no control over a public blockchain is retained by the coder(s) and initiator(s) upon its release. It is open source, so anyone who is able to meet the technical requirements may join such a blockchain. More precisely from a technical perspective, every participant may download the software and maintain a node and may then read the ledger and write into the ledger as part of the network, that means append new transactions. In contrast, private blockchains target a specific group of participants. The selection between eligible participants and non-eligible participants in the case of the latter may be carried out by a set of predefined criteria built into the blockchain code and vetted automatically or even by a specific case-by-case decision of admission on a discretionary basis. From the legal perspective, this criterion is noteworthy as it defines if, for example, an offer is made to an unlimited number of counterparties (in the case of a public blockchain) or if it is made to a limited group of counterparties or even specified individuals (in the case of a private blockchain). It also defines who would be eligible to accept such offer. This could be particularly relevant, for example, in the context of the distribution of financial services as an example for regulated activities over a blockchain. In summary, this distinction mainly defines the potential 'participants'[13] of a blockchain.

The next distinction is whether a blockchain is 'permissionless' or 'permissioned'. This relates to the question of whether a – public or private – blockchain may freely be joined without a specific decision of admission (in which case it is permissionless) or if a dedicated admission decision is applied (in which case it is permissioned) (*how a blockchain can be joined*). This distinction is also frequently called 'open' or 'closed'. The 'permissionless/permissioned' distinction seems to overlap with the 'public/private' distinction. This is correct as far as it relates to the application of an admission decision, and as such the decision may factually make a blockchain 'private' as such. However, in the 'public/private' distinction, the focus is on the target group, that means who may generally join or not, while the 'permissionless/permissioned' distinction focuses on the question of whether a blockchain may freely be joined without the vetting of any further criteria or whether certain criteria must be met for being granted admission. Hence, the focus for this, both factually and legally, is on the question under which conditions a blockchain may be joined. Blockchains may also be 'public permissioned', in which case the blockchain would be addressed to everyone, and everyone could potentially access and read the ledger but not create and participate in transactions. This distinction is mainly defined by the role of the 'nodes' as transaction validators, as in a permissioned environment, these would have to be preselected by a blockchain administrator.[14] From a legal perspective, a permissioned blockchain not only allows for a vetting (up to a full identification) of the

13. In this chapter, blockchain 'participants' will be used as a term for the following persons/roles: 'nodes', 'miners', 'users', 'administrators' and 'coders'. The different roles and their distinctive legal qualification are explained below, *see* §2.04[B].
14. Robby Houben & Alexander Snyers, *Cryptocurrencies and Blockchain, Legal Context and Implications for Financial Crime, Money Laundering and Tax Evasion*, Study requested by the

participants who want to execute transactions but also provides the framework for imposing conditions for participation on the users, which could, for example, consist in the acceptance of certain terms and conditions for participation as a 'rulebook' between the participants. In fact, a permissioned blockchain reintroduces to a certain extent the concept of a (trusted) third party which may exercise a certain level of control, while public blockchains aim at completely removing any such intermediary.

The last distinction, which is not commonly made from a technical point of view, but which may add value to the legal perspective, relates to the question of who initiates and operates a blockchain (*who is behind the blockchain*). In a public permissionless blockchain, there is no control retained by the coders of a blockchain with no possibility for them to interfere at a later stage, so this criterion may look moot in this case. However, the fact that who has programmed the blockchain may matter for a potential participant from the legal perspective. It may in the first place determine whether a potential participant considers the developer to be trustworthy and may therefore create a certain 'presumption of legality', if, for example, a public permissionless blockchain would have been set up by a government. In a public permissioned blockchain, the code has built in a certain admission process for new participants, and participation may be vetted either by automated means or on the basis of a distinct decision by a 'gatekeeper', who then becomes central for the legal regulation perspective as the person factually controlling the blockchain. Such person may be the original coder and initiator of that blockchain, or it may be delegated to another party, or it may be a combination of built-in criteria which are only factually vetted by an 'oracle', i.e., a role that transfers off-chain data as an agent into the blockchain. Finally, in the context of private blockchains, these may also run entirely on private networks as opposed to the public Internet in which case the operators of such blockchain can clearly be identified and held liable for that blockchain's compliance with regulations (so-called enterprise blockchains).

The criteria provided above are by no means exclusive or exhaustive, but they may provide a first orientation on assessing and structuring a blockchain from a legal perspective. Certain legal requirements which may be mandatory prerequisites (e.g., the necessity to know the participants) would have a direct effect on this. Table 2.1 summarizes this categorization for convenience.[15]

TAX3 committee (July 2018), 15, available at: http://www.europarl.europa.eu/cmsdata/150761/TAX3%20Study%20on%20cryptocurrencies%20and%20blockchain.pdf (accessed 10 Mar. 2024).

15. The overview partially follows the scheme suggested by Garrick Hileman & Michael Rauchs, Global Blockchain Benchmarking Study (2017) 20., available at: https://papers.ssrn.com/sol3/papers.cfm?abstract_id=3040224 (accessed 10 Mar. 2024).

Table 2.1 Main Types of Blockchains and Certain Pertinent Legal Key Considerations

	Admission Model	*Operated by*	*Certain Legal Key Considerations (Non-exhaustive)*
Public	Permissionless	All nodes and miners (no control)	Focus on how legal compliance can be achieved w/o responsible party
	Permissioned	All nodes and miners (no control), permission process (partially) controlled by coder(s)/initiator(s), third party or oracle(s)	Focus on how legal compliance can be ensured through design of the code and the permission process applied; permission process allows to introduce T&Cs between participants, but difficulties in surveillance of adherence to the T&Cs
Private	Permissionless	Specified operator(s) retaining control over writing transactions but open to anyone for reading transactions	Focus on legal implications of ledger being readable by anyone
	Permissioned (may be in the form of 'consortium' or 'enterprise')	Specified operator(s) retaining control over reading and writing transactions; may be fully or partially on private network	Focus on the T&Cs that are agreed between the participants

[3] Legal Relevance of the Blockchain Protocol

Blockchains may be further distinguished by their underlying protocol. As a blockchain is a decentralized system with many different participants (e.g., users, nodes, miners), and in the absence of a single central authority which is one of the inherent structural and distinct features of that technology, all participants must follow certain rules for the blockchain to form a working network. Those rules are laid down in software protocols which are developed by software coders called the 'blockchain protocol'. Foremost, the blockchain protocol defines the consensus algorithm which is used to add new blocks of transactions to the blockchain. Most commonly, this is based on a so-called Proof-of-Work concept, in which new blocks are validated on the basis of miners solving a mathematical problem and being rewarded for this ('mining') or a so-called Proof-of-Stake concept, in which more senior participants with higher stakes (e.g., more crypto coins) validate transactions (assuming their intrinsic interest in the integrity of the network for the sake of their stakes). While all blockchains follow the same general technological principles, protocols may be significantly different. There are thousands of protocols, and within the limits of technical viability, coders are free to design new protocols as they wish. However, certain major blockchain protocols have emerged, the most prominent of which is probably the Bitcoin protocol. Other widely used protocols specifically for enterprise use include Ethereum,[16] Hyperledger,[17] Corda[18] and MultiChain.[19]

The blockchain protocol contains the rules that coders have foreseen and that participants have agreed upon, through either their action of joining a blockchain network that was generally open to new participants in a permissionless blockchain or their request for participation and subsequent admission in a permissioned blockchain. The question is if, and if yes, to what extent, the underlying protocol is legally relevant. Typically, as described in the context of the principle of technology neutrality below,[20] regulation applying to technology does not address an individual technology discretely, but rather the specific use of the same more generally. It hence appears to be even less relevant which specific form of the blockchain technology in the form of different underlying protocols is applied. This may be compared to Internet-related regulation. For example, regulations on the usage of cookies on websites would refer to neither the technological solution of how such cookies are included in a webpage nor the specific browser that is used for accessing the website or the Internet protocol.[21] Hence, regulation does – at least so far – not distinguish between different blockchain protocols, and any regulatory paradigm that may apply or may be derived for blockchains would not be distinguished accordingly.

However, a blockchain's protocol has two main legal implications. First, the protocol itself needs to be legally compliant, and coders need to take laws and regulations into account when developing code for a specific protocol. For example, a key requirement is the blockchain's compliance with data protection laws, for Europe namely the General Data Protection Regulation (GDPR),[22] which needs to be ensured through the way in which the protocol is developed in the first place. It is evident that coders hence play a key role in a blockchain's legal compliance. Second, the protocol

---

16. https://ethereum.org (accessed 10 Mar. 2024), for a description of certain Ethereum features and characteristics *see* Chapter 1, §1.10[A], *supra*.
17. https://www.hyperledger.org (accessed 10 Mar. 2024).
18. https://www.corda.net (accessed 10 Mar. 2024).
19. https://www.multichain.com (accessed 10 Mar. 2024).
20. *See* §2.03[A], *infra*.
21. For example, the EU General Data Protection Regulation (GDPR) in describing the nature of 'online identifiers' states broadly: 'Natural persons may be associated with online identifiers provided by their devices, applications, tools and protocols, such as internet protocol addresses, cookie identifiers or other identifiers such as radio frequency identification tags'; Regulation (EU) 2016/679 of the European Parliament and of the Council of 27 Apr. 2016 on the protection of natural persons with regard to the processing of personal data and on the free movement of such data, Recital 30.
22. For more details, *see* Chapter 4, §4.02 through §4.09, *infra*.

is instrumental in defining the roles and responsibilities of the various blockchain participants, thereby fundamentally creating the blockchain governance. It may contain not only technical but also legal rules. These may consist in certain terms and conditions that the participants need to adhere to, imposed either by purely technical means in a permissionless blockchain or by the requirement of express acceptance in a permissioned blockchain upon admittance. In terms of technical rules, it contains the standard on which the blockchain is built and operated, and it ensures that all nodes recognize themselves and thereby 'holds the blockchain together'. From a legal perspective, the entirety of the legal principles in the protocol together with its technical mandatories may be characterized as a blockchain's 'constitution'. And like most constitutions, it may not freely be amended, but parts of it may be unchangeable at all, and others only by a majority vote of all blockchain participants. Hence, the protocol has a key influence on the blockchain network and is the place where legal requirements may be localized and built in.

As we have now seen, the protocol is an instrument which defines the mechanisms and governance in a blockchain, and the protocol may be designed in many ways. However, every blockchain has several characteristics which differentiates it from other database technologies, and according to which the protocol's principles are defined to match the definition of being a blockchain. These characteristics and the pertinent legal implications will be discussed below.

[4] Inherent Characteristics of Blockchains and Their Legal Implications

The blockchain technology has a number of fundamental technical characteristics which differentiate it from other database technologies, specifically traditional database models with a central ledger.[23] At the outset of any legal assessment, it is important to acknowledge that these characteristics are inherent to that technology *as such*, and removing them may devaluate the specific benefit that is attributed to them and the blockchain as a technological means for a certain use case in general. In other words, these characteristics are (among others) likely the main reasons why the blockchain technology is given preference over another database technology in a specific case. Hence, the legal assessment needs to take them into account in principle as given, which also means that a 'showstopper' from the legal perspective may become an overall showstopper for the use case. Hence, it is particularly important to deal with these questions as early as possible in the process of the legal assessment. Three of these 'constituting' principles will be described subsequently: decentralization, immutability and transparency.[24]

Decentralization: In the form of a public permissionless blockchain, a blockchain is completely decentralized; that means it is distributed over a multitude of nodes potentially physically located all over the world. Each participant has the same rights,

23. For database concepts, *see* further Chapter 1, §1.04, *supra*.
24. *See* also Thomas Richter, *Blockchain – Rechtliche Aspekte aus Sicht der Finanzindustrie,* DGRI Jahrbuch 2017, Robert G. v. Briner & Axel Funk (ed.) 2018, 165-178.

and the original coders would not withhold any more rights or control than every other participant. Metaphorically speaking, a public permissionless blockchain is 'released by the coder into freedom' and is then outside its strict control. There are no possibilities of exerting influence, other than through any built-in governance mechanisms by, for example, obtaining or securing more than 50% of the voting rights. In such a public permissionless blockchain, it is claimed that there is no need for a trusted central authority since the consensus mechanism described above *as such* creates the trust in the correctness of the blockchain, solely through technological means.

Immutability: Due to the sequential design of the data blocks, and how they are tied together, it is practically impossible to change a transaction once incorporated into the blockchain at any later point in time.[25] For the legal assessment of – at least a public – blockchain, it must hence be assumed that once a transaction has been created, any later need for changes may simply be impossible from a factual perspective. However, there are technical possibilities to intervene in a blockchain. The so-called forking aims at creating a new 'branch' of the blockchain by sending the proposal of a software update to all participants within the network with the aim of invalidating or at least changing the previous chain or 'splitting off' a transaction branch. Furthermore, the so-called 51-percent attack describes a scenario in which the consensus principle is attempted to be overcome by a party taking over more than half of the computing power of all other participants. Leaving aside the question of probability and feasibility, it should be noted that in both cases the previous blockchain would be 'invalidated' by such action, but the data would still be existent. It is, however, possible to design a blockchain technically from the outset with the possibility to allow certain participants to make changes to previous transactions. Although this could be seen as an interference with one of the general principles of the blockchain technology, it should be considered as a possible means to achieve legal compliance. A very precise definition of the possible rights of intervention would then be necessary since this design would involve the risk of an oligopoly of these privileged participants and would require extending the necessary level of trust to those participants.

Transparency: Each node in the network has a complete copy of the blockchain. The blockchain mechanism requires that each participant also has reading rights. This means that all transactions are visible to every participant and are therefore (de facto) public. While the data record of the individual transaction itself does not contain any clear data because there is a separation between the identification and verification level on the one hand and the transaction level on the other, the data record contains at least certain anonymized addresses of the involved parties, which are verified by the system at network level to carry out the transaction. However, it is not technically impossible to decrypt this data and, for example, to establish a personal reference in the meaning of data privacy laws. For legal purposes, it must hence be assumed that such data is not confidential and may be related back to the actual parties by technical means.

25. On the technical aspects of immutability *see* Chapter 1, §1.06[C], *supra*.

[5] Summary

This section has initially outlined the importance of defining blockchain in generic form for legal purposes. It has then introduced the distinction between public and private blockchains on the one hand and permissionless and permissioned blockchains on the other hand and has also drawn the attention to the operator(s) of a blockchain. It has further found that the underlying blockchain protocol is as such not a decisive factor for the legal assessment but may still have important legal implications to consider. It has finally outlined that decentralization, immutability and transparency are to a certain extent inherent features of the blockchain technology that the legal assessment needs to consider.

These insights allow to summarize blockchain in the broadest sense for legal purposes as being *a public or private, permissionless or permissioned database network, which may or may not be controlled to a certain extent by (an) operator(s), which is based on certain software code (protocol) and which inherent features are that it is decentralized, immutable and transparent.*

[C] The Meaning of 'Regulation' in the Context of Blockchain

The previous section has elaborated on the question of what 'blockchain' means from the factual perspective for legal purposes. This section will now – vice versa – try to answer the question of what 'regulation' means in a blockchain context. Legal questions in connection with blockchains have very much focused on individual legal topics around specific use cases in the last few years or isolated legal questions (e.g., on a blockchain's compliance with specific data privacy requirements such as the right to be forgotten). The following section will elaborate on blockchain as a generic technology in the legal context to address the question of which type of regulations may at all be relevant for a project adopting blockchain from a broad structural point of view.

[1] Which Kind of Regulation Can Be Relevant for Blockchains?

Starting from a very broad point of view, drawing a comparison to the regulation of the Internet which has certain similar aspects, reference can be made to Lawrence Lessig who in a famous book has described four factors which regulate behaviour in the cyberspace: Laws, norms, markets and code.[26] He describes all those factors with their specific mode of operation: Laws, which threaten *ex post* sanctions if not adhered to; norms which if not observed would lead to sanctions imposed by the community; markets, with, for example, charges as being potentially prohibitive for access; and code, as the constraints imposed by the software and hardware.[27] Blockchains are

26. Lawrence Lessig, *Code Version 2.0* 124-125 (2006), available at: https://upload.wikimedia.org/wikipedia/commons/f/fd/Code_v2.pdf (accessed 10 Mar. 2024).
27. *Ibid.*

operating in a very similar context, and when applying these factors accordingly, it can be concluded that these go far beyond the pure body of law. This illustrates that it is always important to understand the full context in which a technology is applied, which includes a reasonable understanding of how it works, how it is applied, and which implications may result from its use in a specific case, or, in other words: 'do not forget the broader picture'.

In further assessing which specific regulation applies to blockchains, there is a fundamental distinction to draw, which may help understanding better the overall legal context. First, there is the legal relationship between the various blockchain participants (mainly nodes, miners, users, administrators, coders and oracles) on a horizontal level. Their relationship will be mainly covered by private law and depend very strongly on the set-up of the blockchain and what those parties have agreed upon in terms of their governance (in which context the blockchain protocol is again of relevance).[28] This could be characterized as 'regulation *in* the blockchain'. An example for this is general contract law or the law of torts. Second, there is the relationship between the participants and the general (mostly mandatory) laws which apply in a vertical perspective, which are mainly public law subjects (including criminal law), and which all those participants mandatorily need to adhere to, and, if they do not, could be sanctioned accordingly. This could be characterized as 'regulation *of* the blockchain'. Examples for this are data protection laws, criminal laws and financial services regulations.

For both categories, in the broadest sense, regulation encompasses all applicable laws, statutes, by-laws, subordinate legislation as well as any regulatory requirements from authorities and regulators. However, while in the case of the horizontal relationship between the participants, which is largely based on contractual arrangements, there is generally contractual freedom and most regulation should be dispositive (further depending on the relevant jurisdiction) and hence subject to the parties' specific agreements, the vertical relationship is dominated by mandatory regulation which is not subject to disposition by the parties and which hence always needs to be taken into account as a prerequisite requirement. The blockchain must be designed, and/or applied, in a way that it is able to meet such requirements as a basic legal requirement.

Applicable regulations may be further classified as follows: (1) all generally applicable regulation (i.e., those laws that apply to everyone and everything within their scope of applicability), (2) regulation that applies by virtue of the specific use case that a blockchain is deployed for (i.e., for *what* it is used), and (3) regulation that specifically addresses the blockchain as a technology (i.e., which applies by virtue of specifically using blockchain technology in a certain case). Further, the current discussion oscillates between determining how the existing applicable legal framework applies in a blockchain context and the question of how future regulation encompassing blockchain should look like, as the conceptual characteristics of this new technology are inspiring legal scholars, lawmakers and practitioners to think about the latter.

28. Section §2.01[B][3], *supra*.

[2] *Which Legal Subjects Can Be Relevant for Blockchains?*

There is no doubt: Blockchain is a cross-divisional topic touching upon many different areas of law. This is the case for many technology-related topics, but due to the unique structure and the variety of the blockchain use cases, the range of implicated legal subject matters seems to be particularly broad. This handbook examines in more detail some of them which we have considered particularly relevant for legal practice. Broadly speaking, and in addition to those, the blockchain technology as such, with its characteristics described above, raises legal questions from many different areas of private law (e.g., liability and enforcement questions, contract law questions, technology regulation questions), criminal law (e.g., in the area of data offences and money laundering) and public and administrative law (e.g., in tax and data protection law). Questions concerning the use of the blockchain in the area of corporate law (e.g., for corporate shareholding matters[29]) and corporate governance[30] are particularly relevant for corporates. This already shows the range of individual topics which are currently discussed, and the list is non-exhaustive.

In addition to the general legal requirements, there may be further special requirements depending on who a blockchain uses (regulation that applies to a party as such) and/or the intended specific use case. This is likely to be particularly true for companies in highly regulated industries. For financial institutions, the main requirements are those imposed by supervisory law. These include, for example, in Germany the provisions of the German Banking Act and the Minimum Requirements for Risk Management[31] ('MaRisk'), which must also be complied with when using blockchain technology. Particular emphasis is placed on cyber security issues as well.[32] For example, being an IT system, the blockchain must fulfil certain technical and organizational standards to ensure the integrity, availability, authenticity and confidentiality of data. Finally, a blockchain will also need to be able to meet statutory archiving requirements which exist in certain jurisdictions and for certain types of information

29. For a US-law discussion, compare, e.g., George S. Geis, *Traceable Shares and Corporate Law*, Virginia Public Law and Legal Theory Research Paper No. 2018-13, 2-50, available at SSRN: https://papers.ssrn.com/sol3/papers.cfm?abstract_id=3129042&download=yes (accessed 10 Mar. 2024), and the German Act on Electronic Securities from 3rd June 2021 (*Gesetz über elektronische Wertpapiere*), available at https://www.gesetze-im-internet.de/ewpg/index.html (accessed 10 Mar. 2024).
30. Compare, e.g., Wulf A. Kaal, Blockchain-Based Corporate Governance, U. of St. Thomas (Minnesota) Legal Studies Research Paper No. 19-10, 1-43, available at SSRN: https://papers.ssrn.com/sol3/papers.cfm?abstract_id=3441904 (accessed 10 Mar. 2024); Anne Lafarre & Christoph Van der Elst, Blockchain Technology for Corporate Governance and Shareholder Activism, SSRN Electronic Journal (January 2018) 1-26, available at: https://papers.ssrn.com/sol3/papers.cfm?abstract_id=3135209 (accessed 10 Mar. 2024).
31. *See* https://www.bafin.de/SharedDocs/Veroeffentlichungen/DE/Rundschreiben/2023/rs_05_2023_MaRisk_BA.html;jsessionid=A295F98875097DDCCD877E42D14EEF30.internet982?nn=19659504 (accessed 10 Mar. 2024).
32. Which will become even more relevant under the requirements of the Digital Operational Resilience Act, Regulation (EU) 2022/2554 of the European Parliament and of the Council of 14 Dec. 2022 on digital operational resilience for the financial sector; available at https://eur-lex.europa.eu/eli/reg/2022/2554/oj (accessed 10 Mar. 2024).

(e.g., in Germany for commercial correspondence and accounting documents under tax laws).

On top of that, additional requirements can also result from the specific design of the blockchain solution. Frequently, a blockchain solution is not developed by the party using it but is built on the basis of standard solutions available on the market ('Blockchain-as-a-Service'). This can in turn result in an additional layer of legal requirements (e.g., if such solutions are offered based on certain standard terms and conditions, not only for the 'purchase' but also for the deployment). If a use case in a financial institution would amount to (regulated) outsourcing (potentially also including a cloud element), then, for example, in Europe, the European Banking Authority's Guidelines on outsourcing arrangements[33] would apply, and the blockchain solution, including the contractual arrangements, would need to meet these requirements.

And finally, in a corporate environment, market standards and internal requirements (e.g., based on corporate policies and guidelines) which implement regulation or supplement it with company-specific standards may apply, which in a stricter sense not only is regulation but also needs to be taken into account early on – ideally already in the phase of structuring and designing the blockchain solution.

[3] 'Code Is Law' and 'Code as Law'

'Code is law' is an expression that was framed in connection with the fundamental importance that software code plays in the shaping of the 'cyberspace', mainly as the underlying and governing structure of the Internet.[34] The idea behind that concept was that if such code constitutes the fundamental structure of the Internet, then building in certain rights and freedoms directly in the code could provide for a 'structural guarantee' of application of those in the cyberspace, in the same way that fundamental rights are built into a constitution.[35] In essence, it expresses the idea that in a digital world, 'code has progressively established itself as the predominant way to regulate the behavior of Internet users'.[36] Consequently, those who program the code play an important role for the sake of the power they factually exercise, and it was emphasized that those should incorporate constitutional principles into the code as the code would finally govern the Internet as a whole.[37]

'Code is law' is also often used when the regulation of blockchains is discussed. There are mainly two types of software code in a blockchain context. The first type is the code of the blockchain network itself. This layer of code could be described as the

33. EBA Guidelines on outsourcing arrangements (25 Feb. 2019), available at: https://eba.europa.eu/sites/default/documents/files/documents/10180/2551996/38c80601-f5d7-4855-8ba3-702423665479/EBA%20revised%20Guidelines%20on%20outsourcing%20arrangements.pdf (accessed 10 Mar. 2024).
34. *See* Lessig, *supra* n. 26, at 1-8.
35. *Ibid.*, at 4-7.
36. Primavera De Filippi & Sanmer Hassan, Blockchain Technology as a Regulatory Technology: From Code is Law to Law is Code, 12 First Monday 21 (2016) 1, https://arxiv.org/ftp/arxiv/papers/1801/1801.02507.pdf (accessed 10 Mar. 2024).
37. Lessig, *supra* n. 26, at 6.

'operating system' of a blockchain. The second type is the code that is used for smart contracts,[38] which in a simplified manner can be seen as dedicated software programs which, depending on the specific type of blockchain, are coded separately and which are then executed on the blockchain network. This layer could be described as the 'program' or – more modernistic – the 'app' level. While the former (operating system) layer determines the structure of the whole blockchain, the latter (app) layer would apply between those blockchain users who agree on it – ultimately by virtue of contractual privity as a quite commonly recognized principle of law.

In the first place, both layers (program code and smart contract code) are shaped by the purpose which they must fulfil, which for a use in a legally compliant way includes compliance with applicable regulation. Further to that, it may be shaped by dedicated legal requirements specific to its use. As an example how complex legal rules are applied to code, the International Swaps and Derivatives Association (ISDA) has defined legal guidelines upon which the complex ISDA documentation, which is a comprehensive framework of legal documents that is applied as a financial industry standard for derivatives trading, should be observed when a smart contract solution for derivatives trading is implemented.[39] But beyond the 'translation' of such (analogous) requirements into (digital) code, blockchain is also called out to potentially constitute a means for governments and authorities to apply their laws and regulations in an automated and self-executing manner.[40] In the context of derivatives regulation, it could, for example, be used to apply margin requirements that are imposed by the U.S. Dodd-Frank Act in an automated manner if coded into a Smart Contract.[41] This shifts the paradigm from 'code *is* law' to 'code *as* law',[42] from blockchain as a 'regulatable technology' to a 'regulatory technology'.[43]

Finally, 'code *as* law' also ties into the discussion of the emergence of a new form of law, which may be described as 'cryptolaw'[44] or '*lex cryptographica*', the latter of which emphasizes the benefits that the use of blockchains could provide in the application of the law, to governments in terms of efficiency of regulation and the society as a whole.[45] This goes back to the idea of a '*lex informatica*', as a 'set of rules for information flows imposed by technology and communication networks [...] that policymakers must understand, consciously recognize, and encourage'.[46] However, in that discussion, it is important to recall that code is basically a way of transporting rules rather than creating rules. While blockchain can be appreciated as a means to more

38. For Smart Contracts *see* Chapter 3, *infra*.
39. International Swaps and Derivatives Association, Legal Guidelines for Smart Derivatives Contracts (January 2019), available at: https://www.isda.org/a/MhgME/Legal-Guidelines-for-Smart-Derivatives-Contracts-Introduction.pdf (accessed 10 Mar. 2024).
40. *See* Primavera De Filippi & Aaron Wright, *Blockchain and the Law: The Rule of Code* (2018) 193.
41. *Ibid.*, at 197-198.
42. *Ibid.*, at 199.
43. Michèle Finck, *Blockchain: Regulation and Governance in Europe* 93 (2018).
44. But note that this has nothing to do as such with 'crypto' asset or 'crypto' currency regulation, which are use case-specific aspects.
45. De Filippi and Wright, *supra* n. 40, at 203.
46. Joel R. Reidenberg, *Lex Informatica: The Formulation of Information Policy Rules Through Technology*, 76 Tex. L. Rev. 553, 555 (1997-1998).

efficiently enforce the law by automated and reliable means, and as such may contribute to more legal certainty and efficiency, it does not as such create a new form of law, and the aforementioned concepts may, from a practical standpoint, rather be understood as a fragment towards the establishment of a more automated, digital overall regulatory framework. Having said this, various specific use cases of blockchain technology raise a magnitude of new legal questions, the answers to which may be described as the emergence of a new subject of law, for example, in the area of crypto assets.[47] Beyond this, it can be doubted that the mere use of software code to transport legal rules rather than statutory textbooks as such would justify calling out a new form of law. This view does not deny the fact that the emergence of blockchain technology could contribute to eventually transform the law and to envision 'a world in which law is created first through legislation or regulation written in words and then implemented through cryptographic, smart-contracting computer code'.[48] In practical terms, this means that the code of a blockchain, as well as the blockchain technology as a whole resulting from that code, is subject to the generally applicable laws and regulations in the first place and may be utilized to apply legal rules (even those that emerge as new subjects of law), but does not as such create a new form of law that blockchains would need to adhere and correspond to and that legal practitioners would need to assess in addition to 'traditional' rules. As it has been stated above, a blockchain does not operate in a legal vacuum,[49] and consequently it has been held that 'code needs law'[50] to underpin its recognition and enforceability from a legal (not practical or factual) perspective.

[4] Summary

This section has distinguished between the horizontal relationship of blockchain participants ('regulation *in* the blockchain') and regulation that is imposed vertically on blockchain participants ('regulation *of* the blockchain'), in both of which cases regulation has a broad meaning. It has then provided certain examples for the broad variety of legal subject matters that blockchains touch upon and should be considered when assessing blockchains from a legal perspective. It has then elaborated on the notions of 'code *is* law' and 'code *as* law' and has concluded that while blockchain may also be instrumental as a 'regulatory technology', code follows the regulation, and not vice versa.

47. Chapter 6 and 7, *infra*.
48. Carla L. Reyes, *Conceptualizing Cryptolaw*, 96 Neb. L. Rev. 384, 400 (2017), full text available at: https://digitalcommons.unl.edu/cgi/viewcontent.cgi?article=3121&context=nlr (accessed 10 Mar. 2024).
49. Section §2.01, *supra*.
50. Finck, *supra* n. 43, at 44.

§2.02 REGULATORY CHALLENGES

Blockchain technology, by the very nature of its features, presents some key challenges to its (effective) regulation, some of which will be discussed in the following section.

[A] Decentralization as Key Challenge

To the same extent that decentralization is a constitutive principle of the blockchain technology,[51] it can be a key challenge for the legal aspects.[52] The fact that through the (potential) cross-border decentralization a multitude of different jurisdictions may be affected does create challenges not only for all legal questions where the specific physical place is decisive but also for the questions of effective enforcement of the law. This seems comparable to the situation of the regulation of the Internet. It is, however, important in this context to recognize that a blockchain's decentralization may vary over its life cycle. A public blockchain, as it is the case, for example, for the Bitcoin blockchain, has its origins in one person who develops it and then releases it, and then it spreads (depending on whether it is permissioned or permissionless, more or less controlled) as new participants, nodes and miners join. The original developer therefore seems to be the natural first addressee for imposing any regulation on the blockchain, which may be in the form of imposing mandatory requirements that the software code needs to contain or to follow. However, it needs to be considered in this context that, as from the point of releasing the public blockchain, the original developer does not retain control over that blockchain; hence, imposing legal duties on the developer for any time after such release would be moot from an enforcement perspective.

It is further important to note that decentralization may have a different meaning in the technical context than in the legal context. Decentralization in the technical meaning denotes a blockchain as a data ledger that is spread over a multitude of nodes (which are essentially computers), irrespective of the question of where these nodes are physically located and by whom they are 'owned', for example, if many or even a majority of nodes is owned by or under the control of one single party. Decentralization from the legal perspective has a normative meaning, which may however vary depending on the legal subject matter, for example, under securities laws[53] or under private international law[54] from the perspective of physical location.

51. Section §2.01[B][4], *supra*.
52. For a use case-based view on the regulatory challenges of 'non-centralisation', *see* The Law Society, Society for Computers & Law and Tech London Advocates, Blockchain: Legal & Regulatory Guidance, 3rd ed., 2023, 276-282, available at https://www.lawsociety.org.uk/topics/research/blockchain-legal-and-regulatory-guidance-report (accessed 10 Mar. 2024).
53. *See* Peter van Valkenburgh, *What Could 'decentralization' Mean in the Context of the Law?* (15 Jun. 2018) available at: https://coincenter.org/entry/what-could-decentralization-mean-in-the-context-of-the-law (accessed 10 Mar. 2024).
54. *See* for an introduction, e.g., Andrea Bonomi, *Blockchain and Private International Law – Some general remarks, Yearbook of Private International Law*, Volume 24, 2022/23, pp. 153-164.

[B] Jurisdiction

The question of jurisdiction in connection with blockchains is manifold. Decentralization is a distinctive and inherent feature of the blockchain technology. It is not the mere fact that blockchains often span across a variety of jurisdictions, which is frequently the case in a globalized world and its cross-border economy and for which private international law provides for the applicable rules, but the fact that blockchains in their purest form as public blockchains may be 'transnational' per se, in which scenario traditional jurisdictional anchors and concepts may not be able to answer the questions. In the case of public blockchains, there is no 'root' in any specific country which could be the starting point to determine jurisdiction and applicable law and no 'anchor' which could serve as a regulatory entry point from the pure technological perspective of the blockchain as such.

It may be useful to draw a distinction again between jurisdiction *in* and *over* blockchains. Jurisdiction *in* a blockchain comprises the question which laws are applicable to transactions that are carried out by the blockchain users and in which court a dispute arising from a transaction would be adjudicated. This is mainly a question of the law of contracts and private international law. Jurisdiction *over* a blockchain includes the question of which countries' laws may be applicable to a blockchain and which authorities could assert jurisdiction over a blockchain and the transactions executed in it. This is mainly a question of public and administrative law.

It is beyond the scope of this chapter to provide answers to all these jurisdictional questions that may arise in the context of blockchains.[55] Nevertheless, for legal structuring purposes, three questions that are particularly important from a practitioner's perspective can be distinguished: (1) what is the law that is applicable between the various blockchain participants and can there be an effective choice; (2) which (state) court may assert jurisdiction over the blockchain, i.e., its participants and potentially a blockchain itself; (3) which countries' authorities and regulators may a blockchain be subjected to in case of a use case in a regulated environment (e.g., financial services)?

While question (1) is a question of private international law and may be answered, for example, for Europe on the basis of the Rome I Regulation, question (2) will (subject to public international law treaties) be answered by the courts by applying their local procedural law, and question (3) finally will be answered by the relevant regulations, which in some jurisdictions may have certain extraterritorial reach.

55. For further reading, *see*, e.g., Katherine West, *Where Is Blockchain: Jurisdictional Issues That May Affect Distributed Ledgers*, available at: https://www.lexology.com/library/detail.aspx?g=35f40e2e-38d8-49d7-81ca-9872d8ab9532 (accessed 10 Mar. 2024); Jaak Poldma, *Dragged To Thee U.S: Courts (Part 1): Jurisdiction and the Location of Blockchain Nodes*, available at: https://blogs.orrick.com/blockchain/dragged-to-the-u-s-courts-part-1-jurisdiction-and-the-location-of-blockchain-nodes (accessed 11 Mar. 2020); Casey Watters, When Criminals Abuse the Blockchain: Establishing Personal Jurisdiction in a Decentralised Environment, Laws 12: 33 (15 Apr. 2023) https://doi.org/10.3390/ laws12020033 (accessed 10 Mar. 2024).

[C] Anonymity

Anonymity can be another major obstacle for effective regulation. The question here is not so much whether anonymity is absolute in a given context but whether such anonymity can be overcome by a regulator with the means as such regulator requires and may be able to reasonably deploy so that this allows for, or at least does not hinder, the effective enforcement of regulation. In many areas where it is particularly important to know the acting party, for example, in the context of financial services for the prevention of money laundering and terrorist financing, mandatory identification of the parties is imposed by the law. Any solution which is not able to meet those requirements would simply not be permissible. Hence, from a regulatory perspective, the question is not whether the participants of a given blockchain can stay anonymous or not but whether such anonymity conflicts with existing (or future) identification requirements. Regulators would, for example, now allow the use of any public permissionless blockchain for a use case in which they require the full identification of the participants unless this could be achieved by other means on a separate layer. It is, however, also argued that there might be a potential dilemma for regulators where there is a strong incentive for the promotion of blockchain solutions that meet the anonymization requirements of data protection laws (namely, the GDPR in the EU), on the one hand, without compromising on the non-facilitation of money laundering and not burdening law enforcement more generally, on the other hand.[56]

There are various options to satisfy identification requirements in the design and set-up of a blockchain solution. For example, in a private permissioned blockchain, a trusted party can be retained to exercise control over the admission of new participants which can include a full identification of new participants. There are technical options which facilitate this being done in a fully digitalized way, for example, in a comparable manner than a bank identifies a new customer through digital channels for the opening of a bank account online. Should it not be necessary to conduct a full identification, permissioning a blockchain may still allow for sufficiently tracing the identity of a participant when required. From a legal advice perspective, it is of key importance that any identification requirements are identified upfront for the specific use case and that such advice can be taken into account to determine the suitable form of the blockchain to be developed or deployed. It is also worth mentioning on this occasion that once a blockchain is up and running, there may be a desire at a later stage to broaden the use case or to add new use cases. This should be anticipated, if possible, in the legal assessment, as at a later stage the configuration of the blockchain may no longer be changed, so otherwise it may not be possible to meet the requirements, and the extended use may not be possible for legal reasons. Finally, identification requirements may also be met through additional parallel off-chain processes.

56. Finck, *supra* n. 43, at 63-64.

§2.03 REGULATORY CONCEPTS

There are various conceptual approaches as to how the blockchain technology should be regulated in terms of both lawmaking and regulatory oversight.[57] The following section describes the common approaches of 'technology neutrality', by taking into account a use case-focused regulation and the sandbox approach.

[A] The Regulatory Principle of Technology Neutrality

The principle of technology neutrality in regulation may be summarized as 'a policy position that the regulatory perimeter and treatment of financial products and activities is unaffected by the technological medium through which the product is offered or activity takes place'.[58] More broadly speaking beyond the area of financial services regulation, it characterizes a position under which the law is neutral and silent as to any specific technology in its scope and application. It is the predominant position scholars, lawmakers and regulators have taken with respect to new technologies for quite some time, especially in the early days of blockchain, 'based on the assumption it promotes statutory longevity and equal treatment of old and new technologies'.[59] This means first of all that, on the one hand, existing regulation applies to the blockchain technology without any restrictions, relaxation or privilege, and a blockchain needs to be designed in a way that it is able to comply with existing regulation. This is, in particular, relevant for the question if, in a specific case, a public versus a private and a permissionless versus a permissioned blockchain model is chosen, as this has a decisive influence over the ability to meet legal and regulatory requirements. On the other hand, this also means that the use of the generic blockchain technology as such compared to using any other technology does not entail any special additional requirements and would also not subject the blockchain technology to any additional authorization requirements as such. Obviously, this only applies to the extent that the specific features of the blockchain technology would not per se trigger any additional elements of a legal norm.

However, the principle of technology neutrality does not mean that regulation would not be considerate of the specific particularities of blockchains at all. For example, the Swiss Government had set out in a report accompanying a new draft bill, concerning the adaptation of Swiss law to the developments of the distributed ledger technology, that Switzerland should continue to pursue a principle-based and technology-neutral legislative and regulatory approach but where required also to

57. Various conceptual approaches are discussed, e.g., by Finck, *supra* n. 43, at 153-165.
58. Rory Copeland, *FCA Final Guidance on Cryptoassets: Jettisoning Tech-Neutrality?*, Oxford Business Law Blog (23 Sep. 2019) available at: https://www.law.ox.ac.uk/business-law-blog/blog/2019/09/fca-final-guidance-cryptoassets-jettisoning-tech-neutrality (accessed 10 Mar. 2024).
59. Brad A. Greenberg, *Rethinking Technology Neutrality*, 207 Minn. L. Rev (2016) 1495, available at: https://www.minnesotalawreview.org/wp-content/uploads/2016/04/Greenberg_ONLINE PDF.pdf (accessed 10 Mar. 2024).

allow for exceptions, in which case the rules should be designed in a competition-neutral way as possible.[60]

Applying the same approach of eliminating potential hurdles for the blockchain technology in existing laws, the State of Delaware in the United States (US), within the context of the 'Delaware Blockchain Initiative' launched by the then-Governor in May 2016 as one of the earliest more comprehensive blockchain law initiatives,[61] has amended its corporation laws already back in 2017 by removing prohibitive wording in the Delaware corporate laws to allow for the record-keeping of share issuance and transfer on the basis of the blockchain technology. However, this was done without addressing blockchain namely in the text, but only in the explanatory synopsis provided with the bill.[62]

As an example for a blockchain-embracing yet technology-neutral overall regulatory and legislative approach, the German Federal Government's Blockchain Strategy may be mentioned. While it had underlined 'the goal of using the opportunities in blockchain technology and of mobilizing the areas of potential that it offers for the digital transformation',[63] a guiding principle for the implementation of the strategy and such new legislation 'is that of technology neutrality. Existing obstacles to the development and application of technologies are being eliminated, provided that doing so is compatible with the existing laws' fundamental objectives',[64] expressly towards the aim of fair competition. It stipulates very clearly as a 'legal framework condition' that '[c]onsistent with technology neutrality, the legal framework must not favour or disadvantage blockchain technology in relation to other technologies'.[65] It resulted, *inter alia*, in a law on electronic securities in 2021 which, while having blockchain-based solutions in mind, is not restricted with respect to the underlying technology that may be used.[66]

60. Botschaft zum Bundesgesetz zur Anpassung des Bundesrecht an Entwicklungen der Technik verteilter elektronischer Register (2019), 7 (1.1.3, III.), available at: https://www.newsd.admin.ch/newsd/message/attachments/59301.pdf (accessed 10 Mar. 2024). Available in German only and translation in the text by the author. The original reads: 'Die Schweiz soll weiterhin einen prinzipienbasierten und technologieneutralen Rechtsetzungs- und Regulierungsansatz verfolgen, jedoch bei Bedarf auch Ausnahmen zulassen; dabei sind die Regeln möglichst wettbewerbsneutral zu gestalten.'
61. *See* https://corpgov.law.harvard.edu/2017/03/16/delaware-blockchain-initiative-transforming-the-foundational-infrastructure-of-corporate-finance (accessed 10 Mar. 2024).
62. Act to Amend Title 8 of the Delaware Code Relating to the General Corporation Law (5.5.2017), Synopsis, section 1, available at: https://legis.delaware.gov/BillDetail/25730 (accessed 10 Mar. 2024).
63. Blockchain Strategy of the Federal Government, We Set Out the Course for the Token Economy (18 Sep. 2019) 4, English version available at: https://www.bmwi.de/Redaktion/EN/Publikationen/Digitale-Welt/blockchain-strategy.pdf?__blob=publicationFile&v=3 (accessed 10 Mar. 2024).
64. *Ibid.*
65. *Ibid.*, at 12.
66. *See* German Act on Electronic Securities from 3rd June 2021 (Gesetz über elektronische Wertpapiere), available at https://www.gesetze-im-internet.de/ewpg/index.html (accessed 10 Mar. 2024) where the central function of a crypto securities registrar is intentionally not related to using a specific technology.

These are only a few examples of many which demonstrate a common way of lawmakers and regulators to approach blockchain regulation under the doctrine of technology neutrality while recognizing the unique and distinctive character of the blockchain technology in the general laws by contemplating appropriate exceptions and eliminating potential hurdles, and by taking the specific features and risks of blockchain into account with respect to exercising regulatory supervision. While there is also a general debate on the utility of the principle of technology neutrality as such,[67] it can be expected that this concept will remain a common approach to regulation in terms of blockchain as a generic technology.

However, certain states have taken an approach to distinctively address blockchain by statutory regulation in an effort to foster the technology while still keeping definitions sufficiently broad and agnostic to avoid that the scope becomes too narrow. Examples for this are the Malta Innovative Technology Arrangements and Services Act 2018[68], the Liechtenstein Token and Trusted Technology Service Provider Act from 2019[69] and the European DLT Pilot Regime (Regulation (EU) 2022/858 of the European Parliament and of the Council of 30 May 2022 on a pilot regime for market infrastructures based on distributed ledger technology).

[B] Regulating the Use Case Versus Regulating the Technology

Against the background of the principle of technology neutrality, most lawmakers and regulators have focused on observing and regulating the specific use cases of the blockchain technology, one prominent being crypto assets, over the last years. In this connection, it has been a guiding principle that specifically financial services regulators[70] would look at the use case and the underlying business model to assess the applicability of regulation, in what a board member of the European Central Bank has described in the past as the 'golden rule of supervision: same business, same risk, same rules'.[71] This, however, also implies that regulators may use the principle of proportionality, on the basis of applying the same rules, where appropriate to account for any differences that the underlying technology including blockchain may make.

67. *See*, e.g., Greenberg, *supra* n. 59, at 1495 et seq. for a critical review of the approach with respect to copyright law.
68. Innovative Technology Arrangements and Services Act (1 Nov. 2018), available at: http://www.justiceservices.gov.mt/DownloadDocument.aspx?app=lom&itemid=12874&l=1 (accessed 10 Mar. 2024).
69. Liechtenstein Token and Trusted Technology Service Provider Act, *supra* n. 9.
70. Including, for example, the German Federal Financial Supervisory Authority (BaFin), *see* https://www.bafin.de/SharedDocs/Veroeffentlichungen/EN/Pressemitteilung/2016/pm_160628_FinTechs_en.html (accessed 10 Mar. 2024).
71. Sabine Lautenschlaeger, *A Supervisory Perspective on 2019 and Beyond*, Speech in Dublin, Ireland, 17 Jan. 2019, available at: https://www.ecb.europa.eu/press/key/date/2019/html/ecb.sp190117.en.html (accessed 10 Mar. 2024).

[C] Regulatory Sandboxing

Several countries have adopted a 'sandboxing' approach in connection with the application of regulation to new technologies, specifically in the area of financial services regulation. In computer science, a 'sandbox' is an isolated testing environment in which new software can be tested without any connection to live systems.[72] The intention thereby pursued is to protect the live systems from anything that may go wrong during the testing, hence allowing more flexibility, which ultimately means risk, to the tests. If such testing is successful, then the software may safely be applied in the real world outside of the sandbox.

This concept has been transferred to the application of regulation. In this context, it means that new technologies and pertinent business models are tested with a limited scope in a program that is closely accompanied and controlled by the relevant regulatory authorities. According to the European Banking Authority, '[r]egulatory sandboxes provide financial institutions and non-financial firms with a controlled space in which they can test innovative FinTech solutions with the support of an authority for a limited period of time, allowing them to validate and test their business model in a safe environment'.[73] In turn, regulatory requirements are sometimes lowered in order to avoid that the entry barrier is set too high, thereby especially allowing new and smaller market participants to enter established markets without the need to meet the full regulatory requirements in the early stage of the development. This concept is particularly applied in the context of financial services regulation and financial innovation ('FinTech') for innovative financial services products. The primary aim is the promotion of new and innovative ideas and technologies, often with the goal of creating an innovation-friendly regulatory place and to foster the establishment of research and development activities in this area. It aims to allow financial technology to grow and regulatory authorities to educate themselves in depth on such new technologies.

However, as much as some countries have promoted this concept in the last years, as much have others been reluctant on changing existing regulatory standards, even in a limited context. While the concept, as a potential advantage, aims to promote innovation, and hence economic growth, it is rejected by others as being potentially unfair to other market participants which, if they do not apply technologies that are eligible for the sandboxing, need to adhere to the full set of regulatory requirements which may amount to regulatory arbitrage. As an alternative to still remain innovation-friendly, but neutral from a regulatory perspective,[74] certain countries and their

72. *See*, e.g., https://searchsecurity.techtarget.com/definition/sandbox (accessed 10 Mar. 2024).
73. European Banking Authority, Discussion paper on the EBA's approach to financial technology (FinTech), EBA/DP/2017/02 (4 Aug. 2017) n. 8, available at: https://eba.europa.eu/sites/default/documents/files/documents/10180/1919160/7a1b9cda-10ad-4315-91ce-d798230ebd84/EBA%20Discussion%20Paper%20on%20Fintech%20%28EBA-DP-2017-02%29.pdf?retry=1 (accessed 10 Mar. 2024).
74. Remaining neutral in this context has no negative connotation but merely refers to the regulatory principle of 'technology neutrality' again.

regulatory authorities rely on the principle of proportionality as an appropriate means to accommodate the differences between the market participants.[75]

Countries which have applied, in various forms, sandbox approaches in the area of financial services are, for example, Denmark, Lithuania, the Netherlands, Poland, the UK, Bermuda, Guernsey and Jersey.[76] Turkey, within the framework of a broader blockchain strategy, has announced to allow for regulatory sandboxing for blockchain projects.[77] This list is non-exhaustive and dynamic, and it should also be noted that in countries which do not apply a sandbox approach, other forms of experimentation may apply.[78] Sandboxes can also aim at establishing regulatory dialogue between lawmakers, regulators and market participants, as it is the case for the European Blockchain Regulatory Sandbox established by the EU Commission. This project is taking in applications from market participants and is then selecting twenty blockchain use cases annually, with a view to facilitating dialogue around legal and regulatory topics of such use cases.[79]

§2.04 ADDRESSEES OF REGULATION

One of the most fundamental legal questions in connection with blockchain is to whom any regulation may actually be addressed to. In order for a regulation to be effective, that regulation needs a specific addressee to whom it is directed and to whom it may assign legal rights and obligations. Certain conceptual aspects of the blockchain technology – namely decentralization and anonymity – challenge both the possibility to clearly identify an addressee and the ability to enforce any regulation upon such addressee. However, this strongly depends on the type and form of the specific blockchain. Behind every blockchain, there are ultimately natural or legal persons. However, once a public blockchain, for example, is 'released', control over such blockchain may be limited or not existent. In a private blockchain, in contrast, this may be possible.

75. *See*, e.g., the answer of the German Government (*Antwort der Bundesregierung*) to a parliamentary request on regulatory sandboxing, Deutscher Bundestag, Drucksache 19/15103 (13 Nov. 2019) at 3 (in German only).
76. According to the answer of the German Government (*Antwort der Bundesregierung*) to a parliamentary request on regulatory sandboxing, *Ibid.*, at 1.
77. https://www.ledgerinsights.com/turkey-blockchain-regulatory-sandbox (accessed 10 Mar. 2024).
78. Experimentation clauses for innovation-driven models are, e.g., not entirely alien to German law. The German Carriage of Passengers Act in section 7(2), e.g., allows for regulatory exemptions with a view, e.g., on autonomous cars: 'In order to allow for the practical testing of new modes or means of transport, the licensing authority may, upon request on a case-by-case basis, authorise exemptions from the provisions of this Act or from provisions adopted on the basis of this Act for a maximum period of four years, insofar as they do not conflict with public transport interests,' translation from the German Federal Ministry for Economic Affairs and Energy, *see* https://www.bmwi.de/Redaktion/EN/Dossier/regulatory-test-beds-testing-environments-for-innovation-and-regulation.html (accessed 10 Mar. 2024).
79. https://ec.europa.eu/digital-building-blocks/sites/display/EBSI/Sandbox+Project (accesses 10 Mar. 2024).

[A] Addressing 'the Blockchain' as Subject of Regulation

Against this background, a discussion has commenced as to whether a blockchain may also be awarded legal personality as such. This discussion may be seen in the context of respective discussions in the area of the 'Internet of things' (IoT) and the potential need to rethink traditional concepts of legal personality in the digital age in a more fundamental way.

[1] Legal Personality of the Blockchain

Traditionally, legal personality as the capacity to be the subject of legal rights and duties has been granted to a natural person. It has further been extended to organized groups of human beings as 'legal persons', for example, by the establishment of corporations which group several natural persons by a commercial purpose predominantly in the context of national commercial and corporation laws and nation states in public international law. Over the last three decades, linked to the progress in computer sciences with the creation of 'intelligent' machines and the rise of AI, a discussion has started as to whether the concept of legal personality should be extended to certain machines and AI systems (which otherwise, by law, are only recognized as 'things' as regards the hardware and 'rights' as regards the software). One of the main aspects in the discussion of a (limited) legal personality for such systems is their presumed capacity to form 'intelligent', or at least independent, decisions.[80] This is perceived as a 'risk of autonomy' if, for example, these decisions lead to contractual or tortious liability.[81] Against the background of this discussion, and with the purpose of addressing these issues as well as the blockchain-specific challenges discussed above, it has been suggested that blockchains may also be granted their own legal personality.

[2] The Malta Innovative Technology Arrangements and Services Act 2018

Malta became one of the first countries to attempt a holistic regulation of the blockchain technology, along with other technology arrangements. The Innovative Technology Arrangements and Services Act (ITAS Act)[82] followed an earlier consultation document issued by the Maltese Government, which has held that:

> '[w]hilst some Technology Arrangements are owned by a corporate structure, other Technology Arrangements may not have such an ownership structure. This

80. For a historically shaped discussion, *see*, e.g., Evan Joseph Zimmerman, *Machine Minds: Frontier in Legal Personhood* (12 Feb. 2015) 35-41, available at https://papers.ssrn.com/sol3/papers.cfm?abstract_id=2563965 (accessed 10 Mar. 2024).
81. For an overview on the discussion for autonomous software agents and potential gaps in the liability system, *see*, e.g., Gunther Teubner, *Digitale Rechtssubjekte? Zum privatrechtlichen Status autonomer Softwareagenten*, 218 AcP 155-205 (2018).
82. For more details on the ITAS Act, *see* Chapter 5, *infra*, §5.11[A].

> could result in the possibility of transacting on and with the Technology Arrangement without a proper "legal person" as counterparty. The proposed TAS Bill will try to provide a solution to such a scenario and it is being proposed that certain Technology Arrangements will be able to register with the Registrar for Legal Persons in Malta and acquire legal personality upon satisfaction of a number of requirements'.[83]

The idea of granting such (limited) legal personality has been considered, with one main argument being the autonomy, for example, because 'such autonomous entities may even survive the life of their designers'.[84] The ITAS Act has finally not included such concept in that specific way, but the discussions in the consultation process demonstrate an increasing willingness generally to at least challenge traditional concepts for blockchain as a technology with unique characteristics. This may be linked to both the general willingness to rethink traditional 'closed shop' concepts (as legal subjectivity is perceived in many legal orders) and an increasing perception of the 'emancipation'[85] of technology systems, the latter of which the blockchain is a prime example.

[3] Decentralized Autonomous Organizations as a New Corporate Form

One specific example which has particularly raised questions over legal personality and corporate form is the Decentralized Autonomous Organization (DAO). Essentially, a DAO is a combination of the blockchain technology with Smart Contracts and crypto assets or tokens and may be characterized in short as 'an association of often anonymous or pseudonymous members with internal capital'.[86] Today's perception of what a DAO constitutes is largely based on a project called 'The DAO', which was launched in 2016. The starting point was the coding of a crowdfunding Smart Contract, following which investors would be furnished with tokens, and such token holders would be given far-reaching voting rights over the administration of the project, especially on how the collected funds would be invested. Such voting was effected by digital means, based on funding proposals for products and services that companies could make to the DAO token holders. Likewise, the DAO was a modular concept with its 'core' kept relatively simple, and the idea that the code, and hence the DAO as such, could be updated over time based on coding proposals by its members and pertinent voting. The proposed mechanism of such a DAO was set out in a whitepaper and realized as an open-source code so that any interested community member could participate and start to create a DAO according to the proposed model. One large community with over five thousand members subsequently created a Smart Contract

83. Cited after Steve Tendon & Max Ganado, *Legal Personality for Blockchains, DAOs and Smart Contracts*, 1 RTDF (2018) 1-2.
84. *Ibid.*, at 1.
85. For an argumentation derived from the concept of 'emancipation', *see* Katrin Becker, Blockchain Matters—Lex Cryptographia and the Displacement of Legal Symbolics and Imaginaries, Law and Critique (2022) 33, p. 118 ff., available at https://doi.org/10.1007/s10978-021-09317-8 (accessed 10 Mar. 2024).
86. The Law Society et al., *supra* n. 52, at 136.

framework, which was put on the Ethereum blockchain and which then became known as 'The DAO'.

One of the key characteristics of a DAO generally is its high degree of autonomy. Once the code of a DAO, or more precisely the conglomerate of Smart Contracts by which it is constituted, has been created and deployed on a blockchain, the coders will not have any advanced control over such DAO but will rather only have voting rights that attach to any tokens they will 'purchase'. The governance mechanism of a DAO will provide for its automated function, and human intervention would only happen through the members voting and the proposals that may be made regarding a DAO's organizational structure (through the proposal of an amendment of its code) or the investment decisions (based on the proposals that may be presented to them). Furthermore, the monies (through cryptocurrency) invested by the members would by means of the technical set-up factually be held by the DAO itself and not by the collectivity of the members anymore. It is obvious that this structure raises immediate questions over its legal status, in particular whether such an organization could or should have legal personality, and the corporate form that would apply.

Against these characteristics, it is discussed whether a DAO should be equipped with its own legal status, potentially as a new corporate form.[87] Yet, most legal regimes have a 'closed shop' of legal personality forms, and it would hence not exist under current regulation as a separate legal form. However, this does not exclude that DAOs may be seen as fulfilling the conditions of an existing corporate form, for example, a partnership. But this will vary based on the relevant jurisdiction. Meanwhile, several countries have revisited, or announced to revisit, their corporation laws with respect to the blockchain technology. However, it is worth noting that most of these initiatives do not aim at creating a new legal form for blockchain-based organizations, but rather at using the blockchain technology for certain corporate housekeeping matters.[88]

DAOs are one of the most complex scenarios within the blockchain ecosystem. Their specific legal characterization depends not only on the jurisdiction that applies but also on how a DAO is specifically structured around its purpose. Accordingly, a specific DAO set-up may trigger a variety of legal and regulatory requirements, e.g., but not exhaustively, with respect to securities laws, authorization and licensing requirements in the financial services sector, and anti-money laundering obligations. Any set-up should therefore be carefully vetted upfront, including with respect to the prospective member's obligations and liabilities.[89]

[4] Summary

It remains to be seen in light of the broader discussion to which extent blockchains may become distinct and separate legal subjects, while in the meantime they qualify as legal

87. *See* for the discussion, as an example with respect to German law, Maximilian Mann, Die Decentralized Autonomous Organization – ein neuer Gesellschaftstyp? NZG (2017) 1024 et seq.
88. For example the State of Delaware, *see supra* n. 62.
89. *See* for a practical typology, a list with pros and cons and a summary of key regulatory obligations: The Law Society et al., *supra* n. 52, at 136 ff.

subjects under the 'ordinary' rules if they fulfil the requirements (e.g., of a certain corporate form). Hence, the focus in the following sections will be to examine the role of the various blockchain *participants* as potential subjects of regulation. However, there is a discussion, embedded into the wider question of IoT, on whether blockchains should be granted legal personality by future legislation, which does not seem to be excluded.

[B] Addressing Blockchain Actors as Subjects of Regulation

Based on the foregoing, the focus is on the blockchain participants in their capability as 'legal intervention point'.[90] These are the nodes, miners, users, coders and oracles in the first place. They may neutrally be called a blockchain 'function'. Behind such function, there may just be a machine (in legal terms, a thing) or a natural or legal person. These functions may also be organized in groups or under a specific governance structure. The following section will provide an overview of the extent, and practical feasibility, that they may be used as such 'intervention points' or 'access points'[91], specifically in using them as addressees for blockchain-related regulation.[92]

[1] Validation Nodes ('Nodes')

Validation nodes, often also just called 'nodes', are computers which are all connected to each other via the Internet based on a predefined, and unchangeable, software protocol. That software protocol may be freely downloadable as open-source software in a public blockchain network or on a restricted basis in a private blockchain network. Each validation node stores the blockchain file (ledger) and constantly sends and receives updates to the blockchain file as new transactions are added. The sending and receiving of data happens automatically; they are a form of 'autonomous system'.[93] Validation nodes are so-called lightweight nodes, that means they only download parts of the blockchain file as is necessary to validate the addition of new blocks (which

90. Usha R. Rodrigues, *Law and Blockchain*, 104 Iowa L. Rev. 679, 682 (2019), available at: https://ilr.law.uiowa.edu/sites/ilr.law.uiowa.edu/files/2023-02/Rodrigues.pdf (accessed 10 Mar. 2024).
91. Thematic Report of the European Blockchain Observatory and Forum, *supra* n. 7, at 6: 'First will be the evolution of legal and regulatory "tools" to assist authorities with some of the novel aspects of blockchain technology. Many of these already exist. As is the case today with the Internet, authorities have recourse to various "access points" – exchanges for example – to help them monitor and enforce legal and regulatory requirements even in highly decentralised, permissionless environments. The blockchain industry itself has also been developing tools that can assist authorities (and blockchain companies) in enforcing regulatory compliance – for example methods to "pierce the veil" of pseudonymity on blockchains and identify network participants.'
92. For an examination of the various roles against data privacy aspects, *see* Chapter 4, §4.03[B], *infra*.
93. John Salmon & Gordon Myers, *Blockchain and Associated Legal Issues for Emerging Markets*, Emerging Markets Compass Note 63 (January 2019) 4, available at: https://hdl.handle.net/10986/31202 (accessed 10 Mar. 2024).

consists of a group of transactions) through a hashing exercise. Validation nodes are hence instrumental for the blockchain's overall integrity.

From the legal perspective, nodes are things (the hardware that is used) and rights (the software that is used). As such, they cannot have any legal personality and hence cannot be addressed directly by regulation. However, there are two factors to consider as potential access points. The first is the (natural or legal) person who owns, controls or operates the hardware and the software which form the validation node. A comparison may be drawn here to cars. A car as such cannot be addressed directly by road traffic regulations but the owner of the car and the driver who is not the owner (or, in some instances, both). For example, the Federal Communications Commission, the telecommunications regulatory authority in the US, has addressed a notification of harmful interference to a person who operated a bitcoin mining device, in a way negatively interfering with the network operator's broadband network, and ordered that person to stop the use of the device on the basis of telecommunication regulations.[94] A second potential access point is the place where the validation node (the computer hardware or software) is physically located. This could be the access point for any regulation where jurisdiction is established by the place where such things are physically located (*territorial jurisdiction*). However, this would only be possible in jurisdictions which recognize the principle of in rem jurisdiction, such that regulatory jurisdiction could be exercised and enforced against the thing as such, for example, by attaching a regulatory notice to the thing and, if not adhered to by the legal persons who owns or controls it, seize it.

It can, however, be difficult, if not impossible, in some cases to identify the persons behind the node. But as shown above, a blockchain transaction is not completely anonymous, and it may be possible to trace back the individual person behind a node through the transactional data or the telecommunications data (in which case Internet service providers would play a role as well). But even if the person behind the node could be sufficiently identified to address regulation to that person, then the question is whether such person could change anything to the blockchain (and specifically, the transactions) at all. This is not the case for individual nodes in a public blockchain, unless they amount to a group of nodes with a certain computational power in the hands of that person. Hence, in the case of a public blockchain, addressing the person behind the node would be remote as it would be factually impossible for that person to interfere with the blockchain other than simply deactivating the node, which would normally have no measurable effect on the blockchain due to its decentralized nature. This is different in private blockchains, and wherever individual responsibility of an addressee is a prerequisite (e.g., in financial services regulation) deploying private blockchains would hence be an option to achieve compliance by retaining and addressing control over the nodes.

However, with all these difficulties, it is important to underline that the persons behind the nodes are of course subject to all applicable laws in the capacity of their very

94. Federal Communications Commission, Enforcement Bureau, Case No.: EB-FIELDNER-17-00025658, Letter dated 15 Feb. 2018, available at: https://transition.fcc.gov/Daily_Releases/Daily_Business/2018/db0215/DOC-349258A1.pdf (accessed 10 Mar. 2024).

person, and 'hiding' behind the node would not relieve them from any of these, as it is the case also for all other functions discussed below as well.

[2] Mining Nodes ('Miners')

Mining nodes, often also just called 'miners', are basically validation nodes which also take part in the process of mining (i.e., trying to solve the 'Proof-of-Work' or 'Proof-of-Stake' exercise). Hence, they are not fundamentally different from the perspective applied here, other than adding any connecting points which may result from the mining. Potential additional entry points may be that miners are often building larger 'mining pools', which are more easily identifiable, and that miners get a reward for the mining exercise (mostly, cryptocurrency) which they may want to eventually convert to fiat money, in which case identifying information may be required. The other way around, as miners are involved as parties in the mining process, they need to be mindful even more than nodes if they would be conducting a regulated activity (e.g., in the case of crypto assets, a regulated financial services activity which may trigger licensing requirements, and if not adhered to may lead to sanctions amounting up to a criminal offence).

[3] Blockchain Users

Blockchain users are the parties to a blockchain transaction, for example, in the case of Bitcoin, the sender and the receiver of the Bitcoins. The best entry point in imposing regulation on them is in a private blockchain, probably the point in time when they join a blockchain (and where legal obligations may then be imposed on them contractually), and in a public blockchain, the point of execution of a transaction, as this may be connected to an off-chain activity (e.g., through an exchange platform which applies full identification requirements).

[4] Coders

As it has already been set out above,[95] coders as the programmers of a blockchain's software code are relevant in various instances. First, there are the coders who program the core blockchain software, which is then deployed as the software protocol to connect the nodes. Second, coders program updates which may alter the blockchain at a later stage and may decide on updates as a core group.[96] Coders can be regarded as a key element in the search for a regulatory access point, as they are the developers of the protocol which may be characterized as the 'constitution', and there is probably no better point in time to account for general regulatory compliance than in the beginning

95. Section §2.01[B][3], *supra*.
96. Finck, *supra* n. 43, at 52.

of a blockchain's design and software development. Of course, there are not necessarily only coders involved in the design of a blockchain, and, for example, in a corporate environment many functions would be involved. However, the coders are the persons actually implementing any requirements directly into the blockchain through the code; hence, they have an instrumental function in this process. It goes without saying again that coders need to act in compliance with all applicable laws both when they program the software and with respect to what the software later does, but this is also the occasion to build in any regulatory requirement by design. This includes the basic question of whether a blockchain should be public or private and permissionless or permissioned.

[5] Intermediaries and Other Parties

The blockchain ecosystem has seen an increasing arrival over the years of intermediary and other parties, e.g., crypto asset trading platforms or crypto custodians. As they are holding client relationships, this seems to be the natural starting point for any of the associated obligations, not only generally (e.g., all of the requirements an institution has with respect to client onboarding) but also with respect to specific regulatory requirements that may apply for the particular subject matter. The regulatory landscape is more and more 'formalizing' the positions of these parties as core regulatory addressees. A preeminent example of comprehensive regulation in the context of crypto assets is the EU Markets in Crypto Assets Regulation (MiCA) which covers, in particular, not only the issuance and offering of crypto assets but also various crypto asset-related services by 'Crypto Asset Service Providers' (CASPs),[97] thereby providing a clear definition of the various actors in scope.

§2.05 FINANCIAL SERVICES PRUDENTIAL REGULATION

Within financial services regulation, the prudential treatment of blockchain-related topics has received increasing attention over the last years specifically for crypto asset exposures. While it is beyond the scope of this chapter to provide an overview on this particular matter, the Basel Committee on Banking Supervision's (BCBS) efforts as a global standard setter for prudential regulation of banks shall be mentioned. The BCBS has first issued a discussion paper for comments on the designing of a prudential treatment for crypto assets in March 2020[98] against the rapid growth of crypto assets over the past years back then and identified the overall size of the crypto capitalization to be meaningful, having the possibility to raise financial stability concerns.[99] This work was intensified over the years, and BCBS has finally endorsed a prudential framework for crypto assets exposure by banks in December 2022 with the aim to

97. For a detailed overview of the MiCA, *see* Chapter 6, *infra*.
98. Basel Committee on Banking Supervision, Discussion paper: Designing a prudential treatment for crypto-assets (December 2019), available at: https://www.bis.org/bcbs/publ/d490.pdf (accessed 10 Mar. 2024).
99. *Ibid.*, at 1.

establish a global prudential standard for mitigating risks to overall financial stability.[100] Further to the release, the BCBS has issued a consultation for certain proposed amendments to the framework, specifically with respect to the treatment of stablecoins in December 2023.[101]

§2.06 OUTLOOK: BLOCKCHAIN, REGULATION AND AI

Blockchain and AI are among the most significant technological developments of the 21st century. In recent times, an increasing convergence between both technologies can be observed,[102] and they have been characterized as the 'new power couple'.[103] This paragraph provides a brief outlook on how the interplay between blockchain and AI could look like and some pertinent regulatory considerations.

As a starting point, one must remember that blockchain is mainly either regulated as a technology in a generic way or because regulation addresses a specific use case that it is deployed for.[104] It is rather not regulated 'simply because it is blockchain'. The underlying approach for the emerging AI regulation landscape is largely different, given that it aims to address AI-specific risks. A good example for this is the Artificial Intelligence Act adopted by the European Parliament in March 2024 ('EU AI Act')[105] which specifically applies to 'AI Systems'[106] based on the reasoning that '[...] depending on the circumstances regarding its specific application, use, and level of technological development, AI may generate risks and cause harm to public interests and fundamental rights that are protected by Union law. Such harm might be material or immaterial, including physical, psychological, societal or economic harm'.[107] This means that AI will be regulated as a technology, or rather method, as such, while still

100. Basel Committee on Banking Supervision, Prudential treatment of cryptoasset exposures (December 2022), available at https://www.bis.org/bcbs/publ/d545.pdf (accessed 10 Mar. 2024).
101. Basel Committee on Banking Supervision, Consultative Document, Cryptoasset standard amendments (December 2023), available at https://www.bis.org/bcbs/publ/d567.pdf (accessed 10 Mar. 2024).
102. For a comprehensive overview on business use cases, *see* Satish Kumar, Weng Marc Lim, Uthayasankar Sivarajah and Jaspreet Kaur, Artificial Intelligence and Blockchain Integration in Business: Trends from a Bibliometric-Content Analysis (Information Systems Frontiers 25, 2023) 871; available at https://doi.org/10.1007/s10796-022-10279-0 (accessed 10 Mar. 2024).
103. https://kpmg.com/us/en/articles/2023/ai-blockchain-new-power-couple.html (accessed 10 Mar. 2024).
104. *See* §2.03[A], *supra*.
105. Artificial Intelligence Act as adopted by the European Parliament on 13 March 2024, *European Parliament legislative resolution of 13 March 2024 on the proposal for a regulation of the European Parliament and of the Council on laying down harmonised rules on Artificial Intelligence (Artificial Intelligence Act) and amending certain Union Legislative Acts (COM(2021)0206 – C9-0146/2021 – 2021/0106(COD))*, available at https://www.europarl.europa.eu/doceo/document/TA-9-2024-0138_EN.html (accessed 19 Mar. 2024).
106. Which is defined as: '[...] a machine-based system designed to operate with varying levels of autonomy, that may exhibit adaptiveness after deployment and that, for explicit or implicit objectives, infers, from the input it receives, how to generate outputs such as predictions, content, recommendations, or decisions that can influence physical or virtual environments', *see ibid.*, Art. 3(1).
107. *Ibid.*, at Recital (5).

taking into account the purposes that it is used for with respect to the specific requirements, meaning that '[t]he different risk levels will mean more or less regulation'.[108] Interestingly, the EU Parliament has also stated that it 'wants to establish a technology-neutral, uniform definition for AI that could be applied to future AI systems'.[109] This should, however, not be misunderstood in a way that the Act would be a technology-neutral regulation. It is clearly addressing AI specifically with the above reasoning. Rather, this means that the definition of an 'AI System' would be kept sufficiently neutral and broad to ensure that future AI technology would still be encompassed. Blockchain or Distributed Ledger Technology is not mentioned in the EU AI Act. The same is the case for the UK's AI regulatory framework[110] or the Blueprint for an AI Bill of Rights in the US.[111] Even if AI and Blockchain may further converge in the future, it is rather unlikely that future AI regulation will expressly include references to Blockchain, as this would not match with the purpose of addressing AI risks from an outcome perspective rather than as from the perspective of any underlying or ancillary technologies that are used.

In terms of a convergence of Blockchain and AI, certain trends can be observed. First, a potential scenario where blockchain and AI converge could be where blockchain technology is used in AI systems as a means to enhance compliance with regulatory requirements of AI, e.g., for identification and verification purposes (transactional records on a blockchain basis in order to create immutable tracking of the ownership of data used in AI models), tracking of IP rights (applying blockchain to label IP protected content in an immutable and transparent way), data privacy compliance[112] or in the area of supporting AI regulatory requirements regarding cyber security (in order to fulfil record-keeping, transparency assurance or access control enforcement requirements).[113] The use of blockchain in AI has been described as 'decentralized AI',[114] and this variant is characterized by using blockchain-specific features for the benefit of AI models.

Second, AI technology could be used in blockchain technologies, where the focus is on enhancing the latter. For example, AI algorithms could be used in the coding and

108. EU Parliament, EU AI Act: first regulation on artificial intelligence (8 Jun. 2023, updated 19 Dec. 2023), https://www.europarl.europa.eu/topics/en/article/20230601STO93804/eu-ai-act-first-regulation-on-artificial-intelligence (accessed 10 Mar. 2024).

109. *Ibid.*

110. *See* the Consultation outcome on *A pro-innovation approach to AI regulation: government response* (6 Feb. 2024); available at https://www.gov.uk/government/consultations/ai-regulation-a-pro-innovation-approach-policy-proposals/outcome/a-pro-innovation-approach-to-ai-regulation-government-response (accessed 10 Mar. 2024).

111. Blueprint for an AI Bill of Rights, *Making Automated Systems Work for the American People* (October 2022); available at https://www.whitehouse.gov/wp-content/uploads/2022/10/Blueprint-for-an-AI-Bill-of-Rights.pdf (accessed 10 Mar. 2024).

112. Examples listed by KPMG, *supra* n. 102.

113. *See* Simona Ramos and Joshua Ellul, Blockchain for Artificial Intelligence (AI): enhancing compliance with the EU AI Act through distributed ledger technology. A cybersecurity perspective, pp. 17 and 18 (Int. Cybersecur. Law Rev. 5 2024), available at https://doi.org/10.1365/s43439-023-00107-9 (accessed 10 Mar. 2024).

114. Kunal Kejriwal, A Comprehensive Review of Blockchain in AI (14 Sep. 2023), available at https://www.unite.ai/a-comprehensive-review-of-blockchain-in-ai/ (accessed 10 Mar. 2024).

operation of blockchains and therefore create some kind of decentralized and immutable but 'living' blockchains. This ties into the various elements of flexibility in blockchain models wherever an interaction through the outside world is required (e.g., through oracles or voting mechanisms in DAOs), where we may see a replacement of the human interaction with an AI, potentially leading to an even more 'isolated' form of blockchains with new challenges over their control. Specific AI regulation will play a key role in this discussion, as it will add to the requirements that need to be observed. It remains to be seen whether the usage of AI for specific blockchain or distributed ledger purposes could eventually become a use case that is specifically accounted for in AI regulation.

Given such potential convergence, it may be useful to compare some of the key elements of the two technologies. Like blockchain, AI technology has some defining characteristics which may not be as deterministic as it is the case for blockchain but still inherent to their model.

Table 2.2 Blockchain and AI Comparison of Certain Key Features

Blockchain	*AI*
Decentral	Centrally operated
Immutable	Evolving (adaptive models learning over time)
Transparent	Transparency requirements, but 'inner core' processes not always fully visible

Table 2.2 shows that certain characteristics of blockchain and AI are quite contrary. While it needs to be emphasized that this is a very simplistic comparison and that there are many nuances to these technologies, it also shows the reason why blockchain and AI are seen as a promising combination. To the same extent that they might complement each other from a technical point of view, they might also show the same potential for resolving issues from a regulatory point perspective. For example, if AI providers may wish to keep their algorithms private, blockchain as a traceability instrument may provide a means in helping to fulfil transparency and explainability requirements.

It is finally worth mentioning in a regulatory context that the EU AI Act introduces an AI sandbox regime (Articles 57 et seq.), under which each member state shall at least establish one AI sandbox on national level (Article 57(1)). This follows the sandbox approach also taken for blockchain with the European Blockchain Regulatory Sandbox regime[115] but on a national level. It will be interesting to see to what extent the convergence between blockchain and AI will be reflected in the use cases once the sandboxes have been established and how the interaction will be for combined use cases. This might exemplarily demonstrate how the various regulatory regimes could then also address convergence topics on a broader level.

115. Section §2.03[C], *supra*.

It can be concluded that a convergence between blockchain and AI is already underway and increasingly discussed with respect to potential use cases. From a regulatory perspective, the combination of both technologies also means a combination of regulatory requirements. Combined blockchain/AI use cases will need to be vetted against regulation which applies to each of them. In certain instances, the features of one of the technologies may help to satisfy regulatory requirements of the other technology. It remains to be seen to what extent regulation might increasingly recognize the convergence and address such use cases more specifically.

§2.07 SUMMARY

This chapter has attempted to provide an overview on the implications that legal regulation has on the blockchain technology and has elaborated on definitional aspects, challenges and actors from a broader perspective of the blockchain as a generic technology rather than from a use case basis. The following chapters of this handbook will dive deeper into the specific legal and regulatory subject matter items on smart contracts (Chapter 3, *infra*), data privacy (Chapter 4, *infra*), capital markets (Chapter 5, *infra*), crypto asset regulation in the Europe and the UK (Chapter 6, *infra*) and the US (Chapter 7, *infra*), intellectual property (Chapter 8, *infra*) and antitrust (Chapter 9, *infra*).

It is important to note that this chapter is by no means exhaustive, and the legal assessment of a specific blockchain remains subject to a comprehensive review on a case-by-case basis. Also, blockchain is a fast-moving technology, and it can be expected that characteristics may change as well over time – most probably not the constituent ones, but in further details, specifically where it is the question of how blockchain can be made compliant with current and future regulation. Hence, a thorough legal review in each individual case is and will remain indispensable.

FURTHER READING

Primavera De Filippi and Aaron Wright, *Blockchain and the Law: The Rule of Code* (2018).

Benedetta Cappiello and Gherardo Carullo (eds.), Blockchain, Law and Governance (2021).

Josias N. Dewey (ed.), *Global Legal Insights Blockchain & Cryptocurrency Regulation* (2nd edition 2020).

Michèle Finck, *Blockchain: Regulation and Governance in Europe* 93 (2018).

Eduard Hofert, *Regulierung der Blockchains* (2018).

Muharem Kianieff, Blockchain Technology and the Law, Opportunities and Risks (2019)

Lawrence Lessig, *Code Version 2.0* (2006), available at: https://upload.wikimedia.org/wikipedia/commons/f/fd/Code_v2.pdf (accessed 10 March 2024).

Carla L. Reyes, *Moving Beyond Bitcoin to an Endogenous Theory of Decentralized Ledger Technology Regulation: An Initial Proposal*, 61 Vill. L. Rev. 191-234 (2016).

Thomas Richter, *Blockchain – Rechtliche Aspekte aus Sicht der Finanzindustrie*, at 165-178, DGRI Jahrbuch 2017, Robert G. v. Briner & Axel Funk (eds) 2018.

Usha R. Rodrigues, *Law and Blockchain*, 104 Iowa L. Rev. 679, 682 (2019), available at: https://ilr.law.uiowa.edu/sites/ilr.law.uiowa.edu/files/2023-02/Rodrigues.pdf (accessed 10 March 2024).

CHAPTER 3
Blockchain and Smart Contracts*

Philip Trillmich, Matthias Goetz & Chris Ewing

§3.01 TERMINOLOGY AND CHARACTERISTICS: WHAT IS A SMART CONTRACT?

[A] History of the Term 'Smart Contract'

Although many believe that blockchain technology evolved earlier than smart contracts, mentions of smart contracting can be traced back to the 1990s.[1] That is when Nick Szabo developed a theoretical concept of computer programs designed to make all stages of contractual relationships less costly, more secure and more functional.[2] He drew on the real-life example of the vending machine to illustrate the characteristics of a smart contract:

> Within a limited amount of potential loss (the amount in the till should be less than the cost of breaching the mechanism), the machine takes in coins, and via a simple mechanism ... dispense change and product according to the displayed price. The vending machine is a contract with bearer: anybody with coins can participate in an exchange with the vendor. The lockbox and other security mechanisms protect the stored coins and contents from attackers, sufficiently to allow profitable deployment of vending machines in a wide variety of areas.[3]

---

* Special thanks go to Monopoly Christiaan-Rakus, Aleksandra Drabek, Elena Blessing, Rachel Thompson and Cameron Lee who assisted with this chapter.

1. Szabo, N., *Formalizing and Securing Relationships on Public Networks*, firstmonday (9 Jan. 1997), available at: http://firstmonday.org/ojs/index.php/fm/article/view/548/469 (accessed on 18 Mar. 2024); *see also* Wilkens, R. & Falk, R., *Smart Contracts – Grundlagen, Anwendungsfelder und rechtliche Aspekte* 3 (2019); Gyr, E., *Blockchain und Smart Contracts – Die vertragsrechtlichen Implikationen einer neuen Technologie* (21 Feb. 2019), available at: https://biblio.unibe.ch/download/eldiss/19gyr_e.pdf (accessed on 18 Mar. 2024).
2. Szabo, *supra* n. 1.
3. *Ibid.*

Thus, three features of the original idea of a smart contract deserve attention: (1) its potential to perform a contract with anyone, (2) the automatic performance of the contractual obligations if a specific condition is met, and (3) security mechanisms which make it unattractive to circumvent the agreed processes to obtain the promised goods or services, due to the potential costs of breaches.[4]

Nevertheless, smart contracts remained a theoretical idea for a number of years because of the absence of technology suitable to realize two of the principal features – a more secure performance of contractual promises and a reduction of transaction costs.[5] As such, despite software development being able to automate contractual relationships, no technology could come as close as traditional contracts in guaranteeing the secure performance of contractual obligations.[6] Software programs used by one party in a traditional client-server-environment, for example, by automating order processes in a web shop,[7] were not transparent enough and could be susceptible to manipulation.

However, it appears this has now changed. The emergence of decentralized blockchain technology is an opportunity to revisit the concept of smart contracts. In practice, we have already seen the first use of smart contracts within the blockchain technology as outlined in §3.02 below. As further described in this chapter, the deployment of smart contracts in blockchain brings with it a number of advantages. These advantages appear to finally fulfil Szabo's idea of smart contracts.

[B] Technical Characteristics of a 'Smart Contract'

Nick Szabo defined smart contracts as 'a set of promises, specified in digital form, including protocols within which the parties perform on these promises'.[8] Max Raskin used a simpler definition to describe the features of a smart contract when indicating that smart contracts are 'agreements wherein execution is automated, usually by computers'.[9] Both of those definitions share similar features. However, no unanimous definition of smart contracts exists. In particular, there is a certain level of disagreement as to the characteristics of smart contracts. The *legal* characteristics will be discussed in more detail in §3.01[C] below. For a detailed description of the technical characteristics and features of a smart contract, *see* Chapter 1 §1.02 above.

---

4. Gyr, *supra* n. 1.
5. Kaulartz, M. & Heckmann, J., *Smart Contracts – Anwendungen der Blockchain-Technologie* 618 (CR 2016).
6. Wilkens, R. & Falk, R., *supra* n. 1, at 4.
7. Paulus, D. & Matzke, R. *Smart Contracts und das BGB – Viel Lärm um nichts?*, 431, 435 (ZfPW 2018).
8. Szabo, N. *Smart Contracts: Building Blocks for Digital Markets* (1996), available at: http://www.fon.hum.uva.nl/rob/Courses/InformationInSpeech/CDROM/Literature/LOTwinterschool2006/szabo.best.vwh.net/smart_contracts_2.html (accessed on 18 Mar. 2024).
9. Raskin, M., *The Law and Legality of Smart Contracts*, 305, 306 (1 Georgetown Law Technology Review 2017).

[C] Terminology

[1] The Meaning of the Term 'Smart' in Smart Contract

The term 'smart' in 'smart contract' implies that such a contract is, in some sense, intelligent and able to adapt to changing circumstances. However, this view is rather misleading. Smart contracts are not 'smart' in the sense of being intelligent or adaptive. In particular, they are not means of autonomous decision-making (e.g., and in contrast, smart home concepts such as a device which automatically optimizes room temperature might apply artificial intelligence (AI) to autonomously gather and analyse data and make autonomous decisions[10]).[11] The term 'smart contract' should rather be understood as a 'buzzword' implying that computer programs and codes are involved, which perform in line with their instructions and the way they are programmed to perform.[12]

Usually, modern smart contracts refer to an application of decentralized blockchain technologies, which enable storing and execution of codes in their database. The decentralized blockchain technology enables smart contracts to develop beyond the vending-machine example discussed above in §3.01[A]. Such a machine is under the control of its owner who can switch it off at any point.[13] This does not apply to a smart contract in a blockchain, which is automatic and autonomously executing.[14] In addition, smart contracts can be programmed in such a way that they can obtain further input from human-controlled processes ('oracle') when certain defined events occur[15]. Therefore, although smart contracts are not 'smart' in an AI sense because they are simply pre-programmed lines of code, it would be fair to say that they have still developed a different kind of 'intelligence'. This is because, due to the use of blockchain technology, they have become more autonomous.

[2] What Does the Term 'Contract' Mean in Smart Contract?

There have been many attempts to assess the extent to which a smart contract actually is a contract in the legal sense. Durovic and Janssen propose that a smart contract is just a 'computer code which is operated by a computer and is self-executing and self-enforcing'.[16] This definition sees smart contracts through the lens of a blockchain,

10. Samsung Newsroom, *A Relaxing Weekend with Samsung's AI-Enabled and Smart Appliances* (28 Nov. 2019), available at: https://news.samsung.com/global/a-relaxing-weekend-with-samsungs-ai-enabled-and-smart-appliances (accessed on 18 Mar. 2024).
11. Kaulartz, M. & Heckmann, J., *supra* n. 5, at 618.
12. *Ibid.*
13. Paech, P., *Law and Autonomous Systems Series: What Is a Smart Contract?* (University of Oxford, 9 Jul. 2018), available at: https://www.law.ox.ac.uk/business-law-blog/blog/2018/07/law-and-autonomous-systems-series-what-smart-contract (accessed on 18 Mar. 2024).
14. *Ibid.*
15. Oracle is an interface that feeds in information about the event, explored in more detail in Chapter 1, §1.11[B], *supra*.
16. Durovic, M. & Janssen, A., *The Formation of Blockchain-Based Smart Contracts in the Light of Contract Law* 753 (26(6) European Review of Private Law, 2018).

indicating that a smart contract is merely a code that can document a contract in the legal sense or automate certain legally relevant processes.[17] However, in its 2021 study of the applicability of existing English law to smart contracts, the Law Commission distinguished a 'smart contract' from a 'smart legal contract': the former being '[c]omputer code that, upon the occurrence of a specified condition or conditions, is capable of running automatically according to pre-specified functions' and the latter being 'a legally binding contract in which some or all of the contractual terms are defined in and/or performed automatically by a computer program'.[18] These distinct definitions exemplify that in order to gain legal force, a smart contract on the blockchain must be structured to comply with specific legal requirements to constitute a legally enforceable contract.[19]

In particular, smart contracts can perform different tasks in the context of contractual relationships, such as: (1) automatically perform certain obligations (unlocking a door to an apartment once payment is made[20] or remunerating employees[21]), (2) providing access to a person's digital identity stored on blockchain during Know Your Client (KYC) processes,[22] (3) automatically effecting a reaction in case a contractual obligation is not performed (e.g., locking a smart lock in the event of a delayed payment or after a contract has ended[23] or using a smart meter to block energy provision as a result of a delayed payment[24]), and (4) recording the effect of contractual relationships (e.g., by recording a change in property ownership).[25]

As such, the wide spectrum of uses encouraged a broader understanding of 'smart contracts' and attempts to use them to execute legally binding declarations or perform legally binding acts.[26] Nevertheless, as the Law Commission's distinct definitions highlight, executing legally binding contracts is dependent upon fulfilling legal requirements, rather than the conditions in a code; how far smart contracts are able to fulfil those requirements is discussed in §3.03 below. The issue of 'applicable law vs code in law' is analysed in more detail in §3.03[A] below.

17. Paulus, D. & Matzke, R., *supra* n. 7, at 433.
18. The Law Commission, *Smart legal contracts: advice to Government*, available at: Smart-legal-contracts-accessible.pdf (cloud-platform-e218f50a4812967ba1215eaecede923f.s3.amazonaws.com) (accessed on 6 Mar. 2024). For the purposes of this chapter, the focus will be on 'smart legal contracts' on a blockchain, which will generally be referred to as 'smart contracts' (such concepts are discussed *intra* at §3.01[C]).
19. *Ibid.*
20. Wilkens, R. & Falk, R., *supra* n. 1, at 19.
21. Rampton, J., *Applications for Blockchain in Your Business* 5 (The Economist), available at: https://execed.economist.com/blog/industry-trends/5-applications-blockchain-your-business (accessed on 24 Feb. 2020).
22. Ambisafe *Smart Contracts: 10 Use Cases for Business*, available at: https://ambisafe.com/blog/smart-contracts-10-use-cases-business/ (accessed on 24 Feb. 2020).
23. Paulus, C. & Matzke, R., *supra* n. 7, at 434.
24. Paulus, C. & Matzke, R. *Smart Contracts und Smart Meter – Versorgungsperre für Fernzugriff* 1905, 1906 (NJW 2018).
25. Davies, A., *10 Uses for Smart Contracts*, available at: https://www.devteam.space/blog/10-uses-for-smart-contracts/ (accessed on 18 Mar. 2024).
26. Paulus, C. & Matzke, R., *supra* n. 7, at 433-434.

[3] The Attempt to Develop a Definition

As indicated above, there is no universal definition of a 'smart contract'.[27] The 2019 legal statement on crypto assets and smart contracts by the UK Jurisdiction Taskforce (UKJT)[28] did not provide a precise definition, pointing out it was 'unlikely to be useful'[29] and instead focused on characteristics and their relevance legally. Indeed, the search for a comprehensive definition is a rather challenging exercise. Like the definition of smart contracts suggested by the Swiss Parliament or the German Federal Financial Supervisory Authority,[30] the conception of smart contracts is often limited to blockchain-related use.

However, it is also important to realize that smart contracts are, in principle, technology neutral and can exist outside of the blockchain framework. For example, a computer program on an e-commerce platform that automates the processes of concluding a contract or an application for a car/bike rental which automatically unlocks the vehicle also fulfils the criteria of a smart contract as developed by Szabo and should therefore be classified as a smart contract.[31] The automatic freezing of a credit card in case of fraudulent activities is cited as a further example of a smart contract.[32]

Therefore, not confining their definition to blockchain, Kaulartz and Heckmann define a smart contract as a software program which performs, controls and/or documents legally relevant acts (in particular, the performance of contractual obligations) that are conditional upon digitally verifiable results.[33]

Evidently, and in line with the definition proposed by Kaulartz and Heckmann, smart contracts can be deployed outside of the blockchain. However, there are a number of advantages of a smart contract existing within the blockchain compared to a smart contract existing outside of the blockchain. Some of these advantages are

---

27. *Ibid.*
28. The UKJT is one of six taskforces under the LawTech Delivery Panel, an industry group which supports the digital transformation of the legal sector. The findings within the legal statement are the result of several rounds of public and private consultations and has the benefit of technical, judicial, legal and academic opinions.
29. UKJT, *Legal Statement on Cryptoassets and Smart Contracts*, The LawTech Delivery Panel (November 2019), available at: https://www.blockchain4europe.eu/wp-content/uploads/2021/05/6.6056_JO_Cryptocurrencies_Statement_FINAL_WEB_111119-1.pdf (accessed on 18 Mar. 2024).
30. The BaFin defined smart contracts as 'programmable contracts, which are defined by the programme code and are automatically executed and enforced in blockchains', *see* Bundesanstalt für Finanzdienstleistungsaufsicht, *Blockchain-Technologie*; the Swiss parliament in a report gives a similar definition of a smart contract as a computer protocol, which – usually based on a decentralized blockchain system – allows for an automated performance of contractual obligations between two or more parties based on previously coded information, *see* Bundesrat der Schweizerischen Eidgenossenschaft, *Rechtliche Grundlagen für Distributed Ledger – Technologie und Blockchain in der Schweiz – Eine Auslegeordnung mit Fokus auf dem Finanzsektor* 85 (14 Dec. 2018), available at: https://www.newsd.admin.ch/newsd/message/attachments/55150.pdf (accessed on 18 Mar. 2024).
31. Paulus, C. & Matzke, R., *supra* n. 7, at 435.
32. Moeslein, F., *Smart Contracts im Zivil- und Handelsrecht* 254, 261 (ZHR 2019).
33. Kaulartz, M. & Heckmann, J., *supra* n. 5, at 618; *see also* Wilkens, R. & Falk, R., *supra* n. 1, at 4.

showcased in §3.03[D] below. Based on this and the below, as well as the significant advantages of smart contracts within the blockchain over smart contracts outside of the blockchain, the analysis of smart contracts in this chapter is limited to smart contracts within the blockchain.

[D] Characteristics of 'Smart Contracts' as an Application of a Blockchain

As indicated above, there are many advantages of utilizing smart contracts within the blockchain environment. One of the key benefits is a guarantee of autonomous performance of contractual obligations. This is in contrast to 'offline' contracts, where despite the very best intentions of both parties, breaches such as delayed payment or delayed delivery can occur. As such, the certainty attributed to blockchain can be a significant advantage.

In addition, smart contracts are effectively 'permanently tamperproof',[34] protected from the influence of third parties or institutions as the blockchain is a decentralized system that can only be amended with the consent of all of its members. This makes it a trustworthy way of doing business. In contrast, when smart contracts exist outside of a blockchain, the software is essentially under the control of one party, thereby making it more likely for data or contracts to be manipulated.

Another key advantage of smart contracts within the blockchain is the inherent possibilities and functionalities. It is possible to program complex functionalities,[35] for example, to make the performance of a smart contract conditional upon a digitally verifiable event. For this purpose, an oracle is needed[36] – for a more detailed discussion of oracles, *see* Chapter 1, §1.11[B] above. A smart contract in a blockchain environment can also be connected to other smart contracts with different functionalities, enabling further development and building of more complex and sophisticated contracts.[37]

Moreover, other aspects of a blockchain environment provide for effective enforcement mechanisms: (1) a virtual currency is available to perform payment obligations, (2) automatic register entries can be generated to document transfers of property rights, and (3) oracles can also be used to cause a real-world output and thus generate more complex legal effects.[38]

However, there are also disadvantages to using smart contracts within a blockchain environment. For example, while the lack of control over blockchain appears to be a significant advantage, there are also difficulties associated with this very feature.

34. Sultan, K., Ruhi, U., & Lakhani, R., *Conceptualizing Blockchains: Characteristics & Applications* (2018), available at: https://arxiv.org/ftp/arxiv/papers/1806/1806.03693.pdf (accessed on 18 Mar. 2024); Bremann, N.-L., *Smart Contracts im Einsatz* 299, 303-304 (DSRITB 2019); Saive, D., *Rückabwicklung von Blockchain-Transaktionen* 371-372 (DSRITB 2018); Paulus, C. & Matzke, R., *supra* n. 7, at 437-438.
35. Wilkens, R. & Falk, R., *supra* n. 1, at 10; Moeslein, F., *supra* n. 32, at 254, 261.
36. Wilkens, R. & Falk, R., *supra* n. 1, at 14.
37. Heckelmann, M., *Zulässigkeit und Handhabung von Smart Contracts* 504, 505 (NJW 2018).
38. Paulus, C. & Matzke, R., *supra* n. 7, at 433; Moeslein, F., *supra* n. 32, at 254, 261.

Unless the option has been pre-programmed, it is essentially impossible to change the code in a blockchain once it has been programmed to perform (as mentioned above).[39] Because such contracts are automatically executed, this can be a detriment for parties wishing to retain flexibility. To resolve this issue, modifiable smart contracts are making an appearance within the technology world, enabling a smart contract to be, to some extent, reversible in some parts of the program, which are stored within a library.[40] However, a significant drawback of such a modifiable smart contract is the need for a trustworthy relationship with anyone who holds access to the library. This dilutes the above-mentioned advantage of the lack of control over a smart contract in a blockchain environment.

It should also be noted that, as the blockchain allows for the anonymous performance of contractual relationships, with very limited information being available online (such as a public key, transaction sum and transaction date),[41] this can create difficulties, especially when attempting to trace and hold them accountable.

Tied in with this is the fact that enforcement in this area must take different forms; in contrast to traditional contractual disputes, whereby one party seeks to receive compensation for lack of or inadequate performance, smart contracting means guaranteed performance and restitutionary claims. The legal difficulties of smart contracts are analysed in more detail in §3.03 below.

However, as shown above, there are a lot of practical advantages to smart contracts within a blockchain that can be utilized in a number of fields; such fields are further elaborated below.

§3.02 FIELDS OF APPLICATION

[A] Legal Profession

A number of possible use cases for smart contracts are being discussed within the legal industry, such as inheritance or family law. For example, with respect to wills and probate, smart contracts could allow for automatic transactions without intermediaries. This could be as follows: (1) a testator lists the relevant assets in a smart contract will[42] and (2) the death certificate's registration then automatically triggers distribution of assets and payment of inheritance tax.[43] The significant advantage of such a smart contract is its security over a physical, written will which could be lost or tampered with.[44] In family law, a smart contract could be linked to a marriage certificate which

39. Paulus, C. & Matzke, R., *supra* n. 7, at 437-438.
40. Wilkens, R. & Falk R., *supra* n. 1, at 12-13.
41. Wilkens, R. & Falk, R., *supra* n. 1, at 14-15. For a more detailed discussion of the blockchain features, please *see* Chapter 1 *supra*.
42. Cheung, A., *Can You Write Your Will onto a Blockchain? Smart Contracts* (16 Oct. 2023), available at: https://www.rocketlawyer.com/gb/en/blog/can-you-write-your-will-onto-a-blockchain-smart-contracts/ (accessed on 18 Mar. 2024).
43. DiMatteo, L.-A., Cannarsa, M. & Poncibo, C., *The Cambridge Handbook of Smart Contracts, Blockchain and Technology and Digital Platforms* 47 (2019).
44. Cheung, *supra* n. 42.

manages the division of accumulated savings during divorce proceedings.[45] Additionally, a smart contract could automatically enforce court orders, such as maintenance payments.[46] This would provide clients with 'greater security, reduced costs and the potential to avoid the need to return to court with an application to enforce the order or an agreement'.[47]

However, blockchain and smart contracts are usually accessible on a public network. Therefore, the lack of privacy could be a possible limitation of using smart contracts for private client or family work.[48] Another problem could arise out of formality requirements. For example, in English law, section 9 of the Wills Act 1837 provides that a will must be in writing and signed by the testator in the presence of two witnesses.[49] Similarly, German law provides that a will must be handwritten and signed by the testator.[50] For a more detailed discussion of formality requirements, *see* §3.03[B][2] below.

Another potential use case of smart contracts could be in the field of legal drafting. For example, lawyers could be filling standard forms to generate smart contracts.[51] Such a process could be termed as 'combined drafting'. Equally, the inalterability of blockchain data could assist notaries seeking to prove the provenance and authenticity of documentation.[52]

Nevertheless, at this stage, such use cases are merely ideas as there are still issues which prevent the widespread utilization of blockchain within the legal profession, one of which is the particularity of subjective expressions, such as 'fair and reasonable' or 'best efforts'. Such expressions are often used by lawyers when drafting traditional contracts and are not easily translated into computer code. For more details on this issue, *see* §3.03[F] below.

[B] Insurance Industry

There is a clear opportunity for automation through smart contracts to improve efficiency for consumers in the field of the insurance industry.[53] It could also create

45. DiMatteo, L.-A., Cannarsa, M. & Poncibo, C., *supra* n. 43.
46. Kempster, K., *How Blockchain Might Transform Family Law*, available at: https://vardags.com/family-law/how-blockchain-might-transform-family-law (accessed on 18 Mar. 2024).
47. *Ibid.*
48. Orcutt, M., *Hate Lawyers? Can't Afford One? Blockchain Smart Contracts Are Here to Help?* (11 Jan. 2019), available at: https://www.technologyreview.com/s/612748/hate-lawyers-cant-afford-one-blockchain-smart-contracts-are-here-to-help/ (accessed on 18 Mar. 2024).
49. Cheung, A., *supra* n. 42.
50. Paragraph 2247 subs. (1) of the German Civil Code (*Bürgerliches Gesetzbuch*) in the version of 2 Jan. 2002.
51. Vinters, T., *Smart Contracts: A Boom or Bane for the Legal Profession?* (24 Sep. 2018), available at: https://www.lexology.com/library/detail.aspx?g=f16551a7-e974-41d2-ba45-37e2dc7f6e41 (accessed on 5 Mar. 2024).
52. *Ibid.*
53. Queen Mary University of London, Centre for Commercial Law Studies, *Triggering Innovation How Smart Contracts Bring Policies to Life* (2019), available at: https://assets.lloyds.com/assets/pdf-triggering-innovation-how-smart-contracts-bring-policies-to-life/1/pdf-triggering-innovation-how-smart-contracts-bring-policies-to-life.pdf (accessed on 5 Mar. 2024).

considerable savings, especially in light of the 'high cost centres of underwriting, claims management, fraud reduction and reinsurance'.[54] Therefore, there is a likelihood that the use of smart contracts will transform the insurance industry, in particular, because smart contracts can be utilized at multiple stages of the insurance process.[55] At the underwriting stage, various sources, including third-party oracles, could gather information regarding prospective customers and risks. This would shift the onus away from customers to provide such information and could result in more specific and bespoke insurance packages and premiums.[56] An example of such a bespoke insurance package could be a smart flood insurance which would work by providing real-time evidence of water damage through its sensors. Such insurance could also automatically trigger an insurance claim after water levels exceeded a certain predefined threshold.[57] In a similar way, crop insurance could be used with sensors monitoring the weather and payment being automated in the event of persistently bad weather.[58]

Another example within the sector could be in relation to customers travelling on significantly delayed flights, who could automatically receive compensation payments without the need to submit a claim.[59] Such automation of claims could enhance transparency and reduce operating costs for the insurance company. The objective nature of claims would provide certainty for customers that payments will be made once the precondition is met and could accordingly reduce disputes.[60]

Nevertheless, the use of blockchain and smart contracts within the insurance industry brings with it a number of concerns. There are fears that the relevant technology would collect sensitive personal data such as race, religion and other discriminatory characteristics, which could subsequently be used to price insurance products. This may result in certain groups of people becoming uninsurable.[61] Similar concerns in relation to data arise regarding the concept of 'pay-per-use' insurance whereby sensors would be used to activate or deactivate policies, and blockchain would record the details. Such insurance would rely on the collection of records or data which could engage data protection issues if location or other personal data were collected; *see* Chapter 4 below. The 'pay-per-use' insurance policy could nevertheless

54. *Ibid.*
55. For a brief discussion of recent use cases of smart contracts and blockchain technology in the insurance industry, *see* Informatics International, *Revolutionizing Insurance with Smart Contracts: Harnessing the Power of Blockchain Technology*, available at: https://www.linkedin.com/pulse/revolutionizing-insurance-smart-contracts/ (accessed on 6 Mar. 2024).
56. Gatteschi, V. et al., *Blockchain and Smart Contracts for Insurance: Is the Technology Mature Enough?* (2018), available at: https://www.the-digital-insurer.com/wp-content/uploads/2018/07/1243-futureinternet-10-00020-v2-1.pdf (accessed on 18 Mar. 2024).
57. Queen Mary University of London, *supra* n. 53.
58. Gatteschi, V. et al., *supra* n. 56.
59. Mlynar, T.-J. and Fettman, R.-M., *Blockchain and Smart Contracts Will Change the Face of Insurance in the U.S.* (23 May 2019), available at: https://www.lexology.com/library/detail.aspx?g=b119f47b-764b-464c-9090-89b8e6e58219 (accessed on 18 Mar. 2024).
60. Savelyev, A., *Contract Law 2.0: 'Smart' Contracts as the Beginning of the End of Classic Contract Law*, Information & Communications Technology Law, 116-134 (2017).
61. Mlynar, T.-J. and Fettman, R.-M., *supra* n. 59.

be an attractive option in a number of fields, for example, in relation to services with respect to which a policy would only be activated when an individual uses the service.

In addition, there are other concerns which relate to the nature of such smart insurance contracts. One of such concerns is whether these contracts are indeed insurance contracts that are subject to a large volume of regulations or whether they could also just be simple derivative contracts.[62]

There are other significant regulatory and compliance issues arising out of the use of smart contracts, some of which are addressed in Chapter 2 §2.01[C][3] above.

[C] Music Industry/Media Industry

The media industry is another area that could benefit from smart contracts. Currently, the music industry suffers from issues regarding ownership and rights.[63] The payment of royalties is often a complex process, with multiple contracts between artists, producers and publishing houses and reliance upon royalty-collection bodies for the distribution of payments. 'Artists regularly sue their labels for withholding payments, and labels often sue streaming services... for unpaid royalties and copyright infringement.'[64] This is also because royalty-collection bodies gather general airplay statistics which are not directly associated with a rights holder, often resulting in inaccurate payments or unfair compensation, especially in relation to lesser-known artists.[65]

By using smart contracts, the process of making royalty payments could be simplified, while also removing the current uncertainty that exists around the ownership of rights in works. For example, downloading a song could activate a smart contract that would arrange an automatic and real-time payment of royalties, with specific distribution percentages, amongst its contributors.[66] This would remove the need for royalty-collection associations, shifting the power to copyright owners,[67] and reducing the cost of, and time taken to process, royalty transactions. Smart contracts could also assist by automating rights management and remove the need for disputes and the courts' involvement.[68] Further, they 'may [also] play a role in standardizing

62. *Ibid.*
63. Hu, C., *Are Smart Contracts Smart Enough For the Music Industry?*, available at: https://breakermag.com/are-smart-contracts-smart-enough-for-the-music-industry/ (accessed on 24 Feb. 2020).
64. *Ibid.*
65. *Ibid.*
66. Finck, M. and Moscon, V., *Copyright Law on Blockchain: Between New Forms of Rights Administration and Digital Rights Management 2.0* (2019), available at: https://www.ip.mpg.de/de/publikationen/details/copyright-law-on-blockchains-between-new-forms-of-rights-administration-and-digital-rights-management-20.html?pk_campaign=newsletter1 (accessed on 18 Mar. 2024).
67. Deloitte, *Blockchain @ Media – A new Game Changer for the Media Industry?*, available at: https://www2.deloitte.com/content/dam/Deloitte/tr/Documents/technology-media-telecommunications/deloitte-PoV-blockchain-media.pdf (accessed on 18 Mar. 2024).
68. Hu, C., *supra* n. 63.

licensing terms and conditions for copyright works across uses and different jurisdictions, similar to the way in which [Creative Commons] licenses are deployed at a global scale'.[69]

However, 'there remain substantial unresolved issues limiting the applicability of smart contracts' in the media industry.[70] For example, assuming an author posts their work on a blockchain, recording ownership and using smart contracts to automate who has access to the records, difficulties immediately arise in relation to who has access to the works and under what conditions. Further, as a blockchain is not tied to any jurisdiction, there could be issues arising as copyright varies by jurisdiction. For example, New Zealand offers protection for the life of the author and an additional 50 years, whereas the European Union, Canada and the United States offer 70 years after the death of the author.[71] Additionally, there are concerns whether smart contracts will resolve the issue of payment because if you cannot accurately identify who owns the music in the first place, you cannot even begin the payment process.[72] Unless there are independent safeguards in place that monitor and verify who can be registered as the owner of rights for certain work, there is also the immediate concern that a person could fraudulently register themselves as the owner of certain rights on the blockchain and incorrectly begin receiving royalty payments.[73]

Another issue arises because smart contracts may not be able to handle the 'sprawling layers of complex, dynamic agreements that pervade the music business today, especially when it comes to digital consumption'.[74] For example, there are complex and subjective clauses in record labels' contracts that are more relational than transactional (such as 'reasonable' and 'good faith'), which cannot be encoded in smart contract form.[75] More detail on the interpretation of terms in a smart contract is found below in §3.03[F].

As such, due to the complexity of these contracts, it is likely that, in the short term, smart contracts will mainly be used for large volumes of simple contracts, for example, licensing music to a TV show[76] that has fewer variables such as the name of a song, name of a TV show, and price of a song. Regarding copyright licences, 'for the foreseeable future, this uncertainty surrounding the legal status of smart contracts is

69. Bodó, Balázs, Gervais, D.† and Quintais, Joao Pedro, *Blockchain and smart contracts: the missing link in copyright licensing?* (25 Sep. 2018), available at: https://academic.oup.com/ijlit/article/26/4/311/5106727 (accessed on 18 Mar. 2024).
70. *Ibid.*
71. *Ibid.* On 23 Jun. 2022, the Canadian Parliament enacted legislation to extend the term of protection of copyrighted works under the Copyright Act from the life of the author plus 50 years to plus 70 years, which came into effect on 30 Dec. 2022. *See* the Copyright Act R.S., 1985, c. C-42, s. 61993, c. 44, s. 582022, c. 10, s. 276.
72. Hu, C., *supra* n. 63.
73. For an interesting example of this in the context of independent verification for artwork and collectibles, *see* the following blog post https://shkspr.mobi/blog/2018/06/how-i-became-leonardo-da-vinci-on-the-blockchain/ (accessed on 18 Mar. 2024) in which Terence Eden explains how he easily convinced a blockchain-based startup called Verisart that he was the creator of the Mona Lisa.
74. Hu, C., *supra* n. 63.
75. *Ibid.*
76. *Ibid.*

likely to limit the emergence of more complex and robust arrangements in the domain of automated copyrights licenses'.[77]

[D] Energy Supply Industry

The energy sector is undergoing significant changes regarding both renewable energy and technology.[78] At a commercial level, smart contracts could affect electricity wholesale trading,[79] particularly in the field of renewable energy production. Currently, wholesale energy markets involve complex third-party intermediaries conducting lengthy activities consolidating and communicating information held by each party. These unnecessary intermediaries naturally inflate the costs of trading and exclude small-scale distributors from the market.[80] Smart contracts could remove these intermediaries, automatically monitoring the demand, delivery and payment of electricity (e.g., requesting electricity when prices are below a threshold or when renewable electricity is available).[81] The objective nature, certainty and reduced costs enabled by smart contracts 'would lead to incentives to invest more in these renewable energies and would also make a completely new product possible'.[82] Indeed, this emerging shift towards Peer-to-Peer (P2P) and community energy trading will be a principal factor in smart contract utilization.[83] For example, a recent systematic review of smart contracts in energy systems hypothesized that a community energy project could in future be assisted by 'blockchain-enabled Decentralised Autonomous Organisations, which use smart contracts to self-enforce mutual agreements between their members'.[84]

At the grassroots level, smart contracts have the potential to affect individuals through smart meters and billing. The combination of smart contracts and the Internet of Things (IoT), discussed below, further broadens the influence of smart contracts within the field of energy supply. Additionally, smart contracts could simplify and reduce the time taken to switch energy suppliers, which, in turn, will increase competition in the energy market and reduce tariffs.[85]

77. Bodó, B. et al., *supra* n. 69.
78. FSR Energy Florence School of Regulation, *Blockchain Meets Energy, Digital Solutions for Decentralized and Decarbonized Sector* (June 2019), available at: https://fsr.eui.eu/wp-content/uploads/Blockchain_meets_Energy_-_ENG.pdf (accessed on 18 Mar. 2024).
79. Electricity wholesale trading refers to a market, where electricity is traded between generators and suppliers. The energy is obtained at wholesale prices to which a markup is added, resulting in electricity being sold at higher prices to consumers. FSR Energy Florence School of Regulation, *supra* n. 78.
80. *Ibid.*
81. *Ibid.*
82. *Ibid.*
83. Kirli, D. et al, *Smart contracts in energy systems: A systematic review of fundamental approaches and implementations*, Renewable and Sustainable Energy Reviews, vol. 158, 112013 (April 2022), available at: https://doi.org/10.1016/j.rser.2021.112013 (accessed on 7 Mar. 2024).
84. *Ibid.*
85. FSR Energy Florence School of Regulation, *supra* n. 78.

[E] Internet of Things

The IoT industry is a computing concept describing 'the idea of everyday physical objects being connected to the internet and being able to identify themselves to other devices'.[86] The industry is growing exponentially, with the number of IoT devices increasing from 8.4 billion to 20 billion from 2017 to 2020 (and estimated to be over 500 billion by 2030).[87]

On a business level, this rapid growth creates a new opportunity to maximize the value of data generated by IoT sensors.[88] 'The IoT will create opportunities for new, exciting applications that will interweave the physical with the cyber world.'[89] Smart contracts would facilitate a novel business model/platform whereby customers can automatically purchase data from IoT sensors (without the need for intermediaries).[90] The smart contract would be entered into between the IoT sensor owner/provider and the customer, whereby payment would automatically provide the customer with a certain quantity of data from IoT sensors. IoT sensors could provide a wide variety of information, and smart contracts would allow the large-scale sharing of that information. Additionally, 'leveraging the trust anchors provided by smart contracts and the underlay blockchain, it should be easier to build open, reliable, and secure distributed applications, as well as novel security, accountability, and charging mechanisms'.[91] This information sharing could have widespread uses, including marketing and research. However, this would also trigger further data protection concerns, expanded on in Chapter 4.

Smart contracts could also enhance IoT at an individual level, providing a 'high degree of coordination and authority. Particularly when it comes to managing transactions and interactions, smart contracts ensure proper cohesion'.[92] They could collaborate with IoT sensors in individual homes to take the 'right amount of action at the right time',[93] and they would automatically facilitate transactions once certain pre-set conditions agreed in the smart contract are met. For example, when an existing light bulb burns out, a smart contract could trigger the purchase of a new one, with the program only allowing orders of a certain price and delivery date.[94]

---

86. Techopedia Internet of Things, available at: https://www.techopedia.com/definition/28247/internet-of-things-iot (accessed on 18 Mar. 2024).
87. Smatz Platform Blog, *How Blockchain and Smart Contracts Can Impact IoT*, available at: https://medium.com/smartz-blog/how-blockchain-and-smart-contracts-can-impact-iot-f9e77ebe02ab (accessed on 18 Mar. 2024).
88. Papadodimas, G., Palaiokrasas, G., Litke, A. and Vavarigou, T., *Implementation of smart contracts for blockchain based IoT applications* (2022), available at: Implementation of smart contracts for blockchain based IoT applications | IEEE Conference Publication | IEEE Xplore (accessed on 18 Mar. 2024).
89. Fotiou, N. and Polyzos, G.-C., *Smart contracts for the Internet of Things: opportunities and challenges* (23 Jan. 2019), available at: https://arxiv.org/pdf/1901.10582.pdf (accessed on 18 Mar. 2024).
90. Papadodimas, G. et al., *supra* n. 88.
91. Fotiou, N. and Polyzos, G.-C., *supra* n. 89.
92. Smatz Platform Blog, *supra* n. 87.
93. *Ibid.*
94. *Ibid.*

Based on the above, there is a chance for smart contracts to eliminate intermediaries and reduce transaction time and expense.

[F] Sharing Economy

The sharing economy enables groups of individuals to cooperate in providing tangible and intangible assets, with the community subsequently evaluating the asset and paying the provider. The sharing economy has expanded rapidly due to the highly regarded combined review structure from both providers and customers and now encompasses some of the largest and most successful companies.[95] Smart contracts could further enhance and digitize the sharing economy by streamlining and further automating transactions.

The involvement of smart contracts creates the chance to remove the detriment of human error and intermediaries and 'facilitate secure transactions or reduce the fees associated with international currency transfers'.[96] For example, in the context of car hire, as a number of ride-hailing services demonstrate, smart contracts could enable an individual to send payment to a car-hire company, unlock the car and drive – such contracts would automatically come to an end once the car-hire contract expires.[97]

To conclude, the utilization of smart contracts within a sharing economy would result in a reduction or even 'no need for third-party intermediaries who would normally serve as the trusted platform providing the services',[98] thereby reducing the cost of these services for customers and service providers. The reduced cost for service providers would also inevitably open the market to smaller start-ups, increase competition and revolutionize the sharing economy by opening it up to other areas beyond accommodation and car hire.

The utilization of smart contracts on a blockchain could bring a number of advantages, such as reducing costs and increasing efficiency. Nevertheless, despite the prospect of revolutionizing the economy and the extraordinary potential of blockchain, smart contracts also create a number of unresolved issues which would need to be dealt with. We have analysed some of these issues in detail in §3.03 below.

95. Miller, D. *The Sharing Economy and How is it Changing Industries* (19 Sep. 2022), available at: https://www.thebalancesmb.com/the-sharing-economy-and-how-it-changes-industries-4172234 (accessed on 18 Mar. 2024).
96. Miller, L. *Blockchain and the sharing economy – a match made in heaven? This startup plans to prove it* (13 Apr. 2018), available at: https://thenextweb.com/cryptocurrency/2018/04/13/blockchain-and-the-sharing-economy-a-match-made-in-heaven-this-startup-plans-to-prove-it/ (accessed on 18 Mar. 2024).
97. Harrington, L. *Sharing Economy 2.0: Can Blockchain Remove the Need for Single-Asset Ownership?* (9 Jan. 2019), available at: https://www.iotforall.com/sharing-economy-can-blockchain-eliminate-single-asset-ownership/ (accessed on 18 Mar. 2024).
98. *Ibid.*

§3.03 CONTRACT LAW ISSUES

[A] Applicable Law Versus 'Code in Law'

As has been mentioned above in §3.01[C][2], smart contracts are often viewed as a means to autonomously exercise certain steps in an already established contractual relationship.[99] As such, they perform existing contractual obligations rather than enable the creation of new legally binding obligations through smart contracts. The terms of a contract in its traditional form, setting out the parties' intentions and expectations, would be coded onto the blockchain via a smart contract, and the blockchain network would then become, for that contract, a 'governance mechanism ... [that] is enforced by a computer'.[100] In such circumstances, it could be argued that the rules governing such contract are the 'self-executing and self-enforcing'[101] code of the smart contract itself. This would also require that the parties' intended remedies in the event of a breach or dispute are coded into the smart contract so that they can be automatically executed if the necessary conditions are satisfied.

However, even if this view of smart contracts as the means of executing and governing previously established contracts in their traditional form is accepted, there are strong arguments that parties should not anticipate relying solely on smart contracts for governance and execution. As discussed in §3.04[A] below, there is always a risk of parties' previously agreed intentions not being given effect to if, for example, there appears to be an error in code. In such circumstances, the terms contained in the 'traditional' contract (and coded in the smart contract) could be the subject of a dispute, which would need to be heard before, and ultimately enforced by, the relevant court.

How this would work in practice where such a contract is executed by, or in the form of, a smart contract is difficult to predict. Smart contracts cannot be amended or terminated once coded and placed on the blockchain and will self-execute once the necessary circumstances arise. In a situation where there has been an incorrect transfer of value executed by a smart contract, '[t]he recourse will probably be in the form of an injunction for return of [that value]',[102] but other, more complex uses of a smart contract may not be so simple to resolve once the contract has been self-executed.

Alternatively, if a smart contract is a legally binding contract,[103] then what must instead be determined is the law that is applicable not to the underlying, 'traditional' contract (which would in any case likely specify the parties' preferred applicable law) but to the smart contract itself. Given that '[o]ne of the key promises of blockchain

99. Durovic, M. & Janssen, A., *supra* n. 16.
100. Grinhaus, A., *A Practical Guide to Smart Contracts and Blockchain Law* 157 (Pema Banigan, Matthew Rappard & Zachary Skeith [eds], 2019).
101. Durovic, M. & Janssen, A., *supra* n. 16.
102. Grinhaus, A., *supra* n. 100.
103. *See* below in §3.03 for a further discussion of the formation of a smart contract.

technology, and by extension smart contracts, is the development of robust, decentralized and global platforms',[104] it is possible that a large number of people across a number of jurisdictions around the world will be making use of a certain smart contract. Therefore, if the relevant parties do not specify an applicable law when entering into a smart contract, it will presumably be difficult to objectively determine, with certainty, which law should be applicable in interpreting that smart contract in the event of a dispute. It would therefore be advisable for the parties to agree and specify the relevant governing law and jurisdiction; otherwise, 'a plaintiff may be relatively unconstrained in choosing where to file a claim or in arguing which substantive law should apply'.[105] This sentiment was recently reinforced by the Law Commission, which advised that contracting parties include a jurisdiction and choice of law clause in their smart contracts in order to mitigate any difficulties in applying conflict of laws principles and other jurisdictional issues.[106]

[B] Formation of a Smart Contract

[1] Contracting Parties

In the context of AI, there are some discussions as to which person declarations and actions are attributable. This problem does not arise in the context of smart contracts.[107] As set out in §3.01[B] above, a smart contract is a computer program with a specific if/then logic. It does not generate autonomous actions but rather performs certain pre-programmed actions. It usually serves as a tool to perform contractual obligations or – under specific circumstances – communicate declarations of the person using it. Thus, even if a smart contract is used in a context in which two software programs interact and exchange transactions, the actions are easily attributable to the person(s) for whom the smart contract performs an action.[108]

However, for contractual agreements that include the use of a smart contract in a blockchain environment, identifying the contracting parties might be more complicated than for traditional contracts. This is because of the use of pseudonyms in a

---

104. Dewey, J.-N., *Blockchain & Cryptocurrency Regulation 2020*, 165 (Global Legal Insights, 2nd ed., 2020).
105. *Ibid.*
106. The Law Commission, *Smart legal contracts: advice to Government*, *supra* n. 18, at 176 and 212. The Law Commission detailed certain jurisdictional issues applicable to smart contracts, including a party's physical location and the place of formation of the contract. For a discussion of such issues, *see* Ma, A. *Blockchain-Enabled Smart Legal Contracts*, available at: https://www.intechopen.com/chapters/86570 (accessed on 6 Mar. 2024).
107. Paulus, D. & Matzke, R., *supra* n. 7, at 446 fn. 111; *see* for a brief discussion of this issue, Paulus, D. & Matzke, R., *supra* n. 7, at 442-445.
108. *See also* Wilkens, R. & Falk, R., *supra* n. 1, at 33; Lupu, R., *Zulässigkeit, Handhabung und rechtliche Grenzen bei der Gestaltung von Smart Contracts* 209, 214 (DSRITB 2019); Paulus, D. & Matzke, R., *supra* n. 7, at 446, noting that this might be different for actions the parties did not want and were caused by faulty programming; in favour of a possible attribution to the programmer, Heckelmann, M., *supra* n. 37, at 506.

blockchain environment which complicates the identification of the contracting parties. Although the identification of contracting parties could be complicated, in the view of UKJT, it will not be an issue since there is 'no doubt that a smart legal contract between anonymous or pseudonymous parties is capable of giving rise to binding legal obligations'.[109]

In addition, it is also argued that parties using a smart contract usually have no particular interest or need in knowing the identity of the other party because a smart contract in a blockchain environment guarantees the immediate performance of the contractual obligations.[110] However, in some jurisdictions, the use of pseudonyms can be an issue particularly in business-to-consumer (B2C) contracts. For example, German consumer-protection law stipulates[111] that businesses must disclose their identity and contact details prior to the formation of the contract. Also, companies would often want to know about the identity of the party they are contracting with. As a consequence, the concept of smart contracts is likely to be more often deployed for simple, low-value transactions rather than complex contracts. With respect to more complex contracts and transactions, it is advisable to provide contact information to the other party in a suitable way.[112]

[2] Form Requirements

A core principle in contract law which applies in most jurisdictions is the principle of 'freedom of contract'. This means that parties are free to write their bargains in the language and form of their choosing.[113] Generally, this also encompasses smart contracts' computer code. However, contract law across jurisdictions very often still has various formalities that will need to be satisfied.

For example, in Germany, a contract can be null and void if certain formalities are not fulfilled.[114] German law stipulates a number of form requirements for certain types of contracts. Common form requirements are text form,[115] written form,[116] official

109. UKJT, *Legal Statement on Cryptoassets and Smart Contracts*, The LawTech Delivery Panel JT, *supra* n. 29.
110. Schawe, N., *Blockchain und Smart Contracts in der Kreativwirtschaft – mehr Probleme als Lösungen?* 218, 220 (MMR 2019).
111. § 312d subs. (1) German Civil Code in connection with Art. 246a s. 1 subs. (1) sentence 1 lit. 2 Einführungsgesetz zum Bürgerlichen Gesetzbuch (Introductory Law to the German Civil Code) in the version of 21 Sep. 1994 (BGBl. I p. 2494; 1997 I p. 1061), last updated by Art. 2 G. v. 18 Dec. 2018 (BGBl. I p. 2648); *see also* Schawe, N., *supra* n. 110.
112. For details regarding suitable means, *see infra* §3.03[D].
113. Durovic, M. & Janssen, A., *supra* n. 16.
114. S. 125 sentence 1 German Civil Code (*Bürgerliches Gesetzbuch*).
115. Text form requires a readable declaration that the person making the declaration be named and that it must be made on a durable medium (s. 126b German Civil Code). As an example, text form is required in the context of a lease contract for a request to raise the rent, s. 558a subs. (1) German Civil Code.
116. Written form requires a document with a signature (s. 126 subs. (1) German Civil Code). As an example, written form is required for declaring a personal guarantee, s. 766 German Civil Code or for a temporary lease contract which is longer than one year, s. 550 sentence 1, s. 578 German Civil Code.

certification[117] and/or notarial recording.[118] It is unclear if and to what extent a smart contract can comply with such form requirements. In any case, a smart contract fulfils the German text form requirement which requires a contract to be readable and submitted on a permanent data carrier.[119] A smart contract in a blockchain is such a permanent medium.[120] In addition, the code of a smart contract is 'readable'.[121] For a contract to be readable, it is irrelevant whether it is only readable with the help of technical means[122] or readable by only a few people, as it can be translated if necessary.[123]

English law usually requires an objectively reached agreement with sufficiently certain terms, an intention to create legal relations and (unless a deed is used) consideration. According to UKJT, there is no reason as to why 'the normal rules should not apply just because a potential contract is a smart contract'.[124] There are further requirements for specific types of contracts; for example, section 2 of the Law of Property (Miscellaneous Provisions) Act 1989 states that contracts for sale, transfer or lease of land must be in writing; similarly, section 90(3) of the Copyright, Design and Patent Act 1977 and section 4 of the Statute of Frauds 1677 have such formalities in relation to assignments or exclusive licences and guarantees, respectively. As the fundamental nature of a smart contract is the underlying computer code, it is uncertain whether this would satisfy the requirement under English law that such a contract must be 'in writing'. However, upon consideration of the Interpretation Act 1978, which serves to interpret common words used in statutes, it becomes clear that such an 'in writing' requirement includes 'modes of reproducing words in a visible form',[125] which arguably encompasses a computer code. As further pointed out by UKJT, the fact that 'the code might not be comprehensible to an ... English speaker without an expert translator is irrelevant'.[126] The Law Commission agreed with the UKJT in principle, as the definition of 'writing' in the 1978 Act is inclusive of all modes (as stated above), but

117. Official certification requires that a notary certifies the signature of the person declaring (s. 129 German Civil Code). As an example, conditions for a land register entry must be provided to the land registry in officially certified form, s. 29 German Land Registration Code (*Grundbuchordnung*) in the version of 26 May 1994 (BGBl. I p. 1114), last updated by Art. 11 G. v. 12 Dec. 2019 (BGBl. I p. 2602).
118. Notarial recording is the strictest form and requires that a notary records offer and acceptance (s. 128 German Civil Code). As an example, notarial recording is required for sale of real estate (s. 311b subs. 1 German Civil Code) or for the renunciation or sale of an inheritance (s. 2348 and s. 2371 German Civil Code, respectively).
119. Heckelmann, M., *supra* n. 37; Wilkens, R. & Falk, R., *supra* n. 1, at 37; Paulus, D. & Matzke, R., *supra* n. 7, at 457; Gerald Spindler, *Recht der elektronischen Medien* at § 126b para. 1 (Gerald Spindler & Fabian Schuster [eds], 4th ed. 2019).
120. Paulus, D. & Matzke, R., *supra* n. 7, at 457.
121. As required by s. 126(b) German Civil Code.
122. Gyr, E., *supra* n. 1; Einsele, D., *Münchener Kommentar zum Bürgerlichen Gesetzbuch* at § 126b para. 4 (Franz Jürgen Säcker et al. [eds], 8th ed. 2018).
123. Against this: Bertram, U., *Smart Contracts – Praxisrelevante Fragen zu Vertragsabschluss, Leistungsstörungen und Auslegung* 1416, 1418-1419 (MDR 2018), arguing that the information purpose is not fulfilled; arguing that this only applies if the parties can understand code, Gyr, E., *supra* n. 1.
124. UKJT, *supra* n. 29.
125. Interpretation Act 1978 section 5.
126. UKJT, *supra* n. 29, at 38.

went on to conclude that the question of whether source code can satisfy a statutory 'in writing' requirement shall ultimately be determined by 'construing the intention of Parliament in the particular context'.[127]

Furthermore, in relation to the execution of smart contracts, there have been concerns as to whether smart contracts' electronic signatures would satisfy the execution requirement and be regarded as a valid signature under English law. However, under the Communications Act 2000, 'an electronic signature has counted [as] if it is incorporated into, or is associated with, an electronic communication'.[128] This has also been confirmed by the Law Commission which has clarified that 'electronic signatures can be used to sign formal legal contracts under English law'.[129] Also, the UKJT is optimistic and points out that private keys are highly likely to meet signature requirements.[130] This is due to the fact that public-key cryptography is a type of electronic signature which generally satisfies statutory signature requirements. The key question is not what the signature looks like but rather whether a party intended to authenticate the document.[131] As such, electronic signatures should not pose an issue for smart contracts.

Another potential difficulty in relation to form requirements in English law relates to the execution of deeds.[132] A deed has to comply with formalistic requirements by virtue of section 1(3) of the Law of Property (Miscellaneous Provisions) Act 1989 under which an executing party must sign a deed in the presence of a witness. This could be an issue in light of the automatic nature of smart contracts. However, in *R (Software Solutions Partners Ltd)* v. *HM Customs & Excise,*[133] it was held that the 'automatic medium for contract formation can result in valid contracts', and the Law Commission confirmed that 'there is scope ... to do even more to make signing formal documents more convenient'.[134] This indicates that the deployment of smart contracts could result in further developments in the legislative sphere, resolving such form requirements and ensuring the validity of such contracts. Indeed, following its reports in 2019 and 2021, the Law Commission recommended that a review of the current requirements of deeds be undertaken in order to account for 'current and emerging technologies' such

127. The Law Commission, *Smart legal contracts: advice to Government, supra* n. 18, at 59.
128. Young, A., *Take note: Emails can be legally binding* (6 Jul. 2021), available at: http://www.contractflooringjournal.co.uk/blog/take-note-emails-can-be-legally-binding/ (accessed on 18 Mar. 2024).
129. The Law Commission, *Electronic Signatures are valid say Government's legal experts,* available at: https://www.lawcom.gov.uk/electronic-signatures-are-valid-say-governments-legal-experts/ (accessed on 18 Mar. 2024).
130. UKJT, *supra* n. 29, at 37.
131. *Ibid.*
132. A deed is a written document which is executed with the necessary formality (i.e., more than a simple signature), and by which an interest, right or property passes or is confirmed, or an obligation binding on some person is created or confirmed. *See*: Practical Law Glossary.
133. *R (Software Solutions Partners Ltd) v. HM Customs & Excise,* 2007, EWHC 971, para. 67.
134. The Law Commission, *Electronic Signatures are valid say Government's legal experts, supra* n. 129.

as smart contracts.[135] Therefore, perhaps it is not for smart contracts to align to the requirements of deeds but for deeds to adapt to the current technological and legal landscape.

[3] Offer and Acceptance

If a smart contract is used to form a contractual relationship, specific questions arise concerning the existence and content of offer and acceptance.

A contract is formed by at least two corresponding declarations of will (offer and acceptance), each with the intention to have a legally binding effect and with the purpose of forming a contract.[136] In this context, technology can be used either to communicate a specific declaration of will – for example, via an e-mail – or to automatically generate a declaration of will. For example, with respect to the latter, the German Federal Court of Justice (*Bundesgerichtshof*) has confirmed that an automated declaration of will issued by a software, according to prior programming, can be legally binding.[137] A transaction via a smart contract might be considered an automated declaration of will. In the context of smart contracts, a computer program will initiate a transaction, validating certain conditions, which would trigger a pre-programmed result, acting within the limits of logic set by prior programming. In this way, the automated declarations arguably express the general will of the individual deploying the computer program.[138] The same applies if a contract is formed entirely without human interaction by two corresponding automated declarations of will, for example, a computer program that detects a fridge is empty and orders certain goods.[139] Usually, in this scenario, the parties would have entered into an underlying contract off-chain (e.g., in the form of a framework contract) before the order is placed via the computer program. In such a situation, the existence and content of contractual obligations must be determined according to the time and circumstances of the previously formed contract and not at the time of the relevant blockchain transaction. If the automated transactions are the first and only communication between the parties, an objective understanding of the specific circumstances could imply that the automated transaction (such as automatic payment or automated delivery of goods) would form an implicit offer and/or acceptance of the respective parties.[140]

However, the termination of offers could cause some issues. Subject to certain requirements, an offer can be terminated by a lapse of time, withdrawal, rejection by the acceptor, failure of a condition precedent or death of the offeror. Smart contracts could easily include in their terms the time period for which the offer will be valid or

---

135. The Law Commission, *Smart legal contracts: advice to Government*, *supra* n. 18, at 71. For a non-exhaustive list of considerations that contracting parties may wish to include in a smart contract, *see Ibid*, Appendix 1.
136. Kaulartz, M. & Heckmann, J., *supra* n. 5, at 621; Wilkens, R. & Falk, R., *supra* n. 1, at 30-31.
137. FCJ, decision of 25 Jan. 2005 – XI ZR 325/03, NJW 976 (2005).
138. Paulus, D. & Matzke, R., *supra* n. 7, at 440-41; Spindler, *supra* n. 119, at. §§ 116 ff. para. 5.
139. For a more detailed discussion on IoT, *see* §3.02[E], *supra*. Wilkens, R. & Falk, R., *supra* n. 1, at 33-34; Paulus, D. & Matzke, R., *supra* n. 7, at 446.
140. Wilkens, R. & Falk, R., *supra* n. 1, at 33-34; Paulus, D. & Matzke, R., *supra* n. 7, at 446.

that the offer is only valid so long as certain condition precedents are met. However, an offer within the smart contract cannot be deleted which makes it impossible for that offer to be withdrawn. Furthermore, as the offeror is a 'cryptographic private key representing an individual',[141] it is exceptionally difficult to track whether the offeror has died. Therefore, the withdrawal of offers may need to be reconsidered or carefully drafted within smart contracts.

[C] Regulatory Issues and Smart Contracts

The use of smart contracts may also be subject to certain regulatory requirements. Some of these are addressed in Chapter 2, §2.01[C][3] above.

[D] Consumer-Protection Laws and Smart Contracts

In certain jurisdictions, consumer-protection laws could pose challenges with respect to B2C smart contracts.

[1] EU Directive 2011/83/EU

In the Member States of the European Union, a number of laws relevant for B2C contracts are based on Directive 2011/83/EU ('Directive' on consumer rights)[142] which has been implemented in the various Member States and was later amended by Directive 2019/2161/EU[143]. For example, in Germany, certain requirements of the Directive are reflected in para 312-312k of the German Civil Code (*Bürgerliches Gesetzbuch*). Subject to certain conditions being met (e.g., the contract being entered into between a business[144] and a consumer[145]), the consumer law provisions apply. Therefore, despite the difficulty of identifying the other party (refer to §3.03[B][1] above for more detail), if such conditions are met, the smart contract itself may be subject to consumer-protection provisions.

Most of the relevant provisions require a distance contract, which means that the contract was negotiated and formed exclusively by means of long-distance communication (e.g., phone, internet, e-mail, or letter) and that the contract was formed under

141. Di Matteo, L.-A., Cannarsa, M. & Poncibo, *supra* n. 43.
142. Directive 2011/83/EU of the European Parliament and of the Council of October 25, 2011 on consumer rights, 22 Nov. 2011, OJ EU L 304/64-88.
143. Directive 2019/2161/EU of the European Parliament and of the Council of November 27, 2019 amending Council Directive 93/13/EEC and Directives 98/6/EC, 2005/29/EC and 2011/83/EU of the European Parliament and of the Council as regards the better enforcement and modernisation of Union consumer protection rules, 18 Dec. 2019, OJ EU L 328/7-28.
144. A business, as defined in para. 14 subs. (1) German Civil Code (*Bürgerliches Gesetzbuch*), is a natural or legal person, which when entering into a contract acts in exercise of his or her trade, business or profession.
145. A consumer, as defined in para. 13 German Civil Code (*Bürgerliches Gesetzbuch*), is a natural person, which when entering into a contract acts predominantly outside of his or her trade, business or profession.

an 'organised distance sales or service-provision scheme'.[146] The application of the Directive to distance contracts executed by blockchain technology has been affirmed by subsequent guidance.[147]

When contracting with consumers and prior to forming a contract, the Directive requires the business to disclose its identity and further information, such as the price, delivery conditions, duration of the contract, existence and procedure of a right to cancellation.[148]

For distance contracts, the business may provide information on a durable or any other medium, provided information is readable and identifies the business.[149] Further, the Directive also necessitates the business to provide information to the customer in plain and intelligible language.[150] With respect to smart contracts, this could be an issue because a computer code is unlikely to be regarded as plain language by most consumers. As such, to get around this, businesses may be required to provide electronic or text forms of the computer code, specifying the obligations of the parties.[151]

Furthermore, as discussed above, providing relevant information to consumers is essential. In the absence of the relevant information, the right to cancel applies for two years and fourteen days from the date of contract formation or delivery.[152]

[2] Unfair Standard Terms

Smart contracts in the B2C space will often include a number of standard terms, especially if they enable transactions with a large number of users. Therefore, in certain

146. Paragraph 312c subs. (1) German Civil Code (*Bürgerliches Gesetzbuch*); Recital 20 of the Directive 2011/83/EU on consumer rights.
147. *See* section 4.1 and footnote 109 of the Commission Notice 'Guidance on the interpretation and application of Directive 2011/83/EU of the European Parliament and of the Council on consumer rights (2021/C 525/01)', 29 Dec. 2021, OJ EU C 525/1.
148. Paragraph 312d subs. (1) German Civil Code in connection with Art. 246a subs. (1) and (3) Introductory Law to the German Civil Code. Even if there is no distance contract, most information must be provided nonetheless. This is because of the 'minimum' information obligation in para. 312 subs. (2) sentence 1 German Civil Code in connection with Art. 246 subs. (1) and (3) Introductory Law to the German Civil Code. This is also a requirement of the Directive 2011/83/EU, Article 8.
149. Article 246a s. (4) subs. (3) Introductory Law to the German Civil Code; however, according to para. 312f subs. (2) German Civil Code, the consumer must receive this information on a durable medium after contract formation. This is also a requirement of Directive 2011/83/EU, Article 7.
150. Directive 2011/83/EU, Article 7.1.
151. Further obligations of the business prior to contract formation include explaining to customers the technical details of how the contract is formed (para. 312i subs. (1) sentence 1 German Civil Code in connection with Art. 246c Introductory Law to the German Civil Code), providing possibilities to correct mistakes and means to access and save the standard terms (para. 312i subs. (1) German Civil Code) and designing the website in a way that makes it clear for customers if they enter into contractual relationship, for example, a payment obligation (para. 312j subs. (3) German Civil Code); otherwise, the contract is invalid (para. 312j subs. (4) German Civil Code).
152. Paragraph 356 subs (3) sentence 2 German Civil Code. According to its sentence 3, this does not apply to contracts for financial services.

jurisdictions, certain rules regarding the use and content of such standard terms will often apply.

In Germany, such rules are applicable if: (a) the terms are pre-formulated,[153] (b) one party 'presents' the terms to the other party, and (c) the terms are not individually agreed.[154]

If previously agreed contractual obligations are performed by the smart contract, no smart contract-specific problems as to the application of such rules (the provisions on unfair standard terms) arise. If the conditions as to such application are met with respect to the previously agreed contractual terms, the provisions regarding unfair standard terms are applicable.[155] For example, this would be the case where a standard insurance contract that includes automated calculation and performance of damage events has been entered into.

If, however, the only communication between the parties is via a blockchain transaction, the identification of contract clauses as being standard terms is likely to be more difficult. Nevertheless, the provisions on unfair standard terms will usually still be applicable if the same smart contract – and thus an identical contractual arrangement – is used for a large number of contracts.[156] There is no reason for such smart contracts not to be subject to the provisions on unfair standard terms.

With respect to the requirements of the application of the provisions on unfair standard terms, it should be noted that a clause in a smart contract will often be pre-formulated. This is the case if a smart contract is programmed with the intention to use it several times. For this purpose, it might be even stored in a library. For the application of these provisions, it is also irrelevant whether the smart contract was programmed by a third party.

In B2C contracts, the party 'presenting' the standard terms must provide reasonable means for the other party to be able to take notice of their content.[157] There are differing opinions as to whether terms in a program code fulfil such a requirement. It has been argued that contract terms only incorporated in the program code are not part of the contractual relationship itself. According to this view, it is necessary for the

153. This is the case if a smart contract is programmed with the intention to use it for several situations. For example, it might be stored in a library. It is irrelevant whether a third party programmed the smart contract, *see* Riehm, Thomas, *Rechtshandbuch Smart Contracts* 104 para. 16 (Braegelmann, T. & Kaulartz, M. [eds], 2019).
154. An individual agreement requires that the negotiation was open-ended. Arguably, there is an individual agreement if parties customize their contract using an automatic generator, *see* Heckelmann, M., *supra* n. 37, at 507.
155. Riehm, T., *supra* n. 153, at 104 para. 15; Berberich, M., *Smart Contracts in der AGB-Kontrolle?* 221, 223 (DSRITB 2019).
156. Kaulartz, M. & Heckmann, J., *supra* n. 5, at 622; Berberich, M., *supra* n. 154, 225-227 (2019), arguing that this follows from para. 306a German Civil Code (*Bürgerliches Gesetzbuch*), insofar as there is no written document; Schrey, J. & Thalhofer, T., *Rechtliche Aspekte der Blockchain* 1431, 1436 (NJW 2017); Paulus, D. & Matzke, R., *supra* n. 7, at 459-60, arguing that in this case, such clauses will never become part of the contract because they are not incorporated; for this as well, Wilkens, R. & Falk, R., *supra* n. 1, at 39; *see*, however, Heckelmann, M., *supra* n. 37, at 507-08.
157. Paragraph 305 subs. (2) German Civil Code (*Bürgerliches Gesetzbuch*): either explicit reference to the standard terms or enabling the other party to reasonably take notice of their content. This provision does not apply B2B, para. 310 subs. (1) sentence 1 German Civil Code.

'presenting' party to provide additional means, such as providing a link or text of the terms to the other party.[158] Others argue that the contract itself is implicit in the program code and therefore contains all relevant contractual provisions.[159]

In any case, where feasible, it appears to be advisable to draft and make available a supplemental document that describes the smart contracts' contractual obligations and standard terms.

[E] Interpretation of Smart Contracts and Their Terms

When interpreting contracts in the event of a dispute, English courts strive to identify the intention of the parties, which should be ascertained objectively. Unless the language is ambiguous, the term will be taken to mean what it actually says.[160] As the computer code would generally be clear and unambiguous, it could be concluded that such contract is an 'extreme example' of a contract from which there is no reason to depart, as the objective meaning is exactly what it says.[161] The Law Commission adopts this objective approach to interpretation in its classification of the 'reasonable coder',[162] asking what the coded term would mean to a 'person with the knowledge and understanding of the code at the time when the codes were written'.[163] Some difficulties could nevertheless arise where the meaning would not be easily ascertainable from the computer code; in such circumstances, it would be determined whether the code was intended to be the complete set of obligations or whether it was merely designed to implement such obligations. In both scenarios, extrinsic evidence may be needed.[164]

Further, many contracts contain non-operational clauses and deliberately leave room for ambiguity, using terms such as 'bona fide', 'good faith' or 'reasonable'. Different legal systems will have varying interpretations of the meaning of these terms as well as other terms, such as 'best endeavours' and 'reasonable endeavours'.[165]

Such subjective terms have generated 'a large number of court decisions and corresponding legislation'.[166] Standard contract linguistic freedom, and the ability of a court to interpret these clauses and solve disputes, allows the flexibility of ambiguous terms and functioning contracts. However, such ambiguous terms do not translate

158. Wilkens, R. & Falk, R., *supra* n. 1, at 38-39; Paulus, D. & Matzke, R., *supra* n. 7, at 459-60; Moeslein, F., *supra* n. 32, at 254, 279 (2019).
159. According to this view, para. 305 subs. (2) German Civil Code (*Bürgerliches Gesetzbuch*) is not applicable, Kaulartz, M. & Heckmann, J., *supra* n. 5, at 622; *see also* FCJ, decision of 27 Oct. 1994 – IX ZR 168/93, 1995 NJW 190 (1995).
160. UKJT, *supra* n. 29, at 34.
161. *Ibid.*, at 35.
162. The Law Commission, *Smart legal contracts: advice to Government*, *supra* n. 18, at 80 and 81.
163. *Ibid.* Ma, A., *supra*, n. 106, at 8.
164. UKJT, *supra* n. 29, at 36.
165. *Yewbelle Ltd v. London Green Developments Ltd & Anor* [2006] EWHC 3166 (Ch); *IBM United Kingdom Limited v. Rockware Glass Limited CA* [1980] FSR 335; *Overseas Buyers Ltd v. Granadex SA* [1980] 2 Lloyd's Rep 608.
166. Woebbeking, M.-K., *The Impact of Smart Contracts on the Traditional Concepts of Contract Law* (2019), available at: https://www.jipitec.eu/issues/jipitec-10-1-2019/4880 (accessed on 18 Mar. 2024).

easily, or do not translate at all, into a self-executing smart contract.[167] As such, challenges arise in relation to the lack of flexibility of computer codes, as they are unable to interpret or execute such terms.[168]

Contracting parties often prefer traditional, non-operational clauses due to the flexibility of 'linguistic expansiveness and expressiveness'.[169] Nevertheless, some argue that it would be advantageous for smart contracts to exclude ambiguous terms, as this lack of ambiguous terms could remove the 'associated risk'[170] of interpretation, thereby improving the certainty of contracts. Ambiguous terms are argued to be the last resort of 'lazy lawyer[s]',[171] and it would be advantageous for smart contracts not to have such ambiguity.[172] Smart contracts could solve the ambiguity problem by either: (1) not including any ambiguous terms at all or (2) including precise and extensive definitions of the various meanings and permutations of ambiguous terms. While it could theoretically be beneficial to remove ambiguity, not only is it not conceivable practically but also ambiguity is a fundamental feature of certain contractual clauses, such as 'reasonableness' or 'good faith'. Further, the adoption of precise and extensive definitions is also not realistic, given it would be impossible to imagine all eventualities and draft language to deal with them. As removing such ambiguous terms may be inadvisable or impossible, it is likely that drafters of smart contracts will have to decipher how to incorporate ambiguous terms within the smart contracts' code and deal with the repercussions.

It has further been suggested that smart contracts could nevertheless incorporate ambiguous terms offline, by creating a 'legal wrapper' which would set out the terms of the contract, incorporating the smart contract code by reference.[173] This would leave 'parts of the agreement outside the blockchain record, as non-smart or modifiable, while other obligations are inserted into the blockchain as self-executory and immutable'.[174] This contract wrapper would also allow terms to be included that permit the smart contract to be terminated and amended in certain circumstances.[175]

Therefore, due to smart contracts' relative novelty and inability to incorporate ambiguous terms in code, 'it becomes clear that smart legal contracts will require, at least for the near future, a blend between code and natural language'.[176]

However, even if non-operational terms, such as 'commercially reasonable' or 'good faith', were somehow incorporated into smart contracts, these could still be

167. O'Toole, M., Kelly, C. and Hahn, D., *Smart Contracts Need Smart Corporate Lawyers* (7 Feb. 2018), available at: https://www.law360.com/articles/1010335/smart-contracts-need-smart-corporate-lawyers (accessed on 18 Mar. 2024).
168. ISDA Linklaters, *Whitepaper Smart Contracts and Distributed Ledger – A Legal Perspective* (August 2017), available at: https://www.isda.org/a/6EKDE/smart-contracts-and-distributed-ledger-a-legal-perspective.pdf (accessed on 5 Mar. 2024).
169. O'Toole, M. et al., *supra* n. 167.
170. Woebbeking, M.-K., *supra* n. 166.
171. ISDA Linklaters, *supra* n. 168.
172. *Ibid.*
173. DiMatteo, L.-A., *supra* n. 43.
174. *Ibid.*
175. *Ibid.*
176. *Ibid.*

subject to dispute. This could add a further layer of complication, as unlike interpreting standard contracts, interpreting a programming language is likely to cause difficulties for the courts.[177] A possible solution to the interpretation of smart contracts could fall on extrajudicial dispute resolution.[178]

[F] Performance and Remedies

As smart contracts are self-enforcing, once agreed, performance is automatic and does not depend on any further approval or action.[179] Generally, the 'performance of a smart contract cannot be stopped neither voluntarily by the parties nor by a central entity, court or any other supervisor'.[180] The advantage of this is that smart contracts eliminate the requirement of trust between parties for performance[181]. There is no 'need to rely on the willingness of the various parties to perform'.[182]

However, smart contracts' automatic nature can cause some issues. One such issue is the automatic performance regardless of real-world external factors. 'Since performance is automatic',[183] smart contracts are unable to adjust their self-performance as events occur, in the sense that a traditional contract can. 'They cannot respond to parties' changes in circumstances.'[184] Therefore, even if parties change their mind regarding performance, the contract will still be executed as programmed. Additionally, smart contracts 'cannot be revoked or amended, meaning that any recession, rectification, or variation is in principle impossible'.[185]

Further, there are wider public policy concerns. For example, if we allow coders to create financial transactions that are 'unreal' in the sense of not being undertaken by a known entity and not allowing for legal redress, there is a threat to the rule of law,[186] in particular in relation to money-laundering regulations.

One potential solution to smart contracts' automatic self-performance would be to allow the modification of smart contracts. Smart contracts could contain clauses stating that future court decisions are incorporated into the contract through leveraging an oracle. Additionally, smart contracts could be programmed to reflect real-world inputs or predefined events,[187] allowing modification depending on the outcome of

177. Woebbeking, M.-K., *supra* n. 166.
178. *Ibid.*
179. Tulsidas, T.-U., *Smart Contracts from a Legal Perspective* 16, available at: https://rua.ua.es/dspace/bitstream/10045/78007/1/Smart_Contracts_from_a_Legal_Perspective_Utamchandani_Tulsidas_Tanash.pdf (accessed on 18 Mar. 2024).
180. DiMatteo, L.-A., *supra* n. 43.
181. Zou, M., Cheng, G., and Heredia, M.-S., *In Code We Trust? Trustless and Smart Contracts* (31 Mar. 2019), available at: https://www.scl.org/articles/10493-in-code-we-trust-trustlessness-and-smart-contracts (accessed on 18 Mar. 2024).
182. DiMatteo, L.-A., *supra* n. 43.
183. Zou, M. et al., *supra* n. 181.
184. DiMatteo, L.-A., *supra* n. 43.
185. *Ibid.*
186. Vos, G., *LawTech, Smart Contracts and Artificial Intelligence* (2 May 2019), available at: https://www.judiciary.uk/wp-content/uploads/2019/05/CHC-speech-LawTech-Smart-Contracts-and-Artificial-Intelligence.pdf (accessed on 18 Mar. 2024).
187. DiMatteo, L.-A., *supra* n. 43.

these predetermined events.[188] One example of this is the Application Programming Interface (API)[189] that would allow smart contracts to be updated.[190] The API would collect updates to important legal provisions which smart contracts could update accordingly to ensure legality.[191] However, modifying smart contracts may be limited as it would require the parties to: (1) acknowledge that their minds may be changed by certain specific future conditions and (2) prepare the contract on such a basis beforehand.[192] In reality, many contracting parties may not have such foresight or predetermined opinions of how their minds may change. Additionally, it would be difficult to ensure that the API makes changes in the interest of both parties rather than making self-serving changes.

Another potential remedy to smart contracts' automatic self-performance and to achieve 'practical justice' would be for the courts to order the contracting parties to enter into a second transaction on the blockchain of an 'equal and opposite' nature.[193] While the first transaction would remain on the blockchain, its effects would be 'reversed' by this second transaction. However, as the Law Commission notes, the specific form of the court order will likely depend on certain factors, such as the smart contract platform itself and the extent to which the code has been performed.[194]

Even if smart contracts are self-enforcing, they must still comply with the fundamental rules of contract law. An unenforceable clause will not be made enforceable by virtue of embedding it into a computer code, and as such, the judicial remedies of adjustment or voidance will continue to be relevant. Furthermore, just because a smart contract is self-executing does not mean that errors will not arise, and accordingly, parties will continue to seek remedies in court. Therefore, traditional contract remedies and defences will still be applicable as 'smart contracts cannot transplant contract law',[195] developed further in §3.03[A] above.

The self-enforcing nature of smart contracts does not eliminate the risk of contract breach or nullity, triggering the need for remedies[196]. The following example, based on English law, demonstrates the irreplaceability of remedies. A smart contract entered into to transfer an asset from Party A to Party B is invalidated due to fraud, illegality or incapacity. Within the blockchain platform, the asset remains Party B's property;[197] however, in reality, the law recognizes the property as belonging to Party A[198]. In this instance, the court should be able to order a remedy of specific performance requiring Party B to (through the blockchain) transfer ownership of the asset

188. Tulsidas, T.-U., *supra* n. 179.
189. Application Program Interface is a set of routines, protocols and tools for building software applications. Webopedia, available at: https://www.webopedia.com/TERM/A/API.html (accessed on 18 Mar. 2024).
190. Tulsidas, T.-U., *supra* n. 179, at 33.
191. *Ibid.*
192. DiMatteo, L.-A., *supra* n. 43.
193. The Law Commission, *Smart legal contracts: advice to Government*, *supra* n. 18 at 131 and 132.
194. *Ibid.*
195. *Ibid.*
196. Sherborne, A., *Blockchain Smart Contracts and Lawyers* (2017).
197. DiMatteo, L.-A., *supra* n. 43.
198. *Ibid.*

back to Party A[199]. This example highlights the fact that remedies remain necessary, even though smart contracts are self-enforcing. Smart contracts could also be breached or invalidated due to glitches or bugs in the code,[200] producing results that are not in the parties' best interests,[201] which could give rise to tortious claims of negligence. For example, the divergence between contract as intended by parties and smart contract as created could result in the emergence of torts 'for negligent coding or negligent updating'.[202]

As such, even though smart contracts are automatic and self-enforcing, this does not eliminate the risk of breaches which may still occur through real-life circumstances or bugs. Therefore, either the legislators or the coders need to be creative and respond accordingly to ensure that smart contracts do not exist in a legal vacuum and that breaches are capable of being remedied.

§3.04 OUTLOOK

[A] Benefits, Opportunities and Limitations of Smart Contracts

In light of the above, it can be concluded that the development of smart contracts not only presents various benefits and opportunities but also is subject to certain limitations.

Smart contracts benefit from an additional level of security compared to traditional contracts. As smart contracts are encrypted and distributed through the blockchain platform, this keeps a permanent record of the contract. Therefore, smart contracts will provide security which traditional contracts are not able to provide. They 'offer a shield against human error, duplicity and malfeasance'[203] as the blockchain is immutable, requiring the consent of all members of the blockchain for any changes to be made once the smart contract is encoded. Furthermore, traditional contracts may be lost or, if stored electronically, deleted or corrupted. As smart contracts are stored on a decentralized blockchain, they are unable to be deleted as the blockchain will store all of the smart contract's data permanently and the parties 'can retrieve any of the information if there's any data loss'.[204] This security is beneficial for the parties' commercial business relationship.

Additionally, smart contracts are able to be viewed by all members of the blockchain. This transparency is advantageous and also ensures that all members are able to access and *see* all agreed details at any point, making miscommunications or

199. *Ibid.*
200. Sherborne, A., *supra* n. 196.
201. DiMatteo, L.-A., *supra* n. 43.
202. *Ibid.*
203. Wan, A., *Blockchain Smart Contracts: Weighing the Pros and Cons* (12 Jul. 2018), available at: https://blocktribune.com/smart-contracts-weighing-the-pros-and-cons/ (accessed on 18 Mar. 2024).
204. Anwar, H., *Smart Contracts: The Ultimate Guide for Beginners* (19 Jul. 2018), available at: https://101blockchains.com/smart-contracts/#7 (accessed on 18 Mar. 2024).

misunderstandings less likely.[205] In theory, this transparency should enhance contractual relationships, as well as reduce confusion and the amount of time and money spent on litigation of disputed terms.

Smart contracts increase the level of trust between contracting parties for the reasons mentioned above and also because they execute automatically once the necessary conditions are met. This 'remove[s] the need to trust another party's willingness and ability to perform'.[206]

Smart contracts' automatic execution also leads to further advantages, namely greater economy and speed. A traditional contract may require the use of third-party intermediaries to assist with the implementation and execution of that contract, but this introduces an added risk that one of these third-party middlemen may cause a fault or interruption which delays or, in the worst case, prevents the execution of the contract. The use of a smart contract should help to mitigate this risk; however, if a smart contract is linked to an 'oracle', the input from which is required for the smart contract to execute, this reintroduces a third-party intermediary, albeit not a human one, which is still at risk of malfunctioning in such a way that it causes a delay in the execution of the smart contract.

Therefore, one must also consider the downsides of smart contracts. The greatest risk when using a smart contract is the effect of errors in the code. As smart contracts require human input for the coding required to 'draft' a smart contract, the inherent risk of human error exists – 'anyone, even the most brilliant engineer, is liable to make a typo here and there'.[207] The effect of an error in software code is often hard to quantify until the program is executed. This may not become apparent in a smart contract until it has been placed on the blockchain network and has begun the process of automatic execution. While the same is true for traditional, written contracts, the effect of a minor error in such a contract is often limited (e.g., a mistake in cross-referencing between clauses), and even in the case of more serious errors, the risk is more easily mitigated. A traditional contract can be amended, restated or terminated by the parties via a further written agreement if an error is identified post-signing (although this idea may be applied to smart contracts through the postulated 'equal and opposite' second transaction, as noted at §3.03[F] above) or, if a dispute arises as a result of an error in the contract, the parties are able to turn to the courts (or arbitrators) to interpret the contract and the surrounding circumstances in order to give effect to the parties' intentions.

Further, it is posited that it may be possible to create smart contracts that may be terminated at any time or more easily amended (although not once executed).[208] While it may appear this is in juxtaposition to the 'immutable and automated nature of smart

205. *Ibid.*
206. DiMatteo, L.-A., *supra* n. 43.
207. Wan, A., *supra* n. 203.
208. Levi, S. D. and Lipton, A., *An Introduction to Smart Contracts and Their Potential and Inherent Limitations* (26 May 2018), available at, https://corpgov.law.harvard.edu/2018/05/26/an-introduction-to-smart-contracts-and-their-potential-and-inherent-limitations/ (accessed on 6 Mar. 2024).

contracts', it is arguable that smart contracts shall not gain wider commercial acceptance if they do not reflect the business reality of contracting parties.[209] Recent legislative developments appear to echo this sentiment. Article 30 of the Regulation (EU) 2023/2854 (the EU Data Act) contains a clause specifically addressing the terminability of smart contracts [for data sharing] within the blockchain, stipulating that the offering party must comply with the requirements of 'safe termination and interruption',[210] which amounts to the ability to reset, pause or interrupt the operation to avoid future inadvertent executions. While the legislation limits the applicability of the provision to agreements to 'make data available', it may provoke further questions on the ownership of termination functions for each smart contract.

Anyone who has ever attempted to translate a traditional contract from one language to another will understand the technicalities and difficulties that arise when attempting to reflect certain words or phrases. As such, it is conceivable that translating language into a computer code would create even more challenges and perhaps lead to errors. Apart from a human error when translating a code, there is also the risk of glitches between the programming language and the machine code, resulting in smart contracts which do not execute or perform as drafters or coders intended. Arguably, there is also a further risk that drafters or coders deliberately draft smart contracts to automatically execute the conduct of illegal activities. The root cause of these issues is that, unlike traditional contracts, smart contracts exist on the immutable blockchain network and are not currently capable of amendment. Smart contracts will therefore permanently retain any errors.

In addition, contracts are often drafted with certain facts or external circumstances in mind, which can easily change. As mentioned above, traditional contracts can be amended or restated should new circumstances arise post-signing. Additionally, 'parties quite often decide not to enforce certain contractual rights to further nurture business relationships'.[211] However, for the reasons given above, this would not be possible once the smart contract is placed on the blockchain network. Therefore, where the parties agree separately that a certain consequence of the contract should not apply in a certain scenario, the smart contract will continue to execute automatically as it has been programmed to do. 'The rigidity of a pre-programmed software code excludes by definition the possibility to adapt an agreement to the mutability of business contracts.'[212] However, as noted in §3.03[F] above, there are potential solutions to this rigidity being contemplated in order to enable smart contracts to better adapt to the practicalities of commercial negotiations.

Although the transparency of smart contracts offers some advantages, some contracts require a certain level of confidentiality, which is not an option if smart contracts are uploaded onto a blockchain network. This lack of confidentiality may not

209. *Ibid.*
210. Regulation (EU) 2023/2854. For a further discussion on the EU Data Act's 'kill switch', *see* Ledger Insights, *EU Data Act requires smart contracts to have kill switch, not be permissionless* (14 Mar. 2023), available at, https://www.ledgerinsights.com/eu-data-act-smart-contracts-immutability-permissionless/ (accessed on 6 Mar. 2024).
211. DiMatteo, L.-A., *supra* n. 43.
212. *Ibid.*

be an issue for simple contracts; however, it will be a limitation to smart contracts' implementation into corporate transactions, such as those relating to insolvency or particularly sensitive acquisitions or divestitures, which require high levels of confidentiality.

As previously discussed in §3.03[F] above, smart contracts are limited by their ability to translate certain contractual obligations into a computer code. Contractual language often has an 'inherent ambiguity'[213] that cannot always be drafted into binary algorithmic software code. This limits the scope of the functions that smart contracts are able to perform and the scenarios to which they can be applied. Furthermore, 'smart contracts do not permit the presence of implied terms and contractual gaps'.[214] It is common for traditional contracts to contain intentional contractual gaps or incorporate implied terms to allow for efficient business relationships in changing environments. Smart contracts' lack of flexibility, and inability to incorporate any ambiguity, means that the parties must negotiate all clauses upfront to take account of the current situation as well as all possible future situations. In most cases, trying to do this will either be impossible or require a large amount of time which the parties may not have. As things currently stand, this limitation will therefore be a major deterrent to using smart contracts. The 'legal world is full of gray areas, and the binary nature of smart contracts as they currently exist makes them maddeningly difficult to adjust in unforeseen circumstances'.[215]

[B] Use of Smart Contracts in the Future

As was discussed above, in §3.01[B], Nick Szabo's original concept of 'smart contracting' highlighted three features of the original idea of a smart contract: (1) its potential to perform a contract with anyone, (2) the automatic performance of the contractual obligations if a specific condition is met, and (3) security mechanisms which make it unattractive to circumvent the agreed processes to get the promised goods or services, due to the potential costs of breaches.[216] Smart contracts on a blockchain, as they have developed since Szabo created his original concept, do fulfil these three features. However, as has been set out in detail throughout this chapter, smart contracts are subject to a number of conceptual and technical limitations. Two important limitations are likely to be driving factors in the slow adoption of smart contracts in the near future.

Legal systems are often slow to adapt to changes and developments in technology and, as we have set out in §3.03 above, it is not yet clear how smart contracts, if we are to view them as legally binding contracts in and of themselves, can satisfy many of the long-standing legal requirements for valid formation of a contract. While this will likely change, such uncertainty will affect the widespread use of smart contracts as a replacement for traditional contracts. Therefore, it has been suggested 'to avoid seeing

213. *Ibid.*
214. *Ibid.*
215. Wan, A., *supra* n. 203.
216. Gyr, E., *supra* n. 1.

[smart contracts] as legal contracts that require offer, acceptance and consideration'[217] to make it possible for smart contracts to be more commonly used alongside traditional contracts. However, as suggested in §3.03[B][2] above, it seems more likely that the legal framework will develop to ensure smart contracts are able to fit within existing legal principles.[218] As noted by the Master of the Rolls, Sir Geoffrey Vos in his keynote speech of July 2022 on the economic value of English law in relation to digital assets, in order for the UK to position itself as a leading legal arena in this area, it should 'commit to a major new project' that demonstrates its 'commitment to the adoption of new technologies', including blockchain-based smart contracts.[219]

In addition, smart contracts are limited by the nature of computer code as binary and inflexible. Traditional contracts of all types typically contain ambiguous terms or otherwise intentionally contain contractual gaps to which smart contracts will be unable to adapt. While this may not be a concern if a smart contract is being used in a simple scenario, in complex transactions, the parties will need to ensure that all potential ambiguous terms, and all possible future scenarios, have been considered, negotiated and agreed before they are coded into the smart contract – this may be an impossible task that drives the continued use of traditional contracts until such technical limitations are overcome.

FURTHER READING

Mateja Durovic & Andre Janssen, *The Formation of Blockchain-based Smart Contracts in the Light of Contract Law* 753 – 771 (2018, 26 European Review Private Law, Issue 6)

Max Raskin, *The Law and Legality of Smart Contracts* 305, 306 (1 Georgetown Law Technology Review, 2017)

Philipp Paech *Law and Autonomous Systems Series: What is a Smart Contract?* University of Oxford, available at: https://www.law.ox.ac.uk/business-law-blog/blog/2018/07/law-and-autonomous-systems-series-what-smart-contract

Savelyev, A., *Contract law 2.0: 'Smart' contracts as the beginning of the end of classic contract law* 116–134 (Information & Communications Technology Law, 2017)

Theodore J. Mlynar and Robert M. Fettman, *Blockchain and smart contracts will change the face of insurance in the U.S.*, available at: https://www.lexology.com/library/detail.aspx?g=b119f47b-764b-464c-9090-89b8e6e58219

Larry A. DiMatteo, Michel Cannarsa and Christina Poncibo, *The Cambridge Handbook of Smart Contracts, Blockchain and Technology and Digital Platforms* (2019)

Maren K. Woebbeking, *The Impact of Smart Contracts on the Traditional Concepts of Contract Law* (10 J. Intell. Prop. Info. Tech. & Elec. Com. L. 105, 2019)

---

217. Grinhaus, A., *supra* n. 100.
218. UKJT, *supra* n. 29, at 36.
219. Sir Geoffrey Vos, *The economic value of English law in relation to DLT and digital assets* (25 Jul. 2022), available at: https://www.judiciary.uk/speech-by-the-master-of-the-rolls-the-economic-value-of-english-law-in-relation-to-dlt-and-digital-assets/ (accessed on 7 Mar. 2024).

Stuart Levi, Alex Lipton & Cristina Vasile, *Legal issues surrounding the use of smart contracts* 155 (Blockchain & Cryptocurrency Regulation, 2020, 2nd ed., Global Legal Insights)

CHAPTER 4

Blockchain and Data Privacy

Lothar Determann, William Long & Matthias Artzt

§4.01 INTRODUCTION AND EXECUTIVE SUMMARY

Blockchain technologies have emerged as a disruptive way of executing business processes in decentralized environments. It was originally created to facilitate cryptocurrency transactions such as Bitcoin, but entrepreneurs and investors have recognized the potential of the underlying technology as a game-changer that can also be used for other applications.

While blockchain technologies emerged, the European Union (EU) updated its data protection laws with the General Data Protection Regulation (GDPR) that was enacted in 2016 and took effect in 2018. The GDPR has the purpose of protecting all EU-citizens' data privacy and empowering them to enforce their rights towards organizations or individual controllers which process personal data. Several articles of the GDPR clash with features of blockchain technology and present compliance challenges that the drafters of the GDPR may not have anticipated in 2016 when the potential of blockchain technologies was less well known than today. The mismatch between the GDPR, albeit technologically neutral, and the blockchain characteristics generates anxiety about the possibility that the regulation might hinder European innovation in blockchain technology.

Privacy laws in the United States and other countries not only present the same challenges but also impose noteworthy compliance obligations that companies and individuals adopting blockchain technologies should carefully consider. In this chapter, the data privacy state of play in relation to the blockchain will be analysed from two different angles: the GDPR and the US privacy perspective.

The GDPR differs from US privacy laws significantly: The European regulation restricts and regulates the processing of personal data comprehensively, which adversely affects all information technologies and particularly presents serious challenges to the adoption of blockchain and distributed ledger technology (DLT), particularly due to restrictions on international transfers of personal data outside the European Economic Area (EEA) and the obstacles to enforcing the right to be forgotten in a blockchain environment; these and other requirements under the GDPR are discussed in the following sections §4.02 through §4.09, *infra*.

By contrast, US privacy laws do not generally restrict or regulate the processing of personal data and seek to apply only proportionately designed sector-, harm- and situation-specific requirements to safeguard individual privacy against concrete harms. US privacy laws are technology-neutral too and do not affect the blockchain technology adversely or specifically by nature. Nevertheless, the sheer volume of federal and state privacy laws impose a huge challenge on businesses, which must allocate resources to identifying which requirements apply to their blockchain use cases, as further discussed in §4.10, *infra*.

This chapter proposes possible ways of achieving GDPR-compliance by leveraging state-of-the-art techniques. Further, it provides useful hints to cope with US privacy laws and related requirements when dealing with blockchain applications.

§4.02 PERSONAL DATA IN THE CONTEXT OF THE GDPR

[A] GDPR Definitions in the Context of a Blockchain

The GDPR applies to businesses and individuals who engage in the 'processing' of 'personal data'. 'Controllers' and 'processors' are subject to different requirements. The GDPR applies to data processing on the territory of the European Economic Area and, under certain circumstances, also extra-territorially.

[1] Personal Data

Most information humans are interested falls under the broad term 'personal data', which is defined as 'any information relating to an identified or identifiable natural person (data subject); an identifiable person is one who can be identified, directly or indirectly, in particular by reference to an identifier ...'.[1] The Court of Justice of the European Union has ruled several times that Internet Protocol (IP) addresses qualify as personal data if they can be connected to a person.[2] Pseudonymization in the sense of partial, temporary, or reversible de-identification is insufficient to remove data from the scope of the GDPR. Full anonymization would require irreversible, permanent de-identification, or aggregation, i.e., reduction to statistical statements that do not allow conclusions with respect to a particular individual.

A blockchain permanently records transaction information concerning every participant. In the interest of integrity, blockchain users must be able to connect blocks to individuals or to devices or legal entities, which in turn can usually be connected to

1. Article 4 s. 1 of the GDPR.
2. *See, e.g.*, CJEU judgment of 19 Oct. 2016, *Patrick Breyer v. Bundesrepublik Deutschland*, Case C-582/14.

individuals. For example, in the context of cryptocurrencies, blockchains can contain information on miners, currency owners, and transaction participants. Each participant or miner has a public key, ensuring identification of the issuer and receiver of a transaction. Additional data relates to a transaction, e.g., who acquired cryptocurrency from someone else. In connection with other blockchain application, blocks may contain references to other information that may qualify as personal data, such as health records or product shipping documentation. If transactional data includes information about a natural person, who can be identified, directly or indirectly, then this data will need to be considered personal data, even if the identification may be difficult or impossible for most people.

As a rule of thumb, one should assume in practice for compliance purposes that data is or contains personal data, unless one can confirm with certainty that the data does not relate somehow to an identifiable person.

[a] Public Keys

In most public blockchains, every published transaction is linked to a public key that represents a user. That key is typically encrypted to avoid another individual who views the blockchain being able to directly identify the individual (or a corporate entity).[3] The user holds a private key (another string of letters and numbers) which allows for the decryption of data which has been encrypted via the public key. The re-use of the public key enables individuals to be singled out by reference to their key, even if the public key does not allow them to be directly identified. This is one of the key purposes of the public key: to ensure that transactions are attributed to the correct persons.

Where a public key is held by a natural person, it constitutes an 'identifier' for purposes of Article 4(1) and Recital 30 of the GDPR. When combined with additional identifiers, the individual can be identified by a public key.[4] For example, for information technology companies and communications services providers involved, and for government authorities with subpoena powers, it is possible to obtain additional information required to identify the individual because it is held by the

3. Note that the public key will only be considered personal data where it relates to a natural person. Public keys used to identify corporate entities will not qualify as personal data and, hence, not subject to the GDPR; Bacon, J. et al., *Blockchain Demystified: A Technical and Legal Introduction to Distributed and Centralised Ledgers* 62 (25 Richmond Journal of Law and Technology 1, 2018).
4. For example, the ICO, in its guidance on encryption, confirms that where a public key is used as an encryption technique, both the process of converting the personal data into a public key and subsequent use of the encrypted personal data would constitute processing of personal data for GDPR purposes, available at: https://ico.org.uk/for-organisations/guide-to-data-protection/guide-to-the-general-data-protection-regulation-gdpr/encryption/what-is-encryption/ (accessed 31 Aug. 2023). Other commentators have noted that 'even if personal information only entails reference ID numbers, such identifiers are typically unique to a specific person. While in all such cases additional information may be necessary to attribute information to the data subject, such information would be merely pseudonymised and count as personal information'. Berberich, M. & Steiner, M., *Blockchain Technology and the GDPR: How to Reconcile Privacy and Distributed Ledgers?* (2 European Data Protection Law Review 422, 2016).

provider or because someone can connect the key to an individual via their Internet Protocol (IP) address.[5] As such, the key would fall under the definition of pseudonymized data as per Article 4(5) of the GDPR and Recital 26 of the GDPR which states that the GDPR applies to personal data which have 'undergone pseudonymisation [and] which could be attributed to a natural person by the use of additional information'.[6] This is also the position taken by regulators such as the French Data Protection Authority (DPA) who considers that public keys will likely constitute personal data under the GDPR in the context of blockchain.[7] Pseudonymization is defined by the GDPR as the 'processing of personal data in such a manner that the personal data can no longer be attributed to a specific data subject without the use of additional information, provided that such additional information is kept separately and is subject to technical and organizational security measures to ensure that personal data is not attributed to an identified or identifiable natural person'.[8] It follows that the key criterion for determining whether the related information is deemed personal is 'identifiability'. As such, the current view[9] is that pseudonymization should be seen as a security measure rather than a method of removing the 'personal' element of the data. Unlike anonymized data, pseudonymized data is considered to be personal data and, thus, is subject to the GDPR.

For the purpose of determining whether a natural person is identifiable, account should be taken of all the means reasonably likely to be used, such as singling out, either by the controller or by another person, to identify the natural person directly or indirectly.[10]

There are examples which show that the possibility of identifying individuals using blockchain applications still exists, either because the data subject has disclosed the information voluntarily or where the off-chain storage of personal data is required to comply with regulatory requirements (e.g., wallet exchanges storing parties' real-world identities to comply with their Know Your Customer and Anti-Money Laundering duties).[11]

On the other hand, the GDPR does not apply to 'information which does not relate to an identified or identifiable natural person or to data rendered anonymous in such a way that the data subject is no longer identifiable'[12] (i.e., anonymized data). It is important to note that pseudonymization is not a method of anonymization because it

---

5. The *Breyer* case has confirmed that temporary IP addresses assigned to a computing address may constitute personal data even where only a third party (e.g., the internet service provider) has the additional data necessary to identify the individual.
6. Recital 26 of the GDPR.
7. Commission Nationale de l'Informatique et de Libertés (6 Nov. 2018) *Blockchain and the GDPR: Solutions for a responsible use of the blockchain in the context of personal data*, 6 available at: https://www.cnil.fr/en/blockchain-and-gdpr-solutions-responsible-use-blockchain-context-personal-data (accessed 31 Aug. 2023).
8. Article 4(5) of the GDPR.
9. Article 29 Data Protection Working Party, *Opinion 05/2014 on Anonymisation Techniques* 3 (WP 216 Adopted on 10 Apr. 2014).
10. Recital 26 of the GDPR.
11. Bacon et al., *supra* n. 3, at. 61.
12. Recital 26 of the GDPR.

'merely reduces the linkability of a dataset with the original identity of a data subject, and is accordingly a useful security measure'.[13]

The basic principle of determining whether data has been effectively anonymized is the reasonable likelihood of re-identification. The process of anonymization must make it impossible to identify a natural person through any of the means 'reasonably likely to be used',[14] and the process must be irreversible.[15] This implies that any reverse engineering must be practically impossible. The Article 29 Data Protection Working Party also acknowledged that it would be very difficult to create a truly anonymous dataset while retaining the underlying information as required for the performance of the task.[16] However, the view of the UK's Information Commissioner's Office (ICO) is that the relevant criterion is not the possibility of identification but rather that the definition of personal data is based on 'the identification or likely identification of the individual'.[17] Companies and public institutions can render the likelihood of identification sufficiently low to avoid the applicability of the GDPR with technical, organizational and administrative measures, including contractual agreements to refrain from re-identifying individuals. The Court of Justice of the European Union and the lower court of first instance, the General Court, have not completely precluded the possibility of qualifying data pertaining to individuals as outside the scope of the GDPR where effective measures were taken and the companies or institutions with a theoretical ability to identify an individual can reasonably be expected to refrain from doing so.[18] Yet, given the relative obscurity of blockchain participants in the context of public blockchain applications, it is more difficult to rely on contractual measures (including smart contracts) than in cases where public sector institutions or heavily regulated companies commit to keeping data de-identified.

[b] Transactional Data

Besides public keys, blockchains contain transactional data (denoting, for example, who transferred ownership to a virtual item to another person) and additional data (denoting, for example, the content of a non-fungible token (NFT)). The Commission Nationale de l'Informatique et de Libertés (CNIL) uses the term 'additional data' in its Blockchain Guidance for data that is contained 'within' a transaction.[19]

---

13. Article 29 Data Protection Working Party, *Opinion 05/2014 on Anonymisation Techniques* 3 (WP 216 Adopted on 10 Apr. 2014), at. 3. It should be noted that this approach was *not* endorsed by the EDPB when it took office in 2018. To view the list of guidance endorsed by the EDPB, available at: https://edpb.europa.eu/node/89 (accessed 31 Aug. 2023).
14. Recital 26 of the GDPR.
15. Article 29 Data Protection Working Party, *supra* n. 9, at 5.
16. *Ibid.*, at 3.
17. UK ICO, *Anonymisation: managing data protection risk code of practice* 16, available at: https://ico.org.uk/media/1061/anonymisation-code.pdf (accessed 31 Aug. 2023).
18. *See* General Court judgment of 26 Apr. 2023 in Case T-557/20, *SRB v. EDPS*, at 99-105, discussing the Breyer decision of the full court in 2016 that also left the door open to such arguments.
19. CNIL, *supra* n. 7, at 6.

In a blockchain ecosystem, information is encrypted and hashed[20] using specific algorithms and functions before being stored in ledgers. In summary, cryptographic hashing is intended to guarantee the reliability and integrity of blockchains. The process involves running an algorithm to turn a block of data into a fixed-length output (the hash). Each block in the chain will contain a hash (a unique identifier). The unique hash or hash digest is next placed inside the data set for the following block together with whatever transaction will be part of the following block. This data, i.e., the hash digest from the previous block together with the transaction data, is subject to the same cryptographic hash function again, generating another unique hash digest for this second block (further detailed in Chapter 1, §1.06[A] *supra*). This measure prevents either block from being changed or another block being added in between the two existing blocks in the interest of data integrity.

Like encryption, hashing is reversible and therefore not suited to de-identify data to a degree that could ensure anonymity. By hashing or encrypting personal data, controllers can secure the data but not typically remove it from the scope of the GDPR, unless they take other organizational, administrative, and technical measure to prevent re-identification.

Not all hashing algorithms are equal.[21] Hashed personal data may be reconstituted in pre-hashed form by using brute-force decryption. A brute-force attack could be successful by reversing the hash value if the original data is of a known and of relatively small size. The Blockchain Observatory and Forum recommends to mitigate this risk by using techniques such as 'salting' or 'peppering' hashes which involve adding extra information to the set of data with the purpose of making the data set large enough that a brute-force attack would be extremely unlikely to reverse the data.[22] But, there might be situations where pattern analysis makes it possible to uncover information regarding a particular data subject. This boils down to linking hashed data back to an individual by examining certain patterns of usage or context or by comparison of other pieces of information off-chain.

Therefore, and based on guidance from data protection authorities and other commentators,[23] it can be concluded that hashing of personal data needs to be

---

20. Hashing in a blockchain refers to the process of having an input item of whatever length reflecting an output item of a fixed length. For example, in a cryptocurrency transaction, transactions of varying lengths are run through a hashing algorithm, and all give an output of fixed length, regardless of the input transaction. The output is called a hash. This allows participants to keep track of a transaction much easier, particularly if otherwise, the transaction would involve large volumes of data. Most importantly, the hashing function provides security capabilities to processed transactions, making them immutable.
21. European Data Protection Supervisor and the Agencia espanola proteccion datos, *Introduction to the Hash Function as a Personal Data Pseudonymisation Technique* 21 (October 2019), available at: https://edps.europa.eu/data-protection/our-work/publications/papers/introduction-hash-function-personal-data_en (accessed 31 Aug. 2023).
22. European Union Blockchain Observatory and Forum, *Blockchain and the GDPR* 22 (16 Oct. 2018) available at: https://www.eublockchainforum.eu/sites/default/files/reports/20181016_report_gdpr.pdf (accessed 31 Aug. 2023).
23. Nisbet, K., *The False Allure of Hashing for Anonymization* (30 Apr. 2018) available at: https://gravitational.com/blog/hashing-for-anonymization/ (accessed 31 Aug. 2023) and

considered a pseudonymization technique[24] and not sufficient on its own as means of achieving true anonymization.

[2] Processing

Under the GDPR, the term 'processing' is defined broadly as 'any operation or set of operations which is performed on personal data or sets of personal data',[25] which essentially means that anything done with personal data would constitute processing, including collection, recording, deletion and even simply storing personal data.

This implies that storing of personal data in a blockchain network constitutes a data processing activity through automated means. For example, the submission of personal data to a blockchain network, the storage of hashes and public keys thereon, the transfer of transactional information containing personal data through nodes all are considered processing of personal data under the GDPR.

More generally, a blockchain must be updated regularly among all participants of the network, so that everyone has the most up-to-date version of the complete database. That update across the network can also include a data processing operation.

[B] Territorial Scope of the GDPR to the Blockchain

As with any novel form of technology, one of the key questions is which data protection regime kicks in and which is the competent regulatory authority.

The GDPR has considerably expanded the territorial scope of the GDPR opposed to its predecessor, the Data Protection Directive 96/46/EC. Article 3 of the GDPR states that the GDPR applies to the processing of personal data in a number of circumstances.[26] First, where the processing of personal data occurs 'in the context of the activities of an establishment of a controller or a processor in the Union, regardless of whether the processing takes place in the Union or not'[27] (the establishment criterion).

It is important to note that the GDPR also applies to the processing of personal data of individuals located in the EEA by a controller or processor not having an establishment in the EEA when the processing activities relate to: (i) the offering of goods or services (irrespective of whether a payment by the individual is required) to such individuals (the goods and services criterion); or (ii) the monitoring of their

---

Felten, E., *Does Hashing Make Data 'Anonymous'* (22 Apr. 2018) available at: https://www.ftc.gov/news-events/blogs/techftc/2012/04/does-hashing-make-data-anonymous (accessed 31 Aug. 2023).

24. Article 29 Data Protection Working Party, *supra* n. 9, at. 20.
25. Article 4(2) of the GDPR.
26. On 12 Nov. 2019, nearly a year after the draft guidelines were published and following a public consultation, the EDPB published its final guidelines seeking to clarify the territorial scope of the GDPR (the Territorial Scope Guidelines). The Territorial Scope Guidelines largely reaffirm prior interpretations of the GDPR's territorial application under the establishment criterion and offer further guidance with respect to the goods and services and monitoring criteria https://edpb.europa.eu/sites/default/files/files/file1/edpb_guidelines_3_2018_territorial_scope_after_consultation_de.pdf (accessed 31 Aug. 2023).
27. Article 3(1) of the GDPR.

behaviour, providing the behaviour takes place within the EEA (e.g., tracking on the Internet for profiling) (the monitoring criterion).[28]

Where a data controller not established in the EEA processes personal data in a blockchain, the GDPR may apply under the goods and services and/or the monitoring criterion. The broad reach of the GDPR's territorial scope can result in the applicability of the GDPR to many blockchain-based use cases which may have a limited nexus to Europe. However, in a blockchain environment, it can be difficult to determine the applicability of the GDPR. While the GDPR is generally considered technologically neutral, it is still conceived with a centralized database in mind. In these scenarios, the entity that is determining the purpose and the means for processing (i.e., the controller) will in many cases also be the entity that has already developed the systems with the purpose of deploying the related data processing activity.[29] On the contrary, a blockchain can be described as a decentralized network in which transactions are being recorded, and the process can involve multiple controllers located around the globe, some of them may be located in so-called third countries.[30] This is problematic when it comes to using public, non-permissioned blockchain systems which are often operated by nodes located in different countries. The creators of such a blockchain network are most likely unable to narrow down the number of users to one single jurisdiction.[31] If it is not possible to fully understand who precisely is involved in the blockchain network, it will be difficult to determine which data privacy regime applies to that particular blockchain and to assess who shall bear any obligations arising from the relevant data protection rules.

Assuming the identity of the relevant controllers can be determined, then, as stated above, the GDPR will apply if the controller is established in the EEA or if a company located outside of the EEA offers blockchain-related services involving the processing of personal data of EU residents. That processing activity will be subject to the GDPR. Notably, the European Parliamentary Research Service comes to the same conclusion.[32] The GDPR may also apply if an operator of a blockchain makes available the blockchain application enabling the users to put personal data onto the related

28. Article 3(2) of the GDPR; Artzt, M., *Territorial Scope of the GDPR from the US Perspective* (26 Jun. 2018) available at: https://iapp.org/news/a/territorial-scope-of-the-gdpr-from-a-us-perspective/ (accessed 31 Aug. 2023) and EDPB Guidelines 05/2021 on the Interplay between the application of Art. 3 and the provisions on international transfers as per Chapter V of the GDPR, Version 2.0, adopted on 14 Feb. 2023, available at: https://edpb.europa.eu/system/files/2023-02/edpb_guidelines_05-2021_interplay_between_the_application_of_art3-chapter_v_of_the_gdpr_v2_en_0.pdf (accessed 31 Aug. 2023).
29. European Union Blockchain Observatory and Forum, *supra* n. 22, at. 17.
30. A third country is a country other than the EU Member States and the three additional European Economic Area countries (Norway, Iceland and Liechtenstein) that have adopted a national law implementing the GDPR. Under the GDPR, personal data can only be transferred to such third countries in compliance with Chapter V (Arts 44-50 of the GDPR).
31. Finck, M., *Blockchains and Data Protection in the European Union* 17 (Max Planck Institute for Innovation & Competition Research Paper No. 18-01, 30 Nov. 2017) available at: https://edpl.lexxion.eu/data/article/12327/pdf/edpl_2018_01-007.pdf (accessed 31 Aug. 2023).
32. European Parliamentary Research Service, *Blockchain and the General Data Protection Regulation, 'Can Distributed Ledgers Be Squared with European Data Protection Law?'* 9 (July 2019) available at: https://www.europarl.europa.eu/RegData/etudes/STUD/2019/634445/EPRS_STU(2019)634445_EN.pdf (accessed 31 Aug. 2023).

blockchain application. Provided the users are located in the EEA, chances are that this is considered offering a service which entails the applicability of the GDPR pursuant to its Article 3(2).[33]

§4.03 IDENTIFYING CONTROLLERS AND PROCESSORS IN A BLOCKCHAIN ENVIRONMENT UNDER THE GDPR

[A] Definition of Controller and Processor

[1] Controllers

Under the GDPR, most compliance obligations apply to every 'controller', defined as a 'natural or legal person, public authority, agency or other body which, alone or jointly with others, determines the purposes and means of the processing of personal data'.[34] This means that individual persons – not just companies or public sector entities – have to comply with the GDPR. A narrow exception applies to 'the processing of personal data … by a natural person in the course of a purely personal or household activity', but courts and data protection authorities have denied the exception to homeowners who covered public pavements with security cameras, grandmothers who posted photos of grandchildren on social media, and members of religious groups who visited neighbours for door-to-door preaching.[35]

In addition, the GDPR provides a new concept of a joint controllership pursuant to its Article 26. Joint Controllers are two or more controllers which jointly determine the purposes and means of processing. When examining the roles of the blockchain participants, the concept of a joint controllership will be taken into consideration.[36]

On public blockchains, even individual participants will typically be responsible as 'controllers' under the GDPR and thus technically required to comply with all GDPR obligations and restrictions, including to adhere to data minimization principles under Article 5 GDPR; find a lawful basis for processing under Article 6 GDPR; issue privacy notices under Articles 12-14 GDPR; respond to data subject requests for access, deletion, correction, and portability under Articles 15 et seq.; ensure data security under Articles 24 and 32 GDPR; prepare records of processing activities under Article 30 GDPR; designate a representative in the EU under Article 27 GDPR (if the participant resides outside the EEA and the GDPR nevertheless applies according to Article 3[2][a]); notify security breaches under Articles 33 and 34 GDPR; conduct and document data protection impact assessments under Article 35 and 36 GDPR; designate

33. Bacon et al., *supra* n. 3, at 25.
34. Article 4(7) of the GDPR.
35. *See*, EDPB guidance 3/2019 on processing of personal data through video devices, https://edpb.europa.eu/sites/default/files/consultation/edpb_guidelines_201903_videosurveillance.pdf at #12-14; www.nytimes.com/2020/05/22/business/facebook-privacy-law-grandmother.html; Court of Justice of the European Union judgment of 10 Jul. 2018, C-25/17, *Tietosuojavaltuutettu v. Jehovan todistajat — uskonnollinen yhdyskunta*.
36. Artzt, M., *Is Blockchain Compatible with the GDPR?* (18 Jun. 2019) available at: https://platform.dataguidance.com/opinion/eu-blockchain-compatible-gdpr-part-1 (accessed 31 Aug. 2023).

a data protection officer under Articles 37 through 39 GDPR; and comply with restrictions and documentation requirements relating to international data transfers under Articles 44 et seq. GDPR. In practice, it is unlikely that many individuals will have the resources and expertise to satisfy these requirements. Anyone who designs a new blockchain project should analyse the requirements and try to address as many of them as possible for individual participants, for example, by implementing 'data protection by design' mechanisms and referencing default privacy notices and cross-border data transfer terms.

[2] Processors

A 'processor' means a natural or legal person, public authority, agency or other body which processes personal data on behalf of the controller based on clear and concise instructions issued by the controller.[37] Processors have to execute a written agreement with the controller that addresses the requirements under Article 28 GDPR, keep personal data secure, and follow the controller's instructions.

In the context of decentralized storage projects, for example, it would seem appropriate for the companies and individuals who offer storage to position themselves as processors. Data processing terms and instructions could be designed with GDPR in mind to help all blockchain participants satisfy applicable requirements and limit individual exposure.

[B] Legal Status of Participants of a Blockchain Network

[1] Static Number of Roles and Responsibilities

One of the key challenges in a blockchain context is the identification of (data) controllers and (data) processors. Given the nature of blockchain technology, it is not always easy to determine the legal status of the different participants in blockchain networks, such as nodes, miners, oracles, users, or developers. Even though developers of blockchain protocols do not process data, they are playing an important role by determining how the data is being processed through blockchain protocols.[38] Blockchain and other decentralized technologies do not completely fit into the concept of predefined roles and responsibilities as set out in the GDPR. The regulation only provides a limited number of roles the participants may take over. Some blockchain participants have a role to play in a blockchain network, but their legal status seems to be obscure from a data protection point of view.

First and foremost, it does not reside with the blockchain participants to arbitrarily allocate roles among them if the factual situation does not underpin that

37. Article 4(8) of the GDPR; EDPB Guidelines 07/2020 on the concepts of controller and processor in the GDPR, Version 1.0, adopted on 2 Sep. 2020, available at: https://edpb.europa.eu/sites/default/files/consultation/edpb_guidelines_202007_controllerprocessor_en.pdf.
38. Blockchain Bundesverband, *Blockchain, Data protection, and the GDPR* 5 (25 May 2018).

specific role. This implies, for instance, that assigning controllership to a blockchain participant is not permissible in the case this participant does not meet the criteria a controller has to meet under the regime of the GDPR.[39] Strictly speaking, the allocation of roles and responsibilities cannot be subject to any arrangements between blockchain users. However, the factual circumstances are driving the determination which role needs to be attributed to each participant. The recommendations of the French DPA, the CNIL, point out that a group of participants may choose to identify one of them who makes decisions for the group and to designate the said participant as a controller.[40] If the selected natural or legal person is empowered to make decisions on behalf of others, this person factually determines the purposes and means of the processing of personal data on a blockchain and, thus, it shall be deemed as a controller.

It is crucial to consider how the notions of the 'means' and 'purposes' ought to be interpreted in relation to blockchain technology. Regarding the means, the first challenge crops up when it comes to identifying the perspective that should be adopted. The parties that create and operate the software, hardware and data centres in order to operate a blockchain application may determine the means of the particular processing activity. Further, the mere use of a blockchain infrastructure made available by others (such as blockchain-as-a-service solutions) may be considered an implicit determination of the means of the related data processing activity.[41] Given that blockchains are distributed databases designed to be operated by many different parties, it is obvious that many actors have stakes in the determination of the means of data processing. With a view to the public or any type of permissionless blockchains, there is certainly not a single legal or natural person that takes the decision which software, hardware or specific data centre needs to be used. Rather, in practice, these decisions are made by a wide range of different users.[42] For illustration, in proof-of-work systems, miners may make the decision of what hardware and which data centre (for mining purposes) shall be used, whereas software developers decide whether and which software should be updated.[43] If a governance body comprising a group of blockchain participants has been established, those group members will agree upon what software has to be implemented in order to carry out transactions in a private blockchain context.

The former Article 29 Data Protection Working Party has emphasized that '*effective means*' must be interpreted as 'substantial questions' that are 'essential to the core of processing' – the how of processing.[44] This includes what data should be processed and for how long, which third parties have access to the data, when and how the data can be altered or manipulated.[45]

---

39. Arning, A. & Rothkegel, T., Article 4 DSGVO, in Taeger, J./Gabel, D. (ed.), *DSGVO, BDSG* 143 (3d ed., Deutscher Fachverlag GmbH, 2019); Article 29 Data Protection Working Party, *Opinion 1/2010 on the Concepts of 'Controller' and 'Processor'* 14 (WP 169 Adopted on 16 Feb. 2010).
40. CNIL, *supra* n. 7, at. 2.
41. European Parliamentary Research Service, *supra* n. 32, at 43.
42. *Ibid.*
43. *Ibid.*
44. Article 29 Data Protection Working Party, *supra* n. 39, at 14.
45. *Ibid.*

The criteria for determining the purposes of data processing are pivotal for making an assessment on who is considered a controller. It is apparent that, particularly in a public blockchain context, there are many actors which independently determine the purpose of a particular data processing operation, whereas a group of blockchain users may form part of a governance body and, therefore, jointly determine the related purpose. Determining the purpose must be interpreted in conjunction with the individual data processing activity on a case-by-case basis rather than the usage of the blockchain technology in general. The latter criterion points to a macro-perspective which would not be in sync with the interpretation of the means of data processing which should be understood as a granular and case-specific determination as shown above. Hence, it is advisable to determine the purpose on a micro level since this approach relates to the individual transaction, i.e., the recording of a transaction onto a blockchain. This is the more appropriate approach, given that data protection laws typically deal with specific items of personal data and touch upon specific data processing activities rather than taking a high-level approach.[46]

It should be noted that not all blockchain users acting as controllers qualify as joint controllers. Particularly, in a public blockchain context, many users independently define the purpose and/or the means of the individual processing operation. They may be considered co-controllers, albeit the co-controllership is not a legal term under the GDPR. From the practical point of view, co-controllership is a commonly used model which can be leveraged in those scenarios where the users have a role to play without being processors or joint controllers.

Overall, it is essential to perform a case-by-case analysis of the factual circumstances in order to clearly allocate roles and attendant responsibilities.

The rationale for evaluating the data protection roles in a blockchain environment is that data subjects, particularly those whose personal data is being recorded on the blockchain, need to know which natural or legal person they can refer to for effectively exercising and enforcing their rights. Furthermore, data protection authorities must have a contact person who may be held accountable for the processing of personal data and for any data breaches occurred.[47] This contact needs to proof compliance with its obligations arising from the GDPR.

[2] Miners

According to the National Institute of Standards and Technology (NIST) which belongs to the US Department of Commerce, mining is defined as the act of solving a puzzle within a proof of consensus model.[48] With that, miners do not decide what data should be written onto a blockchain. They validate transactions which have previously been submitted by blockchain participants. By no means, they are entrusted to make any decisions on details of an individual processing activity. Neither do they determine the

46. Bacon et al., *supra* n. 3, at. 64.
47. Article 29 Data Protection Working Party, *supra* n. 39, at 14.
48. NIST, *Blockchain Technology Overview* 53 (NISTIR 8202, 2018).

specific purpose and means of the processing of personal data being sent to the network by any third party. With that in mind, they do not qualify as controllers.[49]

However, it needs to be acknowledged that miners exercise significant control over the means by making a decision on which version of the protocol needs to run onto the blockchain. Having control over the means is not the decisive factor. The issue of whether a user may have the power to determine the purpose of the processing always prevails. Hence, miners are not controllers.[50]

Another issue must be considered: Given that miners are not controllers, they may act as processors instead, pursuant to Article 4 section 8 of the GDPR. Following the legal definition set out therein, they need to carry out services or any type of task based on the instructions of any other blockchain participants (controller). This usually does not happen, particularly in public blockchains, as miners are being tasked with validating transactions. The validation of transactions does not relate to the performing of services on behalf of any blockchain participants. To add a new block to a blockchain, all miners must come to a consensus over time. With that, the consensus model contradicts the concept of a controller-processor relationship where the processor has a subordinate role to play by following instructions issued by a controller. By contract, miners act independently and make their validation work on equal terms.

The blockchain protocol can be interpreted as an instruction the miners have to adhere to. The protocol is a software designed by developers (*see* §4.03[B][6], *infra*). Developers are not regarded as controllers unless special circumstances necessitate a controversial assessment. Irrespective of that, the blockchain protocol does not contain concise instructions as to how to deal with personal data to be written onto a blockchain. The CNIL is of the view that, in some cases, miners can be considered processors within the meaning of the GDPR, stating that they follow the controllers' instructions when checking whether the transaction meets technical criteria (such as format and a certain maximum size). This is a prerequisite that the related transaction can be carried out according to the chain rules.[51] If one considered this idea thoroughly, miners would need to conclude data protection agreements with those participants deemed as controllers in accordance with Article 28 of the GDPR. In public blockchains, this approach in not feasible since it is typically not clear which persons have laid down the related blockchain rules embedded in the blockchain protocol. Such persons could, in theory, act as controllers if one followed the CNIL approach.

The CNIL only exemplifies a controller-processor relationship applicable to private blockchains. For instance, if several insurance companies decide to create a private blockchain for their processing operation on their 'Know Your Customer' obligations, in such a case, according to the CNIL recommendation, the insurance companies will need to appoint one of them acting as controller. The insurance company which validates transactions would be likely to be considered the processor.[52] Nevertheless, the validation of a particular transaction does not constitute a

49. Blockchain Bundesverband, *supra* n. 38, at 6.
50. European Parliamentary Research Service, *supra* n. 32, at 46.
51. CNIL, *supra* n. 7, at 3.
52. *Ibid.*, at 4.

processing activity within the meaning of Article 4 section 2 of the GDPR (Processing). The processing under the GDPR relates to personal data. The miner's task is, however, limited to checking special technical criteria set out in the blockchain protocol and to resolving a mathematic puzzle for validation purposes. The protocol itself does not provide any personal data to be processed, neither does it include any instructions to be followed by the miners.

Therefore, miners need to be allocated to the blockchain infrastructure without having a role to play under the regime of the GDPR.

[3] Nodes

Nodes are computers that store a full or partial copy of a blockchain and participate in the validation of new blocks. Once a miner finds a valid hash for a block, the node broadcasts its hash to other nodes, which subsequently run a computation to verify whether the hash is valid (i.e., whether it meets the specifications of the protocol) and where this is the case, they add the new block to their own local copy of the ledger. Nodes verify whether transactions have the correct digital signatures and data format.[53]

Some authors have suggested that each node that triggers a transaction and, hence, distributes information to all other nodes or that saves a transaction in its own copy of a database should be considered a controller. They argue that the node pursues its own purpose, especially the participation in the network.[54] The authors are of the view that the node registers, submits and stores data and can freely use the data that is registered on its own computer.[55]

This view can be challenged since a node is simply a computer and may not define means or purposes of a data processing operation. Further, registering and storing of data is an IT operation which goes automatically and is not linked to a decision-making process of a human being. Irrespective of that, the mere participation in a network is too vague since the determination of the purpose must be interpreted in conjunction with an individual data processing activity rather than the usage of the blockchain technology as such (*see* §4.03[B][1], *infra*).

In addition, qualifying nodes as controller would entail considerable complications. It is impossible to determine the exact number, location, and identity of nodes on a blockchain network, given that nodes may be spread over the globe. Furthermore, nodes see the encrypted or hashed version of the data and not the data in the clear and, therefore, are not capable of making any changes thereto. Nodes are decentralized entities that are not able to comply with the obligations arising from the GDPR.

Besides, the enforcement of such obligations against nodes would be a burdensome exercise. For example, for the Bitcoin blockchain, there were approximately

53. European Union Blockchain Observatory and Forum, *supra* n. 22, at 14.
54. Martini, M and Weinzierl, Q, *Die Blockchain-Technologie und das Recht auf Vergessenwerden*, 1251, 1253 (Neue Zeitschrift für Verwaltungsrecht 2017).
55. *Ibid.*, at 1254.

15,000 nodes around the planet as of November 2022. From the practical perspective, nodes belong to the blockchain infrastructure and should not be considered controllers.

[4] Wallets

Wallets are software packages at the application level that allow companies or individual participants to control their own private key and to interact with the blockchain network by sending transactions to miners for validation purposes. The NIST considers wallets as the software used to store and manage asymmetric keys and addresses used for transactions.[56] Even though wallets may pass personal data to miners, it is apparent that this happens under the control of the blockchain participants which determine the purpose of the related data transfer (i.e., creating a new blockchain transaction) as well as the means of such processing (usage of the specific blockchain application). Against this background, wallets have no role to play from the data protection point of view and, hence, must be allocated to the blockchain infrastructure alongside miners and nodes.

[5] Users of a Blockchain

A blockchain transaction represents an interaction between at least two parties. With cryptocurrencies, for example, a transaction represents a transfer of the cryptocurrency between blockchain network users. Broadly speaking, transactions include all kinds of data. In the case of smart contract systems, transactions are being used to send information, process and store it onto a blockchain. Moreover, a blockchain transaction can also be leveraged to change an attribute of a digitized asset within a blockchain technology-based supply chain system.[57]

From the data privacy point of view, it is critical to determine which user should be deemed as a controller under the GDPR.

The CNIL considers that a user may qualify as a controller when (i) the said participant is a natural person; and (ii) the processing is related to a professional or commercial activity; or when the said participant is a legal person that registers personal data to a blockchain network.[58]

This is predominantly in line with the Thematic Report from the Blockchain Observatory and Forum.[59] For private blockchains, the Blockchain Observatory and Forum recommends that a blockchain consortium which needs to be established designates one or more actors to be responsible for the blockchain and will act as a controller or joint controllers. With respect to public blockchains, the Blockchain Observatory and Forum is of the opinion that it remains quite often a grey zone. If

56. NIST, *supra* n. 48, at 54.
57. *Ibid.*, at 10.
58. CNIL, *supra* n. 7, at 3.
59. European Union Blockchain Observatory and Forum, *supra* n. 22, at 18.

network users submit personal data to the blockchain ledger as part of their business activity, they are most likely controllers.[60] If they, however, submit their own personal data to a blockchain network for their own personal use, for example, to buy or sell crypto assets, they most likely fall under the household exemption regulated in Article 2(2c) of the GDPR and, therefore, may not be regarded as controllers.

Recital 18 of the GDPR states that this regulation does not apply to the processing of personal data by a natural person during a household activity and thus with no connection to a professional or commercial activity. Household activities include correspondence and the holding of addresses or social networking and online activities. The household exemption only applies to those activities which are related to the right of privacy of an individual.[61] Neither the size of the data file nor the number of people who might have access to the data being disclosed online are the criteria in terms of determining the applicability of the household exemption.[62]

Some commentators have another view on how to interpret the household exemption. They assert that even if the user's own personal data was disclosed on a public blockchain and, therefore, on-chain data was made available to an indefinite number of people, the household exemption would not apply.[63] Even in the case the user puts personal data of other people on-chain, the user would nevertheless qualify as a controller since the data is being made available to an unlimited number of users.[64]

This rationale shifts the responsibility to the users of the blockchain technology who, particularly with regard to public blockchains, lack the required expertise to make informed decisions regarding the design of the respective technology. The user of a blockchain who, for example, buys or sells Bitcoins only decides to whom and how many Bitcoins are being transferred.[65] The user has certainly no influence on how long data is stored, which third parties have access to and when the data is deleted.[66]

This assumption will not change if the data subjects gain control over their own personal data through their private key, which links to the question of whether the data subjects can qualify as controllers. One may argue that if an individual hashes his or her own personal information to the blockchain, he or she will be both the data subject and the controller. That solution seems to be weird since the GDPR clearly differentiates between the data subject concerned and the controllers whom the data subject rights may be addressed to. In the case both roles are merged, the data subject rights are jeopardized since there is no participant available which can be held liable to respond to them.

In summary, if individuals submit their own personal data to a blockchain, even if they hash their personal information and use private keys and, by doing so, only pursue private purposes, they will not act as controllers since the household exemption

60. *Ibid.*
61. Schmidt, B., Article 2, in Taeger, J./Gabel, D., *supra* n. 39 at 56.
62. Recital 18 of the GDPR.
63. European Parliamentary Research Service, *supra* n. 32, at 49.
64. *Ibid.*, at 48.
65. Buocz, T. et al., *Bitcoin and the GDPR: Allocating Responsibility in Distributed Networks*, 24 (Computer Law & Security Review, 2019).
66. *Ibid.*

kicks in. When they put their own personal data or the data of other individuals in a block to be added to a blockchain and this happens in the context of carrying out a private activity, they will also fall under the household exemption. By contrast, if they pursue commercial purposes, even if this only makes a very small contribution, the GDPR will apply, and they should be treated as controllers. It should be taken into consideration that the household exemption needs to be interpreted strictly and any classification of blockchain users must be vetted on a case-by-case basis.

[6] Developer of Smart Contracts

The question arises as to how developers of smart contracts should be qualified from the data privacy perspective. Smart contracts are pieces of software that can be deployed to a blockchain network and that, once deployed, may be executed independently from their developer (*see* Chapter 3, §3.01, *supra*). This software is only executed when a network user requests to do so. There are three options which should be factored in when making a decision on which role the developer and the user of such software are taking: The software can be seen as being operated by its developer, by the network user or by both.

The CNIL is of the view that, with regard to smart contracts, the software, respectively, the developer of the related algorithm may simply be considered a solution provider without having a particular data protection role to play. When the developer actively participates in the data processing, he or she may be qualified as a processor or controller depending on the capacity to determine the purpose and means of the individual processing operation.[67] The CNIL clearly states that the smart contract developer may be deemed as a processor, provided that he or she processes personal data on behalf of controllers. The following example may specify the CNIL's view: A software developer offers a solution to an airline by virtue of a smart contract that enables passengers to be automatically reimbursed when their flight has been delayed or cancelled.[68]

If one followed the recommendation of the CNIL, the software developer would be deemed as a processor if he or she would interfere in the data processing, while the airline would act as a controller. This solution is indeed acceptable in the light of the GDPR. Nevertheless, it needs to be questioned in which scenarios a software developer has an active role to play in conjunction with the processing of personal data. Typically, the software developer does not participate in any blockchain transaction. When developing and publishing smart contract algorithms, he or she has nothing to do with any type of processing activity. Irrespective of this, the software is not being operated by the developer as he or she only devises a solution to be offered to blockchain users who capitalize on it. They make the decision to leverage the smart contract algorithm by writing personal data to the blockchain. The smart contract

67. CNIL, *supra* n. 7, at 2.
68. *Ibid.*, at 3.

developer only delivers a ready-to-go solution to any potential users which operationalize the smart contract for their own commercial benefit. The software developer neither determines the purpose and means of any data processing activity nor follows any instructions issued by a controller. In the usual way of business, the smart contract developer is, at no point in time, involved in any processing operation in relation to personal data. In the phase of creating an algorithm, there is simply no personal data to be collected or stored.

However, there may be few scenarios where the smart contract developer actively interferes in a processing activity. Hence, its role must be vetted in the light of the GDPR on a case-by-case basis.[69]

[7] Oracles

An oracle is an agent that allows the transfer of external data to the blockchain for on-chain use in conjunction with the use of smart contracts.[70] Oracles allow users to automate business logic and may be used to process real-world events which occur or occurred externally and have been inputted onto the blockchain. The algorithm contained in the blockchain is digesting the data feed and automatically generates an output of information.

An example is a data set, such as prices, information about flight delays or customer claims. Once entered on the blockchain, the data can be used to automate business processes and services. Without oracles, the blockchain would only operate in its own-closed environment, materially limiting its capabilities.

Oracles operate outside the blockchain network by providing external data feeds to the blockchain. There are indeed similarities with smart contract developers as both groups are operating off-chain. The information from the world outside the blockchain is being processed through an algorithm embedded in the smart contract. By doing this, oracles directly interfere in a data processing carried out by the smart contract algorithm. This leads to the question of whether oracles must be deemed as (joint-) controllers.

That legal issue goes hand in hand with various rulings of the Court of Justice of the European Union (CJEU), which further developed the interpretation of joint controllers in the context of Article 26 of the GDPR. The CJEU tends to interpret joint controllership very broadly to ensure the effective and comprehensive protection of data subject rights.[71] On 29 July 2019, the CJEU confirmed that a website owner (Fashion ID) that has embedded a third-party social media plug-in (Facebook), such as Facebook's 'Like' button, into its website may be jointly responsible along with Facebook for the collection and transmission of personal data relating to visitors. This decision is important because the court considered Facebook and the website owner,

69. European Union Blockchain Observatory and Forum, *supra* n. 22, at 18; Chapter 1, §1.11[B], *supra*.
70. Artzt, M., *supra* n. 36.
71. Case C-210/16 *Wirtschafsakademie Schleswig-Holstein* [2018] C-796/17, para. 16; Case *Fashion ID* [2019] C-40/17.

Fashion ID, as joint controllers even though both parties had certainly not reached an upfront determination regarding the purpose and the means of the data processing as required by the regulation.

With respect to oracles, the said ruling implies that blockchain participants connected by way of smart contracts and oracles may act as joint controllers according to Article 26 of the GDPR, even though there has been no legal interaction between them from the outset. The CJEU held that, by inserting a plug-in into its website, Fashion ID had a strong influence on the collection and transmission of personal data of visitors to Facebook, which would not be the case without the plug-in. These processing operations were carried out in the economic interests of both Fashion ID and Facebook: The visibility of Fashion IDon social media has been increased, and, at the same time, Facebook has been enabled to collect personal data of the visitors for its own commercial purposes.

It is worth noting that, unlike the typical smart contract developer, who usually creates an algorithm to be offered to potential blockchain participants, an oracle has a strong influence on the individual data processing operation and its result carried out by the smart contract algorithm.

If an oracle does have a commercial interest in a processing activity or in its outcome, it should be considered a joint controller alongside the blockchain user.

In the majority of cases, the GDPR does not come into play when oracles provide data feeds to the blockchain. The reason for this assumption is that oracles usually do not have a commercial interest in the outcome of a data processing activity.

[8] Governance Bodies and Joint-/Co-controllership

In a private blockchain context, a governance body, comprising a group of natural or legal persons, can be established to oversee blockchain transactions. This group may define the rules for participants upfront. It is possible that, under certain circumstances, such a governance body may act as a processor in the event it establishes a single point of legal contact within the network. If the governance body has control over personal data by determining the purpose and means of processing, it will most likely be considered a controller or the group as joint controllers depending on the factual circumstances.

Whenever a group of participants decides to carry out processing operations on a blockchain for a common purpose, the CNIL recommends identifying beforehand who should be acting as controller. For example, the participants may create a legal person, or they may choose to designate one participant out of them who makes decisions on behalf of the group. In both cases, the appointed legal or natural person will qualify as controller.[72]

This consideration is indeed sensible as otherwise all participants of the private blockchain could be considered joint controllers and, hence, would need to enter into an arrangement or agreement further set out in Article 26 of the GDPR. That

72. CNIL, *supra* n. 7, at 2.

arrangement must be concluded in a transparent way given that data subjects whose data is being recorded on the blockchain must know against which group member they may address their data privacy rights, and data protection authorities must have a contact point which can be held accountable for the processing carried out.[73]

Once one or more members of the group have been nominated to act as (joint-) controllers, the other members of the group are either processors or joint controllers, depending on whether they are processing personal data. This necessitates that all members of the group must enter into a controller-processor data protection agreement according to Article 28 of the GDPR and/or into a joint controller arrangement according to Article 26 of the GDPR. As a result, two types of contracts need to be put in place: a joint controller arrangement and, in addition, a controller-processor data protection agreement.

Certainly, the joint controllership ought to be assessed and determined on a case-by-case basis, given that the EUCJ tends to interpret the legal term of joint controllership very broadly. A use case for a joint controllership would be a consortium of blockchain users established between many actors that are part of the same supply chain. The legal entities created by the consortium would be joint controllers, bearing in mind that they exercise significant control over the purposes and the means of personal data processing, e.g., by leveraging smart contract algorithms. Those companies which have joined the consortium subsequently and are using the blockchain technology to put personal data onto the chain are co-controllers rather than joint controllers.[74]

[C] Frictions Between Controllership and Obligations under the GDPR

Circumstances may occur where single actors qualify as controllers in a blockchain environment. The related blockchain users identified as controllers have very limited influence over the respective means of a data processing. This may result in a situation where controllers may be unable to meet the GDPR obligations since they have no or insufficient control over the data being processed. For example, a blockchain user may not be capable of complying with a data subject's request for access under Article 15 of the GDPR as the relevant data is fully encrypted. The same applies to a request for the erasure of personal data since the blockchain user is, at first glance, not able to delete the data being submitted to the blockchain. Consequently, acting as a controller in a blockchain network may conflict with the factual capability to perform the obligations imposed by the GDPR.

The issue is how to resolve that mismatch. Commentators are of the view that whenever a controller is not able to comply with data subject right request, the controller should make sure that other participants which may act as (joint-) controllers shall respond to those requests equally.[75] In other words, actors who have taken

73. *Ibid.*
74. European Parliamentary Research Service, *supra* n. 32, at 45: joint controllership.
75. European Parliamentary Research Service, *supra* n. 32, at 53.

the decision to use blockchain technology to process personal data must ascertain that there are appropriate governance arrangements with other blockchain users in place that enable the effective exercise and enforcement of data subject rights.[76]

This approach, however, requires the existence of agreements between the related blockchain participants with the purpose of complying with requests raised by data subjects irrespective of whether the users are acting as co- or joint controllers. From the operational standpoint, this is practically not feasible even though, in theory, it is contractually viable to re-allocate responsibilities from one controller to another one. Only in a private blockchain context you may operate with governance models described above,[77] whereas public blockchains clearly exclude the applicability of those models.

§4.04 LEGAL BASIS AND CONSENT UNDER THE GDPR

In order to process personal data in accordance with the first principle in Article 5 of the GDPR, personal data must be processed lawfully, fairly, and in a transparent manner. Taking the first element of these three requirements as our focus: To process personal data lawfully, the processing must be based on one or more conditions specified in Article 6 of the GDPR, known as a lawful (or legal) basis. While the choice of legal basis is an important consideration in and of itself, it is also worth noting that the choice of lawful basis is closely tied to data subject rights,[78] given certain lawful bases provide exemptions to the availability of certain data subject rights. Although not all processing activities will be able to avail themselves of every lawful basis, this is a factor worth bearing in mind from the outset when designing any processing activities. The Article 6 conditions can be summarized as: (i) the data subject having unambiguously given his consent to the processing of his personal data for one or more specific purpose; (ii) the processing is necessary for the performance of a contract to which the data subject is a party or in order to take steps at the request of the data subject prior to entering into a contract; (iii) the processing is necessary for compliance with a legal obligation to which the controller is subject (whether pursuant to EU or national Member State law); (iv) the processing is necessary to protect the vital interests of the data subject or of another natural person; (v) the processing is necessary for the performance of a task carried out in the public interest; or (vi) the processing is necessary for the purposes of the legitimate interests pursued by the controller or by a third party to whom the data is disclosed, except where the processing is unwarranted in any particular case by reason of prejudice to the rights and freedoms or legitimate interests of the data subject, in particular, where the data subject is a child.[79]

---

76. *Ibid.*, at 72.
77. A good example is a company which offers *Blockchain as a Service* (BaaS) acting as a processor on behalf of one or more controllers.
78. For further discussion around data subject rights in the context of the blockchain, please *see* §4.06, *infra*.
79. Article 6 of the GDPR.

In addition, where a controller is processing special categories of personal data (e.g., health data, data revealing racial or ethnic origin, political opinions, etc.),[80] or data related to criminal convictions or offences, an additional legal ground (as well as an Article 6 ground) to reflect a higher level of protection for those categories of personal data, will need to be relied upon. The Article 9 conditions are: (i) the data subject has given his explicit consent; (ii) the processing is necessary for the purposes of carrying out the obligations and specific rights of the controller in the field of employment law, social security law, or social protection law in so far as it is authorized by national law providing for appropriate safeguards; (iii) the processing is necessary to protect the vital interests of the data subject or of another person where the data subject is physically or legally incapable of giving consent; (iv) the processing is carried out by a not-for-profit body with a specific aim and does not involve the disclosure of data to a third party without the data subject's consent; (v) the data subject has deliberately made the information public; (vi) the processing is necessary for establishing, exercising, or defending legal claims; (vii) the processing is necessary for reasons of substantial public interest on the basis of EU or national Member State law; (viii) the processing (by a person subject to the obligation of professional secrecy) is necessary for the purposes of preventative or occupational medicine, the assessment of the working capacity of the employee, medical diagnosis, the provision or management of health or social care systems, and services pursuant to a contract with a healthcare professional; (ix) the processing is necessary for reasons of public interest in the area of public health, such as protecting against serious cross-border threats to health or ensuring high standards of healthcare, medicinal products, or medical devices; or (x) the processing is necessary for archiving purposes in the public interest, for scientific or historical research purposes, or statistical purposes.[81]

On a similar note, in the case of data relating to criminal convictions and offences, controllers must have both a lawful basis under Article 6 of the GDPR and either legal authority or official authority for the processing under Article 10 of the GDPR. The EU Member State and UK implementing legislation sets out specific conditions providing lawful authority to process these types of personal data. For example, the UK Data Protection Act 2018 treats criminal conviction and offences data in a similar way to a special category of personal data.

Therefore, those deemed controllers in a blockchain that are processing personal data[82] will be required to identify and document the lawful basis under which they are processing personal data. As is the case for many of the GDPR requirements (which we will discuss in more detail throughout this chapter), given the decentralized nature of the blockchain network, it is not always straightforward to determine on what legal

80. Special categories of personal data are defined by Art. 9(1) of the GDPR as personal data revealing racial or ethnic origin, political opinions, religious or philosophical beliefs, or trade union membership, and the processing of genetic data, biometric data for the purpose of uniquely identifying a natural person, data concerning health or data concerning a natural person's sex life or sexual orientation.

81. Article 9(2) of the GDPR.

82. Please *see* discussion on processing personal data in the context of a blockchain in §4.02[B], *supra*.

basis personal data in the blockchain is being processed in reliance on. It is considered by some commentators that the 'most likely and hopeful legal grounds for processing are that there is a contract or consent in play'.[83] We discuss these grounds in further detail below, as well as the potential ability to rely upon the controller's legitimate interests and the consent of the data subject.

[A] Contractual Necessity

Article 6(1)(b) of the GDPR provides for the lawful processing of personal data where it 'is necessary for the performance of a contract to which the data subject is party or in order to take steps at the request of the data subject prior to entering into a contract'.[84] Although the GDPR does not provide guidance as to when this ground may be appropriate to rely upon, the EDPB has adopted a strict interpretation of this legal ground in the context of the provision of online services to data subjects.[85] The EDPB takes the view that where a service requested by the data subject can be provided without the specific processing taking place, it is not necessary for the performance of a contract, and it may be more appropriate to rely on another legal ground. The EDPB also introduces an objective assessment of what is considered 'necessary' for the performance of a contract. According to the EDPB, where there are realistic, less intrusive alternatives to achieve the same objective, the processing is not necessary, and an alternative legal ground will be more appropriate. As such, reliance in a blockchain scenario on this ground may be limited, although it may still have some relevance in the context of concluding smart contracts using blockchain technology.

[B] Consent

Personal data can also be processed where the data subject has given clear consent to the processing of their personal data for a specific purpose.[86] The GDPR standard of consent is high, and consent is defined by the GDPR as: 'any freely given, specific, informed and unambiguous indication of the data subject's wishes by which he or she, by a statement or by clear affirmative action, signifies agreement to the processing of personal data relating to him or her'.[87] In order for consent to be freely given, the data subject must have a genuine choice as to whether to consent or not. Controllers must also comply with their transparency obligations in ensuring individuals are appropriately informed about details of the processing, including the identity of the controller, the type of data processed and the specific purposes for which consent is being sought.

83. Ibáñez, L-D., O'Hara, K. & Simperl, E., *On Blockchains and the General Data Protection Regulation*, 3 available at: https://eprints.soton.ac.uk/422879/1/BLockchains_GDPR_4.pdf (accessed 31 Aug. 2023).
84. Article 6(1)(b) of the GDPR.
85. EDPB draft guidelines 2/2019 on the processing of personal data under Art. 6(1)(b) of the GDPR, adopted on 9 Apr. 2019.
86. Article 6(1)(a) of the GDPR.
87. Article 4(11) of the GDPR.

Where consent is used as the legal ground for processing special categories of personal data (e.g., health data), then the consent will also need to be explicit.

A fundamental issue in the blockchain context is that under the GDPR consent can be withdrawn by a data subject at any time.[88] Although the withdrawal of consent does not impact the lawfulness of the processing prior to such consent being withdrawn, if a controller cannot demonstrate reliance on an alternative legal ground following the withdrawal, the processing has to be stopped. This approach is problematic in itself, given guidance from the ICO is clear that reliance on consent should not be used if an alternative legal basis can be relied upon.[89] Further, withdrawal of consent where there is no alternative legal ground to rely upon may be difficult, given the immutable nature of the blockchain: once personal data is included in one of the blockchains' blocks, it may continue to be processed for as long as the ledger exists.

Another key question when looking at the reliance on consent as a legal basis in the context of blockchain is 'who does a user give consent to?' This is important, for one because under the GDPR a controller must be able to demonstrate that consent was given (and the extent to which the consent was given),[90] which in turn will require that accurate records are kept. As discussed further in §4.03, *supra*, one of the key challenges arising from compliance with the GDPR in a blockchain context is the identification of the relevant controllers and processors. There may, in some instances, exist a grey area where it is not possible to identify a controller, for some (but not all) blockchain networks, particularly those in the public sphere. For private blockchains, it will be possible to identify an entity who acts as an intermediary between the user and the blockchain, and so this issue may be easier to resolve. This demonstrates another issue which reinforces the position taken by the CNIL[91] and others: that public blockchains generate the most concerns from a data protection perspective, and private (permissioned) blockchains may be the way forward from a privacy perspective.

On this note, in a public blockchain, the use of consent will be particularly problematic. It is unlikely that an individual will be able to identify which nodes, and to which recipients, their data will be transferred, and it cannot be known which participants may be involved in the network. The process, at least from the perspective of a public blockchain, seems at odds, at least with some elements of GDPR-standard consent, that the consent must be specific and informed.

Overall, it is important to remember that, in most cases, given the inherent difficulties with obtaining valid GDPR-standard consent across the board, which will also apply to processing in the blockchain context, the GDPR has marked a movement away from reliance on consent and controllers are tending to rely on an alternative legal ground for most processing activities to avoid the issues it creates, including those discussed above. It follows that the same reasoning should likely apply where the

88. Article 7(3) of the GDPR.
89. UK ICO, Guide to the General Data Protection Regulation, Lawful basis for processing, available at: https://ico.org.uk/for-organisations/guide-to-data-protection/guide-to-the-general-data-protection-regulation-gdpr/lawful-basis-for-processing/ (accessed 31 Aug. 2023).
90. Recital 42 of the GDPR.
91. CNIL, *supra* n. 7, at 5.

processing of personal data occurs in the blockchain. In many cases, the GDPR standard will be difficult to achieve, and organizations should proceed with caution when looking to rely on the legal ground of consent.

[C] Legitimate Interest

Article 6(1)(f) of the GDPR provides that processing of personal data is lawful where the 'processing is necessary for the purposes of the legitimate interests pursued by the controller or by a third party, except where such interests are overridden by the interests or fundamental rights and freedoms of the data subject which require protection of personal data, in particular where the data subject is a child ...'.[92]

This is perhaps the most flexible of the GDPR's legal grounds and so the legal basis which could be relied upon most frequently in the processing of personal data in a blockchain context. Legitimate interests are not centred around a particular purpose (e.g., the performance of a contract), nor have the data subjects agreed to the processing (e.g., via consent). In short, a controller must be able to demonstrate that its interests are not outweighed by the interests of the data subject. As such, in order to determine whether the legitimate interest as the legal ground can be relied upon, controllers are required to carry out a balancing test (or complex assessment as it is described by the Article 29 Data Protection Working Party[93]) to consider and address the competing interests of the relevant parties. This test can be split roughly into three elements:[94]

(1) *Purpose:* To fulfil the first element, the 'purpose' test, it should be considered whether the parties are pursuing a legitimate interest. In the case of blockchain, it should be considered what the blockchain is trying to achieve, including the potential benefits to the public and the relative importance of those benefits.
(2) *Necessity:* Next is the processing 'necessary' for the purposes of that legitimate interest. Does the blockchain advance the interest identified in the 'purpose test'? Would there be less invasive ways of fulfilling the same interest?
(3) *Balancing Test:* Lastly, the 'balancing test' requires controllers to consider whether the data subject's interest overrides the controller's purported legitimate interest. In this assessment, various factors should be considered, including: (i) what is the relationship between the controller to the data subjects in question; (ii) what type of personal data is being processed; (iii)

92. Article 6(1)(f) of the GDPR.
93. Article 29 Data Protection Working Party, *Opinion 06/2014 on the notion of legitimate interests of the data controller under Article 7 of the Directive 95/46/EC* 33 ff. (WP 217, adopted on 14 Nov. 2014).
94. This 'three-part test' is advocated by the UK ICO in its Guide to the General Data Protection Regulation, *supra* n. 89.

what does the data subject expect to be done with their personal data; and (iv) what is the potential impact on the data subject?

The GDPR does not provide an exhaustive list of what processing activities may constitute a legitimate interest, but it does list fraud prevention,[95] ensuring network and information security[96] or indicating possible criminal acts[97] as constituting legitimate interests. As with any processing activity where the controller seeks to rely on legitimate interests as the legal ground, this assessment should be documented by way of legitimate interest assessment (LIA).[98]

In relation to the 'Balancing Test', the European Parliamentary Research Service has considered whether this could be satisfied in the blockchain context. For example, it is arguable that an individual who purchases a crypto asset would 'reasonably expect' that it would involve the processing of certain personal data (e.g., the public key). In reality, the European Parliamentary Research Service considers it is 'unlikely that most users in fact realize that the public keys are personal data and the transaction may reveal information about the data subject'.[99]

[D] Compliance with a Legal Obligation

Recital 45 of the GDPR states that 'where processing is carried out in accordance with a legal obligation to which the controller is subject ... the processing should have a basis in [EU] or Member State law'. In other words, the obligation must be imposed by law as opposed to a contractual obligation, and it must be based on the laws of the EU or of an EU Member State (i.e., not the laws of a third country). However, Recital 41 of the GDPR makes it clear that it does not have to be an explicit statutory obligation as long as the application of the law is foreseeable to those individuals subject to it. As such, reliance on this lawful basis could include processing to affect compliance with common law obligations. Examples of processing that can rely on this legal ground will include processing for Anti-Money Laundering and Know Your Customer requirements, which are imposed by EU law.[100]

[E] Special Categories of Personal Data

It should also be noted that where participants in a blockchain are processing special categories of personal data, there will be additional considerations, for example,

95. Recital 47 of the GDPR.
96. Recital 49 of the GDPR.
97. Recital 50 of the GDPR.
98. Note that the term LIA or 'legitimate interest assessment' is not explicitly referenced in the GDPR.
99. European Parliamentary Research Service, *supra* n. 32, at 64.
100. Directive (EU) 2018/843 of the European Parliament and the Council of 30 May 2018 amending Directive (EU) 2015/849 on the prevention and use of the financial system for the purposes of money laundering or terrorist financing and amending Directives 2001/138/EC and 2013/36/EU.

obtaining explicit consent from the data subject or relying on the processing being necessary for the purposes of carrying out the obligations and specific rights of the controller in the field of employment law, social security law, or social protection law[101] (e.g., an employer processing employee health data to comply with its employment law obligations). The requirement for an additional legal ground will make the processing of special categories of personal data (e.g., using blockchain in the healthcare sector where large volumes of health data are processed) more challenging.

§4.05 SECURITY OF DATA PROCESSING ON A BLOCKCHAIN IN THE CONTEXT OF THE GDPR

[A] Personal Data Versus Anonymous Data

The GDPR only applies to the processing of personal data unless the data has lost its personal component due to anonymization. Therefore, the GDPR does not apply to anonymized data. The bar for what qualifies as anonymized data is very high. The anonymization technique must make it impossible to identify a natural person through any and all of the means which may likely be used. The process of anonymization must also be irreversible. This implies that it is not possible to reconstitute the original data from the anonymized form.[102] Any techniques that do not comply with this standard are not sufficient to render the data anonymized. Pseudonymized data remains personal and is, therefore, subject to GDPR obligations.

Given the immutability of data in blockchain networks, the storage of personal data in a clear and readable format on a shared ledger, be it on public, be it on private blockchains, is not in line with the GDPR obligations under Article 32 section 1 of the GDPR. Both the controller and the processor must safeguard the data being processed by implementing appropriate technical and organizational measures, e.g., pseudonymization, anonymization or encryption.

[B] Particular Security Techniques

There are many techniques to meet the requirement set out in Article 32 section 1 of the GDPR, for example, data obfuscation, encryption, hashing or data aggregation, all of them aiming to de-identify personal data in a way that makes it impossible to link such data to an individual.

[1] Encryption

Where data is encrypted, the holder of the encryption key can still re-identify each data subject through decryption of the dataset because the personal data is still contained

101. Article 9(2)(b) of the GDPR.
102. Article 29 Data Protection Working Party, *supra* n. 9, at 8.

therein, albeit in an encrypted format. Assuming that a state-of-the-art encryption scheme was applied, decryption is only possible with the knowledge of the key.[103]

As a result, encrypted data remains personal data,[104] at least for the holder of the key. This is confirmed by the former Article 29 Data Protection Working Party in its Opinion on Cloud Computing which pointed out that encryption does not render personal data irreversibly anonymous although encryption may significantly contribute to the confidentiality of personal data if deployed correctly.[105]

There are debates in relation to cloud services as to whether a state-of-the-art encryption may turn personal data into anonymous data when the cloud service provider has no access to the key. This should be vetted with a view to Article 32 section 1(a) of the GDPR, which describes encryption as one technical measure for safeguarding personal data. This implies that encryption may adequately secure personal data but will not turn its legal nature into the status of anonymous data. Another technical aspect should be also taken into consideration: Even if strong encryption is employed on personal data, the result is pseudonymous, not anonymous data. The reason for that assumption is that, as long as the encryption key exists somewhere, the data can always be decrypted and made transparent. It is possible to reverse the process and reconstitute the original data so everyone can read it.[106]

[2] Hashing

Hashing is at the heart of the most important properties of blockchains, providing much of the magic of decentralization.[107] Hashing is a method of calculating a unique output (called a hash digest) for the input of nearly any size of data by applying a cryptographic hash function to the input data. Theoretically, the input data could be stored outside the blockchain because the data's integrity could be verified by re-running the hash function (for further details, *see* Chapter 1, §1.06[B][4], *supra*).

As outlined above, hashing is an encryption technique and typically generates pseudonymous, but not anonymous data, given that the data subject can be re-identified.[108] This is also in line with the view of the former Article 29 Data Protection Working Party, which made clear that the hash function is a useful security measure but not a method of anonymization.[109] Nevertheless, the former Article 29 Data Protection Working Party pondered that the use of deterministic encryption or keyed-hash functions in conjunction with the deletion of the key might reduce the reasonable likelihood of re-identification of a natural person and, consequently, of decryption of

103. *Ibid.*, at 20.
104. Section §4.02[A][2], *infra.*
105. Article 29 Data Protection Working Party, *Opinion 05/2012 on Cloud Computing* 15 (WP 196 Adopted on 1 Jul. 2012).
106. European Union Blockchain Observatory and Forum, *supra* n. 22, at 21.
107. *Ibid.*
108. Section §4.02[A][2], *supra*; Finck, M., *Blockchain: Regulation and Governance in Europe* 93 (Cambridge University Press, December 2018).
109. Article 29 Data Protection Working Party, *supra* n. 9, at 20.

the hash function.[110] Notably, hashing constitutes a state-of-the-art security technique at present.

[3] Multi-layered Blockchains

To the extent that personal data in the clear is stored and processed on a blockchain network, it is essential that the related blockchain is under strict control of the blockchain participants. In this context, personal data should be restricted to a private blockchain with a small number of nodes governed by a consortium whose members need to agree on contractual terms that, *inter alia*, define concisely the privacy policy towards the users as well as the process for amending the data where required.[111]

One additional safeguard is a multi-layered blockchain design which typically involves two interoperable blockchains: A private blockchain involving a consortium, operated by only a limited number of nodes, where the actual real-time processing of personal data or the exchange of crypto assets takes place. This network is fast but not very decentralized, and it is not interoperable with other networks globally.[112] The second layer is a base, public blockchain, operated by a multiple (thousands) of nodes. That network is very decentralized and difficult for anyone to take control of, but, and this is the flipside, not very fast. This base blockchain can be used to store crypto assets or personal data over long periods of time, particularly when that information is not required any more or shall not be subject to further processing.

In such a model, the base, respectively the public blockchain, makes it possible for the private network to interoperate with other networks worldwide. One of the downsides of this model is that personal data which is exchanged back and forth between the two layers may be compromised. Moreover, it remains unclear who will be responsible for data leakage. However, this can showcase a robust technique that allows personal data to be removed from the private blockchain and transferred to the public blockchain when it is no longer needed for carrying out a data processing operation.

[4] Storing Personal Data Off-Chain

Whenever it becomes obvious that it is not necessary to keep storing personal data which form part of a particular transaction or processing activity on the blockchain, those data can be stored in another, off-chain database and linked to the distributed ledger through a hash pointer. This implies that only a hash of the data remains on the blockchain; the hash is linked to a particular transaction. On-chain hashes of off-chain personal data would also qualify as personal data. Personal data can be recorded in a referenced and encrypted database and not on the blockchain itself.[113]

---

110. *Ibid.*, at 21.
111. European Union Blockchain Observatory and Forum, *supra* n. 22, at 30.
112. *Ibid.*
113. Finck, *supra* n. 108, at 94.

The off-chain personal data is kept in a separate database, e.g., in a pdf or Excel file. From that point of time where the data is being stored outside the blockchain, it is non-transactional data that is either too large to be stored on the blockchain effectively or requires the ability to be changed or deleted. Taking bulk data out of the blockchain may also resolve the scalability problem because more transactions can be processed on the blockchain when data which is not used any more is being set aside, namely outside the blockchain whereas only a hash or hash pointer remains on the blockchain. This constitutes a further efficient measure to safeguard personal data.

[C] Principles of Purpose Limitation and Data Minimization

Given that the above-described security techniques under sections §4.05[B][3] and §4.05[B][4] do not alter the nature of personal data which entails the applicability of the GDPR, the legal issue is whether storing personal data onto a blockchain, albeit encrypted or hashed, is in line with the key data privacy principles such as purpose limitation and data minimization.

[1] Purpose Limitation

Article 5 section 1(b) of the GDPR states that personal data shall be collected for specific, explicit and legitimate purposes and not further processed in a manner that is incompatible with the given purposes. Any further processing shall not be permitted unless the data subject has consented to the new purpose. The reason for establishing this principle is to prevent the use of the personal data of individuals in a way or for further purposes that they might find unexpected, inappropriate, or otherwise objectionable.[114]

The former Article 29 Data Protection Working Party describes purpose limitation as the 'cornerstone of data protection' and points out that the principle is designed to offer a balanced approach: 'an approach that aims to reconcile the need for predictability and legal certainty regarding the purposes of the processing on the one hand and the pragmatic need for some flexibility on the other'.[115]

However, there are exceptions to this principle. For example, if the further processing is for archiving purposes in the public interest, for scientific or historical research, or for statistical purposes. According to Article 5 section 1(b) in conjunction with Article 89(1) of the GDPR, such further processing will not be considered '*incompatible*'. Besides, Recital 50 provides further clarity in examining whether the purpose of further processing is compatible with the initial purpose. It states that the data controller should consider: (i) any link between the purposes; (ii) the context in which the personal data is collected; and (iii) the reasonable expectations of the data subject based on the relationship between the parties; (iv) the nature of the personal

114. Article 29 Data Protection Working Party, *Opinion 03/2013 on purpose limitation* 11 (WP 203 Adopted on 2 Apr. 2013).
115. *Ibid.*

data; (v) the consequences of the further processing; and (vi) the existence of appropriate safeguards.

Article 5(1)(c) of the GDPR also requires that personal data must be *adequate, relevant* and *limited* to what is necessary in relation to the purposes for which the personal data is being processed. It should be noted that this is not an obligation to limit data processing to an absolute minimum but rather an obligation to minimize the data collection to an adequate level with regard to the given purpose of the processing operation.

Blockchain, by nature, continuously processes data once it is on the ledger. As a result, It is possible that keeping and storing personal data onto a blockchain post-completion of a particular transaction infringe the purpose limitation principle, bearing in mind that such data is now part of an immutable chain of blocks and remains there albeit not being used any more. The question arises whether the further processing of personal data after the execution and completion of a transaction or a customer complaint (e.g., reimbursement of flight delays) for which it has been initially added to the ledger can be deemed as being compliant with the purpose limitation principle. It may be argued that the personal data is not needed any more since the transaction or complaint has been completed or settled. Given the append-only nature of the DLT, data, in general, will permanently continue to be stored on the blockchain, even in such a case where, for example, a crypto asset transaction has been successfully executed, and the pertaining transactional data was turned into legacy data. As storing personal data is considered a processing operation, it can be argued that this would violate the principle of purpose limitation.

On the other hand, this view can be questioned. It should be taken into consideration that the storage of such data in subsequent transactions forms part of the original purpose of processing and, therefore, meets the purpose limitation principle. In a nutshell: as long as the purpose includes not only the initial transaction but also the subsequent data storage on a blockchain network, the replicated nature of these distributed databases and the continuous storage of data could be qualified to be in sync with the purpose limitation principle.

However, the purpose of the collection must be clearly and specifically identified; it must be detailed enough to determine what kind of processing activity is or is not included within the specified purpose and to allow compliance with the law can be assessed and data protection safeguards applied.[116] A broad and vague purpose description does violate the purpose limitation principle.[117]

This leads to the following legal question as to whether any lack of specification may be cured by a clear communication towards the data subjects that the controller is using the blockchain technology and that the processing of the related personal data is

116. *Ibid.*, at 15.
117. The CNIL imposed a fine on Google LLC amounting to about EUR 50 million on 21 Jan. 2019 for compliance violations under the GDPR. Among others, the CNIL found that Google did not provide users with information relating to the purpose of data processing. Google users had to give their consent in general, for all processing activities and purposes. That does not meet the requirement to gather specific consents in relation to individual processing activities. The purpose description needs to be specific aimed at obtaining valid consents of the users.

not limited to the original transaction, and the data will continue to be stored after the particular transaction has taken place. It goes without saying that those who act as controllers in a blockchain environment must clearly communicate to the related data subjects, at the time of collecting their personal data, how and for what purpose their data is being used, including how it may be processed in the future when new blocks are added.

However, such type of information does not substitute a concise purpose description and, more importantly, is not practically feasible.[118] As a result, storing personal data on the blockchain post-execution of the initial transaction does not stand up to scrutiny and infringes this principle. Transmitting personal data off-chain after the transaction has been completed and, hence, with no need to re-use the data going forward, is the only measure which complies with the principle of purpose limitation. The technical vehicle to implement this requirement in a blockchain network to comply with this principle alongside data subject right requests will be showcased in §4.05[C][3] in greater detail.

[2] Data Minimization

The principle of data minimization essentially means that only this data which is necessary to meet the purpose determined by the controller must be collected and processed. It partly overlaps with the principle of purpose limitation. Particularly, the data minimization principle requires to ensure that the period for which the personal information is being stored is limited to a strict minimum.[119] Two artefacts of a blockchain are clashing with the data minimization principle: First, the ever-growing nature of such databases as data can only be removed in extraordinary circumstances. Second, the data is replicated in a distributed network, where each node stores a full copy of the database. Strictly speaking, personal data is being replicated indefinitely, and the information transmitted through the blockchain is visible to every node, which could be argued to conflict with the principle of data minimization.

Recording transactional data off-chain while minimizing the data would help in this respect. This consideration will be subject to further evaluation in the following section.

[3] Evaluation in the Light of the Principles of Purpose Limitation and Data Minimization: Multi-layered Blockchains Versus Off-Chain Storage

Generally, it is legally possible to keep data on the blockchain indefinitely as long the data has been completely anonymized. Those data do not fall in the applicability of the GDPR. Vice versa, the personal data which is not needed any more, specifically in the

118. European Parliamentary Research Service, *supra* n. 32, at 66.
119. Recital 39 of the GDPR.

case of completion of the related transaction or matter, has to be segregated in order to meet both the data minimization principle and the purpose limitation principle.

The UK ICO has recognized that erasing data from digital systems is not always a straightforward matter. It has, therefore, proposed that putting personal data beyond use may be an alternative to achieve data minimization.[120] If there is no intention of the controller to access or use the data any more, then this may be held to be compliant.[121] Moreover, the ICO's statement clearly underlines what kind of security techniques should be taken into account when dealing with such sort of legacy personal data.

Whenever personal data is not needed any more because, for example, a certain matter (compensation request raised by a data subject) has been settled, such data will turn into legacy data. In the normal way of business, this data is archived in other files or systems. In a blockchain environment, the related data must anyhow be segregated in order to achieve GDPR-compliance.

One technique which could be leveraged to reach GDPR-compliance is the usage of multi-layered blockchains. That measure differs from the other instrument, namely, putting personal data off-chain. The multi-layered blockchain technique boils down to removing data from a private blockchain and transferring it to a public blockchain. Both blockchains are intertwined, and the public blockchain links to the private one.

Even though this mechanism facilitates the interoperability of blockchain technology, the problem remains unsolved in terms of the given principles. Even if the legacy data is being submitted to the public blockchain, it is fully replicated in the distributed network, and, albeit not in use and most likely encrypted, it is still stored there. With that in mind, the usage of multi-layered blockchains does not provide much added value and cannot resolve the GDPR-compliance issue in a satisfactory manner.

In contrast, the most common technique proposed for protecting personal data embedded in transactions is the 'hashing out' technique. It is achieved by storing hashes of data on-chain and keeping the actual (legacy) data off-chain by using a local database. This approach may eliminate several concerns raised by the distributed nature of public blockchains. It also allows to store more data on the blockchain as the size of hashes is much smaller than that of actual data.[122] Most importantly, this technique may also resolve the issue on compliance with the given data protection principles and the data subject right to erasure personal data.

The core concept boils down to keeping only a hash value or hash pointer onto the blockchain which links to the actual data stored in an off-chain database such as Excel or power point. This solution is recognized by several researchers and commentators as an effective privacy-enhancing technology that can lower the risk of liability for GDPR violations. This is true for the following reasons:

---

120. Information Commissioner's Office, *Deleting Personal Data* 4 (26 Feb. 2014), available at: https://ico.org.uk/media/fororganisations/documents/1475/deleting_personal_data.pdf (accessed 31 Aug. 2023).
121. *Ibid.*
122. Belen-Saglam, R., *A systematic literature review of the tension between GDPR and public blockchain systems*, Blockchain: Research and Applications 4 (2023)100129, at 11; available at: https://doi.org/10.1016/j.bcra.2023.100129 (accessed 31 Aug. 2023).

First, off-chain repositories are used to store actual personal data of users, whereas only a hash value remains on the blockchain, pointing to the storage location of the personal data outside the blockchain. In this way, once a data subject requests deletion of personal data, the personal data on the off-chain repository can be deleted, which renders the immutable hash value stored on the blockchain null and void, and thereby, the system becomes GDPR-compliant. By virtue of deleting the data in the off-chain repository, the hash value or hash pointer becomes a meaningless string of numbers.

Second, a cryptographic hash function is a one-way function which implies that it is not possible to recreate or reverse engineer the original file from the hash value (Chapter 1, §1.03[B][3]). Certainly, hashing is generally considered an encryption technique which cannot turn personal data into non-personal information. Notably, the hash value itself qualifies as personal data as it points to the actual data stored off-chain. However, once the actual off-chain data has been deleted, the hash pointer becomes a string of numbers and cannot be leveraged to trace back the actual data. As a result, a request to delete data raised by an individual will be met if the off-chain data is entirely deleted. Third, there are various variations of this concept which are discussed in the literature. One solution is to use a private key to be transmitted to the data subject to encrypt the hash value. Deleting the key is argued to amount to erasure for the purposes of the GDPR. Key destruction allows the service provider to erase the 'linkability' of the blockchain hash pointer to the data located in distributed off-chain repositories.[123] Unlike outright erasure, the encrypted hash values will still exist on-chain but can only be accessed by the data subject through the exclusive control of the private key. With a single point of storage, it is possible to delete the link between the blockchain and the data storage. Moreover, it is practically impossible to apply reverse engineering to restore data from the encrypted hash. It is only important to ensure that the key information required to link hashed data to off-chain data can be shared securely, and deletion can be done reliably.

Nevertheless, the downside is that hashing out results in storing personal data in a database which is under the control of an identifiable controller. This might be vetted as a circumvention of the decentralization concept inherent to blockchains. The main concern is that a certain degree of control on data remains in the hands of a single centralized party which would contradict the core idea of DLT and, hence, would be detrimental to trust and reliability.[124] The same concerns apply to similar techniques such as Chameleon hashing which allows a trusted authority to rectify, amend or overwrite the content of the blockchain. Chameleon-based hash functions include a trapdoor that can be used to alter a data item without changing the corresponding hash value.[125] This approach, however, requires the existence of a third party which is not in sync with the concept of decentralization. Moreover, old copies of blockchain blocks

123. Erbguth, J., *Five ways to GDPR-compliant use of blockchains*, Eur. Data Protect. Law Rev. 5 (3) (2019) 427-433, available at: https://doi.org/10.21552/edpl/2019/3/19 (accessed 31 Aug. 2023).

124. Ibáñez, et al., *supra* n. 86, at 8.

125. Belen-Saglam et al., *supra* n. 122, at. 13.

would still contain the redacted data which makes it highly questionable to consider this technique as GDPR-compliant.

The upside of hashing out is clearly that this technique facilitates compliance with both the principle of purpose limitation and data minimization. Another advantage of this approach is that the information on the blockchain can be used to validate data stored in local repositories, which helps ensure integrity.

In summary, the hashing mechanism is, from a legal point of view and for the time being, the best option for reaching GDPR-compliance with respect to the principles of data minimization and purpose limitation. Besides, taking data off-chain is described as a pruning technique which, once employed, meets the GDPR erasure requirements.[126]

[D] Recommendation for Security Measures in a Blockchain Environment

In the context of private blockchains, the CNIL recommends to:

- determine a minimum number of miners to avoid a coalition that could control over 50% of powers over the blockchain;
- implement organizational and technical measures to mitigate the impact of an algorithm failure on the security of the transactions. This should include a contingency plan to modify algorithms where vulnerability is detected;
- document the governance of changes to the software used to create transactions and to mine; technical and organizational procedures should be set out to ensure alignment between planned permissions and practical application; and
- ensure the confidentiality of the blockchain by implementing appropriate measures.[127]

With respect to public blockchain ecosystems, there are no recommendations of data protection authorities available to date. However, data protection authorities tend to take a broader view by asserting that an encryption technique using keys can be subject to decryption if those keys are obtained.

Furthermore, the so-called linking risk should be factored in when implementing security measures on a blockchain. Pseudonymized data may, with enough research and diligence, be linked to a specific individual and decrypted in that way. It is, therefore, essential that any business which stores personal data outside the blockchain environment has sufficient control and security measures in place to block any kind of linking attempts.

126. *Ibid.*; European Union Blockchain Observatory and Forum, *supra* n. 22, at 31.
127. CNIL, *supra* n. 7, at 10.

[E] Implications in the Case of Security Breaches

Article 33 section 1 of the GDPR states that 'in the case of a personal data breach, the controller shall without undue delay and, where feasible, not later than 72 hours after having become aware of it, notify the personal data breach to the supervisory authority (...)'.

From the practical point of view, the issue boils down to the question as to whether all controllers have to comply with this requirement set out in Article 33 section 1 of the GDPR, given that there are many of them, in particular in the context of public blockchains. In a private blockchain, as outlined under §4.03[B][8], the participants usually appoint a legal or natural person who makes decisions for the group. That person is acting as a controller and, hence, is capable of complying with the notification obligation according to the said provision. In a public blockchain ecosystem, it remains unclear whether all controllers or co-controllers are facing that obligation and, if so, how they can accomplish GDRP-compliance.

It is the view of the European Parliamentary Research Service that in the case a controller is not able to service any kind of data subject right requests, the controller would need to make sure that other participants acting as co-controllers shall respond to those requests accordingly.[128] Consequently, each controller would be obliged to ascertain that there are appropriate governance arrangements with other controllers in place with the purpose of initiating the notification vis-à-vis the competent supervisory authority in the case of a data breach event, such as attacks or scams.

As outlined above, the governance model necessitates the existence of an agreement or, at least, a consensus between individual blockchain participants which is practically not viable in a public blockchain network. The problem is aggravated since each controller who fails to implement the required security measures (Article 32 of the GDPR) and to comply with the seventy-two hours timeline (Article 33 of the GDPR) may be subject to draconic administrative fines up to EUR 10,000,000 or up to 2% of the total worldwide annual turnover of the preceding financial year, whichever is higher (Article 83 section 4 of the GDPR).

§4.06 DATA SUBJECT RIGHTS UNDER THE GDPR

[A] How Do Data Subject Rights Apply to the Blockchain?

Articles 15-22 of the GDPR set out a huge variety of specific rights for data subjects impacted by the processing of their personal data. If a block contains data of individuals albeit encrypted and the individual block is added to the blockchain as described in Chapter 1, §1.06, *supra*, the GDPR will kick in. The storage of personal data in a blockchain environment is considered a processing activity within the meaning of Article 4 section 2 of the GDPR. The question arises as to how these rights may be exercised against any controller. The controller is obliged to comply with the

128. European Parliamentary Research Service, *supra* n. 32, at 53.

rights provided to the data subjects. In theory, it looks very easy: For example, an individual has submitted his or her own personal data to a blockchain and requests information on the purpose of the data processing pursuant to Article 15 section 1a of the GDPR. Such request needs to be addressed vis-à-vis the controller. As outlined under §4.03[B], *supra*, it is not clear which actor qualifies as a controller and, as soon as one or, most likely, more controllers have been identified, whether they may be capable of complying with data subject rights which have been addressed to them (Article 12 section 2 of the GDPR).

In a private blockchain ecosystem, it is much easier for an individual person to identify one or more controllers against whom he or she may exercise the data privacy rights. In this context, the data subject typically needs to approach the governance body, which has been established to oversee the private (permissioned) network. The governance body can be a single controller, a joint controller, or a co-controller provided it has influence over the purpose and means of the data processing operations.[129]

Unlike private blockchains, it is much more difficult to identify one or more controllers in a public blockchain network and enforce any rights against them in accordance with Articles 15-22 of the GDPR. Data protection authorities have to cope with the same issue whenever they envisage to bring action against particular blockchain actors whom they consider controllers.

The problem is aggravated since some data subject rights under the GDPR appear to conflict with a fundamental feature of blockchains: Once a transaction has been recorded to a blockchain, it is not technically possible to alter or delete the entries. These rights which are, at first glance, not in line with blockchain peculiarities are the rights to access personal data, to rectify personal data respectively to have any errors amended and, in certain circumstances, to delete the data from the system. Other data subject rights do not essentially raise any specific problems in the context of blockchain technology. Indeed, one of the most discussed issues concerns the right to erase personal data. The potential need to identify and contact all necessary nodes with a request to delete or even to rectify personal data gives rise to practical obstacles. If a tamper-resistant database such as DLT was to be altered or modified, such changes would erode trust in blockchain technology. However, there are methods of complying with data subject rights without impinging the nature of a decentralized system which is showcased in this chapter.

[B] Right to Access Personal Data

The right to access personal data is a basic right in the European data protection law since it enables, and is often a prerequisite for, the exercise of any other data subject right under the regime of the GDPR. Accessing personal data will help better understand which data is being processed and for what purpose. It is the mandatory first step before executing other rights, such as the right of rectification or deletion.

129. Blockchain Bundesverband, *supra* n. 38, at 7.

The right to access personal data is set out in Article 15 of the GDPR which stipulates that the data subject shall have the right to obtain confirmation from the controller as to whether his or her data is being processed and, where that is the case, to access the personal data concerned.

The right to access personal data can be complied with in a private blockchain context where one or more controllers have been nominated and tasked with performing the obligations under the GDPR. In the case of a joint controllership, any requests for access can be addressed to any of the joint controllers according to Article 26 section 3 of the GDPR.

In a public blockchain, however, the hurdles of the blockchain technology become obvious: Controllers, once identified, are indeed unable to access data being registered to the blockchain as they typically see encrypted or hashed data only. Moreover, controllers may not be able to determine whether the related data is personal or not.

The European Parliamentary Research Service fosters the concept of establishing appropriate governance arrangements between blockchain users/controllers with the purpose of enabling the effective exercise of data subject rights.[130] The flipside is that the GDPR does not allow for putting such sort of arrangements in place in order to execute data subject rights. Neither does it provide room for interpretation in this regard. Irrespective of whether that approach is legally permissible, such governance arrangements are not viable from the practical point of view.

[C] Right to Rectification

The data subject shall have the right to request rectification of inaccurate information concerning him or her. Moreover, the data subject shall have the right to get incomplete personal data completed, factoring in the purposes of the processing (Article 16 of the GDPR).

The impossibility of altering data once submitted to the blockchain may also conflict with the right of rectification under Article 16 of the GDPR. It should be taken into account that blockchains are append-only ledgers which are intentionally created to make it impossible or, at least, extremely burdensome to modify or supplement the data being added to the blockchain. Such immutability is the backbone and the underlying concept of blockchain technology which aims at securing data integrity and trust in the network. By contrast, one of the fundamental principles of the GDPR is that personal data is subject to changes depending on the type of the related data subject right request.

The tension between the right of rectification and the features of blockchain technology makes it difficult or impossible for controllers to comply with requests to rectify personal data. Two aspects exacerbate that tension:

First, encrypted personal data of the requestor, the data subject concerned, is stored in a distributed network of multiple nodes or computers. The blockchain is

130. European Parliamentary Research Service, *supra* n. 32, at 72.

accessible to blockchain users. In public blockchains, everyone with an internet connection to the network has the same right to access and/or update the ledger according to the predefined consensus mechanism. Therefore, all transactions are transparent and visible to all blockchain users.[131] This implies that data submitted to a public blockchain network will evoke legal issues if such data is altered due to errors, inaccuracies or other problems in data entries without changing the consensus mechanism or making those changes transparent to all blockchain users (which is practically not feasible in a public blockchain ecosystem). That is currently one of the most disputed issues – a still unsolved trade-off between transparency on the one hand and privacy on the other hand.[132]

Second, in theory, after having received the request of rectification submitted by a data subject, the controller may copy and paste the correct personal data in a new block and rectify it therein. At first glance, you may consider this as an appropriate remediation operation. Nevertheless, it does not comply with the rectification request, bearing in mind that the preceding blocks still contain the incorrect personal data which remains unchanged. Creating a new block may lead to a secondary chain, resulting in a change of the official blockchain. The node will start selecting new candidate blocks from the memory pool to proceed from that new longest blockchain onwards which can effectively entail further problems as demonstrated in Chapter 1, §1.08[B], *supra*.

The European Commission considers the storage of confidential, sensitive or personal data off-chain or in other databases as a possible solution.[133] The rectified data being stored outside the blockchain would be linked to the blockchain through a hash reference and maintaining the previous records in the blocks unchanged. As outlined in §5.05[C][3], *supra*, hashing out is the state-of-the-art mechanism to comply with that type of request.

[D] Right to Erasure

[1] What Does Erasure Mean?

The right to erase personal data is better known as the right to be forgotten. Essentially, the data subject may demand the erasure of his or her personal data under certain circumstances as laid out in Article 17 of the GDPR. This right provides the data subject with a tool to exercise full control over the personal data provided that one of the grounds listed in Article 17 section 1 of the GDPR applies. This right is multi-faceted and was subject to various judicial reviews.

The CJEU held that the operator of a search engine (Google) has the responsibility to ensure the privacy rights of individuals. Consequently, the GDPR applies to search engine operators rendering them capable of complying with requests of individuals

131. European Commission, *Blockchain Now and Tomorrow*, 17 (July 2019).
132. Finck, *supra* n. 31, at 29.
133. European Commission, *supra* n. 131, at 17.

who request to remove the link in the search results to the page containing sensitive personal information.[134] This implies that the search engine is effectively conducting a data processing activity, which is subject to special restrictions and obligations. With that in mind, the search engine operator needs to gauge whether the individual has a right to request that the information in question is no longer associated with his or her name in the search results. There is a tendency in the jurisdiction of the CJEU to foster the right to erase personal data in social media. As a result, a blockchain user may, under certain circumstances, be considered a controller and, hence, be the addressee of such deletion requests.

It should be noted that erasure is a legal term which gives room for various and contradicting interpretations. While the former Article 29 Data Protection Working Party stated that the destruction of hardware could arguably qualify as erasure in the meaning of Article 17 of the GDPR,[135] some data protection authorities argued that instances where data is being put beyond use can also be an appropriate method for erasure.[136] It is clear that erasure does not automatically mean to expunge or delete personal data, including the corresponding back-up systems. The former Article 29 Data Protection Working Party ruled that other methods may also be considered equivalent in terms of getting the data erased, e.g., overwriting of data.[137]

On the other hand, Article 35 section 1 of the German Data Protection Act (Bundesdatenschutzgesetz as of 30 June 2017, BGBl. I S. 2097) provides that the data subject has no right to erasure if the data processing is not automated, and the specific type of data storage makes the erasure impossible. That provision refers to Article 17 of the GDPR and clearly demonstrates that the GDPR offers, to a certain extent, flexibility when it comes to adopting the right to erasure to the features and possibilities of new technologies which factually restrict the deletion of personal data being submitted to the related application.

[2] At a Glance: The Techniques to Erase Data

A couple of alternative techniques to delete data in a blockchain network are currently under scrutiny. One technique boils down to destructing the private key. The CNIL supports this solution and points out that where the private key is deleted together with information from other systems, erasure and compliance with Article 17 of the GDPR may be achieved.[138]

Notably, the controller can make personal data practically inaccessible by virtue of deleting the hash function's secret (private) key. Proving or verifying which information has been hashed would no longer be possible. In practice, the hash would

134. CJEU 24.09.2019, C-507/17 and C-136/17.
135. Article 29 Data Protection Working Party, *supra* n. 105, at 12.
136. UK ICO, *supra* n. 120, at 4.
137. Article 29 Data Protection Working Party, *supra* n. 105, at 12; the Austrian data protection authority (DPA 5.12.2018, DSB-D123.270/009-DPO/2018) ruled that erasure does not necessarily require the final destruction of the data, and a possible measure of erasure could also be the removal of the personal reference, i.e., anonymization.
138. CNIL, *supra* n. 7, at 8.

not pose a confidentiality risk. According to the CNIL, it is necessary that the information also needs to be deleted in other systems where it has been stored for processing such as other blockchains or even off-chain databases.

Strictly speaking, this solution may be challenged in terms of achieving GDPR-compliance since the related data would still exist in a hashed format onto the blockchain, albeit inaccessible, given that the private key has been erased. However, this technique does not entail erasure in the legal sense.[139]

A similar solution focuses on off-chain, external databases containing personal data in the clear which link to encrypted or hashed data onto the blockchain. Deleting the data on those external databases complies with the right of erasure. The rationale behind this is that, even though the corresponding encrypted data or the hash value remains on the blockchain network since it has nothing to relate to, then it will become a random string of numbers with no meaning. When hashed data remains available on a blockchain, but the corresponding un-hashed data is ultimately deleted off-chain, there is the view that this would meet the right to erasure.

As outlined in §4.05[C][3], *supra* and in accordance with the Blockchain Observatory and Forum, enterprises which envisage establishing blockchain platforms for operating their businesses are well advised to put personal data off-chain for erasure upon request of the data subject concerned.[140] Once successfully employed, this mechanism allows for a maximum of GDPR-compliance with regard to this right.

As long as personal data is stored on-chain, it must be factored in that, from a legal point of view, effective compliance with Article 17 of the GDPR can only be achieved if the personal data in question is erased from all the nodes that participate in the network.[141] This implies that where a data subject addresses a request for erasure vis-à-vis a controller, the controller must not only remove the related personal data from its own server but also from other servers managed by other controllers and processors that also store personal data. It may be argued that, in accordance with Article 17 section 2 of the GDPR, the controller is obliged to incentive other controllers to undertake erasure of personal data. However, the model of establishing a sort of governance between blockchain participants is, practically speaking, not feasible, given the multiple nodes in a public blockchain environment which are typically spread over the whole globe. Overall, the difficulty or impossibility of addressing all the full nodes of the network to make necessary updates imposes an insurmountable barrier for exercising any rights, particularly the right to erasure. In this sense, even if it is possible for a data subject to identify all the nodes or to identify enough nodes (over 50%) to rectify their personal data, coordination among them would be extremely difficult to ensure.

Further, deletion of on-chain personal data can be accomplished by installing a system in which encrypted databases are replicated in nodes, which a hash of each

139. *Ibid.*, at 9.
140. European Union Blockchain Observatory and Forum, *supra* n. 22, at 31; Timmons, J. & Hickman, T., *Blockchain and the GDPR: Co-existing in Contradiction* 211 (Blockchain & Cryptocurrency Regulation, Global Legal Insights, 2020).
141. European Parliamentary Research Service, *supra* n. 32, at 77.

entry stored on a blockchain that can verify the accuracy and creation date for each entry. There could be a process through which the use of corresponding private keys or authorization codes could delete a database entry in every node that hosts the database. To the extent this is all code driven, it may be argued that it is computationally feasible, even though the nodes may be geographically dispersed. The only way a node could elect not to honour a deletion code or 'kill command' would be to stop participating in the pertaining blockchain protocol.

[3] Public Keys/Identifiers

There is another aspect which is worthwhile to consider in the context of deleting personal data in a blockchain setting. That issue may be better illustrated by using the Bitcoin example: In the Bitcoin transactional system, users are represented by individual addresses, the so-called identifiers. You may compare identifiers with a bank account number.

Identifiers are created by using public key cryptography.[142] Each identifier comprises a series of alphanumeric characters which constitute the public key to the participant's account. This public key is linked to a private key, known only by the related participant.[143] Only the public key is visible for blockchain participants, whereas the private key is never disclosed. Both public and private key are tied up via cryptographic means. Public keys cannot qualify as anonymous data according to the GDPR.[144] The prerequisite for switching personal data into non-personal respectively anonymous data is that identification must be irreversibly prevented, and any reverse engineering to the original personal data cannot take place.[145] Practice, however, reveals that this cannot be the case in relation to public keys. They are considered pseudonymous and, hence, personal data.

For example, with Bitcoin, Ethereum and some of their derivative digital assets, blockchain analytics companies can accurately attribute many public keys to entities such as exchanges, dark web markets or gambling sites. The greater the number of transactions and the larger the number of counterparties, the more likely it is that a blockchain analyst may be able to link a pseudonymous public key with a person's real identity. Every form of extensive activity is prone to re-identification. Researchers and law enforcement agencies have already been able to re-identify bitcoin activity through the application of transactional graph analysis to identify bitcoin merchants and customers. In fact, they have applied similar methodologies to smart contract operations as well.

Many blockchains have identifiers that are typically visible, given that this is crucial for their proper functioning. Nevertheless, there are other initiates going on, e.g., privacy coins, which purport to obscure the sender and recipient public keys in a transaction. However, for those blockchains that rely on public keys, this set of data

142. European Commission, *supra* n. 131, at 20.
143. Section §4.02[A][1], *supra*.
144. Finck, *supra* n. 108, at 96.
145. Section §4.02[A][1], *supra*.

can never be deleted as it is contained in each block, which cannot be changed. Therefore, the identifier cannot be effectively erased from the blockchain.[146] Unlike transactional data, public keys cannot be moved off-chain for deletion purposes as outlined above.[147]

The issue of erasure is certainly the most controversial topic discussed in the blockchain community and should be evaluated by the EDPB. The CNIL made a proposal even though it remains unclear how commercially viable this approach might be, but it does provide some hints as to how the regulators attempt to tackle this issue.

§4.07 ACCOUNTABILITY PRINCIPLES UNDER THE GDPR

Organizations are subject to enhanced accountability principles under the GDPR, including requirements such as: (i) conduct data protection impact assessments; (ii) implement data protection by design and by default; (iii) maintain a detailed record of their processing activities; and (iv) appoint a Data Protection Officer (DPO), where required. The specific requirements imposed by the GDPR depend on whether an organization is defined as a controller or a processor. Processors now have specific statutory obligations under the GDPR, such as notifying controllers about personal data breaches without undue delay. The GDPR further includes joint and several liabilities for controllers and processors to compensate affected individuals.

Article 24 of the GDPR broadly addresses the concept of accountability in its requirement for controllers to 'implement appropriate technical and organizational measures to ensure and to be able to demonstrate that processing is performed in accordance with [the GDPR]'.[148]

The concept of accountability is at the core of the GDPR and should, according to the former Article 29 Data Protection Working Party, 'contribute to moving data protection from "theory to practice" along with helping [DPAs] in their supervision and enforcement tasks'.[149]

The European Data Protection Supervisor further defined the principle of accountability as the requirement for controllers to 'put in place internal mechanisms and control systems that ensure compliance and provide evidence - including internal policies and audit reports - to demonstrate compliance to external stakeholders, including supervisory authorities'.[150]

146. CNIL, *supra* n. 7, at 6 stating that the identifiers are always visible and cannot be further minimized as they are essential for its proper functioning.
147. Finck, *supra* n. 108, at 97.
148. Article 24 of the GDPR.
149. Article 29 Data Protection Working Party, *Opinion 03/2010 on the principle of accountability* 2 (WP 173 00062/10/EN, adopted on 13 Jul. 2010).
150. European Data Protection Supervisor, Giovanni Buttarelli, Value of the EU Data Protection Reform against the Big Data challenges, Keynote address, Berlin, 4 May 2015, available at: https://secure.edps.europa.eu/EDPSWEB/webdav/site/mySite/shared/Documents/EDPS/Publications/Speeches/2015/15_05_04_Speech_EDPD_Berlin_EN.pdf (accessed 30 Sep. 2023).

Essentially, the GDPR requires the integration of data protection in business operations. Under the GDPR, controllers and processors need to focus on implementing practical measures and refrain from adopting a tick-box approach to data privacy compliance.

Current blockchain protocols involve continuous duplications of a full copy of the ledger at each validating node, which may make it difficult or impossible to comply with some of the data protection principles laid out in Article 5 of the GDPR. Therefore, organizations using blockchain technology have to make sure they fully understand the requirements under the GDPR and the Article 5 principles described below.

[A] Lawfulness, Fairness and Transparency

Article 5(1)(a) of the GDPR requires that personal data is processed lawfully, fairly, and in a transparent manner. Although neither 'fairly' nor 'lawfully' are defined in the GDPR, both terms have a broad application in practice.

The standard of fairness is an objective standard, so due regard should be given as to how individuals, in general, might reasonably expect their data to be obtained and subsequently processed and whether individuals would consider the systems and processes that are used fair and appropriate.

Recital 39 of the GDPR does, however, provide guidance in relation to the concept of 'transparency' and states that 'any information and communication relating to the processing of ... personal data be easily accessible and easy to understand, and that clear and plain language be used'.[151] It should be noted that there is no requirement to inform data subjects of the specific technology (e.g., blockchain) used to process personal data.

A core component of assessing the transparency of a data processing operation is whether or not there is a legitimate ground for the collection and use of personal data. The method used to obtain and process personal data will determine whether the processing is fair and lawful. Individuals should not be misled or deceived when providing their personal data, nor should the data be used in ways that might have unjustified adverse effects.

In particular, to process personal data lawfully, the processing must be based on one or more conditions laid down in Articles 6 and 9 of the GDPR (*see* §4.04, *supra*).[152]

151. Recital 39 of the GDPR.
152. The Art. 6 conditions include: (i) the data subject having unambiguously given his consent to the processing of his personal data for one or more specific purpose; (ii) the processing is necessary for the performance of a contract to which the data subject is a party or in order to take steps at the request of the data subject prior to entering into a contract; (iii) the processing is necessary for compliance with a legal obligation to which the controller is subject; (iv) the processing is necessary to protect the vital interests of the data subject or of another natural person; (v) the processing is necessary for the performance of a task carried out in the public interest; or (vi) the processing is necessary for the purposes of the legitimate interests pursued by the controller or by a third party to whom the data is disclosed, except where the processing is unwarranted in any particular case by reason of prejudice to the rights and freedoms or legitimate interests of the data subject, in particular where the data subject is a child.

In practice, a controller should assess the legal ground for processing various types of personal data and regularly update all its data protection notices, consents, and policies.

The concept of transparency can be quite challenging to comply with in a blockchain ecosystem. The European Parliamentary Research Service notes that in certain blockchain use cases (e.g., private blockchain), enabling such transparency is still achievable.[153] However, it goes without saying that, in the case any channels of communication between controllers and data subjects are missing, the transparency requirements will be hard to achieve.[154]

[B] Purpose Limitation, Data Minimization and Storage Limitation

The principles of purpose limitation and data minimization and their implications on the processing of personal data in a blockchain network have been analysed in §4.05[C], *supra* in greater detail.

Another principle of the GDPR is the storage limitation principle set out in Article 5(1)(e) of the GDPR which provides that personal data must be kept in a form that permits identification of data subjects for no longer than is necessary for the purposes for which it was processed. Recital 39 of the GDPR requires that the storage of personal data must be 'limited to a strict minimum'.[155] It further obliges the controller to establish certain time limits for erasure of personal data being stored onto an application.

Just like the principle of data minimization, complying with the storage limitation principle may be more challenging in a blockchain setting since it is virtually impossible to remove information from the blockchain. Even worse, blockchain users are most likely not aware of what type of personal data is available onto the blockchain.

However, as with the principle of purpose limitation, there is an exception that permits organizations to store data for longer periods than is necessary, i.e., archiving

---

The Art. 9 conditions include: (i) the data subject having given explicit consent; (ii) the processing being necessary for the purposes of carrying out the obligations and specific rights of the controller in the field of employment law in so far as it is authorized by national law providing for adequate safeguards; (iii) the processing being necessary to protect the vital interests of the data subject or of another person where the data subject is physically or legally incapable of giving consent; (iv) the processing being carried out by a non-profit-seeking body with a specific aim and does not involve the disclosure of data to a third party without the data subject's consent; (v) the data subject having deliberately made the information public; (vi) the processing being necessary for establishing, exercising, or defending legal claims; (vii) the processing being necessary for reasons of substantial public interest on the basis of EU or national Member State law; (viii) the processing (by a person subject to the obligation of professional secrecy) being necessary for the purposes of preventative or occupational medicine, for the assessment of the working capacity of the employee, medical diagnosis, the provision or management of health or social care systems. and services pursuant to a contract with a healthcare professional; (ix) the processing being necessary for reasons of public interest; or (x) the processing being necessary for archiving purposes in the public interest or for scientific or historical research purposes, or statistical purposes.

153. European Parliamentary Research Service, *supra* n. 32, at 65.
154. *Ibid.*
155. Recital 39 of the GDPR.

in the public interest, scientific and historical research, or statistical purposes.[156] Overall, putting personal data off-chain provides a proper remediation measure aimed at complying with the storage limitation principle.

[C] Use of Data Privacy Impact Assessment

Article 35(1) of the GDPR sets out the requirement for a data controller to carry out a data protection impact assessment (DPIA) ahead of the processing operation in the case the processing embeds new technologies and is likely to result in a high risk to the rights and freedoms of the data subject. Article 35(3) of the GDPR states that a DPIA must be carried out in the following scenarios:

- where there is a systematic, extensive evaluation of personal aspects, including profiling; or
- large-scale processing of sensitive personal data; or
- systematic monitoring of a publicly accessible area on a large scale (such as CCTV and other public monitoring).

In addition, organizations acting as controllers must perform a DPIA when:

- using new technologies; and
- the processing is likely to result in a high risk to the rights and freedoms of data subjects.

In essence, a DPIA needs to strike a balance between the interests of the data controller and the interests of individuals. The related interests must be evaluated and weighted. Article 35(7) of the GDPR states that such assessment should contain as a minimum:

- a description of the processing operations and the purposes, including, where applicable, the legitimate interests pursued by the controller;
- an assessment of the necessity and proportionality of the processing in relation to the purpose;
- an assessment of the risks to data subjects; and
- the measures, particularly security, to address the risks to the individuals.

In a blockchain setting, a DPIA is likely to be required in the case of a blockchain use case designed to process personal data. In particular, where the processing of personal data is the purpose of the blockchain use case, protecting personal data must be built in the system from the outset aiming to ensure it does not pose a risk to the rights and freedoms of data subjects.

It is worth noting that the use of new technologies is considered high risk and, thus, triggers a DPIA. Consequently, the UK ICO states that a DPIA must be carried out

156. Article 5(1)(e) of the GDPR.

whenever a new technology is being used.[157] It goes without saying that blockchain technology should be considered a new technology, and, hence, a DPIA must be carried out.

Making use of blockchain technology can have a significant impact on the rights of individuals regarding the processing of their personal data which is stored in a blockchain application. If transactional personal data is registered there, albeit encrypted or hashed, the controller or user will need to perform a DPIA due to the inherent risk to the rights and freedoms of affected data subjects. This applies to all events where the blockchain technology has been implemented with the purpose of processing personal data even if the data is stored off-chain and merely linked to the blockchain through a hash pointer. As outlined, on-chain hashes of off-chain personal data would still qualify as personal data. Even if a DPIA is legally not strictly required, i.e., because there is no likelihood to result in a high-risk exposure to the rights and freedoms of natural persons, organizations are well advised to conduct a DPIA which helps identify and minimize any kind of data privacy risk. The idea of carrying out a DPIA is not to eliminate all data privacy risks inherent to the related blockchain use case. The DPIA is a tool which aims to assist organizations in identifying and minimizing privacy risks, and in determining whether that level of risk identified is acceptable in relation to the benefits of what the organization is striving to achieve. In any case, controllers should document the results of their assessment diligently to demonstrate compliance with Article 35(1) of the GDPR.

[D] Data Protection by Design and Default

The GDPR requires controllers to establish appropriate technical and organizational measures to implement data protection principles and to protect individual rights. This concept is often referred to as 'privacy by design' and is based on Article 25 of the GDPR. Controllers must give thoughts on the appropriateness of the chosen technology prior to implementing a specific processing activity, and they have to choose a format of that technology with the least impact on an individual's rights and freedoms. Recital 78 of the GDPR states:

> When developing, designing, selecting and using applications, services and products that are based on the processing of personal data or process personal data to fulfil their task, producers of the products, services and applications should be encouraged to take into account the right to data protection (…) and, with regard to the state of the art, to make sure that controllers and processors are able to fulfil their data protection obligations.

In November 2019, the European Data Protection Supervisor issued a set of guidelines for public consultation on privacy by design and default pursuant to the GDPR.[158]

---

157. https://ico.org.uk/for-organisations/guide-to-the-general-data-protection-regulation-gdpr/accountability-and-governance/data-protection-impact-assessments/ (accessed 30 Oct. 2023).
158. EDPB Plenary Meeting November 2019, *Guidelines 4/2019 on Article 25 Data Protection by Design and by Default* (Adopted on 13 Nov. 2019).

It is pivotal to bake in privacy considerations from the outset.

Accordingly, the controller needs to implement measures which can include, *inter alia*, the minimization of data to be processed, pseudonymization of data as soon as possible and the improvement of security features.[159] This includes the consideration as to whether personal data should be submitted to the blockchain at all rather than storing it off-chain or anywhere else. Controllers should give thought as to whether it is inevitable to register personal data on the blockchain. Clearly, it is the preferable solution to keep personal data outside the blockchain ecosystem. In this context, the CNIL recommends that whenever it is mandatory to store personal data on a blockchain, the controller should register the data in the form of a hash generated using a hash function with a key, or, at least, in the form of encryption aimed at ensuring the maximum degree of confidentiality.[160]

However, there are multiple use cases which necessitate the storage of personal data on a blockchain. For instance, in the healthcare sector, doctors, patients, hospitals and other healthcare providers could store electronic health records in blockchain-based decentralized management systems in which they can encrypt personal data and/or sensitive information and grant access to records only to authorized parties via appropriate credentials.[161] The capacity to record and authenticate medical data and customize its use for other parties can leverage the information and economic value of such data. It could stimulate new business models in the health sector, i.e., personalized medicine; data sharing for drug, treatment and public health research; or selling and buying medical data for any number of stakeholders. Further, smart contracts can be used for clinical-trial phase control, whereby patients need to consent explicitly for data analysis purposes. Patients could implement dynamic consents through smart contracts, by defining data access rights stating, for example, the type of data to be disclosed, intended uses, authorized third parties or storage limitations. Under these conditions, they could easily share their sensitive records and, among others, ask different doctors for second opinions, etc. Even in the medical sector, data privacy and security are major concerns, so any blockchain-driven solutions must put in place strong privacy mechanisms by default and in compliance with data privacy regulations, e.g., the GDPR.[162] Any security measures must be state-of-the-art[163] and encompass encryption techniques.

Some blockchain developers have tried adding additional layers of privacy to design around the availability of participant and transaction information on the blockchain via 'privacy coins'. For example, Zcash uses a 'zero-knowledge proof algorithm' to verify the transaction without the need to disclose the identity of blockchain participants or the amount of each transaction. Monero is another example

159. Recital 78 of the GDPR.
160. CNIL, *supra* n. 7, at 6.
161. Ekblaw, A. et al., *A Case Study for Blockchain in Healthcare: 'MedRec' Prototype for Electronic Health Records and Medical Research Data* (IEEE Technology and Society Magazine, 2016).
162. European Commission, *supra* n. 131, at 83.
163. EDPB Plenary Meeting November 2019, *supra* n. 158, at 7, 8.

of a blockchain-based network that obfuscates digital currency data, including transaction sources and amounts, by using advanced cryptography, transaction-specific, one-time addresses, and obfuscated signatures. While these approaches can help prevent re-identification, masking network participants makes it more difficult for legitimate businesses to perform Anti-Money Laundering measures to identify illegal transactions.

If (i) it is not possible to put personal data off-chain, (ii) on-chain storage is justified by the purpose of the individual processing operation, and (iii) a privacy impact assessment has proven that the residual risks are acceptable, personal data can be stored on a blockchain network. This necessitates that all appropriate security measures need to be built in, whereby it should be factored in that, as a rule of thumb, a public blockchain has a higher risk exposure in terms of the privacy rights than a private blockchain.

Nevertheless, when implementing technical and organizational measures, blockchain developers must account for the data protection by design and default (DPDD) principle from the outset, irrespective of which kind of blockchain is used.[164] This requires to minimize the processing of personal data, restrict the processing to the given purpose and encrypt personal data in the earliest phase. This also affects the volume of personal data being processed and the period where the data is stored and made accessible.[165]

It is apparent that the GDPR was framed for centralized models of data collection, storage and processing. The blockchain technology, however, is a stumbling block for the enforcement of fundamental privacy rights. It should be noted that some national governments have vetted blockchain technology whether it stands up to scrutiny from the national and European law perspectives.[166]

[E] Record of Processing Activities

The GDPR requires data controllers and data processors to maintain records of their processing activities to help demonstrate compliance with the GDPR (Article 30(1) of the GDPR). These records must include among others:

- the name and contact details of the data controller;
- the purposes of the processing; and
- a description of the categories of data subjects and of categories of personal data.

164. German Government, *Blockchain-Strategie der Bundesregierung* 13 (2019), available at: https://www.bmwi.de/Redaktion/DE/Publikationen/Digitale-Welt/blockchain-strategie.pdf?__blob=publicationFile&v=10 (accessed 31 Aug. 2023).
165. Article 25(2) of the GDPR.
166. For example, the government in the Netherlands has been weighting the pros and cons of the blockchain technology, available at: https://www.lexology.com/library/detail.aspx?g=a8cd5d22-c729-4a5d-a393 (accessed 31 Aug. 2023).

The GDPR requires that records must be held in writing which also encompasses electronic forms and that they must be made available upon request.[167] The obligation to keep records of processing activities does not apply to organizations with fewer than 250 employees unless:

- the processing is likely to result in a risk to the rights and freedoms of data subjects;
- the processing is not occasional; or
- the processing includes special categories of data referred to in Article 9(1) of the GDPR or criminal convictions data in Article 10 of the GDPR.

With blockchain, categorizing data subjects and personal data can be challenging since the controller may not know with certainty what sort of data is stored on the blockchain.

[F] Appointment of a DPO

Another key concept of accountability is the appointment of data protection officers (DPOs). Article 37 of the GDPR requires that data controllers and data processors (where their respective data processing activities fall within specific criteria set out below) appoint a DPO for their organization. It also sets out what that role encompasses and creates employment protection for actions taken in the role as DPO. Article 38(1) of the GDPR requires that the DPO needs to be 'involved, properly and in a timely manner, in all issues which relate to the protection of personal data'.

Irrespective of whether the DPO is an employee of the respective legal entity, the DPO must be able to perform the duties in an independent manner.

The DPO's role includes understanding and upholding data subjects' rights, implementing data protection by design and by default, maintaining and updating records of processing activities, understanding and championing security of the processing of personal data and notification, management and communication of security breaches to the supervisory authority.

Article 37(1) of the GDPR states that a data controller or a data processor shall be required to appoint a DPO in any case where:

- they are public authorities;
- the core activities of the controller or the processor consist of processing operations which require regular and systemic monitoring of data subjects on a large scale; or
- the core activities of the controller or processor consist of a large scale of special categories of data (i.e., sensitive personal data) and personal data relating to criminal convictions and offences.

167. Article 30(3) and (4) of the GDPR.

The above requirements apply to entities operating in the blockchain space, provided that they are operating with the data of individuals.

§4.08 INTERNATIONAL DATA TRANSFERS ON A BLOCKCHAIN UNDER THE GDPR

Under the GDPR, there is a general prohibition against transferring personal data of data subjects to countries outside of the EEA (otherwise known as third countries) that are not considered by the European Commission to offer an 'adequate protection' of personal data unless appropriate safeguards have been adopted to legitimize the transfer of personal data to third countries.

The GDPR provides that an international transfer may take place where the European Commission has decided that the third country in question ensures an adequate level of protection. A finding of adequacy can also be made under the GDPR in respect of a territory or processing sector within a third country or an international organization (e.g., the financial sector). Countries currently deemed adequate by the Commission are Andorra, Argentina, Canada (commercial organizations), Faroe Islands, Guernsey, Israel, the Isle of Man, Japan, Jersey, New Zealand, Switzerland, the Republic of Korea, the United Kingdom, the United States (in respect of commercial organizations participating in and being certified to the EU-US Data Privacy Framework) and Uruguay.[168]

The main safeguards include:

(1) *Consent* – International transfers from the EEA are technically allowed with the consent of the data subject concerned. However, it may be difficult for companies to obtain valid consent (because the requirements for valid consent are onerous as discussed in §4.04[B]) and where, for example, the personal data is received from a third party and not directly from the data subject. Therefore, other exemptions should be considered for systematic international transfers of personal data.

(2) *Model Contracts* – otherwise known as Standard Contractual Clauses (SCC), model contracts are effectively a European standard form of data transfer agreements and were an existing transfer mechanism under the Directive and remain available under GDPR. Model Contracts allow for data exports from the EEA because the data importer and data exporter agree in the Model Contract to be bound by rigorous contractual obligations and EU data protection laws to protect the exported Personal Data. There are four modules of Model Contracts available, and the parties may select them depending on the data transfer scenario concerned.

168. European Commission, Adequacy of the protection of personal data in non-EU countries, available at: https://ec.europa.eu/info/law/law-topic/data-protection/data-transfers-outside-eu/adequacy-protection-personal-data-non-eu-countries_en (accessed 31 Aug. 2023).

(3) *EU-US Data Privacy Framework* – which is the legal successor of the Privacy Shield. The EU-US Data Privacy Framework (DPF) permits entities in the EU to transfer Personal Data to certifying US organizations. By way of background, on 10 July 2023, the European Commission adopted its *adequacy decision* for the DPF. This decision means that the European Commission has concluded that the DPF offers protection for personal data transferred under it to the US that is essentially equivalent to the protection guaranteed by the GDPR. However, only transfers to US organizations that have self-certified their participation in the DPF will be covered by the adequacy decision. In practical terms, it means that data exporters subject to the GDPR transferring data to certified US organizations do not have to rely on an alternative transfer mechanism, such as standard contractual clauses (SCC). US companies that are eligible to the DPF (see below) will be able to join the DPF by committing to adhere to a detailed set of privacy obligations which apply immediately on self-certification.

Certification will follow along similar lines to the DPF's predecessor, the Privacy Shield. Only US companies subject to the enforcement powers of the US Federal Trade Commission or Department of Transportation (controllers or processors) will be eligible, whereas depositary institutions (such as banks), insurers and telcos are among those organizations which will not be able to rely on the DPF. The UK has also adopted the DPF, so data transfers from UK to US companies which participate in the DPF are legitimate and do not require alternative transfer mechanisms such as the SCC. The UK has also published its own form of the SCCs, known as the International Data Transfer Agreement, and an International Data Transfer Addendum to be used when using the SCCs.

(4) *Binding Corporate Rules* (BCRs) – BCRs are given statutory recognition by the GDPR as an appropriate safeguard for transfers of personal data for the EEA. BCRs are effectively a global code of practice and program based on European data protection standards that, once approved by a competent European data protection authority, allow an international organization to transfer personal data to its other group companies in third countries, such as parents and affiliates under common control.

When transferring personal data from the EU to third countries, data exporters also need to carry out a transfer impact assessment (TIA). A TIA, among other things, assesses laws governing access to personal data in the recipient country and considers whether supplementary measures that provide privacy protections additional to those provided under SCCs will need to be implemented to ensure an 'essentially equivalent' level of data protection to that afforded in the EEA. The European Commission's adequacy decision in relation to the DPF, referred to above, will assist data exporters when transferring personal data to the US using other data transfer mechanisms such as SCCs and BCRs. The UK Information Commissioner's Office has also published its version of the TIA and guidance on international transfers, although entities may choose to adopt either the EU- or UK-style TIA.

The international data transfer restrictions in the GDPR apply the same way to blockchain networks. These restrictions are important for blockchain technology since nodes will likely be situated in jurisdictions outside the EU, and, in the case of public blockchains, it is virtually impossible to have an eye on the location of every node. The French DPA, CNIL, warns in its blockchain guidance that using blockchain for cross-border data transfers 'can be particularly problematic, especially in the case of public blockchains'.[169]

One potential solution to resolve this complication would be for blockchain network users to create and agree to a contractually binding governance framework incorporating SCC at the time the blockchain network is created. By including SCC in the governance framework, such clauses would become part of a multilateral agreement between the members of the blockchain. This approach was endorsed by the former Article 29 Data Protection Working Party as a valid means of complying with restrictions on international data transfers.[170]

§4.09 OUTLOOK

It will be interesting to see the position of other DPAs and the EDPB as opportunities of blockchain technology evolve. One of the most pressing questions is how the lack of control over personal data stored on a blockchain can be reconciled with the GDPR and its core principles. In the absence of more detailed guidance issued by the European DPAs, it is advisable to adhere to the rule-of-thumb principles which have been published by the Blockchain Observatory and Forum.[171] In essence, those principles are, in the order showcased on the below:

- start with the big picture: How is user value created and how is data used and do you really need blockchain;
- store personal data off-chain or, if the blockchain cannot be avoided, prefer the private blockchain networks;
- make full use of data hashing, obfuscation, encryption and aggregation techniques in order to safeguard personal data;
- anonymize or, at least, pseudonymize personal data;
- consider personal data carefully when connecting private blockchain with public ones.

In addition, it is key to stick to the basic security requirements which have been fleshed out in the CNIL recommendations, particularly with regard to technical and

169. CNIL, *supra* n. 7, at 2.
170. Article 29 Working Party, Letter to ESMA (14 Jun. 2017), available at: http://ec.europa.eu/newsroom/document.cfm?doc_id=45447 (accessed 3 Aug. 2023).
171. European Union Blockchain Observatory and Forum, *supra* n. 22, at 28-30.

organizational measures aimed at limiting the impact of potential algorithm failure on the security of transactions.

Finally, with private blockchains, it is possible that some of the data protection issues can be satisfactorily addressed, e.g., by suitable contractual arrangements or by installing a 'blockchain gatekeeper', which may, under certain circumstances, be classified as the single data controller.

§4.10 BLOCKCHAIN AND US PRIVACY LAW

While EU data protection laws restrict and regulate all processing of personal data (as discussed in the immediately preceding sections §4.02–§4.09, *supra*), US data privacy laws seek to apply only proportionately designed sector-, harm- and situation-specific requirements to safeguard individual privacy against concrete harms. US privacy laws are technology-neutral and do not affect blockchain or DLT adversely or specifically. Companies have to consider hundreds of federal and state privacy laws to determine which requirements apply to particular blockchain use cases. This §4.10, *infra* provides [A] an overview regarding US privacy law with a comparative perspective in reference to EU data protection regulation, [B] an introduction to federal versus state privacy laws, [C] guidance regarding terminology, [D] a summary assessment of the effects of general and specific privacy laws on blockchain and distributed ledger use cases, and (E) a deeper dive into the effects of the California Consumer Privacy Act (CCPA) on blockchain deployment.

[A] US Privacy Law Versus EU Data Protection Regulation

The terms 'data privacy' and 'data protection' are often used interchangeably, in particular in the context of comparisons of Anglo-Saxon data privacy laws and continental European data protection laws. Actually, the two terms and legislative concepts have quite different origins and purposes.[172]

EU data protection regulations are about protecting individuals (the data subjects) from the effects of automated data processing with a default prohibition. Companies and individuals alike are generally prohibited from processing personal data unless they obtain consent from the data subjects or they find an applicable statutory exemption.[173] Under Article 6(1) GDPR, companies and individual data

172. Determann, L., Determann's Field Guide to Data Privacy Law: International Corporate Compliance Chapter 0.14 et seq. (5th ed., Edward Elgar Publishing Ltd., 2022).

173. Individuals can be subject to data protection law compliance obligations under the GDPR unless they are acting as employees on behalf of companies, *see, e.g.*, Court of Justice of the European Union judgment of 10 Jul. 2018, C-25/17, *Tietosuojavaltuutettu v. Jehovan todistajat — uskonnollinen yhdyskunta*. Governments are also subject to restrictions on data processing under national European data protection laws, but details vary from country to country. In 2014, people in Europe reacted with outrage to revelations about large-scale surveillance regarding electronic communications by the United States National Security Agency (NSA) and European intelligence services. Yet, current drafts of the EU Data Protection Regulation continue to largely exempt data processing for national security purposes, due to different

controllers have to justify the processing of personal data in a blockchain by identifying and disclosing in the privacy notices a 'legal basis'.[174] If they cannot find a compelling legal basis, they must not process personal data in blockchains. This approach affects the deployment of any information technology adversely, including blockchain and distributed ledgers.

The United States and many other countries outside of Europe, by contrast, generally allow data processing. Data privacy laws are primarily intended to protect individuals from intrusion into seclusion and interception of confidential communications. Given this focus, individuals are usually not protected under US privacy laws, unless they have a reasonable expectation of privacy in a particular situation or a policy objective justifies restrictions on individual freedoms to process information.[175] Also, many US data privacy laws are addressed to businesses and do not require individuals to comply. Companies can - and frequently do - negate expectations of privacy by notifying individuals of the companies' data collection and processing activities (e.g., in employee handbooks, website privacy statements and in-store warnings about security cameras).[176] Individuals receive relatively more privacy protection in the sanctity of their homes, for example, but communications and activities outside receive little or no protection (e.g., the information in public records, records shared with third parties, photos taken in public, audible phone conversations in public, postings on the internet or via social networking platforms).[177]

When Hessen and then other German states and European countries started enacting data protection laws in the 1970s, the United States also considered this option but decided against comprehensive regulation of data processing. Congress felt it was too early to appropriately identify and address potential privacy harms and balance privacy interests with freedom of information, innovation, and economic freedoms.[178]

---

views in the 28 EU Member States on this topic. *See* Determann, L. & zu Guttenberg, K.-T., On War and Peace in Cyberspace: Security, Privacy, Jurisdiction 875 et seq. (41 Hastings Constitutional Law Quarterly, 1, 13, 2014).

174. *See* Arts 6(1) and 12-14 GDPR and §4.02 through §4.09, *supra*.

175. *See, e.g., Moreno v. Hanford Sentinel, Inc.*, 172 Cal. App. 4th 1125, 1129 (Cal. Ct. App. 2009) ([T]o prevail on an invasion of privacy claim, the plaintiff must have conducted himself or herself in a manner consistent with an actual expectation of privacy.); Cal. Pen. Code, §632. On the concept of 'reasonable expectations of privacy', *see* Freiwald, S., First Principles of Communications Privacy (2007 Stanford Technology Law Review 3); Determann, L. & Sprague, R., Intrusive Monitoring: Employee Privacy Expectations Are Reasonable in Europe, Destroyed in the United States 979 (26 Berkeley Technology Law Journal 2011).

176. *See, e.g., In re Yahoo Mail Litig.*, 7 F. Supp. 3d 1016, 1028-1032 (N.D. Cal. 12 Aug. 2014) (holding that by agreeing to terms of service, email service provider's users had explicitly consented to provider's practice of scanning and analysing emails, therefore, barring their claim under the federal Wiretap Act).

177. *See, e.g., Evens v. Superior Court*, 77 Cal. App. 4th 320, 324 (Cal. Ct. App. 1999) (holding that teacher had no reasonable expectation of privacy in her communications made in the classroom); *United States v. Standefer*, No. 06-CR-2674-H, 2007 WL 2301760, at *3 (S.D. Cal. 8 Aug. 2007) (there is no reasonable expectation of privacy in financial records such as checks, deposit slips, and financial statements maintained by third-party institutions, such as banks because a depositor takes the risk, in revealing his affairs to another, that the information will be conveyed by that person to the Government).

178. Schwartz, P.M., *Preemption and Privacy*, 902, 910-916 (118 Yale Law Journal 902, 910-916, 2009).

Therefore, the United States resolved to pass sector-, situation-, and harm-specific privacy laws as the need arises at the state and federal levels. This allowed information technology companies in Silicon Valley to grow and become industry leaders in semiconductor technologies, software, e-commerce, cloud computing, social media, big data, and other data-intensive products and services.[179] But, the reactive approach with narrowly crafted, specific laws resulted in hundreds of diverging and constantly evolving privacy laws across the United States. Companies and government agencies find it increasingly difficult to navigate the maze of US privacy laws. Businesses are particularly concerned about the CCPA, which added extensive new disclosure requirements and individual rights to existing laws in order to reign in perceived risks emanating from data selling.[180] A dozen other states have enacted comprehensive privacy laws, but applicable only to consumer data and without rights of private action, namely Colorado and Connecticut (effective since 1 July 2023), Delaware (will take effect 1 January 2025), Florida (1 July 2024), Indiana (1 January 2026), Iowa (1 January 2025), Montana (1 October 2024), Oregon (1 July 2024), Tennessee (1 July 2025), Texas (1 July 2024), Utah (31 December 2023), Virginia (effective since 1 January 2023).[181]

In addition to data privacy laws, the United States have also enacted data security laws. These laws aim to protect individuals from specific harms resulting from unauthorized access to personal information, in particular, identity theft (e.g., criminals using someone's personal data to acquire or charge credit cards). Examples include data security breach notification laws (California passed the first law in 2002, with all US states and many countries following suit thereafter, the EU effective 2018 with Articles 33 and 34 GDPR), detailed prescriptions regarding technical and organizational measures to protect health information in the Health Insurance Portability and Accountability Act (HIPAA), and US state laws in California, Massachusetts, Nevada and New York requiring the encryption of certain data in certain circumstances.

Outside the scope of data protection, data privacy and data security are data residency, data retention and property laws. According to data residency and data retention laws, companies have to retain data in a certain location and for certain minimum time periods to be available in case of government audits; such laws are anti-privacy laws in nature.[182] The United States has not enacted general data retention or residency laws, and companies in the US are generally free to transfer personal data internationally.

---

179. Chander, A., *How Law Made Silicon Valley* 63 (Emory Law Journal 639, 2014), available at: https://ssrn.com/abstract=2340197 (accessed 26 Oct. 2023).
180. Determann, L., *California Privacy Law, Practical Guide and Commentary: U.S. Federal and California Law*, Chapter 2.4.3.1 (5th ed., IAPP, 2023).
181. *See* https://iapp.org/resources/article/us-state-privacy-legislation-tracker/ (accessed 30 Oct. 2023).
182. Determann, L., Data Residency Rules Cutting into Clouds: Impact and Options for Global Businesses and IT Architectures (Bloomberg BNA Data Privacy & Security Law Report, 16 PVLR 496 – 04/03/2017); Determann, L. & Weigl, M., Data Residency Requirements Creeping into German Law (Bloomberg BNA Privacy & Security Law Report, 15 PVLR 529 – 3/14/2016); Bekeschenko, E., et al., Keep Russian Data in Russia and Out of Clouds? 32 (6 Computer & Internet Lawyer 1, 2015).

Like EU data protection laws, US data privacy laws are not concerned with property rights. No one owns personal data.[183]

In summary, US privacy law consists of hundreds of sector-, situation- and harm-specific privacy laws that impose numerous obligations and prohibitions to protect reasonable data privacy expectations of individuals.[184] Companies can satisfy most obligations and overcome most prohibitions by providing notice or seeking consent from data subjects. Without a reasonable expectation of privacy, data subjects do not tend to have many rights under California or US federal privacy laws.[185] Companies can set, qualify and negate privacy expectations by way of notice. Only very few US privacy laws do not recognize notice or consent as an exception to prohibitions.[186] Therefore, privacy notices play a key role in US privacy laws.

Data subjects can enforce most laws by way of individual or class-action lawsuits. The FTC, the California Attorney General, the California Privacy Protection Agency, and other regulators can also bring lawsuits or impose fines and other sanctions, but private lawsuits under data privacy laws are much more prevalent in the United States than in other jurisdictions. US privacy laws have been enforced and complied with more effectively for much of their existence compared to EU data protection laws.[187]

For an overview regarding US privacy laws with the perspective of EU data protection laws, it is also helpful to consider what US privacy law is *not*:

- *No one omnibus statute:* Unlike many European, Latin American and Asian countries, neither the United States nor California has enacted one all-encompassing data privacy statute; commentators refer to the CCPA and other states' laws modelled after CCPA as 'comprehensive' privacy laws, but these laws were added to myriad existing laws, which continue to apply. This presents a practical challenge for all businesses, including those that want to adopt blockchain technologies, because it requires a careful, costly, and time-consuming analysis of numerous applicable laws.
- *No default prohibition of data processing:* In the United States, companies are generally allowed to process personal data. Unless a particular restriction or prohibition applies, data processing is permitted.

183. Determann, L., *No One Owns Data* (70 Hastings Law Journal 1, 2018).
184. Solove, D. & Schwartz, P., *Information Privacy Law* (6th ed., Aspen Publishing Co., 2018) and *Privacy Law Fundamentals* (IAPP, 2019).
185. *See, e.g., Safari Club Int'l v. Rudolph*, 845 F.3d 1250 (9th Cir. 2017); *USA v. Michael Marr et. al.*, Case No. 14-cr-00580-PJH, Pretrial Order No. 3 (N.D. California 2016); Todd, R., *Courthouse Steps Listening Devices Not Illegal, Hamilton Says* (The Recorder, 25 Jul. 2016) and On the concept of 'reasonable expectations of privacy', *see* Freiwald, S., First Principles of Communications Privacy (2007 Stanford Technology Law Review 3); Determann & Sprague *supra* n. 176, at. 979.
186. Exceptions include the Song-Beverly Credit Card Act (Cal. Civ. Code §§1747 et seq.), which prohibits merchants from collecting personal information from credit card users regardless of their consent, except as necessary to process credit card payments, Cal. Lab. Code §435, which prohibits employers from placing security cameras in toilets and locker rooms.
187. Determann, L., Social Media Privacy: 12 Myths and Facts (7 Stanford Technology Law Review 4, 2012); Schwartz, P., Preemption and Privacy 902, 910 et seq. (118 Yale Law Journal 2009).

- *No data protection officers:* Under federal healthcare sector privacy law (HIPAA), covered entities have to appoint a data privacy official and a data security official.[188] Other US privacy laws do not require such appointments. Many US companies have voluntarily appointed data privacy and security officers.
- *No specific restrictions on international data transfers:* California and the United States have traditionally stood for free trade and free information flows. International data transfers are not specifically restricted, unlike under the laws in Europe and an increasing number of other countries. This is particularly important for businesses that want to adopt blockchain technologies, given that the decentralized nature of networks makes it challenging to comply with international data transfer restrictions in the GDPR and similar laws, which require, for example, data transfer agreements and data transfer impact assessments for every country where data may end up in.
- *No general translation requirements:* English is the official language of California.[189] Under California and federal privacy laws, companies are not explicitly required to provide translations of privacy notices, privacy policies or other privacy-related documentation. But, §999.305(a)(2)(c) of the regulations of the California Attorney General pertaining to the CCPA requires that companies issue privacy notices required under the CCPA 'in the languages in which the business in its ordinary course provides contracts, disclaimers, sale announcements, and other information to consumers'. Separately, companies in California have to provide translations of certain types of consumer contracts if they negotiate such contracts primarily in the Spanish, Chinese, Tagalog, Vietnamese or Korean language; this requirement could also extend to privacy-related documentation if it is part of such a contract.[190] Also, government agencies and employers can be required to provide translations under certain circumstances.[191]

188. 45 C.F.R. §164.308(1)(1)(ii)(D)(2): covered entities and business associates have to appoint security official; 45 C.F.R. §164.530(a)(1): covered entity has to appoint privacy official.
189. California Constitution, Art. 3, s. 6.(b): 'English is the official language of the State of California.' The USA has not prescribed an official language by law, but some states have, available at: http://en.wikipedia.org/wiki/Languages_of_the_United_States (accessed 30 Oct. 2023).
190. Cal. Civ. Code §1632. *See* Shikai, Y.M., *Applying the California Translation Act to Consumer Agreements* 11-15 (Los Angeles Lawyer, September 2012).
191. For example, long-term health care facilities, must provide translations of the Patients' Bill of Rights (which could include privacy policies) into any language that is used by at least 1% of the facility's population, Cal. Health & Saf. Code §1599.61. State and local authorities are required to provide written materials in languages other than English, for example, under Cal. Gov. Code §§7290 et seq. (state agencies in general); Cal. Lab. Code, §105 (Dept. of Labor Stds. Enforcement); Cal. Unemp. Ins. Code §316 (unemployment compensation); Cal. Welf. & Inst. Code §19013.5 (Dept. of Rehabilitation) and §10607 (Dept. of Social Services). In *Samaniego v. Empire Today LLC*, 205 Cal. App. 4th 1138 (Cal App. 1st Dist. 2012), the court found an employment contract to be unconscionable where an employer did not provide a Spanish translation of a contract that contained a number of one-sided provisions.

- *No data minimization requirements – except recently under CCPA:* Unlike European laws, California and the United States do not require companies to avoid or minimize the processing of personal data. Companies can collect and process as much data as they want, so long as they comply with applicable consent, notice and security requirements. 'Big data' is generally allowed. In California, the California Privacy Rights Act ballot initiative of 2020 added limitations to the CCPA[192] that resemble GDPR requirements on purpose limitation and data minimization,[193] but it remains to be seen whether the CCPA restrictions on freedom of information will survive constitutional law scrutiny under the 1st Amendment of the US Constitution.[194]
- *No data protection authorities – except recently in California:* Neither the United States federal government nor individual states have established European-style data protection authorities, but in 2020, California voters adopted a ballot initiative that created a new California Privacy Protection Agency (CPPA) that will only enforce the CCPA.[195] Additionally, the California Attorney General continues to enforce the CCPA and other California privacy laws with a Privacy Enforcement and Protection Unit that was created in 2012.[196] In other US states, the attorney general usually enforces state privacy laws. At the federal level, the FTC has protected consumer privacy quite effectively based on its powers to enforce general unfair competition laws and some specific privacy laws, including the CAN-SPAM Act and the Children Online Privacy Protection Act (COPPA).[197]
- *No data protection registries or filings – except for data brokers:* The United States has not established any database registries or filing requirements under

192. California Civil Code s. 1798.100(c) provides: 'A business' collection, use, retention, and sharing of a consumer's personal information shall be reasonably necessary and proportionate to achieve the purposes for which the personal information was collected or processed, or for another disclosed purpose that is compatible with the context in which the personal information was collected, and not further processed in a manner that is incompatible with those purposes.'
193. Article 5(1) of the GDPR requires that '[p]ersonal data shall be: (b) collected for specified, explicit and legitimate purposes and not further processed in a manner that is incompatible with those purposes; further processing for archiving purposes in the public interest, scientific or historical research purposes or statistical purposes shall ... not be considered to be incompatible with the initial purposes ("purpose limitation"); (c) adequate, relevant and limited to what is necessary in relation to the purposes for which they are processed ("data minimisation")'.
194. On 18 Sep. 2023, a federal court in California issued a preliminary injunction against the enforcement of the California Age-Appropriate Design Code Act (CAADCA), because the court found the statute largely unconstitutional (*NetChoice v. Bonta* – Case No. 22-cv-08861-BLF) and some of the arguments seem applicable also to a general minimization requirement regarding information collection.
195. Cal. Civ. Code §1798.199.10.
196. http://oag.ca.gov/news/press-releases/attorney-general-kamala-d-harris-announces-privacy-enforcement-and-protection (accessed 30 Oct. 2023).
197. Serwin, A., The Federal Trade Commission and Privacy: Defining Enforcement and Encouraging Adoption of Best Practices 809 (48 San Diego Law Review 2011).

privacy laws, except that data brokers have to register in Vermont, California, and a few other states.[198]

The fact that US privacy law is conceptually so different from EU data protection laws had made it difficult for authorities and courts in the EU to compare them and assess their effectiveness fairly. 'Adequacy decisions' by the European Commission look at the similarity of statutory wording and fail to measure or consider enforcement, actual compliance levels, or effectiveness for individual privacy in the United States versus the EEA and other 'third countries',[199] leave alone the flaws in EU and national data protection laws.[200] Globally, data privacy legislation is at crossroads.[201] Recent developments in California and other US states indicate a trend towards adoption of EU-style data processing regulations. The EU Commission has issued a third adequacy decision concerning the United States, limited to US companies that voluntarily register under the EU-U.S. Data Privacy Framework.[202]

[B] Federal and State Law

The United States Congress enacts US federal laws, as contemplated by the US Constitution, which allocates specific subject matter areas to federal legislative jurisdiction. To the extent the US Constitution does not provide for federal legislative jurisdiction, the states are generally empowered to make laws.[203]

In California, for example, the California Legislature makes new law in statutes and also codifies court-made law, including, for example, the privacy torts. In the California Civil Code, the California legislature clarifies that it does not mean to ossify the common law through codification, and California courts shall remain in charge of further developing common law.[204]

In the area of data privacy, Congress and state legislatures have enacted numerous laws.[205] Some US federal laws expressly preempt state laws,[206] some

198. *See* Lothar Determann and Teisha Johnson, Data Broker Regulation – Competition v. Privacy Considerations: Trade-offs (TechReg Chronicle, October 2023).
199. Determann, L., *Adequacy of Data Protection in the USA: Myths and Facts* (International Data Privacy Law, 2016); Determann, L., *US-Datenschutzrecht – Dichtung und Wahrheit* 561 (Neue Zeitschrift für Verwaltungsrecht, 2016).
200. Veil, W., *The Emperor's New Clothes: On the Structural Shortcomings of Both the Old and the New Data Protection Law* 686-696 (Neue Zeitschrift für Verwaltungsrecht, 2018).
201. Determann, L., *Healthy Data Protection* (26 Michigan Technology Law Review 229, 2020); Determann, L., *Privacy and Data Protection* ***КОНФИДЕНЦИАЛЬНОСТЬ И ЗАЩИТА ПЕРСОНАЛЬНЫХ ДАННЫХ*** 18-26 (Moscow Journal of International Law 2019 No. 1).
202. Lothar Determann, Michaela Nebel and Michael Schmidl, EU-U.S. Data Privacy Framework and the impact on companies in the EEA and USA compared to other international data transfer mechanisms (Journal of Data Protection and Privacy, Volume 6,2, 2023).
203. US Constitution, Art. I, §8 and Amendment X.
204. *See* Cal. Civ. Code §5.
205. *See* Andrew Serwin, Information Security and Privacy: A Guide to Federal and State Law and Compliance, 2022-23 edition.
206. *See, e.g.*, *People v. Delta Air Lines, Inc.*, 247 Cal. App. 4th 884 (Cal. Ct. App. 2016) and 15 U.S.C. §7707(b)(1). *See* also *Omega World Travel, Inc. v. Mummagraphics, Inc.*, 469 F.3d 348, 353-57 (4th Cir. 2006) (holding that the CAN-SPAM Act preempted an Oklahoma statute insofar as it

expressly uphold existing state laws,[207] and some federal laws are silent on the topic of preemption, creating thorny issues for litigation.[208]

[C] Diverse Terminology

US privacy laws do not typically or uniformly use terms found in the GDPR and addressed in this Chapter,[209] such as 'personal data', 'controller', 'processor', 'processing' or 'data subject'. Ever since Congress decided to react to privacy issues with narrowly crafted, specific legislation, lawmakers at the federal and state level crafted terms and distinctions for every new privacy law. As a result, terminology and definitions in US privacy laws are varied and disparate.

For example, a number of California statutes use the term 'personally identifiable information' but define it differently.[210] In the California Civil Code, you can find different definitions of similarly sounding terms like 'personal identification information',[211] 'personal information'[212] and 'personally identifiable information',[213] each

applied to 'immaterial misrepresentations'); *Gordon v. Virtumundo, Inc.*, 575 F.3d 1040, 1061-1064 (9th Cir. 2009) (holding that plaintiff's claims under Washington Commercial Electronic Mail Act relating to header information were precluded by CAN-SPAM Act's express preemption clause); *Hypertouch Inc. v. ValueClick, Inc.*, 192 Cal. App. 4th 805, 833 (2011) (limiting the application of California's anti-spam laws to deceptive emails); *Beyond Sys., Inc. v. Kraft Foods, Inc.*, No. 13-2137, 2015 WL 451944, *4 (4th Cir. 4 Feb. 2015) (holding that neither Maryland's nor California's anti-spam statutes was preempted by the CAN-SPAM Act because they both 'deal with falsity or deception in the vein of tort').

207. *See* 45 C.F.R. §§160.201-160.205 re. HIPAA and 15 U.S.C. §1681t(a) re. FRCA.

208. *See, e.g.*, regarding the Computer Fraud and Abuse Act, *Hecht v. Components Int'l, Inc.*, 867 N.Y.S.2d 889, 898 (N.Y. Sup. Ct. 2008) ('It appears that the CFAA is not intended to preempt state law claims based on unauthorized access to a computer such as trespass to chattel, conversion, or fraud'); *Pacific Aerospace & Elecs., Inc. v. Taylor*, 295 F. Supp. 2d 1188, 1194 (E.D. Wash. 2003).

209. Sections §4.02-§4.09.

210. Cf. Cal. Bus. & Prof. Code §22577(a); Cal. Str. & H. Code §31499(o).

211. Cal. Civ. Code §1747.08. The Song-Beverly Credit Card Act uses the term 'personal identification information', which courts have interpreted to cover any information relating to a person, even a zip code, *see Pineda v. Williams-Sonoma Stores Inc.*, 51 Cal. 4th 524, 530 (2001). The statutory definition in Cal. Civ. Code §1747.08(3)(b) states: 'For purposes of this section, "personal identification information" means information concerning the cardholder, other than information set forth on the credit card, and including, but not limited to, the cardholder's address and telephone number.'

212. Cal. Civ. Code §1798.83(e)(7). The California Shine the Light Law defines the term 'personal information' with an enumerative list of data categories. Cal. Civ. Code §1798.80(e) contains a much broader definition: 'Personal information means any information that identifies, relates to, describes, or is capable of being associated with, a particular individual, including, but not limited to, his or her name, signature, social security number, physical characteristics or description, address, telephone number, passport number, driver's license or state identification card number, insurance policy number, education, employment, employment history, bank account number, credit card number, debit card number, or any other financial information, medical information, or health insurance information. "Personal information" does not include publicly available information that is lawfully made available to the general public from federal, state, or local government records.' Only a couple of sections further, in Cal. Civ. Code §1798.81.5(d)(1), on data security breach notifications, the term 'personal information' is defined with a enumerated list of data categories.

defined differently. In the Colorado Privacy Act, however, you find more GDPR-like terminology, including 'personal data', 'controller', and 'processor'.[214]

Even within one statute, you can find different definitions for different subsections. For example, the CCPA of 2018, which is only one of the dozens of privacy laws within the California Civil Code, uses two different definitions of 'personal information', a relatively narrow definition in the context of security breach liability[215] and an extremely broad definition for all other subsections.[216] Consequently, for purposes of applying US privacy laws to blockchain applications, one has to consider the scope, definitions and terminology of every applicable statute separately and on its own terms.

[D] General and Specific US Privacy Laws Applied to Blockchain

Blockchain or DLT, as such, is not regulated under US privacy laws. US privacy laws tend to be technology-neutral and focus either on individual privacy (with general privacy laws) or a particular industry sector (such as financial, healthcare), situation (e.g., online privacy, credit card payments, video rental history), data subjects (e.g., children), or harm (e.g., identity theft).

With respect to blockchain deployment, companies and individuals have to comply with [1] general privacy laws, including the California constitutional guarantee of privacy as well as common law, torts, consumer protection and unfair competition laws, and [2] sector-, harm- and situation-specific privacy laws.

---

213. Cal. Civ. Code §1798.81.5(d)(1) not only uses and defines the term 'personal information' but also uses 'personally identifiable information' in subsection [f], without separate definition: 'Any person or business that is required to issue a security breach notification pursuant to this section to more than 500 California residents as a result of a single breach of the security system shall electronically submit a single sample copy of that security breach notification, excluding any personally identifiable information, to the Attorney General.'
214. *See*, 6-1-1303, https://leg.colorado.gov/sites/default/files/2021a_190_signed.pdf (accessed 30 Oct. 2023).
215. According to Cal. Civ. Code §1798.150(a)(1) and §1798.81.5(d)(1)(A), 'Personal information' means either of the following: '(...) An individual's first name or first initial and the individual's last name in combination with any one or more of the following data elements, when either the name or the data elements are not encrypted or redacted: (i) Social security number. (ii) Driver's license number, California identification card number, tax identification number, passport number, military identification number, or other unique identification number issued on a government document commonly used to verify the identity of a specific individual. (iii) Account number or credit or debit card number, in combination with any required security code, access code, or password that would permit access to an individual's financial account. (iv) Medical information. (v) Health insurance information. (vi) Unique biometric data generated from measurements or technical analysis of human body characteristics, such as a fingerprint, retina, or iris image, used to authenticate a specific individual. Unique biometric data does not include a physical or digital photograph, unless used or stored for facial recognition purposes. (vii) Genetic data.'
216. According to Cal. Civ. Code §1798.140(v)(1) 'Personal information means information that identifies, relates to, describes, is reasonably capable of being associated with, or could reasonably be linked, directly or indirectly, with a particular consumer or household.'

[1] General US Privacy Laws

Companies are compelled to provide clear privacy notices by a number of general privacy and consumer protection laws in the United States, including the California Constitution, which contains an explicit guarantee of the right to privacy that also applies between private individuals and companies (whereas the US federal constitution only applies to state actors).[217] Also, under tort and unfair competition laws, companies have to avoid infringing reasonable privacy expectations such as by intrusion upon seclusion, public disclosure of private facts, false light, and misappropriation of name or likeness.[218] Blockchain and distributed ledger technologies do not raise any particular issues pertaining to such general laws. But, like other information technologies, blockchain and distributed ledger technologies involve the processing of personal information, which can result in infringements of privacy expectations.

Companies and individuals should take steps to ensure that they are not violating anyone's reasonable privacy expectations when they use blockchain or DLT. This requires an analysis of potential privacy expectations of persons involved, expected use cases, and potential risks of misuse and harm. With respect to any new technology, a key risk is that users misunderstand functionalities, rules or consequences or misjudge the impact on their privacy or other interests. Most privacy violations on social media platforms are committed by the victims themselves, or their friends and family, often inadvertently, due to insufficient understanding of functionalities;[219] nevertheless, the social media platform operators are publicly blamed and often sued or politically held responsible.[220] Therefore, it is in the best interest of technology companies to educate users of potential privacy harms, to reduce the risk of violations and protect themselves against blame and liability.

The most effective way to qualify privacy expectations and reduce the risk of being held liable for intruding on privacy or engaging in unfair or misleading business practices is for companies to issue clear and simple user manuals and privacy notices, ideally with hands-on technology training, real-time tips and on-the-spot privacy warnings. With respect to cryptocurrencies, individuals should be advised of limits to transaction privacy, security vulnerabilities regarding crypto wallets,[221] the publicity of public key information, and what personal information will end up in a particular

217. Article 1, s. 1 of the California Constitution states: 'All people are by nature free and independent and have inalienable rights. Among these are enjoying and defending life and liberty, acquiring, possessing, and protecting property, and pursuing and obtaining safety, happiness, and privacy.' The people of California added this explicit right of privacy to the California Constitution by a ballot measure in November 1972, *American Acad. of Pediatrics v. Lungren* (1997) 16 Cal. 4th 307, 326.
218. Prosser, W., *Privacy* (48 California Law Review 383, 1960).
219. Determann, L., *Social Media @ Work 2014* (BNA/Bloomberg Social Media Law & Policy Report, 2 SMLR 49, 12/17/2013).
220. Determann, L., *Social Media Privacy: A Dozen Myths and Facts* (2012 Stanford Technology Law Review 7, 2012).
221. *See, e.g.*, Dan Olson, Line Goes Up – The Problem With NFTs. https://youtu.be/YQ_xWvX1n9g?si=Bun4K10fFIRlYEgT.

blockchain (e.g., depending on the use case, health information or education history and credentials).

To achieve this goal, companies have to craft short, situation-specific notices that use plain language. Additional disclosures that companies have to issue under CCPA, GDPR and other regimes may have to be provided separately in the form of supplemental notices (which must track all statutory disclosure requirements and will be referred to by regulators, plaintiffs, journalists, etc., but which cannot be expected to be read or understood by consumers).

When companies issue privacy notices to qualify individual privacy expectations, they have to be careful to avoid misleading consumers or misrepresenting any facts. The FTC, State Attorneys General, City Attorneys and private plaintiffs can pursue claims against companies for unlawful, unfair, or fraudulent business conduct.[222] Particularly, companies should avoid marketing fluff and declarations of good intentions in privacy notices, such as 'We take privacy seriously', 'Your privacy is important to us' or 'We deploy state-of-the-art data security measures.' Such statements do not provide the data subject with meaningful information and merely provide additional ammunition to plaintiffs' attorneys and regulators who believe the company did not, in fact, sufficiently respect privacy interests or comply with laws.[223]

Also, companies should avoid cramming disclosures required for multiple jurisdictions into one global privacy notice, as this will inevitably expand the volume of the notice to an unreasonable length, address topics that do not absolutely have to be addressed in each jurisdiction, and add complexity and unfamiliar terminology. For example, a company that is required under Article 13(1)(f) GDPR to state in a privacy notice to blockchain users in Europe that it 'intends to transfer personal data to a third country or international organization and the existence or absence of an adequacy decision by the Commission, or (...) the appropriate or suitable safeguards and the means by which to obtain a copy of them or where they have been made available' should not include such verbiage in a privacy notice addressed to blockchain users in the US as this would be confusing and detracting from relevant or required disclosures. Conversely, the very detailed lists of personal information categories and counterintuitive terminology that companies have to adhere to under the CCPA of 2018 would render privacy notices for European residents unreasonably long, arguably in violation of Article 12(1) GDPR, which requires that privacy notices be framed in 'concise, transparent, intelligible and easily accessible form, using clear and plain language'.

222. Cal. Bus. & Prof. Code §§17200-17210. More generally *see* Federal Trade Commission, available at: www.ftc.gov/about-ftc (accessed 30 Oct. 2023); Statutes Enforced or Administered by the Federal Trade Commission, available at: www.ftc.gov/enforcement/statutes (accessed 30 Oct. 2023).

223. For example, in *In re iPhone Application Litig.*, 844 F. Supp. 2d 1040, 1072 (N.D. Cal. 2012), the court dismissed most claims under specific privacy statutes but declined to dismiss claims under California unfair competition law because 'Apple makes affirmative representations regarding its protection of user's personal information.'

Thus, most companies are better off with one core privacy statement targeted at the company's home jurisdiction or key market, plus supplemental privacy notices to address technicalities for other jurisdictions.[224]

[2] Specific US Privacy Laws

Congress and state legislatures have not enacted privacy laws particularly focused on the blockchain or DLT. But, many sector-, harm- and situation-specific laws may apply to blockchain applications depending on the businesses, data subjects, and data categories involved.

For example, financial institutions may have to comply with the federal Gramm-Leach-Bliley Act,[225] the Fair Credit Reporting Act,[226] the Fair Debt Collection Practices Act (FDCPA),[227] and the Right to Financial Privacy Act[228] as well as numerous state laws, including California's Financial Information Privacy Act, the California Consumer Credit Reporting Agencies Act,[229] California's Rosenthal Fair Debt Collection Practices Act of 1977 (Rosenthal Act),[230] California's Right to Financial Privacy Act in 1976,[231] the Song-Beverly Credit Card Act of 1971,[232] the Areias Credit Card Full Disclosure Act of 1986[233] and various other laws and industry standards, including the Payment Card Industry Standards for credit card data.[234] Fintech companies may be able to avoid becoming entangled with some or all of the US privacy laws that apply to

224. For more detail on this topic and drafting recommendations for privacy notices, please *see* Determann, *supra* n. 172, at 3.18 et seq.
225. *See* 15 U.S.C. §6809. With regard to the Financial Privacy Requirements of the Gramm-Leach-Bliley Act, *see* Federal Trade Commission, available at: https://www.ftc.gov/business-guidance/privacy-security/gramm-leach-bliley-act (accessed 30 Oct. 2023).
226. 15 U.S.C. §§1681 through 1681x. On the history of credit bureaus and regulation, *see* Rowena Olegario, Credit-Reporting Agencies: Their Historical Roots, Current Status, and Role in Market Development, available at: https://documents1.worldbank.org/curated/en/209261468762614853/pdf/wdr27825.pdf (accessed 30 Oct. 2023).
227. *See* 15 U.S.C. §§1692 et seq. When it passed the FDCPA, Congress was faced with 'abundant evidence of the use of abusive, deceptive, and unfair debt collection practices by many debt collectors', 15 U.S.C. §1692(a).
228. 12 U.S.C. §§3402 et seq.
229. *See* Cal. Civ. Code §§1785.1-1785.36. The law became effective in California in 1975 and has been subject to several amendments, *see, e.g.*: www.leginfo.ca.gov/pub/09-10/bill/sen/sb_0901-0950/sb_909_cfa_20100621_110753_asm_comm.html (accessed 30 Oct. 2023).
230. Cal. Civ. Code §§1788-1788.33. For a history of both the federal and California laws, *see, e.g.*: http://www.leginfo.ca.gov/pub/13-14/bill/sen/sb_0201-0250/sb_233_cfa_20130621_120929_asm_comm.html (accessed 30 Oct. 2023).
231. Cal. Gov. Code §§7460 et seq.
232. Cal. Civ. Code §1747.08. *See* generally Song, Alfred H., Oral History Interview (California State Archives State Government Oral History Program), available at: http://archives.cdn.sos.ca.gov/oral-history/pdf/song.pdf (accessed 30 Oct. 2023) (discussing the history of the Song-Beverly Credit Card Act: State Senator Albert H. Song [Democrat, Monterey Park] drafted the original bill and introduced it with State Senator Robert G. Beverly [Republican, South Bay] and Governor Ronald Reagan signed the bill into law).
233. Cal. Civ. Code §§1748.10 through 1748.14.
234. www.pcisecuritystandards.org/ (accessed 30 Oct. 2023).

financial institutions if they follow the motto 'more tech than fin', e.g., by focusing on technology supply and leaving regulated activities to licensed institutions.[235]

If healthcare providers want to use blockchain technology to promote standardized electronic medical records for patients, healthcare providers, and health insurance providers, they may have to comply with the privacy and security rules under the federal Health Insurance Portability and Accountability Act of 1996 (HIPAA).[236] HIPAA prescribes disclosure and consent requirements, data subject access rights, contract terms for business associates, security measures, and various other requirements. Software and hardware providers that target patients directly may be subject to the California Confidentiality of Medical Information Act (CMIA),[237] which prescribes requirements similar to HIPAA plus additional obligations and details, including a duty for companies to obtain written consent in certain situations that must be handwritten by the person who signs it or in a typeface no smaller than 14-point type; clearly separate from any other language present on the same page; executed by a signature that serves no other purpose than to execute the authorization; signed and dated.[238]

Any company that targets children online with a blockchain use case has to comply with the Children Online Privacy Protection Act (COPPA),[239] which requires parental consent before companies may collect personal information from children under 13 years.

Companies that process video purchase or rental history information have to comply with the Video Privacy Protection Act,[240] which contains specific written consent requirements for disclosures and since 2012 permits companies to obtain customer consent through electronic means using the internet, provided that the consent is in a form that is 'distinct and separate from any form setting forth other legal or financial obligations of the consumer',[241] and video tape service providers give customers a choice between consenting to disclosure: (1) in advance for a set period of time up to two years or until consent is withdrawn by the consumer; or (2) each time disclosure is sought.

Thus, every business has to determine for itself which specific US privacy laws it has to comply with pertaining to a particular blockchain or DLT deployment. For an

235. Determann, L. & Lorenz, M., *FinTech: Ground Rules and Checklist for Starting Up and Going Global* (BNA's Banking Report, 27 Nov. 2017); Determann, L. & Lorenz, M., *Fintechs im Dschungel der Regulierungen* 13 (Börsenzeitung, 1 Apr. 2017).

236. *See* Pub. L. 104-191, 110 Stat. 1936, enacted 21 Aug. 1996; 45 C.F.R. §§160-164; 78 Fed. Reg. 5566 (final omnibus rule), available at: http://www.gpo.gov/fdsys/pkg/FR-2013-01-25/pdf/2013-01073.pdf (accessed 30 Oct. 2023); Hirsch, R. & Deixler, H., Final HIPAA Omnibus Rule Brings Sweeping Changes to the Health Care Privacy Law: HIPAA Privacy and Security Obligations Extended to Business Associates and Subcontractors (BNA Privacy and Security Law Report 12 PVLR 168, 2013).

237. Cal. Civ. Code §§56-57.

238. Cal. Civ. Code §56.11.

239. 16 C.F.R. §§312.1-312.13 (implementing 15 U.S.C. §§6501 et seq.); For children's Privacy, *see* Federal Trade Commission, available at: https://www.ftc.gov/business-guidance/privacy-security/childrens-privacy (accessed 30 Oct. 2023).

240. 18 U.S.C. §2710.

241. 18 U.S.C. §2710(b)(2)(B).

overview regarding sectoral US privacy laws, *see Privacy Law Fundamentals*.[242] For a detailed commentary and guidance on US Federal and California privacy laws, *see California Privacy Law, Practical Guide and Commentary*, which addresses the scope of applicability, compliance requirements and sanctions for every federal and California state privacy law.[243] For a list and summaries of other states' laws, *see Information Security and Privacy: A Guide to Federal and State Law Compliance*.[244]

[E] Blockchain and CCPA

Many companies around the world are currently struggling to meet compliance requirements under the CCPA of 2018, a law that is much broader and more restrictive than most other US privacy laws and frequently compared with the GDPR.[245] Unlike the GDPR, the CCPA is not an omnibus privacy law but one of the hundreds of laws intended to protect individual privacy. Like other US privacy laws, the CCPA is focused on a particular activity that is considered harmful to consumer privacy, namely the selling of personal information. But, unlike other US privacy laws, the CCPA comes with an excessively broad scope due to counterintuitive definitions including 'consumer' (defined to mean any California resident), 'personal information' (defined to mean any information that is related to an individual or household) and 'selling' (defined to mean any sharing of information for any valuable information, thus covering most forms of information exchanges and sharing that one would not normally associate with 'selling'). CCPA applies to companies around the world, Business-to-Business and Business-to-Consumer and in all sectors, except to the extent its exemptions apply.

Jerry Brown, the Governor of California, signed the CCPA into law on 28 June 2018.[246] The legislative process was unusually rushed. The California Legislature debated only six days and passed the bill on the condition that a ballot initiative with a similar focus be withdrawn. For more than 100 years, Californians have voted at general elections not only on candidates for public office but regularly also on various constitutional and legislative ballot initiatives. In fact, in 1972, California added a right to privacy to Article 1 section 1 of the California Constitution by way of a ballot initiative. Such initiatives are often sponsored by special interest groups, businesses and wealthy individuals.[247] In 2017, a real estate millionaire had teamed up with a

242. Solove, D. & Schwartz, P., *Privacy Law Fundamentals*, *supra* n. 184.
243. Determann, *supra* n. 180, Chapter 2.
244. Serwin, A.B., *Information Security and Privacy: A Guide to Federal and State Law and Compliance 2023-2024 ed.*
245. Determann, L. & Gupta, C., *Indian Personal Data Protection Act of 2018: Draft Bill and Its History, Compared to GDPR and California Privacy Law* 37 (Berkeley Journal of International Law 481, 2019).
246. Determann, L., *Broad Data and Business Regulation, Applicable Worldwide* (IAPP Advisor, 02/07/2018); Determann, L., *Datenschutz auf Kalifornisch* (FAZ v. 11/07/2018).
247. Boyd, T.M., *How a Rich Californian Hijacked the Legislature: Threatened with a Ballot Initiative, Lawmakers Pass a Ruinous Data-Privacy Law* (The Wall Street Journal, 04/07/ 2018), available at: www.wsj.com/articles/how-a-rich-californian-hijacked-the-legislature-1530723133 (accessed 30 Oct. 2023).

Central Intelligence Agency analyst and a financial services industry professional to propose measure No. 17-0039 regarding the Consumer Right to Privacy Act of 2018 (the Initiative), seemingly wording and organizing the draft bill in a way to appeal to general voters.[248] By June 2018, it was clear that the proponents of the Initiative had gathered more than the required number of signatures and the Governor would have had to certify the Initiative if not withdrawn by 28 June 2018. As a result, Californians would have voted on the Initiative at the general election on 6 November 2018; had the Initiative passed, it could not have been amended, modified or repealed afterwards, except by another ballot initiative or by a 70% majority in the California Legislature, but then only to further the objectives of the Initiative. To prevent the risk of a largely unchangeable law, the California Legislature hashed out compromise legislation with the proponents of the Initiative. After the Legislature passed and the Governor signed the CCPA, the proponents withdrew their Initiative, and the legislative bill became the law. Since its enactment in June 2018, the California Legislature amended the CCPA several times, while the California Attorney General was issuing regulations under the statute.

The proponents of the 2018 Initiative felt that some of the amendments watered down protections and launched a second initiative in 2020 for a California Privacy Rights Act (CPRA).[249] California voters passed the ballot initiative with a 56% majority at the general US election on 3 November 2020 and CPRA became law on 16 December 2020, with a delayed effective date for many provisions until 1 January 2023.[250] The CPRA voided any conflicting legislation that the California legislature enacted after January 2020[251] and authorizes the legislature to amend the CCPA going forward with a simple majority but only to the extent 'amendments are consistent with and further the purpose and intent of' CCPA, as amended by CPRA.[252]

248. https://www.caprivacy.org/about-us/ (accessed 30 Oct. 2023). Myers, J. & Ulloa, J., *California Lawmakers Agree to New Consumer Privacy Rules That Would Avert Showdown on the November Ballot* (Los Angeles Times, 21/06/2018), available at: www.latimes.com/politics/la-pol-ca-privacy-initiative-legislature-agreement-20180621-story.html (accessed 30 Oct. 2023).
249. Determann, L, *California Privacy Rights Ballot Initiative: Businesses, Watch This Space* (The Recorder 22/05/2020).
250. Cal. Civ. Code §1798.130(a)(2)(B).
251. CPRA s. 25(d): 'The provisions of this act shall prevail over any conflicting legislation enacted after January 1, 2020. Any amendments to this Act or any legislation that conflicts with any provision of this Act shall be null and void upon passage of this Act by the voters, regardless of the code in which it appears. Legislation shall be considered "conflicting" for purposes of this subdivision, unless the legislation is consistent with and furthers the purpose and intent of this Act as set forth in Section 3.'
252. CPRA s. 25(a): 'The provisions of this act may be amended after its approval by the voters by a statute that is passed by a vote of a majority of the members of each house of the Legislature and signed by the Governor, provided that such amendments are consistent with and further the purpose and intent of this Act as set forth in Section 3, including amendments to the exemptions in Section 1798.145 if the laws upon which the exemptions are based are amended to enhance privacy and are consistent with and further the purposes and intent of this Act and amendments to address a decision of a California state or federal court holding that a provision of the Act is unconstitutional or preempted by federal law, provided that any further amendments to legislation that addresses a court holding shall be subject to this subdivision.'

CPRA creates a new agency intended to enforce the amended CCPA called the California Privacy Protection Agency (CPPA)[253] and sets aside a portion of proceeds from fines levied under the CCPA for 'nonprofit organizations to promote and protect consumer privacy'.[254]

On 30 June 2023, however, a California Superior Court judge enjoined enforcement of the CCPA regulations by the CPPA until 29 March 2024.[255]

[1] Scope of CCPA

Principally, all California residents are protected under the CCPA with respect to any information that relates to them. Californians are not just protected in their roles as consumers, but also as employees, patients, tenants, students, parents, children, etc., because the term 'consumer' is defined to mean any 'natural person who is a California resident'.[256] Unlike other sections of the California Civil Code and most other US privacy laws, Cal. Civ. Code § 1798.140(v)(1) defines the term 'personal information' broadly as 'any information that ... relates to ... a particular consumer or household'. Data can be protected even if it does not relate to a single individual (since 'households' are covered) and if it does not contain a name. For example, annual water or energy consumption of a household, a particular employee's job description, an IP address, web browsing history and 'purchasing tendencies' will be regulated as personal information, even if no names are associated. Thus, public and private keys, as well as any information relating to transactions between or involving individuals on a blockchain or sidechain, can qualify as personal information under CCPA.

Excluded from the protection of 'personal information' and 'sensitive personal information' is information that is '*publicly available*'. The scope of this exception was broadened by CPRA to cover not only 'information that is lawfully made available from federal, state, or local government records', as in the 2018 version of the law, but also 'information that a business has a reasonable basis to believe is lawfully made available to the general public by the consumer or from widely distributed media; or information made available by a person to whom the consumer has disclosed the information if the consumer has not restricted the information to a specific audience'.[257] 'Publicly available' does not mean 'biometric information collected by a business about a consumer without the consumer's knowledge', but personal information that a blockchain user includes on publicly visible parts of the blockchain now

253. Cal. Civ. Code §1798.199.10(a).
254. Cal. Civ. Code §1798.160(a)-(c).
255. *California Chamber of Commerce v. California Privacy Protection Agency*, No. 34-2023-800 04106-CU-WM-GDS (Cal. Super. 30 Jun. 2023) (J. Arguelles Minute Order).
256. Cal. Civ. Code §1798.140(i) refers to 'Section 17014 of Title 18 of the California Code of Regulations, as that section read on 1 Sep. 2017, however identified, including by any unique identifier.' According to these regulations, a 'resident' includes (i) every individual who is in the State for other than a temporary or transitory purpose, and (ii) every individual who is domiciled in the State who is outside the State for a temporary or transitory purpose, subject to a number of clarifications and specifications set forth in s. 17014 of Title 18 of the California Code of Regulations.
257. Cal. Civ. Code §1798.140(v)(2).

falls outside the rigid restrictions of CCPA, including deletion rights. This means a significant improvement for blockchain and DLT applications.

Also excluded from the reach of CCPA is information collected from Californians when they are outside the state, and the related 'commercial conduct takes place wholly outside of California',[258] but whether this set of facts applies will not normally be known to blockchain participants.

CCPA also excludes 'aggregate' and 'de-identified' information from the definition of 'personal information'. Aggregate information means statistical information that does not relate to individuals. De-identification standards under CCPA are met only by 'information that cannot reasonably identify, relate to, describe, be capable of being associated with, or be linked, directly or indirectly, to a particular consumer'. By irreversibly encrypting and destroying the personal information related to a public and private key, it may be possible to de-identify information included in a blockchain.

[2] Which Blockchain Participants Must Comply with CCPA?

Compared to the GDPR and other privacy laws, it is important to note that only businesses have to comply with CCPA, not individuals. Also, since the CPRA amendments, fewer businesses may be subject to CCPA because CPRA has clarified and narrowed some of the application thresholds. Even so, the scope of applicability is still very broad: Businesses around the world have to comply with the CCPA if they do business in California, operate for profit, determine purposes and means of data processing and exceed one of three thresholds, or if they are parents or subsidiaries of an entity that meets those requirements and the two use a common brand.

[a] Doing Business in California

A company without a physical presence or affiliate in California may be able to avoid having to comply with the statute if it can ensure that its 'commercial conduct takes place wholly outside of California' for purposes of California Civil Code section 1798.145(a)(7) or that it is not doing 'business in the State of California' for purposes of section 1798.140(d)(1). Commentators note that many companies find it difficult to conclude that they are not doing business in California because economic significance of the state and the fact that the term 'doing business' has been interpreted to require only minimal activities directed at California.[259] State legislatures and courts apply different tests to answer the question of whether foreign corporations are 'doing business' in a state depending on the context, including to determine 'whether the foreign corporation is subject to the state's taxing jurisdiction, whether it is subject to the process of the court within the state and whether or not it has subjected itself to the

258. Cal. Civ. Code §1798.145(a)(7).
259. *See, e.g., Hurst v. Bueczek Enterprises, LLC* (N.D. Cal. 2012); Matthew Stein and Christopher Lisy, *Figuring Out if You Are 'Doing Business' in California Under the CCPA*, Bloomberg Law News, 27 Feb. 2020.

regulatory or qualification statutes of the state'.[260] Courts tend to require relatively more substantial intrastate activity for purposes of submitting foreign corporations to qualification and regulatory requirements than for tax and jurisdictional purposes.[261] According to California Corporations Code sections 191(a), 15901.02(ai) and 17708.03(a), companies outside of California may be subject to the law if they enter 'into repeated and successive transactions' in California, which could occur remotely and online.[262] According to California Revenue and Taxation Code (RTC) section 23101(a), an out-of-state company is 'doing business' in California if it is 'actively engaging in any transaction for the purpose of financial or pecuniary gain or profit' in California. An electronic commerce platform vendor incorporated in Canada or Delaware is not necessarily subject to jurisdiction of California courts merely because it hosts online stores for thousands of California-based merchants and maintains a storefront in Los Angeles.[263] To prevent undue burdens on interstate commerce and businesses outside California, courts should place a relatively high burden on plaintiffs to prove activities took place in California for purposes of showing that the foreign business is 'doing business in California' under CCPA, given the extensive compliance requirements under CCPA.

[b] Operating for Profit or Financial Benefit of Owners

A company is subject to the CCPA as a 'business' if it is organized or operated for the profit or financial benefit of its shareholders or other owners. Non-profit organizations do not have to comply with the CCPA if they are incorporated without owners. Thus, some of the foundations that were incorporated to develop blockchain ecosystems are exempt from CCPA (yet, not from the Colorado Privacy Act, for example). Non-profit corporations that have owners and operate for the financial benefit of their owners may, however, remain covered by the CCPA.[264]

---

260. *Filmmakers Releasing Org. v. Realart Pictures of St. Louis, Inc.*, 374 S.W.2d 535, 539 (Mo. Ct. App. 1964).
261. *See, e.g., Questech, Inc. v. Liteco, AG*, 735 F. Supp. 187, 188 (E.D. Va. 1990).
262. Note, however, that Cal. Corp. Code §191(c) provides that 'a foreign corporation shall not be considered to be transacting intrastate business ... solely by reason of ... (5) Effecting sales through independent contractors. (6) Soliciting or procuring orders, whether by mail or through employees or agents or otherwise, where those orders require acceptance outside this state before becoming binding contracts'. For an overview of state-by-state definitions of 'doing business' for purposes of corporate registration requirements, *see* CT Corporation Staff, *What Constitutes Doing Business By a Corporation in States Foreign to the State of its Incorporation* (Wolters Kluwer 2016), https://www.wolterskluwer.com/en/expert-insights/what-constitutes-doing-business (accessed 30 Oct. 2023).
263. *Briskin v. Shopify Inc.*, No. 21-cv-06269-PJH, 2022 U.S. Dist. LEXIS 81797 (N.D. Cal. 5 May 2022).
264. Cal. Civ. Code §1798.140(d)(1) defines a business as 'legal entity that is organized or operated for the profit or financial benefit of its shareholders or other owners'. On public benefit versus mutual benefit corporations, *see* Gov. Code, §§12585, 12586, subd. (a); Cal. Code Regs., tit. 11, §§300-307; Corp. Code, §§7110 et seq. and the *Attorney General's Guide for Charities*, California Department of Justice Office of the Attorney General, https://oag.ca.gov/sites/all/files/agweb/pdfs/charities/publications/guide_for_charities.pdf (accessed 30 Oct. 2023).

[c] Determining Means and Purposes of Processing

A company is subject to the CCPA as a 'business' only if and to the extent it determines the means and purposes of processing.[265] To the extent companies perform services for a customer, they usually do not determine 'the purposes and means of the processing'; the customer does. Also, as a matter of fact, companies usually cannot satisfy the various obligations that the CCPA imposes on businesses where they act as service providers; for example, service providers cannot inform data subjects about the purposes of processing or sources of information where their customer provides the data and decides its ultimate use. The CCPA differentiates between the roles and duties of businesses and service providers throughout the statute and provides that businesses are not liable if their service providers use information in violation of the CCPA unless the business knew or had reason to believe that the service provider intended to commit violations; likewise, service providers are not liable for violations that their customers commit.[266] Therefore, as service providers, companies generally do not have to satisfy obligations that businesses have under CCPA.[267] But, under amendments introduced by CPRA, service providers, contractors and third parties have additional obligations in these specific roles: Service providers and contractors must cooperate with businesses concerning data subject requests[268] and obey consumer requests to limit the use of sensitive personal information.[269]

[d] Thresholds

Small businesses can be exempt from CCPA compliance requirements if they do not meet any of the following three thresholds: (1) annual gross revenues of USD 25 million; (2) they buy, sell or share personal information of 100,000 or more California residents or households annually; and (3) at least 50% of their annual revenue comes from selling or sharing California residents' personal information.[270] A business that falls below all of these thresholds can still be subject to the CCPA if it controls or is controlled by, and shares common branding with, a business subject to the CCPA.[271]

[i] Annual Gross Revenue Threshold: USD 25 Million

Unlike other California laws, the CCPA does not expressly state whether the USD 25 million threshold includes only California revenue or all global sales.[272] By contrast,

---

265. Cal. Civ. Code §1798.140(d)(1).
266. Cal. Civ. Code §1798.145(i)(1).
267. *See* CCPA Regulations §7050(d).
268. Cal. Civ. Code §§1798.1(c), 1798.130(a)(3).
269. Cal. Civ. Code §1798.121(c).
270. Cal. Civ. Code §1798.140(d)(1)(A-C). 'Sharing' is defined narrowly to cover only disclosures 'to a third party for cross-context behavioral advertising' where no exception applies, Cal. Civ. Code §1798.140(ah).
271. Cal. Civ. Code §1798.140(d)(1).
272. Cal. Civ. Code §1798.140(d)(1)(A) refers to 'annual gross revenues' without an expanding reference to 'worldwide' or limiting references to 'from this state'. The California attorney

California Civil Code section 1714.43(a)(1) defines the scope of the California Transparency in Supply Chains Act expressly in reference to 'annual worldwide gross receipts' and section 17942(a)(2) of the California Revenue and Taxation Code refers to 'total income from all sources derived from or attributable to this state'. In the context of enforcement proceedings, it would seem appropriate to interpret the revenue threshold *in dubio pro reo* as counting only revenue attributable to California, particularly since CPRA added a clarification to the temporal dimension of the revenue threshold[273] but no express statement that revenue derived outside California should count towards the revenue threshold, even though this was a known uncertainty under the original wording of CCPA.[274]

[ii] Number of Data Subjects Threshold: 100,000 Annually

CPRA raised this threshold in several ways effective 1 January 2023, from 50,000 to 100,000, by counting only consumers whose personal information a business buys, sells or shares, and by defining 'sharing' narrowly to require a nexus with cross-context behavioural advertising.[275] Companies can avoid meeting this threshold by refraining from buying, selling or sharing personal information.

[iii] Revenue from Selling or Sharing Personal Information Threshold: 50%

A business can also become subject to CCPA if it derives more than 50% of its annual revenue from selling or sharing personal information of California residents. If a company sells or shares personal information, it has to calculate resulting revenue, which can be difficult, given the broad definition of 'selling' (which includes any disclosure for consideration) and the complex definition of 'sharing' (which requires a

general stated in the context of the rulemaking process that clarifying the territorial scope of the revenue threshold would exceed his authority given that the statute does not contain an express limitation to revenue derived from California, *see Final Statement of Reasons*, Appendix A, Row 5, California Department of Justice Office of the Attorney General (2020), https://oag.ca.gov/sites/all/files/agweb/pdfs/privacy/ccpa-fsor-appendix-a.pdf (accessed 30 Oct. 2023).

273. Businesses are covered only as of 1 January of the next calendar year if they exceed the revenue threshold during the prior calendar year. Cal. Civ. Code §1798.140(d)(1)(A).

274. This was flagged already in one of the first published articles on CCPA, Lothar Determann, *Analysis: The California Consumer Privacy Act of 2018. Broad data and business regulation, applicable worldwide*, IAPP Advisor, 2 Jul. 2018, https://iapp.org/news/a/analysis-the-california-consumer-privacy-act-of-2018/ (accessed 30 Oct. 2023). The California Attorney General stated during its rulemaking process in response to a request for clarification (*see* FSOR Appendix A at 1 (Response 5), https://oag.ca.gov/sites/all/files/agweb/pdfs/privacy/ccpa-fsor-appendix-a.pdf) that 'Civil Code §1798.140(d)(1)(A) does not limit the revenue threshold to revenue generated in California or from California residents. Any proposed change to limit the threshold to revenue generated only in California or from California residents would be inconsistent with the CCPA.' This statement could be read to indicate that the California Attorney General believes revenue generated outside California counts for the CCPA threshold, or simply that CCPA leaves the question only and it is therefore for courts or the legislature to decide. Since CPRA leaves this open, CCPA should be interpreted narrowly in this regard in the context of criminal or administrative sanctions proceedings, *in dubio pro reo*.

275. Cal. Civ. Code §1798.140(d)(1)(B) and (ah).

nexus with cross-context behavioural advertising). As with the number of data subjects threshold, companies can avoid meeting this threshold, however, if they refrain from selling or sharing personal information.

[e] Affiliates

A parent company or subsidiary that controls, or is controlled by, an affiliate that is subject to CCPA and uses the same branding can fall into the definition of 'business' if it shares personal information with the affiliate, even if company itself would not otherwise exceed the applicable thresholds to become subject to CCPA as a business.[276] This could have two consequences: One, the affiliated business becomes subject to CCPA. Two, the affiliated businesses can disclose personal information to each other without triggering opt-out rights because the definitions of 'selling' and 'sharing' require a third party, and the business is by definition not a third party.[277] Yet, the fact that the affiliate becomes part of the business – and thus loses its potential status as a 'third party' under CCPA – means that there is no longer a 'third party' involved that could qualify disclosures as 'sharing' under CCPA, which requires 'communicating orally, in writing, or by electronic or other means, a consumer's personal information by the business to a third party for cross-context behavioral advertising'.[278] Consequently, it seems difficult to imagine a situation where a company becomes subject to CCPA as a 'business' merely because one of its affiliates is covered. At the same time, disclosures among affiliates may not be privileged anymore under CPRA, and it seems prudent to take affirmative steps to eliminate 'selling' or 'sharing' of personal information between affiliates.

'Common branding' means a shared name, service mark or trademark.[279] A company that owns multiple brands, business lines and subsidiaries can position some or all of its subsidiaries as part of the same business by using joint or separate branding. By keeping branding separate among subsidiaries, businesses may be able to keep their ultimate parent company or some subsidiaries outside the scope of CCPA compliance requirements or position only some entities in the group as personal information sellers so that others do not have to post a 'do not sell my personal information' link on their websites.

Before CPRA took effect, companies in a group could position themselves as part of the same 'business' and thus share personal information without triggering opt-out rights by opting for group-wide common branding. One commentator had argued that the CCPA roped in parent companies and subsidiaries on a stand-alone basis, without any privileges for intra-group sharing.[280] According to this interpretation of the CCPA,

276. Cal. Civ. Code §1798.140(d)(2).
277. Cal. Civ. Code §1798.140(ad), (ah) and (ai)(1).
278. Cal. Civ. Code §1798.140(ah).
279. Cal. Civ. Code §1798.140(d)(2).
280. *See* Lydia de la Torre, *Does the CCPA Regulate Internal Transfers?*, IAPP News, 25 Jun. 2019, https://iapp.org/news/a/why-are-we-assuming-ccpa-does-not-regulate-internal-transfers/ (accessed 30 Oct. 2023).

intra-group sharing must be disclosed and covered by opt-out rights just as much as sharing with unaffiliated entities. But, if and to the extent all companies in a group qualify as 'the business', then intra-group information exchanges lack 'another business' or a 'third party' for purposes of the definition of 'selling'.[281] The term 'third party' is defined to exclude 'the business'.[282] Similar privileges for intra-group sharing of information are contained in other laws, including California's Shine the Light Law,[283] on which many CCPA provisions seem to have been based. Therefore, information-sharing between parent and subsidiary companies should be exempt from the definition of 'selling' under the CCPA.

Yet, based on the revisions that CPRA introduced, 'sharing' is defined very narrowly to require a disclosure to a third party for cross-context behavioural advertising,[284] which means that other forms of intra-group disclosures no longer trigger the 'business-by-affiliation' rule.[285] As a result, fewer foreign businesses will be subject to the revised CCPA merely because of affiliation with a parent company or subsidiary due to this narrower definition of sharing,[286] and fewer intra-group disclosures may be privileged based on the argument that the affiliates constitute one business.

Given that the CCPA as amended by CPRA no longer seems to offer privileges for disclosures to affiliates and given that horizontal sharing between subsidiaries is not exempt under either interpretation, companies should consider documenting intra-group transfers as service provider arrangements, i.e., conclude intra-group service agreements according to which one affiliate processes personal information only to provide services for the other affiliate, or seek direction from data subjects. Businesses that take this approach can use more uniform documentation globally because many jurisdictions do not grant specific privileges to intra-group disclosures of personal data but exempt disclosures to service providers or at the request of the data subject.[287]

[f] Exempted Businesses

In addition to exemptions for certain types of information and activities, California Civil Code section 1798.145 exempts certain healthcare providers, credit reporting agencies, furnishers of credit reports and other companies partially or fully from CCPA requirements.

281. Cal. Civ. Code §1798.140(ad)(1).
282. Cal. Civ. Code §1798.140(ai)(1).
283. *See* Cal. Civ. Code §1798.83(f)(1).
284. Cal. Civ. Code §1798.140(ah)(1).
285. Cal. Civ. Code §1798.140(d)(1-2).
286. *See* Lothar Determann and Jonathan Tam, The California Privacy Rights Act of 2020: A broad and complex data processing regulation that applies to businesses worldwide, 11 World Data Protection Report #4, at 13 (2020).
287. *See* Lothar Determann, Reassessing EU Standard Contractual Clauses for Transfers of Personal Data to Processing Service Providers, 11 World Data Protection Report #4, at 1, 2 (2011).

[3] CCPA Compliance Obligations

The harshest CCPA obligations apply to businesses that 'sell' or 'share' personal information. According to CCPA, 'selling' means any 'selling, renting, releasing, disclosing, disseminating, making available, transferring, or otherwise communicating orally, in writing, or by electronic or other means, a consumer's personal information ... to another business or a third party for monetary or other valuable consideration'.[288] 'Sharing' is defined as 'sharing, renting, releasing, disclosing, disseminating, making available, transferring, or otherwise communicating orally, in writing, or by electronic or other means, a consumer's personal information by the business to a third party for cross-context behavioral advertising, whether or not for monetary or other valuable consideration, including transactions between a business and a third party for cross context behavioral advertising for the benefit of a business in which no money is exchanged'.[289] In most cases, 'sharing' also constitutes 'selling' under CCPA. Wherever businesses share data in the context of a contractual relationship, they receive some form of consideration. Consideration is a basic condition to valid contract formation under the US law.[290] Regarding relationships where a company pays a service provider to host data, manage payroll, operate a webpage or perform other services, the parties do not normally view data sharing as 'selling' of information but rather as making data available for the limited purpose of enabling the service provider to perform the work. Yet, given the counterintuitive definition of 'selling' as any 'transferring for any valuable consideration', the services themselves are part of every bargain and potentially to be considered 'consideration'. Also, some service providers price their services differently – or offer services free of charge – based on the value of data they process as part of the arrangement.

The CCPA contemplates very narrow and qualified exceptions for disclosers of personal information to service providers, which implies that service provider arrangements are not generally exempt from rules on 'selling' or 'sharing'. In light of these facts and the broad definition of 'personal information', companies have to prepare for the possibility that more information-sharing activities could potentially be covered by CCPA than arrangements that would commonly be characterized as a sale.

As a countermeasure, companies can expressly clarify with their business partners in written contracts that certain unintentional or incidental information-sharing (e.g., public keys or optional personal data that a blockchain participant added to a block) is not intended to be for consideration. Terms to this effect could be included in smart contracts or blockchain whitepapers, which could clarify, for example, that blockchain or sidechain participants pay for cryptocurrency, not for any personal information exchanged as part of transactions.

Also, companies can try to claim one of the complex definitional exceptions in the CCPA, according to which a business is not deemed to sell personal information if users

288. Cal. Civ. Code §1798.140(ad)(1).
289. Cal. Civ. Code §1798.140(ah)(1).
290. Legal Information Institute, available at: www.law.cornell.edu/wex/consideration (accessed 30 Oct. 2023).

direct the disclosures or the business uses or shares an identifier for a consumer who has opted out of the sale of the consumer's personal information for the purposes of alerting third parties that the consumer has opted out of the sale of the consumer's personal information. Yet, claiming any of these exceptions will require additional efforts and likely revisions to existing contracts, disclosures, internal processes and business practices. Each of the exceptions refers to additional terms that are defined in the statute in counterintuitive and very prescriptive ways.

Many companies will find it difficult to get comfortable that they are not somewhere somehow disclosing personal information in a manner that qualifies as 'selling' under the broad and counterintuitive definition in the CCPA. They are obligated to obtain prior opt-in consent from minors under 16 years of age (and parental consent from minors under 13 years) before they share their information in a manner that qualifies as 'selling'.[291] And, companies must provide a clear and conspicuous hyperlink with the words 'Do Not Sell or Share My Personal Information' that direct users to a web page enabling them, or someone they authorize, to opt out of the sale of the resident's personal information.[292] If a California resident opts out, the company must not approach the person with a request to consider opting in again before at least twelve months have passed since the opt-out.[293] Additionally, the California Attorney General requires businesses to implement measures to recognize opt-out signals that consumers activate on their devices, so-called Global Privacy Controls, [294] which would also have to be recognized by blockchain and DLT applications.

An opt-out could pose difficulties in a blockchain context, as the personal information in existing blocks would normally be transferred to additional users. Therefore, blockchain operators should ensure that blockchains are not used to sell personal information and clarify (smart-) contractually that any consideration paid is for services or items other than personal information. Where this is not practical, operators on blockchains should consider data deletion techniques or de-identification measures also proposed for erasure requests.[295] But, since the CPRA expanded exemptions for 'publicly available' information from the scope of CCPA, the more fundamental concerns raised in the first edition of this book no longer apply, given that information on the public portions of the blockchain are largely exempt now.

Companies must update or supplement their privacy policies with required disclosures, whether or not they engage in 'selling of personal information', and include a description of California residents' data subject rights, including access,

291. Cal. Civ. Code §1798.120(c). Companies can try to obtain parental consent by providing a consent form to be signed by the parent and returned via US mail, fax, or electronic scan, available at: www.ftc.gov/tips-advice/business-center/guidance/complying-coppa-frequently-asked-questions#Verifiable%20Parental (accessed 30 Oct. 2023).
292. Cal. Civ. Code §1798.135(a)(1).
293. Cal. Civ. Code §1798.135(c)(4).
294. CCPA Regulations §7025.
295. Section §4.06[D][2], *supra*.

correction, erasure and portability[296] as well as channels to exercise such rights, including, at a minimum, a toll-free telephone number.[297]

If a California resident exercises any of the new rights, including access, correction, erasure of information, portability or prohibitions on data 'selling', businesses must not discriminate against such resident by denying goods or services, charging different prices, providing a different level or quality of goods or services, or otherwise.[298] Businesses may apply a different price, rate or quality only if that difference is reasonably related to the value of the consumer's data.[299] Businesses also have to post a 'notice of financial incentive' that informs consumers about the value of their data to the business.[300] A company that assigns monetary value to personal information has to consider accounting, tax and other implications. Many companies that have been offering services online free of charge and relied on data monetization for funding may now have to consider introducing user fees, given that consumers are free to opt out or to request erasure of information, and companies must not penalize consumers for the exercise of their rights. Companies will also have to consider alternative business models and web/mobile presences, such as California-only sites and offerings.[301] Such alternatives can help confine the impact of CCPA; however, they are costly to create and maintain.

[4] Data Access and Deletion Rights

As noted with respect to GDPR, data access and deletion rights can pose particular challenges with respect to blockchain and distributed ledger technologies.[302] But, since 'publicly available' information is now excluded from the applicability of CCPA, the restrictions under California law only apply to non-public information conveyed with blockchain and DLT applications, which significantly improves the legal environment for such applications.

If a California resident demands access to data held by a business that is subject to the CCPA, then such business would have to provide information about the personal information it holds and make a copy available. If part of the data is encrypted and the business is unable to decrypt the data, then it may have to make the encrypted information available or refer the data subject to publicly accessible copies of the data. Data access requests may result in additional costs and burdens on resources but do not ultimately have to be prohibitive in most situations. Also, with respect to deletion rights, CCPA offers several exceptions.[303]

296. Cal. Civ. Code §1798.135(a)(2).
297. Cal. Civ. Code §1798.130(a)(1)(A).
298. Cal. Civ. Code §1798.125(a)(1).
299. Cal. Civ. Code §1798.125(a)(2).
300. Cal. Civ. Code §1798.125; CCPA Regulations §7016.
301. Cal. Civ. Code §1798.135(b).
302. *See* this book, section §4.06[D], *supra*.
303. Cal. Civ. Code §1798.105(d).

[5] *Sanctions and Remedies*

According to the new Cal. Civ. Code §1798.155, companies can be ordered in a civil action brought by the California Attorney General to pay penalties of up to USD 7,500 per intentional violation of any provision of the CCPA or, for unintentional violations, if the company fails to cure the unintentional violation within thirty days of notice, USD 2,500 per violation under section 17206 of the California Business and Professions Code. Such penalties collected by the State of California shall be allocated to a new 'Consumer Privacy Fund' to fund and encourage enforcement.

According to a somewhat separate section within the new CCPA,[304] companies that become victims of data theft or other data security breaches can be ordered in civil class-action lawsuits to pay statutory damages between USD 100 and USD 750 per California resident and incident or actual damages, whichever is greater, and any other relief a court deems proper, subject to an option of the California Attorney General to prosecute the company instead of allowing civil suits to be brought against it.

With respect to statutory damages for data security breaches only, the new Cal. Civ. Code §1798.150(a)(1) refers to the definition of 'personal information' in the existing Cal. Civ. Code §1798.81.5(d)(1)(A), which covers: 'An individual's first name or first initial and his or her last name in combination with any one or more of the following data elements, when either the name or the data elements are not encrypted or redacted:

- Social security number.
- Driver's license number or California identification card number.
- Account number, credit or debit card number, in combination with any required security code, access code, or password that would permit access to an individual's financial account.
- Medical information.
- Health insurance information'.

This definition of 'personal information' is much narrower than the broad new definition that applies to the remainder of the CCPA (which covers any information relating to a California resident or household), and it is also narrower than the definition of 'personal information' in the existing California data security breach notification laws, which list similar information plus 'information ... collected through ... an automated license plate recognition system'.[305]

'Encrypted' means rendered unusable, unreadable, or indecipherable to an unauthorized person through a security technology or methodology generally accepted in the field of information security.[306] Courts may also refer to this definition to determine the meaning of 'nonencrypted and nonredacted' in the new law.

304. Cal. Civ. Code §1798.150.
305. Cal. Civ. Code §1798.82(h); Cal. Civ. Code §1798.29(g).
306. Cal. Civ. Code §1798.82(i)(4) and Cal. Civ. Code §1798.29(h)(4).

But the new law does not extend to two situations covered under the existing breach notification laws, namely where individuals are protected with respect to encrypted information if the security of the encryption has been compromised[307] and where a user name or email address, if used in combination with a password or security question and answer, would permit access to an online account.[308] Moreover, the new law does not refer to the existing definition of a data security breach but creates a new concept by referring to 'unauthorized access and exfiltration, theft, or disclosure'.[309]

Companies around the world are already required to notify California residents of data security breaches under California's existing breach notification law, which California enacted in 2002 and has updated several times since then.[310] But, the potential liability resulting from breaches was somewhat contained by the fact that the original 2002 version of the California breach notification law only prescribed notification obligations; there were no penalties or other remedies for the actual breach – only for failures to notify.

Based on existing law, plaintiffs are able to refer to various general causes of action, including torts, consumer protection and unfair competition laws, but often find it difficult to show 'an invasion of a legally protected interest' that is 'concrete and particularized' and 'actual or imminent, not conjectural or hypothetical', as required for standing under federal law according to *Spokeo, Inc. v. Robins*.[311] Particularly in the context of class-action lawsuits, plaintiffs' lawyers prefer to assert general harms potentially associated with security breaches as opposed to concrete, individual injuries, which could prevent class-action certification.[312]

Since 1 January 2016, operators and users of automated license plate recognition (ALPR) systems were subjected to specific data security requirements and notification obligations in case of a data security breach under Cal. Civ. Code §§1798.90.5, 1798.29 and 1798.82; individuals harmed by a violation of the California ALPR law were also entitled to bring a civil action against persons who knowingly caused the harm – including harm by data security breaches – and claim actual damages, liquidated damages in the amount of USD 2,500, punitive damages (upon proof of wilful or reckless disregard of the law), reasonable attorney's fees and other litigation costs, and preliminary and equitable relief.[313]

Now, based on the new cause of action in Cal. Civ. Code §1798.150 for statutory damages, plaintiffs generally do not have to show concrete, individual harm associated with certain data security breaches captured by the new statute, at least not in California courts, where no particular standing requirements apply. Therefore, companies have to prepare themselves for significantly increased liability exposure in cases of data security breaches. For example, if a hospital falls victim to a cyberattack or plain

307. Cal. Civ. Code §1798.82(a).
308. Cal. Civ. Code §1798.82(h)(2).
309. Cal. Civ. Code §1798.150(a)(1).
310. Determann, L., *New California Data Security and Breach Notification Requirements* (Bloomberg BNA Privacy & Security Law Report, 15 PVLR 219, 2 Jan. 2016).
311. 136 S. Ct. 1540 (2016).
312. Determann, *supra* n. 180, at Chapters 2-15:1 and 6-2:2.
313. *Ibid.*, at Chapters 2-5:5, 2-15.1.54 and 2-19:6.9.

old burglary and theft of an appointment calendar with 10,000 patient names for doctor visits (without any sensitive medical history), the hospital could be exposed to damages claims between USD 1 million and USD 7.5 million plus the cost of litigation, even if not one patient suffers any concrete harm of any kind.

FURTHER READING

De Filippi, P. & Wright, A., *Blockchain and the Law, the Rule of Code* (2019).

Determann, L., *Determann's Field Guide to Data Privacy Law: International Corporate Compliance* (Edward Elgar Publishing Ltd., 5th ed., 2022).

Determann, L., *California Privacy Law, Practical Guide and Commentary* (IAPP, 5th ed., 2023).

Ibáñez, L-D., O'Hara, K. & Simperl, E., *On Blockchains and the General Data Protection Regulation*, available at: https://eprints.soton.ac.uk/422879/1/BLockchains_GDPR_4.pdf.

NIST, *Blockchain Technology Overview* (NISTIR 8202, 2018).

Serwin, A.B. *Information Security and Privacy: A Guide to Federal and State Law and Compliance* (2023-2024 ed.).

Solove, D. & Schwartz, P., *Information Privacy Law* (Aspen Publishing Co., 6th ed., 2018).

Solove, D., & Schwartz, P., *Privacy Law Fundamentals* (IAPP, 6th ed., 2022).

Timmons, J. & Hickman, T., *Blockchain and the GDPR: Co-existing in Contradiction* (Blockchain & Cryptocurrency Regulation, Global Legal Insights, 2nd ed., 2020).

CHAPTER 5

Capital Markets

Michael Jünemann et al.

§5.01 CAPITAL MARKETS AND BLOCKCHAIN: INTERNATIONAL CHAPTER

This chapter serves as a guide through the highly regulated field of modern capital markets, focusing on international capital market regulatory issues of Distributed Ledger Technology (DLT) and showcasing the broad differences of its regulatory framework across the world. It will not cover the Regulation (EU) 2023/1114 on Markets in Crypto Assets (Markets in Crypto Assets Regulation – MiCAR)[1] or laws regulating Payment Tokens, Asset-Referenced Tokens, Utility Tokens, Non-fungible Tokens or the like but will centre exclusively on capital markets/securities regulations and will focus solely on legal issues specific to and arising from the use of DLT in this context.

[A] What Makes a Token a Security?

This chapter functions as an overview of the possible regulatory classification of Tokens. In particular, the question of when Tokens are covered by the regulatory concept of securities will be addressed and updated along with the new regulations on this field of law.[2]

The issuance of coins or Token(s)[3] using a type of distributed ledger technology (DLT) such as blockchain technology involves linking rights and value to data

1. *See* Chapter 6, §6.01 (The EU Markets in Crypto Assets Regulation (MiCA)), *infra*.
2. Cf., for example, conference report of the specialist conference 'Blockchain: Chancen, Recht und Regulierung' ['Blockchain: opportunities, law and regulation' by Jean Louis Schiltz, MMR-Aktuell 2018 [news service], 400563].
3. Hereinafter 'Token(s)'.

packages. This is analogous to how traditional securities, such as share bonds or other certificates, are designed. However, not all Tokens are suitable to qualify as (a new kind of) security. In this first section of this chapter (and the corresponding sections of the country reviews), we will discuss the different types of Tokens which can be found in the market and whether their individual design justifies (or makes it mandatory) to treat them like securities.

Tokens vary depending on their technical and legal design. They can be (technically and/or legally) fungible or non-fungible and can be grouped into different (non-legal) categories: Security Tokens, Currency Tokens, Utility Tokens, Unique or Non-fungible Tokens and Hybrid Tokens.

A Token can be linked to various rights and obligations, even accumulate characteristics of more than one of those (non-legal) categories, eventually becoming a 'hybrid' Token. Consequently, they also may fall under various areas of law.

NFTs are unique Tokens verifying authenticity and are distinct from each other due to exclusive Token IDs.[4] They may use protocols like ERC-721.[5] Regulatory bodies globally often assess the classification and regulation of NFTs based on their actual design and function (not only by their technical uniqueness), similar to how they approach Fungible Crypto Tokens (e.g., Currency Tokens). Also, here it is substance over form.[6]

Currency Tokens like Bitcoin (BTC), Ethereum (ETH), and Ripple (XRP) aim for universal acceptance, although the level of acceptance can significantly vary among them. They are intended to function as a form of money replacement.[7] Currency Tokens serve as units of account and may or may not be backed by reserves, which can lead to fluctuations in their nominal value against one or more fiat currencies. Depending on the applicable law, Currency Tokens may be considered money, things, copyrighted software, a personal intellectual creation, or other rights, making them a typical subject to civil law. Regarding financial regulations, Currency Tokens could, for example, be classified as financial instruments, electronic money (e-money), capital investments, units in an investment fund, securities, or other instruments regulated under national law. Stablecoins, such as Tether, are designed as a counterpoint to the high volatility often seen in Currency Tokens. Unlike volatile Tokens such as Bitcoin (BTC), the value of Stablecoins is anchored to a fiat currency, commodity, or other financial instruments, offering more stability.[8] Stablecoins are designed to maintain a

4. BaFin Federal Financial Supervisory Authority, Crypto tokens (9 Oct. 2023), https://www.bafin.de/EN/Aufsicht/FinTech/Geschaeftsmodelle/DLT_Blockchain_Krypto/Kryptotoken/Kryptotoken_node_en.html.
5. ERC-721 Non-Fungible Token Standard (9 Oct. 2023), https://ethereum.org/de/developers/docs/standards/tokens/erc-721/.
6. BaFin, Tokenisation (9 Oct. 2023), https://www.bafin.de/SharedDocs/Veroeffentlichungen/EN/Fachartikel/2019/fa_bj_1904_Tokenisierung_en.html.
7. Michael Jünemann & Johannes Wirtz, ICO: Legal Classification of Tokens: part 3 – Currency Token (9. Oct. 2023), https://www.twobirds.com/en/news/articles/2019/global/ico-legal-classification-of-tokens-3.
8. Thomas Fromherz, Entmystifizierung digitaler Währungen (9 Oct. 2023), https://www.der-bank-blog.de/entmystifizierung-digitaler-waehrungen/technologie/37685573/; Adam Hayes, Investopedia, Stablecoins: Definition, How They Work, and Types (9 Oct. 2023) https://www.investopedia.com/terms/s/stablecoin.asp.

stable value and typically exhibit minimal fluctuations by providing collateral. The stability of Stablecoins can vary based on the type of collateral they are backed by. For example, Tether is pegged at 1-to-1 with a matching fiat currency (e.g., 1 USD₮ = 1 USD) and claims to be backed 100% by Tether's reserves and operates on multiple blockchains such as Algorand, Avalanche, Polka and Polygon.[9]

Unlike Currency Tokens, Utility Tokens like Filecoin (FIL) are a type of crypto asset, both commonly understood and acknowledged under European regulation, designed to provide access to a specific good or service rendered by the Token's issuer.[10] Essentially, Utility Tokens provide digital access rights by offering services or functions solely on a particular platform.[11] They are crafted to function as a kind of digital voucher which is redeemable against an issuer's promised service.[12] Utility Tokens neither grant membership rights nor establish a similar financial relationship.[13] Monetary claims are not substantiated through Utility Tokens.[14] Utility Tokens find acceptance only with the issuer and not third parties, and only the issuer can carry out the promised service.[15] According to certain regulations in many but not all countries, Utility Tokens that operate within a delimited business model, serving to pay for certain goods or services of the issuer or acting as vouchers within such a framework, are not considered crypto assets.[16] Other regulations (like MiCAR) do cover Utility Tokens as well.[17] Furthermore, its specified exchange value typically disqualifies a Utility Token as e-money.[18] While Utility Tokens might be exempt from capital market regulations in certain jurisdictions, it's worth noting that many buyers view Utility Tokens with an investment lens, hoping to profit from trading them on the secondary market.[19] Thus, it is worth noting that the mere labelling of a Token as a 'Utility Token' does not equate to a matching legal qualification.[20] Conversely, a Utility Token is not turned into a security because buyers anticipate profits.[21] Still, some regulators maintain this perspective despite the uncontrollable nature of buyer expectations by

9. Tether (9. Oct. 2023) https://tether.to/en/why-tether.
10. BaFin, Crypto tokens (9 Oct. 2023), https://www.bafin.de/EN/Aufsicht/FinTech/Geschaeftsmodelle/DLT_Blockchain_Krypto/Kryptotoken/Kryptotoken_node_en.html.
11. Financial Conduct Authority, Cryptoassets: Feedback to CP19/3 and final guidance to firms, p. 13 (9 Oct. 2023), https://www.fca.org.uk/publication/policy/ps19-22.pdf.
12. Financial Conduct Authority, Cryptoassets: Feedback to CP19/3 and final guidance to firms, p. 13 (9 Oct. 2023), https://www.fca.org.uk/publication/policy/ps19-22.pdf.
13. BaFin - Crypto tokens (9 Oct. 2023), https://www.bafin.de/EN/Aufsicht/FinTech/Geschaeftsmodelle/DLT_Blockchain_Krypto/Kryptotoken/Kryptotoken_node_en.html.
14. Paul P. Momtaz, Kathrin Rennertseder & Henning Schröder, Token Offerings: A Revolution in Corporate Finance?, p. 49; The Capco Institute Journal of Financial Transformation, 32, 37 (2019); Michael Jünemann & Johannes Wirtz, ICO: Legal Classification of Tokens: Part 4 – Utility Token (9 Oct. 2023), https://www.twobirds.com/en/news/articles/2019/global/ico-legal-classification-of-tokens-utility-token.
15. Jünemann & Wirtz, *supra* n. 7 (9 Oct. 2023).
16. Jünemann & Wirtz, *supra* n. 7 (9 Oct. 2023) for Germany.
17. *See* Chapter 6, §6.01[A][1][a] (The EU Markets in Crypto Assets Regulation (MiCA)), *infra*.
18. Jünemann & Wirtz, *supra* n. 7 (9 Oct. 2023).
19. *Ibid.*
20. *Ibid.*
21. *Ibid.*

the issuer.[22] The negotiability of Utility Tokens on capital markets is also not firmly established.[23] Although Utility Tokens might remain outside of traditional banking and capital markets regulation, this absence does not indicate complete deregulation. In this respect, issuers should exercise caution when emphasizing the utility characteristics of the proposed Token and claiming its non-security and therefore 'unregulated' status. Depending on the legal landscape, Utility Tokens might be governed by (national) contractual, consumer protection, trade, and tax laws. However, the specific regulations can vary widely from one jurisdiction to another, and the legal landscape for crypto assets is still evolving (e.g., Utility Tokens will be partly covered by MiCAR). Additionally, the Utility Token's design, especially if hybrid in nature, adds to their complexity and can influence their supervisory law classification.[24]

The regulation of Tokens depends largely on the answer to the key legal question of whether the Token is recognized as a 'security' under applicable national laws.[25] The regulation of Tokens may trigger prospectus requirements[26] or other publication requirements (e.g., as securities under prospectus regulation; as investment fund under investment funds regulation; as investment instrument under investment instrument regulation, etc.) and/or licensing requirements for the issuer; and/or licensing requirements for persons trading or acting as intermediaries in the trade of the Tokens or offering the safeguarding and/or administration thereof. Essential for the classification of a Token as a security is its nature.[27]

By issuing Security Tokens, the issuer promises some form of return. Depending on the design, Security Tokens can constitute securities. The question of what makes a Token a security is naturally linked to the definition of a security under the applicable national law. This means that different standards apply in the European Union compared to, for example, the United States (US)[28] or Singapore.

Tokens regarded as securities are subject to capital markets law in all major economies. Capital markets law is typically intended to mitigate the structural and systemic weaknesses of the capital markets. These markets are characterized not only by divergent interests among various participants (issuers, investors, shareholders, capital seekers, and management) but also by a strong potential for information

22. Securities and Exchange Commission, Cryptocurrency/ICOs (9 Oct. 2023) https://www.sec.gov/securities-topics/ICO.
23. Jünemann & Wirtz, *supra* n. 7 (9 Oct. 2023).
24. BaFin, Crypto tokens (9 Oct. 2023), https://www.bafin.de/EN/Aufsicht/FinTech/Geschaeftsmodelle/DLT_Blockchain_Krypto/Kryptotoken/Kryptotoken_node_en.html;jsessionid=046EB270C6066285A94EA45CC097A0E6.2_cid500.
25. BaFin, Tokenisation (9 Oct. 2023), https://www.bafin.de/SharedDocs/Veroeffentlichungen/EN/Fachartikel/2019/fa_bj_1904_Tokenisierung_en.html; US Securities and Exchange Commission, Framework for 'Investment Contract' Analysis of Digital Assets (7. Oct. 2023), https://www.sec.gov/corpfin/framework-investment-contract-analysis-digital-assets; Financial Conduct Authority, Guidance on Cryptoassets, p. 40 (9 Oct. 2023), https://www.fca.org.uk/publication/policy/ps19-22.pdf.
26. BaFin, Prospectus requirement (9 Oct. 2023), https://www.bafin.de/EN/Aufsicht/Prospekte/Wertpapiere/Prospektpflicht/prospektpflicht_node_en.html.
27. Financial Conduct Authority, How we define cryptoassets (9 Oct. 2023), https://www.fca.org.uk/firms/cryptoassets (9 Oct. 2023).
28. *See* Chapter 7, §7.02 (Federal Securities Laws), *infra*.

asymmetry between them, particularly between investors and issuers. At times, abusive behaviour is tempting for certain participants, considering the monopoly position of the stock exchange. Consequently, capital markets law aims to ensure the proper functioning of these markets and protect investors. Investor protection encompasses safeguarding both individual investors, which is essentially a special form of consumer protection, and institutional investors. The latter seeks to safeguard the investor community as a whole, thereby ensuring the overall functioning of the capital market. These principles apply equally on national, European and global scales.

The European concept of securities refers to their fungibility which is consequently the central principle used to compare Tokens to other well-established securities. In order to satisfy the concept of a security, a Token must be standardized, negotiable, and transferable in (capital) markets. Unlike US law, which uses 'investment contracts' as a catch-all definition for securities, European law is more specific in its definition of securities.[29] The securities concept of European law originates from the Markets in Financial Instruments Directive II (MiFID II), which aims to counter the weaknesses of the European financial markets that were revealed during the financial crisis. The European Securities and Markets Authority (ESMA) already clarified that certain types of Tokens might qualify as securities under the definitions provided by the Prospectus Directive. This also applies to the Prospectus Regulation which has (gradually) replaced the Prospectus Directive. Securities are those 'classes of securities which are negotiable on the capital market',[30] with the exception of 'instruments of payment'[31] and, for prospectus law, 'money market instruments … having a maturity of less than 12 months'.[32]

Alongside Europe, the US is the other most vibrant region for Token offerings.[33]

According to the US Securities and Exchange Commission (SEC), 'depending on the nature of the digital asset, including what rights it purports to convey and how it is offered and sold, it may fall within the definition of a security under the US federal securities laws'.[34] The term 'security' includes an 'investment contract', as well as 'other instruments such as stocks, bonds, and transferable shares'.[35] The US Supreme Court decided in *SEC v. W. J. Howey Co.* (328 U.S. 293 (1946) – also known as the 'Howey Case') that an 'investment contract' exists where there is the 'investment of money in a common enterprise with a reasonable expectation of profits to be derived from the efforts of others'.[36] Both the SEC and the US federal courts use the so-called

29. US Securities and Exchange Commission, *supra* n. 25 (9 Oct. 2023).
30. Article 4(1) no. 44 directive 2014/65/EU (2014).
31. *Ibid.*
32. Article 2. a) Regulation EU 2017/1129 (2017).
33. Philipp Maume & Mathias Fromberger, *Regulation of Initial Coin Offerings: Reconciling U.S. and E.U. Securities Laws*, 19(2) CJIL, 548, 548 (2019).
34. Bill Hinman, *Statement on 'Framework for "Investment Contract" Analysis of Digital Assets'* (9 Oct. 2023), https://www.sec.gov/news/public-statement/statement-framework-investment-contract-analysis-digital-assets.
35. US Securities and Exchange Commission, *supra* n. 25 (9 Oct. 2023), *See* Chapter 7, §7.02 (*Federal Securities Laws*), *infra*.
36. *See* Chapter 7, §7.02 (*Federal Securities Laws*), *infra*.

investment contract analysis to determine whether a Token is a security subject to US federal securities laws.[37]

Apart from Europe and the US, regions like Asia have also become significant in the Token offering landscape, with countries like Singapore, Hong Kong, and South Korea developing regulatory guidelines for Token offerings. Furthermore, Malta and Switzerland have positioned themselves as friendly hubs for blockchain projects. With the evolving landscape, it becomes increasingly crucial for stakeholders to be well versed with the unique regulations that each of these jurisdictions offer.

However, many questions with regard to the regulation of Tokens remain unanswered. Time will tell whether a regulatory patchwork or a similar framework will develop under US law, European law, the national laws of the Member States of the European Union, and other jurisdictions with large capital markets. The following country reports will answer the question 'What makes a Token a security?' for numerous individual jurisdictions.

[B] Blockchain Finality

In this chapter, we explore the concept of blockchain finality. The technical structure of a Token is flexible, similar to the rights associated with them. A widespread belief is that any transfer of a Token is irreversible and thus technically final.[38] This is further supported by the decentralized design, viewed as tamper-proof.[39] These 'facts' suggest a finality that can also be found in securities trading. However, analysing the historical developments of DLTs reveals many cases that negate such finality.[40] And so far, finality has always been a legal fiction designed to promote the frictionless functioning of capital markets. In this section of this chapter (and the corresponding parts of the country reviews), we will focus on the question of whether blockchain finality actually exists and which consequences this may have from a financial market regulatory perspective.

In case of a 'hard fork',[41] the 'original' chain and the new chain become incompatible. When the underlying right is a security that exists as an individual entity and is traded and negotiated, the law needs to address what happens in the case of two strings of the chain operating the exact same security. Furthermore, '51% attacks'[42] cause all following transactions to rely on falsified information that is subsequently

37. Hinman, *supra* n. 34 (9 Oct. 2023).
38. A Report by UK Government Chief Scientist Adviser: *Distributed Ledger Technology, beyond blockchain* (9 Oct. 2023), https://assets.publishing.service.gov.uk/government/uploads/system/uploads/attachment_data/file/492972/gs-16-1-distributed-ledger-technology.pdf.
39. Marcella Atzori, *Blockchain Technology and Decentralized Governance: Is the State Still Necessary?*, https://papers.ssrn.com/sol3/papers.cfm?abstract_id=2709713 (9 Oct. 2023). *See* Chapter 1, §1.06[A], *supra*.
40. Vitalik Buterin, *On Settlement Finality* (9 Oct. 2023), https://blog.ethereum.org/2016/05/09/on-settlement-finality.
41. Crypto forks, *What are forks in cryptocurrency? Risks, Opportunities and Calendar for a ll 2018 forks* (9 Oct. 2023), https://www.fxstreet.com/cryptocurrencies/resources/what-are-cryptocurrency-forks.
42. *See* Chapter 1, §1.08[G], *supra*.

verified as the leading block.[43] However unlikely these events may or may not be, they do exist.[44] In the event of technical malfunction, the question arises whether legal finality needs to be addressed by the applicable law or should influence the classification of a Token as a security. There is no general rule that transactions have to be legally final. For example, in the event of multiple assignments in a chronologically extended sequence to different assignees (assignment chain), each of the assignees successively acquires the sole legal title to the claim. However, if one of the assignments is void, the following assignments are void as well. Since the title to the claim is not linked to any external evidence, e.g., possession or entry in a public register, typically the assignee cannot rely on a bona fide acquisition rule or concept under applicable law.

But legal finality produces legal certainty as required for the frictionless functioning of trading on capital markets. Establishing legal certainty of bookings and transactions is a particular prerequisite for the success of DLT systems. Most countries have principles to establish legal finality. One of them is the aforementioned bona fide acquisition rule stemming from Roman law.[45] The bona fide acquisition rule protects good faith purchasers who acquire property without notice of misconduct, representing a compromise between the interests of transaction efficiency and the protection of ownership.[46] Bona fide purchasers acquire title to the property free from the risk that the property may be claimed by the 'rightful' owner, resulting in the loss of ownership or title for the 'rightful' owner.[47] Therefore, the 'rightful' owner's remedy is limited to actions against the 'thief'[48] or an otherwise unauthorized person who sold the property to the good faith acquirer. The bona fide acquisition rule is based on the concept that possession strongly hints at ownership.

It is argued that the possibility of bona fide acquisition is the only way to ensure orderly processing and trading on the financial market. MiFID II, for example, lays down the conditions of fungibility and tradability on the financial market but does not state a requirement for bona fide rights protection.[49] In respect of trading on the financial markets, an elaborate chain of title due diligence is not possible. Unlimited negotiability on the market requires that transactions can be processed securely and easily and that there can be no objections from third parties. Therefore, the classic understanding of capital market negotiability is based on the possibility of bona fide acquisition.

However, in transactions involving the purchase of Tokens, there is more than one possible approach to establish legal finality. One approach is to treat all transactions recorded on the blockchain as valid. This is on the basis that blockchains

43. Sarwar Sayeed & Hector Marco-Gisbert, *Assessing Blockchain Consensus and Security Mechanisms Against the 51% Attack* (9 Oct. 2023), https://doi.org/10.3390/app9091788.
44. *See* Chapter 1, §1.08[G], *supra*.
45. Andrew Balthazor, *The Bona Fide Acquisition Rule Applied to Cryptocurrency*, 3 GLTR402, 408 (2019).
46. *Ibid.*, at 408, 409 (2019).
47. *Ibid.*, at 405, 409 (2019).
48. *Ibid.*, at 409 (2019).
49. Hagen Weiß, *Tokenisation* (9 Oct. 2023), https://www.bafin.de/dok/12477346.

permanently record all transactions and therefore allow users to trace transactions. In this way, blockchain technology could provide a substitute for a bona fide purchase. The cryptographic rendition of the chain of ownership allows for each transaction to be transparent in a way that the ownership of the underlying right is inseparably linked to the Token. This could provide sufficient protection against ineffective Token transfers for capital market trading. Accordingly, the data written on the blockchain would be considered similar to a public register, thus subject to public credence. However, difficulties are encountered in cases such as a 'fork', where two strings of the blockchain operating with the exact same underlying right would exist. If this scenario arose in a title-transfer transaction, it would be impossible to determine the true holder of the title. Other problems arise with Token theft, where the unauthorized use of access data may result in dispositions by non-entitled individuals or in a case where the transfer agreement for the Token may be void due to incapacity to contract, e.g., because of a pathological mental disturbance.[50]

Furthermore, if a private key is not kept confidential, an unauthorized person can use the key for further disposure of a Token.[51] Whereas a certificate can only ever be in the direct possession of one person, data can be copied without an original being detectable. The Token would have to be retransferred[52] as the right on which it is based, and its valid transfer must be considered. It could also not be argued that a purchase process could not be reversed due to anonymity and that this resulted in functional equivalence with a bona fide purchase. It would be very much against well-established legal principles to accept a Token transaction, which is based, for example, on a computer crime, as final because of factual difficulties.

The use of permissioned blockchains could solve most of these problems. Although blockchains differ greatly in their technical and governance set-up,[53] common references to 'blockchain' usually mean public and permissionless blockchains. 'Public' means that the reading of blockchain data and the submission of transactions are not restricted, whereas 'permissionless' means that all users are eligible transaction processors.[54] Therefore, such blockchains are – leaving aside the technical and economic restrictions around mining and software governance – characterized by the fact that anyone who downloads the open-source software can join the ledger, read the chain, make legitimate changes or download the ledger without a permission by the gatekeeper.[55] A well-known example of a public and permissionless blockchain is the Ethereum Blockchain.

50. Paul Varul, Anu Avi & Triin Kivisild, *Restrictions on Active Legal Capacity* (9 Oct. 2023), https://www.juridicainternational.eu/public/pdf/ji_2004_1_99.pdf.
51. Michael Jünemann & Johannes Wirtz, *ICO: Legal Classification of Tokens: Part 2 – Security Token* (9 Oct. 2023), https://www.twobirds.com/en/news/articles/2019/global/ico-legal-classification-of-tokens-2.
52. Jünemann & Wirtz *supra* n. 51.
53. Michèle Finck & Valentina Moscon, *Copyright Law on Blockchains: Between New Forms of Rights Administration and Digital Rights Management 2.0*, ILC 50, 77, 90 (2019).
54. *See* Chapter 1, §1.14[A] and [B], *supra*.
55. Finck & Moscon *supra* n. 53 at, 77, 90.

However, there are also private and permissioned blockchains where access and performance of transaction processing require permission by the single party or consortium acting as a gatekeeper.[56] Under this model, only previously selected participants (nodes) are authorized to access the blockchain. Examples of this are R3 Corda and Hyperledger Fabric. Permissioned blockchains are particularly preferred by investors to mitigate the risk of public and permissionless blockchains. That, in particular, makes them suitable for a Security Token. The risk of tampering with permissioned blockchains is expected to be much lower than with public and permissionless blockchains due to the restrictions on access and transaction processing. A licensed state actor could additionally be appointed as gatekeeper. The competent national supervisory authority could, together with a national institute, regularly review the technology used to mitigate the risks related to general information technology (IT) security, tampering and malfunctioning software. Were such a system to be put in place, legal finality could be established by the confidence that all records on the private and permissioned blockchain are valid.

Whether the bona fide acquisition rule can be applied to blockchain transactions and other means of establishing legal finality will be addressed in the country reports.

However, the bona fide purchase of Tokens does not depend on the blockchain technology itself but on the governing law which might base this question on the underlying right (if any). For example, if this right (an interest claim or profit-sharing) is transferred by assignment or by the assumption of contract, a bona fide purchase may be excluded (depending on applicable laws).[57] A conceivable concept may be that crypto securities must be registered in a crypto securities register administered by a licensed service provider. As a result of their registration, crypto securities are deemed to be tangible assets. Thus, they can be transferred by way of transfer of title, making good faith acquisitions possible.

If a bona fide purchase is not possible and no substitutes exist (due to determination), the legal consequence is obvious: if the Token has been transferred by a person who is not entitled to the underlying right, the actual holder of the claim can also demand 'reversal'; i.e., the underlying right has never been validly transferred, but the data packages must be returned by anyone who controls such data. There may be factual difficulties to enforce such claims, but that does not question its existence as long as the applicable law does not stipulate finality.

[C] International Private Law

In this chapter, we examine the private law issues that arise in cross-border transactions involving Tokens. Tokens present a series of intricate challenges when it comes to cross-border transactions.[58] Within this sphere, private international law is emerging

---

56. *Ibid.*; Michèle Finck, *Blockchain Regulation and Governance in Europe* 15-15 (2018).
57. Jünemann & Wirtz *supra* n. 51.
58. Swift, Ground-breaking Swift innovation paves way for global use of CBDCs and tokenised assets (9 Oct. 2023), https://www.swift.com/news-events/press-releases/swift-innovation-enables-global-use-of-cbdcs-and-tokenised-assets.

as a central focus, primarily for its implications on issuers, investors, and the diverse array of service providers associated with Tokens. This section of this chapter (and the corresponding parts of the country reviews) shall focus on the applicable law when it comes to cross-border transactions. Central to the discourse is the question of which private law governs Tokens and the rights they represent.[59]

Historically, when one speaks of traditional securities, the foundational tenets of international private law can be traced back to the Convention for the Settlement of Certain Conflicts of Laws related to Bills of Exchange and Promissory Notes, dated 7 June 1930 in Geneva.[60] Yet, it is essential to understand that this convention doesn't directly encompass securities' certificates, creating a notable area of legal ambiguity.

A distinctive characteristic of international private law is its varied approach to securities, with rules fluctuating based on factors such as their custody and the manner of their issuance. Offering further insight into this complex realm is the Convention of 5 July 2006, centred on the Law Applicable to Certain Rights concerning Securities held with an Intermediary. However, its reach is still somewhat limited, given its current ratification solely by the US, Mauritius, and Switzerland.

Also, on an EU level, there is no clarity on the governing law for Tokens. Rome I Regulation applies to conflict of laws in relation to contractual obligations in civil and commercial matters. It does expressly not apply to obligations arising under bills of exchange, cheques and promissory notes and other negotiable instruments to the extent that the obligations under such other negotiable instruments arise out of their negotiable character. However, this poses the question of whether the Token qualifies as negotiable instrument and where to find the preconditions for such determination.

As we venture further into the digital age, traditional mechanisms to determine the applicable law – methods like *lex cartae sitae* and *lex libri siti* – are confronting the challenges posed by the decentralized nature of blockchain storage. The intricate interplay of laws in cross-border Token transactions demands a comprehensive examination. A focal point of this exploration is understanding how the legal characterization of individual Tokens might influence the applicable law. Once this legal landscape has been mapped out, another layer of complexity arises. The interpretation and valuation of securities vary across jurisdictions, resulting in potential disparities. Such differences can introduce friction in cross-border dealings, emphasizing the pressing need for a unified approach to offer clarity in an environment where private law frameworks are yet to be harmonized. Key questions to answer are whether a Token may change its character as an asset, thing or claim when it or its ownership is transferred to another jurisdiction or remains subject to the laws of the jurisdiction it or its underlying rights were created under. And what happens if the Token is sold and

59. Schwartz, Private International Law and Token Transactions (9 Oct. 2023), https://www.law.berkeley.edu/wp-content/uploads/2021/10/Private-International-Law-and-Token-Transactions.pdf.
60. International Conference for the Unification of Laws on Bills of Exchange, Promissory Notes and Cheques, Geneva, 1930-1931, Convention for the settlement of certain conflicts of laws in connection with bills of exchange and promissory notes. London: H.M.S.O., 1930.

transferred under a law different from the laws governing the Token or its underlying rights.

Moreover, UNIDROIT has adopted the UNIDROIT Principles on Digital Assets and Private Law (the Principles) as its guidelines and best practices concerning digital assets and private law. The Principles are part of UNIDROIT's broader efforts to unify international laws relating to emerging technologies. They have been crafted to be technologically, jurisdictionally, and organizationally neutral to facilitate broader adoption. The Principles provide a comprehensive examination of the main private law challenges that could emerge when transacting with digital assets in the market. They are organized into 19 key principles spread across seven chapters. The Principles apply to 'digital assets', which are defined as any 'electronic records capable of being subject to control'. An 'electronic record' is information stored in an electronic medium and can be accessed later. 'Control' is central to these principles, influencing other legal outcomes as well. A key suggestion is that legal systems should acknowledge digital assets as capable of being subject to ownership rights. The Principles propose a 'waterfall' method for determining the applicable jurisdiction's laws, allowing significant flexibility for individual states. Among other aspects, the Principles address how digital assets can be secured and how a security right in a digital asset can be made effective against third parties. However, the Principles do not specify particular methods for enforcing security rights in digital assets. Instead, commonly available enforcement approaches under existing law, including judicial enforcement, are applicable.

[D] Special Requirements for Prospectuses

This chapter dives into the general requirements for securities which usually involves a prospectus. The issuance of securities is a highly regulated process across many jurisdictions. This holds equally true when issuing Security Tokens: As discussed in section A above, Security Tokens can, for instance, constitute 'securities' within the meaning of the Regulation (EU) 2017/1129 (EU Prospectus Regulation) and under any relevant national prospectus act. Depending on specific regional regulations, Security Tokens might be classified as 'securities' which may necessitate the issuance of an investor information document, like a prospectus, which might require to be approved by the competent supervisory authority. The following section of this chapter (and the corresponding parts of the country reviews) shall focus on the special requirements for prospectuses which arise for Security Tokens.

Many public offerings of securities require the prior publication of a prospectus unless specific exemptions apply under the relevant regulatory framework. Both the product and the issuer must adhere to the regulatory standards of the jurisdiction where the Token is being offered. In essence, the typical prospectus must encompass all essential information for investors to make well-informed assessments of the securities offered and their issuer. The absence of this information places investors' financial interests at risk, as they cannot make informed decisions. Regarding the information that must be included in a prospectus for Tokens and blockchain technology, there's no definitive answer at this time. In general, the prospectus should prominently address the inherent risks associated with blockchain technology and Tokens since without a clear understanding of these specific risks, investors will be unable to make informed decisions. For instance, the prospectus should provide special attention to risks associated with the technical design of the Token, the finality of transactions on the blockchain, the risk of international private law or compatibility issues with wallets.

Since the blockchain on which Tokens are issued can change, the issuer will generally not take any responsibility for the finality of the transfer of Tokens.[61] In particular, blocks may be reset by 'hard forks', which can create considerable risks for the investors. Additionally, the blockchain is susceptible to hacking attacks such as mining attacks and vulnerabilities within smart contracts. After all, smart contracts and other applications used in an STO are, like any other code, prone to errors, and malfunctioning software may cause security gaps. As a result, the risk of hacking attacks leading to unauthorized transactions or 'forks' increases. In case of a 'fork', Tokens would be available on both forks of a chain. In this case, all nodes have to upgrade the software if they want to use the new Token, maintain the existing protocol to run the old Token or run two separate versions of the software.[62]

Malfunction may also lead to a Token being allocated late or falsely in connection with the investments which has been made.[63] A further risk is that not only the issuer of the Token but also the operator in the form of a crypto-exchange can be attacked. The issuer has no control over this event and is dependent on the security procedure of the crypto-exchange operator.[64] Technical hazards like, for example, DDoS attacks may decelerate the STO or pause it.[65]

While the risk of software malfunction is a risk that is not blockchain specific, it is particularly high due to the requirements of blockchain technology, where an issuer may be dependent on key personnel such as programming experts for smart contracts. The loss of key personnel can have a material adverse effect on the issuer's business and the technological function of its business concept.

Risks also emerge concerning protocol amendments and technical advancements. If an issuer uses smart contracts based on a protocol that shifts from a proof-of-work to a proof-of-stake algorithm (like the Ethereum Protocol), Tokens could be lost or stolen.[66] Any changes in the underlying technology or related to smart contracts and STO applications can adversely affect the Token values potentially leading to investor losses. Investors' liability is typically limited to the value of their

61. Crowdlitoken AG, *Prospectus for the Issue/Public Offer of up to 1'000'000'000 Crowdlitokens* (9 Oct. 2023), https://crowdlitoken.com/wp-content/uploads/2022/11/2022_10_24-Crowdlitoken-Prospekt.pdf.
62. *See* Chapter 1, §1.09, *supra*.
63. Crowdlitokens AG, *supra* n. 61.
64. *Ibid.*
65. *Ibid.*
66. *Ibid.*

investment.[67] Additionally, technical advancements such as the advent of quantum computing can pose new threats.

Investors face the challenge of ensuring that the source code running on the blockchain at a specific contract address is congruent with the stipulations of the smart contract set forth in the prospectus. Conversely, Token issuers bear the responsibility of providing comprehensive information in the prospectus, enabling investors to make well-informed decisions about participating in the smart contract. Access to the smart contract's source code is a key element for any dispute over prospectus liabilities; however, it's not the full picture. The intricacy of the smart contract's source code often exceeds the technical expertise of investors and lawyers, essentially making it a sealed book to them.[68] While portals or interfaces can offer a way to read the code, they do not necessarily make it easier to evaluate the encoded rights and obligations effectively. This leaves a gap that can be filled by a trustworthy third party. Such an entity should not only conduct a rigorous verification of the source code but also transparently display the results in the prospectus or in a court proceeding.[69]

Tokens are digital, meaning that they do not require physical storage. However, the private key needed to access the Tokens must be securely stored. Losing or forgetting the private key renders Token access impossible. Malfunctions or incompatibilities in digital wallets can also lead to access issues. Furthermore, Tokens can become inaccessible if the Token holder passes away without passing on the private key to a successor. Such 'lost' Tokens are indefinitely paused.[70] Private keys can be acquired not only by malicious actors through malware and hacking but also by social engineering or coercion because private keys can be stored digitally, offline, encoded in devices or written down on paper.[71]

In this context, it is important to ask who is responsible for the prospectus. Both the IT specialists who wrote the code and the initiators of the respective Token project could be regarded as 'issuers'. However, the contribution of the IT specialists does not go beyond coding. Therefore, under applicable law, only the initiators of the Token project should typically qualify as 'issuers'. Additionally, in many jurisdictions, the prospectus must undergo approval by the appropriate regulatory authority, which may not always be a swift process across all jurisdictions.

[E] Regulatory Specifics for Organized Trade

The usual path a security takes from the issuer to the investor is by way of an intermediary. This intermediary typically takes the form of a regulated financial service provider, usually entities such as bourses, multilateral trading facilities (MTFs),

67. *Ibid.*
68. Gerald Spindler, *Initial Coin Offerings und Prospektpflicht und -haftung*, WM 2109, 2110 (2018).
69. Spindler, *supra* n. 68 at 2115 (2018).
70. Crowdlitokens AG, *supra* n. 61.
71. Max I. Raskin, *Realm of the Coin: Bitcoin and Civil Procedure*, 20(4) Fordham JCFL969, 977, 989 (2015); Balthazor, *supra* n. 45, at 407 (2019).

brokers, among others. Such intermediary is often the subject of regulatory requirements to ensure investor protection. These may include licence requirements, specific limitations on targeted investor groups or reporting to the national financial supervisory authority. In contrast to traditional securities, a blockchain-based Security Token offers the issuer the chance of direct access to investors through the issued Token (if it is not an anonymous product). This may economically be very attractive to the issuer because the regulated intermediary is forced out of the process. This section of this chapter (and the corresponding parts of the country reviews) shall outline regulatory specifics for organized trade, like trading facilities for Tokens.

In such trading facilities for Tokens, the intermediary might be removed, allowing a direct (peer-to-peer) trading. Notwithstanding regulation designed to target the product and the issuer (e.g., as discussed under [D] above), the regulatory requirements targeting the intermediary could, in this course, either be passed on to the issuer, the wallet provider (if the investor does not take the Tokens in self-custody) or become inapplicable. This is particularly true if former clients of financial service providers become direct market participants or contractual counterparties, rendering obsolete the financial service previously provided by intermediaries. Going forward, national regulation might shift to targeting the investor or the issuer who would need to meet certain requirements before entering the crypto market.

Whether the trading of a Token is regulated or not depends on the criteria set out in the respective legal system or supervisory authority. While regulation usually applies to the trade of securities-like Tokens, there might be jurisdictions that do not apply such rules for Utility Tokens: the (organized) trade of any Token is not necessarily subject to regulation. Considering the character of (pure) Utility Tokens as digital vouchers and Currency Tokens, capital markets regulation may not be the choice of regulatory instrument. If the assessment of the Token shows it is a financial instrument, most jurisdictions will use the regulation as usual.

Accessing clients directly through the product may ultimately render certain regulations designed for organized trade obsolete. Notwithstanding the regulation of the issuer or the product itself, regulation of the Token placement could be inapplicable. The basic idea derives from the so-called issuer's privilege. This privilege, possibly varying in each jurisdiction, exempts an issuer from further licence requirements and regulation when placing its own securities products on the market. A broker or other intermediaries usually require an individual licence as they operate with several different securities products and function as the point of contact for the investors requiring protection. Theoretically, an issuer organizing the trade of its own blockchain-based Tokens and acting as its own intermediary could enjoy issuer's privilege and be exempt from licensing requirements.

Another new phenomenon comes into play if the infrastructure to facilitate the organization of the trade is provided through a decentralized exchange (DEX) (according to statista, the largest DEX are: Uniswap, Sushiswap, and Curve).[72] An ideal DEX is

72. Statista, Largest DeFI cryptocurrency exchanges or DEX in the world as of 29 Mar. 2022, https://www.statista.com/statistics/1263110/biggest-dex-in-the-world/.

a trading platform without a single point of failure that is characterized by peer-to-peer interactions. There is no authentication process to be carried out in order to buy and sell on the DEX. The DEX neither acts as a trustee nor stores information about the users, but it is a protocol run by each user individually. Buyers and sellers interact directly on the platform. The exchange is therefore 'decentralized', meaning that the funds remain with the exchanging parties at all times. This is a central feature of a DEX. If the Token is stored by the platform, it is no longer a DEX. In this case, there is a central point of attack (honey pot). Certain regulations could be linked to such storage. DEXs like Bisq (formerly known as Bitsquare) achieve decentralization through the use of or building on 'The Onion Router Network' (TOR).[73] The exchanging parties are the only ones being able to access each other's information because the communication is end-to-end encrypted. As a result of the decentralized structure, a DEX offers hardly any room for attacks. Unlike centralized exchanges (CEX) that have difficulty adequately defending themselves against hacker attacks, particularly as they grow, DEX are unattractive targets as buyers and sellers hold their own money.

One might imagine that the DEX itself could be subject to regulation. However, this would require justification as to why the DEX is acting not simply as an infrastructure but as a new type of intermediary. The question is also who should face the regulatory requirements? The software developer? Whether regulation is being triggered is linked to the presence of a central element as a touchstone of regulation. The degree of (de-)centralization of the exchange depends in particular on the following factors: custody of Tokens or fiat, the way of settlement, the (non-)existence of an order book, the price negotiation and the trading partner. For example, if an order book is available on the platform, there is a central element. Furthermore, if the execution of the transaction by fulfilling the payment obligations and transaction duties is up to the platform, a central intermediary is required to facilitate the transaction. The latter will then also be responsible. This is the touchstone for regulation.

This principle also applies to on-chain price negotiations with regard to inter-blockchain trades. 'On-chain' means transactions recorded directly on the blockchain, while 'off-chain' refers to transactions settled outside the blockchain. Whereas in the event of off-chain price negotiations the calculation is under the control of users who determine privately at which price they want to trade, there is a central element (the smart contract) in on-chain negotiations. Furthermore, the trading partner is usually the other user, but if the platform operated an order-matching system, there would again be a central element because an interim purchase would take place on the platform. Each of those central elements could trigger regulation because, under the applicable law, each of these activities could constitute a (financial) service to the other market participants. Whether these activities are regulated depends on national law; lawmakers and regulators may take different approaches – also depending on their (technical) understanding of the functioning of a DEX. An exchange is only unregulated in the absence of any regulated activity.

73. Bisq, https://bisq.wiki/Frequently_asked_questions#Is_Bisq_open-source_software.3F.

§5.02 CAPITAL MARKETS AND BLOCKCHAIN: COUNTRY REPORT – AUSTRIA

Johannes Frank & Philipp Kinsky[74]

Austrian capital markets law relevant for Security Tokens includes *inter alia* the Capital Markets Act (*KMG 2019*), the Stock Exchange Act (*BörseG 2018*), the Custodian Act (*DepotG*), the Investment Fund Act (*InvestmentfondsG 2011*) and the Banking Act (*BWG*) as well as any respective legislation of the European Union, including the Prospectus Regulation[75] and its delegated Acts. Austria does not provide for certain laws focusing exclusively on Security Tokens and/or crypto assets. However, as of December 2019, there is one law, which partly provides explicit provisions in respect of crypto assets: the Financial Markets Anti Money Laundering Act (*FM-GWG*). The FM-GWG stipulates a registration obligation with the Austrian Financial Market Authority (*FMA*) in respect of virtual currency service providers.[76] Such service providers are required to obtain the aforementioned registration before starting their respective services in Austria. The FMA may refuse to register such service providers in case of indications that they may not be able to comply with the FM-GWG. Further, the FMA may refuse a registration in case of any doubt concerning the personal reliability of the significant shareholders and/or managers or other persons actually providing the respective services of such service providers. This may enable the FMA to examine the business model of such service providers to a certain extent and to mitigate any negative impacts on the capital market in advance.

[A] What Makes a Token a Security?

The Austrian prospectus regime distinguishes between security (*Wertpapiere*) and non-security investments (*Veranlagungen*) and, therefore, provides a security and a non-security prospectus regime.[77]

Austrian laws provide for two different definitions of securities. On the one hand, according to the Austrian securities law definition, a deed (*Urkunde*) is considered to be a security if the enforcement of any rights contained in such security requires its proper holding.[78] On the other hand, securities within the meaning of the Austrian capital markets law (e.g., the Prospectus Regulation) are defined as: all kinds of

74. Co-Founder of the Legal Tech Hub Vienna (LTH) and partner at Herbst Kinsky Vienna, Dr Philipp Kinsky underlines his intricacies of the legal frameworks around start-ups. More than ten years of Banking and Finance, insurance and capital market law expertise enables him to focus on the understanding of the client's needs in today's fast-changing business. Associate at Herbst Kinsky Johannes Frank advises in start-up companies, capital markets, crypto assets, alternative investment funds, as well as securities and payment services.
75. Regulation (EU) 2017/1129 of the European Parliament and of the council of 14 Jun. 2017 on the prospectus to be published when securities are offered to the public or admitted to trading on a regulated market, and repealing Directive 2003/71/EC.
76. § 32a FM-GWG.
77. As the Prospectus Regulation provides for the securities regime, the Austrian capital markets act has been amended and provides for the non-securities investments regime only.
78. Cf. Kalss/Oppitz/Zollner, Kapitalmarktrecht2 § 11 n. 15.

securities, which are negotiable on the capital market, with the exception of instruments of payment, in particular, but not limited to shares and other shares in companies, partnerships or other securities, equity certificates, debentures or other securitized debt securities, etc.

The Austrian civil law and the Austrian capital markets law definitions of securities differ *inter alia* in a certain aspect relevant for Security Tokens. According to the FMA and part of literature, a security shall not necessarily be securitized by way of a physical 'paper'; however, a registration within a certain register should suffice.[79] This opens the possibility to qualify Tokens as a security in case the other prerequisites are met, which is feasible under the current Austrian legal regime.

Non-security investments (*Veranlagungen*) are defined as an economic right (*Vermögensrecht*) which is not securitized (as defined above), derived from the direct or indirect investment of capital of several investors on their common account and common risk or common account and common risk with the issuer, unless the investors are managing the capital invested on their own.

According to this definition, non-security investments may be offered by way of offering of limited partnership shares, shares in a limited liability company or in a real estate investment fund. However, a Token could also be structured in such a way that it qualifies as a non-security investment.

The main differences between a security and a non-security investment prospectus are as follows. The relevant financial market authority is not in charge to approve a non-security prospectus. Instead, a prospectus auditor (as denominated by the financial market authority) shall evaluate such prospectus. On the one hand, the structure of such non-security investment prospectus differs (slightly) from the security prospectus as a security prospectus follows the general European guidelines and the non-security investment prospectus is governed by the Austrian capital markets act (*KMG 2019*), providing for Austrian law specifics. On the other hand, as a significant difference, a non-security investment prospectus is not able to be notified to other countries according to a European scheme and, thus, cannot be offered in other countries of the European Union by way of notification; in case of an envisaged publication of a non-security investment prospectus in several European countries, a respective prospectus has to be set up in every such country, observing the relevant respective regulatory prerequisites of each country.

[B] Blockchain Finality

The Blockchain technology provides a variety of possibilities to store and/or transfer Tokens. These transactions are saved in the protocol of the blockchain (i.e., the respective blocks). Now, it seems to be the common understanding that these transactions may not be deleted or reversed and, thus, are technically final. In terms of

79. Cf. et al., Paulmayer, *Die kapitalmarktrechtliche Einordnung von Token* in Kirchmayr-Schliesselberger et al. (ed.), *Krypowährungen* 324 (2019); Kalss/Oppitz/Zollner, *supra* n. 78 at § 11 n. 15; Völkel, *Initial Coin Offerings aus kapitalmarktrechtlicher Sicht*, ZTR 2017, 013.

blockchain security, however, it may occur that transactions may be 'reversed' by means of certain attacks or changes of the protocol. The possibility of such attacks or changes is typically derived from the (technical) rules of the Blockchain.

Recent history and experience have shown that the following attacks and/or protocol changes are the most important threats to Blockchain finality: forks (hard and soft fork), majority attacks (i.e., double spending), Sybil attacks and 'timejacking'.

While during a fork a new copy of the blockchain is created and – in order to be valid for users – must be accepted by such users, the success of a majority attack is based on the rules of the Blockchain itself. Usually, a Blockchain provides for the rule that the users follow the longest (heaviest) version of the (block-)chain. This means that the version of the Blockchain with the most blocks and with the most difficulty is detected and followed by the clients. If one or more clients acquire more hash power than all other (mining) clients in the network combined, such person may be able to create the longest (heaviest) version of the (block-)chain and, thus, force all other clients to accept his copy of the (block-)chain (containing, as the case may be, some malicious code as, i.e., double-spending transactions).

In case of a Sybil attack, the attacker may achieve a similar result, by introducing nodes in the network, which are controlled by the attacker. In case a user connects to such a node, the attacker may – among others – be able to cause the user to refuse relying on other blocks than such blocks created by the attacker. In effect, this could cause the user to connect to a new copy of the (block-)chain and, thus, he would be threatened with double-spending attacks.

Further, the Blockchain network typically would only accept blocks showing a time stamp, which differs not more than a certain amount of minutes from the network time. In the course of a 'timejacking' attack, an attacker aims basically to utilize this rule of the network by slowing down the target node clock and accelerating the clock of the majority of the mining resources. Further, by sending a block with an adjusted time stamp, the attacker would, thus, cause the target node to reject such block due to the slowed-down clock of the node and to continue using the previous version of the Blockchain. Contrary to that, the miners, having an accelerated clock time, would accept such block. This would isolate the target node from the network processing and enable the attacker to send transaction confirmations to the target node. Such confirmed transactions would cease to be valid in case the attack stops as the target node (again) uses the (block-)chain version used by all the other participants in the network. In such a way, the attacker would be able to double spent Tokens.

However, Austrian (capital market) laws do not particularly address these topics and may be subject to general penal or civil law (proceedings).

[C] Special Requirements for Prospectus

The Austrian financial market authority is in charge of approving any security prospectus, evaluating the coherence, completeness and comprehensibility of the provisions of the prospectus.[80] The issuer itself shall *inter alia* be responsible for the correctness of the content.

However, tokenized securities – due to lack of specific laws – may according to current practice require *inter alia* to draw specific attention to the following issues and topics in respect of the prospectus.

There should be included general and specific risk factors of the relevant Security Token relating to the Token offered. Such factors may differ in case of permissionless or permissioned Blockchains, different types of storage, Masternode implications or the respective proof-of-work/stake mechanisms. Depending on the exact mechanisms of the issuance of the Tokens, specific risks may be associated with the storage of Tokens and a subsequent airdrop and/or other transfer of Tokens in the course of the respective issuance. Further, any investor should be informed about the tradability of any Tokens and/or about any potential (significant) weaknesses of the network in respect of certain scenarios.

The draft of the prospectus shall provide for a detailed description of the technical structure of the offering, the way of potential transfers of Tokens, respectively, of the underlying technology of the Token and/or the company as well as of the business side of the company.

Further, the prospectus shall include information on the taxation treatment of the securities, where the proposed investment attracts a tax regime specific to that jurisdictions where a public offer shall take place.

[D] International Private Law

From an international private law perspective with a focus on capital markets, any crypto assets-related cross-border transaction raises questions about the applicable law of obligations and property law.

Since capital market-related transactions are generally closely managed on the legal and commercial side, and are subject to detailed contracts, this subsection will not focus on legal questions regarding non-contractual obligations but only on contractual obligations and on the respective property law. Further, most of the respective contracts set forth a respective choice of law clause.

[1] Applicable Law: Contractual Obligations

Such choice of law clause basically is valid according to the basic principle in private international law of contractual autonomy. Moreover, Article 3(2) Rome I Regulation provides for the possibility to subsequently change the law applicable. However, such choice of law is restricted by some special conflict-of-law rules contained in the Rome I Regulation,[81] as stated below.

80. Article 20 Prospectus Regulation.
81. Regulation (EC) No. 593/2008 of the European Parliament and of the council of 17 Jun. 2008 on the law applicable to contractual obligations (Rome I).

As stated, the Rome I Regulation provides for exceptions to this general principle for specific fields as follows:

Ordre public. The so-called ordre public clause (Art 21 Rome I Regulation), allows a court to declare certain provisions of the applicable law inapplicable, to the extent the application of such provisions would be incompatible with the public order of the state of the respective court and thus offers protection of the national constitutional order.

Positive ordre public. In contrast to the ordre public clause, which allows a court to omit the applicability of a provision of a certain law, the so-called positive ordre public clause (Art 9 Rome I Regulation) enables a court to actively apply so-called overriding mandatory rules (*Eingriffsnorm*), if the application of such rules or provisions are decisive for the protection of the public interest of that state. From an Austrian perspective, the provision of Section 100 Austrian Banking Act is being discussed,[82] which penalizes the conduct of banking transactions without the required license. This could be applicable as the scope of banking transactions differ between states which could lead to crypto exchanges, wallet providers and similar platforms and service providers conducting banking transactions listed in Section 1 Austrian Banking Act.

Apart from these two general restrictions, Rome I Regulation provides in Articles 5 to 8 for specific requirements for contracts relating to transport, consumer (Article 6) and insurance, individual employment contracts. Generally, consumer contracts are governed by the law of the country in which the consumer has his residence.[83] In case of a different choice of law, the protection of the consumer under the law of the country of his residence may prevail if consumer protection provisions are more advantageous for the consumer. However, Article 6 paragraph 4 of the Rome I Regulation provides for certain exceptions, in particular, but not limited to, contracts in relation to financial instruments and contracts concluded within multilateral systems (Bourse, MTF, OTF). This includes trading of crypto assets, on the one hand, via exchanges and trading platforms and, on the other hand, in case such crypto assets qualify as a security.

Further, from a blockchain perspective, depending on the qualification of the legal nature of crypto assets, the consumer protection provision of section 13a Austrian Consumer Protection Act – KSchG may be relevant. Section 13a KSchG Clause 4 deals with the warranty or guarantee for the purchase or manufacture of movable goods. Depending on the qualification of crypto assets as movable goods, this provision may apply; however, the prevailing literature[84] opines that data are incorporeal objects and therefore do not qualify as movable objects, but its applicability is supported by some authors.[85] According to the latter opinion, the Austrian warranty and guarantee provisions would therefore apply: (i) if an Austrian consumer is involved, (ii) a law of a non-EEA country would otherwise apply and (iii) the Austrian law would be more favourable to the consumer.

82. Cf. Aigner, ZfRV 2020, 211 (218 f). Further, for the applicability of overriding mandatory provisions, the facts of the case must show a sufficient connection to the respective state.
83. Provided that (a) the trader carries out his activities in this country and (b) is at least oriented towards this country.
84. Cf. Eccher/Riss in KBB5 § 293 n. 1; Helmich in Kletečka/Schauer, ABGB-ON1.04 § 293 n. 3.
85. Cf. Völkel in Piska/Völkel, Blockchain Rules n. 3.14.

In addition, pursuant to section 13a (2) KSchG, section 6 KSchG and section 864a and 879(3) Austrian Civil Law Act – ABGB are applicable for the protection of consumers, irrespective of the otherwise applicable law, if the contract in question was concluded by a company that conducts its business in Austria. From the perspective of European law, the provisions cited are to be qualified as overriding mandatory provisions.

[2] Applicable Property Law

The question of the applicable property law poses difficulties for decentralized networks insofar as the classic conflict of laws asks about the usually physically understood seat of the legal relationship. Different solutions are therefore discussed in the literature. As a basic principle, regarding rights in rem to tangible property, the law of the state of the location at the relevant time applies (basic rule set forth in section 31 Austrian International Private Law Act – IPRG) of the connecting factor (*situs rule*). However, as crypto assets are considered intangible[86] (section 292 ABGB), several approaches to determine the applicable law are currently discussed. First, the strongest link to the respective law of the state (section 1(1) IPRG) could be relevant;[87] further and in case crypto assets represent rights, the respective law of obligations could be utilized.[88] The analogous application of sections 31 and 33a IPRG seems to be the current solution of the prevailing opinion in the literature.[89] Section 33a IPRG contains a special conflict-of-law rule for rights in rem to intermediated securities(*Wertpapiere im Effektengiro*), whereby the assessment must be made in accordance with the law of the state in which the relevant wallet is maintained (PRIMA – 'place of relevant intermediary approach').[90]

With regard to the scope of rights in rem to intermediated securities (*Wertpapiere im Effektengiro*), the Hague Conference concluded the Convention of 5 July 2006 on the law applicable to certain rights in respect of securities held with an intermediary,[91] which will take precedence over section 33a IPRG once it enters into force.[92] To date, however, neither Austria nor the EU has ratified the Convention.[93]

A conclusion could be that when determining the applicable property law to a respective crypto asset (transaction), the characteristics of the respective details of the crypto asset must be taken into account. Further, it is important as to whether such crypto asset may be characterized as a security. In this case, the applicable law could be determined in accordance with either section 31 or section 33a IPRG.

86. Cf. Helmich, *supra* n. 84, at 1.07 § 292 n. 8/1 with further references.
87. Cf. general Neumayr in KBB6 § 31 IPRG n. 7.
88. Cf. Anderl/Aigner/Schelling in Anderl, #Blockchain in der Rechtspraxis 57 (76).
89. Cf. Aigner, ZfRV 2020, 211 (220).
90. Cf. Neumayr, *supra* n. 87, at § 33a IPRG n. 1.
91. Treaty text: https://assets.hcch.net/docs/3afb8418-7eb7-4a0c-af85-c4f35995bb8a.pdf (downloaded 10 Nov. 2023).
92. Cf. Neumayr, *supra* n. 87, at § 33a IPRG Rz 3 with further references.
93. Cf. https://assets.hcch.net/docs/ccf77ba4-af95-4e9c-84a3-e94dc8a3c4ec.pdf (downloaded 28 May. 2023).

[E] Regulatory Specifics for Organized Trade

This section shall on the one hand briefly describe which major requirements an issuer shall comply with in case of a direct issuing of Security and Non-security Tokens to investors. On the other hand, it shall provide an overview of potential regulatory implications for (centralized) organized trade of these Tokens.

The initial offering of Tokens typically involves several service providers. If the Token qualifies as a security (*Wertpapier*), these service providers could be subject to the WAG 2018. As the scope of the Regulation (EU) 2020/1503 (ESCPR) covers certain services with regard to certain securities as well, such service providers may fall within the scope of the ECSPR (instead of the WAG 2018). However, ESCPR will not apply if the value of the total issued Tokens does not exceed EUR 5 Million (within twelve months). In case of an issuance of Tokens (in the own issue) without any agents or third-party service providers involved, the stated laws would typically not apply. Nevertheless, as stated above, prospectus regime shall be complied with, as the case may be. In case of any Non-security Investment Token (*Veranlagung*) any such service provider may qualify as investment adviser (*gewerblicher Vermögensberater*) and may be subject to Austrian capital markets act (KMG 2019) or the Austrian alternative financing act (AltFG).

In case Security Tokens shall be traded automatically on an organized trading platform, several further regulatory implications may be triggered.

Depending on the qualification of the Token as a security, such a trading platform may qualify as a 'stock' exchange, an MTF or an organized trading facility (OTF). In such cases, the operation of an exchange may require the respective licence as 'stock' exchange company according to the Austrian stock exchange act (BörseG 2018) or as an investment firm (IF) under the Austrian securities supervision act (WAG 2018). In most cases, a licence as an IF under the WAG 2018 could suffice when such systems organize the trade of these Tokens in the course of a centralized orderbook.

Further, the operators of 'stock' exchanges, MTFs and OTFs shall provide for deposition of all financial instruments (which securities are a part of) with a central depository agency to be traded within their MTF and/or OTF systems.

The DepotG generally requires a physical securitization (except for certain special securities). As such a physical securitization for any Token is technically not feasible, such registration service for Tokens is not (yet) available with the Austrian central depository agency.

Thus, Tokens may only be traded outside MTF, OTF or a regulated market. However, several (private) initiatives aim to change the respective requirement of physical securitization in order to enable a non-physical securitization of securities to foster a more efficient operation of deposition and storage of securities and Tokens.

In case crypto assets qualify as a security and shall be traded on a trading platform (*Handelsplatz*) and/or are admitted on a regulated stock exchange, the anti-market abuse laws could apply.

Further, Regulation (EU) no. 1286/2014 (packaged retail and insurance-based investment products – PRIIPs) may apply inter alia in case the crypto asset may qualify as 'packaged retail investment product'. Such a product qualifies as PRIIP in case the crypto asset qualifies as an investment, regardless of its legal form, where the amount repayable to the retail investor is subject to fluctuations due to exposure to reference values or to the performance of one or more assets, which are not directly purchased by the retail investor.

§5.03 CAPITAL MARKETS AND BLOCKCHAIN: COUNTRY REPORT – BELARUS

Klim Stashevsky & Mikhail Khodosevich[94]

[A] What Makes a Token a Security?

Belarusian regulations[95] specifically outline that legal rules on securities and securitization, alongside the security market activity licence requirements, shall not be applied to operations with Tokens in Belarus. Therefore, from the viewpoint of Belarusian regulatory authorities, a Token cannot be considered a security.

Instead of this, the Belarusian lawmakers decided to create a separate legal framework specifically for operations with Tokens, making such operations valid if they comply with strict requirements and take place within the special regime of the High Technologies Park.

On 21 December 2017, the President of Belarus signed Decree no. 8 'On Development of Digital Economy' that elaborated initial provisions on the legal status of Tokens which put it in a totally new division of objects of civil rights.

This Decree gives a definition of a Token (or a 'digital sign', as it is also qualified) as a record in a transaction block ledger (blockchain) or another distributed information system. Legislation provides two possible qualifying attributes of Tokens:

- it verifies that its owner has a right to certain objects of civil law (for instance, corporate or exclusive rights);
- it is a cryptocurrency. In its turn, a cryptocurrency is defined as a bitcoin, another digital sign (Token) used in international circulation as a universal means of exchange.

94. Head of Arzinger's IT & Media sector group Klim Stashevsky advises his clients with a focus on innovative technologies in data protection and IP having been ranked by Chambers and Legal 500 as a rising star. Working with Arzinger since 2016, Deputy Director Mikhail Khodosevich focuses on the needs of IT companies performing business activities in Belarus. He understands the frameworks around high technologies and his client's admission to the High Tech Park as residents. Both Klim and Mikhail developed and tested legal algorithms of administrative procedures of the Republic of Belarus to be included in the electronic registry establishing an e-government.
95. Decree no. 8 of the President of the Republic dated 21 Dec. 2017 *On Development of Digital Economy*, http://law.by/document/?guid=3871&p0=Pd1700008e (accessed 1 Oct. 2023).

In contrast to some modern legal systems, this definition characterizes Tokens as neither securities nor derivative financial instruments. In the Belarusian legal system, securities are determined as documents or a set of records certifying – per a defined form – proprietary and non-proprietary rights. Each security shall possess obligatory details and requisites, which Tokens cannot have due to their unique legal and technical nature.

Moreover, the Belarusian legislation directly excludes Tokens from the regulation of these legal instruments and categories: securities, securitization, and licensed exchange activities in securities. Therefore, the legislation that regulates these categories is not applied to relations connected to blockchain and Tokens. Legal effect of the currency legislation is excluded as well, which means that Tokens do not have a status of currency values (besides securities, currency values include a national currency and foreign currencies).

At the same time, in certain aspects, Tokens are categorized within the existing legal categories. Tokens now relate to the term 'funds' within the meaning of the legislation on countering laundering of criminal assets, financing terrorism and proliferation of weapons of mass destruction. This means that all entities executing financial transactions with Tokens, such as banks and other financial institutions, notaries, insurance companies, shall apply all internal control measures prescribed for funds, including identification of clients, report to state financial control authorities on suspicious transactions with Tokens, and block these transactions, should certain criteria be met.[96]

From an accounting perspective, Tokens are treated as assets. The Ministry of Finances of the Republic of Belarus adopted a special regulation on proper accounting of Tokens.[97] According to this document, business entities may account Tokens as 'long term or short term financial investments', 'current incomes' or 'goods'. This variety of legal features of Tokens shows an exclusive position of Tokens in the Belarusian legal field.

[B] Blockchain Finality

The finality of blockchain transactions has not received sufficient legal regulation status in Belarus yet. From this perspective, Tokens have a quite similar status with tangible property: the transfer of a Token from one entity to another entails a complete and permanent transfer of rights certified with this Token. A transfer of a Token shall be deemed performed at the moment of reflection of a relevant approved transaction in

96. Law No. 165-Z of the Republic of Belarus dated 30 Jun. 2014, On Measures for Prevention of Laundering of Proceeds from Crime, Financing of Terrorist Activities and Financing of Proliferation of Weapons of Mass Destruction.
97. Resolution no. 16 of the Ministry of Finances of the Republic of Belarus dated 6 Mar. 2018, On Approval of the National Standard of Accounting and Reporting 'Digital Signs (Tokens)' and Amendments and Alterations to Some Resolutions of the Ministry of Finances of the Republic of Belarus.

a transaction block ledger (blockchain) or another distributed information system according to its rules and protocols.

The said principle is not applied to transfers of rights which additionally require a state registration (for instance, rights of ownership in real estate or exclusive rights to a trademark).

For a documentary reflection of a blockchain transaction, each party (business entity) shall draft a primary accounting document. Unlike a significant part of other business transactions, when entities are obliged to draft bilateral or multilateral primary accounting documents (such as acts of acceptance), parties to blockchain transactions may draft unilateral acts based on information of blockchain transactions. A business entity shall attach a documentary evidence (for instance, a printout of blockchain transactions) to this primary accounting document.

[C] International Private Law

Civil law of the Republic of Belarus has not reflected the concept of Tokens in the international private legal aspect yet. As well as a majority of states of the continental law system in Europe, Belarus generally divides private law regulations into two main categories: property law and law of obligations (contractual law).[98] Legal system of Belarus and state institutions unequivocally qualify Tokens as property which allows to make a conclusion that property conflict-of-laws rules do apply to Tokens. Nevertheless, due to a specific material form of existence of Tokens and absence of inseparable connection to any specific state or territory, some traditional conflict-of-laws rules cannot be in practice used by courts. For instance, the principle *lex rei sitae* is not applicable to Tokens.

At the same time, some conflict-of-laws rules might apply to Tokens as to any other type of property with specific reservations. If a Token is a subject of a deal, emergence and termination of property rights shall be specified in accordance with the laws of the state where the deal took place.[99] For protection of the property rights, a claimant may choose laws of a location of the property or the law of the state of the court.[100] *Since lex rei sitae* is not applicable, laws of the state of the court shall be imperatively applied to protection of the property rights to Tokens.

Law of the obligations provides much more optionality for parties of Token-related transactions. Parties are free to choose laws applicable to their deal in the course of conclusion of contracts or afterwards, unless all involved parties are Belarusian citizens or Belarus-based business entities.[101] If the applicable law is not chosen by the parties, court will apply laws of the state of the party which has a decisive impact on performance of the contract.[102] With respect to Tokens, this conflict-of-laws rule may apply as follows:

98. Chapter VII of the Civil Code of the Republic of Belarus dated 7 Dec. 1998.
99. Clause 1 Art. 1120 of the Civil Code of the Republic of Belarus dated 7 Dec. 1998.
100. Clause 1 Art. 1123 of the Civil Code of the Republic of Belarus dated 7 Dec. 1998.
101. Clause 1 Art. 1124 of the Civil Code of the Republic of Belarus dated 7 Dec. 1998.
102. Clause 4 Art. 1125 of the Civil Code of the Republic of Belarus dated 7 Dec. 1998.

- for sale and purchase agreements – law of the state of the seller;
- for donation agreements – law of the state of the donator;
- for services agreements (in relation to Token-related consulting services, cryptobroker services, etc.) – law of the state of the contractor.

As a secondary rule, when courts are unable to specify an applicable law in accordance with the rules described above, a court shall apply laws of a state which has the closest connection to the deal. The Civil Code of the Republic of Belarus establishes that if a contract has been concluded at an auction, by a tender or on a stock exchange, then the law of the location of the respective auction, the tender or the stock exchange shall be applied,[103] which closes a significant gap in Token-related conflict-of-laws regulation.

[D] Special Requirements for Prospectus

A prospectus or a 'White paper' declaration is a document with information on the investment project in the form of a Token offering and participants of this process.[104] Per Belarusian legislation, this is an obligatory document for any Initial Coin Offering (ICO). Ways to amend the white paper after the start of a Token offering are very limited.

There is a certain variability regarding an entity which shall draft a white paper. It can be a customer – an entity particularly interested in a Token offering (hereinafter referred to as the 'Customer') or an ICO organizer – a professional participant in the Token services market arranging and conducting the process of an ICO for a Customer and drafting a white paper based on information provided by this Customer.

An entity may also perform an ICO of its own Tokens, including drafting a white paper, without the participation of an ICO organizer. However, such entity shall have the status of a resident of the High Technologies Park of Belarus and its business plan shall cover activities in the sphere of Tokens as described below in section 4.

Legislation provides an exhaustive list of requirements to a white paper. As a general rule, each white paper shall contain:

(1) information on the Customer, including a title, a legal address, a tax ID number and an email address;
(2) information on the ICO organizer and an entity that has created Tokens (if it is an entity other than the ICO organizer) and a general description of contractual relations between the Customer, the ICO organizer and the entity that has created the Tokens. If there are any interdependence or affiliation relations between the participants of the ICO or an immediate interest of the ICO organizer (its shareholders, affiliated entities) in the Token offering, the white paper shall reflect this information as well;

103. Clause 3 Art. 1125 of the Civil Code of the Republic of Belarus dated 7 Dec. 998.
104. Rules on Rendering Services Connected to Creation and Placement of Digital Signs (Tokens) and Related Transactions, http://www.park.by/content/docs/Regulations-on-Crypto/ICO.pdf (accessed 1 Oct. 2023).

(3) general description of contractual relations between the Customer and/or the ICO organizer and an 'anchor' investor, as well as their interdependence or affiliation relations, if any. An 'anchor' investor is considered a renowned investor having a positive business reputation. Purchase of Tokens by an 'anchor' investor can usually be regarded by other potential investors as an indicator of the reliability of Tokens as investments;
(4) information of financial indicators of the Customer, including its balance sheet, an income statement, a statement of changes in equity, a statement of cash flows, notes to the balance sheet and an audit report for the preceding year. These documents shall be attached to the white paper as its annexes;
(5) description of the main risks of the ICO and major competitors of the Customer;
(6) description of risks to Token holders. The description shall be provided on the title page of the white paper and include information that Tokens are not legal tenders and are not ensured by the state, the ICO organizer is a technology intermediary and that the Customer shall be liable for satisfying rights of Token holders related to creation and placement of the Tokens;
(7) disclosure of information on the Customer: its CEO, shareholders, a chief accountant and an officer responsible for the ICO – at least their names (titles) and states of their residence (incorporation);
(8) information on any court proceedings of the Customer and their outcomes for three preceding years;
(9) facts of administration liability of the Customer for three preceding years and any current administration proceedings;
(10) description of rights of Token holders, a Token circulation period and a possibility of the early performance of rights of Token holders;
(11) description of the main conditions of the Token purchase by the Customer. White papers may also stipulate that the Customer may not purchase Tokens until the full performance of obligations is certified with these Tokens;
(12) description of the essence of the Token investment project, including a reasoned assessment of financial expenses for each stage of the project and expected financial results upon its implementation. Information on the investment project shall also describe its technical part and terms of implementation of its separate stages;
(13) restriction of transfer of Tokens from their first holders to other holders and consequences of violation of this restriction;
(14) information on the applied blockchain or another distributed information system, an opinion on its reliability (potential resistance against technical failures and unlawful interference), a date and results of the last technical audit, if any;
(15) means of securing obligations certified with the Tokens, if any;

(16) information on any breaches related to Tokens committed within three preceding years by the Customer (its shareholders, CEO or the officers responsible for ICO);
(17) description of how Token holders can receive information on the current state of the Token investment project;
(18) other information that may help potential Token holders maximize their risk assessment.

A single white paper may relate to an ICO of Tokens of a single or of several types of Tokens. The general assumption is that Customers may not use objects of civil rights raised with the ICO for the purchase of other types of Tokens or for other purposes than stated in the white paper. However, the relevant white paper may provide otherwise.

The Customer shall maintain a white paper on its website at least until the full performance of all obligations certified with the Tokens is reached.

[E] Regulatory Specifics for Organized Trade

Legal regulation of Tokens in Belarus is expressed in two key characteristics. First, the legal regime of using Tokens for private persons and business entities substantially differs. The second specific feature is that Token activities are closely bound up with a special legal regime – the High Technologies Park of Belarus, with Belarus-based entities enjoying its benefits.

Private persons in Belarus are free to perform mining, purchase and hold Tokens in virtual wallets, exchange Tokens, sell them for national or foreign currency and electronic money, gift and bequeath Tokens. Private persons are not required to declare Tokens and pay an income tax for them until the end of 2024. Token-related activities of private persons are not qualified as their professional business activities (therefore, no business registration is needed).

Professional Token activities in Belarus are mostly concentrated in the High Technologies Park, a special IT cluster for doing business in the sphere of modern technologies. This cluster is open for IT companies and start-ups; however, preliminary approval of their business plans with the perspectives of development and assessment of a team and resources of the company by the Supervisory Board of the High Technologies Park is required. Residents of the Park receive significant tax and other legal benefits, but they shall do business exclusively in the sphere that is specified in their business plan. Arranging and performing an ICO, creating special platforms for trade in Tokens and their exchange in Belarus which are available for residents of the High Technologies Park with respective business plans only. Legislation provides four main types of professional participants of the Token market:

(i) cryptographic platform operators holding and managing platforms designed for trading Tokens;
(ii) cryptocurrency exchange operators conducting the processes of exchanging Tokens;

(iii) entities performing trade deals with Tokens on their own behalf, but in the interest of their clients (hereinafter referred to as the 'Cryptobrokers');
(iv) professional entities working in other Token-related spheres. This category includes ICO organizers, companies which perform ICO of their own Tokens and companies rendering information and consulting services.

Other Belarus-based business entities may trade Tokens, exchange them and perform ICO of their Tokens exclusively via residents of the High Technologies Park.

All potential residents of the High Technologies Park engaged in Token-related activities listed above shall meet stricter criteria to be admitted to the High Technologies Park than other IT companies: they shall prove their previous experience in banking, insurance, professional and exchange activity on securities, or in some other financial spheres, comply with financial ratios established by the High Technologies Park, and perform cybersecurity audit of their information systems. They also face strict requirements to their shareholders and beneficiary owners.[105] Cryptocurrency exchange operators shall keep in Belarusian banks not less than BYN 200,000 to ensure their obligations to their clients. For cryptographic platform operators, the threshold is higher – BYN 1,000,000. Cryptobrokers shall have a share capital of not less than BYN 500,000.

Additionally, the High Technologies Park has elaborated detailed regulation on anti-money laundering (AML) and know-your-customer (KYC) policies for Token activities. Business entities shall approve rules of internal control, identify and verify all their clients, use only a certified software, report to financial controlling state bodies regarding suspicious financial transactions, block these transactions and freeze the funds. Each such company shall appoint a compliance officer or officers whose rank is no lower than a deputy director.[106]

The process of trade in Tokens at a cryptographic platform also has a comprehensive legal regulation. For admission to a platform, a cryptographic platform operator (hereinafter referred to as the 'Operator') shall conclude contracts with potential clients – both private persons and legal entities without reference to a state of their residence/registration.[107] Regarding private persons, an Operator shall collect information on their contact details, full names, date of birth and address of residence, regarding legal entities – their title, legal address and Tax ID number. Operators are prohibited from establishing relations with underage persons and persons involved in terrorist activities. In relation to foreign citizens and entities, Operators are also obliged to check that trade at a cryptographic platform is not prohibited for these potential clients under the legislation of the state of their residence/registration. After the

105. *Regulations on the Requirements to be Met by Certain Applicants for Their Registration as Residents of the High Technologies Park*, https://park.by/content/docs/Regulations-on-Crypto/Applicants%20requirements.pdf (accessed 1 Oct. 2023).

106. *Regulations on the Requirements for the Internal Control Rules of Residents of the High Technologies Park*, https://park.by/content/docs/Regulations-on-Crypto/AML.pdf (accessed 1 Oct. 2023).

107. *Requirements to Cryptoplatform Operators*, http://www.park.by/content/docs/Regulations-on-Crypto/CryptoExchange.pdf (accessed 1 Oct. 2023).

conclusion of a contract, a client receives an account in the cryptographic platform system. The client may not have more than one account.

Private persons – citizens of Belarus – have an additional stage of verification for admission to a bidding process. Preliminarily, an Operator shall check their competence and knowledge in the sphere of the trade in Tokens by filling in the questionnaire. For other categories of clients (legal entities and foreign citizens), an Operator may establish its own requirements to their financial state and business reputation.

The Operator shall provide its clients with comprehensive information on contract provisions, terms and conditions of the work of the cryptographic platform and risks they take by participating in the trade of Tokens. The Operator may not advise clients on any aspects which may induce them to buy or sell particular Tokens.

The Operator is entitled to choose software and technical means in order to provide the clients with the access to the bidding system and give them the right to observe the bidding process for its maximum transparency. The Operator shall prevent bidders from manipulating with Token prices and unfair usage through any insider information that they may have. The Operator shall not admit to the bidding the Tokens that anyhow violate legislation requirements, or which are based on the principle of full anonymity of transactions.

Generally, the process of trade in Tokens contains the following steps. The bidder shall credit money, electronic money or Tokens to a respective account of an Operator. These funds are reflected in the account of the bidder on the trading platform. The Operator shall ensure a separate accounting of funds of all its clients and its own funds. The Operator shall collect information on all cash flows and transactions of the client, prepare daily reports with this data and keep it for five years.

For making a deal, the bidder places an order for purchase, sale or exchange of Tokens. Specific requirements to these orders and to the procedure of their placement are specified in the internal regulations of Operators. After the trading system detects an offsetting order of another bidder with suitable conditions, the Operator shall immediately execute it and transfer funds from the account of one bidder to another. The principle of 'last look' when the execution of orders can be postponed is not applicable.

The Operator may provide bidders with Tokens for participation in bidding subject to the payment of interest by these bidders. For each transaction that these bidders enter, a proportion between borrowed Tokens and their own Tokens shall not be more than 5 to 1.

Upon a client's consent, an Operator may use client's Tokens for entering into transactions on its behalf and for its own benefit if all the following conditions are met:

- the transactions are aimed at increasing liquidity of the Operator;
- counterparties of the Operator under these deals are legal entities having a special licence for Token trade business under the legislation of its registration;
- these deals do not involve more than 50% of all funds of the respective client;
- the Operator has a reasonable belief that these deals will not lead to the Operator's failure to transfer all funds which are due to be paid by the Operator under the contract to the client.

In 2023, the High Technologies Park introduced regulations for a new category of participants in the organized trade in Tokens – Cryptobrokers.[108] Cryptobrokers are entitled to:

- execute deals with Tokens on their own behalf, but in the interest of their clients;
- render consulting services related to deals with Tokens.

With respect to AML and KYC policies and requirements to accounting of funds of the clients, Cryptobrokers shall comply with requirements which are quite similar with those designed for Operators. Additionally, Cryptobrokers shall conclude a commission contract with a client to be entitled to execute deals with Tokens. Also, Cryptobrokers may execute deals in the interest of their clients only through Operators.

Cryptobrokers shall conclude an agreement with an Operator and provide the following assurances regarding the Cryptobroker and the clients of the Cryptobroker:

- the clients are private persons and are not underage; they have capacity to deal with Tokens under the legislation of the state of their residence;
- the clients do not reside in states (territories) where provision of services of the Operator is restricted;
- the clients and their beneficiary owners are not involved in terrorist activities;
- the Cryptobroker is not going to use insider information or manipulate prices.

The Cryptobroker shall receive technical access to the trading system of the Operator, arrange a secure data transmission channel, and ensure access of authorized officers of the Cryptobroker to the trading system. After that the Operator shall create subaccounts in the trading system which will be used by the Cryptobroker for the trade in Tokens in the interest of the clients.

The trading process starts with the transfer of money or electronic money by a client to accounts of the Cryptobroker. The Cryptobroker shall credit the money or electronic money to accounts within the trading system of the Operator. The Cryptobroker executes deals after receiving respective applications from the client. Within the terms prescribed in the commission contract, the Cryptobroker shall create an order for purchase, sale or exchange of Tokens. Type and number of Tokens, minimum and (or) maximum limits of prices, and rates of return for the deals are specified in the applications of the clients.

As seen from above, the sphere of trading Tokens and blockchain technology in the Republic of Belarus continues its developmental path. First introduced in 2017, the blockchain legislation becomes more progressive and develops further each year.

108. Rules on Activities Related to Services Concerning Execution of Deals (Transactions) with Digital Signs (Tokens) in the Interest of Other Entities, https://park.by/content/docs/05%20Правила%20осуществления%20деятельности,%20связанной%20с%20оказанием%20услуг%20по%20осуществлению%20сделок%20(операций)%20с%20цифровыми%20знаками%20(токенами).pdf (accessed 1 Oct. 2023).

§5.04 CAPITAL MARKETS AND BLOCKCHAIN: COUNTRY REPORT – ESTONIA

Kirsti Pent[109]

[A] What Makes a Token a Security?

Estonian law does not include any comprehensive regulation regarding Tokens.[110] Tokens are either qualified as certain financial instruments regulated under European Union law and respective national laws (e.g., a security) or as a 'virtual currency'. The latter is a term introduced by Estonian law and will become obsolete as soon as Regulation (EU) 2023/1114 on markets in crypto assets (MiCAR) fully enters into force. However, currently, virtual currency is a value represented in digital form, which is digitally transferable, preservable or tradable and which natural or legal persons accept as a payment instrument but which is not the legal payment instrument of any country or funds for the purposes of Article 4(25) of the Second Payment Services Directive (*PSD II*)[111] or a payment transaction for the purposes of points (k) and (l) of Article 3 of PSD II.[112]

The definition of a virtual currency only covers digital assets which are accepted as payment instruments, however, which are not the legal currency or any country or a payment instrument under PSD II. The concept of a virtual currency also does not apply if a Token meets the criteria of any other regulated financial instrument, e.g., a share, a fund unit, a derivative instrument, any other type of a security or even a deposit. Therefore, in order to determine the legal classification of a particular Token, the analysis should always start from establishing whether the Token may constitute another regulated financial instrument.

While there is no established case law by the Supreme Court of Estonia to clearly distinguish between virtual currencies and other regulated financial instruments, the Estonian Financial Supervisory Authority (EFSA) has issued an opinion on the classification of Tokens reaffirming that substance should be considered over form.[113]

---

109. Partner at TGS Baltic, Kirsti Pent integrates knowledge of financial institutions in regulatory issues. She heads the financial law committee of the Estonian Bar Association and is thereby involved in providing input to draft legislation. According to Legal 500 (2023), Kirsti is 'considered to be a heavyweight in fintech'.

110. In order to implement MiCAR, a draft law has been prepared in Estonia (Markets in Crypto-Assets Act), however, the current draft is limited to the same instruments as MiCAR, meaning that, among others, Tokens which constitute securities are excluded from the scope of the draft law.

111. Directive (EU) 2015/2366 of the European Parliament and of the Council on payment services in the internal market, amending Directives 2002/65/EC, 2009/110/EC and 2013/36/EU and Regulation (EU) no. 1093/2010, and repealing Directive 2007/64/EC (OJ L 337, 23.12.2015, pp. 35-127).

112. Money Laundering and Terrorist Financing Prevention Act, Art. 3(9) (26 Oct. 2017), RT I, 17.11.2017, 2, https://www.riigiteataja.ee/en/eli/ee/525032019005/consolide/current (accessed 21 Nov. 2023).

113. EFSA, *The Legal Framework of Initial Coin Offering in Estonia*, https://www.fi.ee/en/investment/aktuaalsed-teemad-investeerimises/virtuaalraha-ico/legal-framework-initial-coin-offering-estonia (accessed 21 Nov. 2023).

Most significantly, Tokens may be securities. The definition of securities is set forth in the Securities Market Act, Securities Register Maintenance Act as well as in the Law of Obligations Act. The Securities Market Act defines securities in terms of capital markets. Each of the following proprietary rights, obligations or contracts, if transferable on the basis of at least a unilateral expression of will, constitutes a security, even without a document being issued therefor:

- a share or another similar tradable right;
- a bond, convertible security or another tradable debt;
- a subscription right or another tradable right granting the right to acquire securities specified above;
- an investment fund unit or share;
- a money-market instrument;
- a derivative security or a derivative contract;
- a tradable depositary receipt;
- a greenhouse gas emission allowance.[114]

In 2022, the Securities Market Act was amended to specify that each of the securities listed above may be issued by means of distributed ledger technology (DLT).[115] According to the explanatory memorandum, the provision was added based on Regulation (EU) 2022/858 on a pilot regime for market infrastructures based on distributed ledger technology.[116] In practice, the provision reaffirms that securities may be tokenized; however, whether a Token constitutes a security or not still depends on substance, i.e., the rights and obligations the Token represents.

Although certain provisions of the Securities Market Act also apply to crowdfunding offers made under Regulation (EU) 2020/1503 on European crowdfunding service providers for business (ECSPR)[117] and this regulation includes, in addition to transferable securities, also 'admitted instruments for crowdfunding purposes', the latter are not considered securities.

Other than the above, Estonian national law does not provide further guidance for determining what constitutes a security. Rather, MiFID II and the opinions of the ESMA and the Committee of European Securities Regulators (CESR) are most often used to furnish the definition. Thereby, securities are proprietary rights or obligations which are standardized, negotiable and freely transferrable on (capital) markets. As a result, one practical way to preclude the application of the securities' regulation is to

114. Securities Market Act, Art. 2(1) (17 Oct. 2001), RT I 2001, 89, 532, https://www.riigiteataja.ee/en/eli/522032019007/consolide (accessed 21 Nov. 2023).
115. Securities Market Act, Art. $2(1^1)$, *supra* n. 114.
116. Regulation (EU) 2022/858 of the European Parliament and of the Council of 30 May 2022 on a pilot regime for market infrastructures based on distributed ledger technology, and amending Regulations (EU) No. 600/2014 and (EU) No. 909/2014 and Directive 2014/65/EU (OJ L 151, 2.6.2022, pp. 1-33).
117. Regulation (EU) 2020/1503 of the European Parliament and of the Council of 7 Oct. 2020 on European crowdfunding service providers for business, and amending Regulation (EU) 2017/1129 and Directive (EU) 2019/1937 (*OJ L 347, 20.10.2020, pp. 1-49*).

impose restrictions on the transferability of the Token, e.g., rights of pre-emption or other limitations as to who can acquire the Tokens.

The EFSA has explained that if Tokens are transferable and give the investors certain rights with respect to the issuer or if the value of the Tokens is tied to the future profits or success of the issuer, then the Tokens are likely to be considered securities.[118] For example, Tokens classify as securities if they 'provide voting or decision making rights in the issuer or give the investor a certain return expectation regarding their investment (e.g., a right to a part of the issuer's profit, regular cash flows, or any other promise about future profit), regardless of whether the funds raised are repayable by maturity date or no maturity date exists (e.g., a perpetual bond)'.[119]

If the aim of issuing Tokens is to further invest the funds raised in common interests, the Tokens may constitute a specific type of securities – investment fund units. An investment fund is a legal entity or pool of assets which raises capital from a number of investors with the view of investing it in accordance with a defined investment policy for the mutual benefit of the investors.[120] Thus, Tokens may qualify as fund units depending on the structure and objective of the Token issued – the guidelines issued by the ESMA are used to make the determination.[121] As a general rule, an investment fund must have a fund manager, i.e., a company whose main and permanent activity is the management of one or several funds.[122] Depending first on whether the funds are offered publicly and the volume of assets under management, the fund manager must be either licensed by or registered with the EFSA.

In principle, a Token may also be a derivative instrument: a derivative security or a derivative contract. A derivative security is a tradable security (expressing a right or obligation to acquire, exchange or transfer) the underlying assets of which are other securities or the price of which depends directly or indirectly, for example, on the exchange or market price of a security or a commodity, interest rate, or another financial index or financial indicator.[123] Although this must be assessed on an individual basis, as a general rule, a Token is not a derivative instrument because it is not intended to hedge risks, and it has none of the specific underlying assets set forth in the law.[124] However, the EFSA has noted in their guidance regarding tokenized securities that Tokens which comply with commodity prices can be deemed derivative instruments.[125]

118. EFSA, *supra* n. 113.
119. EFSA, *Information for Entities Engaging with virtual Currencies and ICOs*, https://www.fi.ee/en/investment/aktuaalsed-teemad-investeerimises/virtuaalraha-ico/information-entities-engaging-virtual-currencies-and-icos (accessed 21 Nov. 2023).
120. Investment Funds Act, Art. 2(1) (14 Dec. 2016), RT I 31.12.2016, 3, https://www.riigiteataja.ee/en/eli/ee/527032019004/consolide/current (accessed 21 Nov. 2023).
121. European Securities and Markets Authority, Guidelines on the key concepts of the AIFMD, https://www.esma.europa.eu/sites/default/files/library/2015/11/2013-611_guidelines_on_key_concepts_of_the_aifmd_-_en.pdf (accessed 21 Nov. 2023).
122. *Ibid.*, Art. 2(3) and Art. 3(1).
123. Securities Market Act, Art. 2(3), *supra* n. 114.
124. Kadi Saluste, *Token'ite kvalifitseerimine Eesti õiguse alusel ning kehtiva õiguse sobivus ICO-de reguleerimiseks*, 6 Juridica, 390, 394 (2018).
125. EFSA, *Security Token*, https://www.fi.ee/en/finantsinspektsioon/innovation-hub/security-token (accessed 21 Nov. 2023).

Assuming that a Token is not a derivative instrument, it may constitute a money-market instrument: an unsecured, transferable and marketable (liquid) debt obligation which is normally traded on the money market, including a treasury bond, commercial paper, certificate of deposit, bill of exchange secured by a credit institution and other securities which comply with the conditions provided for in Article 11 of Commission Delegated Regulation (EU) 2017/565.[126] However, it is doubtful if a Token meets the liquidity criterion. A Token may be regarded as a money-market instrument if it can easily be exchanged into fiat currency, but in practice, such an exchange is often complicated and may be restricted by the issuers.[127]

If a Token is deemed to be any of the following securities, it has to be registered with the Estonian register of securities (CSD):

- debt obligation issued by a legal person registered in Estonia, the public offer prospectus of which is registered with the EFSA pursuant to the Securities Market Act;
- the shares of public limited companies registered in Estonia;
- the units and shares of investment funds registered in Estonia, which are admitted for trading on a regulated securities market or in an MTF;
- subscription rights for shares and securities subject to entry in the register which are publicly issued or publicly offered.[128]

Certain other securities may also be registered with the CSD. In any case, the CSD does not register such instruments as Tokens, but rather the registration of the CSD substitutes Tokens.[129] Since third parties can rely on the correctness of the registrations of the CSD,[130] in case the instrument is registered in the CSD, in order to ensure certainty of any transaction, it would not be sufficient to execute it only on the distributed ledger – it would also have to be registered in the CSD. That would render the use of distributed ledger and Tokens quite pointless.

In addition to securities, Tokens may also be qualified as repayable funds if the main business activity of the issuer is to provide loans in its own name and account – such activity is financed through funds received from the public in the form of a Token issue and the Tokens grant their holders the right to get their investment back.[131] Such a business model may be deemed as that of a bank which requires authorization from the EFSA.

If a Token does not give its holder any right to expect a return on the investment (i.e., the Token is not a security or a repayable fund), the Token could be classified as one of the following:

126. Securities Market Act, Art. 2(2), *supra* n. 114.
127. Saluste, *supra* n. 124, at 390, 394 (2018).
128. Securities Register Maintenance Act, Art. 2(1) (14 Jun. 2000), RT I, 26.06.2017, 1, https://www.riigiteataja.ee/en/eli/527032019007/consolide (accessed 21 Nov. 2023).
129. Kristen Leppik, *Krüptovaradest*, Õiguskeel 2020/2.
130. Securities Register Maintenance Act, Art. 9(2), *supra* n. 128.
131. EFSA, *supra* n. 125.

- a virtual currency as defined at the beginning of this chapter. For example, the Supreme Court has ruled that bitcoin is a virtual currency.[132] The courts have explained that bitcoins are virtual currencies since bitcoins' value in fiat is determinable at any time, it is possible to buy and sell bitcoin for fiat and a number of merchants accept bitcoins as means of payment.[133] Specific legislation applies with respect to service providers who offer wallet, exchange, transfer or issuance services in relation to virtual currencies - these are discussed in the subchapter 'Regulatory specifics for organised trade';
- a donation;
- a Utility Token in case it provides its holder access to a platform, the right to use the services or acquire the products of the issuer. In such cases, contract law applies to the Tokens, including provisions regarding prepayments;
- admitted instruments for crowdfunding purposes under the ECSPR.

Contract law (including provisions on concluding agreements online), consumer protection regulations, advertising requirements and tax laws must be complied with when issuing or trading in any Tokens; however, the exact requirements under these laws depend on the classification of Tokens. It is also possible that the tax treatment of a Token does not correspond to its classification for regulatory purposes.

[B] Blockchain Finality

The finality of Token transactions depends on the classification of the Token.

In case Tokens only represent rights, they are assignable irrespective of the debtor's (e.g., the issuer of the Token) consent.[134] Even if the parties have agreed that the claim right may not be assigned (e.g., the issuer has stated so in the white paper), such agreement has no effect with respect to the acquirer, and the assignment is valid regardless.[135] If the creditor (the holder of the Token) assigns the one and the same Token more than once, the earliest assignment is deemed to be valid.[136]

In case Tokens represent both rights and obligations on the issuer and the holder, as a general rule, they can only be transferred in case both parties have agreed to the transfer,[137] i.e., the rules applicable for assigning a contract as a whole would likely apply. However, applicable rules depend on the legal qualification of the specific Tokens - for example, in case of Tokens which constitute securities.

As a general rule, the bona fide acquisition rule does not apply to rights, such as many Tokens. First, bona fide acquisition is possible in case of physical objects and

132. Case no. 3-3-1-75-15 of the Supreme Court of Estonia, https://www.riigikohus.ee/et/lahendid?asjaNr=3-3-1-75-15 (accessed 21 Nov. 2023).
133. Kadri Siibak, *Mõningad virtuaalrahaga seotud õiguslikud probleemid*, V Juridica 326, 330 (2015).
134. Law of Obligations Act, Art. 164(1) (26 Sep. 2001), RT I 2001, 81, 487, https://www.riigiteataja.ee/en/eli/ee/507032019001/consolide/current (accessed 21 Nov. 2023).
135. *Ibid.*, Art. 166(2).
136. *Ibid.*, Art. 164(3).
137. *Ibid.*, Art. 179.

rights entered into public registers if the law prescribes that an entry in a specific register carries such protection for the acquirer. National laws do not specifically provide for such legal protection with respect to Token purchases made by relying on distributed ledger (even if it is a public ledger). Therefore, purely from a legal standpoint, the legitimate holder of the Token has the right to demand the reversal of an unauthorized Token transfer.

In case a Token constitutes a certain type of a security (e.g., a publicly offered debt obligation issued by a legal person registered in Estonia) and it is registered with the Estonian register of securities (CSD), bona fide acquisition of the security is possible. According to the Securities Register Maintenance Act Article 9(2), if a person acquires a security or a right to a security in good faith relying on the CSD, the register is deemed correct.[138]

[C] International Private Law

The Estonian Private International Law Act[139] does not prescribe any specific rules with respect to Tokens or the use of DLT. Thus, applicable law will depend on the legal qualification of the Tokens.

On an EU level and with respect to the application of Rome I Regulation, please see the comments provided in the international part of this chapter.

To the extent the Estonian Private International Law Act applies and provided the Tokens constitute either shares, debt obligations and other rights expressed in the form of an entry in a register (i.e., registered security instruments), such instruments are governed by the law of the country where the register is kept.[140] Where a person (the intermediary) holds a registered security instrument for and on the account of another person in a register other than the aforementioned – or in an account –, the right expressed in the register or in the account is governed by the law of the State where the register or account concerning the intermediated security instrument is kept.[141]

In case the Token may be deemed a convertible bond or other similar right which is related to a holding in a legal person, as a general rule, the law of the country under which the legal person was founded is applied.[142] However, where actual management of the legal person or the person's main activity takes place in Estonia, Estonian law is applied regardless of the country of registration.[143]

138. Securities Register Maintenance Act, Art. 9(2) (14 Jun. 2000), RT I 2000, 57, 373, https://www.riigiteataja.ee/en/eli/ee/524072017013/consolide/current (accessed 21 Nov. 2023).
139. Private International Law Act (27.03.2002), RT I 2002, 35, 217, https://www.riigiteataja.ee/en/eli/ee/522112022001/consolide/current (accessed 21 Nov. 2023).
140. *Ibid.*, Art. 23^1(1).
141. *Ibid.*, Art. 23^1(2).
142. *Ibid.*, Art. 23^1(4) and Art. 14(1).
143. *Ibid.*, Art. 23^1(4) and Art. 14(2).

[D] Special Requirements for Prospectus

Estonian national law does not prescribe any special requirements with respect to the prospectus or other disclosure documents in case Tokens which qualify as securities are offered publicly.

A prospectus must be prepared, registered with the EFSA and published in case Security Tokens are offered publicly in Estonia and the volume of the offer is more than EUR 5,000,000 per all EEA states in total calculated per a one-year period.[144] An offer of securities to the public means communication in any form and by any means, presenting sufficient information on the terms of the offer and the securities to enable an investor to decide on the purchase or subscription.[145] A prospectus is not required in case any of the exceptions set forth in the Securities Market Act or the Prospectus Regulation apply, for example, if the offer is made solely to qualified investors or the denomination of the securities per unit amounts to at least EUR 100,000. Also, no specific disclosure requirements apply in case of an offer of securities in the amount of up to EUR 1,000,000.

In the case of an offer of securities in the amount of EUR 1,000,000-EUR 5,000,000 in Estonia (calculated over a period of one year), the issuer may choose whether to publish the prospectus in accordance with the Prospectus Regulation, a regulation adopted by the Minister of Finance or the disclosure requirements of a regulated trading facility (irrespective if the instruments are actually traded on the facility or not).[146] The requirements of the latter two are somewhat more lenient compared to the Prospectus Regulation. However, such disclosure documents are not valid for the public offer of securities cross-border. According to a draft law, the option to prepare a disclosure document based on national rules will be extended to offers of securities in the amount of EUR 1,000,000-EUR 8,000,000 and the national rules will be unified in Estonia, Latvia and Lithuania so that such smaller public offers will become easier across the Baltic states.

The content and the level of detail of the prospectus depend on the type of the securities offered; for example, the requirements somewhat differ for shares and bonds. Estonian law does not currently provide for exceptions or any special provisions regulating the public offer of Tokens.[147] However, the Prospectus Regulation grants some exceptions for start-up companies when preparing a prospectus (i.e., companies established less than three years ago).

Any prospectus must include information on the risks associated with the issuer, any guarantor, and the securities offered. Thus, the risks posed by the utilization of the blockchain technology should also be described in the prospectus. However, as already noted, certain publicly offered securities must be registered in the Estonian register of

144. Securities Market Act, Art. 15, *supra* n. 114.
145. *Ibid.*, Art. 12 and Regulation (EU) 2017/1129 of the European Parliament and of the Council of 14 Jun. 2017 on the prospectus to be published when securities are offered to the public or admitted to trading on a regulated market, and repealing Directive 2003/71/EC, Art. 2(d) (the '*Prospectus Regulation*').
146. Securities Market Act, Art. 15(6), *supra* n. 114.
147. EFSA, *supra* n. 125.

securities. In such cases, the technological risks related to DLT are probably irrelevant since the safekeeping, transfer and other aspects of such securities are prescribed by the law.

If the prospectus includes false or inaccurate information or is incomplete and this affects the valuation of the securities, the issuer or any other responsible person set forth in the prospectus must compensate the damages caused by the difference between reality and the information included in the prospectus to the owners of the securities, provided the responsible person should have been aware of the shortcoming and the owner of the security was not aware of it. Such liability also arises if the summary of the prospectus or its translation is misleading, inaccurate or in conflict with the other parts of the prospectus.[148] Instead of compensating damages, the responsible person may also acquire the security from its owner for the same price as paid by the owner.[149]

[E] Regulatory Specifics for Organized Trade

Services related to Security Tokens generally require an authorization from the EFSA to operate as an investment firm (*IF*). Among other, the following services involving securities constitute regulated financial services: receipt and transmission of transaction orders, execution of orders, portfolio management, organizing an offer or issue of securities, operation of an MTF or OTF.[150] The main characteristic of both trading facilities is that they bring together interests of different parties for acquisition and transfer of securities under non-discretionary conditions in a way that results in a contract; i.e., they use automated matching of buy and sell orders. This service should be distinguished from, for example, bulletin boards which only provide information on buy and sell offers but do not match them.

Whereas the legislation applicable to Security Tokens derives from MiFID II, Estonia has also adopted a specific regulation applicable to wallet, exchange, transfer and issuance services with respect to virtual currencies as defined in Estonian laws. Such service providers must obtain a licence from the Estonian Financial Intelligence Unit. The main requirements for obtaining the licence are applying AML/KYC procedures to the clients, proving that the management and owners are reputable (including submission of criminal records), minimal share capital of EUR 100,000 (EUR 250,000 in case of providing transfer services), physical location in Estonia, local manager and an account opened with a bank or a payment institution established in the EEA and authorized to provide services in Estonia. Most of these requirements were introduced in recent years to enhance supervision over the service providers which resulted in the number of licensed entities to decrease from thousands to less than a hundred licensed entities. In the past, it was quite easy to obtain the licence which made it very popular

148. Securities Market Act, Art. 25, *supra* n. 114.
149. *Ibid.*, Art. 26.
150. *Ibid.*, Art. 43(1).

with foreign service providers, even though the licence is not automatically passportable for operations in other jurisdictions. Currently, obtaining and maintaining the licence requires significant effort and investment. However, this national law will become obsolete as soon as Regulation (EU) 2023/1114 on markets in crypto assets (MiCAR) fully enters into force.

§5.05 CAPITAL MARKETS AND BLOCKCHAIN: COUNTRY REPORT – FINLAND

Mika Puurunen[151]

The Finnish market saw its first regulatory steps related to issuance and exchange of digital value on a blockchain or distributed ledger technology in 2019, as the Finnish Act on Virtual Currency Providers (572/2019, as amended, the '**VCP Act**') entered into force on 1 May 2019.[152] The VCP Act is applicable to business operations of virtual currency providers, and it stipulates that any natural or legal person issuing virtual currency (e.g., Tokens used as currency/instruments of payment), providing virtual currency exchange services, maintaining a virtual currency market place or offering virtual currency wallets has to register with the Finnish Financial Supervisory Authority ('**FIN-FSA**').[153] Following such registration, service providers have to comply with certain requirements on safekeeping of client assets, customer due diligence (KYC-rules) and marketing. However, as the VCP Act is constructed to regulate the virtual currency service provider, but not to legally categorize the underlying digital asset, the support for legal construction of Tokens in the context of Finnish securities laws remains very limited. The VCP Act includes a reference to the Finnish Securities Markets Act (746/2012, as amended, the '**SMA**') and sets out that if a virtual currency constitutes a financial instrument as referred to in the SMA, the SMA is applicable. The reference is purely clarifying in nature and does not draw any conclusions on the relevant application criteria for Tokens.

After the implementation of the VCP Act, next regulatory steps related to DLT were seen in Finland in 2023 when certain national amendments were implemented, i.e., to the Finnish Investment Services Act (747/2012, as amended), the Finnish Act on the Book-Entry System and Clearing Operations (348/2017, as amended), the Finnish Act on Trading in Financial Instruments (1070/2017, as amended) and the Finnish Limited Liability Companies Act (624/2006, as amended). These amendments were

151. Joining Bird & Bird in 2019 Partner Mika Puurunen focuses on assignments related to capital markets, M&A and corporate law. In addition, Mika has deep sector knowledge on regulatory frameworks around different types of investment funds and is known for rendering business-minded and solution-oriented advice for his clients.

152. The related transition period has ended and all virtual currency providers have been fully subject to the VCP Act as from 1 Nov. 2019.

153. The FIN-FSA supervises that procedures for customer due diligence and risk management comply with statutory requirements. In case of non-compliance, the supervised entity may be subject to administrative sanctions.

related to the implementation of the DLT Pilot Regulation[154] which entered into force on 23 March 2023. The purpose of the DLT Pilot Regulation is to create an EU-wide framework for market operators and competent authorities to experiment with market infrastructures based on DLT. In connection with the related local amendments, the definition of a financial instrument was amended to also cover financial instruments issued on DLT, reflecting the corresponding amendment implemented on the level of MiFID II.[155] As the amendment of the definition refers to 'financial instruments' issued on DLT, the amendment is more clarificatory in nature than actual extension of the definition (instruments issued on DLT still need to be 'financial instruments' to qualify as financial instruments under MiFID II).

Regardless of the above-mentioned DLT Pilot Regulation and the related local law amendments, currently, there have been no such laws enacted in Finland that would regulate either the position of Tokens as digital assets under Finnish securities markets or the applicability of Finnish provisions on securities offerings to any issuance or sale of Tokens. The same conclusion applies to any official guidance or regulation by Finnish public authorities. Thus, any analysis on the applicability of Finnish securities law requirements to Tokens and/or any sale or issuance thereof has to be made on a case-by-case basis.

Given the above introduction, the applicability of specific securities law constructions on Token offerings (such as general good conduct principles, transaction finality, prospectus disclosure and market abuse regime) needs to be analysed based on general premises of Finnish civil law and the applicable EU legislation – in the following, there will be a concise overview of such aspects. Prospectus regime will be discussed only from the perspective of public security offerings and not admissions to trading, as the former can currently be seen more relevant in the context of Tokens.

The Finnish securities laws are nowadays highly harmonized with the applicable EU legislation. For example, due to the EU Prospectus Regulation[156] that became fully effective on 21 July 2019, basically all national Finnish provisions on prospectuses were repealed. The same applies to the national provisions concerning the disclosure of inside information, which have been replaced by the EU Market Abuse Regulation.[157] Accordingly, the definitions of a security and a financial instrument are very much derived from the EU legislative framework and implemented into the Finnish

154. Regulation (EU) 2022/858 of the European Parliament and of the Council of 30 May 2022 on a pilot regime for market infrastructures based on distributed ledger technology, and amending Regulations (EU) No. 600/2014 and (EU) No. 909/2014 and Directive 2014/65/EU (the '**DLT Pilot Regulation**').

155. Directive 2014/65/EU of the European Parliament and of the Council of 15 May 2014 on markets in financial instruments and amending Directive 2002/92/EC and Directive 2011/61/EU (MiFID II).

156. Regulation (EU) 2017/1129 of the European Parliament and of the Council of 14 Jun. 2017 on the prospectus to be published when securities are offered to the public or admitted to trading on a regulated market, and repealing Directive 2003/71/EC (the '**Prospectus Regulation**').

157. Regulation (EU) No. 596/2014 of the European Parliament and of the Council of 16 Apr. 2014 on market abuse (market abuse regulation) and repealing Directive 2003/6/EC of the European Parliament and of the Council and Commission Directives 2003/124/EC, 2003/125/EC and 2004/72/EC (MAR).

legislation basically as such. The following chapter will contemplate the position of Tokens as securities under Finnish law, blockchain finality, international private law in the context of Tokens, the disclosure requirements related to Token offerings in Finland and finally, the applicability of the market abuse regime to Tokens subject to public trading. The definitions of a 'security' and 'financial instrument' are used in parallel, and it is appropriate to note that where all securities are financial instruments, all financial instruments are not necessarily securities.

[A] What Makes a Token a Security?

There are no exemptions in the Finnish capital markets law for any specific Token type or categorization. Any analysis made is very much case specific and needs to be done through examining the Token qualifications in question. Can digital assets (e.g., Utility Tokens, Currency Tokens or Security Tokens) be construed as securities under Finnish law? Intuitively, it seems apparent that the answer to such question is yes. Also, many European regulators recognize that Tokens (especially Security Tokens) may qualify as financial instruments, providing the requirements of fungibility and transferability further as securities under applicable securities laws. However, analysing the circumstances where this might happen requires a systematic approach both to the definition of a security and the characteristics of the specific digital asset in question.

Pursuant to the SMA, a security is negotiable and issued (or meant to be issued) to the public together with several other securities with similar rights (requirement of fungibility[158]). Finnish civil law deems securities as bearer bond documents, and the requirement of negotiability has been construed to mean that a transferee of the bearer bond is protected against any subsequent third-party claims. Holding a security on a book-entry securities account in dematerialized form has traditionally been considered to produce the same protection against third-party claims as the possession of a physical bearer bond document.[159] This analogy might be extended to Tokens held on a blockchain database. Thus, it may be possible to meet the requirement of transferability also in relation to instruments issued in dematerialized form on a blockchain platform (*see* section [B] on Blockchain Finality). However, the negotiability (transferability) of the Token cannot be restricted, for example, in the issuer's Articles of Association - otherwise, the Tokens will not qualify as securities.

Pursuant to the SMA, a security may be:

(i) a share in a limited liability company or a corresponding share of another entity as well as a depositary receipt in respect of such right;
(ii) a bond or other securitized debt as well as a depositary receipt in respect of such right;

158. The fungibility requirement means in practice that no distinction can be made between the issued securities based on the attached rights, i.e., from investor's perspective it does not matter which security he or she owns.
159. There is an established view in the Finnish jurisprudence that the SMA may be applied where a person has the possibility to obtain proof for his or her ownership right, e.g., by requesting an extract from a custody system where such ownership right has been recorded.

(iii) any other security giving the right to acquire or sell a security referred to in items (i) and (ii);
(iv) a security giving rise to a cash settlement determined by reference to a security, currency, interest rate or yield, commodity or other index or measure; or
(v) a unit in a common fund or a unit issued by a collective investment undertaking comparable thereto.

Rights to possess a specific apartment, other premises or real estate have been carved out from the definition of a security. Also, money-market instruments are out-of-scope.[160]

As the issuance of Tokens through blockchain or distributed ledger technology means to assign digital value, the characterization of such Tokens under applicable securities laws needs to be done by examining the nature of the digital value in question, i.e., the rights and obligations attached to the Token. As we can see from the definition of a security, the underlying value of a security can be a number of things. Whether the underlying value of a Token to be issued is made of rights attached to shares or bonds or any other security establishing rights to acquire or sell such rights, it seems clear that such Token can be categorized as a security provided that the Token is negotiable on a securities market (e.g., on a blockchain platform). Where a transferable Token carries profit-sharing rights and/or voting power, it is likely that we are dealing with securities (Security Tokens).

In case of Utility Tokens, the classification as securities is harder to construe, but it cannot be excluded that also Utility Tokens could be securities. This is very much a question of the characteristics of a specific Utility Token and, first of all, its negotiability and settlement mechanisms. If a Utility Token can be settled in cash, for example, based on a reference to a commodity price, such a Token could be construed as a security.[161] In respect of Currency Tokens, ESMA has taken a view that pure payment-type crypto assets are unlikely to qualify as financial instruments under MiFID II.[162] The FIN-FSA is likely to follow such guidance.

[B] Blockchain Finality

Where transactions on securities recorded on the book-entry system maintained by the Finnish Central Securities Depository benefit from statutory legal finality rules, Finnish law does not include any legal finality rules for transactions conducted on blockchain platforms. Also, there is no requirement for a DLT-based settlement system in accordance with the DLT Pilot Regulation to qualify as a securities settlement system

160. The definition of a 'security' in the SMA is based on the definition of a 'transferable security' in item (44) of Art. 4(1) of MiFID II.
161. The preparatory works of the SMA specifically note that also such instruments where the settlement is determined by a reference to commodity products can be securities under the SMA.
162. ESMA, *Advice on Initial Coin Offerings and Crypto-Assets*, https://www.esma.europa.eu/sites/default/files/library/esma50-157-1391_crypto_advice.pdf (accessed 11 Mar. 2020).

designated under the Settlement Finality Directive,[163] and thus an exemption from the rules on settlement finality in the Securities Settlement Regulation[164] is applicable. The question of blockchain finality and the related protection mechanisms against third-party claims should thus be construed under general principles of Finnish civil law.

As security ownership data recorded on a blockchain ledger does not carry public credence (i.e., bona fide third party does not benefit from statutory legal protection in relation to a transaction conducted on the basis of ownership data recorded on the blockchain ledger), the buyer of a Token carries a risk of third-party claims in case there would be a parallel transaction on the same identified ownership right.[165] In such collision of rights, the main principle to be applied would be the time priority rule, i.e., the party whose right of ownership has been established prior to the other party's will gain legal ownership to the Token in question. Evidencing such right could mean in practice that the first buyer (*primus*) of the Token would need to obtain an extract of the conducted transaction validated by several blockchain mining nodes and compare it to the secondary buyer's (*secondus*) corresponding data.

It is possible to deviate from the above-mentioned time priority rule by affording an extinction right to secondus. However, usually such right is based on the requirement that the secondus was bona fide at the time of the transaction and has since taken active steps to validate his/her ownership right (e.g., by registering such right on a public register). However, as transactions conducted on (public) blockchain platforms are all registered automatically by definition of the technology itself, seeking such registration may not offer any additional protection towards primus whose transaction has also been recorded on the blockchain ledger.

As long as there is no legal blockchain finality, the general transaction time priority rule seems to offer the most efficient ultra partes protection for Token transaction participants. Public credence is a difficult concept in the context of decentralized ledger technology, where there is no centralized party who would carry the responsibility of proper functionality of the blockchain protocol. If protection is afforded based on public credence of incorrect ownership data, there would be no one single party to claim damages from for recording such incorrect data or the malfunction of blockchain protocol causing such entry. After all, can you really establish legal finality without a party who takes on the related obligations meant to guarantee the finality creation process?

---

163. Directive 98/26/EC of the European Parliament and of the Council of 19 May 1998 on settlement finality in payment and securities settlement systems ('**Settlement Finality Directive**').
164. Regulation (EU) No. 909/2014 of the European Parliament and of the Council of 23 Jul. 2014 on improving securities settlement in the European Union and on central securities depositories and amending Directives 98/26/EC and 2014/65/EU and Regulation (EU) No. 236/2012 ('**Securities Settlement Regulation**').
165. In normal circumstances within the blockchain network this should not be technically possible, but in case there is a malfunction or change in the blockchain protocol, parallel transaction could happen.

[C] International Private Law

Potential private law issues that may arise in cross-border transactions involving Tokens are numerous. This is, for example, due to the fact that legal characteristics of a Token may differ significantly from one Token to another. Also it might not always be clear who the parties of a cross-border transaction of Tokens are in and which legal jurisdictions these parties are actually based. From the perspective of private international law, the key question is how Tokens with their rights and obligations should be legally construed under private law.

Respectively, Rome I[166] and Rome II[167] regulations are applicable in Finland, governing situations involving a conflict of laws to contractual and non-contractual obligations in civil and commercial matters. These regulations would be the starting point in analysing which private law should be applied to cross-border transactions of Tokens.

Rome I is not applicable to obligations arising under bills of exchange, cheques and promissory notes and other negotiable instruments to the extent that the obligations under such other negotiable instruments arise out of their negotiable character. Thus, it seems that a Token should be negotiable on a securities market. Rome I will not be applied to such obligations that arise out of the Token's negotiable character. However, it might not be always clear which are the actual obligations that arise specifically out of the negotiability of the Token in question. For example, issuers' obligations to distribute assets to a Token holder may be deemed to derive from the underlying profit-sharing rights of the Token in question and not from the Token's negotiability *per se*. Further, pursuant to Rome I, in the case that the law applicable to the contract has not been chosen, a contract concluded within a multilateral system which brings together or facilitates the bringing together of multiple third-party buying and selling interests in financial instruments in accordance with non-discretionary rules and governed by a single law, shall be governed by that law. Accordingly, Tokens should be subject to public trading on a multilateral system and assuming the parties of the transaction did not separately agree on the law applicable in their transaction agreement, pursuant to Rome I, the applicable law would be the one applied to the trading platform. Considering the above-mentioned exclusion from the scope of Rome I, apparently such applicable law of the trading platform would be applied to only such obligations of the transaction contract, which does not arise out of the negotiable character of the Token in question.

Rome II is not applicable to non-contractual obligations arising under bills of exchange, cheques and promissory notes and other negotiable instruments to the extent that the obligations under such other negotiable instruments arise out of their negotiable character. As with Rome I, it seems that a Token should be negotiable on a

166. Regulation (EC) no 593/2008 of the European Parliament and of the Council of 17 Jun. 2008 on the law applicable to contractual obligations ('**Rome I**').
167. Regulation (EC) no 864/2007 of the European Parliament and of the Council of 11 Jul. 2007 on the law applicable to non-contractual obligations ('**Rome II**').

securities market, Rome II will not be applied to such obligations that arise out of the Token's negotiable character.

It shows that there is no absolute clarity on an EU level about the choice of law for Token-related cross-border transactions. Especially when the Tokens that are the subject to the transaction, are negotiable on a securities market, it might be difficult to determine which law is applicable to the obligations arising from the characteristics of the Token in question.

[D] Special Requirements for Prospectus

Assuming we would be offering Tokens categorized as securities under Finnish law – in such an offering we would need to comply with the applicable disclosure requirements related to offering of transferable securities, i.e., prospectus regime and existing good conduct principles of the Finnish securities market. What would be the right prospectus disclosure rules to comply with? There are no specific schedules for Tokens in the Prospectus Regulation or the delegated acts of the Commission, and the FIN-FSA has not issued any guidance on selecting applicable disclosure criteria for public Token offerings. Thus, the appropriate disclosure criteria should be determined based on the underlying value of the Tokens to be offered, i.e., the rights and obligations the Tokens provide for their holders. If the Token provides rights and obligations that of a shareholder (represents a share/equity portion in the issuer) then the prospectus disclosure to be followed would be a one for equity securities. If the Token provides rights and obligations, for example, that of a bondholder (represents a bond/debt instrument of the issuer), the prospectus disclosure to be followed would be one for non-equity securities. These two types of STOs are most likely the most common ones to be seen in the Finnish market in the first place if and when the relevant market picks up.

Offering Tokens under a prospectus would in practice mean preparing a summary, registration document and a securities note based on the selected disclosure criteria (e.g., criteria for equity securities or non-equity securities). Such disclosure criteria include several prospectus content requirements related to the securities offered. For example, the prospectus should include:

(1) description of the material risks specific to the securities being offered;
(2) a description of the type and class of the securities offered;
(3) an indication of whether the securities are in registered form or bearer form and whether the securities are in certificated form or book-entry form;
(4) a description of the rights attached to the securities, any limitations thereof and procedure for the exercise of those rights;
(5) method and time limits for payment and delivery.

The above items are examples of such prospectus content requirements, where the special digital nature of Tokens as instruments held and kept in custody by means of a blockchain technology has special significance. In terms of item (1), risks related to the blockchain technology used to hold and transact with the offered Tokens would be elaborated pursuant to this requirement in the risk factors section of the prospectus. This would mean evaluating the materiality of the recognized risks on the securities offered based on the probability of their occurrence and the expected magnitude of their negative impact. Conducting this assessment in practice can be very challenging and requires a deep understanding of the blockchain technology used. Risk of several blockchain strings operating with the same underlying right (fork), losing one's private key to dispose of Tokens at a given address, risk of being hacked or risk of failure in the Token custody and transaction verification ecosystem are examples of issues that would need to be described in the prospectus.

Pursuant to item (2), one would describe the underlying value of the offered Tokens, i.e., the rights and obligations produced for the holder of the Token. In terms of item (3), the starting point would be to assume that the offered Tokens are in bearer form. However, it appears to be a somewhat problematic question of whether the offered Tokens should be categorized as certificated securities or book-entry form securities. Certificated form would imply issuing a physical certificate on the underlying right (e.g., a share certificate). This would not work in relation to transfers of title in the blockchain ecosystem, as the physical certificate would have to follow the purchaser (this is why there is a requirement to cancel all certificates before issuing any securities relating to such certificates in the book-entry system maintained by the Finnish Central Securities Depository). Then again it seems that Tokens cannot be in book-entry form, as book-entry form securities have been specifically defined in Finnish law to refer to securities that have been registered on a book-entry system maintained by a licensed central securities depositary. Thus, having book-entry form Tokens would imply that the blockchain infrastructure service provider would need to be a licensed central securities depository. However, should Tokens be registered on a DLT-based settlement system in accordance with the DLT Pilot Regulation, the requirement for Tokens to be in book-entry form would not be applicable pursuant to an exemption under the before-mentioned regulation.[168] Accordingly, tokenization of financial assets on a blockchain infrastructure seems to fall somewhere in between of the said categories. In any case it seems that the requirement as per item (3) would need to be adjusted to meet the specifications of the offered Tokens in question (*see* section [B] on Blockchain Finality).

In terms of item (4), the prospectus would need to include a description of the mechanisms through which the rights attached to the offered Tokens are exercised, i.e., there would need to be a description of the actual process for using voting power and/or financial rights attached to the Token. Pursuant to item (5), one would describe the actual technical process of payment and delivery in the blockchain environment to be utilized and the blockchain protocol to be used for transaction validation. The

168. In respect of shares being registered on a DLT-based settlement system, Finnish law stipulates that even though the book-entry form requirement would not be applicable pursuant to an exemption under the DLT Pilot Regulation, the technical implementation of the DLT-based settlement system should nevertheless enable maintaining a share register and exercising rights related to the ownership of the security in the manner stipulated by applicable law.

descriptions could end up being very technical in nature and thus hard to grasp for an individual investor. As the technology used can vary from one offering to another, it might be difficult for investors to understand the process or compare the specifications of different platforms in a meaningful manner.

When contemplating an STO, the issuer should always analyse whether (i) a prospectus exemption is available and whether (ii) the Token offering exceeds the national prospectus threshold of EUR 8 million.[169,170] Where the total offer consideration is between EUR 1 and EUR 8 million, the offering may be made by making available a concise basic information document (no FIN-FSA approval needed). If the total consideration is below EUR 1 million, no mandatory disclosure document is needed, but the offer is governed under general good conduct principles of the Finnish securities market (elaborated further below). In respect of the prospectus exemptions, the most commonly used are offers to qualified investors, offers to less than 150 non-qualified investors and offers with a total consideration of at least EUR 100,000 per investor. By default, these exemptions should be normally available for STO as well.

It should be noted that regardless of the applicability of prospectus exemptions or the fact that the national prospectus threshold is not exceeded in relation to an individual offering, the general good conduct principles of the SMA must be always complied with. This means in practice that regardless of the size of the offering, the issuer of Tokens shall not provide false or misleading information on the offering, the offered Tokens or the issuer itself. Further, pursuant to the good conduct principles, the issuer has an obligation to correct and/or supplement without undue delay in an adequate manner any information which is revealed to be untruthful or misleading in nature and which may be of material significance to an investor. The issuer has also a general obligation to keep sufficient information on factors that may have a material effect on the value of the offered security equally available to all investors. In offerings executed without a prospectus or other official offering document, such general information obligation is usually met with information memorandums and/or company presentations.

[E] Regulatory Specifics for Organized Trade

The FIN-FSA has not issued any official guidance or regulation that would contemplate whether a Token that is subject to public trading should be legally construed based on the fundamental principles of the existing market abuse regime. Such an interpretation

169. Finland has decided to exempt public security offerings from the obligation to publish a prospectus, where the total consideration of public offers in the EU is less than EUR 8 million calculated over a period of twelve months.

170. On 7 Dec. 2022, the European Commission introduced its proposal for the new Listing Act Package which comprises quite significant amendments to the Prospectus Regulation, MAR and MiFID II. Pursuant to the proposal, the threshold to publish a prospectus would be increased to EUR 12 million (the aggregate considerations in the EU in the period of twelve months) when offering securities to the public. The current threshold implemented by Finland is EUR 8 million and hence, in the future, it could be possible for companies to gather EUR 4 million more without having to publish a prospectus.

would mean that information relating to Tokens or issuers of such could constitute inside information as referred to in MAR and further, that provisions concerning, e.g., insider trading, unlawful disclosure of inside information and market manipulation would become applicable. Applicability criteria of MAR is twofold; (i) there needs to be a financial instrument that (ii) has been admitted to trading (or for which a request for admission to trading has been made) on a trading venue referred to in MiFID II. As discussed in section B.1, Tokens may well be categorized as securities under Finnish law depending on their characteristics. In terms of MAR applicability, the key question seems to be the admission to a trading venue.

The European Securities Market Authority has taken a view that where Tokens qualify as financial instruments, any platform trading such Tokens with a central order book (or matching orders under other trading models) is likely to qualify as multilateral system.[171] Pursuant to MiFID II, such platforms should operate as regulated markets, multilateral trading facilities or organized trading facilities (i.e., trading venues under MiFID II). Trading Tokens qualifying as financial instruments on such trading venues triggers the applicability of MAR. This would mean that the issuer of the Token would have an ongoing obligation to disclose all inside information relating to such issuer to the public.

Also, Tokens qualifying as financial instruments subject to public trading on a DLT-based trading venue will be subject to provisions of MAR. As a starting point, the DLT Pilot Regulation does not change the regulation of securities trading or settlement other than by adding a new digital implementation option for the DLT platform service providers. When planning a ramp-up of such an activity, the service provider must establish how it will fulfil the requirements of MAR and other applicable regulations, and on the other hand, the licensing authority (FIN-FSA) has to take a position on whether it considers that the applicable requirements are met.

[F] Conclusion

In Finland, Tokens are a rather new digital asset class, and the market is still very much in its infancy.[172] In terms of regulation, the part of the Finnish securities laws that have not been already repealed are very much aligned with the EU capital markets law. Even though the DLT Pilot Regulation might be a beginning for something new, the existing Finnish securities laws have not been drafted with digital assets or blockchain technology in mind. Thus, it seems clear that there are areas of national law where the categorization of Tokens as securities in the context of capital markets regulation creates a need for a certain level of interpretation to allow a meaningful application of provisions. Also, such scenarios might arise where there are no relevant provisions available at all. The FIN-FSA is likely to follow closely the guidance and advice of ESMA

171. ESMA, *supra* n. 162.
172. According to a thematic review by the FIN-FSA concerning the present state of the use of new digital technologies and related risks published on 25 Apr. 2022, the entities supervised by the FIN-FSA had progressed the furthest in the use of big data and data analytics, but the utilization of blockchain technology is still very limited.

and will most likely adopt best practices from more experienced markets once available. New EU regulation to be adopted will most likely be implemented on a national level without any significant gold-plating.

§5.06 CAPITAL MARKETS AND BLOCKCHAIN: COUNTRY REPORT – FRANCE

Bertrand Levy[173]

[A] What Makes a Token a Security?

France has been very active over the past years in order to create a legal environment which would be favourable to the development of digital technology. In particular, France enacted in 2019 the so-called PACTE (*Plan d'Action pour la Croissance et la Transformation de l'Entreprise*)[174] law governing ICOs and creating a regulatory framework for digital asset service providers, thus setting up the definition of digital assets which can be divided into two main categories: cryptocurrencies and Tokens.

The French Financial and Monetary Code[175] provides a definition of Token: A Token is constituted by any intangible asset representing under digital format one or several rights which can be issued, registered, stored or transferred by means of a shared electronic registration system which enables to identify, directly or indirectly, the owner of such property. A natural tendency might be to assimilate Tokens to financial instruments, which would in the end have the merits of simplicity in terms of legal treatment but would create a rather stringent legal framework. This is not the path that was chosen by the French legislator because French law privileges substance over form. In other words, if a Token falls within the definition of financial instruments, it will follow the legal regime applicable to financial instruments. For instance, if a Token is qualified as a financial instrument as per French law, the relevant provisions regarding prospectus will be applicable in case of public offers. The consequence of this principle is that the terms and conditions of each Token should be reviewed in order to determine whether it can be qualified as a financial instrument.

What is a Security Token under French law? In order to answer this question, we first need to know what a security is under French law. Rather than providing for a theoretical definition of security, the French Financial and Monetary Code[176] provides a list: financial securities are (i) share capital securities issued by stock companies, (ii) debt securities, and (iii) shares of collective investment schemes (CISs). If a Token has characteristics which fall within these categories, it can be qualified as a Security Token.

173. Bertrand Lévy is a corporate partner at Bird & Bird based in Paris. Bertrand has extensive expertise in M&A and LBO transactions with a strong focus on Fintech matters. Bertrand Lévy would like to thank Ms Lina Lahlou for her contribution to this chapter.
174. Law No. 2019-486 dated 22 May 2019.
175. Article L. 552-2 of the French Financial and Monetary Code.
176. Article L. 211-1 II of the French Financial and Monetary Code.

As an example, a Security Token can be constituted by a share of capital which is registered on a shared electronic registration system instead of being registered in a traditional book-entry form as is usually the case in practice. We will see below that French law recognizes such a Security Token with corresponding legal consequences. Some might also name certain Tokens which are not securities that have been digitalized but represent the underlying securities as 'Security Tokens'. This type of Token is more construed as a new type of securitization instrument rather than a pure Security Token. We will base our analysis below on Security Tokens that can actually qualify as securities under French law.

[B] Blockchain Finality

The notion of shared electronic registration system has been introduced in France by two ordinances dated 28 April 2016[177] and 8 December 2017[178] relating respectively to: (i) savings bonds (so-called minibonds) and (ii) financial instruments which were implemented by a Decree dated 24 December 2018.[179]

The 'minibonds' constitute a new category of savings bonds which are intermediated by crowdfunding platforms and can be issued by limited liability companies under certain conditions for an amount not exceeding EUR 2,500,000 per year. Such bonds are nominative and non-negotiable. The provisions of the French Financial and Monetary Code[180] provide that the issuance and transfer of such bonds can be implemented through a shared electronic registration system. In addition, French law implicitly recognizes the validity of the 'smart contract' which is constituted by the transfer of the 'minibonds' in the shared electronic registration system.[181]

More importantly in terms of legal impact, the Ordinance dated 24 December 2018 enables to register, transfer and pledge securities as defined by French law on a shared electronic registration system.[182] However, listed securities are not included in the type of securities which can benefit from these provisions. Nevertheless, this constitutes a significant breakthrough in terms of recognition of shared electronic registration systems for purposes of Security Token issuance. Thus, in theory, French law provides equal legal strength, hence protection for securities which are registered in a traditional book-entry form (the 'old fashion' way) or in a shared electronic registration system. The holders of Security Tokens therefore benefit from the same rights as the holders of a security which is not tokenized.

In particular, the provisions of the French Financial and Monetary Code specifically provide that the bona fide acquisition rule apply to transfer of securities carried out through a DLT.[183] French law recognizes that digital assets can constitute financial

177. Ord. 2016-520 dated 28 Apr. 2016.
178. Ord. 2017-1674 dated 8 Dec. 2017.
179. Decree no. 2018-1226 dated 24 Dec. 2018.
180. Article L. 223-12 of the French Financial and Monetary Code.
181. Article L. 223-13 of the French Financial and Monetary Code.
182. Article L. 221-20, VII of the French Financial and Monetary Code.
183. Article L. 211-16 of the French Financial and Monetary Code.

securities, which is the natural step after dematerialization which occurred quite a long time ago and perhaps the first step towards full digitalization of financial securities. However, we will see below that the will of the legislator to grant the same legal effects for securities registered under a shared electronic registration system and under book-entry form will require a few further legal adaptations.

It should be noted that French law is theoretically neutral from a technical standpoint and does not refer to a specific underlying technology or type of shared electronic registration system (public, private or consortium). However, specific legal requirements might impose the recourse to a private- or consortium-shared electronic registration system on which to register Security Tokens so that certain legal provisions can be enforceable. In particular, French law now provides that it is the responsibility of the issuer, or an agent appointed by the issuer, to keep the register in a book-entry form or in a shared electronic registration system.[184] For instance, French law provides that a seller and a purchaser of shares can freely determine the effective date of transfer for their shares. If there is no account manager, this flexibility can be difficult to achieve, in practice, on a blockchain. Another example is the enforcement of pledges. French law provides that a pledge has to be enforced against the custodian of the securities, which might prove difficult, in practice, against public blockchains.[185] There is also a legal difference in terms of rules regarding the pledge of securities. The legal regime applicable to the pledge of securities is constructed so that it is the account itself which is the subject of the pledge, not the securities, which creates theoretical and practical questions as to how these legal provisions can apply for securities registered in a shared electronic registration system since there is no account anymore.

There is clearly a will from the legislator to grant the same legal effect to the registration of securities in a shared electronic registration system and in the book-entry form, but there is still some fine-tuning to reach full equivalence, but most importantly, confidence from security holders on this new technology must be gained.

[C] Private International Law and Blockchain

The interaction between private international law and blockchain remains an interesting area of doctrine that has not been studied a lot. Yet blockchain technology, which is decentralized and dematerialized, raises major challenges for private international law because of its international nature.

According to the 'Code is Law' paradigm, it could be considered superfluous to look for an applicable national law. This is because each blockchain application is autonomous, operating independently of an external legal regime, comparable to a spontaneous legal order. However, reality dictates the need for regulation, and national legislators have already shown their willingness to intervene, both in France and abroad.

184. Article R. 228 of the French Commercial code, Art. R. 211-2 and R. 211-3 of the French Financial and Monetary Code.
185. Vincent Malassigné, *Blockchain et droit des sociétés*, the principle of equivalence of book-entry registration and registration in a shared electronic recording device.

In the area of financial transactions, blockchain technology poses a real challenge. At the European level, the European Commission has set up a working group on 'Conflicts of laws concerning securities and claims'. Faced with the complexity of harmonizing blockchain with the principles of conflict of laws, part of the working group preferred to avoid the question,[186] deeming it too complex and requiring in-depth consideration.

To compensate for these shortcomings, initiatives are emerging to create virtual jurisdictions integrated into the blockchain, such as the Aragon network[187] and the Kleros adjudication protocol[188] based on game theory. These mechanisms aim to settle internal blockchain disputes without recourse to state courts. Consequently, it is legitimate to question the relevance and effectiveness of these systems compared with traditional mechanisms of private international law.[189]

Furthermore, the impact of blockchain technology on the field of private international law raises complex questions, particularly about determining the applicable law. Despite the autonomous nature of blockchain, states are drawing up recommendations or treaties to regulate its use. National laws, such as those already introduced in France,[190] are beginning to regulate blockchain, with the goal to demonstrate that the idea that 'Code is Law' can be limited. Consequently, private international law must be mobilized to determine the competent jurisdiction and the applicable law. When these exchanges are contractual in nature, the mechanism of party autonomy allows the parties to stipulate in their contract not only the role they intend to give to blockchain but also to choose the law applicable to their contract, in particular by preferring the law of a State that has recognized the blockchain mechanism, a principle recognized by Article 3 of Regulation 593/2008, known as Rome I. Fundamentally, concerns about evidence in the context of cross-border transactions involving *Tokens* raise complex issues in the field of private international law. The procedural effectiveness of acts in France is determined by French law,[191] and the same applies to information obtained via blockchain.

---

186. *Meeting of the Expert Group on conflict of laws on securities and claims*, Brussels, 15-16 May 2017, p. 2: '*Some experts stressed that blockchain raises a lot of legal problems which the expert group might not have the time to analyse as well as technological problems (time which is needed to validate a transaction, high energy consumption, hardware problems due to huge amount of data being transferred) which might lead to moving beyond DLT soon (e.g. to distributed consensus technology)*', available at: https://ec.europa.eu/transparency/regexpert/index.cfm?do=groupDetail.groupDetailDoc&id=33452&n° =2/ (last access: 17 Jun. 2020).
187. *Aragon Network Jurisdiction Part 1: Decentralized Court*, Aragon Network, 18 Jul. 2017, available at: https://blog.aragon.org/aragon-network-jurisdiction-part-1-decentralized-court-c8ab2a675^{e} 82/ (last accessed 3 Apr. 2020).
188. C. Lesaege and F. Ast, *Kleros Short Paper v1.0.6*, November 2018, available at: https://kleros.io/assets/whitepaper.pdf/ (last accessed 3 Apr. 2020).
189. The discussion was subsequently taken up in another forum: *Distributed Ledger Technology and Governing Law: Issues of Legal Uncertainty*, Financial Markets Law Committee, March 2018.
190. Article L. 223-12 Code monétaire et financier, resulting from Ordonnance no. 2016-520 of 28 Apr. 2016, provides for the use of the blockchain in relation to 'minibons' (a type of bond issue for small businesses). *See also* Act 2016-1691 of 9 Dec. 2016 (Sapin II Act) and Order 2017-1674 of 8 Dec. 2017 on the use of a shared electronic recording device for the representation and transmission of financial securities.
191. Civ. 1re, 14 Jun. 1983, no 82-13.247, Suhami c./ Venture.

Nevertheless, the location of encryption operations on blockchain poses challenges for the application of the law of the place where the deed is drawn up. A promising alternative would be to use the law applicable to the substance of the deed in accordance with European regulations such as Regulation (EC) No. 593/2008[192] on the law applicable to contractual obligations (Rome I) and Article 22.2 of Regulation (EC) No. 864/2007[193] on the law applicable to non-contractual obligations (Rome II). Assuming that the parties are identified, they will be able to place their relationship under a law that allows the use of blockchain. This would allow them to choose a law that takes account of the use of blockchain. This demonstrates the legal potential, but also the limitations, of French and international law.

In summary, the complex interaction between private international law and blockchain raises challenges, particularly in determining the applicable law. Although initiatives are emerging to settle domestic disputes, the balance between the technological autonomy of blockchain and the need for legal regulation remains a crucial issue.

[D] Special Requirements for Prospectus

France is of course subject to EU prospectus regulations, and the issuance of Security Tokens should therefore be specifically reviewed in this respect as well as local French requirements. Any public offering of securities requires the prior publication of a prospectus unless the public offering falls under exemptions of the applicable regulation.

If there is no exemption, the prospectus will have to provide the relevant information required by law, with a specific focus on risk factors related to the shared electronic registration system. In particular, the prospectus will have to describe the specificities of the Security Tokens. For instance, how the revenue streams are generated from the underlying asset (dividends, interest, etc.) and distributed to the Token holder. To determine if the Token issued actually is a share, the prospectus will have to describe the type of shares represented by the Token and the various rights attached to the shares, such as dividends (preferred or not), information rights or any other type of rights provided by law or by contract. It could be envisaged that specific shareholders' rights which are usually set forth in a separate shareholders' agreement be included in the Token code in the form of a smart contract (lock-up periods, waivers of preferred subscription rights, right of first offer, audit rights, etc.). Voting rights could also be exercised via the shared electronic registration system.

French law provides an exception to the prospectus requirement which might be of interest in the context of STOs for small- or medium-size companies.

The general regulations of the French FMA provide in Article 211-2 that public offerings below EUR 8,000,000 do not constitute public offers subject to prospectus. The total amount of the offer is calculated on a twelve-month period following the first

192. Article 18.2 of Regulation No. 593/2008.
193. Article 18.2 of Regulation No. 864/2007.

offer. In this specific case, the issuer benefits from a simplified procedure which consists in providing to the subscriber a simplified information document which includes basic information detailed in Article 212-44 of the general regulations issued by the French FMA:

(1) presentation of the issuer and a description of its activity, project and use of proceeds, together with the latest financial statements available, financial forecast, fundraisings, financings and cash position, as well as an org chart of the management and shareholding;
(2) information on the level of commitment of the management in the proposed offer;
(3) comprehensive information on all rights attached to the securities to be issued (voting rights, financial rights and information rights);
(4) comprehensive information on all rights (voting rights, financial rights and information rights) attached to securities not offered to the public as well as the beneficiaries of such securities;
(5) description of the provisions mentioned in the by-laws or shareholders' agreement governing the liquidity of the securities;
(6) the conditions under which copies of the registration of the ownership of the investors in the issuer can be obtained;
(7) description of the risks implied by the activity of the issuer and the contemplated project;
(8) if available, a copy of the reports prepared to the attention of the general assembly of the last financial year and the current financial year as well as the reports prepared by the statutory auditors if any;
(9) the date of the simplified information document.

Such information documents and the communications relating thereto, whatever their format or communication method, have to be provided to the French FMA which can require specific disclaimer to be included. It should, however, be noted that securities listed (or to be listed) on a regulated market or MTF cannot benefit from this exemption.

The new regulations recognizing the registration and transfer of securities in a shared electronic registration system combined with the prospectus exemption referred to above create a favourable legal framework for the development of securities Token offerings in France for transactions below EUR 8,000,000, but such offerings remain confidential for the moment. The legal framework relating to STOs on the primary market will not be in a position to develop if there is no secondary market which actually enables to exchange the Tokens once they are issued.

Several transactions qualifying as STOs were identified on the French market over the past years. In particular, a subsidiary of Société Générale, SG SFH, issued in May 2020 EUR 40,000,000 of covered bonds in the form of digital financial securities on a public blockchain. These securities were fully subscribed by Société Générale and simultaneously paid to the issuer by means of a traditional transfer in euros and reflected by Tokens issued by the French central bank on a blockchain. This transaction represented the first settlement of a financial instrument transaction using central bank digital currency in a developed country.[194]

[E] Regulatory Specifics for Organized Trade

The regulation of the European Parliament and of the Council on a pilot regime for market infrastructures based on distributed ledger technology, known as the 'pilot regime regulation', published in the Official Journal of the European Union on 2 June 2022, came into force on 23 March 2023. The aim of such regulation is to introduce a uniform regime for activities involving *Security Tokens* or tokenized financial securities and to enable the development of distributed ledger technologies. Three categories of market infrastructures are eligible for this regime: DLT multilateral trading facilities (DLT MTF), DLT securities settlement systems (DLT SS), and a new concept of DLT trading and settlement systems (DLT TSS), providing both DLT MTF and DLT SS services.

The regulation provides targeted regulatory exemptions from MiFID 2 and Finality Directives, as well as Regulation 909/2014 on Central Securities Depositories,[195] which were designed without distributed ledger and crypto asset technology in mind. These exemptions, which can last up to 6 years, relate to the market infrastructures previously listed and are offered in return for compliance with certain obligations and compensatory measures. In particular, the regulation provides for exemptions from licensing requirements, as well as from the conditions governing the registration of securities and bookkeeping for each securities settlement system of a DLT SS.

The French so-called DDADUE law[196] amended Articles L. 211-3 and L. 211-7 of the French Financial and Monetary Code. Article L. 211-7 previously provided that financial securities, when admitted to trading by a central depository, could be registered in a securities account held by an authorized intermediary. When they are not admitted to the operations of a central depository, they must be registered, in the name of the owner of the securities, in a securities account held by the issuer or in a shared electronic registration system. The law added a third paragraph to this article, which now sets the legal framework for a new category of securities: 'financial securities admitted to the operations on a "DLT market infrastructure" within the meaning of the pilot regime regulation'. These securities are entered in the shared electronic registration system either by the issuer or by a DLT market infrastructure under the conditions set out in the regulation.

194. Rapport sur les titres financiers digitaux ('Security Tokens') du Haut Comité Juridique de la Place Financière de Paris, le 237 novembre 2020.
195. Regulation (EU) No. 909/2014 of the European Parliament and of the Council of 23 Jul. 2014 on improving securities settlement in the European Union and on central securities depositories.
196. Law No. 2023-71 dated 9 Mar. 2023 called 'loi portant diverses dispositions d'adaptation au droit de l'Union européenne dans les domaines de l'économie, de la santé, du travail, des transports et de l'agriculture'.

Until recently, securities registered in a shared electronic registration system by the issuer could only be in registered form. Now, Decree no. 2023-421 of 31 May 2023 specifies that securities registered in a shared electronic registration system by a DLT market infrastructure under the conditions set out in the pilot regime, must be in bearer form. Bearer securities enjoy greater liquidity, notably because they can be admitted to a multilateral trading facility.

French law currently allows an investor to trade bearer securities through a market infrastructure without an intermediary to provide the custody account-keeping service. Nevertheless, Decree no. 2023-421 of 31 May 2023 specifies that an owner of bearer financial securities registered in a shared electronic recording device in application of the pilot regime may instruct an intermediary mentioned in Article L. 211-3 (i.e., a custodian account keeper) or a 'DLT market infrastructure' to hold the means of access to its securities, including in the form of private cryptographic keys, and to process events concerning these securities, under the conditions set by the general regulations of the French FMA.[197]

In addition, the ESMA has updated its Q&A to clarify the conditions for implementing the regulation.[198] Its responses provide further details, notably on the conditions for exemption under the regulation, and on the asset used as settlement means to pay transactions executed on DLT market infrastructures.

§5.07 CAPITAL MARKETS AND BLOCKCHAIN: COUNTRY REPORT – GERMANY

Dr Michael Jünemann[199] & *Johannes Wirtz*[200]

[A] What Makes a Token a Security?

The answer to the question of what makes a Token a '*security*' in Germany plays a key role in determining the extent to which capital markets and, in particular, securities regulation law apply to it.[201] The German Federal Financial Supervisory Authority (*BaFin*) evaluates Tokens on a case-by-case basis depending on their legal design and existing supervisory laws, none of which were initially framed with Tokens in mind.[202]

197. Article R. 211-4 of the French Financial and Monetary Code.
198. ESMA Questions and Answers on the implementation of Regulation (EU) 2022/858 of the European Parliament and of the Council of 30 May 2022 on a pilot regime for market infrastructures based on distributed ledger technology.
199. Head of international Finance and Financial Regulation Group at Bird & Bird, Dr Michael Jünemann understands the intricacies of the legal frameworks around FinTech and is one of the few to integrate knowledge of technology with capital markets law.
200. As a Finance and Financial Regulation Partner at Bird & Bird, Johannes Wirtz has profound knowledge about the highly regulated financial market and focuses on the EU-regulatory landscape of cryptoassets.
201. *Rüdiger Veil*, Token-Emissionen im europäischen Kapitalmarktrecht, 183 ZHR 2019, 346, 354.
202. BaFin Federal Financial Supervisory Authority, Crypto tokens dated 23 Oct. 2023, https://www.bafin.de/EN/Aufsicht/FinTech/Geschaeftsmodelle/DLT_Blockchain_Krypto/Kryptotoken/Kryptotoken_node_en.html (accessed 14 Nov. 2023).

Although specific regulations exist for digital assets like crypto securities (*Kryptowertpapiere*) in Germany, a comprehensive legal framework covering all common types of Tokens is lacking. One common non-legal category of Tokens is Security Tokens, also referred to as Investment Tokens or as their specialized form Equity Tokens.[203] They exhibit properties akin to traditional financial instruments, such as stocks. In contrast to Security Tokens, 'pure' Utility Tokens or Currency Tokens are not regarded as securities (or capital investments) in Germany.[204] In its supervisory practice, BaFin qualifies Utility Tokens as Tokens that are digital vouchers which can be redeemed against a promised service of the issuer.[205] According to BaFin, Currency Tokens have a money replacement character and serve as decentralized non-governmental, substitute currency.[206] With regard to Hybrid Tokens, the functions that the Token focuses on and the circumstances of the individual case are decisive.[207] Due to their resemblance to certain conventional financial instruments such as 'securities', Security Tokens are frequently considered regulated financial instruments under German law, adhering to the concept of '*substance over form*'.[208] Thus, Security Tokens may potentially fall under the classification as '*securities*' under various German and European legal frameworks, including the Regulation (EU) 2017/1129 (*EU Prospectus Regulation*), the German Securities Prospectus Act (*Wertpapierprospektgesetz* (*WpPG*)), and the German Securities Trading Act (*Gesetz über den Wertpapierhandel* (*WpHG*)).

If a Token is classified as '*security*', this may trigger the requirement to publish a securities prospectus unless exemptions apply. WpPG (the German supplement act) and the EU Prospectus Regulation, '*securities*' has the meaning given to it under point (44) of Article 4(1) of Directive 2014/65/EU (*MiFID II*) with the exception of money-market instruments having a maturity of less than twelve months. Under MiFID II, '*transferable securities*' are classes of securities negotiable on the capital market, with the exception of instruments of payment, like company shares. Within the WpHG (implementing MiFID II for Germany), the definition of '*securities*' encompasses all categories of transferable securities, irrespective of whether they are represented by a certificate, excluding payment instruments that are inherently tradable on financial markets. In order to qualify as a '*security*' the Token must be tradable on financial markets, though not necessarily actually traded.[209] In 2022, '*instruments issued using*

203. *Maute* in Maume/Maute, Rechtshandbuch Kryptowerte, 1st ed., § 6 Verträge über Kryptotoken.
204. BaFin, *Prospektpflicht – Rechtslage seit dem 21.07.2019*, https://www.bafin.de/DE/Aufsicht/Prospekte/Wertpapiere/Prospektpflicht/prospektpflicht_node.html (accessed 7 Dec. 2023).
205. BaFin, Zweites Hinweisschreiben zu Prospekt- und Erlaubnispflichten im Zusammenhang mit der Ausgabe sogenannter Krypto-Token dated 16 Aug. 2019, https://www.bafin.de/SharedDocs/Downloads/DE/Merkblatt/WA/dl_wa_merkblatt_ICOs.html (accessed 14 Nov. 2023).
206. *Ibid.*
207. *Ibid.*
208. BaFin Federal Financial Supervisory Authority, *Crypto tokens*, dated 23 Oct. 2023, https://www.bafin.de/EN/Aufsicht/FinTech/Geschaeftsmodelle/DLT_Blockchain_Krypto/Kryptotoken/Kryptotoken_node_en.html (accessed 14 Nov. 2023).
209. BaFin, *supra* n. 204.

distributed ledger technology' were included in Article 4 I 1 No. 15 of MiFID II (to be implemented into national law by March 2023) reinforcing the interpretation that Security Token can be covered.[210] It must also be transferable to be considered negotiable on capital markets.[211] This is the case if the Token can be transferred to a transferee technically and legally unaltered.[212] Since BaFin adopts the 'substance-over-form' approach of ESMA, securitization in a certificate is not a mandatory requirement for a security under German supervisory law.[213] However, the question remains whether the conceptual similarity of Security Tokens with traditional securities is sufficient for tradability on capital markets or if an additional requirement of legal finality is necessary to make a Security Token a security under German supervisory law (legal finality is discussed further in section §5.07[B] below). Neither the formal name of the Token nor any advertisement with regard to the Token is determinative of its status.[214] Essential to a Token's classification as a '*security*' is the (corporate) membership or financial rights associated with it. The concept of securities is therefore notably fulfilled by Tokens that are functionally similar to 'classic' securities such as stocks, bonds or certificates. Tokenization of corporate membership is possible only in a limited way: Under German law, (only) some types of companies such as civil law partnerships (*Gesellschaft bürgerlichen Rechts – GbR*) can be established on a blockchain.[215] Shares in German limited liability companies (*Gesellschaften mit beschränkter Haftung (GmbHs)*) – which do also not qualify as classic securities in Germany – cannot be issued as Tokens on a blockchain due to strict formal requirements (notarization).[216] However, a hypothetical alternative for GmbHs involves employing a trustee structure:[217] In this set-up, a trustee holds the company shares in their own name but acts for the benefit of the investors. The trustee issues Tokens to these investors, granting them contractual rights, such as a share in the company's profits. These Tokens do not represent direct equity in the GmbH but rather specific rights related to membership benefits. The trustee exercises shareholder rights in accordance with directives from the investors. This approach does not enable the direct tradeability of the GmbH shares themselves but does facilitate the trading of certain associated membership elements. As those Tokens come with a contractual right and membership elements, they are likely to qualify as security.[218] While innovative, this model carries

210. Philipp Maume in *Struktur, Definition und Anwendungs-fälle der Kryptoregulierung*, NJW 2023, 1168 n. 4.
211. Deutscher Bundestag, *Gesetzesentwurf der Bundesregierung, Finanzmarkt-Richtlinie-Umsetzungsgesetz*, Deutscher Bundestag Drucksache 16/4028 53 (2007).
212. BaFin, *supra* n. 204.
213. BaFin, *Initial Coin Offerings: Hinweisschreiben zur Einordnung als Finanzinstrumente 2018*, WA 11-QB 4100-2017/0010.
214. *Hagen Weiß* in *Tokenisation*, https://www.bafin.de/SharedDocs/Veroeffentlichungen/EN/Fachartikel/2019/fa_bj_1904_Tokenisierung_en.html (accessed 14 Nov. 2023).
215. Lena Maute in Maume/Maute, *supra* n. 203, § 6 Verträge über Kryptotoken.
216. *Andreas Fuchs* in Wertpapierhandelsgesetz, 3rd ed. (2024).
217. Philipp Maume in Die Anwendung der Blockchain-Technologie im GmbH-Recht, NZG 2021, 1189.
218. Gerald Spindler in Möslein/Omlor, FinTech-Handbuch, § 25 Effektengeschäft, n. 43.

inherent risks, including the potential for abuse by the trustee, the risk of the trustee's insolvency, and the possibility of enforcement actions against the trustee's assets.

In summary, a Token can only be classified as a '*security*' under German law if it possesses certain essential characteristics: *negotiability*, *transferability* on (capital) markets, and the incorporation of rights comparable to traditional securities.[219] For securities to be considered '*negotiable*', it must be sufficiently standardized: each issued Token must contain the same characteristics to ensure a degree of certainty simply indicated by the number of the Token, making it *fungible*.[220] This is not the case if the issuer offers individual adjustments, such as changes to the maturity, face value, or the basic price of the Token.[221] Concepts for the definition of '*security*' known from other jurisdictions, such as (1) vouchers issued in relation to goods or services not yet available, (2) profit expectations of the Token purchasers or (3) a profit coming from the efforts of a promoter or a third party, are not relevant under German law.

Furthermore, Tokens embodying bearer bonds can qualify as '*crypto securities*' under the German Electronic Securities Act (*Gesetz über elektronische Wertpapiere – eWpG*), provided that certain criteria are met. Additionally, an expansion of the scope of the eWpG is planned (and currently in parliament) to include the issuance of crypto stocks (*Kryptoaktien*). As a result, stock corporations will have the option to offer their stocks either in the form of physical certificates or as crypto stocks in compliance with the eWpG. Crypto securities and crypto stocks qualify as securities.[222]

Tokens may also fall into other categories of regulated financial instruments beyond the category of '*securities*'. They can, for example, qualify as '*debt instruments*' or as '*crypto-assets*'[223] as defined in the German Banking Act (*Kreditwesengesetz – KWG*) and German Investment Firm Act (*Gesetz zur Beaufsichtigung von Wertpapierinstituten* (*WpIG*)). These acts determine whether a service provided in relation to such an instrument is a banking business, a financial service or an investment service. Such businesses or services require an authorization which is granted in Germany by BaFin. According to the KWG and the WpIG, the term '*crypto-asset*' means a digital representation of a value that has not been issued or guaranteed by any central bank or public body, does not have the legal status of currency or money but is accepted by natural or legal persons as a means of exchange or payment or for investment purposes on the basis of an agreement or actual practice which can be transmitted, stored and traded by electronic means. The scope of crypto asset is therefore broader than the term '*security*'.

219. BaFin, *supra* n. 204.
220. *Michael Jünemann & Johannes Wirtz* in *ICO: Rechtliche Einordnung von Token – Teil I*, Zeitschrift für das gesamte Kreditwesen 2018, 27, 28; *Christoph Kumpan*, Kapitalmarktrechts-Kommentar s. 1 § 2 marginal no. 7 WpHG (Eberhard Schwark & Daniel Zimmer ed 2010).
221. *Peter Zickgraf* in Initial Coin Offerings – Ein Fall für das Kapitalmarktrecht? 2018, Die Aktiengesellschaft 293, 299, 300.
222. *Poelzig* in, Kryptoaktien nachdem Referentenentwurf des Zukunftsfinanzierungsgesetz RDi 2023, 333, n. 5.
223. *Behrens/Schadtle* in WM 2019, 2099, 2101.

[B] Blockchain Finality

It is generally agreed that technical finality and immutability are key characteristics of blockchain transactions.[224] However, this popular notion is met with a technical counter: transactions on the blockchain are technically only 'probably final' but not absolute. Potential forks and re-orgs can occur unpredictably, leading to scenarios where transactions might be expunged from a blockchain's history. This uncertainty is especially prevalent in blockchains that use probabilistic finality, like Bitcoin, where the finality of a block increases over time but is never absolute.[225] To mitigate this uncertainty, experts discuss propositions like defining a specific time lapse or a certain number of blocks from which a transaction is considered 'final'.[226]

This technical 'non-finality' of blockchain transactions raises the question of how legal finality of blockchain transactions can be established under German law. Given the rapid pace of individual transactions, even beyond high-frequency trading, legal finality emerges as an indispensable prerequisite for trading on the capital market. Therefore, the classic understanding of *capital market negotiability* is based on the possibility of bona fide acquisition:[227] For the market to function properly, it requires unrestricted title trading and secure, straightforward transaction processing without the possibility of third-party objections. Failing this, buyers of securities would be exposed to incalculable risks, unsure if they had acquired securities from a rightful transferor.[228] This necessity leads to the relevance of concepts such as the bona fide acquisition rules. However, given the nature of a blockchain itself, one could conclude that a blockchain could be considered a (decentralized) register similar to a (centralized) public register (like the land registry administrated by a neutral, independent government body) potentially earning public credence.[229] To achieve this, the blockchain must furnish comprehensive information on the legal relationships with regard to the relevant Tokens. Blockchains record Token transmissions through a cryptographic depiction of ownership chains. This suggests that the ownership of the underlying right and the Tokens are inseparably linked, achieved through the illustration of the specific right on the blockchain (*tokenization*). Nonetheless, the realm of public credence is under the purview of German legislation, which, as *per lege lata,* has not accorded public credence to blockchains.

Furthermore, the bona fide acquisition of Tokens is largely not possible, with very few statutory exceptions, as German law does not accord proprietary rights to

224. *Tobias Zepf* in Blockchain, Technologie, Innovationen und Anwendungen – oder eine Kette, die Ketten sprengt 9-9 2016.
225. Benjamin Samuels The Engineer's Guide to Blockchain Finality (23 Aug. 2023), https://blog.trailofbits.com/2023/08/23/the-engineers-guide-to-blockchain-finality/ (accessed 14 Nov. 2023).
226. *Müller/Pieper* in eWpG/Pieper, eWpG, § 4 n. 81.
227. 17 A Ralf Wehowsky, *Becksche Kurz Kommentar Erbs/ KohlhaasStrafrechtliche Nebengesetze vol 1* D. 30 marginal no. 2 Peter Häberle ed. (226th ed. 2019).
228. Wehowsky, *supra* n. 227, *at* marginal no. 2; Kumpan, *supra* n. 220, at marginal no. 9.
229. Harald Wilsch, *The German 'Grundbuchordnung': History, Principles and Future about Land Registry in Germany*, Zeitschrift für Geodäsie, Geoinformation und Landmanagement 224, 225 (2012).

data. Yet, we must take the underlying right of the Token into account. Should this right be transferred via assignment within the meaning of section 398 German Civil Code (*Bürgerliches Gesetzbuch – BGB*) or by an assumption of contract, a bona fide acquisition is excluded. There is no general statutory provision that makes the right encapsulated in a Token comparable to certificated bonds, which are negotiable on the capital market and subject to bona fide acquisition (even if the certificate has been stolen or lost).[230] However, exceptions to the principle that a bona fide acquisition of Tokens is not possible have arisen from the legislative action taken by the German legislator aiming to give Tokens a '*digital certificate*'[231] status and to abolish the necessity for a security to be represented by a tangible certificate:[232] The former German government's 2019 blockchain strategy[233] created electronic securities through registration and to replace the documentation function of the securities certificate for electronic securities with the recording of the corresponding rights in an electronic securities register which is kept by a central agency, retaining the core elements of electronic securities: legitimation function, liberation effect, and transfer function.[234]

Reflecting these advancements, the adoption of the eWpG in 2021 marked a milestone in the evolution of German securities law, paving the way for the issuance of electronic (including crypto) securities. Among others, it provides for a legally secure transfer of electronic securities. This change allows issuers to choose between traditional certificated issuance and electronic issuance. The eWpG includes a fiction that electronic securities are deemed to be a thing within the meaning of section 90 of the BGB. Thus, they can be transferred by way of transfer of title making bona fide acquisition possible. The eWpG introduced decentralized crypto securities registers, managed with Distributed Ledger Technology (DLT), enabling the issuance and registration of bearer bonds. As early as 2021, it was envisaged to extend the scope of the eWpG to include electronic stocks.[235] In 2023, the German Federal Cabinet and the Bundestag approved the draft of the Future Financing Act (*Zukunftsfinanzierungsgesetz (ZuFinG)*).[236] This draft proposes, among others, key amendments to the

230. Mathias Habersack, *Münchener Kommentar zum Bürgerlichen Gesetzbuch*, s. 793 BGB, marginal. no. 27, Franz Jürgen Säcker, Roland Rixecker, Hartmut Oetker & Bettina Limperg ed. (7th ed. 2017).

231. Robert Oppenheim & Eric Romba, *Initial Coin Offering (ICO) aus rechtlicher Sicht: Der Token als digitale Urkunde?*, https://www.it-finanzmagazin.de/initial-coin-offering-ico-rechtliche-sicht-token-digitale-urkunde-65569 (accessed 14 Nov. 2023).

232. BMF & BMJV, *Eckpunkte für die regulatorische Behandlung von elektronischen Wertpapieren und Krypto-Token*, https://www.bundesfinanzministerium.de/Content/DE/Gesetzestexte/Gesetze_Gesetzesvorhaben/Abteilungen/Abteilung_VII/19_Legislaturperiode/2019-03-07-Eckpunktepapier-Wertpapiere-Krypto-Token/2019-03-07-Eckpunktepapier-regulatorische-Behandlung-elektronische-Wertpapiere-Krypto-Token.pdf;jsessionid=D5779523DB71FD407E8FE439C0A5C0D3?__blob=publicationFile&v=7 (accessed 14 Nov. 2023).

233. *Ibid.*

234. *Ibid.*

235. BT-Drs. 19/26925, p. 39; Philipp Maume, Die Kryptoaktie im Zukunftsfinanzierungsgesetz BKR 2023, 282.

236. German government draft law on financing investments to safeguard the future (*Zukunftsfinanzierungsgesetz – ZuFinG*).

German Stock Corporation Act (*Aktiengesetz – AktG*) and the eWpG, facilitating the issuance of electronic stocks. Electronic stocks, under this proposed law, will not constitute a new category of stocks but will represent an alternative method of issuance. The expanded scope of the eWpG will cover registered bearer bonds, registered shares, and bearer shares. Effective transactions involving electronic securities will necessitate an entry in the electronic securities register,[237] and a bona fide acquisition will be possible. This will grant the holder of an electronic stock the same extensive protection afforded to the owner of a certificated stock, safeguarding them in scenarios of the custodian's insolvency by giving them a segregation right.

In cases where a bona fide acquisition is impossible, the right embodied in the Token has never been transferred. The rights holder can demand reversal of an unauthorized transfer; data packages must be returned, or else the data on the blockchain will not correspond to the legal ownership status of the Tokens under German law. For that reason, a common approach under German law is to peg the digital Token to its underlying rights in the terms and conditions of the Token issuer. Such terms and conditions oblige the holder of a Token not to transfer the Token without transferring the underlying and vice versa. However, such legal technique has effect only *inter partes;* there is no *inter omnes* effect of good faith acquisitions and the legal finality created by it. Consequently, any envisaged transferee of a Security Token should conduct a proper title due diligence regarding the transferor's ownership of the Token before any payment is made – a precaution which is rather difficult to reconcile with the idea of faster and efficient capital markets. For this reason, the logic of BaFin's approach to qualifying financial instruments as securities once they are put on the blockchain must be questioned.

[C] International Private Law

Cross-border transactions involving Tokens can present various international private law issues, owing to the complex interplay between technology and international legal frameworks. One of the first hurdles to overcome is determining applicable law. German law separates between law of obligations and property law. While the law of obligations can be influenced by the parties, there is no choice of property law.[238] In the context of Tokens, several conflict-of-law challenges arise.[239]

Property law is reaching its limits. Tokens, in general, and Security Tokens, in particular, are not corporeal objects. Applicable law cannot be determined pursuant to Article 43 EGBGB which implements *lex rei sitae* into German law. The Token has no place of occupancy. If the Token represents an asset, it is (usually) the intention of the

237. BT-Drs. 19/26925, p. 66.
238. Wolfgang Wurmnest in: Zekoll/Wagner, Introduction to German Law, § 6.01 Introduction, https://www.jura.uni-hamburg.de/media/die-fakultaet/personen/wurmnest-wolfgang/wurmnest-contract-law-in-zekoll-wagner-introduction-to-german-law.pdf (accessed 23. Nov. 2022).
239. Robert Freitag in: Möslein/Omlor, FinTech-Handbuch, § 14 Internationales Privatrecht, n. 30.

parties that the asset shall be transferred if the Token is transferred.[240] The asset embodied in a Security Token is usually a claim. Regulation (EC) 593/2008 (Rome I) generally apply to the governing law of contracts, including those in relation to Tokens. The legal relationship governing the issuance of the Token serves as the focal point for conflict-of-law considerations, as opposed to the act of issuing the Token or its subsequent transfer. The claims represented by a Token are subject to the law determined by the conflict of law rules, especially of Rome I and the Regulation (EC) No. 864/2007 (Rome II). The transfer of the claims is governed by the respective assignment statute which is, however, not regulated by Article 14 of Rome I.[241] Excluded from Rome I are, among others, obligations arising under bills of exchange, cheques and promissory notes and other negotiable instruments to the extent that the obligations under such other negotiable instruments arise out of their negotiable character underscoring that international securities law is a distinct legal field separate from international contract law.[242] '*Negotiable instruments*' means transferable securities where – when the security is transferred – the documented claim is also transferred together with it.[243] The underlying definition of instruments in Rome I is broad. It also applies to dematerialized securities where there is no physical documentation but only a digital entry. This is the case for Security Token, meaning that Rome I is unlikely to apply to the questions of negotiability for Security Token.

For German crypto securities, the eWpG provides a national conflict-of-laws rules as laid out in section 32 of the eWpG.[244] Unless section 17a of the DepotG (which applies *lex libri siti* and *lex conto sitae*)[245] applies, rights to an electronic security and dispositions over an electronic security are subject to the law of the state under the supervision of which the registering entity operates, in whose electronic securities register the security is registered. If the registering entity is not under supervision, the location of the registering entity is decisive. If the location of the registering entity cannot be determined, the location of the issuer of the electronic security is decisive.

Taking from the intention of the rules of the eWpG, it might be considered to apply *lex libri siti* and *lex conto sitae* also to other Security Tokens. Alternatively, *lex registri* could be considered. However, all those efforts fail when it comes to decentralized Tokens. There is not one place where the register or account is held, but the blockchain is decentralized and distributed throughout the world. Finally, it might be suggested that for Security Tokens it should be decisive to take a look at the law governing the embedded claim. The Token itself takes a back seat, but the underlying right directs the applicable law. This opens the general conflict-of-law rules for assignments.[246] Whether the Token is transferred becomes irrelevant – the assignment of the underlying right is decisive.

240. *Ibid.*, at n. 39.
241. *Ibid.*, at n. 40.
242. BeckOGK/Paulus, 1.3.2023, Rom I-VO Art. 1 n. 84.
243. *Ibid.*, at n. 86.
244. *Ibid.*, at n. 46.
245. Skauradszun, ZfPW 2022, 56, 59.
246. Martiny in: Münchener Kommentar BGB, Rom I-VO, Art 1 Rn 64.

[D] Special Requirements for Prospectus

Provided that Tokens are classified as 'securities' under German law (the classification as security has been discussed further in section §5.07[A] above), their public offering/issuance is subject to the requirements of the EUR Prospectus Regulation. This regulation serves as the basis for the approval and validity of securities prospectuses and is complemented by Commission Delegated Regulations (EU) 2019/979 and 2019/980 which specify the content and presentation of such prospectuses. The WpPG contains provisions for exemptions to the prospectus requirement, on prospectus liability, on the securities information sheet, as well as provisions relating to the authority of BaFin and the punishment for offences. According to Article 3(1) of the EU Prospectus Regulation, securities shall only be offered to the public after the prior publication of a prospectus in accordance with the regulation. In Germany, such prospectus needs to be approved by BaFin. This prospectus must contain all information related to the relevant issuer and the securities being offered. The rationale is to provide information to enable an investor to obtain an accurate understanding of the offer and to make an informed investment decision. According to the EU Prospectus Regulation, the prospectus shall in particular contain all information on the assets, liabilities, profits, losses, the financial situation of the issuer and of any guarantor, the rights attached to the securities, the reasons for the issue and the impact on the issuer.[247]

Thus, when encountering advertisements for Tokens, it is prudent for individuals to seek references to an officially approved prospectus. Caution should be exercised concerning advertisements as they may contain misleading or false statements. Advertisements are required by law to be clearly marked as such, aiding in transparent decision-making. Additionally, they should guide potential investors on how to obtain the prospectus. Should advertisements be found online or through other means, it is advisable to cross-reference this information with the prospectus to ensure consistency. All oral or written information about the public offering of securities, even if they are not intended for advertising purposes, must align with the information contained in the prospectus.[248] Ensuring that the information in the advertisement aligns with that in the official prospectus is key to making informed decisions.

The term 'offer of securities to the public' is defined in Article 2(d) of the EU Prospectus Regulation as 'a communication to persons in any form and by any means, presenting sufficient information on the terms of the offer and the securities to be offered, so as to enable an investor to decide to purchase or subscribe for those securities'. There is a connection to Germany if investors resident in Germany are targeted by the offer. According to BaFin, this is the case if the offer is accessible from

247. BaFin, *supra* n. 204; Rüdiger Koch, *Neue Regeln für Wertpapierprospekte*, https://www.bafin.de/SharedDocs/Veroeffentlichungen/DE/Fachartikel/2019/fa_bj_1906_Wertpapierprospekte.html (accessed 14 Nov. 2023).

248. BaFin, PREOS-Token und Aktien der PREOS Global Office Real Estate & Technology AG: Hinreichend begründeter Verdacht für Werbeverstöße, https://www.bafin.de/SharedDocs/Veroeffentlichungen/DE/Verbrauchermitteilung/weitere/2021/meldung_210331_PREOS.html (accessed 14 Nov. 2023).

Germany.[249] In each individual case, BaFin derives from circumstantial evidence whether there is a public offer to the domestic market or not. In this process, BaFin evaluates the facts of the respective case as a whole.[250] If a public offer is made on the internet without restriction of access to the audience addressed, the worldwide public is deemed to be addressed.[251] According to BaFin, the obligation to publish a prospectus in Germany will apply in this case unless certain exemptions (such as private placements) apply.[252] BaFin has pointed out that even if there is no domestic reference, a prospectus requirement may exist if foreign laws provide for it.[253] The whitepapers published in the context of ICOs often do not meet the requirements that supervisory law imposes on securities prospectuses since they lack comparable informative value and structure.[254] Although BaFin has approved securities prospectuses relating to Security Token since January 2019, there remain unanswered questions with regard to the special requirements for prospectuses in relation to Security Tokens. It has not yet been stated which information a Token securities prospectus has to contain – over and above the requirements for a traditional securities offering. So far, BaFin has only made a general statement about the main risks of Crypto Tokens (market liquidity and volatility risks, counterparty and project risks as well as technical and operational risks (e.g., cyber security risks)).[255] However, the risk factors featured in a prospectus shall be limited to risks which are specific to the issuer and/or to the securities and which are material for taking an informed investment decision, according to Article 16 of the EU Prospectus Regulation. ESMA has stated that the prospectus should include detailed information on the features and rights attached to the Tokens, the issuer's venture, the expected timetable of the offer, the use of the proceeds of the offer, the terms and conditions and the specific risks related to the underlying (blockchain) technology.[256]

The kind of special or additional information that has to be contained in Token securities prospectuses according to BaFin can be derived from the Token securities prospectuses already approved by the German regulator: These prospectuses often include details about the key features of the Tokens, where these securities are traded, and any guarantees made for the Tokens. They also specify the rank of the Tokens in case of insolvency and the conditions and timeline for investment, along with any restrictions on the transferability of the Tokens. These prospectuses elaborate on the central risks inherent to blockchain technology, such as the loss of private keys, Token theft or wallet hacking and vulnerabilities in the underlying blockchain protocol and infrastructure (e.g., the Ethereum Network) to hacking that could result in a loss of Tokens, software errors or bugs, exchange or exchange rate losses if an investor has to exchange fiat money or other cryptocurrencies and the possibility that a payout in

249. BaFin, *supra* n. 204.
250. *Ibid.*, at 142.
251. *Ibid.*
252. *Ibid.*
253. *Ibid.*
254. BaFin, *BaFinPerspektiven*, 1 BaFinPerspektiven 1 63 (2018).
255. *Ibid.*, at 65, 66 (2018).
256. ESMA, *Advice Initial Coin Offerings and Crypto-Assets*, https://www.esma.europa.eu/sites/default/files/library/esma50-157-1391_crypto_advice.pdf (accessed 14 Nov. 2023).

cryptocurrencies (e.g., Ether) will not be possible for technical reasons because the network (e.g., the Ethereum Network) is no longer operated and in case of Token-based bonds, where applicable, the limited fungibility of the Token-based bonds.[257] Custody options for the Tokens and limitations on their fungibility, especially for Token-based bonds, are also discussed.

Moreover, there may be a prospectus requirement as well if the Tokens constitute an investment instrument under the German Capital Investment Act (*Vermögensanlagengesetz – VermAnlG*), an investment fund under the German Capital Investment Code (*Kapitalanlagegesetzbuch – KAGB*) or as PRIIPs under the Regulation (EU) No. 1286/2014.

Where a public offer of Tokens is made without a required prospectus, BaFin can prohibit the public offer and initiate an administrative offence proceeding.

[E] Regulatory Specifics for Organized Trade

Security Tokens may qualify as financial instruments under the KWG and WpIG, investments according to the VermAnlG, or as investment funds as defined in the KAGB.[258] Although Security Tokens are traditionally traded on crypto-exchanges, recognized by BaFin as 'capital markets' or 'financial markets',[259] Security Tokens are not currently traded on 'traditional' capital markets. This includes the organized market (section 2 paragraph 11 of the WpHG) as well as off-market trading (non-organized market), i.e., trading via multilateral trading systems (section 2 paragraph 21 of the WpHG) or on the OTC (over-the-counter) market.[260] However, the proposed expansion of the eWpG to include crypto stocks suggests an emerging trend for Security Tokens that qualify as crypto stocks.[261] This legislative development marks a significant shift in the trading dynamics for certain types of Security Tokens.

Trading of Tokens may be subject to approval under the KWG or WpIG if they represent financial instruments. According to BaFin, Tokens which carry rights to dividend-like payments or rights under the law of obligations with regard to property rights against the issuer, which are interchangeable and negotiable, qualify as debt instruments (*Schuldtitel*) and are therefore financial instruments according to the KWG and WpIG.[262] Moreover, since 2020, certain Tokens are also classified as 'crypto assets' (*Kryptowerte*) within the meaning of the KWG.[263] If not covered by other categories of financial instruments under WpHG, the general conduct regulation of MiFID II does not

257. FUND Real Estate, https://fnd.group/de (accessed 14 Nov. 2023).
258. BaFin, *supra* n. 204.
259. BaFin, *Initial Coin Offerings: Hinweisschreiben zur Einordnung als Finanzinstrumente*, WA 11-QB 4100-2017/0010, https://www.bafin.de/SharedDocs/Downloads/DE/Merkblatt/WA/dl_hinweisschreiben_einordnung_ICOs (accessed 14 Nov. 2023).
260. Fuchs, *supra* n. 216, at s. 2 WpHG, marginal no. 16 (2016).
261. Poelzig/von Zehmen, Kryptoaktien nach dem Referentenentwurf des Zukunftsfinanzierungsgesetz, RDi 2023, 333, 343 Fn. 55.
262. BaFin, *supra* n. 204.
263. Bundesregierung, *Regierungsentwurf eines Gesetzes zur Umsetzung der Änderungsrichtlinie zur Vierten EU-Geldwäscherichtlinie RL (EU) 2018/843*, https://www.bundesfinanzministerium.de

apply to such crypto assets. Depending on the specific structure, the trading of Security Tokens on the secondary market can qualify as different investment services, including principal brokering service (*Finanzkommissionsgeschäft*), as underwriting business (*Emissionsgeschäft*), investment brokering (*Anlagevermittlung*), investment advice (*Anlageberatung*), operation of an MTF (*Betrieb eines multilateralen Handelssystems*), placement business (*Platzierungsgeschäft*), operation of an OTF (*Betrieb eines organisierten Handelssystems*), contract brokering (*Abschlussvermittlung*), portfolio management (*Finanzportfolioverwaltung*), proprietary trading (*Eigenhandel*) or asset management (*Anlageverwaltung*).[264] However, the issuer is privileged under German law: The initial offer of Security Tokens by the issuer does not constitute a financial service within the meaning of the German Banking Act. If the issuer carries out the issuance of Tokens without the involvement of third parties, a licence by BaFin is not required even if the Tokens qualify as financial instruments.[265] It is possible for the issuer to buy back the issued Tokens and sell them again, e.g., on his own trading facility. In this case, the aforementioned privilege could also apply. However, the buying and selling of the Tokens could also constitute the financial service of proprietary trading (*Eigenhandel*) under KWG and WpIG. Proprietary trading (also known as dealing on own account in MiFID) is, e.g., the purchase and sale of financial instruments for one's own account as a service for others. The purchase of financial instruments particularly means the conclusion of purchase contracts for financial instruments, and the sale of financial instruments is the conclusion of contracts relating to the sale of financial instruments. For one's 'own account' means that the provider of the service bears the entire price and performance risk.[266] Still, the proprietary trade is 'a service for others'.

To be a service, the trader must have a special relationship with the customer that requires an imbalance between the trader and the customer: The trader has to have better access to the market than the customer, for example, because the trader provides the customer with access to it.[267] This criterion could be fulfilled if the issuer buys and sells Tokens on his own trading facility. Thus, the buying and selling of Tokens by the issuer could qualify as proprietary trading (*Eigenhandel*). Companies aiming to provide investment services in (or to) Germany need authorization under the KWG or WpIG. The primary trading arena of crypto stocks is expected to be the OTC market due to both infrastructural constraints and their emerging presence in exchange trading.[268] For trading on regulated venues, crypto stocks would need to be recorded in a central

/Content/DE/Gesetzestexte/Gesetze_Gesetzesvorhaben/Abteilungen/Abteilung_VII/19_Legislaturperiode/2019-05-24-Gesetz-4-EU-Geldwaescherichtlinie/0-Gesetz.html (accessed 14 Nov. 2023).

264. BaFin, *supra* n. 204.
265. *Ibid.*; 1 A, Sernetz Schäfer, *Kommentar zu Kreditwesengesetz, VO (EU) Nr. 575/2013 (CRR) und Ausführungsvorschriften* marginal no. 113 Karl-Heinz Boos, Reinfrid Fischer & Hermann Schulte-Mattler ed. (5th ed. 2016).
266. BaFin, *Merkblatt – Hinweise zu den Tatbeständen des Eigenhandels und des Eigengeschäfts*, https://www.bafin.de/SharedDocs/Veroeffentlichungen/DE/Merkblatt/mb_110322_eigenhandel_eigengeschaeft_neu.html (accessed 14 Nov. 2023).
267. BaFin, *supra* n. 204, at no. 1.c) cc).
268. Poelzig/von Zehmen, Kryptoaktien nach dem Referentenentwurf des Zukunftsfinanzierungsgesetz, RDi 2023, 333, 339 n. 39.

securities depository system.[269] The current legal framework enforces a strict separation between trading and post-trading activities, presenting potential challenges for the use of DLT-based systems designed for rapid transactions. The DLT Pilot regime allows combination but has merely a limited time of application.

Additionally, access to exchanges and MTFs is typically restricted to professional participants, potentially excluding private investors from direct participation in these markets. Therefore, OTC trading might become a prevalent platform for crypto stock transactions initially. This situation underscores the dynamic nature of regulatory and market adaptations as new digital assets like crypto stocks begin to enter the financial sphere. The above-mentioned criteria that trigger regulation are not met through simply operating decentralized software on a number of computers. Thus, if the infrastructure for the trading is provided through a DEX, the question arises if it is still subject to regulation according to German supervisory law. Centralized trading venues such as stock exchanges offer buyers and sellers certain functionalities (such as an order book or price-fixing mechanisms). Those functionalities (central elements) are typically subject to regulation. However, many of the so-called DEXs are not 'pure' DEX but contain central elements.

The administrator of a DEX operates an MTF within the meaning of the KWG, WpIG and the WpHG if he brings the interests of a large number of people in buying and selling of financial instruments within the system and in accordance with established rules in a manner together which results in a contract for the purchase of such financial instruments. The storage of Tokens on the platform might qualify as crypto custody, which is subject to authorization by BaFin.[270] Furthermore, if the platform operates an order-matching system and an interim acquisition by the platform takes place, the activity of the platform might qualify as a central counterparty. In order to avoid regulation, a 'pure' DEX must not involve any regulated activity. The only task of such a DEX could be to distribute software on different servers or different computers of exchange participants. However, without order matching, the potential contractual partners could perhaps still find each other but would have to conclude bilateral contracts. In the absence of pricing mechanisms, they would have to negotiate an individual price which would at best come close to the best price available at the time (that the parties would never know). Whether the German legislator will introduce regulation also for 'pure' DEXs remains to be seen. A possible trigger for regulation could be programming: The person who puts software into circulation in a targeted manner in order to establish a DEX, or the person who participates in this, could be regulated.

269. Poelzig/von Zehmen, Kryptoaktien nach dem Referentenentwurf des Zukunftsfinanzierungsgesetz, RDi 2023, 333, 340 n. 41.
270. Bundesregierung, *supra* n. 263.

§5.08 CAPITAL MARKETS AND BLOCKCHAIN: COUNTRY REPORT – IRELAND

Niall Esler[271]

[A] What Makes a Token a Security?

Currently, the only Irish legislation addressing the definition of virtual assets is the Criminal Justice (Money Laundering and Terrorist Financing) Act 2010, as amended (CJA), in the context of anti-money laundering. The CJA introduced anti-money laundering registration and compliance requirements for virtual asset service providers (VASP). The CJA does not provide any assistance in assessing whether a particular Token is a security.

The Irish financial services regulator, the Central Bank of Ireland (Central Bank), has issued a number of consumer warnings in relation to crypto assets, and its representatives have regularly discussed the risks and benefits of distributed ledger technology. In the context of the European Commission's Public consultation on EU framework for markets in crypto assets, the Central Bank submitted that it would be 'beneficial to have a harmonised taxonomy at EU level in relation to crypto assets, including a harmonised definition of a Security Token as a transferable security'.[272] The Governor of the Central Bank has also stated that this area should be 'treated no differently to other financial markets with similar rules on the treatment of client funds, and on disclosures, governance, risk management and information exchange'.[273]

In the absence of specific Irish legislation or guidance in relation to the classification of Tokens as securities, one must consider any Token within the context of the existing regulatory regime applicable to securities on a case-by-case basis in order to ascertain how it is regulated or indeed if it is regulated at all.

The primary financial services regulatory legislation relevant to the characterization of a Token as a security in Ireland is the European Union (Markets in Financial Instruments) Regulations 2017 (MiFID II Regulations),[274] which transposed Directive 2014/65/EU (MiFID II) into Irish law. The MiFID II Regulations regulate the provision of investment services or performance of investment activities in relation to 'financial instruments'. Financial instruments include transferable securities, units in collective investment undertakings and certain derivatives, among other things. Notably, the

271. Niall advises domestic and international institutions on all aspects of Irish and EU financial services regulation. A core part of Niall's practice includes advising innovative clients on the regulatory perimeter, licensing, prudential and conduct of business requirements. Niall is ranked by Chambers in Financial Services Regulatory and in FinTech Legal.
272. Central Bank, *Letter of response to the European Commission Consultation on the Market of Crypto Assets* (30 Apr. 2020), https://www.centralbank.ie/docs/default-source/regulation/innovation-hub/response-to-ec-consultation-on-the-market-of-crypto-assets.pdf?sfvrsn = 2.
273. Central Bank, *Crypto and how we can protect the consumer* (5 May 2023), https://www.centralbank.ie/news-media/press-releases/blog-crypto-and-how-we-can-protect-the-consumer.
274. European Union (Markets in Financial Instruments) Regulations 2017, SI No. 375/2017.

definition of financial instrument was recently amended to specifically include where a financial instrument is issued by means of distributed ledger technology.[275] It is important to consider whether any Token meets the definition of a financial instrument.

Under the MiFID II Regulations, transferable securities are defined as those 'classes of securities which are negotiable on the capital market', excluding instruments of payment such as:

(a) shares in companies and other securities equivalent to shares in companies, partnerships or other entities, and depositary receipts in respect of shares;
(b) bonds or other forms of securitized debt, including depositary receipts in respect of such securities; or
(c) any other securities giving the right to acquire or sell any such transferable securities or giving rise to a cash settlement determined by reference to transferable securities, currencies, interest rates or yields, commodities or other indices or measures.

Therefore, first, the Token must be capable of being considered to be a class of securities. This is likely to require consideration of a range of factors, including what rights are granted by the Token to its holders, the identity of the issuer and its fungibility. Second, the Token must be negotiable on the capital market, which the Central Bank has indicated is to be interpreted broadly and not limited to securities listed or traded on regulated markets.[276] The European Commission has published Question and Answers in the context of Directive 2004/39/EC (MiFID I), wherein it is stated that the term capital market includes all contexts where buying and selling interest in securities meet.[277] Finally, if the Token is an instrument of payment, it would be excluded from this definition. ESMA has noted that a crypto asset which is a pure payment-type cryptocurrency is less likely to be considered a transferable security.[278] However, Tokens representing rights traditionally associated with classes of securities (e.g., governance and/or profit rights) and meeting the other requirements are more likely to be transferable securities.

Should the analysis show that a Token is a transferable security, a range of financial services regulatory rules will become relevant. For example, intermediaries will need to consider if their activities fall within the scope of the authorization and conduct of business requirements under the MiFID II Regulations. Subject to certain

---

275. Regulation 3(1), MiFID II Regulations.
276. Central Bank, *Investment Firms Questions and Answers*, 7th Edition (4 Mar. 2019), https://www.centralbank.ie/docs/default-source/regulation/industry-market-sectors/investment-firms/mifid-firms/regulatory-requirements-and-guidance/190229_investment-firms-qa-document-edition-7.pdf?sfvrsn = 2.
277. European Commission, *Questions and Answers on MiFID Directive 2004/39/EC* (22 Feb. 2007), https://finance.ec.europa.eu/system/files/2020-01/mifid-2004-0039-commission-questions-answers_en_0.pdf.
278. ESMA, *Advice on Initial Coin Offerings and Crypto-Assets* (9 Jan. 2019), https://www.esma.europa.eu/sites/default/files/library/esma50-157-1391_crypto_advice.pdf.

exemptions, there are also requirements for the drawing up, approval and distribution of a prospectus when securities are offered to the public or admitted to trading on a regulated market situated or operating within an EU Member State, under Regulation 2017/1129/EU (Prospectus Regulation) and the European Union (Prospectus) Regulations 2019[279] (the Irish Prospectus Regulations). For the purposes of the Prospectus Regulation, a 'security' means a transferable security (as per the MiFID II Regulations defined set out above), with the exception of money-market instruments having a maturity of less than twelve months.

[B] Blockchain Finality

As Ireland has a common law legal system, there is flexibility to address new or novel instruments within the existing legal structures without necessarily legislating for the particular scenario.

The issue of whether Tokens could be seen as property under Irish law has not been directly addressed or settled by Irish courts or legislature. However, the High Court treated a digital wallet of Ethereum as 'property' for the purposes of the Proceeds of Crime Act 1996 when granting a freezing order.[280] Similarly, the Commercial Court has granted an order for the disclosure of certain assets and it appears from the judgment that the court was happy that a disclosure order could be made in respect of cryptocurrency wallets.[281] We expect that case law in this area will continue to develop.

There is currently no specific legislative or regulatory framework which provides for blockchain finality in Ireland. To the extent that there is a contract between one counterparty and another (express or implied), the contractual terms will govern the arrangement. In order for a contract to be legally binding, the essential elements would need to be present, i.e., offer, acceptance, consideration and intention to create legal relations. There is no requirement for a contract to be made in writing,[282] save for certain exceptions, e.g., the sale of land.[283] The Electronic Commerce Act 2000 recognizes electronic signatures as being legally binding; however, there are procedural requirements such as consent which must be complied with.

If a Token is a security, it will also be important to consider whether there are any particular requirements to legally effect the transfer of the particular security, for example, under a company's constitution or under Irish company law. It is notable that, for example, laws governing the registration and transfer of ownership for uncertificated securities do not expressly address Tokens.

Irish law recognizes an equitable defence, in certain circumstances, for a bona fide purchaser for value without notice of another's equitable right in the property. It remains to be seen whether the concept of a bona fide purchaser for value without

279. European Union (Prospectus) Regulations 2019, S.I. No. 380/2019.
280. *Criminal Assets Bureau v. Mannion* [2018] IEHC 729.
281. *Trafalgar Developments Limited v. Mazepin* [2019] IEHC 7.
282. *Richard & Comrie PLC v. FII (Fyffes) plc* (11 Nov. 1988, unreported), Supreme Court.
283. Statute of Frauds (Ireland) 1695.

notice would be invoked in disputes regarding transactions involving Tokens – the individual facts and circumstances of any particular case would be important. Another option might be to specifically extend statutory protections to such purchasers of Tokens. In this context, it is interesting to note that the International Institute for the Unification of Private Law (UNIDROIT) has published the UNIDROIT Digital Assets and Private Law Principle 2(2) (UNIDROIT Principle).[284] The UNIDROIT Principle proposes in its guidance recognition of 'innocent acquisitions', whereby an innocent acquirer would acquire a digital asset free of conflicting proprietary rights in circumstances where they (a) obtain control of a digital asset and (b) comply with requirements equivalent to those found in the relevant good faith acquisition and take-free rules as specified by the relevant State.[285] As case law develops in Ireland, it will be interesting to see whether the UNIDROIT Principle and the guidance therein are referenced and/or followed.

At the date of drafting, we are not aware of any indication in Ireland that a fiduciary duty of care may be owed by cryptocurrency developers; however, there is some indication that this may be considered a possibility in England and Wales, another common law jurisdiction.[286]

[C] International Private Law

As a preliminary comment, we would note that Irish law has not been amended to provide any bespoke provisions for conflicts of law or choice of law in the area of blockchain/distributed ledger contracts. As such, general principles in respect of both apply and are detailed below. We note however that UNIDROIT has adopted Principles on Digital Assets and Private Law which includes a series of factors to utilize to determine the applicable law for any digital asset.

European Union legislation designed to harmonize the laws of the Member States has been adopted in relation to many aspects of private international law within the framework of the European Union. This includes *inter alia*:

(a) Council Regulation (EC) No. 593/2008 of 17 June 2008 on the law applicable to contractual obligations (Rome I) which replaced the Rome Convention on the Law Applicable to Contractual Obligations of 1980 (Rome Convention) from 17 December 2009 and is the focus of this section;

284. UNIDROIT, *Digital Assets and Private Law Principle 2(2)*.

285. *Ibid*.

286. *Tulip Trading v. Wladimir van der Laan and Ors* [2023] EWCA Civ 83. Note that in this particular UK judgment, it was stated that:

> The conclusion is not that there is a fiduciary duty in law in the circumstances alleged by Tulip, only that the case advanced raises a serious issue to be tried … . If the decentralised governance of bitcoin really is a myth, then in my judgment there is much to be said for the submission that bitcoin developers, while acting as developers, owe fiduciary duties to the true owners of that property.

(b) Council Regulation (EC) No. 864/2007 of 11 July 2007 on the law applicable to non-contractual obligations (Rome II);
(c) Regulation (EU) No. 1215/2012 on jurisdiction and the recognition and enforcement of judgments in civil and commercial matters (Brussels I Recast); and
(d) Regulation (EU) 2015/848 of the European Parliament and of the Council of 20 May 2015 (EU Insolvency Regulation Recast).

Of most relevance is Rome I, and an Irish court must apply Rome I (subject to certain derogations and exemptions which must be considered in the context of the specific Tokens) whenever an issue arises before the Irish courts concerning a contractual obligation in any situation involving a choice between the laws of different countries, even where there is no connection with the EU.

If there is no express choice of law, the applicable law is determined by the specific rules which apply to different types of contracts, intended to produce greater certainty. In most cases, the applicable law is that of the country where the party who is to perform the contract has his 'habitual residence'.

Rome I does not preclude parties from incorporating by reference into their contract the law of a non-Member State jurisdiction or the provisions of an international convention. As a result, that party's Member State will apply the rules provided in Rome I to determine the law of contractual obligations, even if the application of those rules results in the law of a non-Member State (e.g., New York law) being applied.

Further, the courts of Member States will also apply Rome I even if some or all of the parties appearing before them are non-European.

[D] Special Requirements for Prospectus

As previously mentioned, should a Token be deemed to be a transferable security for the purposes of the MiFID II Regulations (and is not a money-market instrument having a maturity of less than twelve months), the requirements of the Prospectus Regulation should be considered.

If the Token will be offered to the public or admitted to trading on a regulated market, a prospectus must be prepared and approved by the Central Bank. There are a number of exemptions to this requirement. For example, the obligation to publish a prospectus does not apply to any of the following types of offers of securities to the public:

(a) an offer of securities addressed solely to qualified investors;
(b) an offer of securities addressed to fewer than 150 natural or legal persons per EEA Member State, other than qualified investors;
(c) an offer of securities whose denomination per unit amounts to at least EUR 100,000;

(d) an offer of securities addressed to investors who acquire securities for a total consideration of at least EUR 100,000 per investor for each separate offer.

The Irish Prospectus Regulations also exclude offers to the public where the total consideration for the securities does not exceed EUR 8,000,000 over a 12-month period.[287] Separate exclusions must be considered where a security is to be admitted to trading on a regulated market.

One of the objectives of the Prospectus Regulation is to ensure investor protection. Through mandatory disclosure requirements, the offering document should contain sufficient information to empower a prospective investor to make an informed decision about the risks of investing, the nature of the rights attaching to the securities and the status of the issuer. Details of the issuer and its key financial information are required.[288] A section containing information pertaining to all material risk factors must be included, as set out in Article 16 of the Prospectus Regulation. The responsible person must also be identified, i.e., the offerer if a public offer is being made or the person seeking admission if the securities are being traded.[289] The relevant fee must also be paid to the Central Bank.[290]

The Central Bank will engage in a review process upon receipt of a draft prospectus by email. Any requests to omit information must be submitted in writing and will be considered.[291] Comments raised by the Central Bank will be remitted to the applicant and must be addressed in subsequent submissions.

The Central Bank stated in March 2023 that it is 'highly unlikely' to approve a crypto-based proposal under the Prospectus Regulation. However, the Central Bank noted that this position will be kept under review and informed by regulatory discussions and developments at EU level.[292] Since then, the Central Bank has increased the investment limits for qualifying investor alternative investment funds seeking exposure to digital assets, which may influence the position regarding prospectuses more generally going forward.

Where a Token constitutes a transferable security, it will also be important for intermediaries to be aware of the potential application of the MiFID II Regulations to their activities, including the potential requirement for authorization to provide investment services on a professional basis. For example, investment services for the purposes of the MiFID II Regulations include placing, receipt and transmission of orders and execution of orders.

287. Regulation 3(1)(b), Irish Prospectus Regulations.
288. Article 6(1), Prospectus Regulation.
289. Schedule (3)(2), Irish Prospectus Regulations.
290. Central Bank Act 1942 (Section 32E) Prospectus and Related Documents Fee Regulations 2022, S.I. No. 135/2022.
291. ID 1009, Central Bank, *Prospectus Regulatory Framework Questions and Answers, 1st Edition* (4 Aug. 2017), https://www.centralbank.ie/docs/default-source/regulation/industry-market-sectors/securities-markets/prospectus-regulation/regulatory-requirements-guidance/prospectus-reg-framework-qas-1st-ed-4-aug-2017.pdf?sfvrsn=2.
292. Central Bank, *Securities Markets Risk Outlook Report 2023* (March 2023), https://www.centralbank.ie/docs/default-source/regulation/industry-market-sectors/securities-markets/risk-outlook-reports/securities-markets-risk-outlook-report-2023.pdf?sfvrsn=dc0f991d_2.

[E] Regulatory Specifics for Organized Trade

The CJA provides that a person must not carry on business as a VASP or claim or represent that they are a VASP, unless registered with the Central Bank. A VASP must also comply with the anti-money laundering and countering the financing of terrorism requirements set out under the CJA. The VASP registration is for the purposes of anti-money laundering supervision, rather than amounting to a financial services authorization.

A VASP is defined to mean a person who by way of business carries out one or more of certain activities for, or on behalf of, another person, including:

(a) exchange between virtual assets and fiat currencies;
(b) exchange between one or more forms of virtual assets;
(c) transfer of virtual assets, that is to say, conduct a transaction on behalf of another person that moves a virtual asset from one virtual asset address or account to another;
(d) custodian wallet provider;
(e) participation in, and provision of, financial services related to an issuer's offer or sale of a virtual asset or both.

A 'virtual asset' is defined to mean a digital representation of value that can be digitally traded or transferred and can be used for payment or investment purposes but does not include digital representations of fiat currencies, securities or other financial assets.

A trading platform for virtual asset exchange will typically be required to register with the Central Bank as a VASP under the CJA.

Where a Token falls within the definition of a financial instrument for the purposes of the MiFID II Regulations, the operator of a trading platform may be required to seek authorization to operate a trading venue (either a regulated market, multilateral trading facility (MTF) or organized trading facility (OTF)) under the MiFID II Regulations. It will be important to analyse the Tokens on a case-by-case basis, the identity of the operator, as well as the functionality of the trading platform in order to assess whether authorization is required.

A key aspect of the definition of each type of trading venue for the purposes of the MiFID II Regulations is that the venue is a 'multilateral system'. This is defined to mean any system or facility in which multiple third-party buying and selling trading interests in financial instruments are able to interact in the system. In 2019, ESMA provided Advice on Initial Coin Offerings and Crypto-Assets and provided a preliminary view that where crypto assets qualify as financial instruments, platforms trading crypto assets with a central order book and/or matching orders under other trading models are likely to qualify as multilateral systems and should therefore either operate as regulated markets or as MTFs or OTFs, in accordance with the relevant requirements under MiFID.[293] In the ESMA Opinion on the Trading Venue Perimeter, it is stated that bulletin boards that merely aggregate and broadcast indications of interest are not multilateral systems.[294] ESMA confirmed that where a crypto asset is considered a financial instrument within the meaning of MiFID II, it would be in scope of the ESMA Opinion on the Trading Venue Perimeter.[295]

A close examination of the activities of the operator and the trading platform will be required to assess how these definitions apply in circumstances where the Tokens traded are financial instruments.

As set out above, depending on the particular Token, it will also be necessary to consider whether there are further formalities to complete the registration of the transfer (e.g., if the Token is a security, under Irish company law).

§5.09 CAPITAL MARKETS AND BLOCKCHAIN: COUNTRY REPORT – ITALY

Giuseppe D'Agostino & Stefano Febbi[296]

Italian legislation still does not organically regulate Tokens, the nature of such digital instruments and the provision of services related to their issue, offering or trading.

The first set of rules on the provision of services related to digital assets/values was the introduction in 2017 of a specific regime applicable to 'providers of services related to the use of virtual currency'.[297] In 2019, such regime has been extended also to 'providers of digital wallet services'.[298] However, such legislations were substantially limited to introducing the obligation for persons providing the aforementioned

---

293. ESMA, *Advice on Initial Coin Offerings and Crypto-Assets* (9 Jan. 2019), https://www.esma.europa.eu/sites/default/files/library/esma50-157-1391_crypto_advice.pdf.
294. ESMA, *Final Report On ESMA's Opinion on the Trading Venue Perimeter* (2 Feb. 2023) ESMA70-156-6360, https://www.esma.europa.eu/sites/default/files/library/ESMA70-156-6383%20Final%20Report%20on%20ESMA%27s%20Opinion%20on%20the%20trading%20venue%20perimeter.pdf.
295. *Ibid.*
296. **Giuseppe D'Agostino** is Co-Head of the International Finance & Financial Regulation Practice in Bird & Bird. He is an expert in the economics of financial services, with an extensive knowledge of financial intermediation processes and related international regulatory standards. He worked for the Italian financial supervisory authority for 30 years becoming deputy general manager and representing Consob in several international committees at the International Organization of Securities Commissions (IOSCO), at the European Securities and Markets Authority (ESMA) and, finally, at EU Joint-Committee Sub-Committee on Consumer Protection and Financial Innovation. **Stefano Febbi** is a Partner at Bird & Bird's Finance & Financial Regulation Group and co-head in the Financial Services Group based in Milan. Specialized in financial services legislation, Stefano advises major clients on topics such as measures to comply MiFID as well as the Insurance Distribution Directive (IDD) and AML Directives, with a focus on new technologies and digitalization processes.
297. Reference is made to Legislative Decree 90 of 25 May 2017 that amended Legislative Decree 141 of 13 Aug. 2010.
298. Reference is made to Legislative Decree 125 of 4 Oct. 2019 that amended again Legislative Decree 141 of 13 Aug. 2010.

services to be enrolled in a special register held by a national agency,[299] essentially for the purpose of subjecting them to the obligations provided for by the Italian anti-money laundering legislation.[300]

A second intervention – implemented by Legislative Decree no. 135/2018 – concerned the introduction of a specific regime identifying the validity requirements of contracts concluded through the use of DLT (smart contracts), without however addressing the issue of the nature of digital values on a blockchain or DLT and their legal qualification.

More recently, in order to enable the application and operation in Italy of Regulation (EU) 2022/858 on the pilot regime for market infrastructures based on distributed ledger technology ('**DLT Pilot Regime**'), the Law Decree 25 of 17 March 2023 ('**LD 25/2003**') has introduced specific provisions regulating the issuance and circulation of certain financial instruments in digital form through the use of DLT.

However, even the latter legislation does not fully resolve the issue of the legal nature of all different types of Tokens,[301] which must therefore be addressed in light of the general principles of the legal system and of specific provisions regulating the performance of investment services and the offer of products of a financial nature to the public.

[A] What Makes a Token a Security?

The term 'Token' is generally used as a synonym for 'crypto asset', the definition of which was introduced in the most recent European legislation with Regulation (EU) 2023/1114 on markets in crypto assets (MiCAR).

As MiCAR is a maximum harmonization regulation, binding in all its elements and directly applicable in all Member States, the definition of a crypto asset (or Token) as 'a digital representation of a value or right that can be electronically transferred and stored using distributed ledger technology or similar technology'[302] provided by the same is automatically transposed in the Italian legal framework.

Having said that, for the purposes of Italian law, the question 'What makes a Token a Security?' must be read in the light of the definitions of 'financial instrument' and 'financial product' contained in the Italian Financial Markets Act (FMA),[303] which

299. Italian and foreign service providers must register in a special section of the register of money changers kept by the Organismo per gli Agenti e Mediatori (OAM). This regime was made fully effective by the MEF Decree of 13 Jan. 2022, published in Official Gazette No. 40 of 17-02-2022.

300. According to Art. 3, para. 5, letter i) and i-*bis*) of Legislative Decree 231 of 21 Nov. 2007, providers of services related to the use of virtual currency and providers of digital wallet services are included among the 'obliged entities' required to comply with the obligations on anti-money laundering contained in such decree.

301. The Pilot Regime's scope of experimentation concerns a chosen subset of financial instruments and the notion of 'digital financial instruments' provided by LD 25/2023 reflects the definition of 'DLT financial instrument' set forth in Regulation (EU) 2022/858.

302. *See* Art. 3(1)(5) of MICAR.

303. Legislative Decree 24 Feb. 1998, n. 58 (**FMA**).

transposes into Italian law the provisions of MiFID II[304] and other EU Directives relating to the financial sector. More broadly, the FMA regulates the functioning of financial markets and investor protection.

In fact, the classification of Tokens as 'financial instruments' would imply the full application of rules transposing MiFiD II in Italy and regulating the performance of investment services, while the main consequences of the classification of Tokens as 'financial products' would be the application of FMA's provisions requesting the preparation and publication of a prospectus[305] and regulating the 'remote offering' (*offerta a distanza*) of financial products.[306]

The definition of financial instrument set forth by the FMA perfectly mirrors the definition provided by Article 4(1)(15) of MiFID II, which in turn makes reference to the list of instruments contained in Section C of Annex I to the same MiFID II. Such definition has been recently amended by Article 18 of the DLT Pilot Regime to clarify that the notion of financial instruments also includes the instruments mentioned in the relevant list when 'issued through distributed ledger technology'.

However, even such addition to the definition of financial instrument set forth by MiFID II does not solve all uncertainties on the qualification of Tokens, as both Italian and EU legislation make reference to a non-exhaustive list of financial instruments rather than providing a definition based on clear and final criteria.

Furthermore, it should be noted that, besides the definition of financial instruments, the FMA also contains a broader notion of 'financial products', which are defined as 'financial instruments and any other form of investment of a financial nature'.[307] The latter includes any contract in which the following elements coexist: (1) the use of capital, (2) the expectation of a financial return and (3) the assumption of an associated risk (*see*, in this respect, CONSOB communication no. 0385340 of 28 April 2020). The existence of the transferability requirement is not considered necessary for a contract to fall under the concept of financial product.

Therefore, a crypto asset embodying any contract that gives rise to a right (or value) for the holder, even if it does not embody any administrative, economic or financial right exercisable vis-à-vis the issuer, could fall within the category of 'financial product' under Italian law, if it is construed (and offered) in order to satisfy the investor's expectation of monetary gains/returns, the rationality of which may be based, for example, on the existence of a repurchase obligation by the issuer or on the fact that it is negotiated on a trading platform.

The FMA establishes the regulatory framework for financial products and regulates various aspects, including issuance, offer, disclosure and investor protection.

304. Directive 2014/65/EU of the European Parliament and of the Council of 15 May 2014 on markets in financial instruments (MiFID II).
305. According to Art. 94 of the FMA, any offering of investment products requires the prior publication (and delivery to investors) of a prospectus. For further details, please *see* following s. [D] of this chapter.
306. Pursuant to Art. 32 of the FMA and relevant implementing regulation issued by Consob, only banks and investment firms authorized in accordance with MiFID II rules may carry out the activity of '*remote offering of financial products*'.
307. *See* Art. 1(1)(u) of the FMA.

The Commissione Nazionale per le Società e la Borsa (CONSOB) is designated to supervise and enforce such regulations. Failure to comply with regulatory requirements may result in administrative sanctions, fines or other legal consequences (e.g., prohibition to continue the offering of a product/instrument).

CONSOB has issued numerous warnings and taken enforcement action against entities or individuals engaged in the abusive or unauthorized offering of financial products, including those involving crypto assets, to the Italian public. These actions aim to protect investors from fraudulent schemes, misleading information, and unregulated activities.

The lack of an equivalent notion of financial product in the relevant EU regulation (i.e., MiFID II and the Prospectus Regulation) could create a compatibility problem with MiCAR. Indeed, a crypto asset could be considered an 'other type of investment of a financial nature' under the national regulation, whereas for MiCAR it could be treated as a crypto asset falling under the residual typology of 'other crypto assets'. Indeed, after the implementation date of MiCAR (30 December 2024), the possible conflict of rules applicable to this type of crypto asset should be resolved in favour of the EU regulation, in accordance with its maximum harmonization nature and in line with the principle of primacy of EU law over national law.

However, if a financial product circulates both as a Token (i.e., as a digital representation of a 'financial investment contract' registered in a distributed register) and in traditional form (dematerialized or paper-based), not all issues of discipline attribution would be resolved, with possible asymmetry of treatment due to the coexistence of two disciplines (one EU and the other national).

This issue will therefore have to be addressed and finally resolved at the national level before the date of application of MiCAR.

[B] Blockchain Finality

With regard to Security Tokens, as mentioned in section [A] above, LD 25/2023 introduces into the Italian legal framework a regime for the issuance and transfer of digital financial instruments as an alternative to the paper-based and traditional book-entry regimes, providing that such operations may be carried out through recordings made in a distributed register ('register for digital circulation').[308]

This regulatory regime is effectively linked to the DLT pilot regime but extends its scope to financial instruments not covered by the EU regulatory framework, including financial instruments not intended to be traded on trading venues.

LD 25/2023 deals with legal aspects that are a prerequisite for settlement finality; in fact, it establishes the legal validity of the entries in the 'register for digital circulation', which certifies the ownership, type and number of the digital financial

308. *See* Art. 3(1) of LD 25/2023. The 'register for digital circulation' is the term used in the aforementioned Law Decree to refer to the register referred to in Art. 2(2) of the DLT Pilot Regime (i.e., to a 'repository of information in which transactions are recorded and which is shared by a number of nodes of the DLT network and synchronised between them, through the use of a consensus mechanism').

instruments held by each holder, as well as the transfer of the digital financial instruments (and of the related encumbrances), also for the purposes of the exercise of the related rights.[309]

For digital financial instruments that can be written under the DLT pilot regime, the digital circulation register is managed by the operator of a DLT settlement system (SS DLT or TSS DLT). For digital financial instruments that are not (i.e., cannot) be written on an SS DLT or a TSS DLT, the register for writing shall be kept by a 'register administrator' as defined in the same LD 25/2023.[310]

The person who is the holder of the Security Tokens by virtue of the inscriptions in the register, obtained 'on the basis of an appropriate title and in good faith', has the full and exclusive right to 'dispose of them [...] in accordance with the provisions in force'[311] and 'is not subject to claims or actions by previous holders'.[312]

The system set up by Legislative Decree 25/2023 does not go so far as to provide the 'guarantees' envisaged by Directive 98/26/EC of the European Parliament and of the Council of 19 May 1998 on settlement finality in payment and securities settlement systems (as amended), implemented in Italy by Legislative Decree no. 210 of 12 April 2001 (as amended), which deals with the finality (irrevocability) of transfer orders and netting of transactions in all the financial instruments listed in Section C of Annex I of Directive 2004/39/EC (MiFID II), including 'Security Tokens' if centralized at a CSD, as they are traded on a trading venue within the meaning of MiFID II.

LD 25/2023 does not refer to Legislative Decree 210/2001, which provides, in accordance with Directive 98/26/EC, that the opening of insolvency proceedings shall not have a retroactive effect on the rights and obligations of participants in connection with their participation in a system that arose before the date of the opening of such proceedings.[313]

As a result, the Italian legal system does not foresee a proper settlement finality regime for Security Tokens equivalent to that provided for securities settlement systems under Directive 98/26/EC, except as strictly provided for by the DLT pilot regime for certain categories of digital financial instruments and the cases of exemption

309. *See* Art. 5(1) of LD 25/2023.
310. This 'person in charge' can be the issuer itself or a third party designated by the issuer, provided that it is included in the register of persons in charge of registers for digital circulation referred to in Art. 19(1) of LD 25/2023, on the basis of an authorization issued by the Italian securities market supervisory authority (CONSOB). Among the entities that may be enrolled in the register pursuant to Art. 19(1) of the aforementioned LD 25/2023, a distinction can be made between (i) those who may act on behalf of issuers of digital financial instruments (i.e., on behalf of third parties) (namely banks, investment firms and market operators established in Italy, other entities established in Italy) and (ii) those who may act exclusively with respect to digital financial instruments of their own issuance (i.e., issuers established in Italy; payment institutions; electronic money institutions; collective investment managers; insurance and reinsurance undertakings). Italian central depositories that intend to act as registrars on an ancillary basis will instead be enrolled as of right (Art. 19(2) of LD 25/2023).
311. *See* Art. 5(2) of LD 25/2023.
312. Article 5(4) of Decree Law 25/2023.
313. For these rules to apply, Security Token transactions must, *inter alia*, be cleared in a system or involve transfers between participants in a system designated as such and notified to ESMA by the EU Member State whose law applies.

from the settlement finality rules set forth in Regulation (EU) No. 909/2014, subject to certain compensatory measures, including specific compensatory measures to mitigate the risks arising from insolvency.

Therefore, for all that is not provided for therein, the circulation of securities under Italian law is based on the expression of the parties' consent. Therefore: (a) contractual rules apply and, in particular, the relationship between the parties involved is subject to the principle of good faith; and (b) Italian law has recently addressed the issue of the written form of the circulation of rights and claims through blockchain technology only in relation to smart contracts. Article 8b of Legislative Decree no. 135/2018, on the one hand, defines a smart contract as 'a computer programme operating with distributed ledger-based technologies, the execution of which automatically binds two or more parties on the basis of effects predefined by them' and, on the other hand, provides that, as regards form, 'smart contracts satisfy the requirement of written form through the computer identification of the parties involved, by means of a process that meets the requirements established by the *Agenzia per l'Italia Digitale*, with guidelines to be implemented within ninety days of the entry into force of the law converting this Decree law'.

Neither statute can be applied in practice because: (1) no standards follow the definition other than the specific form; and (2) the rules on the written form require further standards (the guidelines for establishing the requirements of the identification process), which have not yet been published.

[C] International Private Law

The identification of the law applicable to Tokens under Italian private international law is an extremely complex issue, which is difficult to address in general and abstract terms.

In fact, the identification of the applicable law may be driven by several factors, including (i) how the specific type of Tokens qualifies under applicable civil/commercial law, (ii) the possibility of identifying with certainty the parties to the contracts having as their object the subscription or exchange of the Tokens, as well as (iii) the manner in which the circulation of the Tokens takes place.

Having said that, the main rules of international law provided for by the Italian legal system are those set forth in Rome I[314] and Rome II[315] regulations, fully applicable in Italy, which respectively regulate situations involving a conflict of laws to contractual and non-contractual obligations in civil and commercial matters.

As a general principle, Article 3 of Rome I recognizes freedom of choice to the parties, providing that a contract shall be governed by the law chosen by the parties, provided that the choice is made expressly or clearly demonstrated by the terms of the

---

314. Regulation (EC) no 593/2008 of the European Parliament and of the Council of 17 Jun. 2008 on the law applicable to contractual obligations ('**Rome I**').
315. Regulation (EC) no 864/2007 of the European Parliament and of the Council of 11 Jul. 2007 on the law applicable to non-contractual obligations ('**Rome II**').

contract or the circumstances of the case.[316] However, according to the same Article 3, where all other elements relevant to the situation at the time of the choice are located in a country other than the country whose law has been chosen, the choice of the parties shall not prejudice the application of provisions of the law of that other country which cannot be derogated from by agreement.[317]

Following Article 4, paragraph 1, of Rome I provides the criteria to identify applicable law in the absence of choice by the parties, stating that, to the extent that the law applicable to the contract has not been chosen in accordance with previous Article 3, the law governing the contract shall be determined - in particular - in accordance with the following criteria:

- a contract for the sale of goods shall be governed by the law of the country where the seller has his habitual residence;
- a contract for the provision of services shall be governed by the law of the country where the service provider has his habitual residence;
- a contract concluded within a multilateral system which brings together or facilitates the bringing together of multiple third-party buying and selling interests in financial instruments, as defined by MiFID, in accordance with non-discretionary rules and governed by a single law, shall be governed by that law.[318]

Following paragraphs 2 and 3 of the same Article 4 further clarify that:

- where the contract is not covered by any of the criteria set forth in paragraph 1 or where the elements of the contract would be covered by more than one of such criteria, the contract shall be governed by the law of the country where the party required to effect the characteristic performance of the contract has his habitual residence;
- where it is clear from all the circumstances of the case that the contract is manifestly more closely connected with a country other than that identified pursuant to the above, the law of that other country shall apply.

316. The existence and validity of the consent of the parties as to the choice of the applicable law shall be determined in accordance with the provisions of following Arts 10, 11 and 13 regulating, respectively, consent and material validity, formal validity of contracts/terms and incapacity.
317. In particular, where all other elements relevant to the situation at the time of the choice are located in one or more EU Member States, the parties' choice of applicable law other than that of a Member State shall not prejudice the application of provisions of Community law, where appropriate as implemented in the Member State of the forum, which cannot be derogated from by agreement.
318. Following paras 2 and 3 of the same Art. 4 further clarify that:

 - where the contract is not covered by any of the criteria set forth in para. 1 or where the elements of the contract would be covered by more than one of such criteria, the contract shall be governed by the law of the country where the party required to effect the characteristic performance of the contract has his habitual residence;
 - where it is clear from all the circumstances of the case that the contract is manifestly more closely connected with a country other than that identified pursuant to the above, the law of that other country shall apply.

As may be inferred from the foregoing, the identification of the applicable law would depend to a large extent on the nature and characteristics of the Tokens under consideration and the way in which they are traded.

This a fortiori considering that Rome I is in any case not applicable to 'obligations arising under bills of exchange, cheques and promissory notes and other negotiable instruments to the extent that the obligations under such other negotiable instruments arise out of their negotiable character'.[319]

Therefore, where a Token is to be considered a 'negotiable instrument', Rome I would not apply to such obligations that arise out of the negotiable character of the Token (and thus, in the case of contracts 'concluded within a multilateral system which brings together or facilitates the bringing together of multiple third-party buying and selling interests in financial instruments' the law regulating such multilateral system may not apply to such obligations).

However, it might not be always easy to conclude which are the actual obligations that arise specifically out of the 'negotiability' of the Token in question and which are not. In this respect, in the absence of significant case-law precedents, it should be noted that Italian legal doctrine tends to give a restrictive interpretation to the notion of the negotiable character of an instrument; thus, only disputes in which the rules of circulation of the instrument are at issue would be excluded from Rome I and not those that have as their object the rights and obligations of the parties arising out of the instrument.[320]

Lastly, for the sake of completeness, it is worth noting that Rome I provides specific derogations to the above rules in the case that a party to an agreement is a 'consumer'.[321] In this respect, Article 6, paragraph 1, of Rome I regulation provides that a contract concluded by a consumer with a professional[322] shall be governed by the law of the country where the consumer has his habitual residence, provided that the professional: (a) pursues his commercial or professional activities in the country where the consumer has his habitual residence, or (b) by any means, directs such activities to that country or to several countries including that country, and the contract falls within the scope of such activities.[323] Notwithstanding the above, the parties may choose the law applicable to a contract in accordance with Article 3 mentioned above, but such a choice may not have the result of depriving the consumer of the protection afforded to him by provisions that cannot be derogated from by agreement by virtue of the law which, in the absence of choice, would have been applicable on the basis of paragraph 1.

319. Cf. Art. 1, para. 2, letter d) of Rome I regulation.
320. *See* A. Bonomi, *Il nuovo diritto internazionale privato dei contratti*, in BBTC 1992, I, 48 ff.
321. A 'consumer' being a natural person acting for a purpose which can be regarded as being outside his trade or profession.
322. A 'professional' being a person acting in the exercise of his trade or profession.
323. If the requirements in points (a) or (b) are not fulfilled, the law applicable to a contract between a consumer and a professional shall be determined pursuant to the above-referred Arts 3 and 4 of Rome I regulation.

The above derogations would not in any case apply to:

- rights and obligations which constitute a financial instrument and rights and obligations constituting the terms and conditions governing the issuance or offer to the public and public take-over bids of transferable securities, and the subscription and redemption of units in collective investment undertakings in so far as these activities do not constitute provision of a financial service;
- contracts concluded within a multilateral system which brings together or facilitates the bringing together of multiple third-party buying and selling interests in financial instruments, as defined by MiFID, in accordance with non-discretionary rules and governed by a single law (which would remain governed by such law in accordance with the above-referred Article 3).

The rules described above, however, are limited to regulating the relationship between the parties to an agreement involving the subscription, sale and/or circulation of Tokens, but not other instances in which a dispute may arise regarding the ownership of Tokens (such as in cases where the rights of the owner of the Token are to be asserted in the face of hacking or computer fraud).

In such cases, under the rules of Italian private international law, the relevant criterion for identifying the applicable law would be the criterion of *lex rei sitae*,[324] which, however, is not easy to apply to Tokens because of the decentralized structure of DLT-based platforms (particularly in the case of permissionless platforms). Equally complex, in the case of DLT platforms, would be the application of the criterion provided by Italian law for *titoli di credito* (negotiable instruments), to which some Tokens would be assimilable in many respects, which would lead to identifying the law of the state where the instrument was issued.[325]

As correctly noted by some authors, however, in most situations where the contractual linkage criteria set forth by Rome I are not applicable, property claim actions will originate from computer fraud, hacking or other tort cases and, consequently, the criterion of the law of the place where the harmful event occurred would find application in line with the provisions of Article 4 of Rome II for the identification of the law applicable to compensatory obligations.[326]

[D] Special Requirements for Prospectus

If the Tokens can be specifically included in the financial products and are offered to the public, to be intended as:

> every communication to persons in any form and by any means, presenting sufficient information on the terms of the offer and the financial products to be

324. Cf. Arts 51 ff. Law No. 218 of 31 May 1995 ('L. 218/1995').
325. *See* Art. 59, para. 3, L.218/1995.
326. For a discussion of the specific point *see* Andrea Guaccero, Giulio Sandrelli in Bank Securities Exchange, Issue 6, 1 Dec. 2022, pp. 824 et seq.

> offered, so as to enable an investor to decide to purchase or subscribe for those securities, including the placing through financial intermediaries.[327]

The rules set out in Articles 94 et seq. of the FMA, concerning public offerings of financial products (requiring the publication of a prospectus), shall be applied as well as the rules provided for by the Regulation implementing FMA concerning the discipline of issuers of financial products (*Regulation no. 11971/1999*).

Although a general model for the prospectus would not be available, it shall be considered that on the basis of Article 94-bis, §1 of the FMA, the prospectus shall contain (1) the information that, depending on the characteristics of the financial products and the issuer, is necessary for investors to make an informed assessment of the issuer's assets and liabilities, profits and losses, financial position and prospects and of the financial products and related rights and (2) a securities note which briefly gives key information, in non-technical jargon, in the language in which the prospectus was originally drafted, the format and content of which give adequate information on the fundamental features of the financial products in order to aid the investors to decide whether or not to invest in such products.

For the offer of financial products other than transferable securities, the issuer or the offerer may request Consob to establish the content of the prospectus, where this has not been defined in general[328] and (2) if Consob believes, on reasonable grounds, that additional information is necessary, it shall inform the issuer or the bidder.[329]

If, vice versa, the Tokens are deemed to be transferable securities,[330] and are offered to the public, the rules on the prospectus provided for by the FMA and by Regulation no. 11971/1999 are completed by those set out in the Regulation (EU) 2017/1129.

The information set out in the prospectus, then, pursuant to Article 6, §1 of the Regulation (EU) 2017/1129, may '*vary depending on any of the following: (a) the nature of the issuer; (b) the type of* [transferable] *securities; (c) the circumstances of the issuer; (d) where relevant, whether or not the non-equity securities have a denomination per unit of at least EUR 100,000 or are to be traded only on a regulated market, or a specific segment thereof, to which only qualified investors can have access for the purposes of trading in the transferable securities*'. Furthermore, on the basis of the type of interest or claim connected to the Tokens (as transferable security), the format and the content of the prospectus set out in the Annexes of the Commission delegated Regulation (EU) 2019/980 will be applied, completed with the provision provided for by the Commission delegated Regulation (EU) 2019/980.

327. Article 1, lit. t, of the FMA.
328. Article 5 of the Regulation no. 11971/1999.
329. Article 8, §2, of the Regulation no. 11971/1999.
330. As defined '*in point (44) of Article 4(1) of MiFID II le 2 (D), with the exception of money market instruments as defined in point (17) of Article 4(1) of Directive 2014/65/EU, having a maturity of less than 12 months*': Art. 2, lit. a, Regulation (EU) 2017/1129.

However, the exemptions from the obligation to publish the prospectus set out in FMA, as detailed in both Regulation no. 11971/1999 and Regulation (EU) 2017/1129, are applicable.[331]

[E] Regulatory Specifics for Organized Trade

As highlighted in previous sections, distributed ledger technology can embed any right or value into digital information, and crypto assets can take different forms and nature (Security Token, Asset-Referenced Token, E-money Token, Utility Token, Non-fungible Token and also Hybrid Token).

The regulations applicable to organized forms of Token trading, therefore, vary according to the different types of crypto assets under consideration from time to time.

Focusing the analysis on Tokens that qualify as financial instruments assumes central importance the DLT Pilot Regime mentioned in previous paragraphs, which – as part of the European Commission's 'Digital Finance Package' – introduced an experimental regime for market infrastructures based on distributed ledger technology.

The objective of the DLT Pilot Regime is to introduce, for the duration of the pilot period,[332] some exemptions from the current European regulatory framework to enable the establishment of DLT-based market infrastructures. In fact, in the existing regulatory framework, DLT technology could not be used for trading financial instruments without a change in the current European and Italian regulatory framework, including the provision of market infrastructure and an appropriate issuance and circulation regime.[333]

The DLT Pilot Regime aims to overcome regulatory limitations by introducing a specific legal regime for the listing and trading of crypto assets registered on the blockchain that qualify as financial instruments.[334]

331. Basically, prospectuses are expected for the public offerings concerning transferable securities whose total consideration of each offer in the European Union, calculated over a period of twelve months, is between EUR 1,000,000 and EUR 8,000,000 [Art. 34 *ter*, § 01, of the Regulation no. 11971/1999 and Art. 1, §4, of the Regulation (EU) 2017/1129]. In general, the rules set out in the FMA (concerning the appeal to public savings and, in details, the public offering of European Union financial instruments and financial products other than open-end undertaking for the collective investment in units or shares) shall not apply (at least) to the public offerings: (*a*) addressing fewer than 150 persons, other than the qualified investors; (*b*) addressing qualified investors; (*c*) whose consideration for each offer in the European Union, calculated over a period of twelve months, is below EUR 8,000,000; (*d*) for a total consideration of at least EUR 100,000 per investor and per each separate offer; (*e*) of a *minimum* unit nominal value of at least EUR 100,000 (Art. 100 of the FMA and Art. 34 *ter* Regulation no. 11971/1999).
332. The temporary scheme will last for six years from March 2023, but can be renewed or made permanent by the European institutions at the end of this period.
333. This is because the current European regulatory framework includes a requirement to issue financial instruments traded on dematerialized trading venues, and this requirement is a substantial limitation on the development of DLT-based market infrastructures in the European Union.
334. Trading in other crypto assets is therefore excluded from the scope of the DLT Pilot Regime, but will be regulated by MiCAR through the specific regulations introduced regarding crypto asset service providers.

To this end, in addition to modifying – as already mentioned above – the definition of financial instrument under MiFID 2, Article 18 of the DLT Pilot Regime also required Member States to adopt and publish the necessary provisions to allow the issuance of financial instruments in 'digital form' (i.e., by means of distributed ledger technology), thus creating the conditions for the circulation of such instruments through dedicated market infrastructures.

The application of the DLT Pilot Regime is, however, limited only to certain specific types of financial instruments; only (i) shares of an issuer with a market capitalization (or provisional market capitalization) of less than EUR 500 million may be admitted to trading on a DLT-based market infrastructure; (ii) bonds and other forms of securitized debt, or money-market instruments, with an amount in terms of issuance of less than EUR 1 billion (excluding those incorporating a derivative component); (iii) units of collective investment schemes under the UCITS Directive, the assets under management of which is less than EUR 500 million.[335]

The DLT Pilot Regime thus introduces a specific regulatory regime for DLT-based market infrastructure, regulating:

- DLT multilateral trading facilities (DLT MTF), which are equivalent to the multilateral trading facilities under MiFID 2;
- DLT securities settlement systems (DLT SS), which are the settlement systems that settle transactions in DLT-based financial instruments;
- DLT trading and settlement systems (DLT TSS), a notion that encompasses entities that simultaneously offer DLT MTF and DLT SS services.

DLT Pilot Regime essentially provides that DLT MTFs, DLT SSs and DLT TSSs are subject to the same legal framework that applies under MiFID 2 to multilateral trading facilities (MTFs) and securities settlement systems, subject to some limited exemptions.

As a result, only entities holding an authorization to operate an MTF under MiFID2 may operate a DLT MTF, although such authorization may also be granted with exclusive reference to the operation of a DLT MTF.

A significant difference from the trading systems governed by MiFID 2 is that the DLT Pilot Regime allows a DLT MTF to admit entities (natural and legal persons) other than institutional investors to trade on their own account (as members or participants), provided they meet specific requirements.

As for the rules applicable to the trading of digital instruments on a DLT MTF or a DLT SS, the DLT Pilot Regime provides for the application of Regulation (EU) No. 596/2014 on market abuse (MAR), thus making the same obligations applicable to issuers and participants in DLT market infrastructures as those applicable to traditional type markets in terms of transparency and market information.

335. An additional limitation is that the aggregate market value of all financial instruments traded on a DLT market infrastructure cannot exceed 9 billion euros. If this threshold is exceeded, the DLT-based market infrastructure must start a transition process to begin operating as a 'traditional market infrastructure'.

That said, as far as the Italian legal system is concerned, until the approval of the DLT Pilot Regime, there were two orders of limitations to the use of DLT technology for the implementation of infrastructures for the trading of financial instruments. On the one hand, in fact, the rules governing the issuance and circulation of many financial instruments (e.g., company shares, mutual fund shares) were not fully compatible with their digitization by DLT technology.

Second, Article 83-bis of the FMA provided that the obligation of representation in book-entry form required by Article 3(1) of Regulation (EU) No. 909/2014 (Central Securities Depositary Regulation – c.d 'CSDR') could be fulfilled (exclusively) 'by direct issuance, or placement, in dematerialized form, with a central securities depository established in the territory of the Republic, or with a central securities depository authorized to provide cross-border services in the territory of the Republic, pursuant to Article 23 of the same Regulation'. What effectively prevented the use of distributed ledger technology for the trading of instruments admitted to trading on regulated markets.[336]

With the aforementioned Decree Law 25/2022 (also known as the 'Fintech Decree'), Article 18 of the DLT Pilot Regime was implemented in Italy, with the introduction of a general regulation of the issuance and circulation of digital financial instruments, using distributed ledger technology.

Decree Law 25/2023 first amended FMA by specifying that the notion of 'financial instruments' includes instruments issued through DLT, thus implementing the amendment made by the DLT Pilot Regime to MiFID 2.

The new issuance and circulation regime introduced by Decree Law: 25/2023 is actually broader than the scope of the DLT Pilot Regime. However, the new regime does not apply to all financial instruments, but only to: (i) shares and bonds of joint-stock companies, (ii) debt securities issued by limited liability companies, (iii) additional debt securities whose issuance is permitted under Italian law, (iv) depository receipts relating to bonds and other debt securities of non-domiciled issuers issued by Italian issuers, (v) money-market instruments governed by Italian law, (vi) shares or units of alternative investment funds (AIFs) and undertakings for collective investment in transferable securities (UCITS).[337]

In addition, consistent with the European Union's regulatory framework, the rules introduced by L.D. 25/2023 do not apply to crypto assets that do not fall under the notion of financial instruments (e.g., Utility Tokens or Payment Tokens), the trading of which will therefore remain governed by the rules introduced by MiCAR.

336. Article 3 of Regulation (EU) No. 909/2014 of 23 Jul. 2014 on improving securities settlement in the European Union and on central securities depositories provides that '1. Without prejudice to paragraph 2, any issuer established in the Union that issues or has issued transferable securities which are admitted to trading or traded on trading venues, shall arrange for such securities to be represented in book entry form as immobilisation or subsequent to a direct issuance in dematerialised form. Where a transaction in transferable securities takes place on a trading venue the relevant securities shall be recorded in book-entry form in a CSD on or before the intended settlement date, unless they have already been so recorded.'

337. The Italian authority in charge of supervision of financial markets (Consob) has the power to expand the number of financial instruments subject to the regime under Decree Law 25/2023 by its own regulation.

The new regulations introduced by Decree Law 25/2023 provide that the aforementioned financial instruments can be issued and transferred through entries on a register for digital circulation maintained by a registry manager, thus overcoming the previous formal constraints on the issuance of securities through DLT. In other words, the Fintech Decree introduces a 'dematerialized' issuance and circulation system that is not subject, however, to the rules that characterize the ordinary dematerialization regime provided by the aforementioned FMA regulations.

L.D. 25/2023 thus sets specific requirements that must be met to ensure the security and reliability of the records on distributed ledgers[338] and establishes differentiated detailed provisions on issuance according to the category of financial instrument taken into consideration. The entry on the register of digital financial instruments has the effect of fully and exclusively legitimizing the holder of the rights to the instrument (i.e., the person in whose favour the registration is made) to exercise them and to dispose of the digital financial instruments.[339]

As for the regulatory profiles, with respect to financial instruments that fall under DLT Pilot Regime, registers for the issuance of digital financial instruments may only be held by entities authorized to operate a DLT MTF or a DLT SS under the same DLT Pilot Regime.

With reference to financial instruments issued in digital form that do not fall under the scope of the DLT Pilot Regime, Decree Law 20/2023 establishes a specific authorization regime by providing that the register of unscripted financial instruments can only be kept by persons registered in the special list held by Consob.

In this regard, Decree Law 25/2023 provides that registers may be kept only by the following categories of entities: (i) banks, investment firms and market operators established in Italy; (ii) other intermediaries established in Italy limited to instruments of their own issuance or of group entities (financial intermediaries registered in the register as per Article 106 of the Consolidated Banking Act, payment institutions, IMELs, managers of FIAs or UCITS and insurance or reinsurance companies); (iii) other non-financial issuers with registered offices in Italy in relation exclusively to digital instruments of their own issuance; (iv) other companies established in Italy other than the above; and other entities identified by regulation by Consob.[340] Decree Law

338. L.D. 25/2023 stipulates, among other things, that the registries must: (i) ensure the integrity, authenticity, non-repudiation, non-duplicability and validity of the entries attesting to the ownership and transfer of digital financial instruments and the related encumbrances; (ii) allow, directly or indirectly, to identify at any time the persons in whose favour the entries are made, the species and number of digital financial instruments held by each, as well as to make possible their circulation; (iii) allow the entry of constraints of any kind on the digital financial instruments; ensure accessibility by Consob and the Bank of Italy for the exercise of their respective functions.

339. Based on the provisions of Decree Law 25/2023, as mentioned above, a person who has obtained the entry in his favour, based on a suitable title and in good faith, is not subject to claims or actions by previous holders; the establishment of liens on financial instruments issued in digital form must be done only by entry in the register, reporting the information indicated within the same Decree.

340. The Fintech Decree provides additional requirements for non-financial issuers and other non-financial companies established in Italy that wish to register on the registry-also subject to review by Consob as part of the process described above. In particular, there is a requirement

25/2023 specifies that Italian central depositories that intend to perform on an ancillary basis also the activity of registry manager are included in the list of authorized entities upon their request, without the need of a proper authorization procedure.

The time limit for the registration process with Consob is ninety days from the receipt of the complete registration application.

The Fintech Decree delegates to the same Consob the power to adopt implementing provisions regarding the criteria and principles for the establishment and maintenance of the list of managers of such registers. Consob's Regulation issued by Resolution No. 22923 of 6 December 2023 establishes the procedure for registering operators of the list and the requirements they must meet.

For the purposes of inclusion in the list of registry managers, Consob verifies, in particular, the suitability of the registry for which one intends to assume responsibility to ensure compliance with the requirements posed by Decree Law. 25/2023 and the presence of appropriate mechanisms and devices: (i) to prevent the use of digital financial instruments by parties other than those legitimized; (ii) of business continuity and business restoration, which include the external securing of information; (iii) to prevent the loss or unauthorized modification of data and scripts related to digital financial instruments for the entire duration of the script and ensure that the total number of digital financial instruments constituting a single issue is not modifiable.[341]

The person in charge of the registry and the manager of a DLT MTF or a DLT SS must ensure that the registry complies with the characteristics prescribed by L.D. 25/2023, is required to ensure the correctness, completeness, and updating on an ongoing basis of the evidence regarding the information on the issue, and is liable for any damages arising from the maintenance of the registry to the issuer of the financial instruments and to the person in whose favour the entries were made or should have been made, unless he/she provides evidence that he/she has taken all appropriate measures to avoid the damage.

---

to be incorporated as a joint-stock company and to have an initial capital of at least EUR 150,000, to have their financial statements audited, to take out an insurance policy, or other appropriate form of guarantee, to cover liability for damages that may result from taking on the role of registry officer, and to adopt effective policies for the identification, prevention, management and transparency of conflicts of interest. Non-financial companies that intend to act as registry officer vis-à-vis third parties are then required to appoint, as members of the administrative, management and control bodies, individuals with special requirements of honourability and/or competence, as well as to adopt a clear organizational structure, with well-defined, transparent and consistent lines of responsibility, effective internal controls and ICT systems, effective policies for outsourcing, and appropriate administrative and accounting procedures to ensure compliance with the Decree, including by personnel. Additional requirements may be identified by Consob in its own regulations in which the criteria for identifying significant registrants will also be defined.

341. Among the information relevant to Consob's assessment are the technical specifications of the DLT infrastructure used to operate the digital registries, those related to accessibility, security, governance and measure to regulate accesses. Detailed information is also required on smart contracts, financial instrument management, any interoperability mechanisms with other platforms, and security protocols for user identification. Consob is also required to supervise in continuum the compliance with the above-mentioned requirements.

Thus, the legislation introduced by the Fintech Decree enables the adoption of DLT as a tool to simplify the process of issuing, transferring and settling transactions involving financial instruments.

The Fintech Decree does not, however, resolve all issues related to the use of DLT systems for trading digital financial instruments. In particular, one point that is much discussed by early commentators on the new legislation concerns whether the Fintech Decree actually legitimizes the adoption, including by central securities depositories, of DLT-based solutions in relation to listed financial instruments, subject to the aforementioned Article 3 CSDR and Article 83-bis of the TUF, thus eliminating the monopoly of scriptural management for securities traded in regulated markets.[342]

In addition, the interpretative difficulties related to the identification of the applicable law remain unresolved, for all cases in which the existing rules of private international law do not allow the identification of a clear connecting factor as pointed out in the previous paragraph (C).

§5.10 CAPITAL MARKETS AND BLOCKCHAIN: COUNTRY REPORT – LIECHTENSTEIN

Johannes Dür[343]

Liechtenstein is one of the first countries worldwide which has introduced a legal framework for all applications of the so-called Token economy, particularly in order to ensure legal certainty. For that purpose, the Liechtenstein Parliament adopted on 3 October 2019 the Law on Tokens and TT Service Providers (Tokens and TT Service Provider Act, also known as 'Blockchain Act', hereinafter 'TVTG'),[344] which entered into force on 1 January 2020. This country report for Liechtenstein particularly deals with and is based on the legal framework of the TVTG.[345]

The TVTG constitutes a comprehensive legal framework for transaction systems based on so-called trustworthy technologies, which mainly addresses Blockchain or other Distributed Ledger Technologies (TT); TT are the core connecting factor for the applicability of the TVTG. The definition of TT is agnostic and technology-neutral and shall ensure applicability of the TVTG also for subsequent technology generations; it

342. In a favourable sense, *see* U. Malvagna, *Digital securities: first notes on the DLT Pilot implementation decree*, in dirittobancario.it, 20 Mar. 2023. Of an opposite opinion, T. N. Poli, MiCA, *Pilot Regime and Fintech Decree: The Regulation of the Crypto Phenomenon and the Difficulties of Framing It in the Financial System*, in dirittobancario.it, 13 Dec. 2023.

343. Johannes Dür, co-founder and partner at advocatio Attorneys at Law, understands that legal questions make up only one aspect of a business problem. He holds double diploma in Management, and uses his learning to consider economic aspects and impacts in his legal analysis and advice. Johannes is specialized in litigation and advisory in corporate, commercial and banking matters.

344. German: *Gesetz über Token und VT-Dienstleister* (*Token- und VT-Dienstleister-Gesetz; TVTG*).

345. After the editorial deadline, an amendment of the TVTG came into force, primarily to prepare for the upcoming applicability of MiCAR (Regulation (EU) 2023/1114) in Liechtenstein, which is not covered by this chapter at all. Thus, this Country Report regarding Liechtenstein reflects the legal status of the TVTG prior to the amendment of 1 Feb 2024.

suggests that TT must ensure that the correctness and integrity of Tokens cannot be manipulated or at least only with disproportionate efforts.[346]

With the TVTG, the Token as a new legal object is introduced into Liechtenstein law to enable the representation of the 'real' world on TT Systems in a legally secure manner. Under the TVTG, 'Tokens' are understood as a kind of 'container' and are characterized as digital representations of analogous rights, which cannot be transferred or enforced without the Token itself.[347] Tokens can represent claims or rights of membership against a person, rights to property, other absolute or relative rights or even nothing.[348] The TT System shall ensure 'the secure transfer and storage of Tokens and the rendering of services based on this by means of trustworthy technology' (TT System).[349]

Due to its abstract formulation, the TVTG shall apply for all applications of the Token economy, irrespective of the kind of Tokens involved; it regulates mainly the essential aspects of the Token economy, such as generating and storing of Tokens, change and exchange platforms, the public sale of Tokens as well as the transfer of rights represented by a Token. However, it is not a regulation of activities related to the financial market and reaches far beyond financial services.

Financial market regulation is in general technology-neutral and thus also applicable for regulated activities involving TT Systems. The application of financial market regulation laws often depends on terms like 'legal currency', 'security' or 'financial instrument'. Thus, Tokens representing legal currencies, securities or financial instruments are also to be classified as such in accordance with financial market regulation.[350]

The TVTG includes a civil law chapter and a regulatory chapter. The civil law part governs the qualification of Tokens and the disposal over Tokens and their underlying rights under civil law. It follows widely the concept of classic securities law and adapts other pre-existing laws to the Token economy. The civil law provisions play an important role in achieving legal finality and legal certainty of transactions on TT Systems (*see* below).

The regulatory approach of the TVTG is not aimed at a regulation of the technology itself. Instead, it defines several types of professional service providers of the Token economy (TT Service Provider), who are obliged to apply for prior registration in a public register and are subject to (non-prudential) supervision by the Liechtenstein FMA. The requirements for such a registration include among others: personal reliability, technical suitability, a headquarter or place of residence in

346. Government of Liechtenstein, *Bericht und Antrag der Regierung an den Landtag des Fürstentums Liechtenstein betreffend die Schaffung eines Gesetzes über Token und VT-Dienstleister (Token- und VT-Dienstleistergesetz; TVTG) und die Abänderung weiterer Gesetze*, Report and Application no. 54/2019, 135, https://impuls-liechtenstein.li/wp-content/uploads/2019/06/bua_054_2019_tvtg.pdf (accessed 11 Mar. 2020).
347. Government of Liechtenstein, *supra* n. 346, at 59 et seq. and 166.
348. Article 2(1) c) TVTG.
349. Article 2(1) b) TVTG.
350. Government of Liechtenstein, *supra* n. 346, at 44; Liechtenstein FMA, *Faktenblatt 'Initial Coin Offering'*, 2, https://www.fma-li.li/files/fma/fma-faktenblatt-ico.pdf (accessed 11 Mar. 2020).

Liechtenstein, a suitable organizational structure and a procedure to deal with conflicts of interest, appropriate written internal proceedings and control mechanisms.[351] In the course of the registration process, the FMA examines also possible obligations to obtain a licence according to financial markets legislation.[352] Precisely, the TVTG identifies and regulates the following TT Service Providers: *Token Issuer* (person who publicly offers Tokens in its own name or in the name of a client), *Token Generator, TT Key Depositary, TT Token Depositary, TT Protector* (person who holds and disposes over Tokens on TT Systems in its own name on the account for a third party), *Physical Validator* (person who ensures the enforcement of rights represented in Tokens in terms of property law), *TT Exchange Service Provider* (person who exchanges legal currencies against Tokens and vice versa and Tokens for Tokens), *TT Verifying Authority* (person who verifies the legal capacity and requirements for disposal over a Token), *TT Price Service Provider, TT Identity Service Provider* (person who identifies the person in possession of the right of disposal related to a Token and records it in a directory) and *TT Agent* (person who distributes or provides TT Services in Liechtenstein on a professional basis in the name of and for the account of a foreign TT Service Provider).

[A] What Makes a Token a Security?

Ever since, Liechtenstein security law has been strongly influenced by the notion of the connection of a right with a physical carrier (certificate).[353] The securitization of rights in a physical document, however, has been long outdated. Therefore, the concept of genuine book-entry security is introduced into Liechtenstein law[354] together with the adoption of the TVTG. Such uncertificated or book-entry securities (German: *Wertrechte*) have – if properly created – all the functions of a classic security of public faith (bearer or order paper), namely: transport function, legitimation function and liberation function, transaction protection and objection restriction.[355]

Book-entry securities are to be recorded by the debtor in an (electronic) register; they come into legal existence with, and have the legal effects pursuant to, the entry in the register (constitutive effect). The register has to be organized in such a manner that unauthorized intervention of the debtor in the rights of creditors is prevented. It may

351. With certain exemptions for TT Agents.
352. Government of Liechtenstein, *Stellungnahme der Regierung an den Landtag des Fürstentums Liechtenstein zu den anlässlich der ersten Lesung betreffend die Schaffung eines Gesetzes über Token und VT-Dienstleister (Token- und VT-Dienstleistergesetz; TVTG) und die Abänderung weiterer Gesetze aufgeworfenen Fragen*, Report and Application no. 93/2019, 21, https://www.llv.li/files/srk/bua_093_2019_stellungnahme-tvtg.pdf (accessed 11 Mar. 2020).
353. Section 73(1) Final Part of the Persons and Companies Law (PGR); nevertheless, immobilized and dematerialized uncertificated securities have not been completely unknown to the Liechtenstein legal system; cf. Government of Liechtenstein, *supra* n. 346, at 108.
354. Section 81a Final Part of the (amended) Persons and Companies Law (PGR).
355. Government of Liechtenstein, *supra* n. 346, at 110.

also be kept using trustworthy technologies according to the TVTG, such as Blockchain. Hence, with the introduction of genuine book-entry securities into Liechtenstein law, a new interface between the TVTG and securities law is created.[356]

Depending on the specific characteristics of a Token, it may be treated as security or financial instrument under the Liechtenstein financial market legislation (substance over form). As Liechtenstein is a member of the EEA, in principle, the regulatory framework for financial and capital markets of the EU is applicable also in Liechtenstein.

Hence, the question of whether under Liechtenstein financial market laws, a Token is treated as security or not is determined by the respective definition of the European concept of securities, namely in MiFID II.[357,358] Therefore, standardization, transferability and negotiability are the crucial elements for the classification of Tokens as securities also under Liechtenstein law, and the Liechtenstein practice widely conforms to the practice in other EU Member States, such as Germany.[359] Due to the substance-over-form approach, neither certification[360] nor tradability on (traditional) capital markets[361] is necessary for the treatment of Tokens as securities.

According to the current practice of the Liechtenstein FMA, Utility Tokens and cryptocurrencies in Liechtenstein are basically treated as commodities:[362] Therefore, the production and use of cryptocurrencies and Utility Tokens usually do not require a specific licence of the FMA.[363] However, such a licence may be necessary for certain business models related to any kind of Tokens, depending on the characteristics of the business model and the specification of the involved Tokens.

[B] Blockchain Finality

In view of legal certainty of transactions executed on a TT System, the relationship and coordination between the digital representation of rights in a Token and the underlying 'analogous' rights are essential. The aim is that the disposal over the Token shall also

---

356. *Ibid.*, at 108 et seq.
357. Directive 2014/65/EU of the European Parliament and of the Council of 15 May 2014 on markets in financial instruments and amending Directive 2002/92/EC and Directive 2011/61/EU.
358. Liechtenstein FMA, *FMA-Mitteilung 2019/2 – Pflichten für Emittenten von Wertpapieren und Security Token*, https://www.fma-li.li/files/list/fma-mittteilung-2019-2-emittenten-wp-st.pdf (accessed 11 Mar. 2020).
359. Cf. the legal practice in Germany (Michael Jünemann), §5.07[A], *supra*.
360. Liechtenstein FMA, *supra* n. 358, at 4 et seq.
361. For example, the so-called book-entry securities are transferred by entry in the respective register and not on traditional capital markets.
362. Depending on its specific design, a Utility Token may nevertheless fulfil the requirements of MiFID regarding securities and/or financial instruments and are thus treated as such, which is assessed by the FMA on a case-by-case basis.
363. Patrick Bont, Liechtenstein FMA, speech 'Kryptowährungen – und was machen die Regulatoren?', handout sheet no. 13, https://www.fma-li.li/files/fma/fma-digital-banking-liechtenstein.pdf (accessed 11 Mar. 2020); Thomas Nägele & Josef Bergt, Kryptowährungen und Blockchain-Technologie im liechtensteinischen Aufsichtsrecht, 2 Liechtensteinische Juristenzeitung, 65 (2018); Government of Liechtenstein, *supra* n. 346, at 44.

effectuate a valid and effective transfer of the rights represented by the Token. This is achieved in the TVTG, on the one hand, by the provision that the 'disposal over the Token results in the disposal over the right represented in the Token'. This programmatic legal order works particularly with Security Tokens respectively book-entry securities registered in TT Systems and governed by Liechtenstein law.[364]

On the other hand, in cases where such a synchronization of digital and analogous disposal cannot be achieved by law (e.g., the Token represents rights in immovable property or rights governed by foreign law), the person obliged under the disposal over the Token must ensure the following: (1) that the disposal over the Token directly or indirectly procures the effective transfer of the represented right, and (2) that a competing disposal over the represented right is excluded. The obligated person has to take appropriate organizational, structural and/or legal measures to achieve this, e.g., deposition of a physical object with a Physical Validator or other custodians, or – with regard to claims – stipulation of provisions in the underlying contract or in terms of issue of a financial instrument, according to which the transfer of the claim is only possible in accordance with the rules of the TT System.[365]

In this context, the TVTG determines the requirements for a valid disposal over Tokens (the term 'disposal' also includes the creation of limited rights in rem, namely the establishment of securities or of rights of usufruct to a Token): following the principle of title and mode of the Liechtenstein property law, lawful disposal requires a valid contractual agreement between the parties and a transfer of the Token in line with the regulations of the TT System as well as the prerequisite that the transferring party is in possession of the right of disposal over the Token.[366] The right of disposal comes close to the right of ownership of a physical object and may be granted/delegated to a third party (agency).[367]

On TT Systems, such as Blockchain, the TT key (i.e., private key) is required to dispose over a Token; thus, the holder of the private key has de facto the power to dispose over the Token, but he is not necessarily legally entitled to do so; for example, in case of theft of the private key, the thief is not entitled to dispose over the Token, or in case of bankruptcy proceedings regarding the holder of the private key, the right of disposal is withdrawn.[368] For practicability reasons, there is the rebuttable statutory presumption that the holder of the TT key also has the right of disposal over a Token. This means, that in case of unlawful appropriation of the private key, the aggrieved party has to initiate respective court proceedings and prove its legitimate right of disposal.[369]

Under the TVTG it is assumed that, due to the underlying technology (e.g., Blockchain), transactions on TT Systems are largely final (at least in technical terms).[370] Problems arise when the nominal legal situation does not correspond to the

364. Article 7(1) TVTG; Government of Liechtenstein, *supra* n. 346, at 168 et seq.
365. Article 7(2) TVTG; Government of Liechtenstein, *supra* n. 346, at 170 et seq.
366. Article 6 TVTG; Government of Liechtenstein, *supra* n. 346, at 190 et seq.
367. Government of Liechtenstein, *supra* n. 346, at 67 et seq.
368. Article 16(1) Bankruptcy Act.
369. Article 5 TVTG; Government of Liechtenstein, *supra* n. 346, at 184 et seq.
370. Government of Liechtenstein, *supra* n. 346, at 126 et seq. and 135.

factual situation as validated on the TT System. Such a situation is given if a Token is disposed over without a valid legal ground (e.g., unlawful agreement) or if the legal ground subsequently ceased to exist (e.g., in case of bankruptcy proceedings).[371] Due to the inalterability of transactions on TT Systems, the TVTG adopts the principle of abstraction for dispositions of Tokens (as opposed to the principle of causality, according to which dispositions without an underlying legitimate cause are basically void). This, however, does not mean that the unlawful disposition as validated on the TT System is absolutely final. Instead, the transaction has to be reversed according to the law of enrichment: the unduly enriched person has to – by way of a new transaction – transfer back the Tokens to the person unduly deprived of the Tokens. The unduly enriched person may be forced to do so by a court judgment.[372]

However, the TVTG stipulates a bona fide rule which protects those who have in good faith and for valuable consideration acquired a Token or obtained a restricted right in rem, even if the transferring party was not entitled to dispose of the Token. Thus, the disposal over the Token is final and effective. The aggrieved party can only hold liable the party which unlawfully transferred the Token. The bona fide rule is generally applicable in case of a lack of the right to dispose over the Token and not in case this entitlement ceased to exist.[373]

Furthermore, the TVTG clarifies that in general the obliged party regarding the right represented by a Token may pay or perform his duties with debt-discharging effect to the authorized person regarding the Token as identified in the TT System. This rule largely corresponds to the legitimation and liberation function in securities law.[374]

Another means of protection for Token 'owners' is the cancellation of Tokens in case of loss of the private key or inoperativeness of a Token (e.g., because of bugs). For that purpose, the person entitled to dispose over the Token has to file an application with the court and may, in case of success, execute the represented rights without the Token or demand production of a new Token on own costs.[375]

The TVTG does not explicitly deal with forks, material technical malfunctions or hacks; it rather seems that the responsible TT Service Provider has the duty to appropriately deal with such constellations[376] and may be held liable for breach of his duties. One opportunity for TT Service Providers to cope with such risks might be the use of a private/permissioned Blockchain.[377]

The TVTG opens a range of possibilities for Token 'owners' to reduce their risks, particularly the risk of loss or theft. For example, the TT key (i.e., private key) may be securely deposited with a TT Key Depositary, or the Token is held by a TT Token Depositary in the name and on behalf of the Token 'owner' or alternatively by a TT Protector on its own name but on account for the principal ('beneficial Token

371. *Ibid.*, at 68 et seq.
372. Article 6(3) TVTG; Government of Liechtenstein, *supra* n. 346, at 191 et seq.
373. Article 9 TVTG; Government of Liechtenstein, *supra* n. 346, at 208 et seq.
374. Article 8 TVTG; Government of Liechtenstein, *supra* n. 346, at 206 et seq.
375. Article 10 TVTG.
376. Government of Liechtenstein, *supra* n. 346, at 84.
377. *See*: the legal practice in Germany (Michael Jünemann), §5.01[B] Blockchain Finality, *supra*.

owner').[378] Another option is the engagement of a TT Identity Service Provider who identifies and registers the person entitled to dispose over a Token.[379] All these TT Service Providers must comply with minimum standards, are subject to registration and publication duties, are supervised by the FMA and usually have contractual obligations with liabilities in case of breach. Furthermore, Tokens or TT keys deposited with or held by such a TT Service Provider constitute a separate asset in case of bankruptcy or foreclosure proceedings and are therefore protected against creditors of the TT Service Provider.[380]

[C] International Private Law

In the civil law part of the TVTG, 'ownership' of Tokens and the associated legal consequences are regulated autonomously only for TT systems, without affecting the established system of property law. This is because digital data and therefore also Tokens are – at least pursuant to the prevailing doctrine – not subject to Liechtenstein property law.[381,382] As a result, the existing provisions of the International Private Law of Liechtenstein regarding rights in rem are not suitable for legal relationships based on TT systems, such as Tokens.

Against this background, a collision law provision was included in the TVTG, according to which the civil law provisions in the TVTG are applicable: (1) if Tokens are generated or issued by a TT Service Provider with headquarters or domicile in Liechtenstein or (2) if the parties expressly declare applicability of its provisions in a legal transaction over Tokens (choice of law).[383] Such a choice of law is even possible for Tokens that were generated before the TVTG came into force.[384]

In case of such applicability, the Token is considered to be an asset located in Liechtenstein with the effect that the courts of Liechtenstein have jurisdiction in related civil law disputes.[385]

Certainly, said collision law provision regulates only one of a range of legal aspects of cross-border transactions involving Tokens. In particular, the legal consequences of a transfer of Tokens on the rights represented in the Tokens provided for in the TVTG take effect only if these rights are subject to Liechtenstein law.[386]

The question of the applicable law of the represented right is not determined in the TVTG but by the different general rules concerning conflict of laws, depending on

378. Government of Liechtenstein, *supra* n. 346, at 153 et seq.
379. *Ibid.*, at 163 and 209.
380. Article 25 TVTG.
381. Sachenrecht (SR) vom 31. Dezember 1922.
382. *Wolf/Wiegand* in *Geiser/Wolf*, Basler Kommentar zum ZGB^6, II., Art. 641, n. 29; cf. *Thomas Nägele*, Die Rechtsnatur von Token, at 40 et seqq. and 47; Government of Liechtenstein, *supra* n. 346, at 62; Jörg/Layr/Lettenbichler, in: Judith Sild (editor), Grundsatzfragen des liechtensteinischen TVTG, at 216 et seqq.
383. Article 3(2) TVTG.
384. Article 50(2) TVTG.
385. Article 4 TVTG; Government of Liechtenstein, *supra* n. 346, at 183.
386. Government of Liechtenstein, *supra* n. 346, at 69.

the type and legal nature of the represented right.[387] For example, movable property is subject to Liechtenstein law if it is located in Liechtenstein or receivables may be governed by the law agreed by the parties in the underlying contract. In this respect, it is worth mentioning that the Rome-Regulations, particularly Rome I,[388] are not directly applicable in Liechtenstein.[389]

[D] Special Requirements for a Prospectus

For the public offering of Tokens, which are regarded as transferable securities according to MiFID II, the prior publication of an approved prospectus is required, and the provisions of the Prospectus Regulation[390] are fully applicable. If such a public offer shall not be notified to other EU/EEA Member States and if its total consideration does not exceed the amount of EUR 8 million over a period of twelve months, it is exempted from the obligation to publish a prospectus in Liechtenstein.[391]

Due to the applicability of the respective legislative provisions of the EU, reference is made, particularly with regard to the contents of the prospectus, to the respective statements in the country report for Germany, which, in principle, also apply to Liechtenstein.[392]

In view of the strict statutory prospectus liability, it is in any event recommended to describe in the prospectus all the legal, regulatory and technical uncertainties and risks specifically related to the STO, Security Tokens and the underlying Blockchain technology in detail. In the legal practice, specific remarks and warnings regarding legal and technical risks in connection with the STO and the underlying Blockchain technology typically comprise the following issues: restriction of tradability risk and risk of illiquid markets (lack of admission of trading on a regulated or unregulated market), other market risks (such as price manipulation, hacking of the crypto-exchange, systemic risks and correlations within markets for digital assets), risk of invalidity of the transfer of Tokens and finality risks, risk of malfunction, bugs and technical errors of applications and/or smart contracts (including changes of the underlying Blockchain technology), risks due to legal uncertainties with regard to Tokens and due to (future) legal and regulatory developments, wallet and private key risks (e.g., risk of loss or inaccessibility of the private key, risk of wrong wallet address, risk of incompatibility of a wallet), risk of loss of key personnel as well as the risk of

387. Government of Liechtenstein, *supra* n. 346, at 70 and 182 et seq.
388. Regulation (EC) No. 593/2008 of the European Parliament and of the Council of 17 Jun. 2008 on the law applicable to contractual obligations (Rome I).
389. Marxer & Partner, Liechtensteinisches Wirtschaftsrecht, n. 38.1.
390. Regulation (EU) 2017/1129 of the European Parliament and of the Council of 14 Jun. 2017 on the prospectus to be published when securities are offered to the public or admitted to trading on a regulated market.
391. Article 3 EEA Securities Prospectus Implementation Act (EWR-WPPDG).
392. Cf. Michael Jünemann, §5.07[C], *supra*.

hacking and data theft and specific technical risks regarding the execution of the STO.[393]

If there is no obligation to publish a prospectus, the issuer of a Token is at least obliged to compile and publish basic information, including but not limited to information about the Token and the associated rights, the name of the TT system used, the purpose and nature of the legal transaction of the Token issuance, the purchase and transfer conditions and the risks associated with the purchasing of the Tokens.[394] The required level of information is achieved if an interested buyer or other persons are informed within a reasonable time period about the offering, its purpose and the associated opportunities and risks associated with it.[395] The responsible persons are jointly and severally liable to every user for damages that arise as a result of incorrect or incomplete or missing information.[396]

[E] Regulatory Specifics for Organized Trade

Emanating from the applicability of the regulatory framework of the EU for financial markets, the EU provisions for trading are also applicable in Liechtenstein. Thus, trading of Tokens may be subject to the approval of FMA if these are classified as financial instruments according to the definition in MiFID II.[397] Furthermore, the provisions of the MiFID framework regarding the operation of a regulated market or MTF or OTF are also applicable in Liechtenstein.[398]

But even if Tokens do not constitute a security or financial instrument, the trading of Tokens or the provision of related services may be subject to registration requirements under the TVTG: Any person or entity who professionally exchanges (fungible) Tokens against Tokens or legal currencies or vice versa has to apply for registration as TT Exchange Service Provider with the FMA.[399] According to the legislative materials, all service providers who exchange Tokens in the above sense on their own account and who neither hold Tokens nor TT keys of their clients are classified as TT Exchange Service Provider. If the service provider holds Tokens or TT

393. Crowdlitoken AG, *Prospectus for the Issue/Public Offer of Up to 190,000,000 Crowdlitokens*, 12 Apr. 2019, https://crowdlitoken.com/das-produkt/#rechtliche-dokumente (accessed 11 Mar. 2020); Invao Trading AG, *Security Prospectus to Issue 52,500,000 IVO Tokens*, 19 Nov. 2019, https://invao.org/ivo-bond/#downloads_block_5d88da8aa7ab0 (accessed 11 Mar. 2020); Enercom AG, *EEA Growth Prospectus for the Public Offering of 200,000 Enercom Tokens*, 21 Nov. 2019, https://www.enercom.ag/prospectus-approved-by-fma/ (accessed 11 Mar. 2020); Curio AG, *Wertpapierprospekt für die Emmission von CT1 Token*, https://curioinvest.com/templates/assets/docs/CurioProspekt.pdf (accessed 11 Mar. 2020).
394. Articles 30 et seqq. TVTG; (minor) offerings are exempted from this obligation under certain circumstances.
395. Government of Liechtenstein, *supra* n. 346, at 271; Rainer Silbernagl in: Judith Sild (editor), Grundsatzfragen des liechtensteinischen TVTG, at 169 et seq.
396. Article 35 TVTG; Government of Liechtenstein, *supra* n. 346, at 280 et seqq.; *Rainer Silbernagl*, *supra* n. 395, at 201 et seqq.
397. Article 3 Bankengesetz (Banking Act, hereinafter 'BankG').
398. Cf. the respective statements in the country report for Germany (Michael Jünemann) §5.07[D], *supra*.
399. Article 2(1) q) TVTG; Government of Liechtenstein, *supra* n. 346, at 9 et seq.

keys of their clients, they are to be registered as TT Token Depositary or TT Key Depositary.[400] Furthermore, the professional provision of aggregated price information on the basis of purchase and sale offers or completed transactions falls under the definition of the TT Price Service Provider.[401] Therefore, the classification of crypto-exchanges (centralized as well as decentralized platforms, with or without matching function) under the TVTG strongly depends on the concrete business model and may trigger registration duties with the FMA either as TT Exchange Service Provider, TT Token Depositary, TT Key Depositary or TT Price Service Provider.

§5.11 CAPITAL MARKETS AND BLOCKCHAIN: COUNTRY REPORT – MALTA

Nicole Debrincat & Omar Zerafa[402]

[A] What Makes a Token a Security?

On 4 July 2018, Malta was the first country to put forward an official set of regulations for operators in blockchain, cryptocurrency and distributed ledger technology (*DLT*).[403] When tackling this new technology, Maltese legislators could either impose a ban or adopt a regulatory regime. In the light of this debate, the Malta Financial Services Authority (the *MFSA*) forwarded its main policy proposal to implement a regulatory and supervisory framework. This aimed to strike a balance between supporting these novel technologies while ensuring effective investor protection and financial stability.[404] The MFSA is established by Article 3 of the Malta Financial Services Authority Act, and its functions include among others integrity of financial markets, financial stability, and the supervision of all financial services activities. Since Malta is a Member State within the European Union, the MFSA is also one of the European Union's (the *EU*) national competent authorities (*NCAs*). The European Securities and Markets Authority (*ESMA*) is the EU's independent financial markets regulator and supervisor. This European authority shares many of the same functions of the MFSA but has the overarching aim towards supervisory convergence among NCAs and to work closely with the other European supervisory authorities.[405]

400. Government of Liechtenstein, *supra* n. 346, at 102 et seq. and 160 et seq.
401. Article 2(1) s) TVTG; Government of Liechtenstein, *supra* n. 346, at 162.
402. Founder of Zerafa Advocates, Dr Zerafa has worked as an associate with one of the leading financial services law firms in Malta where he was also admitted to partnership, responsible for the structuring and licensing of collective investment schemes, investment vehicles, investment services licence holders including asset management companies and financial institutions. Associate at Zerafa Advocates, Nicole Debrincat has an extensive experience in the gaming and financial services sectors. As an associate, Nicole is primarily focused on Fintech and Gaming. Johannes Frank advises in start-up companies, capital markets, crypto assets, alternative investment funds, as well as securities and payment services.
403. https://www.forbes.com/sites/rachelwolfson/2018/07/05/maltese-parliament-passes-laws-that-set-regulatory-framework-for-blockchain-cryptocurrency-and-dlt/?sh=25f3744349ed.
404. https://doi.org/10.1080/17521440.2018.1524687.
405. https://www.esma.europa.eu/about-esma.

From the proposals put forward by the MFSA, legislators promulgated three new bills, these being: the Virtual Financial Assets Act (VFAA); the Malta Digital Innovation Authority Act (MDIAA); and the Innovative Technology Arrangements and Services Act (the '**ITAS Act**'). The VFAA sets out a regulatory framework which is applicable to operators providing virtual financial assets (*VFAs*) and regulates the public offering of such assets. This framework is applicable to Maltese service providers which offer their products within and from Malta. For the purpose of the VFAA, the competent authority is the MFSA which cooperates with the Malta Digital Innovation Authority (*MDIA*), which is enshrined in the MDIAA and is also the competent authority of the ITAS Act. The affairs and business shall be carried out by a Board, members of which shall have adequate qualifications and experience in terms of these matters.[406] The MDIA is also vested with a wide array of functions which it must fulfil in order to contribute towards achieving the principles and objectives outlined in Article 4 of the MDIAA.[407]

[1] Terminology

While the Maltese framework regarding blockchain features particular terminology, the term 'blockchain' is not featured. This nomenclature comprises a vast array of assets, including cryptocurrency and Tokens, which have as their underlying technology among others DLT. The legislator opted to not include such technical terminology, thus preventing the risk of lacunae in the law. Therefore, the Maltese framework is based on the pivotal term of VFA. These assets are defined as 'any form of digital medium recordation that is used as a digital medium of exchange, unit of account, or store of value'.[408] Additionally, the Maltese legislator included an exclusion list of what cannot be categorized as VFA, one of which being the financial instrument.

[2] Concept of Securities and Transferable Securities

DLT has also been expanding in the capital markets industry and consequently the traditional notion of securities has been intertwined with these modern types of assets. To understand what makes a Token a security, one must first understand the characteristics which make an asset a security.

The Maltese legal framework defines securities in Article 2 of the Financial Markets Act[409] (The *Act*) as being transferable securities. This Act further defines transferable securities as 'those *classes of securities which are negotiable on the capital market*'. Regulators have identified three formal requirements which need to be satisfied for an instrument to qualify as a transferable security, these being transferability, negotiability on the capital markets, and the creation of a class of securities.[410] Article 4 of the Act also comprises a non-exhaustive list of instruments of payments

406. Article 5 Malta Digital Innovation Authority Act (hereinafter referred to as 'the MDIAA').
407. Article 6 MDIAA.
408. Article 2 of the Virtual Financial Act (hereinafter referred to as 'the VFAA').
409. Chapter 345 of the laws of Malta.
410. MFSA feedback on consultation paper on STO issued on the 25 Feb. 2020.

which do not amount to transferable securities. Other exclusions in the definition of securities are defined in Article 4(1) of the Markets in Financial Instruments and amending Directive 2002/92/EC (*MiFID*).

With regard to the notion of fungibility, Tokens are normally classified as being fungible in nature. Fungibility is a traditional concept, despite being discussed in terms of modern instruments. Indeed, Jean Carbonnier discussed this notion as referring to something interchangeable and thus negotiable which can be replaced with one another. Carbonnier also provided examples of monetary instruments corresponding to this definition, in particular, physical money.[411] Although not fungible in nature, there could also be instances where Non-fungible Tokens *(NFTs)* would be classified as financial instruments and therefore Security Tokens. Additionally, the MFSA delves deeper into the definition of 'transferable securities'. This term is only partially harmonized at EU level; thus, interpretation plays an important role in order to determine which instruments fall under the remit of this definition. In an attempt to guide the industry, the MFSA sheds light on what constitutes a transferable security. This is in line with the definition provided in MiFID II concurrently with ESMA's Advice to ICOs and Crypto-Assets as to how ESMA and other NCAs are interpreting the concept of a transferable security.[412]

[3] Regulatory Classification of Tokens

The United States Supreme Court in *SEC v. Howey* set out a test which is pivotal for blockchain as certain cryptocurrencies and initial coin offerings *(ICOs)* fall under the definition of an 'investment contract' under the test.[413] The opinion of the Supreme Court stated that '... an investment contract, for the purposes of the Securities Act means a contract, transaction or scheme whereby a person invests his money in a common enterprise and is led to expect profits solely from the efforts of the promoter or a third part ... .'[414] From this statement, the four criteria used as the Howey test can be extracted: an investment of money, in a common enterprise, with the expectation of profit and to be derived from the efforts of others.[415] With regard to the possible regulatory classification of Tokens in the EU, ESMA adopted the position that Tokens can indeed be securities within the meaning of the Prospectus Directive. Moreover, according to MiFID II and the Prospectus Directive, a security connotes 'classes of securities which are negotiable on the capital market'.[416] The security token offering *(STO)* market is still developing, and despite originating from ICOs they still differ.

411. Jean Carbonnier, 'Droit Civile: Tome 2' (Presses Universitaires de France, 2017) 1608-1610.
412. MFSA feedback on consultation paper on STO.
413. https://www.embroker.com/blog/what-is-the-howey-test-does-crypto-pass/.
414. https://supreme.justia.com/cases/federal/us/328/293/.
415. Michael Mendelson, 'From Initial Coin Offerings to Security Tokens: A U.S. Federal Securities Law Analysis.' https://law.stanford.edu/wp-content/uploads/2019/01/Mendelson_20180129 .pdf Stanford Technology Law Review, vol. 22, no. 1, Winter 2019, p. 66.
416. Article 4(1) no. 44 MiFID II.

Researchers often hold that a Security Token is a digital representation of an investment product recorded on a blockchain which is regulated by the law of securities.[417] In reality, an STO refers to the process of investing funds that represent fractional ownership of real-word assets on the blockchain and powered by DLT. In fact, in 2020, the MFSA issued the feedback statement to the consultation document on STO and addressed several issues. MFSA has clarified its position in relation to the Maltese regulatory framework that shall apply with regard to issuers who seek to issue a DLT asset which is defined as a Virtual Token; a VFA; electronic money; or a *financial instrument* using DLT, all while bearing elements of a security.

The MFSA expects such issuers to be guided by the Financial Instrument test (*FIT*). Alternatively, in cases where classification is not easily classified through a prima facie analysis of the FIT, the MFSA advises that issuers seek independent legal advice demonstrating the legal reasoning behind the classification of a Token as a transferable security in terms of MiFID. Moreover, in such cases, the MFSA retains the discretion to ask issuers to elaborate as to how the proposed Token structure complies with the requirements set out under the Maltese Companies Act. The FIT is a negative test which assesses Tokens in a sequential manner via an elimination method. The Token is assessed, and if it does not qualify as a financial instrument, an electronic money or a Virtual Token, then by elimination, it would classify as a VFA. The result is that it would be regulated in terms of the VFA Act. The FIT is conducted by the issuer along with the VFA Agent,[418] which provides legal services for the Issuer, in a self-assessment manner; nevertheless, in order to ensure compliance, various safeguards are embedded within the VFA Act. Moreover, the issuer needs to obtain a countersignature on the said FIT from its VFA Agent, while the MFSA may, by notice in writing, make its determination as to whether a particular DLT Asset qualifies as a Virtual Token, VFA, electronic money, or financial instrument and whether or not it is issued in or from within Malta.[419] Once a Token is given the go-ahead to be offered to the public in Malta or else admitted to trading on a regulated market, a securities prospectus is to be created and approved by the MFSA prior to the offering.[420] The prospectus shall comprise essential information about the company's 'financial condition, capitalisation and risk factors',[421] business operations,[422] directors, senior management and employees,[423] major shareholders and related-party transactions[424] and financial information.[425]

417. Lambert, Liebau, Roosenboom, P. (2021) 'Security token offerings', Small Business Economics, 59(1) https://doi.org/10.1007/s11187-021-00539-9.
418. Article 2 of the VFAA.
419. Zammit, L. (2020) The Evolution of Traditional Capital Markets Through Blockchain, dissertation.
420. Article 1 Regulation 2017/1129 (hereinafter referred to as 'the Prospectus Regulation').
421. Article 6(1)(a) and Annex I (IV) of The Prospectus Regulation.
422. Annex I (V) of The Prospectus Regulation.
423. Annex I (VII) of The Prospectus Regulation.
424. Annex I VIII of The Prospectus Regulation.
425. Annex I (IX) of The Prospectus Regulation.

[B] Blockchain Finality

[1] The Blockchain

One of the key characteristics of blockchain is that it offers a permanent and unalterable network. Once a transaction is recorded on a blockchain, it cannot be modified or deleted. Consequently, it provides a fair and secure data-sharing environment which enhances negotiations and transactions. Nonetheless, there might be instances whereby a blockchain might lose its consistency and encounter some obstacles which challenge blockchain's technical finality.

[2] European and Maltese Law

In the capital markets world, financial instruments will be traded, thus bringing about an element of legal finality in such trading transactions. This finality is a form of guarantee that the transactions in question cannot be altered, reversed or cancelled after completion. Ultimately, the latency level of the blockchain will affect the chain's finality rate.

The European Union has issued Regulation 909/2014 on improving securities settlement in the European Union and on Central Securities Depositories (*the CSD Regulation*).[426] The CSD Regulation guarantees that transfer orders which enter into such systems are also finally settled, regardless of whether the sending participant has become insolvent or if transfer orders have been revoked in the meantime. It refers to MiFID when defining the term 'transferable securities' which defines these as those securities which 'are negotiable on the capital market'. While acknowledging the importance of finality, ESMA notes that settlement finality would change due to different DLT infrastructures operating in different ways. Lastly, Article 39 of the CSD Regulation[427] provides for adequate protection is offered to all participants while imposing several requirements on the central securities depositaries themselves. In Malta, the Malta Stock Exchange has established a system for clearing and settlement of transactions in financial instruments admitted to the exchange and have not been cleared by international central securities depositaries. This system is known as MaltaClear.[428] All settlements are to be done as dictated by the Transfer of Listed Securities Regulations. It should be noted that for now, MaltaClear may only be used in relation to traditional securities.

Regulation 2022/858 on the pilot regime for market infrastructures based on distributed ledger technology *(the DLTR)* creates two systems, these being the DLT Settlement System *(the DLT SS)* and the DLT Trading and Settlement Systems *(DLT TSS)*. The DLT SS shall be used as a settlement system operated by the CSD to ensure

426. Directive 98/26/EC of the European Parliament and of the Council of 19 May 1998 on settlement finality in payment and securities settlement systems.
427. Regulation (EU) No. 909/2014 of the European Parliament and of the Council of 23 Jul. 2014 on improving securities settlement in the European Union and on central securities depositories.
428. https://www.borzamalta.com.mt/maltaclear.

the settlement of instruments traded on DLT. Meanwhile, the DLT TSS shall combine the services of a Multilateral Trading Facility and of a settlement service. The DLT TSS may be operated by either an investment firm or market operator. So far, Malta has not issued licences for these types of settlement systems.

[C] Special Requirement for Prospectus

[1] The Prospects Regulation

Being a Member State, Malta is subject to Regulation (EU 2017/1129) (*the Regulation*), creating an obligation to publish a prospectus with respect to securities offered to the public or admitted to trading on regulated markets in order to ensure investor protection. This harmonization creates a cross-border passport mechanism which facilitates the effective functioning of the internal market in a wide variety of securities.[429] It can be noted that a prospectus should only be required where those situations are accompanied by a communication constituting an 'offer of securities to the public' as defined in the Regulation. This regulation is an essential step towards the completion of a Capital Markets Union, the aim of which is to help businesses diversify the sources of capital from anywhere within the European Union, make markets work more efficiently and offer investors additional opportunities to put their money to work, in order to enhance growth and create jobs.

Article 1(3) of the Regulation establishes that the Regulation does not apply to an offer of securities to the public with a total consideration in the Union of less than EUR 1 million calculated over a period of twelve months. According to Article 3(2) of the Regulation, Member States may decide to exempt offers of securities to the public from the obligation to publish a prospectus. This is subject to two conditions: that such offers are not subject to notification in accordance with Article 25 of the Regulation and that the total consideration of each such offer in the EU is less than a monetary amount calculated over a period of twelve months which shall not exceed EUR 8 million. Member States are required to notify the European Commission and ESMA of whether and how they decide to apply the exemption in Article 3(2).[430] The EU recognizes that not all companies have the same amount of business, and as such, for the sake of proportionality, the Regulation imposes four exemptions on the need for a prospectus.[431]

[2] Prospectuses in Maltese Law

Malta has in place Prospects MTF which is a multilateral trading facility and is operated by the Malta Stock Exchange. It provides a cost-effective opportunity for small and

429. (3) Regulation 2017/1129.
430. https://www.esma.europa.eu/sites/default/files/library/esma31-62-1193_prospectus_thresholds.pdf.
431. https://www.zerafa.com.mt/the-prospectus-regulation-facilitating-security-token-offerings/.

medium-sized enterprises (*SMEs*) to raise capital by issuing bonds or equity. Companies considering admission to Prospects MTF require the services of a Corporate Advisor prior to and following the admission process. Moreover, Prospects MTF is fully compliant with the EU's MiFID.[432] In Malta, a prospectus is not required below the threshold of EUR 5 million.[433] For offers below this threshold, an issuer may seek admission to trading on the above-mentioned Prospects MTF, operated by the Malta Stock Exchange. In such cases, the issuer would need to prepare an Admission Document for review and approval by the Malta Stock Exchange.[434]

Where a prospectus is necessary, the approval and publication of said prospectus is required to be able to list any securities. In Malta, this process starts with a preliminary meeting with the MFSA during which the person wishing to trade and the MFSA may discuss the former's proposal. Once the meeting is held, the application may be opened, and one month before the application is submitted, a notification letter shall be presented to the MFSA.[435] The application and the prospectus may then be initiated. Within ten working days of the submission of the first draft of the prospectus, the MFSA will notify the applicant whether or not it will be accepting the prospectus. While the MFSA will strive to ensure that the ten-day deadline is achieved, it should be noted that this time limit may be extended in certain cases. One such case is the extension to twenty working days if the offer involves securities which are to be issued by an applicant which does not already have any listed securities. These documents shall ultimately be presented to the Board of Governors of the MFSA which will approve or refuse the prospectus and the application.

The documentation presented to the MFSA must be in line with the Regulation, the applicable MFSA Rules and must also conform with the Prevention of Money Laundering and Counter Financing of Terrorism Regulations.

[3] The Prospectus

Once the instrument is defined as a security, it would fall within the remit of the Regulation. It is clearly stipulated that the prospectus shall contain the necessary information which is material to an investor for making an informed assessment of the assets and liabilities, profits and losses, financial position, and prospects of the issuer and of any guarantor; the rights attaching to the securities; and the reasons for the issuance and its impact on the issuer. This information may vary depending on the nature of the issuer; the type of securities; the circumstances of the issue; where relevant, whether or not the non-equity securities have a denomination per unit of at least EUR 100,000 or are to be traded only on a regulated market, or a specific segment thereof, to which only qualified investors can have access for the purposes of trading in the securities. Article 6 of the Regulation states that the information must be written and presented in an easily analysable, concise and comprehensible form. One of the

432. https://www.borzamalta.com.mt/markets/prospects-mtf.
433. ESMA's list of National Thresholds.
434. Prospects MTF Rules.
435. Article 4.1A of the MFSA Capital Markets Rules.

main features of the prospectus is the summary which shall encompass key information that investors need in order to understand the nature and the risks of the issuer.

In their paper, Boreiko, Ferrarini and Giudici, it was concluded that under European prospectus regulation, Tokens that are negotiable on capital markets have to be considered tradable securities, unless the issuer can show that they have no investment component and present no financial risk. When issuers cannot provide this evidence, they have to comply with European prospectus rules, unless their offer falls within an exception.[436]

[D] International Private Law

[1] International Private Law in Malta

Due to its history, Maltese law has several sources, which, although different, tend to converge. One may categorize the sources into primary, secondary and tertiary, thus creating a hierarchy. In Malta, these are legislative, juridical and the English private international law respectively; hierarchically, the legislative source is the strongest. The Maltese legislative source is not found in one place and is scattered throughout the Maltese law. For example, the Code of Organisation and Civil Procedure *(COCP)* presents rules such as Article 742 which provides for the rules on jurisdiction. Furthermore, the COCP explains how and when foreign judgments may be enforced within Malta. With the accession of Malta to the European Union, all EU law became part of this source. This was especially important as the EU itself has several laws which allow for the harmonization of different laws, removing the need for Private International Law.

Despite not following the rule of precedence, the Maltese law also looks to case law and judgments. In cases such *Spiteri v. Soler*, the Court expounded upon which jurisdiction should be applied when it came to a case of succession. Furthermore, Maltese Courts may also sometimes refer to English case law. Moreover, English Private International Law may also be considered to be a tertiary source of Maltese private international law.

EU Law is another source of the Maltese system. The harmonization of laws which the EU has in place allows for easier dispute resolution. Laws such as Regulation 593/2008[437] on the law applicable to contractual obligations have been fundamental in the way that Member States have dealt with each other in private law matters. With the rapid growth of technology, foreign elements are commonplace when it comes to the blockchain industry.

436. Boreiko, D., Ferrarini, G. and Giudici, P. (2019) 'Blockchain Startups and Prospectus Regulation', European Business Organization Law Review, 20(4), pp. 665-694. https://doi.org/10.1007/s40804-019-00168-6.
437. Regulation 593/2008 (hereinafter referred to as 'Rome I').

[2] *Blockchain in Maltese Law*

A Smart Contract and the Decentralised Autonomous Organizations (*DAOs*) fall under the ITAS Act,[438] defined as innovative technology arrangements.[439] The term is further expanded upon in the First Schedule of the ITAS Act. The smart contract itself may be seen as having the same criteria as traditional legal contracts. Article 966 of the Maltese Civil Code[440] states that a contract may only be considered to be valid where the following four conditions are present: all parties involved must be able to contract. Legal persons are also capable of contracting by virtue of their Memorandum and Articles; all parties must have entered into the contract willingly; the contract must describe the subject matter; and it must have a lawful consideration. Maltese contract law is mainly based on the civil tradition, and as such, the formalities of the contract are important for it to be valid. Furthermore, in the case of any discrepancies between the written agreement and the underlying code, ITAS Act specifically states that 'the English language shall prevail'.[441]

The VFAA actually defines the smart contract and describes it as being 'computer protocol; or an agreement concluded wholly or partly in an electronic form, which is automatable and enforceable by computer code, ... and which may be also enforceable by ordinary legal methods or by a mixture of both'. While this was not tried in a Maltese Court as at the time of writing, it can be inferred that through this definition, a smart contract could fall within the scope of traditional contract law. The Maltese Courts have not yet encountered cases which consider the issue of blockchain within the main background of private international law. The Civil Court has jurisdiction over VFA-related disputes as stated in Article 2 of the VFAA. In 2016, the Arbiter for Financial Services Act established an Arbiter which shall 'deal with complaints filed by eligible customers'. Article 2 of the same act states that an eligible customer means that a person who is a consumer of a financial services provider.

[3] *Blockchain under English Law*

As explained above, the Maltese private international system refers to the English private international law culture, and as such, it is necessary to also look at the English perception of blockchain. In 2019, UK legislators considered the question of dispute resolution and the UK Jurisdiction Taskforce *(UKJT)* issued a legal statement in which the concept of property was discussed. The UKJT concluded that each crypto asset would need to be studied before one could conclude that it may be considered to be property. The fact that the crypto asset is intangible does not fall outside the English idea of private property; however, since crypto assets only exist on a virtual plane, they cannot be considered to be instruments as per the Bills of Exchange Act. In the same document, the UKJT considered the smart contract by comparing it to traditional

438. Chapter 592 of the laws of Malta.
439. Article 2 of Chapter 592 of the laws of Malta.
440. Chapter 16 of the laws of Malta.
441. Article 8(4)(e) of the ITAS Act.

contracts which is when two parties come together to reach an agreement, thereby creating a legal relationship between themselves. The Taskforce reasoned that the aim of the smart contract is to do exactly that, albeit in a virtual space. The legal statement explains that 'English law does not struggle with the concept of anonymous or pseudonymous parties contracting', as such English law is equipped to handle bilateral smart contracts but also those which are created through DAOs. This points towards English law considering smart contracts to fall within the scope of traditional contract law. As such, cross-border transactions wherein a smart contract is involved shall be considered in the same way as a traditional contract. In a decentralized environment, this might not be as clear except when the platform's terms and conditions provide for such. This presents somewhat of a grey area, and knowing in which jurisdiction to open a claim is not the easiest task.

[4] EU Law

The many private law regimes have created some confusion as to which laws should be chosen. Consequently, the European Union adopted Rome 1 in 2008 with the aim of harmonizing how contract law is dealt with. Rome I allows contracting parties the freedom of choosing the law which shall govern their agreement. In the event that parties do not determine the governing law, Rome I has extensive rules catering for such a situation based on the type of contract.

As explained above, in Maltese law, a smart contract may be considered to have all the criteria of the traditional contract, thereby falling within the scope of Rome I. It should be noted that Rome I does not cover the smart contract itself but rather the agreement which is being concluded through the smart contract software. Furthermore, Regulation No. 1215/2012, also known as the Brussels Recast, delves into jurisdiction and the recognition and enforcement of judgment in civil and commercial matters. This regulation provides that their place of domicile shall be the place where they shall be sued. However, Sections 2 to 7 of the Brussels Recast provide for the exceptions to this rule. The Court of Justice of the European Union has been referred to multiple times for the proper interpretation of this law.

In 2021, in Case C-709/19, the Court of Justice considered the case between Vereniging van Effectenbezitters and BP Plc, considering the latter's liability for losses suffered by persons who had bought ordinary shares in BP through an investment account in the Netherlands.[442] The referring court asked about which jurisdiction is the correct one under Brussels Recast. The main question was about Article 7(2) of the Brussels Recast which distinguishes between a sale of goods and the provision of services.[443] The Court considered what would happen in case that one of the elements was not bound by European law. The Court explained that the rule of special jurisdiction must be strictly interpreted and should not be interpreted widely to 'encompass any place where the adverse consequences of an event, which has caused

442. Judgment of 12 May 2021, *Vereniging van Effectenbezitters v. BP Plc*, Case C-709/19.
443. Article 7(2) Brussels Recast.

damage actually arising elsewhere, can be felt.'[444] The place where the alleged damage 'actually manifests itself' would be the place of jurisdiction. In its conclusion, the Court went further to explain that this 'must be interpreted as meaning that the direct occurrence in an investment account of purely financial loss resulting from investment decisions'. Moreover, the Court explained that a listed company can reasonably anticipate legal consequences in the jurisdictions where it has met its regulatory obligations. Through this reasoning, the Court came to the conclusion that an international court could not have jurisdiction over such a case.

[E] Regulatory Specifics for Organized Trade

The Maltese financial industry is governed by Chapter 370 of the laws of Malta which is entitled the Investment Services Act *(the Act)*. Through various European Union regulations and directives, this legislation has developed a number of subsidiary regulations, one of which are the Regulations on Multilateral Trading Facilities and Organised Trading Facilities *(the Regulation)*.[445]

This regulation defines multilateral trading facilities *(MTFs)* and organized trading facilities *(OTFs)* in the same manner as they are defined under *MiFID*, and it requires that companies operating such services must be Maltese investment firms or market operators.[446] Other requirements include transparent rules on how to best execute clients' orders and how to determine which financial instruments may be traded on their systems.[447] Besides the regulations which are stated in the MTF Regulation, operators in Malta must ensure to comply with the following regulations:

Control of Assets Regulations – Provides for the protection of the clients' assets which are in control of the operators. It is emphasized that operators shall always keep the best interest of the clients at the forefront. Should this not be followed, an injured client may present his case in front of the Arbiter for Financial Services.[448]

The MFSA Investment Services Rules for Investment Service Providers – Covers the main requirements of a licence for providing investment services. It is important to note that the MFSA has various rules which pertain to different kinds of investment services firms. Part BI of the Investment Services Rulebook pertains specifically to licence holders which qualify as MiFID firms.[449]

Conduct of Business Rulebook – Sets out a comprehensive framework on how to conduct financial services from Malta, thus ensuring the integrity of the financial sector in Malta and the protection of clients.[450]

444. Judgment of 12 Sep. 2018, Lober. Case C-304/17.
445. The Multilateral Trading Facilities and Organised Trading Facilities Regulations (hereinafter referred to as 'Subsidiary Legislation 370.39').
446. Article 2 of Subsidiary Legislation 370.39.
447. Article 3(a)-(g) Subsidiary Legislation 370.39.
448. Article 21 of Chapter 555 of the laws of Malta.
449. https://www.mfsa.mt/wp-content/uploads/2019/01/20181113_ISPR_Part-BI-Rules-applicable-to-Investment-Services-Licence-Holders-which-qualify-as-MiFID-Firms.pdf.
450. https://www.mfsa.mt/wp-content/uploads/2019/08/20190819-Conduct-of-Business-Rulebook-Revisions.pdf?Ver=10000.

The Financial Markets Act – Particularly Articles 4F and 4G. The former article provides that all regulated markets must have in place effective systems to ensure that all of their trading systems are sufficient to deal with their customer base, and under conditions of severe market stress.[451] Article 4G on the other hand provides that regulated markets will need to adopt tick size regimes for financial instruments.[452]

The EU is encouraging the growth in Distributed Ledger Technology and in May 2022, it issued the DLTR. The DLTR provides for exceptions from restrictions in MiFID, which allow for operators to use DLT. The main aim of this was to create a harmonized regulatory system within the EU, and as such, once an exception is granted in one EU Member State, it shall be valid throughout the Union.

The final text of this new regime was published on the 2 June 2022 and has been applicable since the 23 March 2023. Existing entities as well as new entities fall within the scope of this regulation. Since then, the ESMA has provided the industry with more information on the regulations via its Questions and Answers *(Q&As)* and also its Guidelines.[453]

§5.12 CAPITAL MARKETS AND BLOCKCHAIN: COUNTRY REPORT – POLAND

Aleksandra Widziewicz[454] *& Piotr Lesiński*[455]

[A] What Makes a Token a Security?

In Poland, at the moment of preparing this paper, there is no comprehensive legal regulation creating or facilitating the operation of the digital economy and the development of blockchain technology. However, the Polish legislator is taking an increasing interest in blockchain technology and DLT. This is also largely due to the adoption at EU level of Regulation 2022/858 on a pilot regime for market infrastructures based on distributed ledger technology,[456] the so-called DLT Pilot Regime. Its impact on Polish law is direct and does not differ in this respect from the legal orders

451. Article 4F of Chapter 345 of the laws of Malta.
452. Article 4G of Chapter 345 of the laws of Malta.
453. 'Pilot Regime for use of Distributed Ledger Technology in Capital Markets Infrastructure' *Maolem Weitemeyer* 17 Apr. 2023.
454. Aleksandra Widziewicz is Head of the Compliance Committee at ICC (International Chamber of Commerce) Poland and Head of the Compliance Academy at Lazarski University in Warsaw. She is Of-Counsel in Bird & Bird's Finance & Financial Regulation Group and Compliance & ESG Task Force Leader at Bird & Bird Warsaw. She widely advises on the legal and regulatory compliance, including implementation of integrated ESG & Compliance functions. She is an experienced FinTech lawyer.
455. Piotr Lesiński is a partner in the Finance & Financial Regulation team of Bird & Bird Warsaw. He specialises in financial sector regulations, e.g., CRD, CRR, BRRD, MiFID, PSD and AML, as well as capital market transactions, in particular debt capital market transactions.
456. Regulation (EU) 2022/858 of the European Parliament and of the Council of 30 May 2022 on a pilot regime for market infrastructures based on distributed ledger technology, and amending Regulations (EU) No. 600/2014 and (EU) No. 909/2014 and Directive 2014/65/EU (OJ EU. L. 2022 No. 151, p. 1).

of other EU Member States due to the binding force of the regulations. However, specific national provisions resulting from the implementation of the amendment of Directive 2014/65/EU (MiFID II) to the domestic legal order and related to the DLT Pilot Regime will be discussed later in this chapter.

In April 2018, Poland signed a declaration on participating in the European Blockchain Partnership. The Partnership is designed to be a tool for cooperation between the Member States on exchanging expertise in the technical and regulatory areas and for preparing to launch EU blockchain applications. This will facilitate a more dynamic development and implementation of blockchain applications in Europe and in parallel in Poland.

Despite the lack of any regulation that would fully and comprehensively regulate issues related to blockchain and DLT, some legislation does address the issue in certain provisions. One example may be found in Articles 300(1)-300(134) of the Commercial Companies Code, which introduces the concept of a simple joint-stock company. Article 300(31) §3 of the Commercial Companies Code states that the register of shareholders of such companies may be kept in a dispersed and decentralized database that ensures the security of the data contained therein and the proper performance of the duties of the entity keeping the records. This is a signal that the Polish legislator sees the possibilities offered by blockchain and DLT.

The blockchain technology used to register shareholders of a simple joint-stock company is associated with the latest Polish law concepts of understanding a 'document'. The idea behind this concept is information authorization. Significant importance is placed on the ability to reproduce information, not the form in which the information is provided, i.e., in 2016, the Polish Civil Code[457] was significantly amended with regard to the provisions on the media of declarations of intent and the form of carrying out legal transactions. The legal definition of the term 'document' was then changed, which should be regarded as a systemic change in the private law system.

The Polish definition of a document, provided under Article 77(3) of the Polish Civil Code,[458] places emphasis on the medium. Pursuant to Article 77(3) of the Civil Code, a document is a carrier of information which enables its contents to be recognized and permanently stored. The new definition of a document in Article 77(3) of the Civil Code breaks with the traditional view of a document as information fixed in the form of writing. The mere performance of an action in documentary form requires that the document makes it possible to identify the person making the declarations of intent (Article 77(2) of the Civil Code). This makes it possible to state that Tokens, which are records in a distributed database maintained with the use of blockchain technology (DLT), may constitute 'documents' within the meaning of Polish private law. This is because these records constitute files, allowing their content to be decoded and read and to be attributed to a given entity.

457. Act of 23 Apr. 1964 Civil Code (i.e., Journal of Laws 2023, item 1610, as amended).
458. The document is an information carrier enabling familiarization with its content.

The above-described change in understanding the form of the document brings us to the development of smart contracts. The most important element of contract law is the declaration of will. Article 60 of the Polish Civil Code introduces its legal definition, according to which the behaviour of a person who performs a legal act reveals his will in a sufficient manner, such behaviour aiming at creating, changing or terminating the legal relationship. One's act is qualified as a declaration of will if the effects are actually realized by the entity submitting the statement. The above-mentioned concept of a declaration of will also applies to declarations of will made in electronic form (even in an automated manner).

Polish law provides that the conclusion of a contract requires a mutual expression of intent of the parties. The expression of intent may be explicit or implied. The Polish Civil Code provides that the declaration of will can be expressed by any behaviour. As a result, it is possible to conclude a smart contract, which is inseparable from Tokens and blockchain technology.

In order to establish a legally binding smart contract, all the essential elements of the proposed contract must be clearly provided in the computing program. It should be sufficiently precise, clear and understandable to be validly accepted by all parties. Certain types of legal transactions have a legally prescribed form for their performance. Failure to comply with this form is subject to various negative consequences. For example, the transfer of ownership of real estate requires the form of a notarial deed for its validity. In this case, failure to comply with this requirement and the use of, for example, a smart contract would render the legal transaction invalid. Thus, such contracts would not be valid if they were performed using blockchain technology. In this scope, a change in Polish law would be required.

Having established that, in principle, the Polish private law system allows smart contracts and that qualifies Tokens as documents within the meaning of the Civil Code, it is necessary to consider whether: (i) Tokens can be classified as financial instruments under Polish law and (ii) securities may take the form of Tokens in Poland.

A Token is recognized as a property right (Pol. *prawo majątkowe*) within the meaning of the Civil Code. Thus, they can be the subject of civil law relations/relationships. The key question regarding the application of existing regulations in Poland to Tokens and ICO is whether a Token has the features of a financial instrument in accordance with the applicable legal definition.

Pursuant to Article 921(6) of the Civil Code, a security has the following basic features:

- has the form of a document (see the new definition of the document as presented above),
- embodies the debtor's obligation,
- its possession is necessary to effectively demand that the debtor fulfils the obligation (note, however, that 'possession' in this case should not be understood as physical possession of a property; the traditional 'delivery' of a document in this case should be replaced by making the corresponding entry in a securities account).

Due to the changes in the Civil Code discussed above regarding the definition of document, it can be stated that the Token will meet the first of the criteria. Moreover, if the Token is a source of the obligation between different parties, it will also meet the second criterion. If the possession of the Token is required to meet the commitment, the third criterion will also be met.

Furthermore, following the adoption of the DLT Pilot Regime at EU level, which also amends certain aspects of the MiFID II, the Polish legislator has also taken steps to implement the new EU standards into national law. Accordingly, a provision has been introduced in Article 2(1a) of the Law on Trading in Financial Instruments stating that financial instruments may be recorded by means of distributed registry technology used by a DLT-based market infrastructure operator within the meaning of Article 2(5) of the DLT Pilot Regime, under the rules set out in the provisions of the DLT Pilot Regime. Therefore, the above-mentioned provision explicitly allows for the use of DLT-based financial instruments.

However, the regulations do not allow to definitively state that each Token is a financial instrument. A specific analysis should be carried out each time for a specific type of Token. Depending on the results of such analysis, the ICO process will be covered or not covered by the supervision of the Polish Financial Supervision Authority (PFSA). The issue of delimitation of Tokens that are financial instruments from Tokens that are not financial instruments is not specific to Polish law but is common in all EU Member States. In this respect, it is necessary to wait for the Guidelines to be developed by ESMA on the basis of Article 2(5) of the MiCA Regulation, under which ESMA is to indicate the criteria for the qualification of crypto assets as financial instruments.

However, national law may have specific solutions to an extent not harmonized at EU level. An example of such regulations are as a general rule, legal regulations on securities.

Regarding the question of whether securities may take the form of Tokens in Poland, it should be stated as follows. Under Polish law, securities can be issued in electronic form (with exceptions), i.e., under the Polish Civil Code, securities do not need a material form. This is because the provisions of Articles 921(6) et seq. of the Polish Civil Code indicate that securities may take the form of documents. In our view, given the qualification of Tokens under private law as 'documents' – it should be considered that securities can be Token-based.

The above statement must, however, be accompanied by certain caveats. First, in the case of certain named securities (such as bills of exchange, cheques), the laws define their form in a specific manner so that it is not possible to freely issue them in the form of Tokens.

Second, in the case of equity securities, freedom of issuance is not permitted. This is a consequence of the closed catalogue of commercial law companies in Poland. Thus, it is not permissible to issue Tokens which would not be shares but securities resembling shares. For example, pursuant to Article 174 § 6 of the Commercial Companies Code, limited liability companies cannot issue Tokens to represent shareholders' interests in the company. Therefore, if the legislator does not explicitly permit this (as somewhat in the case of a simple joint-stock company, *see* above), tokenization of shares in limited liability companies under Polish law will not be permitted.

Third, it is not permissible to freely issue Tokens that are intended to be commodity securities, i.e., securities that contain an entitlement to dispose of a commodity in the custody of the issuer of the security, e.g., bills of lading, warehouse receipts (Pol. *dowody składowe*). This is a result of the general lack of freedom to freely create rights in rem. Due to the special nature of rights in rem (i.e., rights related to ownership, transfer of ownership and disposal of things) – the Polish legislator, which is common for continental legal systems, does not recognize the principle of freedom of contract in this respect.

On 29 September 2023, amendments to the Act on Trading in Financial Instruments[459] related to the DLT Pilot Regime came into force. The objective of these amendments is to bring the Polish legislation in line with the DLT Pilot Regime.

According to the amended Act on Trading in Financial Instruments, securities that are DLT financial instruments should be registered in DLT SS or DLT TSS in a DLT account (Pol. *rachunek*) or a DLT register (Pol. *ewidencja*). Rights in securities that are DLT financial instruments arise upon their initial recording in a DLT account or DLT register. The securities are transferred when the relevant entry is made in the DLT account or DLT register.

Shares of a company cannot be simultaneously registered in a DLT account and in the DLT register. Shares of the same company registered in the DLT account or in the DLT register cannot be registered at the same time in the register of shareholders maintained according to the Commercial Companies Code and in the Central Securities Repository of Poland (Pol. *Krajowy Depozyt Papierów Wartościowych – KDWP*). The same rules apply to bonds issued in one series. The new provisions also allow for the secondary DLT registration of shares, i.e., shares of a non-listed company registered in the register of shareholders maintained according to the Commercial Companies Code may be subsequently registered in the DLT account or DLT register.

The registration of securities that are DLT financial instruments and selection of the entity maintaining the DLT account or the DLT register requires a resolution of the general meeting of shareholders.

Shares of a company whose shares are admitted to organized trading (other than DLT MTF or DLT TSS) cannot be traded on the DLT MTF or DLT TSS. Only the securities registered in a DLT account or in the DLT register may be traded on a DLT MTF or DLT TSS.

The DLT SS or the DLT TSS may issue electronic money for cash settlement of transactions concluded on the DLT MTF or the DLT TSS, concerning DLT financial instruments registered in that DLT SS or DLT TSS.

The amended Act on Trading in Financial Instruments sets out detailed rules concerning licensing of DLT MTF, DLT TSS and DLT SS.

459. The Act of Trading in Financial Instruments dated 29 Jul. 2005.

[B] Blockchain Finality

The finality of blockchain transactions has not yet received any sufficient legal regulation in Poland. The finality of blockchain is a situation: 'after the transaction is confirmed. Finality is the state of the blockchain, under which the transaction cannot be cancelled, reversed or changed by any of the participants in this network under any circumstances. In other words, no one can do anything to the transaction and everything that happened within this transaction remains on the blockchain supposedly forever'.[460]

From this perspective, Tokens as property rights (Pol. *prawo materialne*) have a quite similar status with tangible property. According to Article 155 §1 of the Polish Civil Code, a contract of sale, exchange, donation, of property transfer or other contract obliging to transfer ownership of the object specified as to its identity transfers the ownership to the acquiring party unless a specific provision provides otherwise or the parties decide otherwise. Additionally, under Article 555 of the Polish Civil Code, the provisions on the sale of objects apply accordingly to the sale of property rights.

However, as mentioned above, if Tokens are classified as financial instruments (securities), their ownership transfer is regulated in separate legal provisions.

[C] International Private Law

Thus far, no specific legal solutions have been developed in Poland with regard to the use of blockchain technology for cross-border securities transactions. The area can be considered problematic, as it falls outside the existing legal framework of private international law.

The problem of the choice of law as it applies to the assessment of obligations is to some extent related to the choice of contract law (*lex contractus*). Indeed, the parties to a contract can, by mutual agreement, choose to make an obligation arising from a contract between them subject to a set of rules arising not from national law but, for example, from an international agreement.

An example of such *lex contractus* that could regulate the substantive law rules between parties with regard to mutual obligations could be the United Nations Convention on Contracts for the International Sale of Goods (CISG) adopted in Vienna on 11 April 1980 (CISG), which was ratified in Poland, thus becoming part of the domestic legal system.[461] According to Article 1(1) of the CISG – the CISG applies to 'sales' contracts. With regard to the trading of rights deriving from tokenized securities, the CISG would not apply, as Article 2(d) of the CISG stipulates that the CISG does not apply to the sales of stocks, shares, investment securities, negotiable instruments or money.

460. Blockchain Finality, http://alevtina.io/blockchain-finality-explained-what-and-why (accessed 11 Mar. 2020).
461. Journal of Laws of 1997, No. 45, item 286 as amended.

The Convention of 5 July 2006 on the Law Applicable to Certain Rights in Respect of Securities held with an Intermediary (the 'Convention') also does not clarify how this problem should be assessed under Polish law, as Poland has not ratified the Convention.[462]

Regulation (EC) No. 593/2008 of the European Parliament and of the Council of 17 June 2008 on the law applicable to contractual obligations (Rome I)[463] might be taken into consideration as legislation that could be used to determine the law applicable to claims arising from tokenized securities.

Rome I does not regulate the rules for determining the law applicable to an issuer's obligations towards creditors arising from tokenized securities. However, Rome I could serve as the basis for determining the law applicable to obligations arising from trading in tokenized securities.

Polish law distinguishes: registered securities (Polish: *papiery wartościowe imienne*), securities to order (Polish: *papiery wartościowe na zlecenie*) and bearer securities (Polish: *papiery wartościowe na okaziciela*). In case of the registered securities, the trading of receivables takes place by an assignment, and therefore Article 14 of Rome I would apply to the trading of registered tokenized securities. In the case of the securities to order and bearer securities, Rome I would not apply in determining the law applicable to trading in such securities because the receivables from these negotiable securities are not transferred by the assignment (such obligations are excluded from the scope of Rome I (Article 1(2)(d) of the Rome I)).

In searching for a basis for determining the law applicable to obligations arising from Token-based securities and trading in such securities, recourse should be sought in the Act of 4 February 2011 – Private International Law (Journal of Laws 2023, item 503; 'Polish Private International Law Act').

In the case of securities, the law applicable to an issuer's obligations is determined by Article 31 of the Polish Private International Law Act. This provision stipulates that an obligation arising from a security other than a bill of exchange or cheque is governed by the law of the country in which the security was issued.

In the case of trading in receivables arising from tokenized securities, the Polish Private International Law Act provides certain mechanisms for determining the law applicable to the assessment of such obligations. In the case of registered securities, the trading of receivables takes place using the assignment, and thus Article 36 of the Polish Private International Law Act will apply. This Article states that it is the law of the country to which the assigned receivable is subject that determines the effects of the assignment vis-à-vis third parties. In the case of securities to order and bearer securities, there is no provision explicitly stating the basis for determining the law applicable to the trading of claims arising therefrom. In this case, the rule of closest connection applies. It states that the applicable law is the law of the country that is most

462. According to the information published on the website of Hague Conference on Private International Law, only Switzerland, the United States and Mauritius have acceded to the Convention and ratified it [acceded on 15 Jan. 2024 https://www.hcch.net/en/instruments/conventions/status-table/?cid=72].

463. OJ. EU. L. of 2008. No. 177, p. 6 as amended; hereinafter 'Rome I'.

closely connected with the obligation in question (Articles 10 and 67 of the Polish Private International Law Act).

Nevertheless, a question that appears to remain unanswered is the determination of the law applicable to obligations arising from the issuance of securities in the form of tokenized securities by decentralized entities (so-called DAOs). In the case of such obligations, the closest connection to the law of a particular country is hard to be defined, making it difficult to determine the law applicable to them.

[D] Special Requirements for Prospectus

According to the provisions of the Polish Public Offering Act (Public Offering Act) and Regulation (EU) 2017/1129 of the European Parliament and of the Council on the prospectus to be published when securities are offered to the public or admitted to trading on a regulated market (EU Prospectus Regulation), the ICO can be considered a public offer (under Article 2 point d of EU Prospectus Regulation) in the situation when the issued Tokens can be classified as securities.

Confirmation of the above conclusions can be found in the PFSA's position, which in its communication of 22 November 2017 indicated: 'Depending on the structure, ICOs may operate outside the scope of the regulations applicable to the financial market or be offered without the required authorisation, and in connection with this, buyers may be deprived of special legal protection related to this market.'[464]

The PFSA did not indicate whether, in its opinion, the ICO process should be qualified as a public offer within the meaning of Polish and European regulations. The PFSA also did not specify what criterion it would use to assess whether the ICO process should be qualified as a public offer within the meaning of Polish regulations.

As there are no specific legal regulations regarding the collection of funds through ICO, one should think about the possible use of legal instruments belonging to different areas of law. According to the PFSA's position, ICO and the sale of Tokens can be discussed in the context of legal regulations regarding the offering and trading of financial instruments. Appropriate application of the provisions on investment funds is also possible.

Issuers of Tokens under ICOs, if they are covered by the Public Offering Act and EU Prospectus Regulation, would be obliged, *inter alia*, to draw up an issue prospectus or an information memorandum. Imposing stringent requirements related to the public offering on the entities organizing ICO and drawing up a prospectus or information memorandum may decrease the attractiveness of ICOs (especially after considering relatively low own capitals and limited HR of such entities).

[E] Regulatory Specifics for Organized Trade

Since the beginning of 2018, the PFSA has established a new fintech department whose tasks include supporting the development of innovations in the financial markets,

464. The PFSA's statement on Initial Token Offerings – ITOs and Initial Coin Offerings – ICOs.

including managing the sustainable development through integrated activities in the area of financial, regulatory and supervisory technologies.[465]

One of the most important initiatives in the area of the use of blockchain technology in the financial market that has been manifested by public authorities is the launch of the DLT Virtual Sandbox (blockchain). Indeed, on 1 February 2023, the PFSA announced that it was launching the DLT Virtual Sandbox.[466] The DLT Sandbox is aimed at entities operating in various market segments. Innovative entities from the capital, investment, banking or insurance markets can apply to the sandbox. The DLT Virtual Sandbox is a sign of the Polish financial market opening up to new technological solutions. It should be noted that it complements the PSD2 Virtual Sandbox, designed for payment services innovation.

In January 2018, the Polish Banks Association (Pol. *Związek Banków Polskich*) came up with an initiative to use blockchain in cooperation with the National Clearing House (Pol. *Krajowa Izba Rozliczeniowa*) and the Credit Information Bureau (Pol. *Biuro Informacji Kredytowej*). These organizations prepared a joint report on the industry solution relating to a durable medium, in which two of the three solutions suggested for banks are to be based on blockchain technology. Although this study was written several years ago, it has not lost its relevance. The recognition of blockchain and Tokens as possible technological solutions to provide a 'durable medium' is consistent with the private law understanding of Tokens as documents (*see* above). The subject of blockchain usage in banking sector is continued in the works of the Polish Bank Association (*see* among others the Report 'Digitization of Corporate Banking 2021').[467]

Moreover, KDPW has implemented its Blockchain Platform for the Capital Market.[468] According to the public information about the platform, it should be an open, fully secure infrastructure for the capital market that supports post-transaction services. One of its most important applications is to be an eVoting application providing support for general meetings. According to KDPW, the application 'will provide capital market participants – such as KDPW, public companies, as well as banks and brokerage houses – with joint access to data on exercising voting rights in almost real time, as well as access to reliable results of electronic (remote) voting'. Nevertheless, however innovative, this program has not developed as much as one might have hoped. It should be noted, however, that the above-mentioned DLT Sandbox launched by the PFSA takes place with the Central Securities Depository's participation. Furthermore, both the KDPW solution discussed here and the DLT Blockchain Sandbox use the same technological solutions (hyperledger fabric). It is therefore to be expected that work on the implementation of blockchain in the financial sector will continue to develop.

A positive example of such work and the development of blockchain implementation by entities in the financial sector is the Private Market platform opened by the

465. https://www.knf.gov.pl/?articleId=61228&p_id=18 (accessed 6 Oct. 2023).
466. https://www.knf.gov.pl/dla_mediow/galeria?articleId=81045&p_id=18 (accessed 6 Oct. 2023).
467. Cyfryzacja-Bankowosci-Korporacyjnej-13-12-2021-r (zbp.pl).
468. https://blockchain.kdpw.pl/en/ (accessed 6 Oct. 2023).

Warsaw Stock Exchange (WSE). The Private Market platform based on blockchain is designed to connect investors with non-public (unlisted) companies seeking capital.[469] Therefore, it is supposed to be a de facto crowdfunding (social investing) platform, but for companies at every stage of development.[470] The construction of this platform is one of the main points of the WSE's strategy.[471]

The use of blockchain technology results in a change of processes and workflows. It affects business structures and the corresponding regulatory and compliance requirements. Polish banks and financial institutions have recognized the potential of blockchain technology. However, the development of blockchain in Poland has been hindered by a lack of comprehensive legal regulations covering all aspects of this technology, including consumer protection, cyber security (not only the General Data Protection Regulation), business integrity and other compliance-related issues.

§5.13 CAPITAL MARKETS AND BLOCKCHAIN: COUNTRY REPORT – SPAIN

Jose Luis Lorente Howell[472]

[A] What Makes a Token a Security?

To date, there is no specific harmonized law governing initial coin offerings in Spain and no cryptocurrency issuing has been registered, authorized or verified by an official regulator or supervisory agency in Spain.

Following the trend started by the UK regulator in 2016, in July 2018, the Spanish Ministry of Economy and Business published the preliminary draft bill for the Law of 'digital transformation of the financial system' which shall provide for a safe testing environment (commonly known as 'Sandbox').[473] This Sandbox, which is fully operational and has already admitted 11 projects,[474] operates as a testing area

469. https://www.gpwpm.pl/ (accessed 6 Oct. 2023).
470. https://www.stockwatch.pl/wiadomosci/gpw-zastosuje-blockchain-oraz-chce-byc-dostawca-infrastruktury-dla-crowdfundingu,akcje,240997 (accessed 6 Oct. 2023).
471. https://www.bankier.pl/wiadomosc/GPW-prowadzi-zaawansowane-prace-nad-platforma-oparta-na-technologii-blockchain-8459256.html (accessed 6 Oct. 2023).
472. Jose Luis Lorente Howell is partner and head of Bird & Bird's Finance & Financial Regulation department in the Madrid office. He is ranked in Chambers FinTech Guide and was recognized by Legal 500 and Best Lawyers in Spain in 2023 edition and he specializes in the banking, financial and insurance regulation, providing advice to national and foreign banks and other regulated entities in financial regulatory matters, including payment services regulation, electronic banking and virtual financial services, including particularly DLT-based financial products, compliance standards and procedures before Spanish authorities such as the Spanish Central Bank and the Spanish Securities and Exchange Commission (CNMV).
473. Ministerio de Economía y Empresa, *Proyecto de Ley de medidas para la transformación digital del sistema financiero*, https://portal.mineco.gob.es/RecursosArticulo/mineco/ministerio/participacion_publica/audiencia/ficheros/ECO_Tes_180711_AP_Ley_transformacion_digital_sistema_financiero_fin.pdf (accessed 6 Oct. 2023).
474. The status of all the admitted and concluded projects can be accessed at the Fintec & Innovation Portal: https://www.cnmv.es/portal/Fintech/Innovacion.aspx?lang=en (accessed 6 Oct. 2023).

controlled and supervised by the competent authorities to study the viability of new financial projects developed using new technologies. At the conclusion of these projects, the competent authorities publish their conclusions on the website of the Spanish Stock Market Commission (hereinafter 'CNMV' by its initials from '*Comisión Nacional del Mercado de Valores*'). These conclusions serve as a basis and starting point for the development of similar projects.

Spanish market participants are engaging in the implementation of blockchain technology at different levels. Spanish banking, energy and telecommunications companies are participating in an initiative known as *Alastria*, a non-profit consortium – with Banco Sabadell as founding partner – created in order to establish a semi-public blockchain infrastructure. Additionally, many Spanish entities are developing their own innovation laboratories where they are testing distributed ledger technology.

The CNMV is aware of the worldwide proliferation of this phenomenon and, accordingly, has taken an active approach on the implications of blockchain-based cryptocurrencies – and more generically, '*crypto-assets*' – when issued and/or commercialized in Spain. In this sense, the CNMV launched a Fintech & Innovation portal on the website in 2016,[475] through which companies can engage to enquire about different aspects of securities market legislation surrounding the Fintech environment, including the need to obtain an authorization or licence prior to starting certain activities.[476] The CNMV publishes periodically a summary of the questions received through this portal, highlighting the position of the CNMV in relation to specific questions and issues. Such summary of Q&As has become a valuable legal resource for lawyers and entrepreneurs.[477]

On 8 February 2018, the CNMV and the Central Bank of Spain published a joint press statement on '*Cryptocurrencies and Initial Coin Offerings*'.[478] This statement, which remains 'in force', clarified that the concept of initial coin offering or '*ICO*' involves, in the eyes of Spanish securities market regulator, not only the issuance of 'pure' cryptocurrencies (such as Bitcoins or Ether) but also the issuance of other assets commonly referred to as 'Tokens'. The statement of the CNMV describes two categories of 'Tokens':

(1) 'Security Tokens' which are defined as those that generally provide a share in the future revenues or increased value of the issuing venture or business.

475. Fintec & Innovation Portal *supra* n. 475.

476. According to the disclaimer that appears in the CNMV portal 'This document is not regulatory. Its purpose is to transmit to the sector and, in particular, to entities wishing to operate in the FinTech field, interpretation criteria for the proper implementation of the securities market rules that may apply to them.'

477. Q&As addressed to FinTech companies. The last update of this Q&A summary was carried out on 14 Oct. 2022: https://cnmv.es/docportal/Legislacion/FAQ/QAsFinTech.pdf (accessed 6 Oct. 2023).

478. Banco de España & Comisión Nacional del Mercado de Valores (CNMV), *Joint press statement by CNMV and Banco de España on 'cryptocurrencies' and 'initial coin offerings' (ICOs)*, http://www.cnmv.es/Portal/verDoc.axd?t={6f310cc7-6b39-4405-a8f7-70d2b1e682d1}, (accessed 6 Oct. 2023).

(2) 'Utility Tokens' are defined as those granting access to a service or a product, despite the fact that mention is commonly made at the time of offering to the appreciation and liquidity expectation or to the possibility of trading them on specific markets.

Simultaneously to the joint press statement with the Central Bank of Spain, the CNMV published a separate document under the title '*CNMV considerations on cryptocurrencies and ICOs addressed to market professionals*' in February 2018.[479] In this document, the CNMV states that a good number of operations structured as *ICOs* should be legally treated as public offerings of transferable securities and thus be subject to the regulatory requirements under the Previous Spanish Securities Market Act[480] due to the broad definition of '*transferable security*' set forth in its Article 2.

It would appear, from the initial criteria of the CNMV, that both types of Tokens are not necessarily mutually exclusive, and therefore Utility Tokens can also be considered by the CNMV as a speculative investment asset provided that it is offered referring explicitly or implicitly to the expectation that the investor will obtain a profit as a result of its rise in value or of some remuneration associated with the instrument, its liquidity or tradability.

On 20 September 2018, the CNMV published an update on '*Criteria in relation to ICOs*' through the Fintech & Innovation portal,[481] according to which the CNMV confirmed its inclination for excluding from the category of '*transferable securities*' on a case-by-case basis. In these models, it is not reasonable to establish a correlation between the revaluation or profitability expectations of the Token and the evolution of the underlying business or project.

Should an ICO be considered a public offering of transferable securities, the issuance of the relevant Tokens would principally require an authorization of the issuer by the CNMV, approval of a prospectus and full compliance with detailed regulation pertaining to public offerings, including duty to register with the CNMV the issuer's financial statements duly audited and requirements relating to the admission to trading of the securities in regulated markets contained in the LMV. Furthermore, in theory, it would trigger the duty to submit a declaration of responsibility of Directors, relevant information and market abuse monitoring, own-shares regime (Article 126 LMV), and periodic information duties compromising both annual and half-year reports (Article 118-123 LMV) with the indication of significant events and their impact on the financial position of the issuer.

In 2023, Law 6/2023 of 17 March on Securities Markets and Investment Services (hereinafter 'LMV' by its initials from '*Ley del Mercado de Valores*')[482] was passed, has

479. Comisión Nacional del Mercado de Valores (CNMV), *CNMV considerations on cryptocurrencies and ICOs addressed to market professionals*, http://www.cnmv.es/Portal/verDoc.axd?t={62395018-40eb-49bb-a71c-4afb5c966374}, (accessed 6 Oct. 2023).

480. Previous Spanish Securities Market Act: Real Decreto Legislativo 4/2015, de 23 de octubre, por el que se aprueba el texto refundido de la Ley del Mercado de Valores.

481. Comisión Nacional del Mercado de Valores (CNMV), *Criteria in relation to ICO*, http://cnmv.es/DocPortal/Fintech/CriteriosICOsEN.pdf (accessed 6 Oct. 2023).

482. Ley 6/2023, de 17 de marzo, de los Mercados de Valores y de los Servicios de Inversión.

been in force since April of the same year, and sets the criteria for Spanish regulators in relation to the admission of securities represented by distributed registration technology as negotiable securities.

Article 2(2) LMV makes it clear that financial instruments shall continue to be considered negotiable securities 'when they are issued, registered, transferred or stored using distributed registration technology or other similar technologies to support such actions'. Furthermore, throughout this new LMV, traditional negotiable securities are equated with negotiable securities issued using DLT technology.

In relation to the advertising of crypto assets as a means of investment, it is important to note that, in January 2022, the CNMV approved its Circular 1/2022, of 10 January,[483] in which it details the regulations relating to the advertising of this type of crypto asset.

Circular 1/2022, of 10 January, applies to any natural or legal person, whether they are crypto asset service providers, advertising service providers or simply private individuals who carry out advertising activities aimed at drawing the public's attention, directly or indirectly, to crypto assets as a means of investment.

Circular 1/2022 indicates that any advertising activity must be clear, balanced, impartial and not misleading, always using language that is direct and easy to understand. In addition, it includes specific wording that must be included in all communications on the subject, including two mandatory disclaimers contained in Article 5[484] of Circular 1/2022, of 20 January. It also regulates how to refer to past and expected returns. In summary, on expected returns, it is required that they must be shown in a very clear and comprehensible manner, and on past returns (which are preferably not included), the rule indicates that positive returns achieved in the past may be included provided that they are not returns for periods of less than twelve months, indicating the exact period in which they were achieved, mentioning the returns of the intermediate periods between these optimal returns and the present time, and including information on periods in which a greater percentage depreciation would have occurred.

Furthermore, this rule is intended to be adapted to all types of advertising activity, including commercial videos that may appear on social networks or other platforms that limit the duration of the video and are complemented with secondary communications. All essential information about the crypto assets must be mentioned in the main communication and that the advertiser must clearly state at the beginning of the video that it is an advertising activity.

483. Circular 1/2022, de 10 de enero, de la Comisión Nacional del Mercado de Valores, relativa a la publicidad sobre criptoactivos presentados como objeto de inversion, https://www.boe.es/boe/dias/2022/01/17/pdfs/BOE-A-2022-666.pdf (accessed 9 Oct 2023).

484. First mandatory disclaimer: 'Investment in crypto-assets is unregulated, may not be suitable for retail investors and the full amount invested may be lost.' Second mandatory disclaimer: 'It is important to read and understand the risks of this investment which are explained in detail at this location.'

[B] Blockchain Finality

From a civil law perspective, and as an approach to establish legal finality, there have been attempts to consider Blockchain as a (decentralized) register similar to a public register, such as the land registry which is administrated by a neutral and independent government body, and therefore that, in theory, could be subject to public credence and legal presumption of correctness and integrity (*Principio de la Fe Publica Registral*). However, in Spain, the legislator determines what is subject to public credence, and since it has not made any provision in this regard, the blockchain is *lege lata* principally not subject to public credence – and notwithstanding the recent generic recognition under the LMV.

As mentioned above, the recently enacted LMV has introduced a degree of flexibility and provided DLTs with a new level of certainty and legal finality. With regard to the incorporation (Article 10 LVM) and transfer (Article 11 LVM) of securities, the new LMV provides that this will occur with the registration in the system used. Moreover, Article 11(2) LVM provides that 'The transfer shall be effective against third parties from the moment that the registration in the book-entry system or in the system based on distributed registration technology, as the case may be, has been effected.'

In the same vein, Article 13 LVM makes it clear that the rightful holder of the securities shall be presumed to be the one recorded in the DLT-based system. Even the constitution of rights and encumbrances on these securities must be recorded in the DLT system to be valid and enforceable against third parties.

In relation to the registration, regardless of who is the issuer of the securities represented by DLT technology, the entity designated by the issuer as responsible for the administration of the registration and recording of the securities has the obligation to have a contingency plan to ensure adequate management of incidents that may affect the network used and the continuity of the register in situations of failure in its operation or because it is no longer viable, for whatever reason, to use it as a registration system.[485]

All entities responsible for the administration of the registration and recording of securities represented by DLT technology will be listed in an official, freely accessible public register which is managed by the CNMV.[486]

485. Article 5.2 of Real Decreto 814/2023, de 8 de noviembre, sobre instrumentos financieros, admisión a negociación, registro de valores negociables e infraestructuras de mercado. (This Royal Decree is one of the implementing regulations of the LMV.) https://www.boe.es/boe/dias/2023/11/09/pdfs/BOE-A-2023-22764.pdf (accessed 13 Nov. 2023).

486. Article 2, letter 'b', of Real Decreto 815/2023, de 8 de noviembre, por el que se desarrolla la Ley 6/2023, de 17 de marzo, de los Mercados de Valores y de los Servicios de Inversión, en relación con los registros oficiales de la Comisión Nacional del Mercado de Valores, la cooperación con otras autoridades y la supervisión de empresas de servicios de inversión. (This Royal Decree is one of the implementing regulations of the LMV.) https://www.boe.es/boe/dias/2023/11/09/pdfs/BOE-A-2023-22765.pdf (accessed 13 Nov. 2023).

[C] Special Requirements for Prospectuses

There are cases under which an ICO may not be considered a public offering of securities under Spanish law, depending on the volume and the addressees, cases in which in turn the prospectus will not be required.

The CNMV, in the aforementioned document '*CNMV considerations on cryptocurrencies and ICOs addressed to market professionals*', points to two factors in assessing whether an ICO should be considered to be offering tradable securities:

- That the Tokens attribute rights or expectations of participation in the potential revaluation or profitability of revaluation or profitability of businesses or projects, or, in general, that they present or confer rights equivalent or similar to those attaching to shares, debentures or other financial instruments; and
- For Utility Tokens, those which refer, explicitly or implicitly, to the buyer's or investor's expectation of a benefit from its revaluation or from some remuneration associated with the instrument.

According to Article 35(2) of the LMV, an ICO will not be considered a public offering:

- If it is exclusively addressed to qualified investors.
- If it is addressed to less than 150 natural or legal persons per EU Member State, without including qualified investors.
- If it is addressed to investors who acquire securities for a total consideration of at least EUR 100,000 each.
- The unit nominal value amounts to at least EUR 100,000.
- It is issued for a total amount of less than EUR 5 million in the European Union, which limit shall be calculated over a period of twelve months.

However, irrespective of whether or not the ICO qualifies as a public offering, if the Tokens themselves can be considered tradable securities, the applicable regulation will be that of the investment services. Particularly, if the placement and commercialization comprise tradable securities generally addressed to the public and is carried out using any form of media communication or advertising, a financial institution authorized to provide investment services (placement and/or underwriting, as the case may be) must intervene for the purposes of marketing.[487] The CNMV in its report '*Questions and Answers on the prospectus regime to be published in public offers and admissions to trading on regulated markets*' recommends that, in case of doubt, a prospectus should be filed and points out that the CNMV will cooperate as far as possible.

Also, it should be pointed out that, irrespective of the place of issuance of the Tokens, if they qualify as transferable securities, their active marketing in Spain (for

487. Article 35(3) Previous Spanish Securities Market Act (Real Decreto Legislativo 4/2015, de 23 de octubre, por el que se aprueba el texto refundido de la Ley del Mercado de Valores), https://www.boe.es/buscar/act.php?id=BOE-A-2015-11435 (accessed 9 Oct. 2023).

instance, the availability of websites in the Spanish language offering the Tokens) would also be subject to the rule of intervention by an authorized financial institution.

When preparing a prospectus for an ICO, difficulties may be encountered due to the absence of a harmonized model at European level, which, in turn, may lead to dysfunctions with other European authorities. However, when a prospectus is necessary due to the characteristics of the transaction, as already mentioned, the CNMV has made public its intention to take a flexible approach, bearing in mind the principle of proportionality (especially when it is foreseeable that the transactions will not be large) in order to reduce the complexity and length of the document to the extent possible.

[D] International Private Law

As earlier noted, the Spanish authorities and local legislators have recently decided in relation to securities represented by DLT technology to level and ensure consistency with the existing treatment of traditional marketable securities. Therefore, it is not astonishing that the regulation of cross-border transactions shall be in principle the same for both types of securities.[488]

On the one hand, Spanish investment firms that would like to provide their services in other countries will always need prior authorization from the CNMV and will be subject to its control and inspections. When it comes to investments in third countries outside the EU and EEA, they will have to comply with all the regulations of the destination country.

On the other hand, in the case of companies from EU or EEA countries, they will continue to be governed and subject to regulation and the competent authorities of their home countries. These competent authorities will merely have to notify the CNMV in advance. In the case of investment institutions and credit institutions from third countries, they will require authorization from the CNMV and the Bank of Spain, as appropriate, and will be fully equivalent to Spanish institutions in this respect. In any case, the CNMV will be able to intervene whenever the stability of the Spanish market is endangered.

[E] Considerations in Relation to Organized Trade and Platforms

According to the criteria of the CNMV as published through the Fintech & Innovation portal,[489] securities market trading regulations should apply to platforms that carry out trading activities of financial products. Accordingly, should the relevant crypto asset be considered a financial instrument, in theory the platform should request an authorization, including where appropriate, authorization as trading venue (such as a regulated market, a multilateral trading system or an organized trading facility). Furthermore, the management of the trading venue should be carried out by an investment firm or

488. The regime is set out in Articles 142 to 151 LMV.
489. Comisión Nacional del Mercado de Valores (CNMV) Fintec & Innovation Portal, *supra* n. 475.

a market operator and would be subject in general to market regulations and CNMV's supervisory scope.

However, the expectations of the CNMV towards platforms where cryptocurrencies or other crypto assets are traded go beyond the trading of regulated financial products. In this sense, CNMV has clarified that in its view these trading platforms should be subject to rules related to custody, registration, management of conflicts of interest between clients and transparency on fees, as well as anti-money laundering requirements.[490]

Two projects related to financial asset trading platforms have already been admitted to the Sandbox. The first, promoted by Renta 4 Banco, S.A. Grupo Lar Inversiones Inmobiliarias, S.A. Iobuilders Blockchain Tech & Ventures, S.L., aims to develop a DLT-based platform for issuing, trading and settling financial instruments in the real estate sector. The second, promoted by Adventurees Global Group S.L., seeks to create a similar platform but applicable to any sector, and products issued by all types of companies, especially small- and medium-sized enterprises. Both projects are at a very early stage, pending the start of testing, but their development and the conclusions drawn by supervisors will undoubtedly be a key element in the question of how DLT-based securities trading platforms will operate.

Other aspects that have been the subject of much discussion are, on the one hand, the applicability of the standard securities market regulation, and, on the other hand, the impossibility to grant rights independently from the underlying smart contract.

First, the applicability of the standard securities market regulation has been challenged by certain Spanish scholars arguing that most of the Token-based projects which have been launched recently did not comply with the key feature required under Article 5 of the Previous Spanish Securities Market Act for tradable securities, that is, the requirement of being represented by either book entries or certificates, neither of which apply to Tokens precisely because crypto assets are essentially decentralized data structures.

Second, Tokens – as opposed to tradable securities – do not necessarily incorporate autonomous credit rights that allow trading independently from the underlying smart contract. Moreover, it has been also argued that as long as the Token solely confers a right to access a digital usage, platform or service, it should not be considered a security.

However, the new LMV has settled these discussions with its Article 6(1): 'Transferable securities may be represented by book-entry securities, certificates *or systems based on distributed record-keeping technology*.' Therefore, and as already announced by the CNMV, the possibility of registering rights that may be considered transferable securities through distributed ledger technology or blockchain cannot be legally excluded.

Another new consequence of this Article 6(1), together with Articles 8(4) and 7,[491] is that Tokens are now tradable on Spanish regulated markets, multilateral trading

490. Q&As addressed to FinTech companies, *supra* n. 477.
491. Articles 6(1), 7 and 8 of LMV, *supra* n. 485.

facility (MTF) or organized trading facility (OTF). However, following the criteria of the CNMV, when Tokens are traded on markets other than Spanish one, it is the law (and the competent authority) of the country where the Tokens are traded the one that determines the specific form of representation of the securities required and, where applicable, whether or not it is necessary to keep the records in a central securities depository.

Overall, it becomes essential a close analysis of the features and rights embedded in each project where Tokens are issued in order to assess whether or not beyond acting as a digital voucher of a future product or service, it also entails the right to benefit from a potential revaluation of the market price of the Token.

Therefore, our recommendation based on experience would be to, prior any attempt of implementation of a Token-based project in Spain, engage in educational lobbying efforts with key officials of the CNMV in order to explain the business model behind and clarify the regulatory applicable framework in Spain. Also, this dialogue would give the opportunity to test arguments used in other jurisdictions and benefit from any endorsements received from other European authorities.

§5.14 CAPITAL MARKETS AND BLOCKCHAIN: COUNTRY REPORT – SWITZERLAND

Olivier Favre & Fabio Elsener[492]

Switzerland can be considered an early adopter and pioneer of the blockchain technology and is home to an active 'crypto-industry'. This development was possible, thanks to a favourable regulation and a pragmatic approach of the Swiss Financial Market Supervisory Authority (FINMA) and the Swiss legislator. FINMA applies the general regulatory framework for financial market activities based on a 'same risks, same rules' approach. At the same time, FINMA takes a technology-neutral approach when applying existing regulations to new technologies.

Swiss law was recently updated to bring Asset Tokens and Utility Tokens representing enforceable rights into the scope of Swiss securities regulation. For such purpose, the 'Federal Act on the Amendment of Federal Law to Developments in Distributed Ledger Technology'[493] (DLT Act) introduced various amendments to Swiss laws to take account of the potential offered by the distributed ledger technology (DLT). In particular, the DLT Act introduced 'DLT Rights' as the digital equivalent to certificated securities and 'DLT Trading Facilities' as a new type of licence category for trading venues for the trading of 'DLT Rights'. Moreover, the DLT Act amended Swiss

492. Olivier Favre is a Banking & Finance Partner at Schellenberg Wittmer. He advises clients on financing and capital markets transactions and regulatory matters. He co-heads the Blockchain Technologies and FinTech group at the firm. Fabio Elsener is a Senior Associate in the Banking & Finance Group at Schellenberg Wittmer and specializes in advice on Blockchain Technology.

493. *Bundesgesetz zur Anpassung des Bundesrechts an Entwicklungen der Technik verteilter elektronischer Register vom 25. September 2020*, Federal Gazette 2020, 7801.

bankruptcy law by introducing additional segregation rights for crypto assets held in custody by a third party (e.g., by a wallet provider).

[A] What Makes a Token a Security?

According to its guidelines of February 2018 (ICO Guidelines),[494] FINMA classifies Tokens from a regulatory perspective into the following three categories:[495]

(1) Payment Tokens or cryptocurrencies: Means of payment that do not confer any claims against the issuer or third parties. Payment Tokens may be used as private means of Payment if agreed between the parties to a transaction. The issuance and exchange of Payment Tokens are subject to the Swiss AML regulation.
(2) Utility Tokens: Tokens that provide rights to access or use a digital application or service, provided that such application or service is already operational at the time of the Token sale. Such Tokens must not have an investment purpose.[496] The issuance and exchange of Utility Tokens are usually subject to the Swiss AML regulation.[497]
(3) Asset Tokens: Tokens which are the digital representation of an asset, for instance, a debt or equity claim against the issuer or a third party, or a right regarding an underlying asset.

FINMA clarified that Tokens may take a hybrid form, including elements of more than one of these categories. Such Hybrid Tokens must comply cumulatively with the regulatory requirements applicable to each relevant Token category. FINMA also acknowledges that the classification of a Token may change over time.

In addition to the ICO Guidelines, FINMA also provided its views on the regulatory classification of stablecoins. These are Tokens backed by an underlying asset, e.g., a pool of fiat currency or other assets. They are not a separate type of Token category in Swiss regulation.[498] Depending on the rights that investors have according to the terms of the stablecoins, these may be classified as Asset Tokens or as a hybrid between cryptocurrencies and Asset Tokens. In respect of stablecoins that are pegged to a specific fiat currency with a fixed redemption claim that can be exercised against the issuer or a third party as the asset owner, FINMA confirmed that such stablecoins

494. FINMA, *Guidelines regarding the regulatory framework for ICOs published 16 February 2018.*
495. Note that the classification largely corresponds with the distinction between different Token categories as defined in (1) above.
496. If such an investment purpose exists, such Tokens usually fall under the Asset Tokens category.
497. An exemption from the scope of the Swiss anti-money laundering regulation is available if any payment function of a utility Token is considered to be only of ancillary nature (exception applied restrictively by FINMA).
498. FINMA, *Supplement to the guidelines for enquiries regarding the regulatory framework for initial coin offerings (ICOs)* (11 Sep. 2019).

qualify as a deposit under Swiss banking regulation[499] and, thus, not as securities (*Effekten*). To the extent that they do not represent any enforceable right, but the issuer just holds an asset pool without being obliged to satisfy redemption claims of investors from such asset pool, they may also be classified as a Payment Token. With this approach, a case-by-case analysis of stablecoins is needed to assess their regulatory implications under Swiss law.

Asset Tokens would be classified as securities (*Effekten*) under Swiss law if they:

(1) confer an enforceable right against the issuer or a third party;
(2) are issued as uncertificated security, derivative or book-entry security; and
(3) are offered with identical terms to more than twenty investors.

A classification of the Tokens as securities must, for instance, be considered when issuing Tokens on behalf of third parties[500] and for secondary market trading activities. In addition, any Tokens classified as securities (*Effekten*) may require a prospectus in accordance with the Swiss Financial Services Act (FinSA) if they were offered to the public in Switzerland or admitted to trading on a stock exchange, MTF or DLT Trading Facility in Switzerland.[501]

The classification of Tokens as securities under Swiss law does not depend on the legal finality of a transfer of Tokens. However, such legal finality of the transfer of Tokens is of importance for the valid transfer of the legal title in Tokens.[502]

[B] Blockchain Finality

As regards the civil law classification of Tokens, it is decisive whether a Token confers enforceable rights to the Token holder or not.

[1] Payment Tokens and Utility Tokens Without Claims

The majority of the Swiss legal scholars as well as the Swiss Federal Council qualify Payment Tokens and Utility Tokens that do not digitally represent an enforceable claim against an issuer or a third person as factual immaterial assets (*immaterielle Vermögenswerte*).[503] Since such Tokens are not the digital representation of any enforceable rights or claims, they are not subject to any particular Swiss law requirements regarding entitlement and transfer. As a consequence, the title in and transfer of such Tokens result solely from the rules applicable to the blockchain concerned.

499. *See* FinSA, §.5.14[D], *infra*.
500. However, the issuance of own Asset Tokens is not subject to a licence requirement in Switzerland, except for the issuance of Asset Tokens qualifying as derivatives.
501. Article 35 paras 1 et seq. FinSA.
502. *See* §5.14[B], *infra*.
503. Federal Council, *Rechtliche Grundlagen für Distributed Ledger-Technologie und Blockchain in der Schweiz*, 54, 67, https://www.newsd.admin.ch/newsd/message/attachments/55150.pdf (accessed 11 Mar. 2020); for a detailed analysis of the legal qualification of bitcoins, *see* Samuel Zogg, *Bitcoin als Rechtsobjekt – eine zivilrechtliche Einordnung*, 2 recht, 95 et seq. (2019).

[2] *Asset Tokens and Utility Tokens Conferring Claims Issued in the Form of DLT Rights*

Under Swiss law, the legal finality of a transfer of such Asset Tokens and Utility Tokens that confer claims is achieved if they are issued in the form of DLT Rights.

DLT Rights were introduced by the DLT Act in February 2021 by amending the provisions of the Swiss Code of Obligations (CO) regulating securities. They are the digital equivalent of certificated securities in the sense of tying a right to a blockchain-based register instead of a certification in a document. Once created, DLT Rights and the rights represented therein follow the principle of 'Blockchain Finality' and can only be transferred by a transfer of the relevant Tokens on the relevant distributed ledger. Moreover, holders of the DLT Rights benefit from *bona fide* protection rights similar to the protection of the owner of a certificated security.[504]

As regards the scope of DLT Rights, any rights that could be issued as certificated or uncertificated securities may be issued as DLT Rights. Therefore, they may be used to represent fungible contractual claims (e.g., debt obligations), non-fungible contractual claims (e.g., claims arising from a licensing agreement), membership rights that can be issued as certificated or uncertificated securities (e.g., shares in stock corporations), and rights in rem that can be issued as certificated or uncertificated securities (e.g., mortgage certificates). Also, book-entry securities in the sense of the Federal Intermediated Securities Act (FISA) may be issued in the form of DLT Rights. However, cryptocurrencies or the possession or factual control of assets could not be issued as DLT Rights.

Furthermore, DLT Rights may be used to create traditional book-entry securities with DLT Rights as the underlying assets. To hold DLT Rights in the form of book-entry securities under the FISA, as amended by the DLT Act, the DLT Rights would have to be transferred to an eligible financial institution acting as securities custodian which will keep the DLT Rights in custody to immobilize them. In addition, such custodian must credit the entitlements of the relevant DLT Rights to a securities account.[505] Once created, DLT Rights held as book-entry securities may only be transferred as book-entry securities under the rules of the FISA, and no transfer of the DLT Rights on the distributed ledger is possible.

The issuance of DLT Rights requires the registration of a right on a distributed ledger based on an agreement between the issuer and the first holder stipulating the registration of the relevant rights on a distributed ledger and the undertaking that such rights may only be transferred and exercised on the relevant distributed ledger. As a result of such registration, the DLT Rights may only be transferred and exercised on such blockchain. Moreover, it is advisable that the parties explicitly specify in the terms governing the DLT Rights that they wish to create DLT Rights and that Swiss law shall be the applicable law. In the absence of such a choice of law, the Swiss Private

504. Cf. Art. 973e CO; Federal Council, report on the DLT Act (*Botschaft zum Bundesgesetz zur Anpassung des Bundesrechts an Entwicklungen der Technik verteilter elektronischer Register*) of 27 Nov. 2019, 52.
505. Article 6 para. 1 let. d FISA.

International Law Act (PILA) as amended by the DLT Act stipulates that the laws of the place of incorporation or residence of the issuer would apply.[506]

In order to create DLT Rights, the designated distributed ledger must meet the following requirements:

(1) it must create a link between the DLT Rights and the distributed ledger in the sense that the holders of the DLT Rights (but not the debtor) must have the power to dispose of the DLT Rights;
(2) it must protect the integrity of the DLT Rights by appropriate technical and organizational measures against unauthorized access and changes;[507]
(3) its terms of operation, the terms of the DLT Rights and the terms governing the registration must be recorded on, or be accessible through, the distributed ledger; and
(4) the creditors of the DLT Rights must be able to consult independently the integrity of the entries relating to the DLT Rights in the distributed ledger.[508]

The Swiss rules governing DLT Rights do not prohibit keeping, in addition to the registration of the DLT Rights on the distributed ledger, an off-chain record of the relevant holders (e.g., for debt instruments, a register of investors held by the issuer). However, in the event of any conflicts, the records of the DLT Rights of the distributed ledger must prevail. The terms and conditions of the relevant instrument could not depart from such principle.

[3] Asset Tokens and Utility Tokens Conferring Claims Issued in Other Form Than DLT Rights

If such Asset Tokens and Utility Tokens are governed by Swiss law but are not issued as DLT Rights, a transfer of such rights would require, in addition to a valid transfer on the relevant distributed ledger, that also such rights represented in the Tokens are validly transferred to the transferee. As a result, the legal finality of a transfer depends on the validity of the transfer of the underlying asset. It would not be sufficient to consider the transfer as final only based on the rules governing the relevant distributed ledger.

506. *See* Art. 145a PILA.
507. Such measures include cryptographic validation procedures for the access to, and transfer of, DLT Rights. However, there is no minimum number of participants in the ledger (i.e., a permissioned distributed ledger may meet this requirement even with only few participants), and there are no restrictions regarding the applicable consensus mechanism (e.g., proof-of-work, proof-of-stake, etc.).
508. Article 973d para. 2 CO.

[C] International Private Law

Issuances of Tokens often involve parties from various jurisdictions and, therefore, give rise to questions regarding the applicable law and the determination of the competent courts regarding any disputes on a matter. Under Swiss law, these questions are governed by the PILA and international treaties on these subjects to which Switzerland is a party. To the extent there is an international treaty, it takes precedence over the PILA.[509] In connection with cross-border cases involving Switzerland and Member States of the European Economic Area, the Lugano Convention[510] is relevant and governs *inter alia* the international jurisdiction.

In connection with Asset Tokens and Utility Tokens conferring claims, the DLT Act introduced the following specific provision to the PILA to determine the applicable law: Pursuant to Article 145a paragraph 1 PILA, the laws specified to apply to a claim determine whether such claim is represented by a certificate or by other equivalent means, such as a blockchain-based register, where a Token is registered.[511] In the absence of such a choice of law, the laws of the place of incorporation or residence of the issuer would apply. Such applicable law determined pursuant to Article 145a paragraph 1 PILA also governs the transfer of the Token.[512]

Please note that the choice of law provisions for movable property pursuant to Articles 100 et seq. PILA or for intermediated securities pursuant to Article 108a PILA in connection with the Convention on the Law Applicable to Certain Rights in respect of Securities held with an intermediary of 5 July 2006 (the Intermediated Securities Convention) are not relevant for such Tokens since they do not qualify as movable property under Swiss law or intermediated securities under the Intermediated Securities Convention. Therefore, from a Swiss international private law perspective, the law chosen by an issuer in terms of Asset Tokens and Utility Tokens conferring claims would govern the relevant Tokens, including the blockchain finality of transactions thereof. In the absence of such a choice of law, the law of the place of incorporation or residence of the issuer would apply.

In connection with Payment Tokens and Utility Tokens that do not digitally represent an enforceable claim against an issuer or a third person, the above-mentioned provision of Article 145a PILA for claims that are represented in paper or equivalent form does not apply as they do not represent any claims. In addition, the Federal Council and legal scholars are of the view that Payment Tokens do not qualify

509. *See* Art. 1 para. 2 PILA.
510. Convention on jurisdiction and the recognition and enforcement of judgments in civil and commercial matters, OJ L 339, 21.12.2007, p. 3-41 (the **Lugano Convention**).
511. *See* Federal Council, *supra* n. 503, 67; for Swiss law governed Tokens, it would be necessary that such Tokens are issued as DLT Rights (*see* §5.14[B][2] *supra*).
512. For securities (certificated securities uncertificated securities or intermediated securities), please note that the transfer requirements remain subject to the governing law as determined pursuant to the relevant other rules of the PILA or the relevant international treaty (e.g., the *lex chartae sitae* for certificated securities or, for intermediated securities, the rules of the Convention on the Law Applicable to Certain Rights in respect of Securities held with an intermediary of 5 Jul. 2006).

as currencies within the meaning of Article 147 PILA.[513] However, such Tokens that do not confer enforceable rights, the title in and transfer of such Tokens are, from a Swiss law perspective, solely subject to the rules applicable to the blockchain concerned,[514] irrespective of the applicable law.

Moreover, the law applying to contractual claims that may arise in respect of Tokens (e.g., between a holder of Tokens and a wallet provider) has to be determined in accordance with the provisions regarding the applicable law for contracts pursuant to Articles 116 et seq. PILA.

As regards the competent forum, Swiss courts would be competent if they were validly chosen or otherwise competent in accordance with any applicable international treaty,[515] if applicable, or PILA. Therefore, it is recommended for Asset Tokens and Utility Tokens conferring claims to define – in addition to the applicable law – also the place of jurisdiction.

[D] Special Requirements for Prospectuses

Any Tokens classified as securities (*Effekten*)[516] require a prospectus in accordance with the Swiss Financial Services Act (FinSA) if they were offered to the public in Switzerland or admitted to trading on a stock exchange, MTF or DLT Trading Facility in Switzerland, subject to the exceptions defined in Articles 36 to 38 FinSA. In this context, an offer to the public is defined as any invitation to acquire such Tokens that is made to an unlimited circle of investors, and that contains sufficient information on the terms of the offer and the Tokens itself.[517] However, an offer of Tokens classified as securities (*Effekten*) would not require a prospectus in accordance with FinSA if they were only offered within a private placement to investors that classify as professional clients within the meaning of the FinSA and to no more than 500 investors that classify as retail investors within the meaning of the FinSA.[518] In addition, a public offer would also be exempt from a prospectus obligation if such Tokens had a minimum investment amount of CHF 100,000, such Tokens had a minimum denomination of CHF 100,000 or the total value of the offered Tokens was not more than CHF 8 million over a period of twelve months.[519]

If such exemptions are not available and a FinSA prospectus requirement applies, a prospectus must be prepared in accordance with the rules of the FinSA and the Swiss Financial Services Ordinance (FinSO). In addition to the inclusion of the relevant Swiss disclosure, this also requires an approval by a Swiss prospectus review body (e.g., SIX

513. *See* Federal Council, *supra* n. 503, 82; Felix Dasser, in: Pascal Grolimund/Leander D. Loacker/Anton K. Schnyder (Hrsg.), Basler Kommentar Internationales Privatrecht (IPRG), Basel 2020, Art. 147 N 9.
514. *See* §5.14[B][1] *supra*.
515. For example in accordance the Lugano Convention.
516. *See* §5.14[A] *supra*.
517. *See* Art. 3 let. g and h FinSA.
518. Article 36 para. 1 let. a and b FinSA; *see* for the qualification of investors as professional clients Art. 4 para. 3 and Art. 5 FinSA.
519. Article 36 para. 1 let. C to e FinSA.

Exchange Regulation Ltd.). Alternatively, prospectuses that have been approved in certain jurisdictions that are eligible for passporting under the Swiss passporting regime[520] may, subject to certain requirements, be registered with a Swiss review body. At present, in particular, a prospectus that has been approved in the EEA under the regime of the EU Prospectus Regulations by the competent EU authority is eligible for such passporting into Switzerland.

[E] Regulatory Specifics for Organized Trade

[1] Payment Tokens and Utility Tokens

Organized trading services for Payment and Utility Tokens which operate in or from Switzerland are subject to the Swiss AML regulation as such activities usually qualify as payment services. Swiss AML regulation requires *inter alia* the affiliation with an authorized self-regulatory organization (SRO) as well as KYC and reporting obligations in connection with suspicious transactions and client relationships. Furthermore, to the extent that the trading facility provides for routing of such payment and Utility Tokens to third parties, the identity of such third party must be verified.[521] As regards decentralized trading facilities, the Swiss AML regulation only applies to the extent that the trading facility can dispose of the traded Tokens. Thus, the mere intermediation of buyers and sellers without involvement in the transaction is not subject to the Swiss AML regulation.[522] Yet, FINMA has adopted a restrictive practice, and it should be clarified on a case-by-case basis whether a decentralized trading application falls under the Swiss AML regulation.

[2] Asset Tokens

Organized trading services for Asset Tokens which usually qualify as securities under Swiss regulation require, depending on the offered trading structure, either a licence as a stock exchange or as an MTF, or as a DLT Trading Facility or as an OTF.

However, licence categories of stock exchanges or MTFs, which allow the offering of multilateral trading services according to non-discretionary rules (i.e., matching of trades according to rules of the facility without discretion of the operator) in respect of securities, are ill-suited in relation to Asset Tokens, since the eligible participants are limited to prudentially supervised persons (no retail participants). Furthermore, the involvement of separate central counterparties and central securities depositories for the purpose of clearing and settlement of transactions is mandatory. This would not allow post-trading activities, which are integrated into the trading

520. Pursuant to Art. 54(2) FinSA, the Swiss prospectus review bodies may define certain jurisdictions for which prospectuses may be recognized without approval procedure in Switzerland ('passporting') if such prospectuses have been approved in accordance with the laws of such jurisdictions and are drafted in an official Swiss language or English.
521. FINMA, *Guidance 02/2019, Payments on the blockchain.*
522. *See* Federal Council, *supra* n. 503, 146 et seq.

platform, as is usual with the trading of Tokens. Therefore, only the licence categories for a DLT Trading Facility and an OTF are available in practice for offering organized trading services in respect of Asset Tokens.

Due to the above-mentioned difficulties in establishing a stock exchange or MTF for Asset Tokens that qualify as securities, the DLT Act introduced the DLT Trading Facility as a new licence category for the offering of multilateral trading services according to non-discretionary rules in relation to DLT Rights and similar Tokens represented on a distributed ledger.[523] Such DLT Trading Facility must have at least one of the following characteristics:

(1) trading is allowed by unregulated participants;
(2) the operator of the trading system centrally deposits the eligible Tokens on the basis of uniform rules; or
(3) the operator of the trading system performs the post-trading activities in relation to the eligible Tokens on the basis of uniform rules and procedures.[524] Thereby, the DLT Trading Facility is designed as a tailor-made licence category for offering multilateral trading services according to non-discretionary rules. However, the DLT Trading Facility licence category is aimed at centralized exchanges and is not designed for decentralized trading facilities.[525]

An OTF is a trading facility providing either for multilateral trading of securities according to discretionary rules or of other financial instruments[526] according to discretionary or non-discretionary rules or for bilateral trading between the participants and the operator of the OTF.[527] OTFs can only be operated by supervised banks, securities dealers, stock exchanges or MTFs that are authorized by FINMA to operate an OTF. Therefore, in relation to Tokens which qualify as securities, an OTF is only suitable if the trading between participants is executed according to discretionary rules; i.e., the trading facility must have discretion regarding the matching of a trade.[528] Subject to this limitation, banks, securities dealers, stock exchanges or MTFs may at present offer organized trading services in relation to Asset Tokens that qualify as securities. The licence category of an OTF applies also to decentralized trading facilities, provided that such decentralized structures qualify as an OTF. Please note that FINMA specified that systems not providing for the execution of trades, e.g., bulletin boards or order-routing systems, do not constitute an OTF.[529] However, the

523. *See* Federal Council, *supra* n. 503, 40 et seq.
524. Article 73a of the Swiss Financial Market Infrastructure Act (FMIA).
525. *See* Federal Council, *supra* n. 503, 41.
526. Financial instruments are defined in Art. 3 lit. a of the Swiss Financial Services Act and comprise, in particular, debt and equity securities, derivatives, structured products and index or exchange-linked deposits which do not qualify as securities (*see* §5.14[A]), *supra*, and the definition is in in particular relevant for derivatives.
527. Article 42 FMIA.
528. Article 23 of the Swiss Financial Market Infrastructure Ordinance.
529. FINMA *circular 2018/1, organized trading facilities*, no. 10.

Federal Council emphasized that such decentralized trading facility are deemed to facilitate the transfer of assets and, therefore, should fall under the AML regulation.[530]

[3] Travel Rules

In the FINMA Guidance 02/2019 on payments on the blockchain dated 26 August 2019, FINMA introduced travel rules for blockchain transactions that apply to financial intermediaries supervised by FINMA (including, without limitation, DLT Trading Facilities or OTFs) as well as financial intermediaries affiliated with a self-regulatory organization (SRO) for AML purposes (together, the Swiss VASPs). These travel rules are relevant for Swiss providers of organized trading services as they also qualify as Swiss VASPs.

Under these travel rules, when a Swiss VASP transfers Tokens from a client wallet hosted by itself to an external client wallet, the relevant Swiss VASP has to transmit the same information as required for wire transfers in fiat money or, alternatively, it must:

(1) identify the transferee in accordance with the Swiss AML rules as if the transferee was a client of the relevant Swiss VASP (only relevant for transfers to third parties); and
(2) verify the transferee's power to dispose of the wallet address used by it through appropriate technical measures as defined by the relevant Swiss VASP.

§5.15 CAPITAL MARKETS AND BLOCKCHAIN: COUNTRY REPORT – BRITISH VIRGIN ISLANDS

Sara Hall[531]

[A] Introduction

The BVI is a common law jurisdiction with its own parliament, constitution and legislature. It is not part of the UK and nor is it part of the EU. There are links to the UK, particularly in relation to legal matters. For example, legislation made by the UK

530. Federal Council, Explanatory Report on the consultation draft regarding amendments to Swiss federal law in connection with the developments with the distributed ledger technology (*Erläuternder Bericht zur Vernehmlassungsvorlage des Bundesgesetzes zur Anpassung des Bundesrechts an Entwicklungen der Technik verteilter elektronischer Register*) of 22 Mar. 2019, 24 et seq.

531. Sara Hall Sara Hall is a partner in Walkers' Global Regulatory & Risk Advisory Group. With over thirty years' experience in global senior in-house roles as well as in private practice, Sara now practises Cayman Islands, British Virgin Islands and Bermuda law. She specialises in all aspects of financial services and international regulation. Since joining Walkers, she has expanded her practice to advise on digital assets, DAOs, cryptocurrencies and NFTs.

Parliament may be extended to the BVI. As a practical matter, however, the principal instances of this in the context of financial services are in the realm of foreign policy, with UK sanctions extended to the BVI by Orders in Council. To give another example, the final appeal court for BVI cases is the Judicial Committee of the Privy Council which sits in London, England. While English law court cases are not binding on the BVI courts, English law decisions of the appeal courts of England & Wales are persuasive. The same is true for appeal court decisions of other Commonwealth countries. In the realm of the licensing of financial services activity conducted in or from within the BVI, the BVI passes its own legislation, and financial services laws and regulations implemented in the UK and the EU do typically not form part of BVI law.

[B] What Makes a Token a Security?

Financial services activity conducted in or from within the BVI falls under the supervision of the BVI's sole financial services regulator, the Financial Service Commission (FSC). To determine the question of what makes a Token a security, we must consider relevant BVI legislation and the FSC's regulatory guidance, plus any relevant case law.

Although the BVI has legislation regulating the conduct of services related to 'virtual assets',[532] that legislation does not consider whether a Token (or any other form of crypto asset) would be a 'security'. The principal BVI legislation to determine whether a Token might be a 'security' is the Securities and Investment Business Act (2020 Revision) as amended (SIBA). This legislation regulates the conduct of defined activities carried out in or from within the BVI in respect of 'investments' and does define a 'security'. SIBA does not refer to Tokens or indeed to virtual or crypto assets. Nor is there any test established in BVI case law to determine whether a negotiable instrument such as a Token, crypto asset or financial instrument is a 'security'. The FSC has however issued guidance to assist with assessing when activities involving virtual assets (such as Tokens) might fall within the regulatory perimeter. This is the '*Guidance on Regulation of Virtual Assets in the Virgin Islands (BVI)*' published in July 2020 (the 'FSC Guidance'). As the FSC is the competent regulator responsible for licensing, approving, or recognizing a person conducting securities investment business as well as supervising licensees, and taking enforcement action for non-compliance, its guidance is therefore key to interpreting this question.

The FSC Guidance is clear that Tokens may be considered 'investments' despite the absence of any express reference to virtual assets in SIBA. The FSC Guidance clarifies that if the rights and obligations of a Token mean it is conceptually synonymous to debt or equity securities or an embedded derivative on debt or equities, that Token might be characterized as an 'investment'. Certain Tokens that include profit-sharing and/or governance rights could meet the test. A simple coin or Token used as a medium of exchange or payment with no rights against any issuer would not normally be an 'investment'.

532. The Virtual Asset Service Providers Act, 2022.

For example, the FSC Guidance observes:

(i) 'Coins, for example Bitcoin, do not in of themselves typically grant the holder rights synonymous with shares. However, there have been instances where the manner in which the coin or Token is used, and the rights attached thereto would grant the holder a share or equity interest. Where a Token is therefore issued in this manner and confers such rights, the activity would be considered an investment as prescribed by schedule 1 of SIBA.

(ii) Careful analysis of the terms and features of any virtual asset product is critical. An assessment of the characteristics of the Token and token holder's rights, for example, whether there is a right to vote and determine the manner in which the proceeds raised will be utilised or a right to receive dividends declared or a share of the profit, would aid [the determination].'

Whether a Token is an 'investment' therefore depends on an analysis of the rights, entitlements and obligations (if any) embedded in the relevant instrument by either protocol/smart contract or external terms and conditions to see if it is akin to any of the categories of investments in SIBA. Given the financial instruments defined as 'investments' in SIBA are comparable to those within the definition of 'security' in SBIA, in our view, whether a Token is a 'security' requires the same analysis.

SIBA has a definition of 'security' which includes:

- a share of any kind;
- a debt obligation of any kind;
- an option, warrant or right to acquire a share or debt obligation.

The definition excludes an interest or right that the Public Issuer's Code specifies is deemed not to be a 'security'. To date, there have been no such exclusions specified. SIBA also states that for the purposes of Part V of SIBA (which relates to market abuse), 'security' has the meaning specified in Schedule 5 of SIBA. The instruments specified in Schedule 5 are as follows: shares and stock in the share capital of a company; debt securities; warrants to subscribe for shares or debt securities; depositary receipts; options to acquire or dispose of any security in Schedule 5; futures; and contracts for differences. The net effect of this means that a Token which has none of the characteristics of any of these categories of financial instrument (such as a Token with no enforceable rights) has a low risk of being considered a 'security' under BVI law.[533]

By way of illustration, we consider a number of the principal categories of 'securities' in a crypto assets context below.

533. Such a Token may be a 'virtual asset'. In this case, activities that relate to virtual assets if carried out in or from within the BVI may require consideration under the Virtual Assets Service Providers Act, 2022.

Shares, of any kind

There is no definition in SIBA of 'shares' and the concept of 'shares in and stock in the share capital of, a company' within the meaning of SIBA has not been tested in the BVI courts.

However, shares and other equity interests often give voting rights, management rights and/or rights to a share in profits that is conditional on the relevant entity or legal arrangement being solvent. The BVI's Business Companies Act (2020 Revision) as amended (BCA) does not define a 'share' although it specifies that a share in the capital of a company confers on its holder the following default rights (which may be modified in the memorandum of the company):

(i) the right to one vote at a meeting of the members of the company or on any resolution of the members of the company;
(ii) the right to an equal share in any dividend paid in accordance with the BCA; and
(iii) the right to an equal share in the distribution of the surplus assets of the company.

A Token which has one or more of these rights in relation to an issuer or indeed any other company would be more likely to be considered a security under BVI law. This might be intended by the issuer, for example, in the case of tokenized representations of shares in a BVI company or the tokenization of interests in a fund for example.

Turning to partnerships, and taking a prudent approach, a Token may be akin to an interest in a partnership and thus could be a 'share of any kind' depending on the rights if any that it gave to its holder and the goals of the token holders. There are a number of different kinds of partnership under BVI law including general partnerships and limited partnerships, with differing degrees of formality required for their establishment. The Limited Partnership Act, 2017, for example, specifies a partnership interest of a partner as the partner's:

(i) share of the assets of the limited partnership, if any;
(ii) right to receive distributions from the limited partnership, if any;
(iii) right to vote, if any;
(iv) right to any other benefit conferred by the limited partnership agreement.

It includes any liability of the partner in relation to the limited partnership. Given the rights certain token holders enjoy as part of many DAOs, it is not inconceivable that a Token with one or more of the above characteristics could by analogy be seen as a security, not least as a partnership agreement need not be in writing or signed by the partners. As a Limited Partnership under BVI requires certain formalities to be observed, it would be unlikely such a partnership would unintentionally be formed by DAO token holders, but general partnerships may be formed without any formality required. When designing and marketing a Token, therefore, it is necessary to take advice on whether this might be a risk for a particular project and, if so, how best to mitigate this risk.

Fund interest

An interest in a fund may also be a type of security under BVI. For example, SIBA defines 'fund interest' as the rights or interests, however described, of the investors in a mutual fund with regard to the property of the fund (but does not include a debt). Section 40 of SIBA defines 'mutual fund' as:

> a company or any other body, a partnership or a unit trust that is incorporated, formed or organised, whether under the laws of the British Virgin Islands or the laws of any other country, which:
>
> (a) collects and pools investor funds for the purpose of collective investment, and
> (b) issues fund interests that entitle the holder to receive on demand or within a specified period after demand an amount computed by reference to the value of a proportionate interest in the whole or in a part of the net assets of the company or other body, partnership or unit trust, as the case may be [...].

If a Token were to give its holder redemption rights such that the Token entitles its holder to receive on demand to an amount computed by reference to a proportionate interest in the assets of any of the kinds of entities referenced above (being a company, other body, partnership or unit trust) the Token might then be 'fund interest' and thus a security. This may be the case where Tokens are staked and the person staking receives another Token representing the staked Tokens if that Token gives its holder the right to redeem it at any time. An analysis of the rights (if any) which such a Token may enjoy and the computation of the amount paid out would need to be conducted to assess whether a Token in this scenario might be a security under BVI law.

Debt instruments

A Token which creates or acknowledges a debt and gives rights to claim that debt against another person would usually be considered a debt instrument and thus could be at risk of being a security. That said, a Token may have no rights to redeem against any person or legal arrangement and will provide its holder with nothing more than the opportunity to effect an interaction with a protocol rather than against any legal person or arrangement. As such, this would reduce the risk of such a Token being a security under BVI law (absent any other factors to the contrary).

Other factors

An assessment of whether a Token is a security will typically take into account statements made in marketing materials (whether these are formal such as whitepapers or less formal such as in Discord or Telegram messages) as well as terms and conditions. Well-drafted marketing materials and terms and conditions (e.g., on any website) are key elements in ensuring that the prospective purchasers and eventual token holders understand the issuer's or sponsor's intentions and will be one element that the FSC (or a court) is likely to consider in making its determination. Key to the analysis is the functionality of the particular Token and any rights that it gives holders, rather than any particular name (such as 'Utility Token') given to the Token.

[C] Blockchain Finality

There are currently no BVI laws or regulations explicitly governing the legal standing of blockchain transactions and their finality. To the extent that there is a contract between one counterparty and another (express or implied), it will be the contractual terms that govern the arrangement. Where the Token is a security or gives rights to a security (such as a share in a BVI business company), regard must also be had to the applicable BVI statute for that particular instrument (such as the BVI Business Companies Act in the case of shares in a BVI business company).

That said, as the BVI is a common law system, there is nothing particular to transfers on blockchains or distributed ledger systems that would prevent such transactions being recognized as settled with finality as a matter of BVI law. In other words, it is not necessary for the BVI to pass any law so as to give effect to transactions which are settled on a blockchain, as there is no law prohibiting settlement on a blockchain. The challenges that might be brought to such transfers apply equally to transactions in traditional financial instruments that are conducted and settled entirely off-chain. Such challenges may include transactions purportedly made at an undervalue in an insolvency context, for example. They could also include disputes as to ownership (which may then involve consideration of the proper law to determine this question). Despite blockchain being in its infancy and blockchain-specific case law being necessarily at an early stage of development, BVI cases are beginning to establish the principles applicable to such disputes. See, for example, the BVI case of *Philip Smith and Jason Kardachi (in their capacity as joint liquidators of Torque Group Holdings Limited) (in liquidation) v. Torque Group Holdings Limited (in liquidation).*[534] In this case for interim relief, the BVI court considered the UK Jurisdiction Taskforce (UKJT) publication, 'Legal statement on cryptoassets and smart contracts' and the decision in the High Court of England & Wales in *AA v. Persons Unknown.*[535] The Court confirmed that crypto assets should be treated as 'assets or property' and that the test of legal and beneficial ownership of such crypto assets was determined by ascertaining who had control of the private keys enabling control, maintenance and disposition of the crypto assets in question. As blockchain is in its infancy, and cases that are not interlocutory but full hearings on the merits will eventually be decided, this aspect of the law is expected to continue to develop.

[D] International Private Law

Questions involving private international law often arise in the context of disputes. Disputes involving Tokens and other crypto assets may be particularly complex as they often involve parties who are physically present or domiciled in different jurisdictions and thus trigger issues of private international law due to multiple legal systems being

534. *Philip Smith and Jason Kardachi (in their capacity as joint liquidators) v. Torque Group Holdings Limited* [2021] BVIHC (COM) 0031.
535. *AA v. Persons Unknown* [2019] EWHC 3556 (Comm).

in play. Where crypto assets are issued from and settled on permissionless, decentralized systems and are held in unhosted wallets (e.g., on a physical device such as a mobile phone) rather than on centralized exchanges, it may be challenging to establish applicable law – and the appropriate jurisdiction – to resolve the dispute. Each of the jurisdictions of potential relevance may take a different approach to characterizing the crypto asset in question and the associated rights (and may see the asset simply as a bundle of rights), resulting in conflict-of-law issues.

Where the parties have agreed to contractual terms, or a contract can be inferred from the conduct of the parties, this is the starting point under BVI law to determine the applicable law for such disputes. The fact that a contract is a smart contract would not invalidate such a contract, unless exceptionally, BVI law provided that the particular kind of contract had to be made by deed and have a 'wet ink' signature or comply with certain other formalities due to its subject matter.

It may not however be possible to establish the existence of any contract, or the dispute may relate to non-contractual matters such as fraud, succession or tort. The BVI would in such cases follow common law rules in determining the applicable law. This may require an assessment of whether the assets in question were movable or immovable property – or a third category of property – before any related rights could be considered. The nature of the property may be specified in a BVI statute (*see* for example *Sheikha Amena Ahmed H.A. Al-thani et al v. Sheikha Aisha Mohammed Ali Abdullah Al Thani et al*[536] which considered this issue in the context of shares in a BVI business company). In the case of Tokens that are not securities, there is no BVI statute specifying whether such Tokens are movable or immovable property or indeed a different kind of property. Therefore, regard must be had to the common law which does recognize a third category of property.[537] This has established that certain kinds of Tokens such as those on distributed, public, permissionless systems (e.g., bitcoin) are a third kind of personal property.

That said, some kinds of disputes need only decide that crypto assets are property without assessing the kind of property before a ruling can be made. The BVI courts in the context of interim relief granted in disputes involving crypto assets (and in line with a series of interlocutory decisions decided in the English courts) have ruled without needing to decide if the assets in question were moveable or immovable property or a third kind of property.

On the horizon are potential changes to private international law specifically focused on digital assets. These potential changes are included in the proposals of the International Institute for the Unification of Private Law (UNIDROIT) which included this topic in a consultation issued in January 2023.[538] The resulting rules may bring greater certainty to this area in the future.

536. BVIHC(VAP) 2021/0001 available at https://www.eccourts.org/judgment/sheikha-amena-ahmed-h-a-al-thani-et-al-v-sheikha-aisha-mohammed-ali-abdullah-al-thani-et-al.
537. *See* the consideration of this topic in the report of the Law Commission of England & Wales issued in June 2023 available at: https://www.lawcom.gov.uk/project/digital-assets/.
538. Available at https://www.unidroit.org/wp-content/uploads/2023/01/Draft-Principles-and-Commentary-Public-Consultation.pdf.

[E] Special Requirements for Prospectus

The Virtual Assets Service Providers Act, 2022, has no requirement for a prospectus to be published for Token or virtual asset issuances as a matter of BVI law. By contrast, while SIBA has no express requirements that a prospectus be issued for virtual asset or Token issuances, it does however specify prospectus requirements for the issuance of different types of 'investments'. Therefore, the SIBA provisions must be considered if the Token or virtual asset is such an 'investment' under BVI law. These provisions govern whether a prospectus must be issued for the particular kind of 'investment' and if so the specific requirements to be included in such prospectuses for different categories of 'investment'.[539] The characteristics of a Token or other kind of virtual asset must therefore be considered on a case-by-case basis to determine whether a prospectus is required by SIBA and if so the contents of such a prospectus.

Separately, whether or not a Token is a 'security' under BVI law, a 'VASP' registered as such with the FSC is also subject to the prohibitions in the Virtual Assets Service Providers Act, 2022 regarding the issuing of false or misleading marketing materials (including materials that contain an incorrect statement of fact) and dishonestly concealing a material fact (whether in marketing materials or otherwise). The BVI is not prescriptive in detailing what facts must be included, and therefore it is a question of objective judgment which information to include.

Whether a prospectus is required is also a question of the jurisdiction where the marketing, distribution or sale of the Token is to be conducted. This is typically not the BVI (or not solely the BVI). As a result, BVI issuers must consider non-BVI prospectus laws when planning their overall strategy to ensure that the proceeds of sale are lawfully obtained by the BVI issuer.

[F] Regulatory Specifics for Organized Trade

BVI law does not mandate that Tokens or virtual assets be traded on a regulated or indeed any exchange. Tokens may be traded on or off exchange. It does however require that 'VASPs' who carry out certain specified services (defined as 'virtual asset services') in relation to virtual assets in or from within the BVI for or on behalf of a customer (or user) as a business must be registered with the FSC before they are permitted to conduct those activities. The registration regime is set out in the Virtual Assets Service Providers Act, 2022 (the 'VASP Act') as supplemented by the BVI's Regulatory Code. A VASP must also comply with the BVI's anti-money laundering and countering the financing of terrorism requirements for VASPs. Although the registration does not result in a licence for the VASP, many of the requirements to obtain the registration are comparable to those required of an applicant for a licence from the FSC. In line with its risk-based approach, the FSC establishes more stringent requirements for higher-risk activities such as custodians, and trading platforms that come into control or custody of a user's virtual assets.

539. As at the date of this publication, not all of the provisions of SIBA are in force.

[1] *Virtual Assets*

The first question for a business is whether the activity is conducted in respect of a 'virtual asset' within the meaning of the VASP Act. 'Virtual asset' is defined as a digital representation of value that can be digitally traded or transferred, and which can be used for payment or investment purposes. Certain NFTs may be in scope if used for such purposes.

Digital representations of fiat currencies (essentially, legal tender) and digital records of a credit against a financial institution of fiat currency, securities or other financial assets that can be digitally transferred are specifically excluded. Also excluded are certain closed-loop items such as airline miles and credit card awards.

Depending on the type of virtual asset, an analysis may be needed to determine whether the associated activities of a crypto business fall within scope of the Securities and Investment Business Act, Revised Edition 2020 (as amended) (SIBA) as well as the VASP Act.

[2] *Definition of a Virtual Assets Service*

A 'virtual assets service' is defined in the VASP Act as the business of engaging, on behalf of another person, in any VASP activity or operation (as outlined in the definition of VASP) and includes:

- hosting wallets or maintaining custody or control over another person's virtual asset, wallet or private key;
- providing financial services relating to the issuance, offer or sale of a virtual asset;
- providing kiosks (such as automatic teller machines, bitcoin teller machines or vending machines) for the purpose of facilitating virtual asset activities through electronic terminals to enable the owner or operator of the kiosk to actively facilitate the exchange of virtual assets for fiat currency or other virtual assets; or
- engaging in any other activity that constitutes the carrying on of the business of a virtual assets service, pursuant to the issuance of guidelines (no such guidelines have been issued to date).

The definition of 'VASP' means the conduct of one or more of the following activities or operations for or on behalf of another person:

- exchange between virtual assets and fiat currencies;
- exchange between one or more forms of virtual assets;
- transfer of virtual assets, where the transfer relates to conducting a transaction on behalf of another person that moves a virtual asset from one virtual asset address or account to another;
- safekeeping or administration of virtual assets or instruments enabling control over virtual assets;

- participation in, and provision of, financial services related to an issuer's offer or sale of a virtual asset; or
- any such activity or operation as may be specified in the VASP Act or prescribed by regulations.

The net effect of this means that any activity involving virtual assets that is conducted in or from the BVI if carried out as a business for a customer or third party must be assessed by reference to these five activities as it may trigger a VASP registration with the FSC.

The sole act of issuing a virtual asset is not a VASP activity under the VASP Act and does not require registration with the FSC as a VASP. Nor does the FSC require an issuer to 'pre-clear' virtual asset issuances. This has made the BVI a popular choice for Token issuances.

Of note is the fact that the VASP Act provides a specific definition of a 'virtual assets exchange'. This means a trading platform that is operated for the purpose of allowing an offer or invitation to be made to buy or sell any virtual asset in exchange for money or any virtual asset and which comes into custody, control, power or possession of, or over, any money or any virtual asset at any point in time during its course of business.

As a result of the definition, virtual assets exchanges will typically have to be registered with the FSC as a VASP to provide virtual assets custody services and comply with the additional VASP Act obligations in this respect, including appropriate capital requirements.

[3] On the Horizon

The VASP Act came into force on 1 February 2023. This granted VASPs operating as such on 1 February until 31 July 2023 to file a VASP registration application with the FSC. The FSC received over 70 registration applications. The FSC did not grant any VASP registrations during 2023, and the first successful applications are expected to be granted in 2024.

The FSC has not yet issued any guidance to support the interpretation of the VASP Act although this is expected at a future date. As the VASP Act derives from the FATF standards and in particular its guidance for virtual assets, the FSC will interpret the VASP Act in the light of these standards and guidance, including any changes that are made.

The FSC will also take into account the principles and standards issued by IOSCO. In particular, IOSCO's consultation on digital assets[540] resulted in new principles for DeFi which may result in additional guidance from the FSC in 2024.

540. https://www.iosco.org/news/pdf/IOSCONEWS706.pdf.

§5.16 CAPITAL MARKETS AND BLOCKCHAIN: COUNTRY REPORT – CANADA

Daniel Fuke & Mike Stephens[541]

Until 2017, the use of blockchain technology and digital assets in fundraising transactions was almost unheard of in Canada. Since then, however, Canadian founders have increasingly used blockchain technology and digital assets both for fundraising and for related business lines or digital commerce and consumer products, such as cryptocurrency exchanges, video games, investment funds invested in digital assets, and advisory services relating to such businesses.

We have seen the emergence of new asset classes such as the Non-Fungible Token and breakthrough projects such as 'CryptoKitties' (which was a Canadian project spearheaded out of Vancouver and represented the first real-world use case of the Non-Fungible Token, which was, at the time, only a theoretical digital asset). Since 2017, blockchain companies in Canada have weathered at least two pronounced Crypto Winters, and a continued regulatory uncertainty continues to hamper some aspects of the industry and broad consumer adoption in Canada. Since 2017, regulatory challenges and Crypto Winters have caused the failure of many blockchain businesses in Canada.

There has, however, been some regulatory progress in Canada over this period, but regulators have favoured a more piecemeal and reactionary approach to regulations. Often preferring to publish regulatory guidance or notices in an attempt to plug holes in the existing regulatory framework (and, ultimately, to try to avoid harm to the investing public), rather than leaning on legislature to push for and enact a regulatory overhaul on these fast moving and ever-evolving businesses and technologies. Regulatory reactions to the Quadriga CX[542] debacle and, more recently, the FTX fiasco have made it clear that the regulators in Canada intend to bring digital assets (including crypto trading platforms) into their jurisdiction and represent a clear indication that they will assert domain with respect to how the Canadian capital markets will incorporate blockchain technology and digital assets, and how the related industries will be regulated.

As the industry has evolved in Canada, it has become clear that the regulation necessarily engages multiple levels of government (both the federal government and

541. Recognized leader in the British Columbia technology ecosystem, Mike Stephens works as a Partner at Fasken. He advises start-ups, executives and company boards on corporate and business issues, with particular focus on early-stage entrepreneurs in understanding the potential of Blockchain & Distributed Ledger Technology to transform into businesses. Daniel Fuke is Partner at Fasken in Securities and M&A group and is related to investment funds and Blockchain technologies. He holds Fasken Seminars on 'Blockchain and the Gold Industry – A Digital Certificate at the end of the Rainbow?' combined with publications on 'Regulatory Net Tightening on the "Wild West" of the Blockchain and Cryptocurrency Industry' which underlines his expertise in share and asset purchase transactions, investment fund formations and ICOs.

542. https://www.reuters.com/article/us-quadrigacx-crypto-canada/ontario-securities-regulator-looking-into-digital-platform-quadriga-idUSKCN1PX26G (accessed 11 Mar. 2020).

the relevant Provincial and Territorial governments) and different agencies within those levels of government.

Notwithstanding the piecemeal and reactionary approach to crypto regulation in Canada, Canadian regulators have been open to consultation with industry participants and have shown a desire to understand the technology and work creatively with industry participants to find a path towards commercialization (beating the US to approving crypto ETFs, for example, and providing 'no-action' style letters on multiple ETH based ICOs and NFT projects in the past), which, together with Canada's stable democracy, promotion of technological innovation, and secure infrastructure, have led to making Canada a leader in the blockchain and digital asset industry.

The Canadian blockchain and digital asset industry must still overcome certain obstacles to maintain its position on the global stage for blockchain, including reputational issues. For every CryptoKitty and Dapper Labs, there is a cautionary tale. As a result, the incorporation of blockchain technology and digital assets into Canadian capital markets will remain a very rewarding, but slow, process.

[A] What Makes a Token a Security

Throughout the first half of 2017, we saw what we have come to view as the 'ICO 1.0' phase of the market in Canada, and, during that phase, Canadian securities regulators were silent as to the application of securities laws on ICOs and cryptocurrencies. The key regulatory question in Canada during this period was whether cryptocurrencies and other digital assets should be considered securities and regulated accordingly (this is still frequently the most critical question often asked on new blockchain projects in which a Cryptographic Token is to be issued). Applying securities laws to the blockchain and digital asset industry would have imposed significant time and cost obligations on participants, such as requiring ICO issuers to prepare prospectuses, requiring cryptocurrency exchanges to be regulated as 'marketplaces',[543] and requiring

543. Per s. 1(1) of *Securities Act*, RSO 1990, c-S.5, 'Marketplace' means any of the following, but does not include an inter-dealer bond broker:

1. An exchange.
2. A quotation and trade reporting system.
3. A person or company not included in paragraph 1 or 2 that, i. constitutes, maintains or provides a market or facility for bringing together buyers and sellers of securities or derivatives, ii. brings together the orders for securities or derivatives of multiple buyers and sellers, and iii. uses established non-discretionary methods under which the orders interact with each other, and the buyers and sellers entering the orders agree to the terms of a trade.
   i. constitutes, maintains or provides a market or facility for bringing together buyers and sellers of securities or derivatives,
   ii. brings together the orders for securities or derivatives of multiple buyers and sellers, and
   iii. uses established non-discretionary methods under which the orders interact with each other, and the buyers and sellers entering the orders agree to the terms of a trade.
4. With respect to securities, a dealer who executes a trade of an exchange-traded security outside a marketplace described in paragraph 1, 2 or 3; ('marché').

advisory firms to be registered with Canadian Securities Administrators (CSA) as 'dealers'[544] or 'advisers'.[545]

Notwithstanding the cost and scrutiny that would come with being subject to securities regulation, many industry participants would have welcomed regulation as a means to legitimize the developing industry and keep out bad actors. Others, however, took the position that silence from securities regulators meant their activities were entirely unregulated. For some, these decisions came with harsh consequences, as described below under 'Enforcement'.

In North America, securities regulatory action first came from the SEC, which published in July 2017 an investigative report on the ICO of the Decentralized Autonomous Organization (DAO Report) which concluded that the DAO's USD 150 million ICO in May 2016 was a non-compliant securities offering that was not registered under US securities laws.[546]

The CSA, an umbrella organization of Canada's provincial and territorial securities regulators, issued CSA Staff Notice 46-307 – *Cryptocurrency Offerings* (Staff Notice 46-307) on 24 August 2017, shortly after the publication of the DAO Report. In it, the CSA concluded that 'in many cases' cryptocurrency coins and Tokens 'should properly be considered securities',[547] a position that was consistent with the SEC's analysis in the DAO Report.

Canadian securities legislation defines a 'security' to include, among more commonly used categories like shares and bonds, 'any investment contract'. The test in Canada for when a particular instrument is an investment contract, and therefore a security, comes from the 1978 Supreme Court of Canada case *Pacific Coast Coin Exchange of Canada v. Ontario (Securities Commission)* (Pacific Coast Coin). The test states that 'an investment contract will be found where there is: (a) an investment of money; (b) with an intention of expectation of profit; (c) in a common enterprise, in which the fortunes of the investor are interwoven with and dependent upon the efforts and success of those seeking the investment or of third parties; and (d) that the efforts made by those other than the investor are the undeniably significant ones, those essential managerial efforts which affect the failure or success of the enterprise'.[548]

While Staff Notice 46-307 was encouraging because it meant that Canadian regulators were alive to the securities law issues presented by cryptocurrencies, it was also disappointingly vague. Cryptocurrencies and other digital assets are inherently different from the traditional investment structures discussed in Pacific Coast Coin and

544. 'Dealer' means, except for the purposes described in subsection (1.2) of the *Securities Act*, a person or company engaging in or holding himself, herself or itself out as engaging in the business of trading in securities as principal or agent ('courtier').

545. 'Adviser' means a person or company engaging in or holding himself, herself, or itself out as engaging in the business of advising others as to the investing in or the buying or selling of securities.

546. https://www.sec.gov/litigation/investreport/34-81207.pdf (accessed 11 Mar. 2020).

547. https://www.osc.gov.on.ca/documents/en/Securities-Category4/csa_20170824_cryptocurrency-offerings.pdf (accessed 11 Mar. 2020).

548. *Pacific Coast Coin Exchange v. Ontario (Securities Commission)*, 1977 CanLII 37 (SCC), [1978] 2 SCR 112 at 128.

other case law, yet Staff Notice 46-307 made no such distinction, forcing industry participants and their advisors to apply a 45-year-old test to revolutionary technology.

Some industry participants chose to accept the notion that digital assets are securities and applied to CSA for exemptions from or specialized categorization within securities laws in order to proceed with their businesses. The decisions in Token Funder[549] and Impak[550] both resulted in the applicable company obtaining exemptions in order to conduct ICOs or run (exempt) 'marketplaces' for the secondary sale of digital assets that are securities, and investment fund managers First Block Capital[551] and Majestic Asset Management[552] expanded their securities registrations in order to allow them to launch investment funds exposed to cryptocurrencies.

Others, however, took the position that the digital assets with which they were dealing were not captured by Pacific Coast Coin because the digital assets in question had utility (Utility Tokens) within an online ecosystem and were, therefore, inherently distinguishable from securities.

[B] Crypto Winter(s)

The bull market for cryptocurrencies and the momentum behind ICOs came to an abrupt halt in 2018. After reaching its (then) all-time high of approximately USD 20,000 per coin in December 2017, the price of bitcoin fell by 67% in the two months of 2018 to approximately USD 7,000 and continued a steep slide over the year.[553] By the end of 2018, bitcoin's market capitalization had shrunk by 80%.[554]

The actions of Canadian regulators in early 2018 may also have contributed to the slowdown in the blockchain and digital asset industry in Canada as many 'crypto nomads' were dissuaded from pursuing their business objectives within the jurisdiction of Canadian regulators. On 11 June 2018, CSA published Staff Notice 46-308 – *Securities Law Implications for Offerings of Tokens*[555] (*Staff Notice 46-308*), in which it took the position that most, if not all, offerings of crypto assets would be an issuance of securities. Staff Notice 46-308 took a purposive look at crypto assets and took the position that the economic reality on an offering must be considered, regardless of how the instrument was characterized and regardless of an asset being a Utility Token.

549. https://www.osc.gov.on.ca/en/SecuritiesLaw_ord_20171023_token.htm (accessed 11 Mar. 2020).
550. https://www.osc.gov.on.ca/documents/en/Securities-OSCB/20170824_oscb_4034_toc.pdf at 18 (accessed 11 Mar. 2020).
551. https://www.theglobeandmail.com/investing/globe-wealth/article-high-net-worth-investors-now-able-to-hold-bitcoin-in-registered (accessed 11 Mar. 2020).
552. https://news.coinsquare.com/investing/csa-authorizes-three-digital-currency-investment-funds (accessed 11 Mar. 2020).
553. https://www.theguardian.com/technology/2018/nov/20/bitcoin-price-plunges-2018-low-cryptocurrency-value (accessed 11 Mar. 2020).
554. https://coinmarketcap.com/currencies/bitcoin/historical-data/?start=20130428&end=20191031 (accessed 11 Mar. 2020).
555. https://www.osc.gov.on.ca/documents/en/Securities-Category4/csa_20180611_46-308_implications-for-offerings-of-tokens.pdf (accessed 11 Mar. 2020).

This meant that, in CSA's view, virtually all businesses dealing with crypto assets, whether they be ICO issuers, cryptocurrency exchanges, or advisory firms, would be subject to securities laws, even if they had been operating their businesses prior to Staff Notice 46-308.

The blockchain and crypto asset industry was in a difficult place at the end of 2018. Not only were cryptocurrency markets down considerably but tightened regulatory scrutiny forced industry participants to reconsider how to approach their businesses. Crypto asset issuers in particular faced two principal alternatives: (i) redesign their crypto asset to avoid securities regulatory application which, based on Staff Notice 46-308, would be difficult, or (ii) pivot to a security token offering (STO).

[C] Special Requirements for Prospectus

As mentioned above, some industry participants valued regulatory certainty so much that they embraced the idea that their crypto assets were securities and actively complied with securities regulations. A good example of this is issuers who, rather than undertaking an ICO, undertook an STO.

As the name suggests, Security Tokens are securities by nature, representing ownership of a company, debt obligation, value of underlying assets, or an investment contract. Security Tokens share almost all of the same characteristics as traditional securities, except that they are distributed digitally rather than in certificate or book-entry form.

STOs take advantage of many of blockchain technology's benefits, including ease of communication between management and security holders, greater transparency, ease of transfer among security holders, and lowering transaction costs by eliminating intermediaries.

Although they exist on the blockchain, Security Tokens are subject to all Canadian securities laws. Token issuers have the same obligation when distributing to prepare a prospectus or rely on an exemption from the prospectus requirement, such as those available in respect of accredited investors and where an offering memorandum is prepared. Security Tokens distributed in Canada pursuant to a prospectus exemption are subject to resale restrictions prescribed by National Instrument 45-102 – *Resale of Securities*, including that the first sale of which requires a prospectus or a further exemption in respect of the secondary seller.

[D] Regulatory Specifics for Organized Trade

[1] Regulatory Environment and Oversight

The securities and derivatives laws of the Provinces and Territories of Canada impose regulation on certain digital asset industry participants. In addition, the federal government of Canada might also have jurisdiction over such industry participants where their activities invoke the federal anti-money laundering legislation.

Businesses that are in the business of trading in securities, including receiving a commission for arranging for certain Token purchasers, are required to be registered as a dealer. Exchanges that facilitate secondary trading of certain Tokens (or derivatives) are required to be recognized as marketplaces by CSA and are subject to the oversight of the Financial Transactions and Reports Analysis Centre of Canada (FINTRAC).[556]

[2] *Enforcement*

Canadian securities regulators play an important role in protecting investors and preserving the integrity of capital markets and must walk a fine line between that mandate and promoting efficient capital markets. To this point, Canadian securities regulators have understandably taken a conservative approach to this new industry.

While CSA and other Canadian enforcement agencies have put the entire digital asset industry on notice that securities laws apply to most digital assets, their enforcement actions have generally been limited to seeking out instances of fraudulent ICOs[557] and advisors who promoted ICOs while not registered as an investment dealer. The OSC has issued hundreds of letters to organizations that have led to various orders, rulings and decisions for issues based on their regulatory disclosure documents or business activities in 2019 alone.[558]

One such example is the recent July 2019 OSC settlement with CoinLaunch Corp., a provider of various ICO-related services to ICO issuers. Following an investigation by the OSC, it was determined that CoinLaunch engaged in and held itself out as engaging in the business of trading in securities without registration under securities law as they advertised and marketed promotional services to two ICO issuers. The services CoinLaunch provided to the issuers included creating and preparing promotional materials for the issuers' Token offerings, directly introducing the issuers to potential investors, and taking the offerings on roadshows to help solicit investors. CoinLaunch and the OSC settled, and CoinLaunch agreed to cease their cryptocurrency business and pay over CAD 50,000 in penalties.

Another interesting story from the industry, while not originating from an enforcement action, involved the now-defunct cryptocurrency exchange Quadriga CX. This unregulated exchange (because it ostensibly did not list for trading any crypto assets that are securities) was once one of Canada's largest cryptocurrency exchanges, but after the sudden death of its CEO, it was found that he had moved roughly CAD 180 million of client assets into personal accounts only he could access.[559]

The OSC ultimately began looking into the matter in February 2019 as there was harm to Ontario investors, and their investigation exposed the regulatory vacuum in

556. http://www.gazette.gc.ca/rp-pr/p2/2019/2019-07-10/html/sor-dors240-eng.html (accessed 11 Mar. 2020).
557. https://www.coindesk.com/police-freeze-bank-accounts-seize-luxury-cars-in-probe-of-22-million-ico-promoter-vanbex (accessed 11 Mar. 2020).
558. https://www.osc.gov.on.ca/en/5610.htm?query=registration&x=16&y=17 (accessed 11 Mar. 2020).
559. https://www.reuters.com/article/us-quadrigacx-crypto canada/ontario-securities-regulator-looking-into-digital-platform-quadriga-idUSKCN1PX26G (accessed 11 Mar. 2020).

the crypto assets industry over who would be held accountable if an unregulated cryptocurrency exchange suddenly prevented its customers from accessing their assets.

Perhaps to address this vacuum, on 14 March 2019, CSA and the Investment Industry Regulatory Organization of Canada (an SRO of investment dealers) published the Joint Securities Administrations/Investment Industry Regulatory Organization of Canada's Consultation Paper and Proposed Framework for Crypto Asset Trading Platforms,[560] which sought input from the industry regarding how best to regulate cryptocurrency and digital asset exchanges.

[3] Digital Asset Trading

Given the speed with which the blockchain and digital asset industry has developed, it is not surprising that comprehensive regulation dealing with all aspects of the industry has not yet been implemented. The decentralized nature of blockchain technology allows cryptocurrencies to be traded between users with great efficiency, but any exchange that lists digital assets that are securities and provides a facility to bring together multiple orders and buyers and sellers for such orders of such digital assets would be a 'marketplace' for the purposes of Canadian securities legislation, and be subject to the same regulation as major stock exchanges such as the Toronto Stock Exchange.

(i) Securities Marketplaces

Securities marketplaces are regulated by Provincial and Territorial securities legislation; exchanges are regulated pursuant to their applicable provincial securities statutes and National Instrument 21-101 *Marketplace Operation* (NI 21-101) and National Instrument 23-101 – *Trading Rules* (NI 23-101).

While there has been much discussion in the Canadian blockchain industry about the advantages of pursuing the recognition as an exchange for the purpose of NI 21-101 and NI 23-101, to date, there have not been any such digital asset 'marketplaces' recognized in Canada. There have, however, been examples of certain exchanges seeking and receiving exemptions from the requirements of NI 21-101 and NI 23-101 to facilitate the buying and selling of digital assets that are securities on a private placement or on an exempt market basis.

(ii) Crypto Trading Platforms

In the absence of definitive legislation to address the trading of digital assets in Canada, the Provincial and Territorial securities regulators in Canada have sought to fill in the regulatory gaps by publishing Staff Notices on how they intend to regulate Canadian crypto trading platforms or crypto trading platforms operating in Canada.

560. https://www.osc.ca/en/securities-law/instruments-rules-policies/2/21-402 (accessed 12 Jan. 2024).

On 14 March 2019, CSA and the Canadian Industry Regulatory Organization (CIRO) published the Joint Securities Administrations/Investment Industry Regulatory Organization of Canada's Consultation Paper and Proposed Framework for Crypto Asset Trading Platforms,[561] which sought input from the industry regarding how best to regulate cryptocurrency exchanges (Consultation Paper 21-402).

The Consultation Paper 21-402 culminated in the publication of Staff Notice 21-329 – *Guidance for Crypto-Asset Trading Platforms: Compliance with Regulatory Requirements* (Staff Notice 21-329)[562] and Staff Notice 21-327 – *Guidance on the Application of Securities Legislation to Entities Facilitating the Trading of Crypto Assets* (Staff Notice 21-327)[563] and Staff Notice 51-363 – *Observations on Disclosure by Crypto Assets Reporting Issuers* (Staff Notice 51-363).[564]

According to Staff Notice 21-327, any entity that facilitates transactions relating to crypto assets will be subject to securities legislation, including crypto trading platforms that facilitate transactions in crypto that the CSA does not even consider to be a security (i.e., BTC or ETH or other digital assets that are commodities).

There are certain circumstances where a crypto trading platform will facilitate transactions in digital assets where the user's digital asset will remain on the platform or reside in a platform wallet, even following the clearing and settling of trades by the platform for the user. The CSA has taken the position that if the digital asset is not immediately delivered to the user's wallet post-trade, the platform user's rights in their digital assets will be considered a derivative for the purposes of securities legislation.

The CSA's expectation is that a crypto trading platform operating in the Canadian market with services offered to Canadian retail investors should be registered with CIRO as 'investment dealers'. Acknowledging that the registration burden would be time-consuming and costly to some crypto trading platforms operating within Canada, the CSA provided a transitional path towards registration as an 'investment dealer' by permitting such platforms to first seek registration as a 'restricted dealer' for an 'interim period' (where they would be unable to offer any margin or leverage trading) until the platform is able to satisfy the rigours of registering as an 'investment dealer' and comply with the ongoing requirements associated with such registration.

In the later stages of 2022 and in early 2023, a number of crypto trading platforms started to experience liquidity issues in the face of increasing volatility in digital asset values. In order to further their mandate in such circumstances, the CSA quickly introduced measures to further enhance Canadian investor protections in the digital asset trading space. The CSA published Staff Notice 21-332 – *Crypto Asset Trading Platforms: Pre-Registration Undertakings – Changes to Enhance Canadian Investor*

561. https://www.osc.ca/en/securities-law/instruments-rules-policies/2/21-402 (accessed 12 Jan. 2024).
562. https://www.osc.ca/en/securities-law/instruments-rules-policies/2/21-329 (accessed 12 Jan. 2024).
563. https://www.osc.ca/en/securities-law/instruments-rules-policies/2/21-327 (accessed 12 Jan. 2024).
564. https://www.osc.ca/en/securities-law/instruments-rules-policies/5/51-363 (accessed 12 Jan. 2024).

Protection[565] on 22 February 2023 (Staff Notice 21-332). The purpose of Staff Notice 21-332 was to ensure that Canadian crypto trading platforms or foreign crypto trading platforms operating in the Canadian retail market could continue to operate while either pursuing their 'dealer registration' or an exemption therefrom, provided that they tendered a pre-registration undertaking (a PRU) to regulator and complied with additional measures introduced to improve Canadian retail investor protections.

In the face of Staff Notice 21-332, such crypto trading platforms had to their PRU or (alternatively) comply with all the additional, operational Canadian retail investor protections by the end of March 2023. Failing that, the CSA's expectation was that non-compliant crypto trading platforms would block Canadians from accessing the platform and seek to disable the accounts of Canadian resident users.

[4] Crypto Dealer Registration

In Canada, any person or entity either who is actively trading securities or derivatives or advising on trades of securities or derivatives for a business purpose is subject to the requirement to register as either an 'investment dealer' or an 'investment advisor'.

Therefore, where a person or entity person is engaged in soliciting investors for a sale in digital assets (either online or personally) and raising large amounts of capital from a sale of digital assets to a large amount of investors, and where such person or entity is compensated for such activity (i.e., the 'business purpose'), then such person or entity will need to register as an 'investment dealer' (or seek out an applicable exemption from such registration, where available).

Obviously, the main question engaged when it comes to crypto dealer registration is whether or not the digital asset in question is a security or not for the purposes of securities law. In the current regulatory environment, the likelihood of a particular digital asset being considered a security is still overwhelmingly large, and, therefore, the safest path for a person or entity conducting such activities in the Canadian capital markets would be to seek to become registered as an 'investment dealer' or to engage the services of an already registered 'investment dealer' with the necessary digital asset experience.

[5] Money Services Businesses and Anti-money Laundering Laws

On 1 June 2021, amendments to the regulations under the federal *Proceeds of Crime (Money Laundering) and Terrorist Financing Act* (the PCMLTFA) came into effect. These amendments ushered in rules and definitions concerning virtual currency and other related subjects.

In the PCMLTFA, a 'virtual currency' is now defined as: (a) a digital representation of value that can be used for payment or investment purposes that is not a fiat

565. https://www.osc.ca/en/securities-law/instruments-rules-policies/2/21-332/csa-staff-notice-21-332-crypto-asset-trading-platforms-pre-registration-undertakings-changes (accessed 12 Jan. 2024).

currency and that can be readily exchanged for funds or for another virtual currency that can be readily exchanged for funds; or (b) a private key of a cryptographic system that enables a person or entity to have access to a digital representation of value referred to in paragraph (a). Persons or entities that *deal in* virtual currencies are considered money services businesses (MSBs) and are subject to the corresponding requirements.

There are also now requirements relating to virtual currencies that apply to other types of reporting entities, including record-keeping, identification and reporting requirements for large virtual currency transactions (i.e., the receipt of USD 10,000 or more in a single transaction), subject to certain exceptions.

The amendments to the PCMLTFA differentiate between domestic and foreign MSBs. Both need to register with the Financial Transactions Reports and Analysis Centre of Canada (FINTRAC) and are subject to similar, though not identical, requirements.

Foreign MSBs are defined as persons or entities that do not have a place of business in Canada but direct prescribed services to persons or entities in Canada. The term 'direct' in this context includes targeting, advertising or having a Canadian domain name.

Any person or entity (Canadian or foreign where such foreign entity is directing prescribed services to persons or entities in Canada) is required to adopt a compliance program in accordance with the PCMLTFA (such as adopting a program of keeping records, reporting, KYC and other related requirements under the regulation).

The amendments to the PCMLTFA do not specify what it means to 'deal in' virtual currency, but FINTRAC later provided guidance that the legislation is intended to capture the activities of virtual currency exchanges and exchanges facilitating transactions in virtual currencies. Transactions of virtual currencies to acquire goods or services are not covered by the legislation.

[E] Conclusion

The use of blockchain technology and digital assets in Canadian capital markets experienced multiple bull and bear markets since 2017. Those entities or persons who were attracted to the industry seeking an unregulated 'wild west' in which to get rich quickly are largely gone, leaving industry participants who believe that blockchain technology and digital assets have a crucial role to play in making Canada's capital markets more efficient.

Canadian securities regulators have come a long way, from standing on the sidelines in 2017 to positioning crypto assets as a securities law jurisdiction, to the decisions in TokenGX and 3iQ, where they embraced novel concepts and found ways for those to work within existing regulatory frameworks.

While it may be several years before blockchain technology and digital assets are used in mainstream Canadian capital markets transactions, they have the ability to improve the efficiency and transparency of such markets and as a result should continue to be pursued by industry participants and regulators alike.

§5.17 CAPITAL MARKETS AND BLOCKCHAIN: COUNTRY REPORT – UNITED STATES

James Gatto[566]

[A] What Makes a Token a Security?

In the US, there are both federal and state laws and regulations that apply to digital assets (including cryptocurrencies and Tokens). At the federal level, there are no new laws that have been passed. Rather, the relevant agencies have issued guidance on how the existing law and legal principles apply to digital assets, and they have engaged in various enforcement actions. Some states have passed new laws that apply to digital assets. This report will primarily cover federal issues but will highlight some of the state law issues.

Various federal agencies have exerted jurisdiction over digital assets. Their jurisdiction seems to be overlapping, at least for now. In part, this is due to the fact that these different agencies have classified various digital assets, and cryptocurrency in particular, in conflicting ways. This table shows a high-level summary of these classifications:

Agency	*Classification*
SEC	Security
CFTC	Commodity
FinCEN	Money
IRS	Property

A more detailed explanation of the legal issues that these agencies address is set forth below.

[1] US SEC

The SEC has been one of the most active agencies in this area. The SEC regulates securities and securities exchanges. The mission of the SEC is to protect investors; maintain fair, orderly, and efficient markets; and facilitate capital formation. The SEC strives to promote a market environment that is worthy of the public's trust.

566. Leading the Blockchain and Fintech Team and its Artificial Intelligence Team and Partner at Sheppard Mullin, James G. Gatto leverages his unique combination of over thirty-five years of IP and technology law experience, business insights and attention to technology trends. James' leadership on Blockchain & Cryptocurrencies has been selected for a National Law Review Go-To Thought Leadership Award by acknowledging his insightful, helpful and timely insight for NLR readers in these complicated areas of law, as well as the digital media industry and technology trends.

The SEC has been primarily focused on whether digital assets are securities. The term 'securities' is defined to include a number of things (including stocks, bonds and transferable shares).[567] None of these traditional types of securities seem to cover most cryptocurrencies and Tokens although in some cases they can. However, the definition of security further includes the term 'investment contracts'. When analysing whether cryptocurrencies and Tokens are securities, the SEC has focused most of its analysis on this category of security.

The primary test that the SEC uses to determine if a Token is an investment contract (and thus a security) is the *Howey* test.[568] This test defines an offering as an investment contract if there is: (i) an investment of money; (ii) in a common enterprise; (iii) with a reasonable expectation of profit; (iv) derived solely from the efforts of others.[569]

According to the SEC, the focus of the *Howey* analysis is not only on the form and terms of the instrument itself (in this case, the digital asset) but also on the circumstances surrounding the digital asset and the manner in which it is offered, sold, or resold (which includes secondary market sales). It has indicated that labels do not matter, but the totality of the facts and circumstances do. For example, calling a Token a 'Utility Token' will not exclude it from being a security. The SEC has stated that most Token offerings that it has seen, in particular ICOs, are securities, but bitcoin and ether are not.

The federal securities laws require all offers and sales of securities, including those involving a digital asset, to either be registered under its provisions or to qualify for an exemption from registration. The registration provisions require persons to disclose certain information to investors, and that information must be complete and not materially misleading. This requirement for disclosure furthers the federal securities laws' goal of providing investors with the information necessary to make informed investment decisions.

The SEC has issued various guidance to help assess whether a digital asset is a security. The most recent is its *Framework for 'Investment Contract' Analysis of Digital Assets*, April 2019.

The SEC has engaged in a number of enforcements through litigation. Some of the more high-profile recent decisions in the US have clarified the applicability of *Howey* to digital assets. A U.S. District Court in New York granted the SEC's motion for summary judgment against an issuer of digital assets.[570] Another District Court found that LBRY offered its LBC Tokens as securities based on how it marketed the Tokens.[571] This

567. The term 'security' is defined in s. 2(a)(1) of the Securities Act of 1933 (the 'Securities Act'), s. 3(a)(10) of the Securities Exchange Act of 1934, s. 2(a)(36) of the Investment Company Act of 1940, and s. 202(a)(18) of the Investment Advisers Act of 1940.
568. *SEC v. W.J. Howey Co.*, 328 U.S. 293.
569. The *Howey* case limited the fourth prong of the test to profits derived 'solely' from the efforts of others. Over time, the courts relaxed this requirement. Thus, according to the SEC, it is not necessary that the profit comes solely from the efforts of others.
570. *SEC v. Kik Interactive Inc.*, 492 F. Supp. 3d 169 (S.D.N.Y. 2020).
571. https://www.nhd.uscourts.gov/sites/default/files/Opinions/2023/23NH082.pdf.

decision clarified that a Token can be a security even if it has utility.[572] Another District Court in NY ruled that Ripple's sales of XRP on cryptocurrency exchanges were not offers of securities because purchasers did not have a reasonable expectation of profit that depended on Ripple's efforts, yet Ripple's direct sales of XRP to investors were securities.[573]

In June 2023, the SEC charged Coinbase, Inc. with operating its crypto asset trading platform as an unregistered national securities exchange, broker, and clearing agency. The SEC also charged Coinbase for failing to register the offer and sale of its crypto asset staking-as-a-service program. Coinbase vigorously denies these allegations. This matter is pending.[574]

The SEC's actions are not limited to crypto currencies. The SEC announced enforcements against two Non-fungible Token (NFT) projects for allegedly violating securities laws. In both cases, two SEC Commissioners dissented. In each case, the SEC focused on how the NFTs were marketed as investments, more so than what the NFT represented.[575]

[2] The Commodities Futures Trading Commission

The mission of the Commodities Futures Trading Commission (CFTC) is to foster open, transparent, competitive, and financially sound markets. By working to avoid systemic risk, the Commission aims to protect market users and their funds, consumers, and the public from fraud, manipulation, and abusive practices related to derivatives and other products that are subject to the Commodity Exchange Act (CEA). The CFTC has asserted jurisdiction over various types of digital assets based on its view that they are commodities. According to the CFTC, the definition of 'commodity' in the CEA is broad and includes 'all services, rights, and interests ... in which contracts for future delivery are presently or in the future dealt in'. This nebulous language allegedly covers most cryptocurrencies.

The CFTC's jurisdiction is implicated when a virtual currency is used in a derivatives contract or if there is fraud or manipulation involving a virtual currency traded in interstate commerce. Beyond instances of fraud or manipulation, the CFTC generally does not oversee 'spot' or cash-market exchanges and transactions involving virtual currencies that do not utilize margin, leverage, or financing.

According to the CFTC, a smart contract, depending on its structure, operation, and relevant facts and circumstances, could be a Commodity, Forward Contract, Futures Contract, Option on Futures Contract or a Swap.

572. *Federal Court Rules LBRY Offered Security and Rejects Arguments SEC Did Not Provide Fair Notice, https://www.nhd.uscourts.gov/sites/default/files/Opinions/2023/23NH082.pdf.*
573. https://www.nysd.uscourts.gov/sites/default/files/2023-07/SEC%20vs%20Ripple%207-13-23.pdf.
574. https://www.sec.gov/files/litigation/complaints/2023/comp-pr2023-102.pdf.
575. *SEC Enforcements Against NFTs – Are You Next?*, https://www.lawoftheledger.com/2023/09/articles/nfts/sec-enforcements-against-nfts-are-you-next/#more-2584.

The CFTC has issued various guidance documents, including *A CFTC Primer on Virtual Currencies* and *A Primer on Smart Contracts*.

[3] The Financial Crimes Enforcement Network

Financial Crimes Enforcement Network's (FinCEN's) mission is to safeguard the financial system from illicit use, combat money laundering, and promote national security through the strategic use of financial authorities and the collection, analysis, and dissemination of financial intelligence. FinCEN is responsible for administering regulations relating to the Bank Secrecy Act (BSA) and its amendments. The BSA is focused on AML and CFT.

FinCEN was quite forward-looking and issued initial guidance in 2013 '*Application of FinCEN's Regulations to Persons Administering, Exchanging, or Using Virtual Currencies*', and various updates to that guidance, including on 9 May 2019 '*Application of FinCEN's Regulations to Certain Business Models Involving Convertible Virtual Currencies*'.

According to its guidance, FinCEN 'In contrast to real currency, "virtual" currency is a medium of exchange that operates like a currency in some environments, but does not have all the attributes of real currency.' Its guidance addresses 'Convertible' Virtual Currency (CVC). This type of virtual currency either has an equivalent value in real currency or acts as a substitute for real currency.

This guidance refers to the participants in generic virtual currency arrangements, using the terms 'user' 'exchanger' and 'administrator'. A user is a person who obtains virtual currency to purchase goods or services.[576] An exchanger is a person engaged as a business in the exchange of virtual currency for real currency, funds, or other virtual currency. An administrator is a person engaged as a business in issuing (putting into circulation) a virtual currency, and who has the authority to redeem (to withdraw from circulation) such virtual currency.

A user who obtains CVC and uses it to purchase real or virtual goods or services is not a Money Services Business (MSB) under FinCEN's regulations. An administrator or exchanger that (1) accepts and transmits a CVC or (2) buys or sells CVC for any reason is a money transmitter under FinCEN's regulations unless a limitation to or exemption from the definition applies to the person.[577] FinCEN interprets these exemptions strictly. Therefore, a person may not take advantage of a particular exemption if the activity he or she engages in does not conform fully to an exemption.

FinCEN's regulations define the term 'money transmitter' as a person that provides money transmission services or any other person engaged in the transfer of

576. FinCEN notes that how a person engages in 'obtaining' a virtual currency may be described using any number of other terms, such as 'earning', 'harvesting', 'mining', 'creating', 'auto-generating', 'manufacturing', or 'purchasing', depending on the details of the specific virtual currency model involved.
577. FinCEN's regulations provide that whether a person is a money transmitter is a matter of facts and circumstances. The regulations identify six circumstances under which a person is not a money transmitter, despite accepting and transmitting currency, funds, or value that substitutes for currency. 31 CFR s. 1010.100(ff)(5)(ii)(A)-(F).

funds. The term 'money transmission services' means 'the acceptance of currency, funds, or other value that substitutes for currency from one person and the transmission of currency, funds, or other value that substitutes for currency to another location or person by any means'.[578]

The label applied to any particular type of CVC (such as 'digital currency', 'cryptocurrency', 'crypto asset', and 'digital asset') is not dispositive of its regulatory treatment under the BSA. Additionally, transactions denominated in CVC will be subject to FinCEN regulations regardless of whether the CVC is represented by a physical or digital Token, whether the type of ledger used to record the transactions is centralized or distributed, or the type of technology utilized for the transmission of value.

According to FinCEN, a person still qualifies as a money transmitter if that person's activities include receiving one form of value (currency, funds, prepaid value, value that substitutes for currency – such as CVC) from one person and transmitting either the same or a different form of value to another person or location, by any means. Similarly, a money transmitter may accept and transmit value in either order. That is, a person is still a money transmitter under FinCEN regulations if the person transmits value first and only later accepts the corresponding value for this transfer.

FinCEN has made it clear that, in its view, persons accepting and transmitting value that substitutes for currency, such as virtual currency, are money transmitters. Persons accepting and transmitting CVC are required (like any money transmitter) to register with FinCEN as an MSB and comply with AML program, record-keeping, monitoring, and reporting requirements, including the filing of suspicious activity reports (SARs) and Currency Transaction Reports (CTRs). These requirements apply equally to domestic and foreign-located CVC money transmitters doing business in whole or in substantial part within the US, even if the foreign-located entity has no physical presence in the US.

Most recently, the leaders of the CFTC, FinCEN and the SEC issued a joint statement to remind persons engaged in activities involving digital assets of their AML and CFT (AML/CFT) obligations under the BSA. This joint statement provides further clarity on some of the many laws potentially applicable to cryptocurrency and other digital assets and highlights the need for anyone operating in the space to obtain legal advice to understand their legal compliance obligations. According to the statement, AML/CFT obligations apply to entities that the BSA defines as 'financial institutions', such as futures commission merchants and introducing brokers obligated to register with the CFTC, MSBs as defined by FinCEN, and broker-dealers and mutual funds obligated to register with the SEC. Among those AML/CFT obligations are the requirement to establish and implement an effective AML Program and record-keeping and reporting requirements, including SAR requirements.

578. 31 CFR s. 1010.100(ff)(5)(i)(A).

[4] FINRA

FINRA is a government-authorized not-for-profit organization that oversees US broker-dealers. It issued a report, *'Distributed Ledger Technology: Implications of Blockchain for the Securities Industry'* in January 2017. The report notes that DLT has the potential to affect various aspects of the securities market, including market efficiency, transparency, post-trade processes and operational risk. The report highlights many of the potential implications of DLT on broker-dealers. The report is not intended to express any legal position, and it does not create any new legal requirements or suggest any change in any existing regulatory obligations. Nor does it provide relief from any regulatory obligations. Rather, the report highlights certain operational and regulatory areas that broker-dealers may wish to consider as they explore adopting DLT.

[5] The IRS

The Internal Revenue Service (IRS) issued initial guidance in 2014 and updated guidance in 2019. The guidance addresses how existing general tax principles apply to transactions using virtual currency. According to the IRS, for federal tax purposes, virtual currency is treated as property. General tax principles applicable to property transactions apply to transactions using virtual currency. It is not treated as a currency that could generate foreign currency gain or loss for US federal tax purposes. One of the ramifications of this is that, according to the IRS, a taxpayer who receives virtual currency as payment for goods or services must, in computing gross income, include the fair market value of the virtual currency, measured in US dollars, as of the date that the virtual currency was received. If the fair market value of property received in exchange for virtual currency exceeds (is less than) the taxpayer's adjusted basis of the virtual currency, the taxpayer has taxable gain (loss).

A taxpayer generally realizes capital gain or loss on the sale or exchange of virtual currency that is a capital asset in the hands of the taxpayer. For example, stocks, bonds, and other investment property are generally capital assets. Arguably, this applies to cryptocurrencies that are deemed securities or other investment property. A taxpayer generally realizes ordinary gain or loss on the sale or exchange of virtual currency that is not a capital asset in the hands of the taxpayer. Inventory and other property held mainly for sale to customers in a trade or business are examples of property that is not a capital asset.

Few people have reported taxable gains on the disposition of cryptocurrencies. The IRS has announced an enforcement campaign to educate taxpayers and compel compliance.

[6] State Laws

Most states have money transmitter laws that require companies to obtain a licence in that state if they engage in money transmission services. Some states, such as New York, impose a separate requirement to obtain a 'BitLicense.' Subject to certain exceptions, anyone engaging in any of the following activities may be required to obtain a BitLicense in New York: (i) virtual currency transmission; (ii) storing, holding, or maintaining custody or control of virtual currency on behalf of others; (iii) buying and selling virtual currency as a customer business; (iv) performing exchange services as a customer business; (v) or controlling, administering, or issuing a virtual currency.

Delaware is the most popular state for incorporation in the US. Recent changes to the Delaware General Corporate Law expressly permit the keeping of corporate records in the form of electronic networks and databases. These changes permit a corporation to maintain the required stock ledger using DLT/blockchain technology.

Space constraints limit the ability to address in this report much more about the many state laws that have been passed that relate to digital assets. The National Conference of State Legislatures maintains a very helpful collection of blockchain-related state laws.

§5.18 CAPITAL MARKETS AND BLOCKCHAIN: COUNTRY REPORT – JAPAN

Takashi Itokawa[579]

Over the past years, there have been several security tokens offerings (or digital securities) in Japan. Approximately all Tokens issued in Japan are real estate Security Tokens or corporate bond Security Tokens. Those are small-lot products targeting mainly individual investors and are realized by combining the existing structure of real estate funds or corporate bond with the blockchain technology.

Unlike the real estate small-lot securities used to date for raising capital from individual investors, such as the Japan Real Estate Investment Trust (*J-REIT*)[580] and real estate crowdfunding, the real estate Security Tokens continue to gain special attention since it can be expected to differentiate itself in terms of improving liquidity using digital technologies if the secondary market develops. Additionally, the amended laws and regulations, including the Financial Instruments and Exchange Act in Japan *(the FIEA)* that came into effect on 1 May 2020, have clarified the status of Security Tokens under the FIEA and have improved legal certainty regarding regulations.[581] Furthermore, amendments to the Act on Strengthening Industrial Competitiveness on 2 August 2021 are expected to lead to further developments for the Security Tokens practices.

579. Takashi Itokawa is a partner at Nagashima Ohno & Tsunematsu. His practice focuses on finance transactions and relevant regulatory matters, especially securities offerings by various issuers including Security Token offerings, including J-REITs, M&A finance, securitization, and structured finance. In addition, he also has extensive experience with real estate and M&A transactions and regularly handles cross-border transactions for both Japanese and foreign clients.

580. Japan Real Estate Investment Trusts, https://j-reit.jp/en/about/ (accessed 14 Nov. 2023).

581. Also, amendments to the FIEA that come into effect within one year from 29 Nov. 2023 start regulating under FIEA a tokenized right based on a specified joint real estate venture contract prescribed in Art. 2, para. (3) of the Specified Joint Real Estate Ventures Act in Japan.

Even though Security Tokens are primarily regulated by the FIEA, Security Tokens also fall under potential Japanese self-regulations of the Securities Dealers Association *(JSDA)* and the Japan Security Token Offering Association *(JSTOA)*.

[A] What Makes a Token a Security?

Tokens backed by securities under the FIEA are also categorized as securities.[582] Although the equity in the collective investment scheme (*CIS – shudan toshi suki-mu mochibun*) is categorized as securities under the FIEA,[583] the law remains vague since it covers a variety of investment products such as partnership,[584] implied or not. The risk of being classified as securities and regulated by the FIEA as such product is relatively high. More importantly, even though some Tokens are not treated as securities, they might be regulated under the Payment Services Act *(PSA)*.

Generally, in Japan '*Security Tokens*' and *digital securities* represent rights or securities under civil law which can be digitally managed such as blockchain (so-called tokenized). In Japan Security Token Offering (*STO*) refers to the method of financing by issuing Security Tokens. Real estate Security Tokens are Security Tokens backed by real estate. Both *Security Token* and *digital securities* are no official legal terms. The amendment of the FIEA in 2019 stipulates that 'electronically recorded transferable rights that must be indicated on securities' (*Denshi kiroku iten yuka shoken hyoji kenri to*),[585] which are the official legal term equivalent to *Security Token* and *digital securities* under the FIEA.

In addition, Security Tokens that are categorized as equity in the CIS are defined as the official legal term of Electronically Recorded Transferable Rights (ERTF – *Denshi kiroku iten kenri*)[586] with certain exceptions and have been more strictly regulated, similar to listed stocks in Japan.

[B] Blockchain Finality

Since Security Tokens only deal with rights (or securities) and are recognized as rights under civil law, including the Civil Code and the Company Act in Japan, the most important issue has been how to ensure that those rights under civil law that Security Tokens pegged reach the final perfection of the transfer of rights.

There is always the risk of double transfer if the fulfilment/perfection of the transfer is delayed. Furthermore, considering the order of priority of the right to attachment by a third party, including the taxation authority, or the order of priority of the right to the trustee in bankruptcy in the event of bankruptcy, the issue is whether the requirement for assertion against a third party has been satisfied. As mentioned

582. Article 2, paras (1) and (2) of the FIEA.
583. Article 2, para. (2), item (v) of the FIEA.
584. Article 2, para. (2), item (v), the first sentence of the FIEA.
585. Article 1, para. (4), item (xvii) of the Cabinet Office Order on Financial Instruments Business, etc.
586. Article 2, para. (3) of the FIEA.

before, the transferee of the Security Tokens has a major interest in ensuring that the requirements for the assertion of a third party can be satisfied without any delay. Therefore, the certainty and immediacy of the requirements for the perfection of the transfer of rights is a major issue from the viewpoint of securing liquidity and enhancing the market prices and merchantability of the Security Tokens.

It would be legally possible for a third party to acquire the rights, which Security Tokens are backed, outside the blockchain by seizure or the like. Therefore, the issue of how much further examination the chain of the title for rights in addition to and beyond the ledger on the blockchain is required is also a major concern.

Since Security Tokens are tokenized only when the rights under civil law are digitally managed by technology such as blockchain, the requirements for generating Security Token rights, valid transfer requirements, and countervailing requirements are subject to the law such as treatment of the rights.

Currently, the issued Security Tokens are mainly backed by corporate bonds and securitization of real estate. Since a trust issuing beneficiary certificates and a silent partnership are most popular for Security Tokens among other types of structures for the securitization of real estate, we will focus on these structures.[587]

[1] Corporate Bonds

Corporate bonds can be traded using corporate bond registry. The entry and record in the corporate bond registry constitute requirement to perfection under the Company Act.[588] Such entry and record can employ the blockchain technology, and the finality can be realized by the blockchain technology.

[2] Securitization of Real Estate

[a] A Trust Issuing Beneficiary Certificates with Stipulating in the Trust Agreement That the Beneficiary Certificates Shall Not Be Issued

Currently, the beneficial interest in trust issuing beneficiary certificates (*jueki sho-ken hakko shintaku*) under the Trust Act in Japan is mainly used for the publicly offered real estate Security Token.

Even if it is a trust issuing beneficiary certificates by stipulating in the trust agreement that the beneficiary certificates shall not be issued, the beneficial interest can be transferred only by the agreement of the parties, and the entry and record in the beneficial interest registry constitute a requirement for perfection.[589]

This trust is advantageous in that it can be implemented digitally by using technology such as blockchain for the management of the beneficiary rights registry.

587. Recently another type of real estate Security Tokens appears. Ultimately backed by real estate is the same, but tokenized are limited partnership interests backed by investment units of a J-REIT.
588. Article 688, para. (1) of the Companies Act.
589. Article 194, Art. 185, para. (2), Art. 93, para. (1), Art. 195, para. (2) of the Trust Act.

Therefore, even under civil law, the transfer of rights that Security Tokens are backed by and the fulfilment of requirements to perfection can be implemented within the platform in a manner that does not cause any time lag.

[b] Investor's Right in the Silent Partnership (Tokumei Kumiai Shusshi Mochibun Kenri)

Silent partnership rights have been typically used in various real estate funds. In other words, it has been used to invest in the *Godo-Kaisha*,[590] a type of LLC in Japan, by establishing *Godo-Kaisha* as a real estate holding vehicle and then having investors enter into silent partnership agreements,[591] known as GK-TK schemes. When a *Godo-Kaisha* holds real estate as a beneficial interest in trust, which is typical in order to avoid further strict regulation, the investor's right in the silent partnership is categorized as an equity in the collective investment scheme.[592] With respect to the investor's rights in the silent partnership, the Commercial Code in Japan, which is the governing law of the silent partnership, does not have the explicit provision for the validity of the transfer and the requirement to perfection. Thus, it is generally accepted that the validity of the transfer and the requirement to perfection are handled in the same manner as the transfer of the claims falls under the Civil Code. In other words, the agreement of the parties may be the condition for validity of a transfer of the right.[593] However, the transfer of the investor's right in the silent partnership usually requires the transfer of the obligation at the same time, so that it is normal for the transfer of the rights to take the form of a transfer of the contractual status. In that case, the prior consent of Godo-Kaisha is required for the validity of transfer.[594] In addition, in order to meet the requirements to perfection, the Civil Code requires a notice or consent based on notarial deed,[595] including the transmission of an officially attested date and authentication as the simplest of several possibilities.

For this reason, it is difficult to manage the transfer of the rights in silent partnerships digitally on the platform due to the requirement of a notice or consent based on a notarized instrument including the transfer of an officially attested date and authentication. In the event of the transfer of the tokenized rights in silent partnerships, there is a time lag in obtaining notarization. Therefore, there is a risk that the requirements may not be met.

[c] Article 11-2 of the Act on Strengthening Industrial Competitiveness

The amendment to the Act on Strengthening Industrial Competitiveness was enacted on 2 August 2021, implementing a special measure concerning the requirement to

590. Article 2, para. (1), item (i) of the Companies Act.
591. Article 535 of the Commercial Code.
592. Article 2, para. (2), item (v), the first sentence of the FIEA.
593. Article 466, para. (2) of the Civil Code.
594. Article 539-2 of the Civil Code.
595. Article 467, para. (2) of the Civil Code.

perfection for the transfer of claims. With this enactment, the digital infrastructure is being developed to meet the requirement to perfection, which previously required physical procedures such as the notarization mentioned above.

As earlier noted, the transfer requirements to perfection must be based on an instrument with notarization, including the transfer of an officially attested date and authentication. Although such notarization can be done electronically, which is currently active, the physical signing procedure cannot be omitted.

On the other hand, the amendment to the Act on Strengthening Industrial Competitiveness has been enacted so that such perfection can be satisfied only by a licensed digital platform.

However, as far as we know, there are several in the demonstration phase, but none have yet been put into actual use in Security Tokens though one platformer has obtained the licence.

[C] Special Requirements for Prospectuses

[1] Real Estate Security Tokens

In case of publicly offered Real Estate Security Tokens, special requirements for prospectuses are provided under the Cabinet Office Order on Disclosure of Information on Regulated Securities and the Cabinet Office Order on Disclosure of Information on Corporate Affairs in Japan.

If preparing a Securities Registration Statement, which must be submitted to the authority pertaining public offering of Real Estate Security Tokens, it is required to state the following matters in a concrete and easily comprehensible manner. The content of the Securities Registration Statement approximately coincides with the requirements for prospectus:[596]

(i) name, details and reason for selection of the technology used for recording and transfer;
(ii) name, details and reason for selection of the platform used for solicitation or offering, or acquisition or disposition;
(iii) name, operational role and the contents of the related business of the asset custody company (including information about a person who manages the cryptographic assets);
(iv) name, operational role and the contents of the related business of the technical provider of the technology used for recording and transfer, if any;
(v) name, operational role and the contents of the related business of the platform provider of the platform used for solicitation or offering, or acquisition or disposition, if any;

596. Form 6-5 of the Cabinet Office Order on Disclosure of Information on Regulated Securities.

(vi) asset outflow risks and other risks inherent in Security Tokens, and risk management systems related thereto; and
(vii) remuneration and fees to technical providers and platform providers.

Additionally, while using the white paper (brief solicitation material) for solicitation, it is mandatory to attach it to the Securities Registration Statement.[597]

[2] *Corporate Bond Tokens*

Regarding corporate bonds, there are no particular matters stated under the Cabinet Office Order on Disclosure of Information on Corporate Affairs in Japan, but the above items in relation to Real Estate Tokens are normally also identically described in the prospectus.

[3] *Self-regulation Guidelines*

In addition, the JSDA has established guidelines as to the content of the explanation of important matters. The following explanation is normally required.[598]

[a] *Technologies Used for Tokenized Securities*

(1) Whereas listed shares and similar securities transfer and record rights through Book-entry Transfer Institutions (Securities Custody and Book-Entry Transfer Organization), tokenized securities transfer and record rights using electronic data processing systems using blockchain technology and similar technology.
(2) Each of the tokenized securities may use different technology (depending on the method of transferring or recording rights).
(3) There may be cases where the person who provides the technology pertaining to the transfer/recording of rights and the person who provides the platform to distribute said tokenized securities using said technology are different.

[b] *Risks of Technology Used in Tokenized Securities*

(1) There are risks to the uncertainty of technology pertaining to the transfer and recording of rights and to the uncertainty of technology and operation pertaining to platforms.
(2) Since the mechanism of the transfer and recording of rights differs from existing securities, meaning securities other than tokenized securities, there is

597. Article 12, para. (1), item (i) of the Cabinet Office Order on Disclosure of Information on Regulated Securities.
598. Regulations Concerning Transactions, etc. of the Right to Electronically Record and Transfer Electronic Records, etc. of JSDA, Approach to Art. 3.4 of the Regulations Concerning Investment Solicitation, Client Management, etc. by Association Members of JSDA.

a risk that the outflow of tokenized securities and validity of the transfer of rights, settlement, and perfection requirements are different from existing securities.

(3) In the event of the outflow of tokenized securities, the transfer of rights will become impossible for a certain period, payment of dividends will cease, and all or part of the rights related to the tokenized securities may be lost.

[c] The Application of Regulations and the Like According to the Type of Securities and the Transaction

The laws and regulations applicable according to the type of securities and the transaction apply to tokenized securities in the same manner as existing securities.

[D] Regulatory Specifics for Organized Trade

[1] Reclassification as Securities under the FIEA

As mentioned before, the majority of Tokens issued in Japan are Real Estate Security Tokens or Corporate Bond Security Tokens. A trust issuing beneficiary certificates and a silent partnership are most popular for Real Estate Security Tokens. A corporate bond and a trust issuing beneficiary certificates were strictly regulated even before the amendment to the FIEA. They are categorized as securities under Article 2, paragraph (1) (paragraph (1) securities) of the FIEA. On the other hand, a silent partnership, which is not categorized as securities under Article 2, paragraph (1) and is treated as securities under Article 2, paragraph (2) of the FIEA that is less regulated (paragraph (2) securities). However, in a case it is tokenized, unless otherwise excluded pursuant to the provisions of the FIEA, they fall under the category of electronically recorded transferable rights (*Denshi kiroku iten kenri*) and are classified as securities under Article 2, paragraph (1) of the FIEA.[599] Consequently, Security Tokens backed by a silent partnership must be handled by a Type I Financial Instruments Business Operator (so-called securities companies).[600] Nevertheless, Security Tokens differ greatly from traditional securities, as they are managed by blockchains. Therefore, it is necessary for securities companies to establish operational systems such as examination practices in response to segregation management, advertising regulations, and obligations to explain. Furthermore, deepening of operations based on the examples of problems in the future will be awaited.

The establishment of a securities company specializing in the sale, purchase, and deposit of Security Tokens is also envisaged, and it is expected that the standard for secondary transactions of Security Tokens will become more common in Japan.

599. Article 2, para. (1) of the FIEA.
600. Article 28, para. (1) of the FIEA.

[2] Limitations for Improving the Liquidity

The liquidity of the Security Tokens appears to be considerably lower than secondary trading in the listed market (e.g., corporate stocks and J-REIT units are traded on a daily basis as in the stock market based on market prices). Experts believe a possible cause for the current sluggish liquidity of the Security Tokens could be the lack of a secondary trading market.[601] From the viewpoint of securing opportunities for return on invested capital of general investors, it is now awaiting the development of secondary trading market.

When considering secondary trading market of Security Tokens, it is necessary to consider the FIEA. There are three types of secondary trading platforms that are planned under the FIEA:

(i) financial instruments markets;[602]
(ii) private trading systems (PTS);[603] and
(iii) over-the-counter trading (OTC).[604]

(i) The establishment of a financial instruments market requires a licence for the financial instruments market that is quite difficult to obtain. (ii) Not only registration of Type I Financial Instruments Business but also the approval of the Proprietary Trading System (PTS) Business are required to conduct the Private Trading System (PTS) Business. Obtaining such registration and approval is substantially difficult, although not as difficult as in the case of obtaining a licence for the financial instruments market. Furthermore, (iii) in cases where the over-the-counter trading (OTC) business is conducted, it is necessary to obtain the registration of the Type I Financial Instruments Business. However, the question of how to handle and describe Security Tokens operations of over-the-counter trading (OTC) in the registration form remains open in current practice. Further progress in the future must be awaited.

[3] Other Regulations under the FIEA

When the Security Token can be transferred for custody independently or jointly with its outsourcee without the involvement of their customer, such as custody under delegated authority holding a secret key sufficient to transfer the customer's Security Token, the custody is basically entrusted with a customer's Token, and therefore falls under the category of a Type I Financial Instruments Business, which requires registration process.[605] Therefore, attention should be always paid when examining the structure for securing liquidity.

601. Osaka Digital Exchange Co., Ltd. started trading by using PTS in 25 Dec. 2023. However, transaction execution timings are only twice daily so far.
602. Article 80, para. (1) of the FIEA.
603. Article 30, para. (1) of the FIEA.
604. Article 28, para. (1) of the FIEA.
605. *Ibid.*

§5.19 CAPITAL MARKETS AND BLOCKCHAIN: COUNTRY REPORT – SINGAPORE

Kim Kit Ow[606] *& Gerard Ng*[607]

[A] What Makes a Token a Security?

As a global financial hub, Singapore has also been a frontrunner in the Fintech scene, and it has certainly been making headlines in Asia for being a staunch promoter of innovation while embracing a balanced and calibrated regulatory approach towards the application of blockchain in capital markets. This can be evidently seen in the Singapore government's attitude towards the regulation of blockchain-based digital Tokens, such as virtual currencies. The use of blockchain technology in itself is not new and has been commonly used in smart contracts and decentralized operations to facilitate trade and transfer of digital assets. Virtual currency or cryptocurrency is one of the many uses of blockchain technology.

The focus on the use of blockchain technology in capital markets in Singapore has been on the offering or issuance of digital Tokens. Unlike some other jurisdictions, Singapore has not classified nor regulated digital Tokens on a standalone basis, deciding against regulating them based on their characteristics and the activities which they are used for. Therefore, depending on its characteristics and what it is used for, a digital Token could be considered a security, a commodity or a utility.

In 2017, the Monetary Authority of Singapore (MAS) clarified that if a digital Token (e.g., blockchain-based) constitutes a product under Singapore's securities laws, then the offer or issuance of such digital Token shall comply with the relevant securities laws under the Securities & Futures Act of Singapore 2001[608] (SFA). The MAS is the integrated regulator and supervisor of financial institutions in Singapore in the banking, capital markets, insurance and payments sectors. This clarification was seen as necessary against the backdrop of a slew of ICOs, heightened concerns over anti-money laundering (AML) and countering the financing of terrorism (CFT) and the potential risks that such activities may negatively impact consumers. In developing a more targeted regulatory approach, the MAS issued a 'Guide to Digital Token Offerings' on 14 November 2017, which has since had three revisions, with its latest version dated 26 May 2020 (the DTO Guide).

Where capital markets are concerned, it is important to consider the situation when a digital Token falls under the definition of 'capital markets product' under the SFA and its regulatory treatment. As stated clearly by the MAS in the DTO Guide, an

606. Kim Kit Ow is a Partner at Blackletter LLC. She specialises in financial services, FinTech, and banking (regulatory). In 2009, she was announced as the Asian regional director for the International Chamber of Commerce (ICC) and in 2018 appointed onto the ICC Commission on Arbitration and ADR. She would like to thank her colleague Shueh Chien Lai for his assistance.
607. Gerard Ng is the Managing Partner at Blackletter LLC. His core practice focuses on transactional banking and finance, structured finance, capital markets, and digital assets.
608. Media release 'MAS clarifies regulatory position on the offer of digital tokens in Singapore' (Monetary Authority of Singapore 1 Aug. 2017).

offer or issuance of digital Tokens may be regulated by the MAS if the digital Tokens are 'capital markets products'.[609] Capital markets products may include securities, derivatives contracts as well as units in a CIS (e.g., an investment fund). The MAS in a non-exhaustive manner set out some instances in the DTO Guide when a digital Token may constitute a 'capital markets product'. The following are five examples listed therein:[610]

(1) a share,[611] where it confers or represents an ownership interest in a corporation, represents liability of the Token holder in the corporation, and represents mutual covenants with other Token holders in the corporation *inter se*;
(2) a debenture, where it constitutes or evidences the indebtedness of the issuer of the digital Token in respect of any money that is or may be lent to the issuer by a Token holder;
(3) a unit in a business trust,[612] where it confers or represents ownership interest in the trust property of a business trust;
(4) a securities[613] -based derivatives contract, which includes any derivatives contract of which the underlying thing is a share, debenture or unit in a business trust; or
(5) a unit in a CIS, where it represents a right or interest in a CIS, or an option to acquire a right or interest in a CIS.

MAS further stated in the DTO Guide that it will 'examine the structure and characteristics of, including the rights attached to, a digital Token in determining if the digital Token is a type of capital markets products under the SFA'.[614] We would observe that such an approach is indeed very measured, looks beyond mere labels and does not seek to over-regulate. Given that Singapore already has extensive laws and regulations in the SFA, its subsidiary legislation and MAS-issued notices and guidance, to the extent that a digital Token has characteristics and risks that are associated with a capital markets product or such regulated activity (e.g., dealing in capital markets

---

609. *See* Guide to Digital Token Offerings at para. 2.1. Also *see* s. 2(1) of the SFA which defines 'capital markets products' to include any securities (which includes shares, debentures and units in a business trust), units in a CIS, derivatives contracts (which includes derivatives of shares, debentures and units in a business trust), spot foreign exchange contracts for the purposes of leveraged foreign exchange trading, and such other products as MAS may prescribe as capital markets products.
610. *See* Guide to Digital Token Offerings at para. 2.3 where examples are provided by the MAS on how digital Tokens may be considered 'capital markets products'.
611. *See* s. 2(1) of the SFA, read with s. 4(1) of the Companies Act 1967. The term 'share' means 'a share in the share capital of a corporation and includes stock except where a distinction between stocks and share is expressed or implied'.
612. *See* s. 2(1) of the SFA, read with s. 2 of the Business Trusts Act 2004. Under s. 2 of the Business Trusts Act 2004, a 'unit', in relation to a business trust, means a 'share in the beneficial ownership in the trust property of the business trust'.
613. Includes shares, debentures and units in a business trust. *See* s. 2(1) of the SFA for the definition of 'securities' under the SFA.
614. *See* Guide to Digital Token Offerings at para. 2.2.

products) in connection thereto, then it will accordingly be regulated under current laws.

[B] Blockchain Finality

There are no specific statutory provisions governing the legal status of blockchain transactions in Singapore at the moment. This is unlike traditional capital market products such as listed shares, which transfers have for many years now had both legal and technical finality. A transfer of listed shares now would typically take the form of book entries which are lodged, registered and finally recorded in an electronic central ledger, held at The Central Depository (Pte) Limited (CDP), which is a wholly owned subsidiary of SGX which provides integrated clearing, settlement and depository services for many products in the Singapore securities market. Insofar as Digital Payment Tokens (DPT) are concerned, 'cryptocurrency' which is a form of DPT (as defined under the Payment Services Act 2019) has been expressly recognized as a form of property capable of being the subject matter of an enforcement order. In Order 22 of the Rules of Court 2021, which deals with the enforcement of judgments and orders, Order 22 Rule 1(1) defines 'movable property' to include 'cash, debt, deposits of money, bonds, shares or other securities, membership in clubs or societies, and *cryptocurrency or digital currency*'. It remains to be seen whether this definition will apply to DPTs other than cryptocurrencies.

In terms of common law, Singapore courts have ruled that cryptocurrencies may be treated as property that can be held on trust. The issue of whether cryptocurrencies are property was first considered in the case of *B2C2 Ltd v. Quoine Pte Ltd* [2019] 4 SLR 17 (*B2C2 v. Quoine*) by the Singapore International Commercial Court[615] but was not explored in detail as the parties proceeded on the common ground that cryptocurrencies were a species of property that was capable of being the subject of a trust.[616] The General Division of the Singapore High Court confirmed this position in the case of *ByBit v. Ho Kai Xin and others* [2023] SGHC 199 (*ByBit v. Ho Kai Xin*) in July 2023 and further characterized cryptocurrencies as a 'thing in action'. The learned Justice Philip Jerayetnam found that cryptocurrencies were property on the following grounds:

(1) MAS issued a consultation paper titled '*Response to Public Consultation on Proposed Regulatory measures for Digital Payment Token Services*' on 3 July 2023 which reflected that it was possible to identify and segregate digital assets, and thus supports the view that it is legally possible to hold such digital assets on trust.[617]

---

615. The Singapore International Commercial Court is a division of the General Division of the High Court and part of the Supreme Court of Singapore. It was established relatively recently in 2015 and aims to be a trusted neutral forum to meet the growing demand for effective transnational dispute resolution through litigation due to Singapore's strategic location within Asia and the reputation of its world-class judiciary known for efficiency, competence and integrity.
616. *See B2C2 Ltd v. Quoine Pte Ltd* [2019] 4 SLR 17 at [142].
617. *See ByBit Fintech Limited v. Ho Kai Xin and others* [2023] SGHC 199 at [29].

(2) The Rules of Court 2021 in Order 22 Rule 1(1) recognized cryptocurrency or other digital currency as 'movable property' for the purposes of defining property capable of being the subject matter of an enforcement order under Order 22.[618]

(3) Crypto assets meet Lord Wilberforce's *dictum* in *National Provincial Bank v. Ainsworth* [1965] 1 AC 1175 at 1248 that:[619]

> Before a right or an interest can be admitted into the category of property, or of a right affecting property, it must be definable, identifiable by third parties, capable in its nature of assumption by third parties, and have some degree of permanence or stability.
>
> The learned Justice Philip Jeyaretnam went on to consider whether the subject of the dispute, Tether, was a thing in action. He accepted that the category of things in action was expanded from its origin as a category of rights enforceable by actions to include other incorporeal rights of property and followed Fry LJ's dictum in *Colonial Bank v. Whinney* (1885) 30 Ch D 261 (*Colonial Bank v. Whinney*) that: 'All personal things are either in possession or action. The law knows no *tertium quid* between the two.'[620]

It is noteworthy that the UK Law Commission published its final report on crypto Tokens and other digital assets on 28 June 2023 (Final Report on Digital Assets)[621] where it was concluded that the law in England and Wales had moved towards the explicit recognition of a 'third' category of things to which personal property rights can relate, and that certain digital assets should be treated as such third category things.[622] By way of background, the Final Report on Digital Assets is the end product of a 3-year project the UK Law Commission undertook from the UK Ministry of Justice to review the law and consider reform to ensure that the law of England and Wales can accommodate digital assets, including crypto assets.[623] The recommendations made in the Final Report on Digital Assets may potentially translate into statutory reform in the UK and may also in itself be persuasive in common law jurisdictions worldwide.

The UK Law Commission agreed with views received from consultees that the reasoning in *Colonial Bank v. Whinny* turned on the interpretation of the bankruptcy statutes then in force and had been taken out of context and used as authority for a proposition that it was not meant to support. Finally, it expressed the view that considering things in action as a wider, residual category of things encompassing everything that was not a thing in possession would risk confusing the defining features of things in action (in the narrow sense), and it would be cleaner to recognize a separate third category of property, rather than multiple 'sub-categories' of a broad

618. *See ibid.*, at [30].
619. *See ibid.*, at [33].
620. *See ibid.*, at [34] and [35].
621. The Final Report on Digital Assets may be downloaded from the following link: https://www.lawcom.gov.uk/project/digital-assets/.
622. *See* Final Report on Digital Assets at para. 3.3.
623. *See* Final Report on Digital Assets at para. 1.9.

residual category.[624] Unfortunately, the Final Report on Digital Assets and its salient observations on the type of property digital assets fell under was not considered in *ByBit v. Ho Kai Xin*, and the subject may well be re-visited in a future case, especially in view of the in-depth analysis conducted by the UK Law Commission on this issue.

Taken together, given that cryptocurrencies have been recognized as property by the High Court in *B2C2 v. Quoine* and *ByBit v. Ho Kai Xin*, as well as in the Rules of Court 2021, there is a high possibility that certain parties who rely on the blockchain records may be afforded some measure of protection in practice.

A bona fide purchaser for value in a blockchain transaction may have relied on the blockchain records and be entitled to keep the property in this case. It is worth noting that it is not the entry in the blockchain record itself that confers this limited extent of finality, but the bona fides of the purchaser, which may be established through reliance on the record.

In the absence of any specific legal authorities, blockchain records have no particular legal significance in Singapore. Entries in the blockchain record do not confer or amend legal rights in themselves. Ultimately, one will have to look at the underlying legal transactions to determine if the blockchain record is an accurate reflection of legal status. There is no reason to doubt that the legal doctrines of mistake and rectification will apply in the same way to this context, such that a court may give a remedy to 'correct' an 'inaccurate' entry on the blockchain record.

The *nemo dat* rule is likely to be applicable in this context, such that assignments of legal rights reflected in the blockchain record will only be valid insofar as the assignors actually had the requisite legal rights to assign, regardless of what may be reflected in the blockchain record.

In summary, blockchain records are not currently a recognized registry, and for now, no legal rights arise from entries into the blockchain records in themselves.

[C] Private International Law

It is important when considering private international law issues involving cross-border transactions of Tokens to determine what is the applicable law. A key question that arises in determining the applicable law in Singapore is whether the claim arises out of property that is located in Singapore.

A recent Singapore High Court decision in the case of *Cheong Jun Yoong v. Three Arrows Capital Ltd and others* [2024] SGHC 21 (*Cheong Jun Yoong*) sets out the following principles with regard to determining the location of crypto assets:[625]

(a) the location of a crypto asset is best determined by where it is controlled;
(b) control over a crypto asset lies with the person who controls the private key to the crypto asset linked to the key; and

624. *See* Final Report on Digital Assets at paras 3.35 and 3.36.
625. *See Cheong Jun Yong v. Three Arrows Capital Ltd and others* [2024] SGHC 21 at [60] to [65].

(c) the residence of the person controlling the private key should be treated as the *situs* of the crypto asset linked to that private key.

The claimant in this case made an application to serve originating documents out of jurisdiction on the defendants in the British Virgin Islands (BVI) for a dispute involving crypto assets. The application was taken out on the basis that the Singapore Court is the appropriate court to hear the action. To this end, the claimant needed to show, *inter alia*, that there is a good arguable case that there is sufficient nexus to Singapore.[626] In turn, one of the factors that shows sufficient nexus to Singapore is if 'the claim is made for a debt secured on immovable property situated in Singapore, *or is made to assert, declare or determine proprietary or possessory rights, or rights of security, in or over movable property, or to obtain authority to dispose of movable property, situated in Singapore*'.[627]

The Singapore High Court found that the residence of the person controlling the private key was the more appropriate test for determining the *situs* of the crypto assets rather than the domicile of the said person as the residence of a person is a better indicator of where the control is being exercised.[628] This is a significant judgment as prior to this case, there were no reported Singapore decisions on the issue of *situs* of crypto assets.[629] One remaining question is whether the test set out in this case will also be applied in a conflicts-of-laws situation when determining whether Singapore law is applicable in situations where the proprietary rights in crypto assets are disputed. This will have to be left to a future court to decide if and when the issue arises.

[D] Special Requirements for Prospectus

In the examples set out above under §5.13[A], offers or issuance of digital Tokens which constitute securities, securities-based derivatives contracts or units in a CIS will be subject to the same regulatory regime and treatment under Part XIII of the SFA as offers of securities, securities-based derivatives contracts or units in a CIS. To this end, there are several aspects that one has to be concerned with, including how an 'offer' is made and its accompanying prospectus requirements.

An offer of digital Tokens which constitute securities, securities-based derivatives contracts or units in a CIS can only be made if it complies with the requirements under Part XIII of the SFA.[630] The offer must also be made in or accompanied by a prospectus that is prepared in accordance with the SFA and is registered with MAS (*Prospectus Requirements*) unless specifically exempted. Where an offer is made in relation to units in a CIS to retail investors, the CIS is further subject to authorization

626. *See* Supreme Court Practice Directions 2021 at para. 63(2).
627. *See* Supreme Court Practice Directions 2021 at para. 63(3)(i).
628. *See Cheong Jun Yong v. Three Arrows Capital Ltd and others* [2024] SGHC 21 at [63].
629. *See Cheong Jun Yong v. Three Arrows Capital Ltd and others* [2024] SGHC 21 at [52].
630. *See* ss 240 and 296 of the SFA.

or recognition requirements[631] prescribed by the MAS. An authorized CIS or a recognized CIS under the SFA must comply with various conditions and restrictions set out under the Code on CISs, published by the MAS.

Under Part XIII of the SFA, an offer as described above may be exempt from the Prospectus Requirements,[632] where, among others:

(1) the offer is a small (personal) offer that does not exceed SGD 5 million (or its equivalent in a foreign currency) within any twelve-month period, subject to certain conditions;
(2) the offer is a private placement offer made to no more than fifty persons within any twelve-month period, subject to certain conditions;
(3) the offer is made to institutional investors only; or
(4) the offer is made to accredited investors, subject to certain conditions.[633]

There are no exceptions made insofar as a digital Token is concerned in this regard. To the extent that a digital Token constitutes a security and its offer is required to be made in or accompanied by a prospectus that is prepared in accordance with the SFA and is registered with MAS, it will have to comply with all the relevant guidelines. As a matter of practical observation, given that the underlying specifics to a digital Token are not as common as traditional capital markets product (e.g., listed shares), it is even more important for those specifics, especially the risks associated with the product, to be fully disclosed.

Another aspect that a person who offers digital Tokens that constitute securities, securities-based derivatives contracts or units in a CIS needs to be concerned with is whether the said digital Token is also traded on the market (e.g., on an exchange). This is because a person who establishes or operates a trading platform in Singapore in relation to digital Tokens which constitute securities, derivatives contracts or units in a CIS may be considered to be establishing or operating an organized market.[634] A person who establishes or operates an organized market, or holds himself out as operating such a market, must be approved by MAS as an approved exchange or recognized by MAS as a recognized market operator under the SFA unless otherwise exempted.[635]

In the DTO Guide, MAS sets out eleven case studies, wherein it assesses how (if at all) the current legislation and regulations in respect of financial markets may apply to the offers of digital Tokens and the activities related thereto. While MAS makes it

631. *See* ss 286 and 287 of the SFA, read with Part II of the Securities and Futures (Offers of Investments) (Collective Investment Schemes) Regulations 2005.
632. In the case of units in a CIS, exempt from the authorization and recognition requirements.
633. *See* Guide to Digital Token Offerings at para. 2.7.
634. *Ibid.*, at para. 2.11 and also *see* Part I of the First Schedule to the SFA for the definition of an 'organised market'.
635. Also *see* Guidelines on the Regulation of Markets (Guideline no. SFA02-G01) https://www.mas.gov.sg/-/media/MAS/resource/legislation_guidelines/securities_futures/sub_legislation/Guidelines_Regulation_of_Markets.pdf (accessed 11 Mar. 2020) for guidance.

clear that these case studies are merely for illustrative purposes,[636] it does provide some guidance on MAS' regulatory approach on how it would deal with similar situations – to assess each underlying digital Token to see if it may fall within the definition of 'capital markets products', and if so, then apply the relevant legislation and regulations applicable traditionally to such products to the said digital Token.

When intermediating digital Tokens (i.e., dealing, buying and selling or broking), it is also important to note that even if a digital Token is not to be considered a 'capital markets product', it may still be caught as a 'Digital Payment Token' under the Payment Services Act 2019 (PS Act). Under Section 2 of the PS Act, 'digital payment token' is broadly defined as:

> 'digital payment token' means any digital representation of value (other than an excluded digital representation of value) that –
>
> (a) is expressed as a unit;
> (b) is not denominated in any currency, and is not pegged by its issuer to any currency;
> (c) is, or is intended to be, a medium of exchange accepted by the public, or a section of the public, as payment for goods or services or for the discharge of debt;
> (d) can be transferred, stored or traded electronically; and
> (e) satisfies such other characteristics as the authority may prescribe.

Therefore, to the extent that a person facilitates the exchange of digital payment Tokens, that person will need to be regulated under the PS Act.[637] The definition of digital payment Token service was further expanded by the Payment Services (Amendment) Act 2021 (PS Amendment Act) to include the following services: (a) transfer of digital payment Tokens, (b) provision of custodian wallet services for digital payment Tokens and (c) facilitating the exchange of digital payment Tokens without possession of moneys or digital payment Tokens by the digital payment Token service provider.[638] The expansion of the definition of 'digital payment token service' was done in order to align Singapore's regime with enhanced Financial Action Task Force (FATF) standards adopted in June 2019 applicable to digital payment Token service providers aimed at addressing money-laundering and terrorist financing risks of VASPs.[639]

This has been part of the wider policy considerations that MAS dealt with in the earlier consultation periods for the PS Act, wherein MAS considered the AML/CFT risks associated with digital payment Tokens/virtual currency and accordingly the appropriateness of regulating these intermediaries.[640] This is elaborated below.

---

636. *See* Guide to Digital Token Offerings at para. 4.1.
637. *See* s. 5 of the PS Act read with First Schedule Parts 1 and 3.
638. *See* s. 7 of the PS Amendment Act for the full version of these definitions. The PS Amendment Act was passed on 4 Jan. 2021, but has not come into force as of the time of writing.
639. *See* 'Explanatory Brief for Payment Services (Amendment) Bill' published by MAS dated 2 Nov. 2020 at para. 6.
640. *See* 'Response to Feedback Received on the Proposed Payment Services Bill' published by MAS dated 19 Nov. 2018 at para. 3.19.

[E] Regulatory Specifics for Organized Trade

When a security is issued, investors would go through an intermediary to access the investment. In Singapore, this intermediary must be a regulated entity, such as a broker or similar. Such an intermediary shall be subject to regulatory requirements that aim to ensure investor safeguards. These would include licences, specific limitations on specific investor groups and reporting to the MAS, etc. Similarly, where a blockchain-based Security Token is offered through such intermediaries, the same regulatory expectations would apply. To the extent that the underlying product that is offered for investment is a 'capital markets product' (e.g., a security), then an intermediary which is dealing in such products shall be required to hold a Capital Markets Services Licence under the SFA.

The heightened concerns surrounding the use of blockchain in digital Tokens in recent times have centred on money-laundering and terrorism-financing risks. Singapore has on all fronts been very vigilant and has also been very particular in complying with the recommendations and standards of the FATF in this regard.[641]

MAS has through the DTO Guide emphasized that all persons who are deemed to be an intermediary conducting regulated activities shall be bound to comply with the relevant MAS Notices on Prevention of Money Laundering and CFT which are applicable to them.[642] This is also now bolstered by the AML/CFT requirements that will also apply to digital payment Tokens intermediaries which will be regulated under the PS Act, where their Tokens are not regulated as 'capital markets products' under the SFA. Digital payment Token intermediaries are *'the points of intersection that provide gateways to the regulated financial system and nodes through which value may be moved'*. In order to ensure that MAS is equipped to implement appropriate measures to counter the evolving ML/TF risks with regard to certain digital payment Tokens which are gaining traction quickly, the PS Amendment Act further provides MAS with new powers to impose:

(a) user protection measures on certain digital payment Token service providers to ensure the safekeeping of customer assets held by the digital payment Token service provider, where necessary; and
(b) measures on certain digital payment Token service providers where it is in MAS' view necessary or expedient in the interest of the public or a section of

641. http://www.fatf-gafi.org/publications/fatfrecommendations/?hf=10&b=0&s=desc(fatf_releasedate) (accessed 11 Mar. 2020). *See* para. 2 of 'Anti-money laundering and counter-terrorist financing measures – Singapore, Enhanced Follow-up Report and Technical Compliance Re-Rafting' published by the FATF in 2019. Singapore is rated as 'compliant' with Recommendation 15 of the FATF which relates to ML/TF risks posed by new technologies, including by blockchain.
642. *See* Guide to Digital Token Offerings at para. 3.1.

the public, the stability of the financial system in Singapore, or the monetary policy of MAS.[643]

In connection with the new section 21A of the PS Act, MAS proposed amendments in a consultation paper to the Payment Services Regulations 2019 (PS Regulations) to implement key segregation and custody requirements for digital payment Token services under the PS Act.[644] These amendments include, *inter alia*, requirements for a digital payment Token service provider to:

(a) ensure its customers' assets are properly segregated from its own assets and held on trust for the benefit of its customers;
(b) safeguard its customers' monies with financial institutions in Singapore;
(c) conduct daily reconciliation of customers' assets and customers' money at the entity-level;
(d) keep transaction records, and maintain separate books and records for each customer with details of the customer's assets at all times;
(e) provide monthly statements of account to the customers;
(f) implement risk management controls to safeguard the private keys and storage of the customer's DPTs; and
(g) maintain adequate systems, processes, controls, human resources, and governance arrangements to ensure the integrity and security of customers' assets and mitigate the risk of any loss of customers' assets, in a manner that is commensurate with the nature, scale, and complexity of their business.

These are the collective efforts by the MAS to ensure that most of the money-laundering and terrorism-financing risks associated with digital payment Tokens/virtual currency may be addressed based on whether the Tokens are 'capital markets products' or not. This approach is in line with other general obligations imposed under Singapore law to combat money laundering and terrorism financing, including:

- an obligation pursuant to section 45 of the Corruption, Drug Trafficking and Other Serious Crimes (Confiscation of Benefits) Act 1992 to report suspicious transactions to the Commercial Affairs Department; and
- prohibitions from dealing with or providing financial services to designated individuals and entities pursuant to the Terrorism (Suppression of Financing) Act 2002 and various regulations that give effect to the United Nations Security Council Resolutions.[645]

643. *See* Explanatory Brief for Payment Services (Amendment) Bill published by MAS on 2 Nov. 2020 at para. 10. *See also* ss 3 and 4 of the PS Amendment Act for the addition of a new s. 21A to the PS Act and amendments to s. 23 of the PS Act.
644. *See* Consultation Paper on Proposed Amendments to the Payment Services Regulations published by MAS on 3 Jul. 2023 at Annex B for the full list of draft amendments to PS Regulations.
645. *See* Guide to Digital Token Offerings at paras 3.3.1 and 3.3.2.

Following the enhanced FATF standards, the Financial Services and Markets Act 2022 (FSM Act) was passed on 5 April 2022,[646] and MAS imposed licensing and ongoing requirements on VASPs to ensure that such VASPs must have a meaningful presence in Singapore.[647] Importantly, the FSM Act imposes a licensing requirement on digital Token service providers providing digital Token services *outside* Singapore from a place of business in Singapore.[648] The same licensing requirement is imposed on Singapore corporations providing digital Token services outside Singapore.[649] The licensing of such digital Token service providers is timely, given a spate of high-profile collapses in 2022 of several cryptocurrency operators registered in Singapore.[650]

[F] Conclusion

The fast-paced developments and evolution of blockchain technology must be seen to be both a boon and bane to our financial world. While innovation should not be stymied, it cannot be allowed a free reign without any regulations and control. The approach that Singapore has adopted in relation to accommodating blockchain in its capital markets has been a calibrated one, ensuring that our laws keep pace with innovation and that Singapore continues to be at the forefront without compromising any global regulatory standards.

§5.20 CAPITAL MARKETS AND BLOCKCHAIN: COUNTRY REPORT – SOUTH KOREA

Jongbaek Park[651]

[A] What Makes a Token a Security?

At this moment, there is no law or administrative regulation that specifically defines the concept of 'Token' in Korea. Under the Act on Reporting and Using Specified

646. The FSM Act will be implemented in phases. The first phase commenced on 28 Apr. 2023, and the remaining phases are targeted to be implemented between the second half of 2023 and 2024.

647. *See* Explanatory Brief for Financial Services and Markets Bill 2022 published by MAS on 14 Feb. 2022 at para. 12. These requirements in the FSM Act include (i) having a permanent place of business in Singapore [s. 143(1)]; (ii) appointing at least one person to be present, on such days and at such hours as MAS may specify by notice in writing, at the licensee's permanent place of business to address any AML/CFT related queries or complaints from any person that uses any digital Token service provided by the licensee or is a customer of the licensee [s. 143(2)]; (iii) keeping and making available the licensee's transactions in relation to any digital Token service provided to authorities in Singapore in a timely manner upon request [s. 145(1)]; (iv) satisfying financial requirements that may be prescribed or specified by MAS by notice in writing [s. 138(6)].

648. *See* s. 137(1) of the FSM Act. For comparison, the PS Act governs persons providing payment services in Singapore.

649. *See* s. 137(3) of the FSM Act.

650. https://www.ft.com/content/e7b85235-87e8-44c7-a97f-2d2ffa253465 (accessed on 15 Aug. 2023).

651. Jongbaek Park is a partner at Bae Kim & Lee leading the Blockchain & Cryptoasset Team and works on crypto assets, fintech, capital market and relevant regulations. He was recognized as

Financial Transaction Information (*AML Act*), which has the legislative purpose to prevent money laundering, 'virtual assets' are broadly defined as 'electronic certificates ("*Jeungpyo*" in Korean) with economic value that can be transferred electronically'.[652] It is worth noting that the criteria of 'transferred electronically' within the definition of 'virtual assets' suggests that the scope of virtual assets is not limited to virtual assets using blockchain or distributed ledger technology for the electronic method of transfer.

In general context, a data package created based on the blockchain technology that has economic value, whether or not it is linked to an existing underlying asset, is understood to be what is meant by a 'Token'. There is no law that stipulates the types of Tokens, but the industry has progressed to categorize certain types of Tokens into Utility Tokens, Payment Tokens, and Security Tokens, depending on the function of a Token.

Under the Financial Investment Services and Capital Markets Act (*FISCMA*), financial investment instruments are divided into two large classes, which are securities and derivative financial instruments. The securities class are further divided into six categories: debt securities, equity securities, beneficiary certificates, investment contract securities, derivative-linked securities, and depository receipts.

Under the FISCMA, a 'financial investment instrument'[653] means a right acquired by an agreement to pay money or any other things with property value (*money or value*) at present or at a specific point of time in the future, with the intention to earn a profit or avoid a loss, with the investment risk that the total amount of such money or value paid or payable to acquire the right may exceed the total amount of money or value already recovered or recoverable from such right.

The class of 'securities'[654] refers to financial investment instruments for which an investor pays money or value at the time of the acquisition of the relevant right, and the investor does not owe any further obligation to make an additional payment on any ground. In contrast, the class of 'derivative financial instruments' refers to financial investment instruments for which an investor might have to bear further obligations to make additional payments.

The definition of 'investment contract securities'[655] under the FISCMA is analogous to the *Howey Test* under the laws of the US. 'Investment contract securities' takes the form of a contractual right for an investor to receive profits and losses based on the performance of a common enterprise with other persons in which the investor invests and which that other person primarily manages.

The key distinction between the *Howey* test and the definition of 'investment contract securities' under the FISCMA is the criteria of considering whether the

---

Leading Practitioner for Fintech&Blockchain in Who's Who Legal (2023), Leading Individual in The Legal 500 Asia-Pacific (2023), and was awarded with the Client Choice Awards Lexology (2024). Jongbaek Park would like to extend his appreciation to Mr Eric Jeong for his contribution to the Korean Country Report.

652. Article 3 of the AML Act.
653. Article 3(1) of the FISCMA.
654. Article 4(1) of the FISCMA.
655. Article 4(6) of the FISCMA.

investor has a reasonable expectation of receiving profits resulting from the common enterprise or whether the investor has a contractual right to receive such profits.

There are two overarching aspects regarding how Security Tokens can be incorporated into the current legal regime. The first aspect involves whether the traditional types of securities under the FISMCA, such as shares, corporate bonds, and beneficiary certificates, can be issued in the form of a Token instead of paper or electronic registered securities (as currently regulated under the Electronic Securities Act). The second aspect pertains to whether certain Crypto-Native Tokens and Tokens linked to real-world assets can be legally categorized as 'investment contract securities' under FISCMA.

As to whether traditional types of securities under the FISCMA can be issued in the form of a Token, there have been some meaningful guidelines published by the Financial Services Commission of Korea (*FSC*) which have helped the industry to better understand the direction in which the financial regulators are navigating towards. On 29 November 2022, the FSC issued the 'Guideline for New Securities Business, including Fractional Investment (known as the *Fractional Investment Guideline*)'. Through the Fractional Investment Guideline, the FSC accepted that certain fractional investment products, which involve multiple individuals sharing ownership of a single asset, may be categorized as 'investment contract securities'. The guideline states that the determination of whether a fractional investment product can be attributed as 'investment contract securities' is based on the substantive content of the rights associated with the fractional investment products, regardless of the method and formality (paper media, description on a depository account book, electronic registration on an electronic register, Tokens on a distributed ledger, etc.) of expressing such rights, and the adoption of specific technologies. Additionally, in January 2022, the FSC announced that the legal characteristics of NFTs are not determined by their underlying technology or name per se but rather by the substantive content of the rights associated with each NFT, and thus, if an NFT possesses the substantive content of 'investment contract securities', such NFT may be considered a security.

Furthermore, in March 2023, the FSC issued the 'Guideline for the Issuance and Distribution System for Securities Tokens (known as the *STO Guideline*)'. The main point of the STO Guideline is that the existing six types of securities under the FISCMA will be permitted to be issued in the form of Distributed Ledger-Based Tokens, and these Distributed Ledger-Based Security Tokens will be incorporated as a new type of electronic registration method under the Electronic Securities Act. In accordance with the STO Guideline, the FSC has submitted proposed amendments to the FISCMA and the Electronic Securities Act to the National Assembly, which are to be reviewed by the National Assembly. The proposed amendments to the FISCMA extend the regulations applicable to security types other than investment contract securities in order to regulate the distribution of investment contract securities in the same manner as the post-issuance distribution of other types of securities, since under the current FISCMA, 'investment contract securities' is treated as 'securities' class only for its issuance stage. Additionally, the amendments propose permitting an over-the-counter market where multiple parties may trade Security Tokens through investment brokers. The proposed amendments to the Electronic Securities Act newly introduce the definition of 'distributed ledgers' and 'distributed ledger registered securities'. Moreover, the amendments propose to recognize an issuer as the account management institution so that an issuer of a Security Token meeting certain requirements will be permitted to record the transfer details of securities.

The term 'distributed ledger' refers to a ledger and its management system where information relating to shares, etc., is jointly recorded in chronological order by multiple participants. It is protected against unauthorized deletion and ex post facto changes through joint management and technical measures. 'Distributed ledger registered securities' means securities electronically registered in an electronic register (including the proprietary account book for an account management institution opened at the electronic registry, which is the Korean Securities Depositary, and customer account books prepared by the account management institution) which is a distributed ledger.

The term 'account management institution as an issuer' refers to an institution that intends to electronically register the securities it issues by using a distributed ledger and is registered with the FSC, meeting certain personnel and facility requirements and has a capital of KRW 1 billion or more.

[B] Blockchain Finality

As a generally accepted understanding, transaction details recorded on a blockchain distributed ledger are designed to be final and irreversible; therefore, the records cannot be arbitrarily modified (hence, technologically final). However, there is no law or regulation in Korea that stipulates regulations regarding blockchain-based distributed ledger or registration of securities on a distribute ledger in order to give effectiveness to the issuance, registration, transfer of, or creation of a pledge on securities with an irrevocable effect (i.e., finality). As discussed in Part 1 above regarding the proposed amendments to the Electronic Securities Act, the proposed amendments include distributed ledger registered securities as a type of electronically registered securities, and the proposed amendments do not distinguish the validity and effectiveness of registration on a distributed ledger from that of the existing conventional electronic registration framework. Therefore, if the proposed amendments pass, the provisions relating to the validity and effectiveness of the existing conventional electronic registration and effective transfer of electronically registered securities, etc., under the current Electronic Securities Act will apply to distributed ledger registered securities.

The key provisions relating to the issue of validity and effectiveness for electronic registration of securities under the current Electronic Securities Act of Korea are as follows:

- For the electronic securities held by an account management institution, the securities shall be registered in the proprietary account book for the account management institution managed by an electronic registry. For the electronic securities held by ordinary customers, the securities shall be registered in the customer account book managed by the account management institution (customer account book and proprietary account book, together the 'electronic register account book'). Any person registered in the electronic register account book may rely on the presumption that such person has lawfully acquired the legal right to the relevant electronically registered securities.[656]

- In the case of transferring electronic securities, the effectiveness of the transfer occurs at the time when the transferor's account is debited and the transferee's account is credited in the electronic register account book.[657]
- The creation of a pledge on electronic securities shall take effect after the registration in the electronic register account book of the fact that the electronic securities are subject to the pledge and the pledgee's details.[658]
- Regarding securities that are electronically registered as a trust property, the relevant trustee may rely on the effectiveness of the registration to defend against any third-party claims towards the registered securities.[659]

In order to find legal finality of blockchain records, one should acknowledge that all records entered on a blockchain are effective and valid. However, the caveat for such acknowledgement is that if a blockchain is forked to create two separate blockchains for the same underlying asset, there may be cases of mismatch between the actual right holder and the right holder recorded on the blockchain. For example, due to branching of a blockchain from forking, there may be instances where the blockchain is recorded with a contract entered with a party who lacks the legal capacity or transactions, such as in cases where Tokens that are acquired through hacking or theft are disposed by a person without lawful rights. Consequently, this raises the question of whether bona fide acquisition rule can be recognized even if any of the above events occur in transactions involving Security Tokens.

If bona fide acquisition rule is not recognized for the purpose of Security Token transactions, the legal consequence borne by a transferee, who receives Security Tokens from a transferor without actual rights, is that the actual legitimate right holder of the relevant Security Tokens may demand reversal of the transaction, and thus require return of Security Tokens based on the ground that the registered transferor of the Security Tokens had no actual rights. However, it could be argued that if the efficiency and stability of the transactions recorded on a blockchain are prioritized over the protection of genuine owners with actual rights, bona fide acquisition rule may be recognized even with respect to Security Tokens.

The principles found in the proposed amendments to the Electronic Securities Act lean favourably towards recognizing the bona fide acquisition rule to a degree. Under the proposed amendments, if a person relies on the details of the rights to Security Tokens shown in the electronic register in good faith and without gross negligence, and

656. Article 35(1) of the Electronic Securities Act.
657. Articles 35(2) and 30 of the Electronic Securities Act.
658. Articles 35(3) and 31 of the Electronic Securities Act.
659. Articles 35(4) and 32 of the Electronic Securities Act.

the person is registered in the electronic register as the owner or pledgee for the relevant Security Tokens, such person shall be deemed to have legally acquired the right to the relevant Security Tokens.[660]

Moreover, with respect to Security Tokens electronically registered on a distributed ledger using blockchain technology, there remain questions on whether both private and public blockchains can be adopted. The technical steps and structure in registering on a distributed ledger as stipulated in the STO Guideline suggest participation of authorized nodes on a private blockchain. The requirements for the aforementioned distributed ledger are that: (i) a transaction must be confirmed and verified by multiple participants before being recorded, (ii) it cannot be arbitrarily changed retrospectively, and (iii) no virtual assets are needed to record the transaction, which means that the relevant blockchain platform does not demand gas fees for transaction records. In simple terms, this means that a public blockchain, which requires gas fees to be paid in the form of virtual assets, is prohibited. Similarly to the operation of an existing electronically registered securities regime, the Korea Securities Depository will take the role of reviewing the issuance and managing the total amount of securities registered in a distributed ledger. According to the STO Guideline, and unlike an issuer of existing general electronic securities who may not act as the account management institution of its own electronic securities, an issuer of a Security Token may become the account management institution for the securities registered on a distributed ledger by meeting certain requirements. Issuers that qualify as an account management institution will be permitted to directly manage the records on the distributed ledger of the Security Token.

[C] Private International Law[661]

With respect to Token issuance, transactions, and services provided through the use of Tokens on a cross-border basis, issues arise regarding the applicable law for the Token, rights represented by the Token, and Token transactions. Since there is no civil law definition of Tokens, in order to discuss the applicable governing law, the legal character of Token must be first established by distinguishing between the types of Tokens. In Principles on Digital Assets and Private Law announced in May 2023, UNIDROIT defines digital assets as 'electronically recorded objects capable of being subject to governance' and classifies Tokens into Crypto-Native Tokens and Non-native Tokens. UNIDROIT's definition of digital assets and its classification are not legally adopted in Korea, but it is endorsed for the purpose of the below discussion.

A Crypto-Native Token exists purely online without any underlying asset, whereas a Non-native Token represents or evidences a specific underlying asset, such as corporeal assets, bonds, membership rights, and securities.

660. Article 35(5) of the Electronic Securities Act.
661. Jongbaek Park would like to extend his appreciation to Professor Inho Kim at Law School of E-Wha Women University for his contribution to this chapter.

The prevailing view is that both types of Tokens are not considered movable assets (corporeal property) under the Civil Act[662] because they exist in the form of data in the virtual world and thus are not considered subjects of property law. Hence, Article 33 of Act on Private International Law (PILA), which states that property rights concerning movable and immovable property shall be governed by the lex situs, does not apply to Tokens.

Article 35 of PILA[663] sets out the governing law in relation to bearer securities for private international law purposes. However, as Tokens are not issued in physical form and cannot constitute bearer securities, Article 35 of PILA does not apply to Tokens.

At present, Native Tokens may be considered a special form of property right that does not exist within the traditional legal framework except some of them constituting a security as defined as investment contract securities under the FISCMA, whereas Non-native Tokens may retain the legal characteristics of their relevant underlying assets, such as bonds, membership rights, securities, etc.,[664] and the governing laws for the underlying assets are applicable for the Tokens. If the underlying assets are claims, the applicable law may be the law designated by the parties; the law of the place of incorporation of the issuer for Tokens representing membership right; and the law of the location of the property for Tokens representing property rights.

However, in cases where a Non-native Token represents a right that does not fall within any of the existing form of legal right, the most relevant laws can be governing laws for such Token, and thus we need to determine the most relevant law for such Tokens.

The blockchains on which Tokens are issued are categorized into either 'permission required/private' or 'permissionless/public' blockchain. Tokens on 'permission required/private' blockchain, representing rights not classified into existing types of rights, are recorded on a system shared by a limited number of authorized people. As such, the law of the place where the entity or person operating the relevant system is located is likely to be deemed the most relevant law in addressing issues related to Token ownership, transfer, security interest and other property rights.

For Tokens on 'permissionless/public' blockchain that represent rights not classified into existing types of rights, it could be purported that the law of the place where the individual holder of the private key is located, or where the company holder is incorporated, at the time of the disputed transaction, is appropriate and valid. Nonetheless, it is arguable that such determination of applicable law is not enforceable against a third party because private keys are not publicly disclosed.

It should be noted that if an owner of a Token does not keep the Token in a private wallet but instead entrusts it with a VASP, the rights held by the owner is a

662. Article 98 of the Civil Act: 'Things mentioned in this Act shall mean corporeal things, electricity, and other natural forces which can be managed.'

663. Article 35 of the PILA: 'The acquisition or loss of, or changes in rights to bearer securities shall be governed by the lex situs of the securities at the time of the completion of the causal act or fact.'

664. 'Choice of Law Regarding Proprietary Aspects of Digital Asset Transactions', Chun Chang-Min, Korea Private International Law Association, Private International Law Studies Vol. 29, No. 2 (December 2023) p. 181.

claim for asset transfer or assignment against the VASP. The owner does not possess direct ownership of the Actual Tokens considered to be held by the owner. Therefore, the applicable law regarding the right to claim by the owner can be determined as agreed upon between the relevant parties under Article 45 paragraph 1 of PILA.[665]

[D] Special Requirements for Prospectus

As illustrated above, given that the current laws of Korea do not provide for the legal regime of issuance of Security Tokens, there are no laws or regulations in relation to prospectus in case of Security Token issuance.

The 'Additional Q&A for the STO Guideline' published by the FSC in February 2023 alludes a plan to build a regulatory framework regarding the submission of securities registration statements for the issuance of Security Tokens. Accordingly, the issuance of Security Tokens for public offering will entail the requirement to submit a securities registration statement, as is specifically provided for paper securities and general electronic securities, depending on the types of the underlying security (equity securities, debt securities, investment contract securities, etc.). Furthermore, it should be highlighted that the content of the securities registration statement varies depending on the classification of the underlying securities, and the form of issuance being paper registration, electronic registration, or registration on a distributed ledger is not relevant for the purposes of composing the securities registration statement. Hence, there is no difference arising by virtue of registration on a distributed ledger for securities of the same kind. Since the realm of Security Token is at its infancy, the details required for securities registration statements for issuance of a Security Token will continue to be supplemented by the FSC to ensure that matters necessary for investors will be included in consideration of the characteristics of any new securities that securitize rights that had not been securitized previously. Regarding DAOs (Decentralized Autonomous Organizations), the FSC has emphasized that the organizational structure of a DAO and its ownership right must first be recognized under the Civil Act and the Commercial Act before any equity right of the DAO may be issued in the form of a security.

Pursuant to the provisions under the current FISCMA, upon public offering of a security, the issuer must file a securities registration statement with the FSC, and the filing takes effect after seven days from the date of filing.[666] In addition, the issuer must file a prospectus of the security with the FSC on the day on which the filing becomes effective and make the prospectus available for public access.[667] Once the securities registration statement becomes effective, no one shall sell the relevant securities to any

665. Article 45 of the PILA: 'A contract shall be governed by the law chosen, explicitly or implicitly, by the parties.'
666. Articles 119(1) and 120(1) of the FISCMA.
667. Article 123(1) of the FISCMA, Art. 13 of the Enforcement Decree of the FISCMA.

other person (excluding professional investors[668]) unless the seller delivers a prospectus, in which its content satisfies the requirements under Article 123 of the FISCMA, to the purchasing person in advance;[669] provided however that, if the public offering amount is less than KRW 1 billion (equivalent to around USD 750,000), the requirements for submission of a securities registration statement and delivery of prospectus are exempted.

The aforementioned prospectus needs to be prepared in two separate sections, titles and main text.[670]

The titles section must include the following matters:

- The effective date of registration of securities.
- The offering price or sales price of the relevant security.
- The subscription period.
- The payment period.
- A copy of the securities registration statement and how to access the relevant prospectus.

The main text section must include the following matters:

- General matters concerning the offering and sale.
- Details on the offering of securities and the rights of the securities sold.
- Investment risks involved in participating in the offering and for the acquisition of the securities sold.[671]
- Purpose of use of funds.
- Regarding the issuer: overview, business details, financial matters, accounting auditor's opinion, matters concerning the company and its affiliates, such as the board of directors, matters concerning officers and employees, details of transactions with interested parties, etc.

In the case of any small-size public offering of an amount less than KRW 1 billion, the issuer is exempt from the submission of securities registration statement and prospectus, but it shall disclose matters concerning its financial status and perform the following tasks:[672]

- Submission of documents specifying the issuer's financial status and business performance to the FSC prior to the offering/sales.
- If the issuer solicits subscriptions for securities, disclosure of matters concerning the offering/sales, matters concerning the issuer, price of offering or sales of securities, subscription period, payment period.

668. Professional investors must meet the requirements of at least KRW 100 million based on income and at least KRW 500 million based on assets.
669. Article 124(1) of the FISCMA.
670. Article 131 of the Enforcement Decree of the FISCMA.
671. Although there is no provision on the inherent risks of Security Tokens, various risks arising from the blockchain technology, such as loss of private keys, hacking, errors in blockchain programs, and network disruption, can be considered.
672. Article 130 of the FISCMA, Art. 137(1) of the Enforcement Decree of the FISCMA.

Under the STO Guideline, the threshold for full exemption from submission of securities registration statement is increased to KRW 3 billion (equivalent to around USD 2.3 million), and public offering between KRW 3 billion to 10 billion (equivalent to around USD 7.5 million to USD 25 million) is permitted as tier 2 small-size public offering with stricter requirements for investor protection like prior filing, review and request for amendments. Furthermore, the STO Guideline specifies that issuers of public offerings only targeting professional investors, who will be subject to a restriction on resale to non-professional investors for at least one year, will be exempted from the submission of securities registration statement. It is emphasized in the STO Guideline that Security Tokens, even if issued with restrictions on resale, will be considered having been publicly offered. This prevents the use of high liquidity in Security Tokens as a means to circumvent public offering regulations.

Any person who publicly offers securities in violation of the obligation to submit a registration statement and a prospectus or who makes a false statement with respect to any material matter in the registration statement or prospectus shall be punished by imprisonment for not more than five years or by a fine not exceeding KRW 200 million.[673]

In sum, if the FISCMA and the Electronic Securities Act are amended by adopting the principles and frameworks suggested in the STO Guideline to permit the issuance of Security Tokens, public offering of Security Tokens of an amount less than KRW 3 billion and public offerings of Security Tokens only targeting professional investors will be exempted from the requirement to file securities registration statements and prospectus. However, in cases where this exemption does not apply, even if the Security Tokens are subject to restriction on resale, the issuer of a Security Token must submit a securities registration statement and a prospectus consisting of all of the existing items included in the securities registration statement and the prospectus of the corresponding type of the Security Token. Of course, there is a possibility for the amended Acts to introduce new items for securities registration statements and/or prospectus, or modify existing items therein, depending on the characteristic of a Security Token.

As a general rule, issuers should be aware that the above requirements for the submission of securities registration statement and prospectus to the FSC apply to public offering of securities issued in a foreign country with effects that extend to Korea.[674] For instance, public offerings of securities targeted at Koreans are generally acknowledged to have an effect on Korea.

[E] Regulatory Specifics for Organized Trade

Under the FISCMA, a 'financial investment instruments market' is defined as a market for trading of securities,[675] and a 'financial investment instruments market' may be

673. Article 444(12) and (13) of the FISCMA.
674. Article 2 of the FISCMA.
675. Refer to Art. 8-2 of the FISCMA.

established and operated only by a person who has obtained the relevant exchange permit from the FSC.[676] Currently, in Korea, the Korea Exchange (KRX) is the only exchange permitted by the FSC, and KRX is the market where listed securities can be traded. To this day, KRX operates the following markets: the KOSPI market (securities market), the KOSDAQ market (market for IT and venture companies), and the KONEX market (market for early-stage small and medium-sized enterprises and venture companies). Unlisted stocks can be traded over-the-counter on a separate platform (K-OTC), which has been established by the Korea Financial Investment Association under the FISCMA.[677] Security Tokens cannot be traded in any of the aforementioned markets or K-OTC. Therefore, the only way for anyone to operate a trading platform where Security Tokens can be traded is by becoming designated as an innovative financial service. The Special Act on Support for Financial Innovation (*Financial Innovation Act*) provides the grounds for applying for a regulatory sandbox, which grants exceptions from financial regulations for innovative financial services that are recognized to be differentiated from the existing financial services in terms of the services provided, methods of service, and forms.[678]

The structure of the STO, which has been designated as an innovative financial service to operate within the regulatory sandbox, involves issuing trust certificates by real estate trusts that are electronically registered while simultaneously offering Tokens with equivalent right to the trust certificates to investors through public offering. The Tokens issued to the investors can be traded on a distributed ledger-based trading platform. With respect to this regulatory sandbox, the exemption from the requirement of obtaining the permit from the FSC to establish a securities market was granted.[679]

Moreover, on 13 December 2023, the 'Unconventional New Securities Market' service, where trading of unconventional securities is permitted within the securities market, was designated as a regulatory sandbox service for KRX. The Unconventional New Securities Market is planned to launch service in the first half of 2024. The Unconventional New Securities Market aims to provide services, including the trading, listing, disclosure, and settlement of unconventional new securities, such as investment contract securities and non-monetary trust certificates.

Securities in the form of a Token based on distributed ledger technology can be listed in the Unconventional New Securities Market, but not directly in the form of a Token. In order to be listed, the relevant Security Token must be first converted into general electronic securities form before listing. The reason for this conversion is that the processing of payment and transfer of Tokens through blockchain technology cannot match the efficiency of the current centralized computing system. It is expected that securities companies, as a member of the KRX, will provide brokerage service for the Unconventional New Securities Market, and non-professional investors may

676. Refer to Art. 373(1) of the FISCMA.
677. Article 286(1)5 of the FISCMA. The Korea Financial Investment Association conducts 'the duties relating to over-the-counter trading of share certificates not listed on the securities market'.
678. Refer to Art. 4-6 of the Special Act on Support for Financial Innovation.
679. Press release issued by the FSC on 26 May 2021.

participate in the Unconventional New Securities Market in the same manner as conventional stock trading by using the existing securities trading accounts held at securities companies.

A multilateral trading company is a type of alternative trading systems (ATS) where a company uses information and communication networks or electronic data processing systems to simultaneously trade securities with multiple parties, or act as counterparty or intermediary in the trading of securities, such as listed stocks, on a securities market.[680] In other words, an ATS is deemed as an investment trader or investment broker under the FISCMA. In order to establish an ATS, it is required to obtain the relevant licence from the FSC and invest the minimum capital of KRW 20 billion (equivalent to around USD 15 million) (for investment brokerage business) or KRW 30 billion (equivalent to around USD 23 million) (for investment trading business). While ATS itself is not specifically designed with Token securities trading in mind, there is an emerging opinion that it is necessary to actively review ways to allow trading of Security Tokens through ATS to ensure stable transactions and investor protection.

According to the STO Guideline, the FSC plans to introduce a new licensing system for over-the-counter brokers for Tokens if beneficiary certificates or investment contract securities, among the categories of securities under the FISCMA, are permitted to be issued in the form of a Token. The new system aims to permit non-professional investors to trade such Tokens over-the-counter through over-the-counter brokers. An over-the-counter broker may facilitate transactions by using multilateral trading method, whereby transactions are executed whenever bid and ask prices match between customers. In the cases where a securities registration statement or disclosure documents for small public offering are submitted at the time of the issuance of a Security Token, the issuer is exempted from the obligation to submit additional securities registration statements for public disclosure when the already-issued Security Token is sold to more than 50 individuals through over-the-counter brokers. Considering the small scale of intermediary trading platforms, where certain disclosure requirements are being exempted as above, trading on these platforms will be limited to small-size investors holding Tokens for less than 5% of the total Token issuance, and participation of intuitional investors will be restricted.[681][682]

Additionally, a lower investment limit will be set for investment contract securities compared to beneficiary certificates since investment contract securities are expected to have more unconventional rights than beneficiary certificates. Another factor considered in lowering the investment limit for investment contract securities is that with respect to investment contract securities, the operating business entity owns the relevant assets, whereas the underlying assets of beneficiary certificates are owned

680. Article 8-2(5) of the FISCMA.
681. In this regard, there is a view that influx of institutional investors will enhance liquidity, providing greater market liquidity for retail investors, and it will help improve the transparency and safety of the market.
682. Seil Lee at '*Considerations for Introduction of OTC brokerage system II – Great STO Digital Transformation*' seminar held at 9 Nov. 2023.

by the trustee. Thus, if the operating business entity becomes bankrupt, the trust assets can be insulated from the bankruptcy, while investment contract cannot enjoy the same benefit.

As we have discussed in Part 1 above, a Security Token issuer can issue Tokens either by acting as its own account management institution or through another investment broker who is an account management institution. However, to prevent conflicts of interest, the issuance of Tokens and the distribution for Token must be strictly separated, which means that an investment broker who was involved in the issuance, acquisition, or arrangement of a Security Token is not allowed to engage in the distribution of the Security Token. Therefore, as distribution of Security Tokens requires brokerage services by an investment broker, it appears difficult to trade Security Tokens without the involvement of an investment broker.

The STO Guideline contemplates cases where Security Tokens of investment contract securities and beneficiary certificates can be listed on the KRX, in which case, in consideration of the limitations in the transaction processing speed of distributed ledgers (currently, the KRX's centralized settlement processing speed is significantly faster), the Tokens will be listed after first being converted into the general electronic securities form. The listing requirements and disclosure obligations of material information for the listed Security Tokens will be relaxed compared to when listing traditional types of securities; however, the existing trading, settlement, and payment infrastructures of traditional electronic securities will continue to be used.

§5.21 CAPITAL MARKETS AND BLOCKCHAIN: COUNTRY REPORT – UNITED ARAB EMIRATES

Gregory Man & Jessica White[683]

[A] What Makes a Token a Security?

The United Arab Emirates (*UAE*) is a constitutional federation comprised of seven Emirates in which there are three distinct legal jurisdictions for the provision of financial services. These are the two financial freezones, being the Abu Dhabi Global

683. Gregory Man is the head of Bird & Bird's Finance & Financial Regulation team in the Middle East and also the global head of Islamic finance. He specializes in Islamic and conventional debt capital markets, banking, structured finance and restructuring and has experience advising clients across a range of jurisdictions including the Middle East, Europe, the UK, Turkey, Africa and Asia. His debt capital markets experience has involved advising on the full range of securities offerings, including corporate and sovereign bonds and sukuk, medium term note and sukuk programs, securitization, structured products, liability management, regulatory capital issuances, projects bonds and sukuk and asset finance. He acts for both arrangers and issuers and has advised on issuances for sovereigns, government-related and supra-national entities, airlines, financial institutions, Premier League football clubs and technology-related entities. He also provides financial services regulatory advice across the traditional financial services, technology, virtual assets, and fintech sectors.

Market (*ADGM*) and the Dubai International Financial Centre (*DIFC*), and the mainland jurisdiction which encompasses the seven Emirates except for the ADGM and the DIFC (*Federal*).[684]

The regulation of Tokens and other virtual assets has been a hot topic in the UAE for some time. The regulation in this area has progressed with major regime implementations occurring over time including the ADGM framework being implemented in 2018, the DIFC framework in 2021 and the Federal framework being overhauled in 2023. All jurisdictions have also been subject to several regular updates and iterations since their initial commencement.

As set out below, the concept of a Token being a security is not uniform across the UAE.

[1] Federal Jurisdiction

The Federal jurisdiction is supervised and regulated by the Emirates Securities and Commodities Authority (*SCA*). The SCA previously set out the relevant regime for Security Tokens under Chairman of the Authority's Board of Directors' Decision No. (23) of 2020 Concerning Crypto Assets Activities and the Administrative Resolution No. (11) of 2021 on Approval of the Illustrative Guide of the Crypto Assets System. However, this regime was repealed recently by the Securities and Commodities Authority Decision No. (26) of 2023.

At the time of drafting, the definition of Virtual Assets in the Federal jurisdiction,[685] expressly excludes 'digital representations of securities or other assets'. Although Security Tokens are therefore not classified as Virtual Assets and the previous regime for Security Tokens has been repealed, there has been no subsequent guidance issued by the SCA as to the status of how it currently regulates Tokens which are digital representations of securities in the Federal jurisdiction. There is speculation in the market that the SCA may make subsequent changes to its regime with respect to Security Tokens.

Jessica White is an associate in the UAE Finance & Financial Regulation practice group. She specialises in financial regulation for both traditional and digital asset types in the Middle East, with a particular focus on the United Arab Emirates in the technology, payments and fintech sectors. She has experience advising on a wide range of financial services regulations, compliance matters and financial crime laws including those issued by the UAE Central Bank, the UAE Securities and Commodities Authority, the ADGM's Financial Services Regulatory Authority, the DIFC's Dubai Financial Services Authority and Dubai's Virtual Asset Regulatory Authority.

684. The Dubai Virtual Asset Regulatory Authority (VARA) has been excluded from this analysis as the UAE Cabinet Decision No. (111) of 2022 on the Regulation of Virtual Assets and Their Service Providers expressly excludes 'digital representations of securities or other assets' from the definition of Virtual Assets under the SCA Virtual Asset Regime which has empowered VARA to regulated virtual assets in the Emirate of Dubai.

685. UAE Cabinet Decision No. (111) of 2022 on the Regulation of Virtual Assets and Their Service Providers.

As a result of the current state of flux of laws in the Federal jurisdiction with respect to Security Tokens, the following sections for the UAE do not refer to the Federal jurisdiction, except for the section concerning International Private Law.

[2] DIFC Jurisdiction

The DIFC jurisdiction is supervised and regulated by the Dubai Financial Services Authority (*DFSA*). The DFSA defines a Token as a cryptographically secured digital representation of value, rights or obligations, which may be issued, transferred and stored electronically using DLT or other similar technology.[686] A Token that is an investment (i.e., either a security or a derivative) is defined as an Investment Token in the DIFC.[687]

Investment Tokens are defined as either a Security Token or a Derivative Token as follows:

(a) *Security Token*: is an Investment Token that is the same as, or substantially similar in nature, purpose or effect to, a share, a debenture, a warrant, a certificate, a unit or a structured product;
(b) *Derivative Token*: is an Investment Token that is the same as, or substantially similar in nature, purpose or effect to, an option or a future.[688]

The DFSA also has discretionary power to declare by written notice that any financial instrument or class of financial instruments is a particular type or a new or existing Security or Derivative, and it may do so on such terms and conditions it considers appropriate.[689] Such a determination can be made upon written application by an issuer or on the DFSA's own initiative.

[3] ADGM Jurisdiction

The ADGM jurisdiction is supervised and regulated by the Financial Services Regulatory Authority (*FSRA*). The FSRA defines a Digital Security as a Digital or Virtual Token that has the features and characteristics of a security (i.e., a share, a debenture or units in a collective investment fund). Digital Securities are deemed to be securities under the FSRA laws.[690]

686. DFSA Glossary Rulebook Module.
687. DFSA General Rulebook Module, Rules A2.1.1(2)(b) and (c).
688. The DFSA sets out additional guidance with respect to its regulatory analysis of what types of Tokens are Investment Tokens in the DIFC in Appendix 6 of the DFSA General Rulebook Module.
689. DFSA General Rulebook Module, Rules A2.4.1(1) and (2).
690. Financial Services and Markets Regulations 2015, s. 58(2)(b) sets out that the FSRA may, by written notice, 'deem any investment which is not a Security to be a Security for the purposes of these Regulations and the Rules made under these Regulations'.

The FSRA will assess whether the Digital or Virtual Token an issuer intends to issue in or from the ADGM exhibits the features and characteristics of a security on a case-by-case basis in keeping with the FSRA's treatment of 'conventional' securities.

Derivatives and collective investment funds of: (i) virtual assets; (ii) Digital Securities; and (iii) Utility Tokens are carved out from the definition of Digital Securities by the FSRA and are instead regulated as specified investments (i.e., as 'conventional' securities).

[B] Blockchain Finality

[1] DIFC Jurisdiction

Prior to the implementation of the DIFC Investment Token regime, the DFSA released a public consultation paper which recognized that issues could arise in relation to the clearing and settlement of Tokens which revolve around settlement and counterparty risks.[691] As a result of this, the DFSA implemented specific rules for firms providing financial services relating to Investment Tokens with respect to technology, governance and the operating of an Alternative Trading System (*ATS*)[692] for Investment Tokens that permits direct access to members.

Where Security Tokens are admitted to trading on an ATS or other facility, the relevant prospectus should confirm whether smart contracts are being used or executed on the facility, and if so:

(a) what form those smart contracts take;
(b) how the legal rights and obligations arising under the smart contracts are performed, including when contract or settlement finality occurs – whether by the smart contract itself, an underlying natural language contract or a combination of both; and
(c) details of the relationship between those smart contracts and any underlying natural language contract.

In addition, the DFSA implemented clearing and settlement arrangements for ATS Operators such that they must: (i) ensure that there are satisfactory arrangements in place for securing timely discharge of the rights and liabilities of the parties to transactions conducted on or through its facility; and (ii) inform its members and other persons having access to its facility through members of details relating to such arrangements.[693]

An ATS Operator is not authorized to provide clearing and settlement services under its licence in the DIFC. Therefore, it must make suitable arrangements relating to clearing and settlement of transactions that are undertaken on its facility. The DFSA

691. DFSA Consultation Paper 138 on the Regulation of Security Tokens published 29 Mar. 2021.
692. An ATS is defined in the DFSA General Rulebook Module in Rule 2.22.1 as including the operation of a Multilateral Trading Facility or the operation of an Organised Trading Facility.
693. DFSA Conduct of Business Rulebook Module, Rule 9.6.11.

recognizes that ATS Operators may arrange for its members to obtain such services from an appropriately licensed person.

This area of law is constantly evolving, and at the time of drafting, the DIFC Authority (the non-financial regulator) has two open consultation papers[694] which propose to introduce a comprehensive new framework in the DIFC for 'digital assets' and digital asset collateral arrangements.[695] The proposals include the legal concept of a transfer of title of digital assets in which it is proposed that an *inter vivos* transfer of title to a digital asset from the transferor to the transferee shall occur when: (i) there is a change in control of the digital asset to the transferee; and (ii) the transferor intends to transfer title to the transferee.[696] It remains to be seen how the proposed framework will be implemented and applied by the relevant DIFC Courts in the event of a dispute.

[2] ADGM Jurisdiction

At the time of drafting, the FSRA had not issued any laws or guidance with respect to blockchain finality in relation to Digital Securities. However, the FSRA has stated that it expects that the particular use and surrounding controls related to the use of DLT will have implications for how Digital Securities are offered, issued, traded, and ultimately settled. The FSRA regime with respect to clearing and settlement of conventional securities has been applied to Digital Securities and only amended slightly to permit for the concept of Digital Settlement Facilities and MTFs using Virtual Assets.

[C] International Private Law

As indicated previously, the Federal regime relating to Security Tokens in the UAE was repealed. However, it is unlikely that any new Federal legislation concerning Security Tokens or digital assets will consider the conflict of law or international private law position in any detail. As such, general provisions of international private law, outlined in the UAE Federal laws, have been considered in this section.

The UAE regime does not have a standalone set of private international laws. This means that there are no specific laws that govern any conflict-of-law issues that arise in cross-border transactions involving Security Tokens or virtual assets more generally. This creates a level of uncertainty for parties dealing with Security Tokens, as it would be difficult to determine the rights that the Security Tokens embody. This also means that the nature of the individual Security Token does not impact what is or becomes applicable law.

A further complication with determining the applicable law and jurisdiction arises due to the existence of multiple financial services jurisdictions within the UAE as set out previously, namely the Federal, ADGM and DIFC jurisdictions.

694. DIFC Consultation Papers No. 4 and No. 5 of 2023 are open for a public consultation period which ends on 5 Nov. 2023.
695. Digital Assets are defined broadly in s. 8 of the proposed Digital Assets Law and may include Investment Tokens, cryptocurrencies, NFTs and stablecoins.
696. Proposed Digital Assets Law, s. 12.

Given the different existing ADGM and DIFC jurisdictions, the potential internal conflict will also need to be considered when it comes to cross-border transactions. This means that in addition to determining any international conflict-of-law issues, steps will need to be taken to consider the applicability of the Federal, ADGM and DIFC laws.

The general conflict-of-law rules that are outlined in Federal Law No. 5 of 1985 On the Civil Transactions Law of the United Arab Emirates State (*Civil Code*) provide some level of guidance.

According to Article 23 of the Civil Code, the Federal UAE courts can apply general principles of private international law to determine the appropriate conflict rule. However, the rule being applied needs to be widely recognized, such as an international treaty.

Despite the above, in practice, if the Federal UAE courts find that they have jurisdiction of a matter concerning Security Tokens, they will apply the Federal laws of the UAE to that dispute. This is cemented by Article 10 of the Civil Code which states that the 'law of the State of the United Arab Emirates shall be the authoritative source in determining relationships when the nature of such relationships requires being determined in a suit in which there is a conflict of laws as to the law to be applied between the parties'.

Separately, when it comes to conflict of laws and property, Article 18 of the Civil Code states that the rights relating to a property 'shall be governed by the law of the location with regards to the real estate, and the law of the party where the moveable property is located upon the achievement of the reason entailing the acquisition, ownership or other in kind rights, or the loss thereof, and such with regards to such moveable property'.

According to the above provision, movable property rights will be governed by the law of the country where the movable property was located at the time of the occurrence of the situation that gives rise to the rights or claims. Arguably, Security Tokens can be described as moveable assets which therefore means that the interpretation under Article 18 of the Civil Code will be applicable in the event of a conflict.

The lack of specific rules relating to Security Tokens or virtual assets means that the courts require flexibility in their interpretation and application of the relevant Civil Code provisions in order to achieve a reasonable outcome. Such an approach is likely to produce non-uniform results, which is arguably what is required given the rapidly evolving industry.

Additionally, it should be noted that precedents are not judicially binding in the Federal UAE courts, although they are used as persuasive argument before the court. Once again, the lack of a precedent system might provide the required flexibility to achieve creative solutions for the conflict-of-law disputes that arise in respect of digital assets.

If a matter concerning Security Tokens is submitted to the jurisdiction of the DIFC, then the relevant courts will apply common law principles such as that of England and Wales or Singapore. If the matter is referred to the ADGM Courts, then they would apply the England and Wales conflict-of-laws rule.

The circumstances of each case are likely to be considered in detail when it comes to deciding whether the Federal, ADGM or DIFC courts have jurisdiction over a matter. However, based on prior cases in the UAE, the proximity of the deal and the location of the involved parties play a substantial role in deciding whether an ADGM or DIFC court has jurisdiction or not.

[D] Special Requirements for Prospectus

[1] DIFC Jurisdiction

The requirements for offers of 'conventional' securities to the public in, or from, the DIFC apply to offers for all types of securities, including Security Tokens (but excluding Derivative Tokens in accordance with the conventional securities regime in the DIFC). Issuers wishing to make an offer of Security Tokens in or from the DIFC or to have Security Tokens admitted to trading on an ATS must comply with all applicable requirements, including the obligation to publish an approved prospectus (unless it is an Exempt Offer[697]).[698]

The DFSA sets out a broad and comprehensive range of required disclosures for inclusion in an approved prospectus.[699] In addition, the DFSA sets out additional content requirements for a prospectus for Security Tokens which include:[700]

(a) *token characteristics*: including the rights and obligations conferred by the Security Token, how these rights are exercised and the type (or types) of investment which the Security Token constitutes;
(b) *accessibility*: of the Security Token including details of the DLT used to issue, store or transfer the Security Token, whether it will be admitted on a trading platform or transferred off-chain;
(c) *capital raising*: details are required if the capital to be raised from issuing the Security Token is to be used to fund the creation of a new Token;
(d) *title*: information setting out how title to the Security Token is established, certified, or otherwise evidenced;
(e) *risks*: specifically in relation to cybersecurity risks or its underlying technology and how steps that have been, or can be taken, to mitigate these risks. Risks associated with the use of the DLT application particularly those relating to digital wallets and the susceptibility of private cryptographic keys to misappropriation;

697. DFSA Markets Rulebook, Rule 2.3 sets out the range of circumstances in which the DFSA prescribes that an offer is an Exempt Offer. These include, for example: (a) an offer made to or directed at only Professional Clients other than natural persons; (b) an offer from the DIFC which is directed at few than 50 Persons in any 12-month period, excluding Professional Clients who are not natural persons; (c) an offer where the total consideration to be paid by a Person to acquire the Securities is at least USD 100,000.
698. DIFC Markets Law No. (1) of 2012, s. 14.
699. DFSA Markets Rulebook Module, Appendix 1.
700. DFSA Markets Rulebook Module, Appendix 7.

(f) *other*: information relevant to the Security Token that would reasonably assist a prospective investor in making an informed decision about investing in the Security Token.

[2] ADGM Jurisdiction

In a similar manner to the DIFC, the requirements for offers of 'conventional' securities to the public in, or from, the ADGM apply to offers of all types of securities, including Digital Securities. Issuers wishing to make an offer of Digital Securities to the public in, or from, the ADGM must comply with all applicable requirements, including the obligation to publish an approved prospectus (unless it is an Exempt Offer[701]).[702]

The FSRA sets out a broad and comprehensive range of required disclosures for inclusion in an approved prospectus.[703] However, a prospectus related to the offering of Digital Securities is only required to include such disclosures as applicable to their Digital Security.[704]

Guidance published by the FSRA[705] indicates that the following disclosure requirements are key for a prospectus related to Digital Securities:

(a) *prospectus language*: must be easily analysable and comprehensible to ensure that the prospectus is true, accurate and not misleading;
(b) *risk factors*: should exclude generic or boilerplate disclosures and grouped together in a coherent manner with those of greatest or most immediate significance disclosed prominently at the beginning of the section;
(c) *responsibility*: of the offer and the disclosures contained in the prospectus remains with the issuer or the person making the offer;
(d) *general information*: with respect to the issuer is included (i.e., incorporation details and whether a special purpose vehicle has been established for the purpose of issuing asset-backed securities);
(e) *actual and proposed business activities*: of the issuer are set out in the prospectus including its corporate history. Where the issuer is newly incorporated, information should be included regarding any preceding entity which conducted similar operations or was controlled by the same parties;
(f) *historical financial information*: prepared in compliance with IFRS;

701. FSRA Market Rulebook Module, Rule 4.3 sets out that an offer will constitute an Exempt Offer where: (a) the offer is directed at Professional Clients other than natural persons; (b) the offer is directed at fewer than 50 persons in any 12-month period, including professional clients who are not natural persons; or (c) the total consideration to be paid by a person to acquire the securities is at least USD 100,000, or an equivalent in another currency.
702. Financial Services and Markets Regulations 2015, s. 61.
703. FSRA Market Rulebook Module, Appendix 1.
704. Noting that a request for a waiver/modification of the required disclosures must be submitted to the FSRA at the time of submission of the draft prospectus.
705. FSRA Guidance – Regulation of Digital Securities Activities in the ADGM, 24 Feb. 2020.

(g) *securities note*: to include specific information relevant to the type of security the Digital Security has the features and characteristics of. Such information could include the existence of voting rights or other rights.

Due to the complexities associated with offers of Digital Securities, from a technology perspective and considering the relative infancy and resulting heightened risks of the Digital Securities sector, the FSRA generally expects that an issuer intending to make the offer will be incorporated in the ADGM.

[E] Regulatory Specifics for Organized Trade

[1] DIFC Jurisdiction

A person or entity who carries on certain activities in or from the DIFC is required to obtain approval or authorization from the DFSA and/or comply with the applicable requirements under the DFSA laws.

The relevant activities that require approval or authorization from the DFSA currently include:[706]

(a) carrying on a financial service which relates to an Investment Token[707] (such as operating a facility on which Investment Tokens are traded or cleared (i.e., an ATS), or giving advice on, or arranging deals in such Investment Tokens);[708]
(b) making a financial promotion in relation to an Investment Token;
(c) making an offer to the public of an Investment Token; and
(d) applying for a Security Token to be admitted on the Official List of Securities.

Persons or entities seeking to carry out the activities set out in paragraphs (a)-(b) above are required to engage with the DFSA in an iterative process to request approval or authorization prior to conducting such activities. This process includes: (i) initial due diligence and discussions with the DFSA team; (ii) submission of a formal application; (iii) granting of an in-principle approval; (iv) granting of final approval; and (where applicable) (v) operational launch testing. Alternatively, persons or entities which already hold a financial services permission from the DFSA and want to expand their services into those which relate to Security Tokens are required to only do so in accordance with their existing authorization or after approval from the DFSA to do so.

706. As set out in the DFSA General Rulebook Module, App 6 Investment Token Guidance, para. 1.
707. Which as set out under §5.21[A][b], *supra*, includes a Security Token.
708. We note that the definition for a 'financial service' in s. 2.2 of the DFSA General Rulebook module is broad and the activities set out in brackets here have been extracted by the current DFSA guidance. However, persons seeking to carry out financial services in or from the DIFC should seek financial advice to assess whether the proposed services meet the definition on s. 2.2 of the DFSA General Rulebook module.

Authorization and supervision fees will also be applicable that vary on the activity being applied for.

Persons or entities intending to make an offer to the public of an Investment Token should refer to the guidance set out above under section [D][1].

Persons or entities applying for a Security Token to be admitted on the Official List of Securities are required to submit an application to the DFSA through the DFSA ePortal. Application fees apply and are due at the time of submission of the application.

[2] ADGM Jurisdiction

In the ADGM, all financial services activities in relation to Digital Securities, such as operating primary/secondary markets, dealing/trading/managing investments in or advising on Digital Securities which are conducted in or from the ADGM are subject to the relevant regulatory requirements under the FSRA laws. Market intermediaries and market operators dealing or managing investments in Digital Securities need to be licensed or approved by the FSRA pursuant to the Financial Services and Markets Regulation 2015 (FSMR).

The FSRA recognizes three types of trading venues for Digital Securities and two types of settlement and custody avenues for the same. These types of activities are regulated under the FSRA laws and require prior approval or authorization from the FSRA in order for these to be established in the ADGM.

Trading venues:

(a) Recognized Investment Exchanges (*RIEs*): which are defined in the FSMR as an investment exchange or MTF operating outside the ADGM which has been granted a Recognition Order by the FSRA.[709]
(b) Multilateral Trading Facilities (*MTFs*): which are defined in the FSMR as a multilateral system, operated by an Authorized Person (i.e., a person or entity which holds a financial services licence from the FSRA) or an RIE, which brings together multiple third-party buying and selling interests in financial instruments, in the system and in accordance with non-discretionary rules, in a way that results in a contract in accordance with its rules.
(c) Organized Trading Facilities (*OTFs*): which are defined in the FSMR as a multilateral system which is not an RIE or an MTF and in which multiple third-party buying and selling interests in financial instruments are able to interact in the system in a way that results in a contract in accordance with the provisions of its rules.

Settlement and custody services:

(a) Recognized Clearing Houses (*RCHs*): which are defined in the FSMR as a clearing house which provides clearing services in the ADGM in relation to which a Recognition Order by the FSRA is in force.

709. Noting that the FSRA may require RIEs to engage the services of a RCH or a DSF for the clearing and settlement of Digital Securities.

(b) Digital Settlement Facilities (*DSFs*): which are recognized in the FSRA guidance[710] as being suitable for the purposes of settlement and custody of Digital Securities. Where a DSF holds a financial services permission from the FSRA for providing custody, it may provide custody and settlement services in Digital Securities for RIEs and MTFs (as applicable).

In addition, MTFs licensed to conduct activities with respect to Virtual Assets which seek to expand their offering to include Digital Securities have the option to apply to the FSRA to either (i) extend into the trading of Digital Securities; or (ii) become a Digital Securities RIE. Similarly, Virtual Asset custodians can apply to the FSRA to become a DSF.

Persons or entities seeking approvals to operate as intermediaries, RIE, MTF, OTF, RCH or DSF with respect to Digital Securities must engage in an iterative process with the FSRA throughout the application process which can broadly be broken down into five stages, namely: (i) initial due diligence and discussions with the FSRA team; (ii) submission of a formal application; (iii) granting of an in-principle approval; (iv) granting of final approval; and (where applicable) (v) operational launch testing. Alternatively, persons or entities which already hold a financial services permission from the FSRA and want to expand their services into those which relate to Digital Securities are required to only do so in accordance with their existing authorization or after approval from the FSRA to do so. Authorization and supervision fees will also be applicable that vary on the activity being applied for.

710. FSRA Guidance – Regulation of Digital Securities Activities in the ADGM, 24 Feb. 2020.

CHAPTER 6

Crypto Asset Regulation in Europe and in United Kingdom

Laura Douglas

§6.01 THE EU MARKETS IN CRYPTO ASSETS REGULATION

Regulation (EU) 2023/1114 on markets in crypto assets[1] (MiCA) introduces a harmonised framework for the regulation of crypto assets and related activities across the European Union (EU). It was first proposed by the European Commission in September 2020 as part of a broader EU digital finance strategy and has since been published in the Official Journal of the EU on 9 June 2023, entering into force on 29 June 2023.

MiCA is the first comprehensive framework for regulation of crypto assets developed globally and has influenced the development of other national and international frameworks for regulation of crypto assets. *See* section 6.03 below for an overview of the developing UK regulatory regime for crypto assets and Chapter 7 for the US approach to crypto asset regulation.

MiCA regulates the issuance and offering of crypto assets, including stablecoins, introduces a licensing and conduct of business regime for crypto asset service providers (CASPs) and sets out a broad market abuse regime with respect to crypto assets. This section provides an overview of the MiCA, its scope and the main regulatory obligations imposed.

1. Regulation (EU) 2023/1114 of the European Parliament and of the Council of 31 May 2023 on markets in crypto assets, and amending Regulations (EU) No. 1093/2010 and (EU) No. 1095/2010 and Directives 2013/36/EU and (EU) 2019/1937.

[A] Scope of MiCA

In order to understand the scope of MiCA, it is necessary to consider both the types of crypto assets it applies to and the types of persons and activities falling within its scope.

In summary:

- MiCA seeks to regulate crypto assets and related activities that fall outside of other pre-existing regulatory frameworks. Therefore, it does not apply to crypto assets that qualify as financial instruments under the recast EU Markets in Financial Instruments Directive[2] (MIFID2), such as tokenised transferable securities.[3] For crypto assets that do fall within scope, MiCA introduces regulatory obligations that are often very similar to those that apply in pre-existing financial services regulatory frameworks.
- MiCA imposes obligations on persons issuing, offering or providing services relating to in-scope crypto assets, including in structures where there is an element of decentralisation. Fully decentralised structures where activities or services relating to crypto assets are provided without involvement of an intermediary are not yet regulated under MiCA, but the EU Commission is required to present a report by the end of 2024 crypto asset related developments including 'an assessment of the necessity and feasibility of regulating decentralised finance'.[4]

[1] Types of Crypto Assets Regulated under MiCA

[a] Definition of 'Crypto Assets'

MiCA regulates activities relating to 'crypto assets', which are defined as 'a digital representation of a value or a right that uses cryptography for security and is in the form of a coin or a token or any other digital medium which may be transferred and stored electronically, using distributed ledger technology or similar technology'.[5]

The key elements of this definition are therefore that:

- the crypto asset must be a digital representation of value or a right;
- cryptography must be used as part of the crypto asset's security mechanism; and
- it must be possible to transfer and store the crypto asset electronically using DLT or similar technology.

2. Directive 2014/65/EU of the European Parliament and of the Council of 15 May 2014 on markets in financial instruments and amending Directive 2002/92/EC and Directive 2011/61/EU (recast).
3. Instead, *see* Chapter 6 (*Capital Markets and Blockchain*) for an overview of how security tokens are regulated in various EU jurisdictions.
4. *See* §1.01 (*Decentralized Finance*) for an introduction to decentralised finance, or DeFi.
5. Article 3(5) MiCA.

This is a very broad definition which is capable of capturing regulated financial instruments that use DLT or similar technologies (e.g., tokenised securities) as well as unregulated crypto assets such as cryptocurrencies, stablecoins, utility tokens and non-fungible tokens (NFTs).

However, certain types of crypto assets are expressly carved out of the scope of MiCA, as set out in section (b) below.

[b] Exclusions from Scope

Article 2 MiCA expressly excludes from its scope crypto assets that:

- are unique and not fungible with other crypto assets (i.e., NFTs); or
- qualify as regulated financial instruments, deposits and certain other types of regulated financial products.

With respect to NFTs, the recitals to MiCA indicate that the concept of non-fungibility should be interpreted narrowly, based on crypto asset the de facto features and use of crypto assets rather than their form or label as NFTs.[6] A crypto asset will not be considered unique and non-fungible simply because it has been assigned a unique identifier, and issuance of NFTs in a large series or collection is an indicator of their fungibility for the purposes of MiCA. In addition, where NFTs are fractionalised, the fractional parts will not be considered unique and non-fungible.

The types of regulated financial products excluded from the scope of MiCA are:

- financial instruments, as defined in MiFID2;
- deposits, as defined in the Deposit Guarantee Schemes Directive[7] (including structured deposits, as defined in MiFID2);
- funds comprising banknotes, coins, scriptural money and electronic money, as defined in the Payment Services Directive[8] (PSD2), unless they are also e-money tokens;
- securitisation positions in the context of a securitisation as defined in Article 2(1) of the Securitisation Regulation;[9]
- non-life or life insurance contracts;
- pension products or schemes; and
- social security schemes.

6. Recital (11) MiCA.
7. Directive 2014/49/EU of the European Parliament and of the Council of 16 April 2014 on deposit guarantee schemes (recast).
8. Directive (EU) 2015/2366 of the European Parliament and of the Council of 25 November 2015 on payment services in the internal market, amending Directives 2002/65/EC, 2009/110/EC and 2013/36/EU and Regulation (EU) No. 1093/2010, and repealing Directive 2007/64/EC.
9. Regulation (EU) 2017/2402 of the European Parliament and of the Council of 12 December 2017 laying down a general framework for securitisation and creating a specific framework for simple, transparent and standardised securitisation, and amending Directives 2009/65/EC, 2009/138/EC and 2011/61/EU and Regulations (EC) No. 1060/2009 and (EU) No. 648/2012.

[c] Categories of Crypto Assets and Stablecoins

MiCA identifies three main categories of crypto assets. Two of the three categories capture different types of stablecoins, defined as 'electronic money tokens' (EMTs) and 'asset-referenced tokens' (ARTs), respectively.

EMTs and ARTs are defined as follows:

- EMTs are defined in Article 3(7) MiCA as 'a type of crypto asset that purports to maintain a stable value by referencing the value of one official currency'; and
- ARTs are defined in Article 3(6) MiCA as 'a type of crypto asset that is not an electronic money token and that purports to maintain a stable value by referencing another value or right or a combination thereof, including one or more official currencies'.

The final category includes all other types of crypto assets, such as cryptocurrencies and utility tokens. This final category also includes certain types of crypto assets that may commonly be referred to as 'stablecoins' but which do not meet the definition of an EMT or ART (e.g., algorithmic stablecoins).

[2] Activities and Persons Regulated under MiCA

MiCA regulates:

- the issuance and offering of crypto assets by persons who offer crypto assets to the public or seek the admission of such crypto assets to a trading platform for crypto assets as outlined in sections [B] and [C] below; and
- the provision of various crypto asset-related services and activities by CASPs, as further described in section [D] below.

Other persons including investors in crypto assets are also subject to the broad market abuse regime discussed in section E.

However, Article 2 MiCA provides certain limited exemptions for intragroup service provision and public entities due to their lower risk profile concerning financial stability and investor protection.

[B] Issuance and Offering of Crypto Assets (Other Than EMTs and ARTs)

MiCA introduces a regulatory framework for the issuance and offering of crypto assets to the public in the EU, including requirements to publish a crypto asset white paper. The regime has various similarities with the EU prospectus regime for public offers of financial instruments to the public under the Prospectus Regulation[10] and seeks to provide greater transparency, increase investor protection and support integrity and confidence in markets in crypto assets.

This section provides an overview of the core regime that applies to crypto assets other than EMTs and ARTs, effective from 30 December 2024. Issuers of EMTs and ARTs are subject to a slightly different regime, as outlined in section [C] below.

[1] Scope: Offerors and Persons Seeking Admission to Trading

The regime for issuance and offering of crypto assets applies to persons who:

- offer crypto assets to the public in the EU; and/or
- seek admission of crypto assets to a trading platform for crypto assets operated by an EU-regulated CASP (which could include the operator of the trading platform if crypto assets are admitted to trading on the initiative of the platform operator).

For convenience, these persons are referred to collectively as 'issuers and offerors' of crypto assets below.

The regime has various similarities with the EU prospectus regime for public offers of financial instruments to the public under the Prospectus Regulation[11] and seeks to provide greater transparency, increase investor protection and support integrity and confidence in markets in crypto assets.

[2] Requirements for Public Offers or Admission to Trading of Crypto Assets (Other Than EMTs and ARTs)

[a] Overview

Title II MiCA prohibits persons from offering crypto assets (other than EMTs and ARTs) to the public in the EU or seeking their admission to trading on an EU crypto asset trading venue, unless the issuer or offeror:

- is a legal person (i.e., natural persons are not eligible to act as issuers or offerors of crypto assets under MiCA);
- has drafted a white paper that describes relevant information about the issuer or offeror, the crypto asset and associated risks, notified the white paper to its competent authority (i.e., regulator) and published the white paper in a

10. Regulation (EU) 2017/1129 of the European Parliament and of the Council of 14 June 2017 on the prospectus to be published when securities are offered to the public or admitted to trading on a regulated market, and repealing Directive 2003/71/EC.
11. Regulation (EU) 2017/1129 of the European Parliament and of the Council of 14 June 2017 on the prospectus to be published when securities are offered to the public or admitted to trading on a regulated market, and repealing Directive 2003/71/EC.

publicly accessible manner on their website, in accordance with Articles 6, 8 and 9 of MiCA;
- has drafted and published relevant marketing communications relating to the crypto assets as required under Articles 7 and 9 of MiCA; and
- complies with requirements for offers or persons seeking admission to trading set out in Article 14 MiCA,

as discussed further in section [2] below.

A person seeking admission to trading may agree in writing with the operator of the relevant crypto asset trading platform that the platform operator is responsible for complying with some or all of the requirements above. In this case, the person seeking admission to trading must also agree to provide all necessary information to the platform operator to enable them to comply with the requirements above.

[b] Exemptions

MiCA sets out various exemptions from the requirements relating to the white paper and requirements to publish marketing communications.

Some of these exemptions are similar to those available under the Prospectus Regulation. In particular, Article 4(2) MiCA provides that crypto asset offerors are exempt from white paper and publication of marketing communication requirements where:

- an offer is made to fewer than 150 natural or legal persons per Member State, provided that such persons are acting on their own account;
- over a period of twelve months, the total consideration of an offer to the public of crypto assets in the Union does not exceed EUR 1,000,000, or the equivalent amount in another currency or in crypto assets; or
- an offer is solely addressed to qualified investors, and the crypto assets can only be held by such qualified investors.

Article 4(3) MiCA sets out additional exemptions, which are specific to the MiCA framework, which apply if:

- the crypto asset is offered for free (though this does not include offering of crypto assets in exchange for processing of personal data);
- the crypto asset is automatically created as a reward for the maintenance of the distributed ledger or the validation of transaction such as mining activity;
- the offer concerns a utility token providing access to goods or services that already exist or are already in operation;
- the crypto asset can be used only in exchange for goods and services in a limited network of merchants with contractual arrangements with the offeror (similar to the limited network exemption under the PSD2 framework).

[c] Form and Content of the White Paper

MiCA sets out detailed requirements for the form and content of the crypto asset white paper. It should, among other things:

- provide information about the offeror or person seeking admission to trading and, if different, the issuer of the crypto assets;
- describe the crypto asset project and the main participants;
- describe the terms of the offer to the public or admission to trading;
- set out the rights and obligations attached to the crypto assets in question;
- disclose the key risks associated with the crypto assets;
- describe the underlying technology and any principal adverse impacts on the climate and other environmental-related adverse impacts of the consensus mechanism used for the crypto asset; and
- contain a summary to help potential purchasers make an informed decision regarding their investment.

The white paper must also contain certain prescribed statements about who is responsible for the white paper, and certain warnings about the future value, transferability and liquidity of the crypto asset and the fact that losses are not covered by investor compensation schemes or deposit guarantee schemes. The white paper must be fair, clear and not misleading, must not contain material omissions and must be presented in a concise and comprehensible form.

White papers must be made available in a machine-readable format, and the European Securities and Markets Authority (ESMA) and the European Banking Authority (EBA) have been tasked with developing regulatory technical standards further specifying certain elements of the required content and format of the white paper.

[d] Notification and Publication of the White Paper

Issuers and offerors of crypto assets are required to notify the white paper to the competent authority of their home Member State at least twenty working days before publication of the white paper. The notification must also be accompanied by an explanation of why the crypto asset referred to in the white paper is not an EMT and ARTs or excluded from the scope of MiCA altogether and confirm the intended start date of the public offer or admission to trading (and of any change to that date).

For EU-incorporated issuers and offerors, their home Member State is the EU Member State in which they have their registered office. For firms with no registered office in the EU but one or more EU branches, the issuer or offeror can choose their home Member State from among the Member States where they have branches. Finally, if the issuer or offeror is a non-EU firm with no EU branches, they can choose as the home Member State either the EU Member State where the crypto assets are intended to be offered to the public for the first time or the EU Member State where the first application for admission to trading of those crypto assets is made.

Where the offeror or issuer intends to offer their crypto assets to the public or intend to seek admission to trading in any other EU Member State, they must provide a list of any such 'host' Member States as part of the notification to the home Member State. The home Member State is then required to provide a copy of the white paper to each host Member State and notify ESMA of the information provided to it.

After the twenty-working day period has elapsed, the white paper can be published and the crypto asset offered to the public and/or admitted to trading in all relevant EU Member States (as notified to the home Member State competent authority). Publication requires the issuer or offeror to make the white paper publicly available on their website. The white paper must remain available on the website for as long as the crypto assets are held by the public in the EU and must match the version notified to competent authorities.

While there is no requirement for formal approval by the competent authority before publication, the relevant competent authority may require amendments to the white paper or suspend the offer or trading of the crypto assets if it does not comply with relevant requirements.

[e] Marketing Communications

Any marketing communications relating to an offer to the public or to admission to trading of a crypto asset (other than an EMT or ART) must be clearly identifiable as such. All information must be fair, clear and not misleading and must be consistent with the white paper (where a white paper is required).

Marketing communications must clearly state that a white paper has been published (unless this is not required) and provide contact details of the relevant issuer or offeror of crypto assets. They must also contain a statement with prescribed wording stating that the marketing communications have not been reviewed or approved by a competent authority.

Unless an exemption applies, no marketing communications can be disseminated prior to publication of the white paper, and marketing communications must also be published on the issuer or offeror's website in a publicly accessible manner and remain available on the website for as long as the crypto assets are held by the public in the EU.

[f] Changes to White Papers and Marketing Communications

Issuers and offerors are required to modify their published crypto asset white papers and, where applicable, their published marketing communications whenever there is a significant new factor, material mistake or material inaccuracy that is capable of affecting the assessment of the crypto assets, which arises during any offer to the public or any period when the crypto assets are admitted to trading.

Where issuers or offerors need to modify a white paper or marketing communications, they must notify their home competent authority at least seven working days before publication, together with an explanation of the rationale for the change. Modified white papers and marketing communications must be timestamped and marked as the applicable version upon publication. However, previous versions must remain publicly available for at least ten years after their publication date, marked with a prominent warning stating that they are no longer valid and a hyperlink to the dedicated section on the issuer or offeror's website where the most recent version of those documents is published.

[g] Liability for Content of the White Paper

Issuers and offerors of crypto assets are responsible for the content of white papers they draw up and publish. Article 15 MiCA provides that issuers and offerors are liable to holders of crypto assets for losses suffered by the holder as a result of incomplete or misleading information in the crypto asset white paper. It is not possible to contractually limit or exclude such liability, though the burden of proof lies with crypto asset holders. However, issuers and offerors shall not be liable for losses incurred as a result of reliance only on the information provided in a white paper summary, unless the summary is misleading, inaccurate or inconsistent with the rest of the white paper or does not provide key information.

Where a crypto asset trading venue operator prepares a white paper on the basis of information provided to it by a person seeking admission to trading, the person seeking admission to trading shall also be held responsible to the extent the information provided is not complete, fair or clear, or is misleading.

[h] Application to Crypto Assets Already Traded on EU Venues

As noted above, requirements applicable to persons seeking admission to trading of crypto assets under MiCA may apply to the operator of a crypto asset trading venue, where the relevant crypto asset is admitted to trading on the initiative of the venue operator. However, by way of exception, the operator of a crypto asset trading venue is not subject to requirements to draw up, notify to its competent authority and publish a white paper where:

- the crypto asset is already admitted to trading on another trading platform for crypto assets in the EU; or
- a crypto asset white paper has been drawn up, notified, published and kept up to date in accordance with MiCA and the person responsible for drawing up such a white paper consents to its use in writing.

There are also specific transitional provisions that apply in relation to crypto assets (other than EMTs and ARTs) that were admitted to trading before the relevant provisions of MiCA started to apply on 30 December 2024. These provide that the requirements of Title II MiCA do not apply in respect of public offers or admission to trading of those crypto assets, except that:

- marketing communications published after 30 December 2024 must comply with relevant requirements; and

- operators of trading platforms to which relevant crypto assets are admitted must ensure that a crypto asset white paper is drawn up, notified, published and kept updated in accordance with relevant requirements by 31 December 2027.

[i] *General Obligations on Issuers and Offerors*

The general obligations on issuers and offerors of crypto assets (other than EMTs and ARTs) under Regulation 14 MiCA require them to:

- act honestly, fairly and professionally;
- communicate with holders and prospective holders of the crypto assets in a fair, clear and not misleading manner;
- identify, prevent, manage and disclose any conflicts of interest that might arise;
- maintain all of their systems and security access protocols in conformity with the appropriate EU standards; and
- act in the best interests of the holders of such crypto assets and shall treat them equally, unless any preferential treatment of specific holders and the reasons for that preferential treatment are disclosed in the crypto asset white paper and, where applicable, the marketing communications.

Offerors of crypto assets (other than EMTs and ARTs) to the public are also required to publish the number of units of the crypto assets in circulation on their website on at least a monthly basis or, if they set a time limit on the public offer, they must publish the results of the public offer on their website within twenty working days of the end of the subscription period. Offerors must have effective arrangements in place to monitor and safeguard the funds or other crypto assets raised during the offer to the public and ensure they are custodied with a bank or CASP providing crypto asset custody services, as appropriate.

[j] *Withdrawal and Reimbursement Rights*

Where crypto assets are sold to retail investors as part of a public offer in the EU, retail holders of crypto assets have a statutory right to withdraw from their purchase of crypto assets within fourteen calendar days from the date on which they agreed to purchase crypto assets. Where a retail holder exercises this right of withdrawal, they are entitled to a prompt reimbursement of payments received, without incurring fees or costs, with the reimbursement to be made through the same means of payment used for the initial transaction, unless the retail holder agrees otherwise. Offerors must inform retail holders of this right in their crypto asset white paper.

However, the right of withdrawal does not apply if the crypto assets have been admitted to trading before purchase or after the end of the subscription period if offerors set a time limit on their public offer.

Where an offer to the public is cancelled, offerors shall ensure that any funds collected from holders or prospective holders are duly returned to them no later than twenty-five calendar days after the date of cancellation.

[C] Regulation of Stablecoins: EMTs and ARTs

Issuers of EMTs and ARTs are subject to similar requirements to those described in section [B] above for other types of crypto assets, including requirements for white papers and marketing communications. However, relevant requirements start to apply six months earlier, from 30 June 2024 (subject to relevant transitional provisions), and issuers of EMTs and ARTs are also subject to licensing and other additional regulatory requirements under MiCA, as summarised below.

[1] Asset-Referenced Tokens (ARTs)

[a] Requirements for Public Offering or Admission of ARTs to Trading

The regulatory regime for ARTs and their issuers is set out in Title III MiCA. Article 16 MiCA prohibits the public offer or admission to trading of ARTs by any person other than an authorised ART issuer, unless an exemption applies or the person seeking to publicly offer or admit the ART to trading has obtained the issuer's permission.

For this purpose, relevant exemptions include offering of ARTs solely to qualified investors (where EMTs can only be held by such qualified investors) and small issuances of EMTs that do not exceed EUR 5 million on average over a twelve-month period.

Even where ART issuers rely on an exemption from licensing requirements, they are still required to draw up an ART white paper, notify the white paper to their competent authority and publish the ART white paper.

[b] Authorisation Regime for ART Issuers

In order to be eligible for authorisation, a prospective ART issuer must be a legal entity incorporated in the EU. It must also meet minimum prudential requirements, including regulatory capital requirements and comply with various organisational, risk management, governance and conduct of business requirements.

Among other things, ART issuers are subject to detailed requirements in respect of treating customers fairly, ongoing disclosure, complaints handling. They are required to hold reserve assets backing the ART in custody on certain prescribed terms. Reserve assets can only be invested in highly liquid financial instruments with minimal market, credit and concentration risk. ART issuers are also required to maintain a recovery plan setting out measures to be taken by the issuer to restore compliance with the requirements applicable to the reserve of assets in certain circumstances.

MiCA sets out the process for granting authorisation as an ART issuer, as well as circumstances in which a competent authority may withdraw authorisation. There are transitional provisions for existing issuers that issued ARTs before MiCA started to apply on 30 June 2024. Provided that they apply for authorisation before 30 July 2024, these existing issuers may continue issuing ARTs until they are granted or refused authorisation under MiCA.

By way of exception, EU-authorised credit institutions (i.e., banks) seeking to issue ARTs do not require a separate authorisation but will still need to draw up a white paper and provide prescribed information about their proposed ART issuance to their home competent authority at least ninety days before issuance of the ART.

[c] ART Redemption Rights

MiCA requires ART issuers to grant holders a permanent right of redemption of the ART. Issuers must establish clear policies setting out redemption conditions, mechanisms and principles for valuation. Issuers can generally allow holders to redeem ARTs by either referenced by the asset-referenced token to the holder or by delivering to the holder the reserve assets that stabilise the value of the token.

[d] ART White Paper and Marketing Requirements

The requirements on ART issuers to draw up, notify to their competent authorities and publish white papers are similar to those applicable to other types of crypto assets. However, ART white papers must be approved by the relevant competent authority before the issuer is permitted to start issuing its ARTs (subject to transitional provisions for ARTs issued prior to 30 June 2024).

Materials must also include certain information specific to ARTs, such as a requirement for the white paper summary to set out details and conditions relating to holders' redemption rights. ART issuers are responsible and liable for the content of white papers in a similar way to other crypto asset white papers.

Where a person other than the issuer is publicly offering an ART or seeking its admission to trading, the white paper must identify them and explain why they are making the public offer or seeking admission to trading. The other person must also comply with relevant requirements relating to marketing communications under MiCA.

[e] Reporting Requirements and Restrictions on Issuance of Widely Used ARTs

Issuers of ARTs with an issue value exceeding EUR 100 million must provide quarterly reports to their competent authorities setting out the number of holders, token value, transaction details and estimates related to its use as a means of exchange within a currency area. Competent authorities also have the discretion to apply this requirement to ARTs under the EUR 100 million threshold.

CASPs providing services relating to these ARTs must also provide information to the ART issuer for reporting purposes.

Article 23 MiCA also imposes restrictions on the issuance of widely used ARTs where quarterly transaction numbers and values within a single currency area exceed 1 million transactions and EUR 200 million, respectively. In this case, the ART issuer must stop issuing the ART and submit a plan to its competent authority within forty working days to control the usage of the ART. The competent authority must approve the issuer's plan and may impose modifications (e.g., minimum denomination) that aim to reduce the use of the ART as a means of exchange. The issuer can only resume issuing the ART when it has evidence that usage has fallen below these thresholds.

[f] *Significant ARTs*

If an ART meets specific criteria, it is deemed 'significant', triggering an enhanced regulatory regime. This entails stricter requirements, such as remuneration and liquidity management, overseen by the EBA as the lead regulator for significant ARTs.

To be classified as significant, an ART must meet at least three of the following criteria (with further details to be specified in technical standards developed by the EBA):

- there are more than 10 million holders of the ART;
- the total value in issuance exceeds EUR 5 billion;
- daily transactions surpass 2.5 million in number or EUR 500 million in value;
- the issuer meets criteria relating to international significance of its activities;
- the ART or issuer meets criteria relating to its interconnectedness with the financial system; and
- criteria relating to other ARTs or EMTs issued by the same issuer or providing crypto asset services.

The EBA may classify an ART as significant based on information provided from competent authorities in relation to the above criteria and once classified as significant, supervisory responsibilities shift from the ART issuer's home competent authority to the EBA. ART issuers may also voluntarily notify their competent authority that they wish for their ART to be classified as significant. In this case, the ART issuer must demonstrate that the ART is likely to meet at least three of the relevant criteria for designation of the ART as significant.

Issuers of significant ARTs are subject to additional obligations, including requirements to have a remuneration policy focused on sound risk management, the ability for the ART to be held in custody by various providers, and the establishment of a liquidity management policy and regular liquidity stress testing for the ART. Regular liquidity stress testing is mandatory. The EBA is mandated to develop technical standards further specifying governance arrangements, liquidity requirements, and adjustment procedures for own funds for significant ART issuers. The EBA is also tasked with issuing guidelines for significant ARTs in collaboration with ESMA and the European Central Bank (ECB).

[2] E-Money Tokens (EMTs)

[a] Requirements for Public Offering or Admission of EMTs to Trading

The regulatory regime for EMTs and their issuers is set out in Title IV MiCA. Article 48 MiCA prohibits the public offer or admission to trading of EMTs by any person other than an authorised EMT issuer, unless an exemption applies or the person seeking to publicly offer or admit the EMT to trading has obtained the EMT issuer's permission. EMTs that reference an official EU currency are deemed to be offered to the public in the EU.

Save where an exemption applies, an EMT issuer must:

- be licensed either as a credit institution (i.e. a bank) under the Capital Requirements Directive[12] (CRD) or as an electronic money institution under the Electronic Money Directive[13] (EMD); and
- have published a white paper for the EMT, which it has notified to its competent authority.

For this purpose, relevant exemptions include offering of EMTs solely to qualified investors (where EMTs can only be held by such qualified investors) and small issuances of EMTs that do not exceed EUR 5 million on average over a twelve-month period, as well as relevant exemptions from licensing under the EMD such as the 'limited network' exclusion.

Even where EMT issuers rely on exemptions from licensing, they are still required to draw up an EMT white paper, notify the white paper to their competent authority and publish the EMT white paper.

[b] Requirements for EMTs and Issuers

EMTs must amount to a claim on the issuer and must be redeemable at par. Granting of interest in relation to EMTs is prohibited and any remuneration or benefit linked to the duration of EMTs is considered interest for this purpose.

All EMTs are deemed to qualify as 'electronic money' for the purpose of the EMD. This means that transactions in EMTs are generally regulated as payment transactions under the EU payment services regulatory regime. Funds received by EMT issuers in

12. Directive 2013/36/EU of the European Parliament and of the Council of 26 June 2013 on access to the activity of credit institutions and the prudential supervision of credit institutions and investment firms, amending Directive 2002/87/EC and repealing Directives 2006/48/EC and 2006/49/EC.
13. Directive 2009/110/EC of the European Parliament and of the Council of 16 September 2009 on the taking up, pursuit and prudential supervision of the business of electronic money institutions amending Directives 2005/60/EC and 2006/48/EC and repealing Directive 2000/46/EC.

exchange for EMTs must be safeguarded in accordance with the requirements of the EMD. Article 54 MiCA further specifies that at least 30% of such funds must be deposited in separate accounts in credit institutions and that the remaining funds may be invested in secure, low-risk assets that qualify as highly liquid financial instruments, with minimal market risk, credit risk, and concentration risk. These investments must be denominated in the same currency as the one referenced by the EMT.

EMT issuers are also required to maintain recovery and redemption plans similar to those for ARTs. EMT issuers are required to notify the competent authority of their recovery plan within six months of offering to the public or admission to trading (as applicable) of the relevant EMT.

[c] EMT White Paper and Marketing Requirements

The requirements on EMT issuers to draw up, notify to their competent authorities and publish white papers are similar to those applicable to other types of crypto assets. Competent authorities are not required to approve EMT white papers.

Materials must also include certain information specific to EMTs, such as a requirement for the white paper summary to state that holders of the EMT have a right of redemption at any time and at par value and to set out the conditions for redemption. EMT issuers are responsible and liable for the content of white papers.

Where a person other than the issuer is publicly offering an EMT or seeking its admission to trading, the white paper must identify them and explain why they are making the public offer or seeking admission to trading. The other person must also comply with relevant requirements relating to marketing communications under MiCA.

[d] Significant EMTs

As for ARTs, if an EMT meets specific criteria, the EBA may classify it as 'significant', triggering an enhanced regulatory regime. These criteria are the same as for ARTs (as set out in section [C][1](f) above), and again, an EMT must fulfil at least three of these criteria in order to be classified as 'significant'.

The EBA may classify an EMT as significant based on information provided from competent authorities in relation to the above criteria and once classified as significant, supervisory responsibilities shift from the EMT issuer's home competent authority to the EBA (unless the EMT is denominated in an EU official currency other than the euro and at least 80 % of the number of holders and of the volume of transactions of the significant EMT is concentrated in its home Member State).

EMT issuers may also voluntarily notify their competent authority that they wish for their EMT to be classified as significant. In this case, the EMT issuer must demonstrate that the EMT is likely to meet at least three of the relevant criteria for designation of the EMT as significant.

Electronic money institutions that issue significant EMTs are subject to additional obligations similar to those applicable to authorised issuers of significant ARTs.

[D] Regulation of Crypto Asset Service Providers

[1] Regulated Crypto Asset Services

MiCA regulates provision of the following crypto asset services, many of which mirror or closely resemble investment services and activities under MiFID2. These services are defined in Article 3 MiCA as follows:

Crypto Asset Service	*Definition*	*Corresponding MiFID Activity*
Providing custody and administration of crypto assets on behalf of clients	The safekeeping or controlling, on behalf of clients, of crypto assets or of the means of access to such crypto assets, where applicable in the form of private cryptographic keys	Safekeeping and administration of financial instruments for the account of clients[14]
Operation of a trading platform for crypto asset	The management of one or more multilateral systems, which bring together or facilitate the bringing together of multiple third-party purchasing and selling interests in crypto assets, in the system and in accordance with its rules, in a way that results in a contract, either by exchanging crypto assets for funds or by the exchange of crypto assets for other crypto assets	Operating a multilateral trading facility or an organised trading facility
Exchange of crypto assets for funds	The conclusion of purchase or sale contracts concerning crypto assets with clients for funds by using proprietary capital	Dealing on own account
Exchange of crypto assets for other crypto assets	The conclusion of purchase or sale contracts concerning crypto assets with clients for other crypto assets by using proprietary capital	Dealing on own account

14. Note: this is a MiFID ancillary service which means that it is only regulated under MiFID where provided in connection with a MiFID investment service or activity.

Crypto Asset Service	*Definition*	*Corresponding MiFID Activity*
Execution of orders for crypto assets on behalf of clients	The conclusion of agreements, on behalf of clients, to purchase or sell one or more crypto assets or the subscription on behalf of clients for one or more crypto assets, and includes the conclusion of contracts to sell crypto assets at the moment of their offer to the public or admission to trading	Execution of orders on behalf of clients
Placing of crypto assets	The marketing, on behalf of or for the account of the offeror or a party related to the offeror, of crypto assets to purchasers	Placing of financial instruments on a firm commitment basis or placing of financial instruments without a firm commitment basis
Reception and transmission of orders for crypto assets on behalf of clients	The reception from a person of an order to purchase or sell one or more crypto assets or to subscribe for one or more crypto assets and the transmission of that order to a third party for execution	Reception and transmission of orders in relation to one or more financial instruments
Providing advice on crypto assets	Offering, giving or agreeing to give personalised recommendations to a client, either at the client's request or on the initiative of the crypto asset service provider providing the advice, in respect of one or more transactions relating to crypto assets, or the use of crypto asset services	Investment advice
Providing portfolio management of crypto assets	Managing portfolios in accordance with mandates given by clients on a discretionary client-by-client basis where such portfolios include one or more crypto assets	Portfolio management
Providing transfer services for crypto assets on behalf of clients	Providing services of transfer, on behalf of a natural or legal person, of crypto assets from one distributed ledger address or account to another	None (but broadly corresponds to execution of payment transactions under PSD2)

[2] *Authorisation Regime for CASPs*

Firms seeking to provide crypto asset services in the EU must be authorised as a CASP, unless they are already licensed under existing EU financial services legislation as further described in section [3] below. This is subject to certain limited exemptions, for example, with respect to custody and transfer services provided in relation to crypto assets (other than EMTs and ARTs) benefiting from an exemption from relevant requirements under Title III MiCA.

In order to apply for authorisation as a CASP, the applicant must be a legal person with its registered office and effective place of management in the EU. At least one director must also be resident in the EU.

Applicants must submit an application for authorisation as a CASP to the competent authority of their home Member State containing certain prescribed information. ESMA is tasked with preparing standard forms, templates and procedures for CASP authorisation applications, in close cooperation with the EBA. The prescribed information that must be included as part of an authorisation application includes:

- the applicant's name, legal identifier, website and contact details;
- the applicant's legal form and articles of association;
- a programme of operations, setting out the types of crypto asset services that the applicant crypto asset service provider intends to provide, including where and how those services are to be marketed;
- evidence that the applicant has relevant prudential requirements, including minimum capital requirements;
- a description of the applicant's crypto asset service provider's governance arrangements;
- evidence that members of the applicant's management body are of sufficiently good repute and possess appropriate knowledge, skills and experience;
- information about direct and indirect shareholders or members that hold at least 10% of the voting rights or capital of applicant or which can otherwise exercise significant influence over the applicant, and evidence that those persons are of sufficiently good repute;
- a description of relevant anti-money laundering internal control mechanisms, policies and procedures and risk framework;
- technical documentation and descriptions of relevant ICT systems and security arrangements;
- information on the segregation of clients' crypto assets and funds; and
- certain other information specific to the crypto asset services intended to be provided.

Once authorised, CASPs are subject to ongoing prudential, organisational and general conduct of business requirements, including minimum capital requirements; governance arrangements; an overarching requirement to act honestly, fairly and professionally in the best interests of clients; rules on safekeeping of client crypto assets and funds; requirements to establish a complaint handling procedure; maintain effective conflicts of interest policies and procedures; outsourcing requirements and requirements for wind-down plans. In common with other types of EU-authorised entities, CASPs are also subject to rules on the acquisition of qualifying holdings.

Authorised CASPs are able to exercise passporting rights to provide crypto asset services throughout the EU either on a cross-border basis or via establishment of a local branch.

There are optional transitional measures for CASPs that provided services in accordance with applicable law before 30 December 2024. Under these measures, Member States can allow CASPs to continue providing their services until 1 July 2026 (or until their application for authorisation has been determined, if sooner) and provide a simplified application procedure for these firms.

[3] Provision of Crypto Asset Services by Licensed Financial Entities

Firms do not need to seek authorisation as a CASP if they are:

- already authorised under EU financial services legislation as a credit institution, central securities depository, investment firm, market operator, electronic money institution, UCITS management company, or an alternative investment fund manager; and
- permitted to carry on relevant crypto asset services under Article 60 MiCA.

Article 60 MiCA sets out the types of crypto asset services that different types of financial entities are able to provide without a separate CASP licence, as follows:

- firms authorised as credit institutions are able to provide any crypto asset services;
- investment firms are able to provide crypto asset services corresponding to the MiFID activities covered by their authorisation (as per the table in section [1] above);
- central securities depositories are able to provide custody and administration of crypto assets on behalf of clients;
- electronic money institutions are able to provide custody and administration of crypto assets on behalf of clients and transfer services for crypto assets on behalf of clients with regard to the EMTs they issue;
- UCITS management companies and alternative investment fund managers are able to provide portfolio management of crypto assets and other crypto asset services corresponding to non-core services for which they are authorised; and
- market operators authorised under MiFID2 are able to operate a trading platform for crypto assets,

in each case, provided that the relevant entity notifies its competent authority of the crypto asset services it intends to provide at least forty working days before starting to provide those services and provides the competent authority with certain required information about its provision of services.

The required information includes a programme of operations for the provision and marketing of crypto asset services, a description of relevant anti-money laundering internal control mechanisms, policies and procedures and risk framework, technical documentation and descriptions of relevant ICT systems and security arrangements, information on the segregation of clients' crypto assets and funds and certain other information specific to the crypto asset services intended to be provided.

[4] Cross-Border Provision of Crypto Asset Services

As noted above, non-EU firms are not eligible to apply for authorisation as a CASP. Article 61 MiCA provides that non-EU firms are able to provide crypto asset services and activities to EU clients where the relevant service or activity is provided at the 'own exclusive initiative' of the EU client (i.e., reverse solicitation).

This reverse solicitation exemption is not available where the non-EU firm has solicited EU clients, regardless of the means of communication and whether or not EU clients are solicited directly by the non-EU firm or via an entity acting on its behalf. It is not possible to override this restriction through use of disclaimers or contractual provisions.

This reverse solicitation exemption applies on a per service or activity basis, meaning that non-EU firms are not able to market new services or activities to existing EU clients under this regime.

ESMA is mandated to develop guidelines on the scope of this reverse solicitation exemption from licensing for non-EU firms.

[5] Ongoing Obligations for Provision of Crypto Asset Services

Firms providing crypto asset services under MiCA are subject to ongoing obligations with respect to the provision of these services. These requirements apply to both CASPs authorised under MiCA and regulated financial entities providing relevant crypto asset services under Article 60 MiCA. In many cases, ESMA and/or the EBA has been tasked with developing technical standards to provide further details of the requirements outlined below. References in this section to CASPs therefore refer broadly to all such entities providing the relevant crypto asset service under MiCA.

[a] Provision of Crypto Asset Custody Services

Crypto asset custody is defined broadly as 'safekeeping or controlling, on behalf of third parties, crypto assets or the means of access to such crypto assets, where applicable in the form of private cryptographic keys'. The reference to 'controlling' in addition to 'safekeeping' means this is broader than the equivalent concept of safekeeping and administration of financial instruments under MiFID2.

Crypto asset custodians are required to put in place detailed agreements with their clients, specifying information such as the identities of the parties to the agreement, the nature of services being provided, the CASP's custody policy, relevant information on communication methods, security systems used, fees, costs and charges and the applicable law governing the agreement.

Custodians must also maintain a register of positions opened in the name of each client, promptly recording changes to positions, have a custody policy, a summary of which must be available to clients on request, ensure segregation of custodied crypto assets from the custodian's own assets so they are protected in case of the custodian's insolvency and provide quarterly statements to clients on their holdings.

MiCA introduces specific liability requirements for custodians of crypto assets in relation to losses. In particular, a custodian will be liable for loss of crypto assets (or their means of access) resulting from an incident attributable to provision of the service or operation of the service provider, capped at the market value of the crypto assets lost. This is in contrast to the position for custody of financial instruments under MiFID, where liability for loss is not generally imposed.

Custodians holding reserve assets for an ART issuer are also subject to liability standards similar to those imposed on fund depositaries under relevant EU frameworks. In particular, a custodian holding reserve assets for an issuer of ARTs must, if financial instruments or crypto assets are lost, return identical assets or their value to the ART issuer without undue delay, unless it can prove the loss arose from an external event beyond its reasonable control, the consequences of which would have been unavoidable despite all reasonable efforts to the contrary.

[b] Operation of a Trading Platform for Crypto Assets

A CASP operating a crypto assets trading platform under MiCA must establish transparent platform rules covering issues including approval processes for crypto assets, categories of types of crypto assets (if any) excluded from trading, fees, objective, non-discriminatory rules and proportionate criteria for participation on the platform, conditions setting out when crypto assets can remain available for trading or may be suspended and procedures to ensure efficient settlement of transactions executed on the platform.

CASPs operating a trading platform must also carry out suitability assessments on crypto assets admitted to trading on the platform and ensure that an associated white paper has been published. Their trading procedures must also prevent admission to trading of crypto assets with an inbuilt anonymisation function.

Platform operators must have in place robust and resilient trading systems and meet various other requirements similar to those for traditional financial instrument trading venues, including with respect to transparency, publication and retention of trading data. Platform operators are prohibited from dealing on their own account and may only engage in matched principal trading subject to client consent.

[c] *Exchange of Crypto Assets for Funds or for Other Crypto Assets*

CASPs exchanging crypto assets for funds of other crypto assets must establish a non-discriminatory commercial policy that indicates the type of clients they agree to transact with and the conditions that shall be met by such clients. They are also required to publish a firm price of the crypto assets or a method for determining the price of the crypto assets that they propose to exchange, execute client orders at the prices displayed at the time when the order for exchange is final and publish information about the transactions concluded by them.

[d] *Execution of Orders for Crypto Assets on Behalf of Clients*

CASPs executing orders for crypto assets are subject to requirements similar to those applicable to MiFID investment firms when executing client orders in financial instruments. These include best execution requirements, requirements to provide clients with appropriate and clear information to their clients on their order execution policy, requirements to obtain express consent of their clients before proceeding to execute their orders outside a trading platform and requirements to monitor the effectiveness of their order execution arrangements.

[e] *Placing of Crypto Assets*

CASPs carrying on placing activities are required to provide certain information to the offeror or person seeking admission to trading (or anyone acting on their behalf) before entering into a placing agreement. This includes information on the type of placement under consideration, fees, expected timing and process and information on the targeted purchasers.

Conflicts of interest policies and procedures must also cover specific situations that may arise in the context of placing activity, including placing of crypto assets with the CASP's own clients, considerations where the price has been over- or underestimated and incentives that may be paid or granted by the offeror in the context of placing activity.

[f] *Reception and Transmission of Orders for Crypto Assets on Behalf of Clients*

CASPs carrying on reception and transmission of orders for crypto assets:

- must establish efficient procedures for order transmission to trading platforms or other service providers;
- are prohibited from receiving any form of remuneration, discount or non-monetary benefit for directing client orders to specific platforms or providers; and

- must not misuse information on pending client orders and prevent employee misuse of such information.

[g] *Advising on and Providing Portfolio Management of Crypto Assets*

CASPs advising on crypto assets or providing portfolio management services relating to crypto assets are again subject to similar ongoing conduct of business requirements similar to those applicable to the corresponding investment services under MiFID.

Among other things, CASPs are required to assess the suitability of relevant crypto asset services or crypto assets for their clients, taking into account clients' knowledge and experience, investment objectives, including risk tolerance and their financial situation. Crypto asset advisers are required to disclose if their advice is independent, with additional requirements applicable to independent advice.

CASPs providing advice or portfolio management services relating to crypto assets are also subject to requirements to disclose fees, costs and charges and are subject to rules and restrictions relating to inducements. They must also provide clients with specific risk warnings in respect of crypto assets and provide periodic statements to clients.

[h] *Providing Transfer Services for Crypto Assets on Behalf of Clients*

CASPs offering transfer services for clients must enter into agreements with their clients specifying their duties and responsibilities. These agreements are required to set out provisions detailing the parties to the agreement, modalities of the transfer service, information about the CASP's security systems, fees and the applicable law governing the relationship.

[E] Market Abuse Regime for Crypto Assets

Crypto assets that do not qualify as financial instruments under MiFID2 fall outside the scope of the EU Market Abuse Regulation[15] (MAR). However, Title VI MiCA sets out its own market abuse regime applicable to crypto assets that are admitted to trading on a trading platform for crypto assets operated by a CASP authorised under MiCA (or which is authorised under MiFID and is able to provide relevant crypto asset services under Article 60 MiCA).

Similar to MAR, the market abuse regime under MiCA includes requirements relating to the disclosure of inside information, the prohibition of insider dealing, the prohibition of unlawful disclosure of inside information and the prohibition of market manipulation, as outlined below. The European Supervisory Authorities (ESAs) are

15. Regulation (EU) No. 596/2014 of the European Parliament and of the Council of 16 April 2014 on market abuse (market abuse regulation) and repealing Directive 2003/6/EC of the European Parliament and of the Council and Commission Directives 2003/124/EC, 2003/125/EC and 2004/72/EC.

also mandated to develop technical standards and guidelines fleshing out the requirements of the market abuse regime under MiCA.

[1] *Inside Information Relating to Crypto Assets*

Inside information is defined in Article 87 MiCA as information:

- of a precise nature,
- which has not been made public,
- relating, directly or indirectly, to one or more issuers, offerors or persons seeking admission to trading or to one or more crypto assets; and
- which, if it were made public, would be likely to have a significant effect on the prices of those crypto assets or on the price of a related crypto asset.

This is similar to the definition of inside information under MAR but refers to crypto assets rather than financial instruments and expands the definition to refer not only to 'issuers' of crypto assets but also to offerors and persons seeking their admission to trading.

When executing orders concerning crypto assets, inside information also covers information conveyed by a client and relating to the client's pending orders in crypto assets, which is of a precise nature, relating, directly or indirectly, to one or more issuers, offerors or persons seeking admission to trading or to one or more crypto assets, and which, if it were made public, would be likely to have a significant effect on the prices of those crypto assets or on the price of a related crypto asset.

Key concepts used in the definition include:

- *Information of a precise nature*: Information is of a precise nature when it indicates a set of circumstances which exists, or which may reasonably be expected to come into existence, or an event which has occurred, or which may reasonably be expected to occur, where it is specific enough to enable a conclusion to be drawn as to the possible effect of that set of circumstances or event on the prices of the crypto assets.
- *Information with a significant effect on crypto asset prices*: Information has a significant effect on the price of a crypto asset where a reasonable holder of crypto assets would be likely to use as part of the basis of their decisions.

Where an event or circumstances result from a protracted process, intermediate steps in that process may be inside information.

The ESAs are mandated to develop technical standards and guidelines in respect of the market abuse regime under MiCA.

[2] *Obligation to Disclose Inside Information to the Public*

Issuers, offerors and persons seeking admission to trading of crypto assets are subject to an obligation to disclose inside information to the public as soon as possible. Such information must be posted and available on their website for a period of at least five years.

Issuers, offerors and persons seeking admission to trading may delay disclosure of inside information where immediate disclosure is likely to prejudice their legitimate interests, the delay is not likely to mislead the public and the person delaying disclosure is able to ensure the confidentiality of that information.

Where an issuer, offeror or person seeking admission to trading of crypto assets delays disclosure of inside information, they must inform their competent authority that the disclosure was delayed and explain how the conditions for delay were met, immediately after the information is disclosed to the public.

[3] Prohibitions Relating to Market Abuse

[a] Prohibition on Insider Dealing

Insider dealing occurs where a person possesses inside information and uses that information by acquiring or disposing of, for its own account or for the account of a third party, directly or indirectly, crypto assets to which it relates. It also includes the use of inside information to cancel or amend orders related to such assets placed before the individual had access to inside information.

MiCA prohibits individuals from engaging in or attempting to engage in insider dealing, recommending or inducing others to engage in insider dealing or acting on such a recommendation or inducement. In this context, recommendations or inducements amount to insider dealing where the person recommending or inducing knows or ought to know that it is based on inside information.

If someone uses a recommendation or inducement based on inside information and knows or should know that it is inside information, it constitutes insider dealing. This regulation applies to various scenarios, including those who have inside information due to their roles in an organisation, ownership in the issuer, access to information through employment or professional duties, or involvement in criminal activities. It also covers individuals possessing inside information under other circumstances if they are aware or should be aware that it is inside information.

[b] Unlawful Disclosure of Inside Information

No person in possession of inside information shall engage in the unauthorised disclosure of such information to any other individual, unless such disclosure occurs within the normal scope of their employment, profession, or duties.

[c] Prohibition on Market Manipulation

MiCA prohibits any person from engaging in or attempting market manipulation. Market manipulation encompasses a range of activities, including actions that give false or misleading signals about crypto asset supply, demand, or price, securing prices at abnormal levels, employing deceptive tactics in transactions and disseminating false information through various means.

Specific examples of market manipulation set out in Article 91 MiCA include securing a dominant position in a crypto asset market in a way that creates or is likely to create unfair trading conditions, placing or cancelling orders on a trading platform in a way that does or is likely to have the effect of disrupting or delaying the platform's functioning, making it more difficult to identify genuine orders and eating a false or misleading signal about the supply of, or demand for, or price of, a crypto asset. The final example given refers to exploiting media access to voice an opinion about a crypto asset, where the relevant person has taken an existing position in the crypto asset leading to personal gain, unless they have simultaneously and effectively disclosed their conflict of interest.

[4] Prevention and Detection of Market Abuse

Any person professionally arranging or executing transactions in crypto assets must have in place effective arrangements, systems and procedures to prevent and detect market abuse. Such persons must report reasonable suspicions of market abuse related to orders, transactions, or aspects of distributed ledger technology to the competent authority of the relevant Member State where they are registered, headquartered, or have branches, as appropriate. Competent authorities receiving these reports must immediately share the information with the relevant trading platforms' authorities.

[F] Status and Future Developments

MiCA was published in the Official Journal of the EU on 9 June 2023. It entered into force twenty days later, empowering the ESAs to start work on the various technical standards and guidelines that they are mandated to develop. The provisions of Title III and IV relating to EMTs and ARTs apply from 30 June 2024 with remaining provisions starting to apply from 30 December 2024.

As discussed above, there are various transitional and grandfathering provisions, including for existing firms that provide crypto asset services or issue ARTs.

There are also processes hardwired into MiCA for its review and revision to take into account future developments. These review and reporting requirements include requirements for:

- the European Commission to present a report by 30 December 2024, following consultation with ESMA and the EBA, on matters not addressed by MiCA including decentralised finance, feasibility of regulating lending and borrowing of crypto assets, treatment of services associated with the transfer of e-money tokens (where not addressed as part of the review of PSD2) and whether there needs to be a specific development covering the regulation of NFTs;

- ESMA to provide a report by 31 December 2025 and annually thereafter on development of crypto asset markets to the EU Parliament and the Council of the EU;
- the European Commission to present an interim report by 30 June 2025 and a final report by 30 June 2027, following consultation with ESMA and the EBA on the application of MiCA, to be accompanied by a legislative proposal if appropriate.

§6.02 AML REGULATION RELATING TO CRYPTO ASSETS IN THE EU

[A] The MLD5 Registration Regime for Virtual Currency Service Providers

In June 2018, the fifth Money Laundering Directive[16] (MLD5) was published in the Official Journal of the EU. Among other things, this introduced a harmonised regime across the EU, extending the scope of anti-money laundering (AML) regulation to firms carrying on certain activities relating to 'virtual currencies'. EU Member States had until 10 January 2020 to amend their national laws to implement its requirements.

As such, this regime pre-dates MiCA, and the concepts and definitions used are slightly different from those used under MiCA. In addition, because MLD5 is a Directive requiring national implementation, there is some variation in the way different Member States have implemented its requirements.

[1] Virtual Currencies

MLD5 defines virtual currencies as 'a digital representation of value that is not issued or guaranteed by a central bank or a public authority, is not necessarily attached to a legally established currency and does not possess a legal status of currency or money, but is accepted by natural or legal persons as a means of exchange and which can be transferred, stored and traded electronically'.

This definition captures various types of cryptocurrencies and stablecoins, noting that the requirement for a virtual currency to be 'accepted … as a means of exchange' means that it is narrower than the corresponding definition of 'crypto asset' under MiCA. However, certain EU Member States took a broader approach when implementing MLD5 into national laws, extending the requirements to activities relating to a broader range of crypto assets.

16. Directive (EU) 2018/843 of the European Parliament and of the Council of 30 May 2018 amending Directive (EU) 2015/849 on the prevention of the use of the financial system for the purposes of money laundering or terrorist financing, and amending Directives 2009/138/EC and 2013/36/EU.

[2] *Requirements on Virtual Currency Exchange Providers and Custodians*

MLD5 extended the definition of 'obliged entities' required to comply with relevant AML requirements to include:

- providers engaged in exchange services between virtual currencies and fiat currencies; and
- custodian wallet providers, defined as any entity that provides services to safeguard private cryptographic keys on behalf of its customers to hold, store and transfer virtual currencies.

Under MLD5, these virtual currency exchange providers and custodian wallet providers are subject to requirements to register with their national AML regulator and are required to comply with AML-related requirements, including with respect to customer due diligence, risk assessments, monitoring and reporting of suspicious transactions and record-keeping requirements.

Again, there has been some variation in the national implementation of this registration requirement under MLD5, with certain Member States imposing more stringent requirements for successful registration.

[B] The EU 'Travel Rule' for Crypto Asset Transfers

The EU published the revised Transfer of Funds Regulation[17] (TRF3) in the Official Journal of the EU on 9 June 2023, alongside MiCA. TFR3 implements the so-called travel rule for crypto asset transfers set out in Financial Action Task Force (FATF) Recommendation 16,[18] which requires crypto asset transfers to be accompanied by certain identifiable information on the transferor and transferee.

It will apply from 30 December 2024, in line with the application of most MiCA provisions.

[1] *Scope and Definitions*

The travel rule requirements under TRF3 apply in respect of transfers of crypto assets, as defined under MiCA. The rules apply to CASPs, including financial institutions offering crypto asset services, that are subject to regulation under MiCA.

Person-to-person transfers, defined as 'a transaction between natural persons acting, as consumers, for purposes other than trade, business or profession, without the use or involvement' of a CASP are out of scope. In addition, crypto asset transfers

17. Regulation (EU) 2023/1113 of the European Parliament and of the Council of 31 May 2023 on information accompanying transfers of funds and certain crypto assets and amending Directive (EU) 2015/849.
18. *See* the FATF Recommendations at https://www.fatf-gafi.org/en/.

are out of scope where both the originator and the beneficiary are CASPs acting on their own behalf.

However, there is no minimum transfer amount for application of the rules, in contrast to the provisions of FATF Recommendation 16 itself, which provided for a EUR 1,000 *de minimis* threshold.

[2] Travel Rule Requirements for Crypto Asset Transfers

For in-scope transfers of crypto assets, TRF3 requires the originator's CASP to ensure that the crypto asset transfers are accompanied by specified information about the originator and beneficiary of the crypto asset transfer, including the:

- originator's name, distributed ledger address, crypto asset account number, physical address, official personal document number and customer identification number or date and place of birth and, where relevant, their legal entity identifier (LEI) or equivalent official identifier; and
- beneficiary's name, distributed ledger address, crypto asset account number, LEI or equivalent official identifier.

In most cases, the originator's CASP is required to verify the accuracy of information about the originator on the basis of documents, data or information obtained from a reliable and independent source.

The beneficiary's CASP is required to implement effective procedures to detect missing or incomplete information accompanying the crypto asset transfer. Before making the crypto assets available to the beneficiary, the beneficiary's CASP is required to verify the accuracy of the relevant information on the beneficiary accompanying the transfer on the basis of documents, data or information obtained from a reliable and independent source. The beneficiary's CASP must also establish effective risk-based procedures for determining whether to execute, reject, return or suspend a transfer of crypto assets lacking the required information on the originator and the beneficiary and for taking appropriate follow-up action.

Where there is an intermediary CASP involved in the crypto asset transfer, intermediary CASP is required to ensure that relevant information is transmitted alongside the crypto asset transfer and records of such information are retained and made available on request to the competent authorities. Intermediary CASPs are also required to detect missing or incomplete information and establish effective risk-based procedures for determining whether to execute, reject, return or suspend a transfer of crypto assets lacking the required information on the originator and the beneficiary and for taking appropriate follow-up action.

With respect to data protection, CASPs are required to ensure that the transmission of any personal data occurs in compliance with the requirements of the General

Data Protection Regulation[19] (GDPR). Among other things, CASPs are required to put in place appropriate measures to protect personal data against accidental loss, alteration, or unauthorised disclosure.

TFR3 does not itself address how CASPs are expected to comply with certain aspects of its requirements in the context of crypto asset transfers using public Blockchains, such as the feasibility of rejecting or suspending transfers of crypto assets with missing or incomplete information. However, the EBA is mandated to publish guidelines on various aspects of TFR3 by 30 June 2024 and has general powers to publish Q&A relating to the practical interpretation of various EU regulations, including TFR3.

§6.03 UK REGULATION OF CRYPTO ASSETS

As at the beginning of 2024, there is no specific UK regulatory regime for firms carrying on crypto asset-related activities other than in relation to financial promotions and anti-money laundering obligations and financial promotions (as outlined in section [B] below as well as in §6.04 below, respectively). However, certain types of crypto assets may fall within existing financial services regulatory frameworks based on analysis of their substantive characteristics.

Looking ahead, the UK is taking a phased approach to the development of a more comprehensive regulatory regime for crypto assets. Phase one is expected to introduce licensing and regulation of firms issuing and providing services related to fiat-backed stablecoins used for payments in the UK. The UK regulators are expected to consult on draft rules during 2024 and have targeted implementation of phase one (i.e., fiat-backed stablecoin regulation) during 2025. Phase two will regulate activities relating to other types of crypto assets on a longer implementation timetable.

[A] Scope of UK Regulation of Crypto Assets

[1] Regulatory Characterisation of Crypto Assets

In 2019, the UK Financial Conduct Authority (FCA) published its final Guidance on Crypto-Assets[20] (the '2019 Guidance'), setting out the UK's approach to identifying whether crypto assets may fall within an existing regulatory regime. According to the 2019 Guidance, a case-by-case analysis of the relevant crypto asset's substantive characteristics is required to determine whether crypto asset qualifies as:

- security tokens (i.e., crypto assets which meet the definition of a 'specified investment' under the Financial Services and Markets Act 2000 (Regulated

19. Regulation (EU) 2016/679 of the European Parliament and of the Council of 27 April 2016 on the protection of natural persons with regard to the processing of personal data and on the free movement of such data, and repealing Directive 95/46/EC (General Data Protection Regulation).
20. Available at https://www.fca.org.uk/publication/policy/ps19-22.pdf.

Activities) Order 2001 (RAO), such as shares, debentures or units in a collective investment scheme);

- e-money tokens (i.e., crypto assets which meet the definition of electronic money[21] under the Electronic Money Regulations 2011 (EMRs)); or
- unregulated tokens (i.e., crypto assets which do not qualify as security tokens or e-money tokens).

Security tokens and e-money tokens are subject to the usual UK regulatory requirements applicable to securities and e-money, respectively. In some cases, they may also be subject to crypto asset-specific regulation, as discussed in the following sections.

Crypto assets that currently fall within the 'unregulated' category include fiat-backed stablecoins and other crypto assets that will become subject to regulation as part of the UK's phased approach to development of a comprehensive regulatory framework for crypto assets. They may also fall within the scope of existing UK financial promotions restrictions and anti-money laundering rules discussed in sections [B] and §6.04, respectively.

In a cross-authority roadmap on innovation in payments published in November 2023,[22] the UK regulators also confirmed that 'tokenised' bank deposits will continue to be regulated in the same way as other types of bank deposits rather than under a crypto asset-related regulatory regime.

[2] Extending the Authorisation Regime under FSMA to Stablecoins and Other Crypto Assets

The Financial Services and Markets Act 2000 (FSMA) is the cornerstone of the UK financial services regulatory framework. Among other things, it sets out the statutory framework for authorisation of firms carrying on regulated activities in the UK and empowers the regulators to supervise authorised firms and make regulatory rules.

The Financial Services and Markets Act 2023 (the '2023 Act') amended FSMA to introduce new powers for HM Treasury (HMT) to bring stablecoins and other types of crypto assets within the scope of the UK financial services regulatory perimeter and FSMA authorisation regime. As noted above, the UK intends to take a phased approach to regulation of crypto assets, starting with fiat-backed stablecoins in phase 1 and other crypto assets in phase 2.[23]

21. Electronic money is defined for this purpose as electronically (including magnetically) stored monetary value as represented by a claim on the issuer, which is issued on receipt of funds for the purpose of making payment transactions and is accepted as a means of payment by persons other than the issuer (subject to certain exclusions set out in the EMRs).
22. Available at https://www.bankofengland.co.uk/paper/2023/cross-authority-roadmap-on-innovation-in-payments.
23. For an overview of the UK's phased approach to regulation of crypto assets and how this compares with the EU approach, *see* 'The Developing Regulatory Landscape for Crypto-assets in the EU and UK', published in The International Journal of Blockchain Law, Volume V, March 2023, available at https://gbbcouncil.org/wp-content/uploads/2023/03/March-2023-IJBL-Volume-V-1.pdf.

[a] Regulation of Fiat-Backed Stablecoins

The 2023 Act introduces the defined term 'digital settlement asset' (DSA) to refer to stablecoins that are used for payments.

A DSA is defined broadly as a 'digital representation of value or rights, whether or not cryptographically secured, that – (a) can be used for the settlement of payment obligations, (b) can be transferred, stored or traded electronically, and (c) uses technology supporting the recording or storage of data (which may include distributed ledger technology)'.[24]

HMT initially intends to use its powers to regulate DSAs that are fiat-backed stablecoins,[25] although the broader DSA definition provides flexibility for further regulation in future. HMT is also granted powers to amend the DSA definition.

HMT is granted a range of powers to regulate services and activities relating to DSAs under the 2023 Act, including power to:

- establish an FCA authorisation and supervision regime for DSA issuers and service providers;
- recognise operators of systemic DSA payment systems and service providers to those systems, bringing them within the scope of supervision by the Bank of England (BoE);
- extend the financial market infrastructure special administration regime to systemic DSA firms, with appropriate modifications; and
- disapply conflicting regulatory rules for systemic DSA firms in areas relating to financial stability.

The Payment Systems Regulator will also have powers to regulate payment systems using DSAs, including powers to give directions relating to direct and indirect access to such systems.

HMT intends to develop the statutory regime for regulation of DAR issuers and service providers during 2024.[26] In parallel, the UK regulators intend to consult on detailed policy proposals and regulatory rules during 2024, with the regime expected to start to apply during 2025.[27]

24. Section 23 of the 2023 Act.
25. As per HMT's policy paper 'Update on Plans for the Regulation of Fiat-backed Stablecoins' published in October 2023, available at https://www.gov.uk/government/publications/update-on-plans-for-the-regulation-of-fiat-backed-stablecoins.
26. *See* HMT's policy paper 'Update on Plans for the Regulation of Fiat-backed Stablecoins' published in October 2023, available at https://www.gov.uk/government/publications/update-on-plans-for-the-regulation-of-fiat-backed-stablecoins.
27. *See* the Cross-authority roadmap on innovation in payments published in November 2023, available at https://www.bankofengland.co.uk/paper/2023/cross-authority-roadmap-on-innovation-in-payments.

[b] *Regulation of Other Crypto Assets*

Section 69 of the 2023 Act also amended FSMA to clarify that other types of crypto assets could be brought within the scope of the FSMA regulatory framework. Section 417 FSMA defines 'crypto assets' as 'any cryptographically secured digital representation of value or contractual rights that – (a) can be transferred, stored or traded electronically, and (b) uses technology supporting the recording or storage of data (which may include distributed ledger technology)'.[28]

In reliance on these powers and as part of phase 2 of the UK's developing regulatory framework for crypto assets, HMT and the UK regulators intend to introduce a comprehensive regulatory framework for crypto assets, similar in scope to MiCA.

In February 2023, HMT published a consultation[29] outlining its intention to create various new regulated activities relating to crypto assets. This means that firms would need to be authorised (or exempt) under FSMA in order to carry on those activities by way of business in or into the UK. Many of these proposed activities mirror, or closely resemble, regulated activities under the existing FSMA regime, though there are also some novel crypto asset activities proposed, such as 'operating a crypto asset lending platform'.

HMT also indicates it may use the new 'designated activities regime' (DAR) that will be introduced into FSMA under the 2023 Act to regulate certain activities relating to crypto assets where it is not necessarily appropriate to impose licensing requirements. Similar to MiCA, HMT's proposals include a regime for the issuance, offering and admission to trading of in-scope crypto assets and a crypto assets market abuse regime, where certain rules may be introduced using the DAR.

HMT confirmed in October 2023 that it intends to proceed with the approach to regulation of other crypto assets broadly as consulted upon. However, the exact scope of the regime, including whether there will be exclusions for certain types of crypto assets (such as NFTs) or activities (such as intragroup activity), is not yet clear.

[B] Financial Promotions Relating to Crypto Assets

[1] The UK Financial Promotion Regime

Section 21 FSMA prohibits persons from communicating a financial promotion unless:

- an exemption applies (for example, if the financial promotion is directed only to 'investment professionals'); or
- the financial promotion has been made or approved by a firm authorised under FSMA.

28. Section 417 FSMA.
29. The consultation and response published in October 2023 are available at https://www.gov.uk/government/consultations/future-financial-services-regulatory-regime-for-crypto assets.

For this purpose, a financial promotion is any invitation or inducement to engage in an investment activity, where an investment activity is defined as a controlled activity that is performed in respect of a controlled investment. The Financial Services and Markets Act 2000 (Financial Promotion) Order 2005 (FPO) sets out the types of controlled activities and controlled investments falling in the scope of the regime and the applicable exemptions.

[2] Extension of the Regime to Crypto Asset Financial Promotions

Effective from 8 October 2023, the Financial Services and Markets Act 2000 (Financial Promotion) (Amendment) Order 2023 amended the FPO to bring 'qualifying crypto assets' within the scope of the regime.

For this purpose, a 'crypto asset' is defined as 'any cryptographically secured digital representation of value or contractual rights that – (a) can be transferred, stored or traded electronically, and (b) uses technology supporting the recording or storage of data (which may include distributed ledger technology)'. This is the same definition as used in the 2023 Act. A 'qualifying' crypto asset is one that is both fungible and transferable but is not an existing controlled investment (such as a security token), an e-money token or a digitally issued fiat currency (such as central bank digital currency).[30]

The Financial Services and Markets Act 2000 (Financial Promotion) (Amendment) Order 2023 also introduced a new temporary exemption in Article 73ZA FPO for firms that are registered with the FCA as a crypto asset service provider under the Money Laundering, Counter-Terrorist Financing and Transfer of Funds (Information on the Payer) Regulations 2017 (MLRs). This exemption allows these FCA-registered crypto asset firms to communicate their own financial promotions without being authorised under FSMA, on the basis that the UK has not yet developed a comprehensive regulatory regime for crypto asset activities. However, they are not allowed to approve other firms' financial promotions.

[3] FCA Rules and Guidance for Crypto Asset Financial Promotions

The FCA has also published rules and guidance relating to crypto asset financial promotions, which apply to authorised firms and FCA-registered crypto asset firms. These rules are set out in Chapter 4 of the FCA's Conduct of Business Sourcebook of the FCA Handbook, supplemented by Finalised Non-handbook Guidance on Crypto-Asset Financial Promotions[31] published in November 2023.

30. For further discussion of the extension of the UK financial promotions regime to crypto assets and how this compares with the US approach to crypto asset regulation, *see* 'New UK Rules, While Strict, Nonetheless Avoid America's Securitarian Trap', published in The International Journal of Blockchain Law, Volume 7, October 2023, available at https://gbbcouncil.org/wp-content/uploads/2023/10/International-Journal-of-Blockchain-Law-Volume-VII.pdf.
31. FG23/3, available at https://www.fca.org.uk/publication/finalised-guidance/fg23-3.pdf.

Some applicable rules are common to all types of financial promotions, such as a requirement for financial promotions to be clear, fair and not misleading. However, others are specific to crypto asset financial promotions. In particular, the rules set out prescribed risk warnings that must be displayed to customers, and refer-a-friend bonuses and similar inducements are banned.

Additional requirements apply to direct offer crypto asset promotions, which specify how the recipient can respond to the financial promotion. These include client categorisation requirements, appropriateness assessments and the introduction of a 24-hour cooling-off period before new customers of a firm can invest or otherwise act upon the financial promotion.

§6.04 AML REGULATION RELATING TO CRYPTO ASSETS IN THE UK

[A] Registration Regime for Crypto Asset Service Providers

[1] Scope and Definitions

The UK implemented MLD5 via the Money Laundering and Terrorist Financing (Amendment) Regulations 2019 (the '2019 Regulations'), which amended the MLRs with effect from 10 January 2020, shortly before the UK left the EU.

The 2019 Regulations introduced a broad definition of 'crypto asset', defined as 'a cryptographically secured digital representation of value or contractual rights that uses a form of distributed ledger technology and can be transferred, stored or traded electronically'.[32] This is wider than the definition of 'virtual currency' in MLD5 referred to in §6.02[A][1] above.

The 2019 Regulations extended the application of the MLRs to:

(i) 'crypto asset exchange providers', which are firms or sole practitioners who by way of business provide one or more of the following services (including where acting as creator and issuer of crypto assets involved):
   - exchanging, or arranging or making arrangements with a view to the exchange of, crypto assets for money or money for crypto assets;
   - exchanging, or arranging or making arrangements with a view to the exchange of, one crypto asset for another; or
   - operating a machine which utilises automated processes to exchange crypto assets for money or money for crypto assets;[33] and

(ii) 'custodian wallet providers', who are firms or sole practitioners who by way of business provide services to safeguard or to safeguard and administer:
   - Crypto assets on behalf of their customers; or
   - private cryptographic keys on behalf of their customers in order to hold, store and transfer crypto assets.[34]

32. Regulation 14A(3) MLRs.
33. Regulation 14A(1) MLRs.
34. Regulation 14A(2) MLRs.

[2] *Requirements on Crypto Asset Exchange Providers and Custodian Wallet Providers*

Under the MLRs, crypto asset exchange providers and custodian wallet providers which carry on their activities by way of business in the UK are subject to requirements to register with the FCA. This applies even if they are already authorised or registered with the FCA for other purposes (for example, if they are also already authorised under FSMA).

The FCA has set rigorous standards in evaluating applications from crypto asset firms seeking registration under the MLRs and may refuse to register an applicant if the FCA is satisfied that the applicant or any associated individual is not a fit and proper person to carry on that business.

Registered crypto asset firms are required to comply with various requirements of the MLRs, including with respect to customer due diligence, risk assessments, monitoring and reporting of suspicious transactions and record-keeping requirements.

The Joint Money Laundering Steering Group (JMSLG) has provided further guidance on the interpretation and practical application of these requirements in Part II of the JMSLG Guidance.[35]

[B] The UK 'Travel Rule' for Crypto Asset Transfers

The UK has also implemented 'travel rule' for crypto asset transfers set out in FATF Recommendation 16[36] via amendments to the MLRs which took effect on 1 September 2023. The UK travel rule requirements are set out in Part 7A MLRs.

[1] *Scope and Definitions*

The UK travel rule applies to crypto asset exchange providers and custodian wallet providers that are registered with the FCA under the MLRs (referred to in this section as registered crypto asset businesses).

Similar to the scope of the EU travel rule under TRF3, this means that person-to-person transfers that do not involve registered crypto asset businesses are out of scope. In addition, crypto asset transfers where both the originator and beneficiary are registered crypto asset businesses acting on their own behalf are out of scope.[37]

[2] *UK Travel Rule Requirements for Crypto Asset Transfers*

The UK travel rule requires in-scope crypto asset businesses to collect, verify and share information about crypto asset transfers.

35. Available at https://www.jmlsg.org.uk/guidance/current-guidance/.
36. *See* the FATF Recommendations at https://www.fatf-gafi.org/en/.
37. Regulation 64A MLRs.

The information required depends on the value of the crypto asset transfer and whether all crypto asset businesses involved operate within the UK. For crypto asset transfers that take place entirely in the UK or which do not exceed EUR 1,000 in value, only basic information is required, comprising:

- the name of the originator and beneficiary (including the registered or trading name where the originator or beneficiary is a firm); and
- the account number of the originator and beneficiary (or unique transaction identifier if there is no account number).

Additional information is needed where at least one crypto asset business involved in the transaction is outside the UK and the value of the crypto asset transfer exceeds EUR 1,000. This additional information includes customer identification numbers or addresses, depending on whether the originator is a firm or an individual.

The beneficiary's crypto asset business is required to check whether it has received all the information required by regulation 64C MLRs and whether the information on the beneficiary corresponds with the information verified by it as part of its customer due diligence before making the crypto assets available to the beneficiary. If the beneficiary's crypto asset business detects any missing or non-corresponding information, it must:

- request the originator's crypto asset business to provide the missing information,
- consider whether to make enquiries about any discrepancies in the information about the beneficiary, and
- consider whether to delay making the crypto assets available to the beneficiary or, if the information is not received or discrepancy is not resolved within a reasonable time, to return the transfer of crypto assets to the originator's crypto asset business.

When deciding what action to take, the beneficiary's crypto asset business must have regard to the risk assessments it has carried out and take into account various factors in assessing the level of the risk relating to the crypto asset transfer in question.

Intermediary crypto asset businesses are subject to similar requirements with respect to missing information.

The FCA has acknowledged[38] the challenges in practical compliance with the UK travel rule, particularly for cross-border crypto asset transfers with jurisdictions that have not yet implemented the travel rule. In the meantime, the FCA expects firms to take all reasonable steps and exercise all due diligence to comply with the travel rule.

Annex 22-I of Part II JMLSG Guidance[39] also sets out further practical guidance on the implementation of the UK travel rule.

---

38. *See* https://www.fca.org.uk/news/statements/fca-sets-out-expectations-uk-crypto-asset-businesses-complying-travel-rule.
39. Available at https://www.jmlsg.org.uk/guidance/current-guidance/.

CHAPTER 7

Regulation of Crypto Assets in the United States

Kayvan B. Sadeghi

§7.01 INTRODUCTION

The crypto industry faces a complex patchwork of laws and regulations in the United States, overseen by multiple regulatory agencies with overlapping authority at both the federal and state levels. The requirements to comply with these overlapping legal regimes remain unclear and hotly contested among legislators, regulators, and industry participants.

Parsing the regulatory requirements in the United States is particularly difficult because, unlike many other jurisdictions, regulation of financial markets is divided among various federal agencies. At the national level, prominent federal regulatory regimes include securities laws overseen by the U.S. Securities and Exchange Commission (SEC), commodities laws overseen by the Commodities Futures Trading Commission (CFTC), a sanctions regime overseen by the Office of Foreign Assets Control (OFAC), and laws governing money services businesses overseen by the U.S. Treasury's Financial Crimes Enforcement Network (FinCEN). Furthermore, a presidential Executive Order on digital assets issued by the Biden administration called on the Consumer Financial Protection Bureau, the Federal Trade Commission and other agencies to attend inter-agency meetings on digital asset regulatory questions, each of which has its own regulatory ambit that may be implicated by certain digital asset activities.[1] This chapter does not delve into tax law, overseen by the Internal Revenue Service (IRS), though taxes are of course a primary consideration for many activities as

1. "Executive Order on Ensuring Responsible Development of Digital Assets" (Mar. 9, 2022), at https://www.whitehouse.gov/briefing-room/presidential-actions/2022/03/09/executive-order-on-ensuring-responsible-development-of-digital-assets/ (last accessed Jul. 4, 2022).

well. Further complicating the analysis, many states have their own laws governing securities, commodities, and money transmitters, which often overlap imperfectly with each other and with federal law.

In the United States, relatively few laws or regulations have been enacted specifically to address crypto assets, so in most instances, the core questions concern how to fit crypto assets and services into laws and regulations developed for established financial markets. There are notable exceptions, however, including laws specifically tailored to govern the licensing and supervision of crypto asset businesses in New York and California.[2]

Identifying the relevant regulatory regimes begins with the nature of the business or activity. Fundraising is often governed by the securities laws, and this may be true regardless of what type of asset the transaction involves. The regulation of secondary markets may depend on the nature of the asset itself, regardless of whether the initial issuance of that asset implicates securities laws. Payments businesses and custodial services, meanwhile, are likely to implicate banking and money transmission laws. And United States sanctions laws apply regardless of the nature of the asset or activity.

The SEC has been the most active federal regulator in the crypto asset industry. Because its authority is limited to securities, for many years, the crypto industry has grappled with threshold questions of whether and when crypto assets can be classified as securities, or transactions involving those crypto assets can be considered securities transactions.

If tokens are securities, businesses offering services with respect to those tokens must consider potential application of a wide range of securities laws and regulations applicable to securities issuers, exchanges and alternative trading systems (ATS), broker-dealers, and investment advisers, among others. If crypto tokens are not securities, many activities related to the tokens may fall outside the securities laws but within the CFTC's authority over commodities markets. Moreover, even if tokens themselves are not securities, certain transactions involving tokens (including fundraising transactions and others) may be subject to securities registration requirements.

If tokens are not securities, they are presumed to fall within the broad definition of commodities. As a result, some crypto businesses may be subject to oversight by the CFTC, but the CFTC is primarily concerned with regulating margin, leverage, and derivative products. As a general matter, the CFTC does not directly regulate "spot" commodity markets (i.e., transactions in the commodities themselves) nor require registration of spot market participants. Thus, businesses that deal with crypto assets themselves, but not futures or derivatives of those assets, may not be required to register with the SEC or CFTC if the assets are classified as commodities. Legislative proposals in the United States have proposed multiple different ways to either bring crypto assets within the definition of securities in order to subject them to oversight by the SEC or to expand the CFTC's authority over spot markets in order to bring them within regulation of the CFTC.[3]

---

2. *See* 23 NYCRR § 200 (New York); Digital Financial Assets Law, A.B. 39 (California).
3. *See, e.g.*, Responsible Financial Innovation Act, S. 2281, 118th Cong. (2023); Clarity for the Payment Stablecoins Act of 2023, H.R. 4766, 118th Cong. (2023); The Financial Innovation and

Regardless of whether tokens are securities or commodities, FinCEN has taken the position that many crypto asset businesses are money services businesses, subject to federal registration and a host of state regulatory requirements as money transmitters, including anti-money laundering (AML) requirements, among others. As a result, many large crypto asset trading platforms and service providers in the United States are registered as money services businesses and money transmitters in many or most states.[4] In addition, all U.S. persons, individuals and businesses must comply with United States sanctions laws, regardless of whether they fall into one or more of the above regulatory regimes.

Because many crypto asset businesses and activities intersect with overlapping regulatory requirements, the multiple enforcement agencies often work together in joint investigations and enforcement actions. A noteworthy recent example of sanctions enforcement is the widely publicized settlement and plea agreement entered into by Binance Holdings Limited (Binance) and its former Chief Executive Officer Changpeng Zhao. As described by the U.S. Department of Justice, Binance admitted "it engaged in anti-money laundering, unlicensed money transmitting, and sanctions violations in [the] largest corporate resolution to include criminal charges for an executive."[5] The plea was part of "coordinated resolutions with the Department of the Treasury's Financial Crimes Enforcement Network (FinCEN) and Office of Foreign Assets Control (OFAC) and the U.S. Commodity Futures Trading Commission (CFTC)."[6]

While this chapter covers many of the most prominent topics concerning regulation of blockchain and crypto assets in the United States, there are many other laws and regulations that must be considered, depending on the nature of the business or activity. Relevant legal regimes that fall outside the scope of this chapter include federal and state tax laws, banking laws, the Uniform Commercial Code and equivalent state laws, and a variety of consumer protection laws at the federal and state levels, among others.

§7.02 FEDERAL SECURITIES LAWS

Federal securities laws trace back to the Great Depression, with the introduction of the Securities Act of 1933 ("Securities Act"), and the Securities Exchange Act of 1934 ("Exchange Act"). Generally speaking, the Securities Act governs issuers and other participants in new securities issuances, while the Exchange Act is directed primarily

Technology for the 21st Century Act, H.R. 4763, 118th Cong. (2023); Securities Clarity Act, H.R. 3572, 118th Cong. (2023); Blockchain Regulatory Certainty Act, H.R.1747, 118th Cong. (2023).

4. *See, e.g.,* https://www.coinbase.com/legal/licenses; https://www.gemini.com/trust-center; https://support.kraken.com/hc/en-us/articles/360031282351-Is-Kraken-licensed-or-regulated-.
5. Press Release, Binance and CEO Plead Guilty to Federal Charges in $4B Resolution, Nov. 21, 2023, https://www.justice.gov/opa/pr/binance-and-ceo-plead-guilty-federal-charges-4b-resolution; *see also* https://www.justice.gov/criminal/case/united-states-v-binance-holdings-limited-dba-binancecom (providing links to the underlying plea agreement and Information statement).
6. Press Release, Binance and CEO Plead Guilty to Federal Charges in $4B Resolution, Nov. 21, 2023, https://www.justice.gov/opa/pr/binance-and-ceo-plead-guilty-federal-charges-4b-resolution.

to the regulation of secondary markets, including intermediaries as well as the issuers' conduct after issuance. In addition, classifying crypto assets as securities implicates a host of additional securities laws overseen by the SEC, including the Investment Company Act, the Investment Advisers Act, and others.

[A] Defining "Securities"

The term "security" is defined in section 2(a)(l) of the Securities Act and section 3(a)(10) of the Exchange Act, and courts have held that the term has "essentially identical in meaning" in both statutes.[7] Per section 2(a)(1) of the Securities Act, a security is:

> [A]ny ***note***, stock, treasury stock, security future, security-based swap, bond, debenture, evidence of indebtedness, certificate of interest or participation in any profit-sharing agreement, collateral-trust certificate, preorganization certificate or subscription, transferable share, ***investment contract***, voting-trust certificate, certificate of deposit for a security, fractional undivided interest in oil, gas, or other mineral rights, any put, call, straddle, option, or privilege on any security, certificate of deposit, or group or index of securities (including any interest therein or based on the value thereof), or any put, call, straddle, option, or privilege entered into on a national securities exchange relating to foreign currency, or, in general, any interest or instrument commonly known as a "security," or any certificate of interest or participation in, temporary or interim certificate for, receipt for, guarantee of, or warrant or right to subscribe to or purchase, any of the foregoing. [8]

The enumerated items in the list of assets that qualify as securities include many items that one might typically consider a security, including stock, bonds, and the like. In addition, the definition includes the term "investment contract," which applies to a wide variety of investment transactions or schemes not otherwise captured in the statutory definition. It is this "investment contract" category into which the SEC places many crypto asset transactions.

The test for what constitutes an "investment contract" was set forth in the Supreme Court case SEC v. Howey. As the court stated and the SEC maintains today, the term "investment contract," as used to define a security, "embodies a flexible rather than static principle, ... capable of adaptation to ... countless and variable schemes."[9] Howey creates a four-part test that the SEC has used to determine whether a digital asset offering is a securities offering. Although there are slightly different articulations of the test, for a transaction or scheme to constitute a securities offering, it must generally involve (1) an investment of money, (2) in a common enterprise, (3) with a reasonable expectation of profits, (4) derived from the effort of others. The Howey test

---

7. *S.E.C. v. Edwards*, 540 U.S. 389, 393 (2004). The SEC has taken the position that the definition of "security" is somewhat broader under the Investment Company Act. *See, e.g.*, Expanding the Investment Company Act: The SEC's Manipulation of the Definition of Security (1999), College of Law, Faculty Publications 92; https://digitalcommons.unl.edu/lawfacpub/92.
8. 15 U.S.C. § 77b(a)(1) (emphasis added).
9. SEC v. Howey, 328 U.S. 293, 299 (1946).

has guided the SEC's position on digital assets as that position has evolved across a series of reports, enforcement actions, and public speeches.[10]

Separately, the SEC and others have argued that certain crypto asset products and services may fall within the definition of securities as a "note," under the test set forth by the Supreme Court in *Reves v. Ernst & Young*, 494 U.S. 56 (1990).

[1] "Investment Contracts" and the **Howey** *Test*

The Supreme Court of the United States set forth the test for determining what constitutes an "investment contract" in the seminal case *S.E.C. v. Howey*, 328 U.S. 293 (1946) (the "*Howey* test"), noting that the term "embodies a flexible rather than a static principle, one that is capable of adaptation to meet the countless and variable schemes devised by those who seek the use of money of others on the promise of profits." The *Howey* test holds that an investment contract is "a contract, transaction, or scheme" that involves an investment of money in a common enterprise with an expectation of profits based on the essential managerial efforts of others.[11]

Nearly 30 years later, in *United Housing Foundation, Inc. v. Forman*, the Supreme Court emphasized that the "touchstone" of an investment contract is "the presence of an investment in a common venture premised on a reasonable expectation of profits to be derived from the entrepreneurial or managerial efforts of others."[12] In contrast, "when a purchaser is motivated by a desire to use or consume the item purchased" rather than "the prospects of a return on [the] investment . . . the securities laws do not apply."[13]

The *Howey* test is often analyzed as consisting of four elements: (1) an investment of money; (2) in a common enterprise; (3) with a reasonable expectation of profits; (4) derived from the efforts of others.

[a] "Investment of Money"

This prong is interpreted broadly to capture investors who have undertaken some degree of economic risk.[14] It focuses on whether investors "chose to give up a specific

10. The SEC's first substantial action relating to cryptocurrencies was its July 2017 "Report of Investigation Pursuant to Section 21(a) of the Securities Exchange Act of 1934: The DAO" (*see* https://www.sec.gov/litigation/investreport/34-81207.pdf (last accessed Jul. 11, 2022)), in which the SEC staff made clear that they viewed the sale of DAO tokens as a securities offering. In June 2018, the director of the SEC's Division of Corporations gave prepared remarks at a cryptocurrency summit, in a speech titled "Digital Asset Transactions: When Howey Met Gary (Plastic)," which was interpreted as conveying the SEC's staff's position at the time—*see* https://www.sec.gov/news/speech/speech-hinman-061418 (last accessed Jul. 11, 2022). The SEC also has brought dozens of enforcement actions, a list of which is maintained at https://www.sec.gov/spotlight/cybersecurity-enforcement-actions (last accessed Jul. 11, 2022).
11. *See Howey*, 328 U.S. at 298-299; *Revak v. SEC Realty Corp.*, 18 F.3d 81, 87 (2d Cir. 1994) (applying the *Howey* test).
12. 421 U.S. at 852.
13. *Id.*, at 853-54 (citing to *Howey*, 328 U.S. at 300).
14. *See Reves v. Ernst & Young*, 494 U.S. 56, 67 (1990) (discussing the relationship between risk and the necessity of application of the Securities Acts).

consideration in return for a separable financial interest with the characteristics of a security."[15] It does not matter whether the consideration provided by the investor is conventionally characterized as "money," and in the blockchain context, courts have consistently held that exchanging a token for another token satisfies this prong of the *Howey* test.[16]

[b] "Common Enterprise"

Courts disagree on the precise contours of the "common enterprise" element of the *Howey* test. Broadly speaking, it considers the extent to which there is "some ongoing relationship or nexus among individuals with respect to a transaction."[17] Courts have adopted several tests to assess the nature and degree of commonality that an investment must exhibit, including: (a) a continuing contractual obligation; (b) horizontal commonality; and (c) vertical commonality.

[i] Continuing Contractual Obligation

Several federal courts have suggested that a "common enterprise" cannot exist between purchaser and seller without some continuing contractual obligation between the parties.[18] Applying this approach, courts have held that even where a seller made promises or had ongoing obligations outside a contract, the purchaser failed to

15. *S.E.C. v. SG Ltd.*, 265 F.3d 42, 48 (1st Cir. 2001) ("The determining factor [for the first *Howey* prong] is whether an investor 'chose to give up specific consideration in return for a separable financial interest with the characteristics of a security'") (*quoting Daniel*, 439 U.S. at 559).
16. *See Balestra v. ATBCOINS LLC*, 380 F. Supp. 3d 340, 353 (S.D.N.Y. 2019) (noting there was no dispute that the first prong of *Howey* was satisfied because exchange of ETH for ATB Coins was an "investment of money"); *United States v. Zaslavskiy*, 2018 WL 4346339, at *5 (E.D.N.Y. Sep. 11, 2018) (emphasizing that even where purchasers exchanged other virtual currencies for RECoin or Diamond, these transfers constituted "investments of money").
17. Maura K. Monaghan, *An Uncommon State of Confusion: The Common Enterprise Element of Investment Contract Analysis*, 63 Fordham L. Rev. 2135 (1995), *available at* https://ir.lawnet.fordham.edu/cgi/viewcontent.cgi?article=3173&context=flr.
18. *See Hart v. Pulte Homes of Michigan Corp.*, 735 F.2d 1001, 1003 (6th Cir. 1984) (*Howey* test not met where "defendants were under no contractual duty to develop the subdivisions" and "plaintiffs had no right to share in the profits of successful development"); *Woodward v. Terracor*, 574 F.2d 1023, 1025 (10th Cir. 1978) (contract for real property was not an "investment contract" because "the mere fact that the plaintiffs bought lots from [the seller] does not mean that by such acquisition they were thereafter engaged in a common venture or enterprise"); *S&S NY Holdings, Inc. v. Able Energy, Inc.*, 2012 WL 3084112, at *5 (S.D.N.Y. Jul. 27, 2012) (finding no investment contract where the governing agreement was no longer valid); *Davis v. Rio Rancho Estates, Inc.*, 401 F. Supp. 1045, 1050 (S.D.N.Y. 1975) (finding no investment contract where promoter was not contractually obligated to manage or "run the development and distribute profits to the plaintiff, as did the operators of the orange groves in *Howey*"); *De Luz Ranchos Inv., Ltd. v. Coldwell Banker & Co.*, 608 F.2d 1297, 1300-1301 (9th Cir. 1979) (finding no investment contract despite marketing materials emphasizing promoter's efforts to develop surrounding land).

establish a common enterprise that satisfied *Howey* absent a contractual obligation from the seller to purchasers.[19]

[ii] Horizontal Commonality

To determine whether a common enterprise exists, the United States Court of Appeals for the Second Circuit ("Second Circuit") and many other federal courts apply the "horizontal commonality" test, which requires "the tying of each individual investor's fortunes to the fortunes of the other investors by a pooling of assets, usually combined with the pro-rata distribution of profits."[20] In an enterprise marked by horizontal commonality, "the fortunes of each investor in a pool of investors" are tied to one another and to the "success of the overall enterprise."[21]

[iii] Vertical Commonality

Many courts also find that a common enterprise may be established through "strict vertical commonality," which requires that "the fortunes of investors be tied to the fortunes of the promoter."[22] The Second Circuit expressly rejected the "broad vertical commonality" test, which is met when "the fortunes of the investors [are] linked only to the efforts of the promoter," and other courts consistently criticized this test as inconsistent with *Howey* because it essentially eliminates the common enterprise requirement.[23]

---

19. *See Alunni v. Dev. Res. Grp., LLC,* 445 F. App'x 288, 292-293, 298 (11th Cir. 2011) (oral promises made during promotional efforts were insufficient to create investment contract where written contract was entire agreement between the parties); *Rodriguez v. Banco Cent. Corp.*, 990 F.2d 7, 10 (1st Cir. 1993) (seller's "strong and repeated suggestions" that surrounding land would develop did not create investment contract as there was no contractual obligation to develop the land); *Happy Inv. Grp. v. Lakeworld Props., Inc.*, 396 F. Supp. 175, 181 (N.D. Cal. 1975) (finding no investment contract "when there are promises of the general nature made by defendants in their literature and handouts, but no actual commitments to perform specific services").
20. *Revak v. SEC Realty Corp.*, 18 F.3d. 81, 87-88 (2d Cir. 1994) (adopting horizontal commonality and citing approvingly to cases from several other circuits holding to like effect); *see also S.E.C. v. SG Ltd.*, 265 F.3d 42, 49 (1st Cir. 2001) (describing "horizontal commonality" as "a type of commonality that involves the pooling of assets from multiple investors so that all share in the profits and risks of the enterprise").
21. *S.E.C. v. Telegram Grp.*, 2020 WL 1430035, at *10 (S.D.N.Y. Mar. 24, 2020); *Balestra*, 380 F. Supp. 3d at 354; *Hart*, 735 F.2d at 1004 ("In fact, a finding of horizontal commonality requires a sharing or pooling of funds") (internal quotation omitted); *In re J.P. Jeanneret Assocs., Inc.*, 769 F. Supp. 2d 340, 359 (S.D.N.Y. 2011) (*quoting Revak*, 18 F.3d at 87); *see also Kaplan v. Shapiro*, 655 F. Supp. 336, 339-340 (S.D.N.Y. 1987) ("Courts espousing a theory of horizontal commonality require plaintiff[s] to show a pooling of the investors' interests in order to establish a common enterprise").
22. *Revak*, 18 F.3d at 87-88 (citation omitted); *see also In re J.P. Jeanneret Assocs., Inc.*, 769 F. Supp. 2d at 360 (stating "that strict vertical commonality (like horizontal commonality) is sufficient to establish a common enterprise under *Howey*").
23. *Revak*, 18 F.3d at 87-88 (collecting cases); *see e.g., S.E.C. v. Continental Commodities Corp.*, 497 F.2d 516, 522 (5th Cir. 1974); *Savino v. E.F. Hutton & Co.*, Inc., 507 F. Supp. 1225, 1237-1238 n. 11 (S.D.N.Y.1981) (noting broad vertical commonality is inconsistent with *Howey*); *Berman v. Bache, Halsey, Stuart, Shields, Inc.*, 467 F. Supp. 311, 319 (S.D. Ohio 1979) ("[A] finding of a

[c] "Reasonable Expectation of Profit"

Purchasers possess a "reasonable expectation of profit" when their motivation to partake in a transaction or scheme is the "prospect of a return on their investment."[24] This element does not require that the investment provide any distributions or dividends and can be satisfied by an expectation of "capital appreciation resulting from the development of the initial investment."[25]

The expectation of profits need not be the only motive of purchasers,[26] but a transaction will generally fail to satisfy this element where a purchase is made with "a desire to use or consume the item purchased" (i.e., motivated by consumptive intent).[27]

Courts conduct an objective inquiry focused on the promises and offers made to investors rather than a search for the precise motivation of individual participants.[28] Courts examine the "terms of the offer, the plan of distribution, and the economic inducements held out to the prospect."[29] They often also look to the promotional and marketing materials used by a seller leading up to a sale and whether those materials emphasized opportunities to profit.[30] Evidence of actual purchasers' intent is also relevant to courts' evaluation of the hypothetical reasonable purchaser,[31] but "[t]he mere presence of a speculative motive on the part of the purchaser or seller does not evidence the existence of an 'investment contract' within the meaning of the securities acts."[32]

[d] "Efforts of Others"

The final factor of *Howey* is whether the expectation of profits would be derived from the efforts of others. *Howey* suggests that the investor must expect profits derived

common enterprise based solely upon the fact of entrustment by a single principal of money to an agent effectively excises the common enterprise requirement of *Howey*") (internal citations omitted).

24. *S.E.C. v. Howey*, 328 U.S. 293, 301 (1946).
25. *S.E.C. v. Edwards*, 540 U.S. 389, 395 (2004); *see also Aldrich v. McCulloch Properties, Inc.*, 627 F.2d 1036, 1039 (10th Cir. 1980) ("That the plaintiffs did not expect to realize any tangible gain until they sold their property does not preclude investment intent").
26. *S.E.C. v. Aqua-Sonic Products Corp.*, 687 F.2d 577, 582 (2d Cir. 1982); *see S.E.C. v. Hui Feng*, 935 F.3d 721, 730-731 (9th Cir. 2019) (finding the requisite expectation of profit even when this investment intent was secondary to a motive unrelated to profit).
27. *United Hous. Found. v. Forman*, 421 U.S. 837, 852-53 (1975).
28. *Warfield v. Alaniz*, 569 F.3d 1015, 1021 (9th Cir. 2009) ("Under Howey, courts conduct an objective inquiry into the character of the instrument or transaction offered based on what the purchasers were 'led to expect'") (internal citation omitted).
29. *S.E.C. v. C.M. Joiner Leasing Corp.*, 320 U.S. 344, 352-353, 355 (1943).
30. *See, e.g., Forman*, 421 U.S. at 853-854; *Edwards*, 540 U.S. at 392.
31. *S.E.C. v. Texas Gulf Sulphur Co.*, 446 F.2d 1301, 1305 (2d Cir. 1971) (finding that the testimony of individual investors "was relevant to whether [a document] was misleading to the 'reasonable investor'"); *Slevin v. Pedersen Assocs., Inc.*, 540 F. Supp. 437, 441 ("The original intention of the parties is crucial to the classification of their contract") (S.D.N.Y. 1982).
32. *See Sinva, Inc. v. Merrill, Lynch, Pierce, Fenner & Smith, Inc.*, 253 F. Supp. 359, 367 (S.D.N.Y. 1966) (*citing Joiner*, 320 U.S. at 348).

"solely from the efforts of the promoter or a third party,"[33] but later decisions have clarified that "the word 'solely' should not be construed as a literal limitation; rather, we 'consider whether, under all the circumstances, the scheme was being promoted primarily as an investment or as a means whereby participants could pool their own activities, their money and the promoter's contribution in a meaningful way.'"[34]

On the other hand, there is no investment contract if a buyer's expectation of profit turns on his or her "own decision and on market forces."[35] This is because "[a]n investor who has the ability to control the profitability of his investment, either by his own efforts or by majority vote in a group venture, is not dependent upon the managerial skill of others."[36] Conversely, where the seller maintains complete control over the scheme from which the purchaser is expecting to profit, the scheme is likely an investment contract.[37]

Sellers' and promoters' efforts both before and after receiving funds from purchasers are relevant to the analysis, and courts recognize that "investment schemes may often involve a combination of both pre- and post-purchase managerial activities."[38] Courts also look to marketing materials in this factor and investigate whether these materials advertised sellers' professional and managerial expertise to facilitate development of the digital asset or associated platform for consumption.[39]

[2] "Notes" and the **Reves** *Test*

Separate from the "investment contract" analysis under *Howey*, certain crypto asset products and services may fall within the definition of securities as a "note" under the test set forth in *Reves v. Ernst & Young*.[40] Official guidance applying *Reves* in the crypto

33. *S.E.C. v. Howey*, 328 U.S. 293, 299 (1946).
34. *United States v. Leonard*, 529 F.3d 83, 88 (2d Cir. 2005) (*quoting S.E.C. v. Aqua-Sonic Prods. Corp.*, 687 F.2d 577, 582 (2d Cir. 1982)).
35. *Long v. Shultz Cattle Co.*, 881 F.2d 129, 137 n. 8 (5th Cir. 1989).
36. *Gordon v. Terry*, 684 F.2d 736, 741 (11th Cir. 1982).
37. *See Balestra v. ATBCOINS LLC*, 380 F. Supp. 3d 340, 355 n. 14 (S.D.N.Y. 2019) (finding purchasers relied on the efforts of the seller because "potential profits stemming from the future valuation of the ATB Coins were entirely reliant on the success of Defendants' new blockchain"); *United States v. Zaslavskiy*, 2018 WL 4346339, at *7 (E.D.N.Y. Sep. 11, 2018) ("Though [defendant] suggested that [ ] investors could trade [digital] coins on an external exchange and make more profit, there is no indication that investors were to have any control over the management of [defendant's business]").
38. *S.E.C. v. Mut. Benefits Corp.*, 408 F.3d 737, 743-744 (11th Cir. 2005) ("[N]either *Howey* [n]or *Edwards* require such a clean distinction between a promoter's activities prior to his having use of an investor's money and his activities thereafter") (internal citations omitted).
39. *See Zaslavskiy*, 2018 WL 4346339, at *7 (*citing Glen-Arden Commodities, Inc. v. Costantino*, 493 F.2d 1027, 1035 (2d Cir. 1974) (noting that investors depended on promoters' "expertise in selecting the type of [product] to be purchased . . . to make the tangible investment pay off")); *Balestra*, 380 F. Supp. 3d at 355 (finding an investment contract where "[d]efendants conveyed to purchasers of ATB Coins that the anticipated return on their investment would be the result of Defendants' efforts to commercialize the ATB Blockchain and ATB Coins").
40. 494 U.S. 56 (1990).

context is lacking, but SEC staff have increasingly invoked *Reves* in public remarks[41] and in enforcement actions such as the settled action against BlockFi.[42]

"Notes," like "investment contracts," are a specific category of asset explicitly enumerated as part of the definition of securities. Courts have recognized that "notes" is a broad term, and not all notes should be construed as securities. Accordingly, the *Reves* test is designed to distinguish notes that are securities from notes that are not.

In *Reves*, the Supreme Court addressed promissory notes payable on demand, with variable interest adjusted monthly. The notes were marketed as an investment, and purchasers lost money when the issuer filed for bankruptcy. The court noted that securities laws are intended to regulate investments and distinguished "notes issued in an investment context (which are 'securities') from notes issued in a commercial or consumer context (which are not)."[43]

The *Reves* test, referred to as the "family resemblance test," begins with the rebuttable presumption that every note is a security but recognizes that some notes should not be construed as securities.[44] To determine whether a "note" constitutes a "security," a court will analyze the following four factors: (a) motivation of the buyer and seller; (b) plan of distribution with respect to the instrument or transaction at issue; (c) reasonable expectations of the investing public as to whether an instrument or transaction is a security; and (d) the existence of factors, such as a regulatory scheme, which would reduce the risk of the instrument or transaction.

In *Reves,* the court found the motivation of the parties supported "security" status because the issuer "sold the notes in an effort to raise capital for its general business operations, and purchasers bought them in order to earn a profit,"[45] and thus "the transaction is most naturally conceived as an investment in a business enterprise rather than as a purely commercial or consumer transaction."[46]

With respect to the plan of distribution, *Reves* held that no secondary-market trading was required; it was sufficient that the notes were offered and sold broadly to unsophisticated members of the public. *Reves* also rejected the argument that notes payable on demand were inconsistent with the risk ordinarily associated with securities.

With respect to investor expectations, *Reves* focused on advertisements marketing the notes as investments and the absence of countervailing factors.

With respect to risk-reducing factors, the court rather focused on the facts that the notes were "uncollateralized and uninsured" and "would escape federal regulation entirely if the [Securities] Acts were held not to apply." *Id.*, at 69. The court also rejected the argument that the liquidity offered by a demand note sufficiently reduced risk. *Id.*

41. *See, e.g.*, https://www.sec.gov/news/speech/crenshaw-sec-speaks-20211012#_ftnref12.
42. *See* https://www.sec.gov/files/litigation/admin/2022/33-11029.pdf.
43. 494 U.S. at 63.
44. 494 U.S. at 65.
45. 494 U.S. at 77.
46. 494 U.S. at 68.

[B] The SEC's Approach to Digital Assets

The SEC has not issued any rulemaking or other definitive guidance concerning its approach to crypto assets. Instead, the SEC has revealed an evolving position through a combination of investigation reports, settled enforcement actions, public speeches, guidance documents, [47] and positions taken in contested litigation.[48]

The SEC's first major action on blockchain tokens was its Section 21(a) Report of Investigation concerning the DAO (the "DAO Report"), released in July 2017.[49] The DAO functioned as an investment club or decentralized venture capital fund. By purchasing DAO tokens, purchasers pooled their funds and gained the right to vote on whether or not to spend the pooled funds on investment proposals presented by third-party "contractors." Any profits from the investments would then either be distributed to DAO holders in proportion to the amount of tokens they held or be reinvested, again conditioned on a DAO vote.[50]

The SEC's DAO Report walks through the SEC's application of the *Howey* test to conclude that the initial offering of the DAO token was an unregistered securities offering. The DAO Report was followed by a string of SEC enforcement actions, primarily concluding that various initial coin offerings were unregistered securities offerings.[51]

Approximately one year later, in June 2018, the Director of the Division of Corporation Finance, William Hinman, made a landmark speech discussing the SEC's approach to digital assets and the possibility that a digital asset determined to be a security in one context might no longer be deemed to be a security in a subsequent analysis.[52]

The following year, in April 2019, the SEC released a *Framework for "Investment Contract" Analysis of Digital Assets* ("SEC Framework").[53] The SEC Framework provides a more comprehensive statement of factors that the SEC may take into account in applying the *Howey* test to digital assets. The SEC Framework is caveated as representing "staff views" rather than a binding standard.[54] It not only offers factors to

---

47. The SEC is an independent agency of the United States government created by Congress following the stock market crash of 1929. It holds primary responsibility for enforcing the federal securities laws, proposing securities rules, and regulating the securities industry. As a result, the SEC staff's interpretations of the securities laws may be persuasive, but those interpretations are not binding on the courts, and courts do not always agree with the SEC, as discussed herein.
48. The SEC maintains a running list of its enforcement actions in the crypto space at: https://www.sec.gov/spotlight/cybersecurity-enforcement-actions.
49. U.S. Securities and Exchange Commission, *Report of Investigation Pursuant to Section 21(a) of the Securities Exchange Act of 1934: The DAO* (Jul. 25, 2017) (the "*DAO Report*"), *available at* https://www.sec.gov/litigation/investreport/34-81207.pdf.
50. *Id.*, at 6.
51. *See S.E.C. Cyber Enforcement Actions, supra* n. 17 (collecting SEC enforcement actions).
52. William Hinman, *Digital Asset Transactions: When Howey Met Gary (Plastic)* (Jun. 14, 2018), *available at* https://www.sec.gov/news/speech/speech-hinman-061418.
53. U.S. Securities and Exchange Commission, *Framework for "Investment Contract" Analysis of Digital Assets* (Apr. 3, 2019), *available at* https://www.sec.gov/corpfin/framework-investment-contract-analysis-digital-assets.
54. William Hinman, Director of Division of Corporation Finance, Valerie Szczepanik, Senior Advisor for Digital Assets and Innovation, *Statement on "Framework for 'Investment Contract'*

consider in analyzing whether a digital asset has the characteristics of an investment contract but also recognizes that the *Howey* test focuses on the circumstances surrounding the digital asset and, therefore, "issuers and other persons and entities engaged in the marketing, offer, sale, resale, or distribution of any digital asset will need to analyze the relevant transactions to determine if the federal securities laws apply."[55] The SEC Framework then purports to analyze both "whether a digital asset is an investment contract *and* whether offers and sales of a digital asset are securities transactions."[56] The SEC Framework also identifies "some of the factors to be considered in determining whether and when a digital asset may no longer be a security."[57]

The SEC Framework does not provide guidance on how to weigh the many identified factors. It was subject to public criticism from SEC Commissioner Hester Pierce, who noted that the SEC Framework's "Jackson Pollock approach to splashing lots of factors on the canvas without any clear message leaves something to be desired, so we still have work to do in clarifying what factors are the most important in making that determination [of how to apply *Howey* to digital assets]."[58] Nevertheless, the SEC Framework is informative as to how the SEC views the *Howey* analysis and particular factors that the SEC will consider.

The SEC's positions in contested litigation have revealed an evolving position as to when tokens themselves may be considered securities and when transactions involving tokens may be securities transactions. In earlier enforcement actions, the SEC took the position that if a token offering satisfies the *Howey* test, the token itself should be considered a security. For example, on September 30, 2019, the SEC announced a settled enforcement action against Block.one, concluding that its "ERC-20 Tokens were securities under the federal securities laws" based on the circumstances of the initial coin offering (ICO).[59] In 2021, current SEC Chairman Gary Gensler has made clear that he views many if not most tokens themselves as securities. As he said in August 2021, "I believe we have a crypto market now where many tokens may be unregistered securities" and "[w]hile each token's legal status depends on its own facts and circumstances, the probability is quite remote that, with 50 or 100 tokens, any given platform has zero securities."[60]

Analysis of Digital Assets" (Apr. 3, 2019), *available at* https://www.sec.gov/news/public-statement/statement-framework-investment-contract-analysis-digital-assets. The SEC has repeatedly made clear that it views staff statements as non-binding. *See, e.g.*, Jay Clayton, Chairman of SEC, *Statement regarding SEC Staff Views* (Sep. 13, 2018), *available at* https://www.sec.gov/news/public-statement/statement-clayton-091318 ("The Commission's long-standing position is that all staff statements are nonbinding and create no enforceable legal rights or obligations of the Commission or other parties").

55. *Framework for "Investment Contract" Analysis of Digital Assets*, *supra* n. 54, at 1.
56. *Id.*, at 2 (emphasis added).
57. *Id.*
58. Hester M. Pierce, Commissioner of S.E.C., *How We Howey* (May 19, 2019), *available at* https://www.sec.gov/news/speech/peirce-how-we-howey-050919.
59. *Block.one*, Order Instituting Cease-and-Desist Proceedings Pursuant to Section 8a of the Securities Act of 1933, Making Findings, and Imposing a Cease-and-Desist Order, Release No. 10714, at 2 (Sep. 30, 2019), *available at* https://www.sec.gov/litigation/admin/2019/33-10714.pdf.
60. SEC Chairman Gary Gensler's prepared Remarks Before the Aspen Security Forum (Aug. 3. 2021), *available at*: https://www.sec.gov/news/public-statement/gensler-aspen-security-forum-2021-08-03.

More recently, the SEC has taken the position that secondary market transactions in many crypto assets are securities transactions, even if the token itself is not necessarily a security. On that basis, the SEC has alleged that trading platforms operate as unregistered securities exchanges, clearing agents, and brokers (each of which is addressed below).[61]

For example, in 2023, the SEC filed suit against Coinbase, alleging that it operated as an unregistered securities exchange, clearing agent, and broker.[62] On March 27, 2024, Judge Katherine Polk Failla of the S.D.N.Y. denied in part and granted in part Coinbase's motion for judgment on the pleadings, which sought dismissal of the SEC's case. In doing so, the court recognized that "the SEC does not appear to contest that tokens, in and of themselves, are not securities."[63] The court held, however, that the SEC's complaint sufficiently alleged that secondary market purchases of tokens on the Coinbase platform were investment contracts under *Howey* and thus that Coinbase was subject to SEC registration requirements as an exchange, broker, and clearing agent.[64]

The SEC also alleged that Coinbase Wallet products operated as an unregistered exchange, broker, and clearing agency.[65] Notably, the court dismissed those allegations concerning the Wallet service.[66] Among other things, the court noted that the Wallet service was non-custodial in that Coinbase could not effect transactions on a user's behalf and that the Wallet did not perform the sort of discretionary tasks typically associated with a broker.[67] The allegation that the Wallet played a part in the transaction and charged a fee measured as a percentage of the transaction was insufficient to allege that it acted as a broker.[68]

Meanwhile, there remains limited federal court precedent conducting the *Howey* analysis in the context of digital assets or digital asset offerings past the pleading stage, and no binding precedent from any federal appellate court.

[1] Issuers and Token Offerings

The trial courts that have considered the issues have generally faced challenges to unregistered token offerings and concluded that the offering was a securities offering in violation of section 5 of the Securities Act but have not clearly adopted (and have arguably rejected) key aspects of the SEC's analytical approach.

[a] Telegram and Kik

In 2020, the SEC's approach to digital assets was articulated most clearly in two contested enforcement actions against *Telegram* and *Kik*, both in the United States

61. *See* Order, *SEC v. Coinbase, Inc.*, No. 23-CV-4738 at 46 (S.D.N.Y. Mar. 27, 2024), ECF No. 105 ("Coinbase Order").
62. *Id.*, at 29.
63. *Id.*
64. *See id.*, at 84.
65. *See id.*, at 12-13.
66. *Id.*, at 81-84.
67. *See id.*
68. *See id.*

District Court for the Southern District of New York (S.D.N.Y.). Both cases involve coin offerings conducted through a simple agreement for future tokens (SAFT) with accredited investors, followed by a planned distribution of those tokens after which the tokens would be available to the general public. As discussed below, the courts adopted some, but not all, of the SEC's reasoning with respect to application of the *Howey* test, leaving open the possibility that tokens may not be securities even if the circumstances in which they were offered constituted a securities offering.

In the *Telegram* case, the SEC sought and obtained a preliminary injunction to prevent Telegram from distributing Gram tokens. The Gram token was previously the subject of a SAFT, through which accredited investors purchased the tokens in advance of distribution. The SEC took the position that the initial SAFT sales and the subsequent token distributions were part of a single unregistered securities offering and distribution of the tokens to the public, or in the alternative that the two transactions should be considered an integrated offering subject to registration requirements. Telegram took the position that the initial SAFT sales were a securities offering exempt from registration because those sales were limited to accredited investors and that the subsequent distribution of tokens was a separate transaction and not a securities offering.

Judge Castel ruled in favor of the SEC, but his approach to the *Howey* analysis made clear that while the SEC had established a likelihood of proving that Telegram conducted an unregistered securities offering, the token itself was not the security:

> While helpful as a shorthand reference, *the security in this case is not simply the Gram*, which is little more than alphanumeric cryptographic sequence. *Howey* refers to an investment contract, i.e. a security, as "a contract, transaction or scheme," using the term "scheme" in a descriptive, not pejorative, sense. This case presents a "scheme" to be evaluated under *Howey* that consists of the full set of contracts, expectations, and understandings centered on the sales and distribution of the Gram.[69]

The proper question was whether "the scheme, viewed as a whole, amounts to a security."[70] Castel granted the preliminary injunction because he was satisfied that the SEC had established a likelihood of proving that "the series of understandings, transactions, and undertakings between Telegram and the Initial Purchasers were investment contracts satisfying the *Howey* test and, therefore, are securities."[71]

In a subsequent decision denying a motion for clarification, Judge Castel made even more explicit that the security at issue was "neither the Gram Purchase Agreement nor the Gram but the entire scheme . . . including the expectation and intention that the Initial Purchasers would distribute the Grams into a secondary public market."[72]

69. *See S.E.C. v. Telegram Grp.*, 2020 WL 1430035, at *18 (S.D.N.Y. Mar. 24, 2020) (emphasis added).
70. *Id.*, at 9.
71. *Id.*
72. *See S.E.C. v. Telegram Grp.*, 19-cv-09439-PKC, at *2 (S.D.N.Y. Apr. 1, 2020).

Subsequently, in deciding the SEC's case against Kik Interactive, the Southern District again applied the *Howey* analysis to a digital asset offering, weighing whether the Kin token ICO constituted a securities offering. In granting the SEC summary judgment, Judge Hellerstein found that the Kin ICO was a securities offering under the *Howey* test because (i) purchasers invested their money in Kin; (ii) all purchasers benefited from increases in the value of Kin, which derived from the Kik's pooling of purchasers funds after the ICO; and (iii) purchasers expected to profit from Kik's efforts in light of Kik's marketing efforts, and retention of 30% of the Kin issued.[73]

In conducting this analysis of the Kin token, Judge Hellerstein did not make the same explicit distinction that Judge Castel had made between the token and the investment scheme, but he also did not expressly reject the distinction.

[b] SEC v. Ripple Labs

In July 2023, Judge Analisa Torres of the S.D.N.Y. issued a summary judgment ruling in *SEC v. Ripple Labs, Inc.*, holding (among other things) that the XRP was not itself a security and that the SEC had failed to establish that Ripple's transactions in the secondary market were securities transactions. The SEC's complaint had alleged that the XRP token was a security under the *Howey* test and that multiple categories of sales of the XRP token by Ripple Labs constituted unregistered sales of securities in violation of the Securities Act.[74]

On summary judgment, the court held that the XRP token was "not in and of itself" an investment contract and that the *Howey* analysis must be conducted based on the circumstances of each set of transactions.[75] The court then applied the *Howey* test to three different types of transactions: (i) Institutional Sales; (ii) Programmatic Sales; and (iii) Other Distributions (such as distributions to Ripple employees as a form of compensation).[76]

The court held that "Institutional Sales," which were sold directly to sophisticated investment entities through written contracts, were a security under *Howey*.[77] However, it also held that "Programmatic Sales," through which Ripple Labs sold XRP through secondary-market platforms in "blind bid/ask" transactions where the purchaser and seller did not know who the other party was, were not securities transactions.[78] The court held that in these transactions, the buyers "could not reasonably expect" that "Ripple would use the capital it received from its sales to improve the XRP

73. *See S.E.C. v. Kik Interactive Inc.*, 492 F. Supp. 3d 169, 177-80 (S.D.N.Y. 2020).
74. Amended Compl., *SEC v. Ripple Labs*, No. 20-CV-10832 (Feb. 18, 2021) Dkt. 46.
75. Order, *SEC v. Ripple Labs*, No. 20-CV-10832 at 15 (S.D.N.Y. Jul. 13, 2023) Dkt. 874 ("Ripple Order").
76. The court held that the Other Distributions failed the first *Howey* prong because the recipients did not pay money or provide other consideration to Ripple in exchange for these distributions. Ripple Order at 26.
77. Ripple Order at 16-22.
78. Ripple Order at 23.

ecosystem and thereby increase the price of XRP."[79] Indeed, the court said "many Programmatic Buyers were entirely unaware of Ripple's existence."[80]

The court held that "the economic reality is that a Programmatic Buyer stood in the same shoes as a secondary market purchaser who did not know to whom or what it was paying its money."[81] Notably, the court held that because "the record does not establish the third *Howey* prong as to the Programmatic Sales," the court "does not reach whether the first [investment of money] or second [common enterprise] *Howey* prongs have been satisfied."[82]

[c] SEC v. Terraform Labs

On December 28, 2023, Judge Jed Rakoff of the S.D.N.Y. granted partial summary judgment in the SEC's case against Terraform Labs, seemingly at odds with the *Ripple* decision issued a few months prior. Here, the court did refer to multiple tokens sold by Terraform as securities, remarking that "There is no genuine dispute that UST, LUNA, wLUNA and MIR are securities because they are investment contracts."[83]

Perhaps most notably, the Terraform decision characterized the stablecoin UST as a security. While stablecoins are often considered not to meet the *Howey* test because there is no expectation of profits in holding a stablecoin, Judge Rakoff held that "UST in combination with the Anchor Protocol constituted an investment contract." Even if not all holders of UST deposited tokens in the Anchor Protocol, the court asserted that it was "of no legal consequence" that "some holders 'ch[o]se not to accept the full offer of an investment contract.'"[84]

[2] ***Trading Platforms***

The SEC has taken the position that crypto asset trading platforms are required to register as exchanges, clearing agencies, and broker-dealers, including in notable enforcement actions against Coinbase,[85] Binance,[86] and Kraken.[87] Because these transactions must involve securities to fall within any of these categories, the above analysis of whether crypto assets are securities, or whether certain transactions involving those assets are securities transactions, is a threshold issue to classification as a securities broker or dealer.

Brokers and dealers encompass a broader range of activities as well and so are addressed in the following subsection.

79. *Id.*, at 23.
80. *Id.*, at 24.
81. *Id.*, at 23.
82. *Id.*, at 25 n. 17.
83. *SEC v. Terraform Labs Pte. Ltd.*, 2023 WL 8944860 (S.D.N.Y. Dec. 28, 2023).
84. *Id.*, at *14.
85. *SEC v. Coinbase, Inc.*, No. 1-23-cv-04738 (S.D.N.Y.).
86. *SEC v. Binance Holdings Limited*, No 1:23-cv-01599 (D.D.C.).
87. *SEC v. Payward Inc.*, No. 3:23-cv-06003 (N.D. Cal.).

[a] Exchanges

Section 5 of the Exchange Act[88] requires an organization, association, or group of persons that meets the definition of "exchange" under section 3(a)(1) of the Exchange Act, unless otherwise exempt, to register with the Commission as a national securities exchange pursuant to section 6 of the Exchange Act.

Section 3(a)(1) of the Exchange Act[89] defines "exchange" to mean "any organization, association, or group of persons, whether incorporated or unincorporated, which constitutes, maintains, or provides a market place or facilities for bringing together purchasers and sellers of securities or for otherwise performing with respect to securities the functions commonly performed by a stock exchange as that term is generally understood, and includes the market place and the market facilities maintained by such exchange."

Exchange Act Rule 3b-16(a)[90] further defines certain terms in the definition of "exchange" under section 3(a)(1) of the Exchange Act, including "[a]n organization, association, or group of persons," as one that: "(1) [b]rings together the orders for securities of multiple buyers and sellers; and (2) [u]ses established, non-discretionary methods (whether by providing a trading facility or by setting rules) under which such orders interact with each other, and the buyers and sellers entering such orders agree to the terms of a trade."

Apart from the SEC's enforcement actions against centralized trading platforms, there remains an open question of whether and how these rules apply to decentralized exchanges. The SEC has taken the position that decentralized exchanges do fall within the rules, but at the same time has proposed revisions to the definition of "exchange" in Rule 3b-16(a),[91] in what has been widely recognized as an effort to "bring decentralized finance (DeFi) systems under the definition of exchange."[92]

[b] Clearing Agencies

Section 17A(b) of the Exchange Act [15 U.S.C. § 78q-1(b)] generally makes it unlawful "for any clearing agency, unless registered in accordance with this subsection, directly or indirectly, to make use of the mails or any means or instrumentality of interstate commerce to perform the functions of a clearing agency with respect to any security."

Section 3(a)(23)(A) of the Exchange Act [15 U.S.C. § 78c(a)(23)(A)] defines the term "clearing agency" as "any person who acts as an intermediary in making payments or deliveries or both in connection with transactions in securities or who provides facilities for comparison of data respecting the terms of settlement of

---

88. 15 U.S.C. § 78e.
89. 15 U.S.C. § 78c(a)(1).
90. 17 C.F.R. § 240.3b-16(a).
91. *See* https://www.sec.gov/files/rules/proposed/2022/34-94868.pdf.
92. Letter from Members of the House Committee on Financial Services to the SEC, Re: File No. S7 02-22, Reopening of Comment Period for Amendments to Exchange Act Rule 3b-16 Regarding the Definition of "Exchange", at 2. https://financialservices.house.gov/uploadedfiles/fsc_gop_letter_on_the_secs_proposed_definition_of_an_exchange_final.pdf.

securities transactions, to reduce the number of settlements of securities transactions, or for the allocation of securities settlement responsibilities," as well as "any person ... who (i) acts as a custodian of securities in connection with a system for the central handling of securities whereby all securities of a particular class or series of any issuer deposited within the system are treated as fungible and may be transferred, loaned, or pledged by bookkeeping entry without physical delivery of securities certificates, or (ii) otherwise permits or facilitates the settlement of securities transactions or the hypothecation or lending of securities without physical delivery of securities certificates."

[3] Brokers & Dealers

[a] Brokers

"Brokers" are defined as "any person engaged in the business of effecting transactions in securities for the account of others."[93] Courts look for multiple factors to determine whether an organization constitutes a broker, typically including whether a person: (1) works as an employee of the issuer, (2) receives a commission rather than a salary, (3) sells or earlier sold the securities of another issuer, (4) participates in negotiations between the issuer and an investor, (5) provides either advice or a valuation as to the merit of an investment, and (6) actively (rather than passively) finds investors.[94]

The SEC has published a guide for financial organizations to determine whether they are considered brokers, which indicates that in the SEC's broad view, the following activities demonstrate that an organization is acting as a broker:

- Finding investors or customers for, making referrals to, or splitting commissions with registered broker-dealers, investment companies (or mutual funds, including hedge funds) or other securities intermediaries.
- Finding investment banking clients for registered broker-dealers.
- Finding investors for "issuers" (entities issuing securities), even in a "consultant" capacity.
- Engaging in, or finding investors for, venture capital or "angel" financings, including private placements.
- Finding buyers and sellers of businesses (i.e., activities relating to mergers and acquisitions where securities are involved).[95]

93. 15 U.S.C. § 78c(4)(A).
94. *S.E.C. v. Hansen*, 1984 WL 2413, *10 (S.D.N.Y.1984); *see also Cornhusker Energy Lexington, LLC v. Prospect St. Ventures*, 2006 WL 2620985, *6 (D. Neb. 2006) (Bataillon, J.) (identifying as evidence of broker activity a person's "analyzing the financial needs of an issuer," "recommending or designing financing methods," discussing "details of securities transactions," and recommending an investment); *S.E.C. v. Margolin*, 1992 WL 279735 (S.D.N.Y.1992) (Leisure, J.) (finding evidence of "brokerage activity" in the defendant's "receiving transaction-based compensation, advertising for clients, and possessing client funds and securities").
95. https://www.sec.gov/reportspubs/investor-publications/divisionsmarketregbdguidehtm.html.

The SEC also gives examples of organizations likely to constitute brokers under the Securities Act:

- investment advisers and financial consultants;
- persons that operate or control electronic or other platforms to trade securities;
- persons that market real-estate investment interests, such as tenancy-in-common interests, that are securities;
- persons that act as "placement agents" for private placements of securities;
- persons that market or effect transactions in insurance products that are securities, such as variable annuities or other investment products that are securities;
- persons that effect securities transactions for the account of others for a fee, even when those other people are friends or family members;
- persons that provide support services to registered broker-dealers.[96]

Lastly, the SEC provides inquiries that if answered in the affirmative further indicate to the SEC that an organization is acting as a broker:

- Do you participate in important parts of a securities transaction, including solicitation, negotiation, or execution of the transaction?
- Does your compensation for participation in the transaction depend upon, or is it related to, the outcome or size of the transaction or deal? Do you receive any other transaction-related compensation?
- Are you otherwise engaged in the business of effecting or facilitating securities transactions?
- Do you handle the securities or funds of others in connection with securities transactions?[97]

Of the above factors, a core inquiry is whether an entity facilitates securities transactions and recoups compensation from transaction-based fees. In addition to the above factors, classification as a broker arguably requires more than merely administrative or ministerial tasks in the process of effecting or facilitating securities transactions, and the SEC has granted or denied no-action relief in certain circumstances with reference to whether the activity of the party seeking relief rose above the level of administrative or ministerial role.[98]

96. *Id.*
97. *Id.*
98. *See* Letter from Ezra Weiss, Chief Counsel, Division of Market Regulation, to Harold J. Smotkin, Clearing Service, Inc. (Jan. 3, 1972) (Clearing Service was required to register as broker-dealer, inasmuch as the services it performed went beyond those of a purely clerical or ministerial nature); Letter from Ezra Weiss, Chief Counsel, Division of Market Regulation, to William F. Clare, ESE Stock Transfer Corp. (Oct. 21, 1971) (ESE Stock Transfer Corp. was required to register because the services it intended to perform went beyond those which are merely clerical or ministerial in nature); cf. Universal Pensions, Inc., SEC No-Action Letter (Jan. 30, 1998) (granting no-action relief to a pension plan administrator performing record-keeping and other administrative services, subject to conditions); Applied Financial Systems, Inc., SEC No-Action

[b] Dealers

Dealers are defined under the Securities Act as "any person engaged in the business of buying and selling securities . . . for such person's own account through a broker or otherwise."[99] Under the "trader exception," an organization that buys or sells securities "not as part of a regular business" is not considered a dealer.[100] The definition of "dealers" has received less attention in federal courts than "brokers," but courts generally construe it to require that an entity buys and sells securities for its own accounts with "a certain regularity of participation in securities transactions."[101]

The SEC also offers examples of dealer organizations:

- a person who holds himself out as being willing to buy and sell a particular security on a continuous basis;
- a person who runs a matched book of repurchase agreements; or
- a person who issues or originates securities that he also buys and sells.[102]

Like their broker analysis, the SEC also provides inquiries that if answered in the affirmative indicate that an entity is acting as a dealer:

- Do you advertise or otherwise let others know that you are in the business of buying and selling securities?
- Do you do business with the public (either retail or institutional)?
- Do you make a market in, or quote prices for both purchases and sales of, one or more securities?
- Do you participate in a "selling group" or otherwise underwrite securities?
- Do you provide services to investors, such as handling money and securities, extending credit, or giving investment advice?
- Do you write derivatives contracts that are securities?[103]

In determining whether an entity is acting as a dealer, the focus will again be on whether an organization engages in transactions with assets that are considered securities and if so on whose behalf these transactions are completed.[104]

Letter (Sep. 25, 1971) (granting no-action relief to entity providing certain shareholder servicing and record-keeping functions as clerical and ministerial).

99. 15 U.S.C.A. § 78c.
100. 15 U.S.C. § 78c (a)(5)(B). "Traders are excluded from the definition of dealer. A trader is someone who buys and sells securities, either individually or in a trustee capacity, but not as part of a regular business. Individuals who buy and sell securities for themselves generally are considered traders and not dealers." https://www.sec.gov/fast-answers/answersbdregishtm.html.
101. *United States Sec. & Exch. Comm'n v. River N. Equity LLC*, 415 F. Supp. 3d 853, 858 (N.D. Ill. 2019); citing *Mass. Fin. Servs., Inc. v. Sec. Investor Prot. Corp.*, 411 F. Supp. 411, 415 (D. Mass. 1976), aff'd, 545 F.2d 754 (1st Cir. 1976); *SEC v. Offill*, 2012 WL 246061, at *7 (N.D. Tex. Jan. 26, 2012).
102. https://www.sec.gov/reportspubs/investor-publications/divisionsmarketregbdguidehtm.html.
103. *Id.*
104. *See, e.g., Couldock & Bohan, Inc. v. Societe Generale Sec. Corp.*, 93 F. Supp. 2d 220, 229 (D. Conn. 2000) (finding that entity was a dealer because it "was not merely matching buyers and sellers, but rather was placing itself squarely in the middle of each transaction in order to reap

[4] *Crypto Asset Lending*

The SEC has taken the view that certain crypto asset lending arrangements are also securities transactions, invoking both the *Howey* test for "investment contracts" and the *Reves* test for "notes," even if the underlying crypto asset is not a security.

For example, in February 2022, the SEC announced a settlement with BlockFi in relation to its crypto lending product.[105] As described in the Consent Order, BlockFi "offered and sold BlockFi Interest Accounts ('BIAs') to investors, through which investors lend crypto assets to BlockFi in exchange for BlockFi's promise to provide a variable monthly interest payment. BlockFi generated the interest paid out to BIA investors by deploying its assets in various ways, including loans of crypto assets made to institutional and corporate borrowers, lending U.S. dollars to retail investors, and by investing in equities and futures."[106] The SEC asserted that this made BIAs securities under both *Reves* and *Howey* and thus that BlockFi was in violation of the Securities Act's registration requirements.[107]

§7.03 FEDERAL COMMODITIES LAWS

Although the SEC views many digital assets as securities, there appears to be consensus that Bitcoin is a commodity, and many other crypto assets are also likely to be commodities according to the Commodities Futures Trading Commission (CFTC). Furthermore, just because one digital asset is part of a securities transaction does not necessarily mean that it cannot also be a commodity, thereby creating the potential for overlapping regulation.

[A] Scope of CFTC's Authority

The CFTC asserts authority over any digital assets that constitute commodities pursuant to the Commodities Exchange Act (CEA). However, the CFTC is primarily directed at regulating the market for derivatives of commodities, not the spot market for commodities themselves.[108] In an August 23, 2021 statement, CFTC Commissioner Dawn DeBerry explained:

---

the profits from the spread, i.e., the price difference between the buy and sell sides of the transactions, for its own account").

105. BlockFi Agrees to Pay $100 Million in Penalties and Pursue Registration of its Crypto Lending Product, SEC Release 2022-26, https://www.sec.gov/news/press-release/2022-26.
106. Order Instituting Cease-and-Desist Proceedings at 1, *In the Matter of BlockFi Lending* LLC, www.sec.gov/files/litigation/admin/2022/33-11029.pdf.
107. *Id.*, at 8-9. The SEC also asserted that BlockFi was an Investment Company. *See id.*
108. *See* 7 U.S.C. §§ 6(a), 6d(a); 7 U.S.C. § 2(c)(2)(D); Bats BZX Exchange, Inc., Release No. 34-80206 (Mar. 10, 2017), at 28 ("[a]lthough the CFTC can bring enforcement actions against manipulative conduct in spot markets for a commodity, spot markets are not required to register with the CFTC, unless they offer leveraged, margined, or financed trading to retail customers").

> Even if a digital asset is a commodity, it is not regulated by the CFTC. However: The CFTC does regulate derivatives on digital assets, just like it regulates other derivatives. That includes the regulation of trading, clearing, etc., of futures contracts and swaps on digital assets (such as the futures contracts on Bitcoin and Ether listed for trading on various CFTC-regulated exchanges).

While the CFTC does not directly regulate spot markets, any activity concerning swaps, futures or other derivatives are likely to fall under the regulatory authority of the CFTC, which pursues enforcement against organizations that fail to register as swap execution facilities or future commission merchants.[109] Likewise, if an organization is a commodity trading adviser or commodity pool operator, the CFTC requires registration, record-keeping and disclosure.

The CEA also applies to "retail commodity transactions"—i.e., those involving a person that is neither an eligible contract participant nor an eligible commercial entity ("retail")—where the transaction is conducted on a leveraged or margined basis or financed by the offeror, the counterparty, or a person acting in concert with the offeror or counterparty on a similar basis. Absent an applicable exception, such transactions must be executed on a designated contract market (generally in a manner similar to regulated futures contracts), and intermediaries offering such transactions must be registered as futures commission merchants.[110]

[B] Registration Requirements

The CFTC requires registration of, and oversees, as Swap Execution Facilities (SEF), Future Commission Merchants (FCM), Commodity Pool Operators (CPO), or Commodity Trading Advisors (CTA).[111]

SEFs are defined as any organization that provides users a trading platform in which users can execute or trade swaps with other market participants,[112] whereas FCMs are entities that either solicit or accept orders to buy or sell futures contracts or options on futures or swaps in exchange for a fee.[113]

In contrast, a CPO is an organization that operates a commodity pool and solicits funds for that pool.[114] A commodity pool "is an enterprise in which funds contributed by a number of persons are combined for the purpose of trading futures or options on futures, retail off-exchange forex contracts, or swaps, or to invest in another commodity pool."[115] However, CPOs not only operate commodity pools but also "make[]

109. *See, e.g.*, https://www.cftc.gov/PressRoom/PressReleases/8433-21 (last accessed Jul. 4, 2022).
110. *See id.*
111. https://www.natlawreview.com/article/cftc-s-approach-to-virtual-currencies. ("[T]he CFTC has brought nineteen enforcement actions from 2015 to the end of June 2020, with an uptick in 2018 after its Division of Enforcement formed a specialized Virtual Currency Task Force").
112. https://www.cftc.gov/IndustryOversight/TradingOrganizations/SEF2/index.htm.
113. https://www.nfa.futures.org/registration-membership/who-has-to-register/fcm.html.
114. https://www.nfa.futures.org/registration-membership/who-has-to-register/cpo.html; 7 U.S.C. § 1a(11).
115. https://www.nfa.futures.org/registration-membership/who-has-to-register/cpo.html.

trading decisions on behalf of the pool or engage[] a [CTA] to do so."[116] Like CPOs, CTAs must provide advice on commodity trading or exercise discretion over customer accounts to qualify.[117]

CPO registration is not required if various exemptions apply under 17 CFR § 4.5 or § 4.13. The exemptions of section 4.5 apply to registered investment advisers, banks, insurance companies, and trustees,[118] whereas the exemptions of section 4.13 apply to operators of pools with either minimal participants (less than 15 at any time) or operators that run a single pool and do not collect a fee for operating the pool.[119]

One notable exception exists for contracts that fall within an "actual delivery" rule. This exception exists for contracts of sale issued on a leveraged or margined basis or financed by the offeror, the counterparty, or a person acting in concert with the offeror or counterparty, resulting in "actual delivery" within "28 days or such other longer period as the Commission may determine by rule or regulation based upon the typical commercial practice in cash or spot markets for the commodity involved."

The Commission issued guidance in 2013 as to the meaning of "actual delivery" as used in CEA section 2(c)(2)(D) (the "2013 Guidance").[120] The 2013 Guidance provided examples of actual delivery, particularly those that involve transfer of title and possession of the commodity to the purchaser or a depository acting on the purchaser's behalf. The Commission followed up in 2020 with interpretive guidance applying the actual delivery requirement to virtual currencies.[121] In short, the guidance suggests that actual delivery will occur upon a transfer of control and not upon a book entry or transfer to a wallet remaining within the seller or intermediaries' control.

[C] Enforcement Actions

While the CFTC has not been as aggressive as the SEC in pursuing enforcement actions in the crypto asset industry, it has brought several notable enforcement actions against crypto industry participants for failure to register as required by the rules set forth above.

The CEA also confers broad anti-fraud and anti-manipulation mandates on the CFTC, which are wide in scope and do extend to the spot markets for commodities in which futures are dealt. For example, the CFTC pursues enforcement action against a variety of potentially deceptive trading practices, such as "spoofing," in which market

116. Futures Glossary, CFTC, https://www.cftc.gov/ConsumerProtection/EducationCenter/CFTC Glossary/index.htm.
117. Futures Glossary, CFTC, https://www.cftc.gov/ConsumerProtection/EducationCenter/CFTC Glossary/index.htm.
118. 17 CFR § 4.5.
119. 17 CFR § 4.13.
120. *Retail Commodity Transactions Under Commodity Exchange Act*, 78 Fed. Reg. 52,426 (Aug. 23, 2013), *available at* https://www.govinfo.gov/content/pkg/FR-2013-08-23/pdf/2013-20617.pdf.
121. *Retail Commodity Transactions Involving Virtual Currency*, available at https://www.cftc.gov/sites/default/files/2020/06/2020-11827a.pdf.

participants place orders they do not intend to complete, and manipulation of commodity or foreign-currency benchmark prices.[122]

The CFTC's crypto enforcement actions include:

- *Plutus Financial, Inc. d/b/a Abra* (July 2020): Penalty order against entity for entering into illegal off-exchange swaps in digital assets and foreign currency with U.S. and overseas customers.
- *Bitfinex* (October 2021): Penalty order for engaging in illegal, off-exchange retail commodity transactions operating as an unregistered futures commission merchant (FCM).
- *Blockratize, d/b/a Polymarket.com* (January 2022): Penalty order for operating an unregistered binary options events market.
- *bZeroX and Ooki DAO* (September 2022): Penalty order for offering leveraged positions whose value was determined by the price difference between two digital assets.
- *Digitex Futures* (October 2022): Penalty order for offering futures transactions on a platform other than a designated contract market and also attempting to manipulate the price of the Digitex Futures native token.

The CFTC's enforcement action in late 2022 against Ooki DAO, which the CFTC alleged operated as an unregistered exchange,[123] raised novel issues about regulators' ability to pursue enforcement against the anonymous and decentralized actors common in the digital assets space. The CFTC sued Ooki DAO as an entity, despite the fact that it is a "decentralized autonomous organization" (DAO) with only anonymous online participants and no centralized governing structure. A court held that the case could proceed because the DAO was an unincorporated association and the CFTC was allowed to effect service on the DAO by posting documents through Ooki's message boards.[124] The case illustrates how U.S. regulators implement novel approaches to existing frameworks to respond to the fluid circumstances of these still-emerging technologies. Since the Ooki DAO action, numerous cases have been filed asserting similar theories that DAOs constitute either a partnership or unincorporated association.

In late 2023, the CFTC used three enforcement actions to send a message to the DeFi community in September 2023 with the coordinated announcement of three settled enforcement actions, against Opyn, ZeroX, and Deridex.[125] These three actions were noteworthy because they each involved different relief, providing some guidance as to the CFTC's expectations for compliance.

122. *See, e.g.*, https://www.cftc.gov/PressRoom/PressReleases/8534-22 (last accessed Jul. 11, 2022); https://www.cftc.gov/PressRoom/PressReleases/7181-15 (last accessed Jul. 11, 2022).
123. *See* https://www.cftc.gov/PressRoom/PressReleases/8590-22.
124. *See CFTC v. Ooki DAO*, No. 3:22-cv-05416-WHO, 2022 WL 17822445 (N.D. Cal. Dec. 20, 2022).
125. Press Release No. 8774-23, CFTC, CFTC Issues Orders Against Operators of Three DeFi Protocols for Offering Illegal Digital Asset Derivatives Trading (Sep. 7, 2023), https://www.cftc.gov/PressRoom/PressReleases/8774-23

Opyn developed and deployed a blockchain-based digital asset trading platform (the "Opyn Protocol") that offered trading of digital asset derivatives to traders in the United States and abroad. The CFTC Order noted that while Opyn had instituted measures to block U.S. users, including "blocking users with U.S. internet protocol addresses, those steps were not sufficient to actually block U.S. users from accessing the Opyn Protocol." The Order further noted that since the CFTC's investigation began, "Opyn took additional steps to block U.S. users' access to the Opyn Protocol and voluntarily provided relevant information to Division staff," and as a result, the CFTC imposed a relatively modest $250,000 penalty.[126]

Zerox developed a protocol and front-end interface "marketed to retail investors as a decentralized exchange ('DEX') as well as a DEX aggregator." A wide variety of crypto assets could be accessed through the interface and those "assets included certain leveraged tokens, which provided traders approximately 2:1 leveraged exposure to digital assets such as ether (ETH) and bitcoin (BTC)." The CFTC noted that ZeroX undertook remedial measures in cooperation with the CFTC including "immediate steps to prevent Leveraged Tokens from being traded through Matcha." As a result, the CFTC imposed a relatively modest $200,000 penalty.[127]

Deridex deployed and maintained a digital asset trading platform available in the United States and abroad that allowed users to "establish and liquidate positions in 'perpetual contracts,' a leveraged derivative product whose value was based on the relative price difference between two digital assets." The CFTC noted that after being contacted by the SEC "Deridex took immediate steps to set the Deridex Protocol into a wind-down mode so that no new deposits or positions could be made or created."[128]

The actions against Opyn, ZeroX, and Deridex demonstrate that paths to compliance with commodities laws may include substantial steps to block U.S. users beyond IP blocking, or measures to exclude leverage, margin and derivatives products, or simply shutting down. Notably, the CFTC's Order and announcement concerning Opyn did not identify the additional measures that were taken to block U.S. users, leaving industry participants to guess as to what more is expected of them.

§7.04 MONEY SERVICES BUSINESSES & MONEY TRANSMITTING

The Financial Crimes Enforcement Network (FinCEN), an enforcement body under the United States Treasury Department, has established regulation and compliance requirements for companies that move money as a business, such as currency dealers or check cashers. Money services businesses and money transmitters must register with FinCEN, and those businesses must ensure compliance with anti-money laundering regulations under the Bank Secrecy Act (BSA) of 1970.

126. *In re Opyn, Inc.*, CFTC No. 23-40, 2023 WL 5937238, at *2 (Sep. 7, 2023), *available at* https://www.cftc.gov/media/9211/enfopynorder090723/download.

127. *In re ZeroEx, Inc.*, CFTC No. 23.41, 2023 WL 5937239, at *2 (Sep. 7, 2023), *available at* https://www.cftc.gov/media/9216/enfzeroexorder090723/download.

128. *In re Deridex, Inc.*, CFTC No. 23-42, 2023 WL 5937236, at *2 (Sep. 7, 2023), *available at* https://www.cftc.gov/media/9221/enfderidexorder090723/download.

The money laundering risks of cryptocurrency are a high priority for the Treasury Department and an area of increasing scrutiny and growing regulation. For example, in April 2023, the Treasury Department issued a report concluding that "decentralized finance" (DeFi) is presently creating opportunities for illegal conduct and reminding DeFi service providers that BSA obligations apply equally to them.[129]

FinCEN has released specific guidance stating that money transmitter regulation applies equally to the national currencies of sovereign states and to cryptocurrencies.[130] Guidance issued in 2019 by FinCEN analyzed various virtual currency business models and concluded that many of them would qualify as money transmitters and thus fall under the registration and other requirements.[131] Cryptocurrency businesses that transmit value between persons or entities are likely to be subject to FinCEN regulation. Additionally, most states have their own registration requirements for money transmitters, thus requiring money services businesses to register in each state in which they do business (with some exceptions).

FinCEN has established registration and compliance requirements that apply to "money services businesses" (MSBs) and "money transmitters" under the Bank Secrecy Act (BSA). "Money services businesses" include currency dealers or exchangers; check cashers; issuers of traveler's checks, money orders or stored value; sellers or redeemers of traveler's checks, money orders or stored value; and money transmitters.[132] Any money services business must register with FinCEN, unless acting as an agent for a registered money services business.[133]

"Money transmitters" are businesses that offer "money transmission services." "Money transmission services" are defined as the acceptance of currency, funds, or other things of value that substitute for currency from one party and the transmission of the same to another location or person by any means.[134] There are a few exceptions, including a person that only "[a]ccepts and transmits funds only integral to the sale of goods or the provision of services, other than money transmission services, by the person who is accepting and transmitting the funds."[135] There are three conditions to this exemption: 1) the money transmission component must be part of the provision of a good or a service that is distinct from money transmission itself; 2) the exemption can only be claimed by the person who is engaged in the provision of goods or services

129. https://home.treasury.gov/news/press-releases/jy1391.
130. https://www.fincen.gov/sites/default/files/shared/FIN-2013-G001.pdf (last accessed Jul. 4, 2022).
131. https://www.fincen.gov/sites/default/files/2019-05/FinCEN%20Guidance%20CVC%20FINAL%20508.pdf (last accessed Jul. 11, 2022).
132. 31 CFR 1010.100(ff).
133. 31 C.F.R. § 1022.380(a)(1) and (3). Banks and organizations that are registered with and regulated by the SEC or Commodity Futures Trading Commission ("CFTC") are specifically exempt from regulation as "money services businesses."
134. 31 CFR § 1010.100(ff)(5)(i)(A); *see also* § 1010.100(m) (defining currency as "[t]he coin and paper money of the United States or of any other country that is designated as legal tender and that circulates and is customarily used and accepted as a medium of exchange in the country of issuance. Currency includes U.S. silver certificates, U.S. notes and Federal Reserve notes. Currency also includes official foreign bank notes that are customarily used and accepted as a medium of exchange in a foreign country.").
135. 31 CFR § 1010.100(ff)(5)(ii)(F).

distinct from money transmission; and 3) the money transmission component must be integral (that is, necessary) for the provision of the goods and services.[136]

FinCEN has released guidance that "the definition of a money transmitter does not differentiate between real currencies and convertible virtual currencies"[137] and that it takes a broad view that any "administrator or exchanger that (1) accepts and transmits a convertible virtual currency, or (2) buys or sells convertible virtual currency for any reason is a money transmitter."[138] This guidance further explains that an organization "is an exchanger and a money transmitter if [it] accepts . . . de-centralized convertible virtual currency from one person and transmits it to another person as part of the acceptance and transfer of currency, funds, or other value that substitutes for currency."[139] FinCEN also clarifies that "a user who obtains convertible virtual currency and uses it to purchase real or virtual goods or services is not [a money services business]."[140] A digital asset trading platform that facilitates transfers between third parties, however, is a money services business.[141]

In 2019, a new FinCEN guidance document specifically addressed the analysis of various virtual currency businesses as money transmitters.[142] It noted that "whether a person is an MSB will not depend on whether the person: (a) is a natural person or legal entity; (b) is licensed as a business by any state; (c) has employees or other natural persons acting as agents; (d) operates at a brick-and-mortar branch, or through mechanical or software agents or agencies; or (e) is a for profit or nonprofit service," and "a person still qualifies as a money transmitter if that person's activities include receiving one form of value (currency, funds, prepaid value, value that substitutes for currency—such as CVC, etc.) from one person and transmitting either the same or a different form of value to another person or location, by any means."[143] FinCEN also clarified that money transmitter status may apply to businesses operating on an account basis, such that they "maintain an account for the transactor to store funds or value that substitutes for currency, from which the transactor can instruct the money transmitter to transfer them in whole or in part." [144]

FinCEN's 2019 Guidance directly addressed hosted wallets, which it described as "account-based money transmitters that receive, store, and transmit CVCs on behalf of their accountholders, generally interacting with them through websites or mobile

136. *See* FIN-2014-R011, "Request for Administrative Ruling on the Application of FinCEN's Regulations to a Virtual Currency Trading Platform," FinCEN (Oct. 27, 2014).
137. FIN-2013-G001, "Application of FinCEN's Regulations to Persons Administering, Exchanging, or Using Virtual Currencies," FinCEN (Mar. 18, 2013), https://www.fincen.gov/sites/default/files/shared/FIN-2013-G001.pdf.
138. *Id.*
139. *Id.*
140. *Id.*
141. *See* FIN-2014-R011, "Request for Administrative Ruling on the Application of FinCEN's Regulations to a Virtual Currency Trading Platform," FinCEN (Oct. 27, 2014).
142. *See* FIN-2019-G001, "Application of FinCEN's Regulations to Certain Business Models Involving Convertible Virtual Currencies," FinCEN (May 9, 2019).
143. *Id.*, § 2.
144. *Id.*

applications."[145] It contrasted hosted wallets with unhosted wallets, which are "software hosted on a person's computer, phone, or other device that allow the person to store and conduct transactions in CVC" and "do not require an additional third party to conduct transactions," in which case neither the person using the wallet nor the software developer is a money transmitter. Similarly, security providers that offer multi-signature or similar services will not be money transmitters where the value still belongs to the owner, who still initiates their own transactions, and where "the person participating in the transaction to provide additional validation at the request of the owner does not have total independent control over the value." [146]

Although the 2019 guidance sets out FinCEN's most complete statement—as of this date—on how it understands the applicability of money transmitter regulation to the crypto space, the 2019 guidance does not present itself as the final word on the matter, and it leaves open the possibility that earlier, pre-cryptocurrency FinCEN guidance may "remain instructive . . . to assist in understanding FinCEN's current interpretation of its MSB regulations" for crypto-related questions that are not directly addressed in crypto-specific FinCEN guidance or rulings.[147] Analogies to activities outside the crypto space may therefore remain persuasive as FinCEN grapples with new developments in the crypto world. For example, FinCEN's 2013 guidance built upon a 2008 guidance document to analogize entities exchanging fiat currency for cryptocurrency to traditional foreign-currency traders, and it stated that such transactions did not make the entities money transmitters so long as they engaged only in a one-sided transaction with the customer and did not pass currency or cryptocurrency to a third party.[148]

As an additional complexity, pre-2011 FinCEN guidance on exemptions to money transmitter status construes an old version of the money transmitter regulations that are no longer in force. FinCEN has indicated that the new regulations remain conceptually the same in that they provide an exemption to money transmitter status for transmissions integral to another transaction *that is not itself money transmission*.[149] However, the text of the money transmitter exemption most likely to be relevant to crypto platforms has seemingly been narrowed from an open-ended inquiry into "a transaction other than the funds transmission itself" into a specific exemption for fund transmissions "integral to the sale of goods or . . . services, other than money transmission."[150] Thus, FinCEN has both indicated the continued informative power of

145. *Id.*, § 4.2.1.
146. *Id.*
147. *See id.*, § 1.2.3 n. 14.
148. *See* FIN-2013-G001, "Application of FinCEN's Regulations to Persons Administering, Exchanging, or Using Virtual Currencies," FinCEN (Mar. 18, 2013) at 3-4, https://www.fincen.gov/sites/default/files/shared/FIN-2013-G001.pdf.
149. *See* FIN-2013-G001, at 4 n. 15.
150. *Compare* 75 Fed. Reg. 65,815 ("Generally, the acceptance and transmission of funds as an integral part of the execution and settlement of a transaction other than the funds transmission itself (for example, in connection with a bona fide sale of securities or other property), will not cause a person to be a money transmitter."), *with* 76 Fed. Reg. 43,596 ("The term 'money transmitter' shall not include a person that only . . . [a]ccepts and transmits funds only integral

pre-2011 guidance on money transmitter exemptions to the crypto space[151] and also signaled that it "interprets [the] exemptions strictly. Therefore, a person may not take advantage of a particular exemption if the activity in engages in does not conform fully to an exemption."[152] The question for applying this exemption will be evaluation of identifying the product or service to which the fund transmission is integral, and determining whether or not that service is itself a money transmission service.

§7.05 SANCTIONS

The Office of Foreign Assets Control (OFAC), another unit of the Treasury Department, is responsible for enforcing trade and economic sanctions. OFAC enforces economic sanctions programs primarily against countries and groups of individuals, such as terrorists and narcotics traffickers. The sanctions can be either comprehensive or selective, using the blocking of assets and trade restrictions to accomplish foreign policy and national security goals.[153] OFAC also has a dedicated page on its website devoted to explaining its position with respect to virtual currencies.[154]

As part of its enforcement efforts, OFAC publishes a list of individuals and companies owned or controlled by, or acting for or on behalf of, targeted countries. It also lists individuals, groups, and entities, such as terrorists and narcotics traffickers, designated under programs that are not country-specific. Collectively, such individuals and companies are called "Specially Designated Nationals" or "SDNs." Their assets are blocked, and U.S. persons are generally prohibited from dealing with them.[155] The SDN List is publicly available at: https://ofac.treasury.gov/specially-designated-nationals-and-blocked-persons-list-sdn-human-readable-lists.

OFAC adds digital currency addresses to the SDN List when those addresses have been associated with a blocked person. Digital currency addresses listed on the SDN List include their unique alphanumeric identifier (up to 256 characters) and identify the digital currency to which the address corresponds (e.g., Bitcoin (XBT), Ethereum (ETH), Litecoin (LTC), Neo (NEO), Dash (DASH), Ripple (XRP), Iota (MIOTA), Monero (XMR), and Petro (PTR)). That list is not exhaustive, however, in that parties who identify wallets that they believe are owned by, or otherwise associated with, an SDN should take the necessary steps to comply with the sanctions rules regardless of whether that wallet address is on the SDN List.[156]

In 2022, OFAC garnered significant attention for including the blockchain addresses of smart contracts associated with an anonymity tool (known as "mixer") called Tornado Cash that was determined to be means by which North Korean actors

to the sale of goods or the provision of services, other than money transmission services, by the person who is accepting and transmitting the funds").

151. *See* FIN-2019-G001, § 1.2.3.
152. *Id.*, § 2.
153. https://ofac.treasury.gov/about-ofac.
154. https://ofac.treasury.gov/faqs/topic/1626.
155. https://ofac.treasury.gov/specially-designated-nationals-and-blocked-persons-list-sdn-huma n-readable-lists.
156. https://ofac.treasury.gov/faqs/topic/1626.

engaged in money laundering.[157] This action was controversial and prompted litigation, with plaintiffs arguing that Tornado Cash as a mere software tool is not the type of person or entity on which sanctions can be levied.[158] The court ruled in favor of OFAC, finding that Tornado Cash could be considered an entity within the meaning of the relevant laws.[159]

OFAC and the Department of Justice have also brought numerous enforcement actions for violation of sanctions requirements in the crypto industry. In 2020, for example, OFAC settled an enforcement action against BitGo asserting failure "to prevent persons apparently located in the Crimea region of Ukraine, Cuba, Iran, Sudan, and Syria from using its non-custodial secure digital wallet management service."[160] In 2021, OFAC settled an enforcement action against BitPay asserting failure to utilize location data to prevent purchases from sanctioned buyers.[161]

The most noteworthy recent example of sanctions enforcement is the widely publicized settlement and plea agreement entered into by Binance Holdings Limited (Binance) and its former Chief Executive Officer Changpeng Zhao, as noted above.[162]

As described by the U.S. Department of Justice, Binance admitted "it engaged in anti-money laundering, unlicensed money transmitting, and sanctions violations in [the] largest corporate resolution to include criminal charges for an executive."[163] The plea was part of "coordinated resolutions with the Department of the Treasury's Financial Crimes Enforcement Network (FinCEN) and Office of Foreign Assets Control (OFAC) and the U.S. Commodity Futures Trading Commission (CFTC)."[164]

---

157. https://home.treasury.gov/news/press-releases/jy0768; https://home.treasury.gov/news/press-releases/jy0916.
158. *See* Plaintiffs' Memorandum in Support of Motion for Summary Judgement at 12-22, *Coin Center v. Yellen*, No. 3:22-cv-20375-TKW-ZCB (N.D. Fla. May 26, 2023), ECF No. 36-1; Plaintiffs' Reply in Support of Motion for Partial Summary Judgment and Response to Defendants' Cross-Motion for Summary Judgment at 3-12, *Van Loon v. Dep't of the Treasury*, No. 1:23-cv-312-RP (W.D. Tex. May 24, 2023), ECF No. 87.
159. *Van Loon v. Dep't of the Treasury*, No. 1:23-cv-312-RP (W.D. Tex. Aug. 17, 2023), ECF No. 94, at 13-16.
160. *See* OFAC Enters Into $98,830 Settlement with BitGo, Inc. for Apparent Violations of Multiple Sanctions Programs Related to Digital Currency Transactions, Enforcement Release: Dec. 30, 2020, https://ofac.treasury.gov/media/50266/download?inline.
161. *See* OFAC Enters Into $507,375 Settlement with BitPay, Inc. for Apparent Violations of Multiple Sanctions Programs Related to Digital Currency Transactions, Enforcement Release: Feb. 18, 2021, https://ofac.treasury.gov/media/54341/download?inline.
162. *Supra* n. 78.
163. Press Release, Binance and CEO Plead Guilty to Federal Charges in $4B Resolution, Nov. 21, 2023, https://www.justice.gov/opa/pr/binance-and-ceo-plead-guilty-federal-charges-4b-resolution; *see also* https://www.justice.gov/criminal/case/united-states-v-binance-holdings-limited-dba-binancecom (providing links to the underlying plea agreement and Information statement).
164. Press Release, Binance and CEO Plead Guilty to Federal Charges in $4B Resolution, Nov. 21, 2023, https://www.justice.gov/opa/pr/binance-and-ceo-plead-guilty-federal-charges-4b-resolution.

§7.06 STATE REGULATIONS

Many crypto asset trading platforms and service providers in the United States are registered as money transmitters in many or most states.[165] Registering as a money transmitter has varying requirements depending on the state and are outside the scope of this chapter. Certain states, however, have enacted and/or are actively considering enacting licensing regimes and regulations specifically targeted to the crypto industry.

Two notable examples are New York, which introduced a business license for virtual currency activities effective 2015 (commonly known as the "BitLicense"),[166] and California which passed legislation to create a similar licensing regime, signed into law on October 13, 2023.[167] Other states are considering similar measures. In addition, Wyoming has enacted well over a dozen laws related to blockchain technology and crypto assets and passed a law in 2023 forming a Wyoming Stable Token Commission to assess issuance of a stablecoin.[168]

[A] New York

Organizations that operate in the state of New York may also be required to maintain a BitLicense if the business engages in "virtual currency business activity."[169] This includes: (1) receiving virtual currency for transmission or transmitting virtual currency, except where the transaction is undertaken for non-financial purposes and does not involve the transfer of more than a nominal amount of virtual currency; (2) storing, holding, or maintaining custody or control of virtual currency on behalf of others; (3) buying and selling virtual currency as a customer business; (4) performing exchange services as a customer business; or (5) controlling, administering, or issuing a virtual currency.[170]

There are two specific exemptions to the BitLicense requirement for "persons that are chartered under the New York Banking Law and are approved by the superintendent to engage in virtual currency business activity; and merchants and consumers that utilize virtual currency solely for the purchase or sale of goods or services or for investment purposes."[171]

New York State's regulatory body clarified on its website in regard to the licensing requirements for software and service developers that:

> [T]he development and dissemination of software (as a purely technical service) in and of itself does not require a BitLicense … . The use of your product or service,

165. *See, e.g.*, https://www.coinbase.com/legal/licenses; https://www.gemini.com/trust-center; https://support.kraken.com/hc/en-us/articles/360031282351-Is-Kraken-licensed-or-regulated-.
166. 23 NYCRR § 200.
167. Digital Financial Assets Law, A.B. 39.
168. https://wyoleg.gov/Legislation/2023/SF0127; https://stabletoken.notion.site/Wyoming-Stable-Token-Commission-a24290df29cd4eaa897c6d628b007930.
169. 22 NYCRR 200.2(q).
170. *Id.*
171. 22 NYCRR 200.3(c).

however, may involve licensable Virtual Currency Business Activity. As an example, writing software that allows customers to self-custody Virtual Currency in a wallet would not, in and of itself, require a BitLicense. However, building a wallet service in which you kept custody of other people's funds on their behalf likely would require a BitLicense.[172]

The New York Attorney General has also been active in pursing enforcement action in the crypto industry, including a notable action against KuCoin,[173] for numerous alleged violations, including under New York's Martin Act.[174] The Martin Act is notable because it covers both securities and commodities. The alleged violations by KuCoin included, for example, holding itself out as an "exchange," which one cannot do under the Martin Act if they are engaged in the sale of any securities *or* commodities, unless they are registered with either the SEC or CFTC.[175]

[B] California

The California Digital Financial Assets Law (DFAL), originally introduced as Assembly Bill 39 (AB-39), and Senate Bill No. 401 (titled "Digital Financial Asset Transaction Kiosks") were signed into law on October 13, 2023.[176]

The DFAL authorizes the California Department of Financial Protection & Innovation (DPFI) to regulate certain virtual currency activity "of a person …who engages in or holds itself out as engaging in [digital financial assets] with or on behalf of a [California] resident." The DFAL defines "digital financial asset" as "digital representation of value that is used as a medium of exchange, unit of account, or store of value, and that is not legal tender, whether or not denominated in legal tender."

The DFPI invited public comment on topics related to the DFAL license application, licensure requirements, and stablecoin approval, to be submitted through January 12, 2024, and the requirement to be licensed will become effective beginning July 1, 2025.[177]

Regulation of the blockchain industry and crypto assets is a complex and evolving tapestry in the United States. The stakes are high as the industry faces an aggressive culture of enforcement. Nothing in this chapter should be construed as legal advice for any particular person, business, or activity, and anyone acting in the space or considering doing so should consult a qualified U.S. lawyer with particular expertise in this industry.

172. https://www.dfs.ny.gov/apps_and_licensing/virtual_currency_businesses/bitlicense_faqs.
173. *People v. Mek Global Ltd.*, No. —(N.Y. Sup. Ct., Mar. 9, 2023).
174. *See id.*
175. Martin Act, GBL § 352-c(3).
176. https://dfpi.ca.gov/dfal/.
177. *Id.*

CHAPTER 8

Blockchain and Intellectual Property

Andreas Holzwarth-Rochford

§8.01 INTRODUCTION

Blockchain and Distributed Ledger Technology (DLT) have a lot of different aspects and have become more and more relevant for ample applications and use cases. Beside financial applications like cryptocurrencies, these technologies are usable in a huge variety of fields to increase the cryptography and record-keeping. Some are smart contracts, supply chain management, data sharing, digital voting, and food safety.

However, the legal area of Intellectual Property (IP) also provides a lot of different aspects and ample possibilities on how to protect non-tangible assets.

In the following chapters, it is tried to show how and in which way these two areas match with each other. The aim is to clear out different prejudices often experienced in industry sectors not customarily being in contact with the field of IP rights, also called the green field.

Often, companies are giving up the possibility to delimit themselves from competitors and to hinder competitors from entering the same market based on a monopoly right only due to unknowingness of what is protectable in which way.

In the following subchapters, an overview of the protective right that might be of relevance for the different aspects of blockchain and DLT technologies and use cases is summarized. Probably surprisingly for the one or the other, there are a number of registered IP rights that can be used to protect products and services in these technologies, in addition to copyrights that can be used to protect creations like texts, software and three-dimensional objects.

Such registered IP rights are (a) trademarks – used to signal the origin of products, (b) designs – used to protect how a product looks, and (c) patents/utility models – used to protect the abstract technical teaching of inventions in all fields of technology, for example, Information Technology (IT).

A first overview of how the registration/creation of the different registered IP rights is taking place can be found on the webpage of the European Union Intellectual Property Office (EUIPO).[1]

The focus of the following subchapters will, however, be the protection by patents and utility models and its prerequisites and impacts.

IP rights are territorially restricted, and thus the regulations on how to reach protection, the scope of protection and the enforcement are different country to country, but general rules exist. These rules are specially defined in a plurality of regional and multilateral agreements. Examples of such agreements are the Paris Convention for the Protection of Industrial Property, the Trade-Related Aspects of Intellectual Property Rights (TRIPS) agreement, the Patent Cooperation Treaty (PCT), the European Patent Convention (EPC) and since June 2023 the UE Agreement.[2]

In this chapter, such general rules will be summarized from a European/German perspective. Furthermore, for some aspects, particularities in respective other jurisdictions will be outlined.

Furthermore, multinational organizations executing and administrating such international and multilateral agreements are existing in the IP area. These organizations provide the infrastructure to implement these agreements.

To be mentioned specially is the World Intellectual Property Organization (WIPO) (www.wipo.org) hosting (a) the Madrid System for registering and managing trademarks in up to 130 countries (https://www.wipo.int/madrid/en/) being based on the Madrid Agreement, (b) the Hague System for International Registration of International Designs in 79 contracting parties covering 96 countries (https://www.wipo.int/hague/en/) being based on the Hague Agreement, and (c) the Patent Cooperation Treaty (PCT) system assisting applicants in seeking patent protection internationally for their inventions in up to 157 contracting states.[3] Furthermore, regional organizations exist. Examples are:

- the European Patent Office (EPO) (www.epo.org) for granting patents being valid in countries of the European Union (EU) as well as in a variety of further European and non-European countries, for example, Switzerland and Turkey;
- the already mentioned European Union Intellectual Property Office (EUIPO) (www.euipo.europa.eu/) for the registration of EU wide designs and trademarks; and
- as non-European regional organizations the Eurasian Patent Organization (EAPO) (https://www.eapo.org/en/) for providing legal protection for inventions in the Contracting States on the basis of the single Eurasian patent.

1. European Union Intellectual Property Office, *The Intellectual Property Metro*, available at: https://euipo.europa.eu/tunnel-web/secure/webdav/guest/document_library/contentImages/rcd_design_definition/intellectual-property-metro.zip (accessed on 12 Nov. 2023).
2. EU Regulation No. 1257/2012 (OJ EPO 2013, 111) creates a 'European patent with unitary effect', commonly referred to as 'Unitary Patent' available at https://www.epo.org/en/legal/official-journal/2013/02/p111.html.
3. All numbers of parties/countries as of 12 Nov. 2023.

§8.02 TRADEMARK

[A] Definition

The WIPO generally defines a trademark as 'a sign capable of distinguishing the goods or services of one enterprise from those of other enterprises'.[4] A registered trademark thus comprises a reproduction of the sign together with a list of goods and services for which the sign is protected.

[B] Duration

In comparison to other registered rights discussed later, a trademark has the advantage of a generally unrestricted protection duration. Generally, the trademark is registered for an initial duration of five years or ten years, depending on the jurisdiction. This term can be extended by payment of renewal fees. Most jurisdictions do not provide a limit for the number of such renewal fees.

[C] Territory

As all IP rights, trademarks also are territorial protective rights, i.e., providing protection only in a restricted territory.

Beside national trademarks regional trademarks, especially the European Community trademark, are also existing. Such regional trademarks have the advantage to allow to reach protection for the entire territory/region by one single registration. However, also the trademark can be invalidated for the complete region in a central revocation procedure being advantageous for third parties aiming to revoke the trademark but increasing the risk for the trademark holder.

The EU Member States allow, however, parallel protection of the identical sign by a national trademark and European Community Trademark. This is in contrast to the protection of a national patent on the one hand and a national part of a European patent on the other hand in some countries, for example, in Germany. When the Agreement on a Unified Patent Court (UPC) was enacted on 1 June 2023, parallel protection by a national patent granted by the German Patent and Trademark Office (GPTO) and a patent granted by the EPO is allowed for a European Patent with unitary effect (UP) according to Article II §8 IntPatÜbkG.[5]

4. WIPO, *Trademarks*, available at: https://www.wipo.int/trademarks/en/ (accessed on 12 Nov. 2023).
5. Gesetz zu dem Übereinkommen vom 27. November 1963 zur Vereinheitlichung gewisser Begriffe des materiellen Rechts der Erfindungspatente, dem Vertrag vom 19. Juni 1970 über die internationale Zusammenarbeit auf dem Gebiet des Patentwesens und dem Übereinkommen vom 5. Oktober 1973 über die Erteilung europäischer Patente.

Furthermore, the WIPO offers the Madrid System for International registration in up to 130 countries by a single application.[6] Although the registration leads to independent national registrations, it significantly eases the registration, renewal and amendment procedure for the respective national registrations.

[D] Goods and Services

A sign can be protected as a trademark for specific types of goods and services. These types of goods and services need to be defined with the filing of the trademark application. The goods and services have been standardized in the so-called Nice Classification.[7]

For products and services being based on blockchain and DLT technologies due to a variety of possible use cases, a plurality of classes might also be possible. Noteworthy are especially:

- (good) class 9 that 'includes mainly apparatus and instruments for (...) information technology equipment ...'[8] with regard to hardware and software used in blockchain and DLT applications, for example, security tokens being encryption devices;
- (service) class 36 that 'includes mainly services rendered in financial and monetary affairs and services rendered in relation to insurance contracts of all kinds'[9] with regard to cryptocurrencies and issuance of tokens of value;
- (service) class 38 that 'includes mainly services that allow at least one party to communicate with another, as well as services for the broadcasting and transmission of data' with regard to the transmission of tokens, for example, relating to cryptocurrencies or distribution chains,[10] and
- (service) class 42 that 'includes mainly services provided by persons in relation to the theoretical and practical aspects of complex fields of activities, for example ... computer programming ...'[11] with regard to data encryption services.

[E] Types of Trademarks

As signals to identify the origin of a product can be directed in various ways to the different human senses, also different trademark types exist. According to the EUIPO,[12] trademarks can especially have the following forms:

6. WIPO, *Madrid System*, available at: https://www.wipo.int/madrid/en/ (accessed on 12 Nov. 2023).
7. WIPO, *Nice Classification*, available at: https://www.wipo.int/classifications/nice/en/ (accessed on 12 Nov. 2023).
8. Explanatory note for Class 9 published by WIPO.
9. Explanatory note for Class 36 published by WIPO.
10. Explanatory note for Class 38 published by WIPO.
11. Explanatory note for Class 42 published by WIPO.
12. EUIPO, *Trade mark definition*, available at: https://euipo.europa.eu/ohimportal/en/trade-mark-definition (accessed on 12 Nov. 2023).

- wordmark (comprising solely words or letters, numerals, other standard typographic characters or a combination thereof) – protects the word in any outer appearance like font, colour or size;
- figurative trademark (comprising only figurative elements and/or non-standard characters, stylization or layout, a graphic feature or a colour);
- shape mark (a sign that relates to a three-dimensional shape of, for example, a product itself, containers, package);
- position mark (the special manner in which a sign is located or attached to a product);
- colour mark (using exclusively a single colour or a combination of colours as an indication of origin);
- pattern mark (a plurality of elements arranged in a regular manner);
- motion mark (sign is represented by a movement or a change of a position of an element of the sign);
- multimedia mark (a sign that is formed by a combination of visual and audible elements);
- sound mark (mark that consists exclusively of a sound or a combination of sounds); and
- hologram mark (sign having holographic properties).

Depending on the respective national regulations and jurisdictions in some countries, only a part of the above-listed trademark forms is accepted. The representation of the trademark is often seen differently in the respective jurisdiction.

[F] Registration Process

In the following, the registration process of a trademark is outlined exemplarily based on the registration process of the EUIPO.

Once the trademark application has been filed,[13] the trademark will run through an examination period and opposition period before the trademark will be registered.

In the examination period, the respective patent office, here the EUIPO, will check the trademark application for formal requirements and the trademark for so-called absolute grounds. In this step, it is assessed whether the general public has an interest in using the sign. For example, the sign is describing the goods and services it is filed for. This covers also wordings being similar to such descriptions and/or similar products. Such concerns against the registration of the trademark might also be brought forward by third parties in the form of a so-called third-party observation.

For example, an absolute ground should be given to register the trademark 'Distributed Ledger' for IT services, especially in the area of banking and finance. The general public has an interest in being able to use this wording without restrictions.

13. EUIPO, *Registration process*, available at: https://euipo.europa.eu/ohimportal/en/registration-process (accessed on 19 Nov. 2023).

In this regard, it is important to note that the descriptiveness obviously depends on the mother tongue of the person assessing the descriptiveness. For example, 'gedistribueerd grootboek' would not necessarily be understood as descriptive for an English language-speaking person although it has the same meaning as a distributed ledger, albeit in Dutch.

However, it is possible to register trademarks including, *inter alia*, the wording 'blockchain' provided that the other parts of the trademark or the combination of this wording are recognized by the informed users as indication for the origin and for the specific layout and no public interest is given to hold the specific wording free. This is more likely the case for figurative trademarks like:

This figurative trademark 'foreverontheblockchain' has been registered as European Community trademark *inter alia* for advertising and IT services.[14]

In case of absolute grounds, the trademark application is (partly) refused. Partly refused means that the trademark is refused only for a part of the goods and services for which protection was applied for. In such a case, the applicant has to at least partly remove the respective goods and services from the list of goods and services.

In the opposition period as well as later nullification proceedings, third parties can raise concerns against the registration of the trademark for so-called relative grounds. Such relative grounds are especially the risk of confusion with existing trademarks registered for the same or similar goods and services. For example, a trademark might be identical to a trademark already registered before, and the goods and services might be similar to each other. To that end, in the case the goods and services are identical and the signs are tonally and visually written in a similar manner, such a relative ground might be given. Also, the opposition proceedings might lead to a revocation of the trademark as a whole or partly for respective services and goods.

[G] Post-registration

For a legal validity, it is furthermore necessary to use the trademark for the registered goods and services. In most jurisdictions, any third party might request the revocation for the goods and services not being used for a respective duration after the registration, for example, the past five years for European Community trademarks.

Thus, after the registration of the trademark, it should be continuously checked, on the one hand, whether the trademark is used for registered goods and services. In case the trademark is planned to be used for further services and goods, a further trademark also covering these additional goods should be applied for. On the other

14. EUIPO, *eSearch*, available at: https://euipo.europa.eu/eSearch/#details/trademarks/018441368 (accessed on 19 Nov. 2023).

hand, it should be vetted on a regular basis whether the trademark is used for all the registered services and goods. Ahead of the end of the duration period the use should be extended to services and goods for which the trademark has not been used so far aimed at reducing the risk of a (partly) cancellation of the trademark in relation to these goods.

[H] Enforcement

The trademark gives its holder the exclusive right to use the trademark sign for the registered goods and services. However, depending on the strength and popularity of the trademark, so-called distinctiveness, this protection also extends to similar signs and/or similar goods and services.

Signs may be deemed similar based on a phonetic similarity, visual similarity and/or similarity of the content of meaning. For the similarity of goods and services, it is *inter alia* assessed whether the consumers for the registered and the used goods and services are at least overlapping and whether the goods and services are usually produced/provided by the same companies.

The similarity is decided by a judge being tasked with assessing whether there is a risk of confusion between the registered and the used trademark for the respective (similar) goods and services from the informed customer perspective. In case the judge rules that there is, indeed, a risk of confusion, the trademark holder can be sued for a cease and desist, for damages and for providing the accounting.

[I] Examples and Practical Hints

Also, market actors in the area of blockchain and DLT are similar to traditional technical and industrial sectors active in the area of registration of trademarks for the offered products and services. A plurality of trademarks has already been registered for a variety of goods and services.

For example, the wordmark 'CORDA'[15] of the open-source blockchain platform is registered in the (goods) class 9, *inter alia* for computer programs. The wordmark 'TETHER'[16] of the Tether Operations Limited issuing the stablecoin Tether is registered for (service) class 36, *inter alia* for issuance and redemption of digital/virtual currency for currency as well as tokens of value, and (service) class 38, *inter alia* providing access to an online peer-to-peer (digital/virtual) currency or valuable token financing platform.

An example for a trademark that has been filed but has not been registered, obviously in view of oppositions by third parties is the trademark 'Libra' applied for by the Libra Association in the (good) class 9 *inter alia* for '... software for sending,

15. EUIPO, *eSearch*, available at: https://euipo.europa.eu/eSearch/#details/trademarks/W01302565 (accessed on 19 Nov. 2023).
16. EUIPO, *eSearch*, available at: https://euipo.europa.eu/eSearch/#details/trademarks/017053307 (accessed on 19 Nov. 2023).

receiving, accepting, buying, selling, storing, transmitting, trading and exchanging digital currency, virtual currency, cryptocurrency, digital and blockchain assets, digitized assets, digital tokens, crypto tokens and utility tokens …' as well as the (service) classes 35 ('… networking services for investors to conduct business, namely, financial trades and exchange of digital currency, virtual currency, cryptocurrency, digital and blockchain assets, digitized assets, digital tokens, crypto tokens and utility tokens …'), 36 ('… digital currency, virtual currency, cryptocurrency, digital and blockchain asset, digitized asset, digital token, crypto token and utility token trading services …'), 41 ('… News reporting services in the field of financial news …') and 42 ('… providing software enabling users to invest in digital currency, virtual currency, cryptocurrency, digital and blockchain assets, digitized assets, digital tokens, crypto tokens and utility tokens …'). The applicant has withdrawn the application in the course of the opposition proceedings.[17]

These few examples show that before a new product or service is put on the market, surveillance of existing trademarks in the specific area should be carried out before deciding on the sign for the product/service. A search can be carried out, for example, with the help of the database TMview[18] allowing access to the trademark registers of ample European, African, Asian, Oceanic and American patent offices via a single webpage. Interestingly, the database has been using distributed ledger technology for internal use since early 2020.[19]

Once an appropriate sign is found for the products/services, it should be protected in the relevant markets by national and/or regional trademarks. In this process, all available types of trademarks should be taken into consideration, especially also colour marks, motion marks and multimedia marks due to the nature of the offered goods and services in the area of blockchain and DLT technology.

One strategy could be that first, a trademark application is filed for the most relevant market. According to Article 4 of the Paris Convention, such a first trademark application allows the applicant or the successor in title to claim the priority of this first filing for further filings in one of the Member States of the Paris Convention within a six-month time period. When claiming the priority, the further filing 'cannot be invalidated by reason of any acts accomplished in the interval, in particular, another filing, … the use of the mark, and such acts cannot give rise to any third-party right or any right of personal possession'.[20]

Furthermore, a trademark surveillance should be installed to timely identify trademark applications that may challenge the trademark based on relative grounds in an opposition procedure aimed at keeping the area of the own trademark free of similar

17. EUIPO, *eSearch*, available at: https://euipo.europa.eu/eSearch/#details/trademarks/018083389 (accessed on 19 Nov. 2023).
18. EUIPO, *TMView*, available at: https://www.tmdn.org/tmview/#/tmview (accessed on 19 Nov. 2023).
19. https://euipo.europa.eu/ohimportal/en/web/guest/-/news/poland-and-italy-join-the-ip-register-in-blockchain-1-1?p_p_id=csnews_WAR_csnewsportlet&journalId=2121627/sv (accessed on 19 Nov. 2023).
20. Paris Convention for the Protection of Industrial Property, Art. 4(B), accessible for example under https://www.wipo.int/wipolex/en/text/288514 (accessed on 19 Nov. 2023).

trademarks. Such trademarks should be attacked in an opposition. By such a surveillance, the registers of the respective patent offices are checked to determine whether any trademark application has been filed that is close to the own trademark and/or the goods and services for which the trademark is registered. Usually, a service provider is entrusted with such a surveillance and provides on a regular basis like weekly or monthly a report on relevant trademarks, giving enough time to start legal remedies against a registration of a trademark based on the application.

§8.03 DESIGNS

[A] Definition

According to the definition of the WIPO, 'in the legal sense an industrial design constitutes the ornamental or aesthetic aspect of an article. An industrial design may consist of three dimensional features, such as the shape of an article, or two dimensional features, such as patterns, lines or color'.[21]

For example, Article 3(a) of the Design Regulation for European community designs[22] defines a design to be 'the appearance of the whole or a part of a product resulting from the features of, in particular, the lines, contours, colours, shape, texture and/or materials of the product itself and/or its ornamentation'.

[B] Duration/Territory

In comparison to trademarks, the maximum protection duration of designs is limited.

The duration is different country by country. For example, for design applications filed with the US Patent and Trademark Office (USPTO), designs for which a design application has been filed on or after 13 May 2015 have a term of fifteen years, according to 35 U.S.C., §173. According to the Manual of Patent Examining Procedure (MPEP) at the USPTO, 'However, patents issued from design applications filed before 13 May 2015 have a 14-year term from the date of grant.'[23]

In Europe, national laws also provide for national design protection. In addition, the EUIPO provides a system to protect industrial designs within the EU Member States by one single design right. This protection can be reached by a registration with the EUIPO in the form of a so-called Registered Community Design (RCD) but also in the way of an unregistered Community Design (CD). The maximum duration of a CD is, according to Article 11 of the Design Regulation,[24] three years, whereas the maximum duration of an RCD is, according to Article 12 of the Design Regulation, by the payment

21. WIPO, *Industrial Designs*, available at: https://www.wipo.int/designs/en/ (accessed on 19 Nov. 2023).
22. Council Regulation (EC) No. 6/2002, of 12 Dec. 2001, on Community designs (OJ EC No. L 3 of 5.1.2002, p. 1) amended by Council Regulation No. 1891/2006 of 18 Dec. 2006 (OJ EC No. L 386 of 29.12.2006, p. 14).
23. MPEP at the USPTO, Ninth Edition, Revision 07.2022, Chapter 1500, section 1505.
24. Council Regulation (EC), *supra* n. 21.

of renewal fees every five years to a maximum duration of twenty-five years from the date of filing.

Thus, it can be applied for design protection as national designs, regional designs, like the RCD.[25] Furthermore, the WIPO offers in a central procedure under the so-called Hague System,[26] the possibility to file a design application that can include up to 100 designs[27] covering 96 countries. Following a positive check for formal requirements of the international application, the design is registered in the International Register of the WIPO and represents a bundle of national/regional applications that are independent of each other, especially regarding examination, revocation and renewal. However, a central renewal procedure is possible. The term of protection is five years from the date of the international registration, but the international registration can be renewed 'for one or more additional terms of five years, in respect of each designated Contracting Party, up to the expiry of the total term of protection allowed by those Contracting Parties' respective laws'.[28] The maximum duration varies between ten and twenty-five years.[29]

Also, for designs, the Paris Convention provides under Article 4 for a first design application for an applicant or the successor in title to claim the priority of this first filing for further filings in one of the Member States of the Paris Convention within a six-month time period. When claiming the priority, the further filing 'cannot be invalidated by reason of any acts accomplished in the interval, in particular, another filing, (...) the putting on sale of copies of the design (...) cannot give rise to any third-party right or any right of personal possession'.[30]

Thus, an appropriate filing strategy might be to first file a design application in the core jurisdiction and use the following six months to decide where to apply for further foreign designs.

[C] Registration/Invalidity Procedures/Protection Requirements

In the following, the most important aspects of the protection requirements, as well as the registration process for an RCD at the EUIPO, will be outlined. The registration process in the respective other countries varies; however, in the Member States of the EU, the national design laws have been harmonized by Directive 98/71/EC[31] to the regulations for the RCD given in the Design Regulation.

25. EUIPO, *Designs in the European Union*, available at: https://euipo.europa.eu/ohimportal/en/designs-in-the-european-union (accessed on 19 Nov. 2023).
26. WIPO, *Hague – The International Design System*, available at: https://www.wipo.int/hague/en/ (accessed on 19 Nov. 2023).
27. WIPO, *Frequently Asked Questions: Hague System*, available at: https://www.wipo.int/hague/en/faqs.html (accessed on 19 Nov. 2023).
28. *Ibid.*
29. Declarations Made by Contracting Parties under the 1999 Act and the Common Regulations under the 1999 Act and the 1960 Act (Revised August 2023), available at: https://www.wipo.int/hague/en/declarations/.
30. Paris Convention for the Protection of Industrial Property, Art. 4(B).
31. Directive 98/71/EC of the European Parliament and of the Council of 13 Oct. 1998 on the legal protection of designs, Official Journal of the European Communities, L 289/28.

For the registration of an RCD to allow the EUIPO to carry out an examination of whether the application is directed to a subject matter being a design in accordance with the above definition (and not for example a living plant wherein the outer appearance is naturally given) and to define the scope of protection, an applicant has to file a reproduction of the design. In most cases, it comprises a plurality of views on the design and a description of the product representing the design, including, similar to trademarks, an indication of a product class. In comparison to trademarks which are categorized in the Nice classification system, designs are categorized in the so-called Locarno Class. The Locarno Classification is the international classification system for industrial designs and is administered by the Word Intellectual Property Organization (WIPO).[32]

Once the formal requirements, as well as the substantive requirements (is the application directed to a design and does the design contain an element that goes against public policy and morality[33]), have been positively examined, the design is registered.

As already mentioned before, the Design Regulation also provides protection by an unregistered community design (CD). Such a CD is generated by the first publication of the design within the EU.

Until this point of the registration procedure of the RCD and the generation of the CD respectively, the further protection requirements are not examined. For the RCD and CD to be legally valid, it has, *inter alia*, to be novel and has to have individual character according to Article 4(1) of the Design Regulation.

To be novel, the design has not been made available to the public, wherein designs shall be deemed to be identical if their features differ only in immaterial details (Article 5 of the Design Regulation). The Design Regulation, however, also allows for a so-called grace period. That means that a disclosure 'shall not be taken into consideration (...) if a design for which protection is claimed under a registered Community design has been made available to the public by the designer, his successor in title, or a third person as a result of information provided or action taken by the designer or his successor in title (...) during the 12-month period preceding the date of filing of the application or, if a priority is claimed, the date of priority'.[34]

Regarding the second requirement of individual character, it is important to notice that this does not mean that respective creativity or artistic height has to be given. According to Article 6 of the Design Regulation, 'a design shall be considered to have individual character if the overall impression it produces on the informed user differs from the overall impression produced on such a user by any design which has been made available to the public beforehand'.

The EUIPO does not assess whether the registered design fulfils these protection requirements. The EUIPO describes disputes on the legal validity as follows: 'unlike

32. WIPO, *Locarno Classification*, available at: https://www.wipo.int/classifications/locarno/en/ (accessed on 19 Nov. 2023).
33. For further details, it is referred to EUIPO, *Registration process*, available at: https://euipo.europa.eu/ohimportal/en/rcd-registration-process (accessed on 19 Nov. 2023).
34. Directive 98/71/EC, Art. 7(2).

trademarks, where disputes can arise before registration of the trademark, designs can only be challenged once registered. This challenge is called – in legal jargon – an application for a declaration of invalidity'.[35] Such an attack against the legal validity of the design can be brought forward not only in national courts, especially during infringement procedures, but also in a central procedure at the EUIPO.

In the case that neither the design owner surrenders the Community design nor the invalidity applicant withdraws the application, for example, based on a settlement, the EUIPO issues a decision that concludes the proceedings. This decision might be (partly) the rejection of the design or the rejection of the invalidity application. In case the Community design is declared invalid, it will be deemed never to have existed.

The decision on the invalidity is subject to an appeal with the court-like division of the EUIPO called Board of Appeal for the party being negatively influenced by the first instance decision. Decisions of the boards of appeal are, in turn, under specific circumstances appealable to the Court of Justice of the European Union.

[D] Enforcement

A design right, especially the RCD and CD, gives according to the summary of the WIPO the holder the 'right to prevent third parties from making, selling or importing articles bearing or embodying a design which is a copy, or substantially a copy, of the protected design, when such acts are undertaken for commercial purposes'.[36]

For the RCD and CD, this is further defined in Article 19(1) of the Design Regulation that 'the (...) use shall cover, in particular, the making, offering, putting on the market, importing, exporting or using of a product in which the design is incorporated or to which it is applied, or stocking such a product for those purposes'.

For the CD, the contested use is restricted in Article 19(2) of the Design Regulation to a use that results from copying the protected design. In this regard, 'the contested use shall not be deemed to result from copying the protected design if it results from an independent work of creation by a designer who may be reasonably thought not to be familiar with the design made available to the public by the holder'. Thus, the CD does not only differ from that RCD by way of its creation and duration but also by the given scope of protection.

The rights of the design holder can be enforced in court actions at the respective civil courts of the EU Member States.

[E] Examples and Practical Hints

The definition of industrial design on the first view does not really allow to detect a link to blockchain technology and DLT technology services, as these are usually not embodied in tangible elements.

35. EUIPO, *Disputes*, available at: https://euipo.europa.eu/ohimportal/en/disputes (accessed on 19 Nov. 2023).
36. WIPO, *supra* n. 20.

However, it is well accepted that this definition also covers virtual elements like the design of characters and font sets as well as pictograms, graphical user interfaces (GUI) and the like. As such elements are often part of products or services using blockchain technology or DLT, the protection of these elements should be taken into consideration before launching or publishing the details of the service that might be protectable as a design.

In this regard, it is important to recall that for the legal validity of the design, it has to be novel. Although a grace period is provided in some jurisdictions, the design application should be filed as soon as possible. It is not uncommon that identical or similar designs are generated by designers independently. In this case, the grace period does not take effect, and the design that has been filed after the other independently developed design has been published will not be novel anymore.

Thus, the rule should be to first file before publishing the design.

As most jurisdictions allow the filing of multiple applications combining a plurality of different designs within the same class, providing cost benefits in comparison to single applications, a plurality of designs differing to such an extent that the overall impression they produce on the informed user differs should be filed. In this way, the protection of a core design could be extended to reach broad protection.

On the other side, before developing a design, it should be checked whether similar designs are already existing that might be infringed by the planned design. A search can be carried out, for example, with the help of the database Design View[37] allowing access and search to the design registers of ample European, African, Asian, Oceanic and American patent offices via a single webpage. Like TM View also Design view is internally using distributed ledger/blockchain technology.[38]

For the user of the design, it is furthermore important that the rights in the design are transferred to the user by the designer. Generally, the designer is the initial holder of the rights, and respective agreements with the designer have to be made to transfer the rights to the user. For example, respective regulations with an employee should be made by the employer to ensure that the rights are transferred. This can be reached in most jurisdictions by respective clauses in the employment agreement.

In case the design is designed by an external designer as commission work, respective agreements should be made with the designer or the employer of the designer that the rights in the design are transferred to the user.

Of course, such agreements can be realized as smart contracts having the advantage that the respective right holder could be identified in the blockchain by any third party.

37. EUIPO, *DesignView,* available at: https://www.tmdn.org/tmdsview-web/#/dsview(accessed on 19 Nov. 2023).
38. https://euipo.europa.eu/ohimportal/en/web/guest/-/news/poland-and-italy-join-the-ip-register-in-blockchain-1-1?p_p_id=csnews_WAR_csnewsportlet&journalId=2121627/sv (accessed on 19 Nov. 2023).

§8.04 COPYRIGHT

[A] Definition

Blockchain protocols and blockchain frameworks can be used as a basis for the new blockchain developments, especially to be adapted to the respective applications.

As a software tool, the blockchain protocols are generally falling under copyright law.

The WIPO defines a Copyright (or author's right) to be '(...) a legal term used to describe the rights that creators have over their literary and artistic works. Works covered by copyright range from books, music, paintings, sculpture, and films, to computer programs, databases, advertisements, maps, and technical drawings'.[39]

For example, the German copyright law (Urheberrechtsgesetz, UrhG)[40] defines under §2(1) *inter alia* that by the UrhG 'literary works, such as [...] computer programs' are protected. This means that the author of the work enjoys a certain right. In §2(2) UrhG, it is further specified that 'only the author's own intellectual creations' are protected.

[B] Rights Given by Copyright, Duration and Practical Hints

In most jurisdictions, especially being the Member States of the Bern Convention,[41] like most of the EU states, especially Germany, the United Kingdom, France, as well as the US, Japan, and China, copyright protection is obtained automatically without special formal requirements like a registration or the like. Anyhow, some countries provide a voluntary system for copyright registration, for example, the USA.[42] Such an official system is, for example, not available in Germany so that it is important to document the date of creation and publication to have evidence in the case of later disputes on the creation or ownership situation of the copyright. In Germany, only private registers are available to ease a prove of the date of creation.

The protection under the copyright gives the author so-called moral rights, *inter alia*, the right to decide whether and how his work shall be published, communicate or describe the content of his work to the public and be identified as the author of the work. Also, the author might oppose changes to a work that could harm the creator's reputation.

39. WIPO, *Copyright*, available at: https://www.wipo.int/copyright/en/ (accessed on 19 Nov. 2023).
40. https://www.gesetze-im-internet.de/englisch_urhg/englisch_urhg.html#p0018 (accessed on 19 Nov. 2023).
41. Berne Convention for the Protection of Literary and Artistic Works of 9 Sep. 1886, completed at PARIS on 4 May 1896, revised at BERLIN on 13 Nov. 1908, completed at BERNE on 20 Mar. 1914, revised at ROME on 2 Jun. 1928, at BRUSSELS on 26 Jun. 1948, at STOCKHOLM on 14 Jul. 1967, and at PARIS on 24 Jul. 1971, and amended on 28 Sep. 1979.
42. The United States Copyright Office, available at: https://www.copyright.gov/recordation/ (accessed on 19 Nov. 2023).

Furthermore, the author is granted with the exclusive right of reproduction, of distribution and of an exhibition of the work. This means that the author can agree upon the owner of a copy of his work, how and to which extent the acts of reproduction and distribution can be realized.

As summarized by the WIPO, 'economic rights have a time limit, which can vary according to national law. In those countries which are members of the Berne Convention, the time limit should be equal to or longer than 50 years after the creator's death. Longer periods of protection may be provided at the national level'.[43]

Regarding the blockchain technology and DLT technology, relevant fields of software, such rights are usually regulated in software licence agreements between the author or the successor in the title, on the one hand, and the user of the software, on the other hand.

However, it should be kept in mind that also other works might be of relevance for applications of blockchain technology and DLT technology. For example, a manual or Financial Product Prospectus in most cases will also fall under copyright law.

Similar to design rights, it is important that the party that wants to exploit the work becomes the successor in title for the work. Thus, respective agreements with employees and external service providers should be made to ensure that the respective rights are transferred. This is, for example, important for private blockchains. Here, external software developers are engaged often, and the contracting authority should ensure that rights on the work result are transferred, too.

§8.05 OPEN SOURCE

As being software, the blockchain Protocols are developed based on these Protocols. They generally fall under the copyright law; *see* section §8.04 above. The use and exploitation rights are generally ruled by licence agreements. Like 'usual' software, open-source software is provided under the so-called open-source software licences.

Publicly available blockchain protocols like 'Ethereum', 'Hyperledger Fabrics' or 'R3 Corda' are widely applied as being suitable as a basis for the development of a Blockchain-based software solution. Under these protocols, software solutions can be developed and tested quickly and easily. However, the use of these protocols is restricted by open-source licences.

As being an open source, the protocols can be supplemented, improved, redacted or used in any other way by developers – without a licence fee being charged. In this regard, opens source software needs to be distinguished from copyright-free software. Such non-copyrighted software 'allows people to share the program and their improvements ... but it also allows ... to convert the program into proprietary software'.[44] As this proprietary application software being developed based on the copyright-free software is then not any more freely distributable due to the own developments

43. WIPO, *supra* n. 35.
44. GNU project, *What is Copyleft*, available at: https://www.gnu.org/licenses/copyleft.en.html (accessed on 19 Nov. 2023).

although being based on the non-copyrighted software the idea of making the initial software available to the general public is not be reached anymore.

Thus, open-source software is subject to copyright obligations being defined in the open-source software licence. Such open-source software licences often include restrictions and obligations that might heavily influence how the software which has been developed based on the open-source software can be used and exploited.

Some open-source licences might include a so-called copyleft obligation. This obligation might heavily influence the value and use of the own developed software as explained below. In particular, a business model might be based on the confidentiality of the details of the software to not make it possible for third parties to reproduce the software and its functionalities. Thus, in case the software has to be disclosed to the public, the complete business model might be put in question, in particular when being mainly based on the own developed software.

By the copyleft obligation, the user of the open-source software is forced to make available any edits like changes, further developments or adaptations of the open-source software created by the development of the application software. This publication of the edits has to be conducted under the same open-source licence as the basic software in the form of the protocol.

In the open-source software licences, it is furthermore defined what 'editing' means. Depending on the respective licence, 'editing' might cover the entire self-developed software. This might, for example, be the case when the newly developed software does not include code of the open-source software but only provides an interface to the open-source software.

Thus, the developer of the application software being based on or using the open-source software being subject to strict copyleft regulations is forced to make the own developed software available as an open source.

By this obligation, commercial use of the application software would not be possible anymore, and thus, the complete business model might be questioned.

Thus, it is essential that before the developing of software, further checks are initiated and carried out. For example, it should be checked whether the development of application software is based on an open-source software. The use of in particular such open-source software often includes or is subject to a licence agreement including strict obligations like copyleft obligations.

There is, however, open-source software being provided under a so-called Apache 2.0 licence.[45] The Apache 2.0 licence is described as 'Permissive Licence'.[46] This means that it does not contain a copyleft, i.e., no obligation on the part of the licensee to publishing software created using the licensed software under the Apache 2.0 licence. The Apache 2.0 licence, therefore, does not prevent the use of these blockchain protocols from creating proprietary applications.

45. Apache Software Foundation, *Apache License, Version 2.0*, available at: https://www.apache.org/licenses/LICENSE-2.0 (accessed on 19 Nov. 2023).
46. Wikipedia, *Permissive software license*, available at: https://en.wikipedia.org/wiki/Permissive_software_license (accessed on 19 Nov. 2023).

Examples of such open-source software under Apache 2.0 licence are Hyperledger Fabrics[47] and the Corda open-source platform.[48]

However, for Ethereum, one of the most commonly used protocols, it is unclear which open-source licence is used. The various components of Ethereum were published under different open-source licences, including the so-called GPLv3. This licence is also a free, copyleft licence.[49] Thus, the developing of proprietary software code for commercial use might not be possible depending on the specific components used in the application software.

Therefore, both when selecting a blockchain protocol for a proprietary development and when investing in a blockchain-related business, it must be very carefully examined which licensing regulations apply to the software used and to what extent this can 'infect' the proprietary software code.

Another problem with the use of open-source platforms could be that there are isolated open-source offers that are only sufficient for the creation of test applications. Once the test application has been further developed to go live into regular operation, the problem might arise that a chargeable 'Enterprise Version' of the open-source platform has to be used to implement essential functions, for example, with regard to IT security, which is missing in the test version. These 'Enterprise Versions' are often made available under stricter licence fee and further licence conditions.

This results in a dependency on the provider of the open-source software since a change to a different blockchain protocol might not be easily possible. Most of the protocols lack compatibility with the different blockchain protocols so that the application software might have to be newly developed to be usable with other blockchain protocols.

The same principles apply to software that is required for essential business functions irrespective of the use of blockchain technology or DLT. The long-term availability of the software with sufficient cost control must be ensured.

Thus, a check regarding open-source compliance should be carried out before the proprietary application software is planned and developed to make sure not to be bound to one-sided licence agreements or agreements, including the obligation not to use the developed software as proprietary software.

§8.06 PATENTS/UTILITY MODELS

[A] Definition/Content of Patent Application

According to the summary of the WIPO, 'a patent is an exclusive right granted for an invention, which is a product or a process that provides, in general, a new way of doing something, or offers a new technical solution to a problem'.[50]

47. Hyperledger Foundation, *FAQ*, available at: https://wiki.hyperledger.org/display/HYP/FAQ (accessed on 19 Nov. 2023).
48. Corda, *Open Source*, available at: https://www.corda.net/ (accessed on 19 Nov. 2023).
49. GNU Operating System, *GNU General Public License*, available at: https://www.gnu.org/licenses/gpl-3.0.en.html (accessed on 19 Nov. 2023).
50. WIPO, *Patents*, available at: https://www.wipo.int/patents/en (accessed on 19 Nov. 2023).

To get a patent, technical information about the invention must be disclosed to the public in a patent application. To fulfil this purpose, a European patent application and a patent, respectively, comprise the following obligatory elements:[51]

(1) a description in which:
   - the technical field to which the patent application/patent is relating;
   - the state of the art existing before;
   - the technical problems existing in the state of the art;
   - the proposed solution of these problems; and
   - examples of how this solution can be realized are described
(2) patent claims, in which the subject matter for which protection is requested (patent application) or granted (granted patent) is defined;
(3) in case it is referred to drawing in the description and/or the claims, these drawings; and
(4) an abstract describing in a limited number of words for what protection is requested/granted – the abstract does only fulfil informative purposes for evaluating if it is worth considering the whole content of the application[52] and does not have any limiting effect, in fact, does (not even) form a part of the disclosure of the patent application.

[B] Rights Provided by a Patent

A patent provides the exclusive right to the patent holder to prevent or stop others from commercially exploiting the patented invention as defined in the claims. In other words, 'patent protection means that the invention cannot be commercially made, used, distributed, imported or sold by others without the patent owner's consent'.[53]

Thus, it is important to note that a patent does not give a positive right to use but only a negative right to prohibit one party from making use of the claimed invention.

To that end, the following example gives a bit more flavour: A patent might have been granted on a car with a brake (assuming that this was not known before and thus is seen as: (i) novel, and furthermore (ii) inventive, *see* below) for a party I. A party II further develops the brake of the car in an inventive way. A patent on a car with a brake, including the further development, is awarded to party II. Now, the situation arises that party I can prohibit party II from using a car with a brake, including the further development as party II will inevitably use a car with a brake. Thus, party II, although having been awarded a patent, does not have the positive right to use the claimed subject matter of the own patent. This situation is called dependent patents. Party I is probably interested in leveraging the further development of party II.

---

51. EPO, *Art 78 EPC of 5 October 1973 as revised by the Act revising Article 63 EPC of 17 December 1991 and the Act revising the EPC of 29 November 2000*, available at: https://www.epo.org/en/legal/epc/2020/a78.html(accessed on 19 Nov. 2023).
52. EPO, Guidelines, F-II-2.1, available at: https://www.epo.org/law-practice/legal-texts/html/guidelines/e/f_ii_2_1.htm (accessed on 22 Dec. 2019).
53. WIPO, *supra* n. 46.

However, party II can prohibit party I from using further development. The situation is usually solved by a cross-licence. That means party I gives party II a licence to use a car with a brake, whereas party II gives party I the right to use further development.

[C] Territory

The patent protection can be applied for by filing national, regional or international patent applications.

A national patent application is examined by a respective national patent office, wherein the examination procedure ends with a refusal of the application or a grant of a patent given the before-described negative prohibition right.

Regional patent applications can be filed with the following regional patent offices:[54]

- European Patent Office (EPO);[55]
- African Intellectual Property Organization (OAPI);[56]
- African Regional Intellectual Property Organization (ARIPO);[57]
- Eurasian Patent Organization (EAPO);[58] and
- Patent Office of the Cooperation Council for the Arab States of the Gulf (GCC Patent office).[59]

The above offices provide a centralized search and examination procedure. The result of the examination, however, differs.

[1] European Patents/Newly Implemented European Unitary Patent

An examination at the EPO leads to a grant of a so-called European Patent. A European patent is granted based on the European patent convention (EPC).[60] All (as of November 2023) twenty-seven Member States of the EU are Member States of the EPC. In addition, the group of EPC Member States also comprise non-EU states, namely

54. WIPO, *Examination by a Regional Patent Office*, available at: https://www.wipo.int/patents/en/topics/worksharing/regional-patentoffices.html (accessed on 19 Nov. 2023).
55. European Patent Office (EPO), available at: https://www.epo.org/index.html (accessed on 19 Nov. 2023).
56. African Intellectual Property Organization (OAPI), available at: http://www.oapi.int/index.php/en/ (accessed on 19 Nov. 2023).
57. African Regional Intellectual Property Organization (ARIPO), available at: https://www.aripo.org/ (accessed on 19 Dec. 2023).
58. Eurasian Patent Organization (EAPO), available at: https://www.eapo.org/en/ (accessed on 19 Nov. 2023).
59. Patent Office of the Cooperation Council for the Arab States of the Gulf (GCC Patent office), available at: https://www.gccpo.org/DefaultEn.aspx (accessed on 19 Nov. 2023).
60. EPO, *The European Patent Convention*, available at: https://www.epo.org/law-practice/legal-texts/epc.html (accessed on 19 Nov. 2023).

Albania, Switzerland, Island, Liechtenstein, Monaco, North Macedonia, Norway, Serbia, San Marino, United Kingdom and Turkey.[61]

However, this does not mean that the patent impacts all Member States of the EU and EPC, respectively. A grant of a European patent does not lead to automatic protection in all EPC Member States. The Member States have agreed upon to accept the decision of the EPO to grant a patent and also grant a national patent. Thus, after the grant of a European Patent and probably its confirmation in an opposition procedure, the national patent offices will accept the legal validity of the patent. After the patent grant by the EPO, the national patent offices also register a national patent upon a further step of the applicant/patent holder, the so-called validation. For such validation in some Member States, translations of the claims or the complete patent need to be filed and/or in some Member States a national representative must be appointed.

Beside the EPC Member States, the European Patent might also take effect in additional states, so-called extension states[62] and validation states,[63] accordingly. Such validation states are not restricted to the European continent, but validation states are the African countries Morocco and Tunisia, and the Asian country Cambodia. A further validation agreement has been signed by the European Patent Organisation with the East European / West Asian country Georgia in 2019, the date of entry of which is not yet certain. To reach an effect in these extension and validation states during the examination procedure, respective validation and extension fees have to be paid, and after the grant, respective validation and extension steps have to be taken.

Due to these validation and extension steps, it is said that a European Patent becomes a bundle of national (independent) patents.

Thus, the designation as regional patent is generally misleading for the European Patent, except for a patent for which unitary effect is requested as explained below. Generally speaking, European patents can only be enforced and revoked in national legal procedures being directed to the validated national parts of the European Patent without any direct effect for the other parallel national parts arising from the same European Patent. Also for each of the states, separate national annuity fees have to be paid on a yearly basis to extend the duration of the patent to a maximum of up to twenty years.

Since the beginning of the establishment of the European Patent Organization (EPO), it has been its aim to provide a procedure to reach a grant of a patent having a unitary character in all EU Member States. All the initiatives failed, however, due to the discussions on the languages. Especially, Italy and Spain did not accept that their national languages would not have become additional official languages at the EPO besides German, French and English. They did not want to accept that a patent in one

61. EPO, *Member states of the European Patent Organisation*, available at: https://www.epo.org/about-us/foundation/member-states.html (accessed on 19 Nov. 2023).
62. EPO, *Extension states*, available at: https://www.epo.org/about-us/foundation/extension-states.html (accessed on 19 Nov. 2023).
63. EPO, *Validation states*, available at: https://www.epo.org/about-us/foundation/validation-states.html (accessed on 19 Nov. 2023).

of these three languages will have effect without obligatory translations into Italian and Spanish, respectively.

A solution was found when the EU decided that irrespective of a unanimity at least nine EU Member States can agree upon enhanced cooperation in the respective legal areas. The enhanced cooperation was, for example, used to find a common regulation in a part of the Member States regarding divorce right in 2008.

In 2011, the tool of enhanced cooperation was then used to bring the Unitary Patent (UP), formally called European patent with unitary character,[64] on its way. The cooperation entered into force in 2013 for twenty-five EU Member States (except Italy and Spain).[65] In 2015, Italy also joined the cooperation, but the United Kingdom left the EU and thus the enhanced cooperation so that up-to-date (as of November 2023) all EU Member States, besides Spain and the later joining Croatia, are participating in the UP.

The UP, however, only applies to the participating Member States in case the respective state has also ratified and enacted the related Agreement on a UPC[66]. This happened for 17 states, namely Austria, Belgium, Bulgaria, Denmark, Estonia, Finland, France, Germany, Italy, Latvia, Lithuania, Luxembourg, Malta, the Netherlands, Portugal, Slovenia, and Sweden (as of November 2023).[67]

The Agreement on a UPC entered into force on 1 June 2023, after the German government ratified the agreement on the UPC in February 2023 following a dismissal of a complaint against the agreement by the German constitutional court. The UPC handles as international court all questions regarding patentability and infringements of UPs as well as European bundle patents for the participating seventeen Member States. With the UPC Agreement coming into force, the rules on the UP are deployed. The patent applicant has to make additional decisions now. For European Patents granted before 1 June 2023, the applicant and owner of a new patent 'only' had to make the decision in which countries to validate the patent.

For any European Patent granted on or after 1 June 2023, now further decisions have to be made. For the states participating in the UP, the patent proprietor has to decide within one month after the grant has been published whether for these countries a unitary effect has to be established. In case this due date passes, the patent proprietor then has to decide whether within a three-month time limit after the publication of the grant separate validations in all or a part of these participating countries are wanted. For all Member States of the EPC not participating in the UP, irrespective of being an EU Member State or not, validations as known before the enactment of the UPC have to be made to secure protection in these states.

There are further specialities for a UP. For the UP, a further translation of the complete patent specification has to be filed. Furthermore, annuities have to be paid also for the UP. The annuity fee of a UP amount to the sum of national annuity fees for

64. EPO, *Unified Patent Court,* available at: https://www.epo.org/law-practice/unitary/unitary-patent.html (accessed on 19 Nov. 2023).
65. EPO, *Unitary Patent,* available at https://www.epo.org/en/applying/european/unitary/unitary-patent (accessed on 25 November 2023).
66. *Ibid.*
67. EPO, *Unitary Patent,* available at https://www.epo.org/en/applying/european/unitary/unitary-patent (accessed on 25 November 2023).

about three national parts of a European patent. Thus, the costs for a UP are significantly lower for protection in the group of 17 participating states compared to separate validations.

However, UP can be revoked in a central procedure for all states.

This will most likely open up, for example, in Germany, the possibility to have protection for an invention based on a national German patent that is litigated in front of national German courts and in parallel by virtue of an UP litigated in front of the UPC. Particularly, in Germany such a coexistence of national patents and UP as national German parts of EP patents being litigated in front of the UPC is possible.

[2] Further Regional Patents European Patents/Planned European Unitary Patent

The initial system of the European Patent Organization that a granted patent leads to a bundle of national patents in specifically designated countries is also applied for patents granted by the ARIPO. Thus, an applicant has to designate the countries of the total of twenty-two Member States (as of November 2023) in which protection is intended.[68]

To that end, the grant system of the EAPO is comparable to the EPO system when it comes to bundling patents. In a central examination procedure, a patent is granted for all seventeen Member States being a former Member State of the Soviet Union. However, the grant does not lead to a patent with unitary character. It is possible to uphold the patent in only a part of the Member States, and invalidation is also possible for single states by national courts.[69]

In contrast to the EPO, ARIPO and EAPO, a grant of a patent of the OAPI leads to unitary protection being extended to all seventeen, most of them Francophobe Member States.[70] Also, a patent granted by the GCCPO leads to a UP being valid in all six Arabic Member States.[71]

[D] Protection Requirements EPO

[1] Novelty/Grace Period

For a patent to be legally valid, the claimed subject matter has to be, *amongst others*, novel and inventive. Novelty means that there has been no publication before the filing of the application disclosing all of the claimed features to persons not being bound by

68. ARIPO, *Patents*, available at: https://www.aripo.org/ip-services/patents/ (accessed on 26 Nov. 2023).
69. EAPO, *Procedures*, available at: https://www.eapo.org/en/feature.html (accessed on 26 Nov. 2023).
70. WIPO, *African Intellectual Property Organization (OAPI)*, available at: https://www.wipo.int/export/sites/www/patent_register_portal/en/docs/oapi.pdf (accessed on 26 Nov. 2023).
71. *Gulf Cooperation Council Patent Office* available at: https://www.gccpo.org/defaultEn (accessed on 26 Nov. 2023).

confidentiality. In most countries, the absolute novelty must be given, i.e., any publication, so-called disclosure, is taken into consideration, especially written disclosure, oral disclosure, disclosure by use or in any other way, as, for example, codified in Article 54(2) EPC.[72]

However, the date until when disclosures are taken into consideration differs from jurisdiction to jurisdiction. For a European Patent and most of the national European patents, any disclosure also by the applicant until the filing date of the application is taken into consideration as long as it is not based on abuse in relation to the applicant or has occurred on specific exhibitions like world exhibitions.

In other countries, for example, the US, Russia and Japan, a so-called grace period is granted. That means that specific disclosures by the applicant or the successor in the title are not taken into consideration as long as they have taken place a specific time before the filing date of the application, in some countries six months and other countries twelve months.[73]

Although the grace period might be granted in respective jurisdictions, it is always advisable to file the patent application before the invention is disclosed to third parties, especially published. This has basically two reasons. First, it is quite often that developments are made independently of each other in parallel to solve a technical problem. In case one inventor publishes the invention, another inventor cannot rely upon the grace period for the same invention as the publication is not based on an own publication. More importantly, the first country might grant a grace period, but in other countries, a parallel foreign national patent application may not provide such a grace period. For these applications, the own publication of the applicant forms state of the art used to assess the patentability of the subject matter claimed with the application. This means that in case the claimed subject has been made publicly available before the filing date, although this was made by the applicant or based on his information, no patentability is given. The requirement of absolute novelty is then not fulfilled anymore.

[2] Priority

To comply with the novelty requirement, an applicant would generally be forced to apply for a patent simultaneously in all countries in which protection is intended. With that, it is advisable to document the filing date that is as early as possible to avoid that disclosure of the claimed subject matter takes away novelty from the claimed subject matter. This would especially mean that a plurality of patents would have to be filed in parallel without having certainty on the patentability.

72. EPO, *Art 54 EPC of 5 October 1973 as revised by the Act revising Article 63 EPC of 17 December 1991 and the Act revising the EPC of 29 November 2000*, available at: https://www.epo.org/en/legal/epc/2020/a54.html (accessed on 26 Nov. 2023).
73. WIPO, *Certain aspects of national/regional patent Laws, (4) Grace period* (status as of October 2019), available at: https://www.wipo.int/export/sites/www/scp/en/national_laws/grace_period.pdf (accessed on 26 Nov. 2023).

To avoid this procedure which is unsatisfying and expensive for the applicant, a total of 180 states signed the Paris Patent Convention back in November 2019.[74] One of the central provision of this convention is the right of priority:

> The Convention provides for the right of priority in the case of patents (and utility models where they exist), marks and industrial designs. This right means that, on the basis of a regular first application filed in one of the Contracting States, the applicant may, within a certain period of time (12 months for patents and utility models; 6 months for industrial designs and marks), apply for protection in any of the other Contracting States. These subsequent applications will be regarded as if they had been filed on the same day as the first application. In other words, they will have priority (hence the expression 'right of priority') over applications filed by others during the said period of time for the same invention, utility model, mark or industrial design.[75]

Thus, an applicant can first file a national patent application in one of the contracting states of the Paris Convention and can await the first examination report for the first application, giving a first indication for the patentability before spending costs on filings in other countries and jurisdictions. Within the priority year, the applicant can make a decision on whether and in which foreign countries or regions patent protection should be aimed for.

[3] International Patent Applications

Under some circumstances, however, also this twelve-month time limit is too short for making a final decision on the election of the countries.

This is one of the reasons why the PCT system[76] was established by the WIPO. This system allows so-called international patent applications. The description 'international' is, however, also misleading as by such applications only, a centralized search and examination procedure is carried out, not leading to a patent grant. The international patent application can be considered as a place holder for national/regional patent applications in the 157 (as of November 2023) Member States of the PCT.[77]

The international examination procedures allow the applicant to have the claimed subject matter examined by a further patent office to get a second independent opinion on the patentability of the claimed subject matter in the form of an International Preliminary Report on Patentability (IPRP) which is not binding for the PCT Member States. It means that in the IPRP, the patentability might be admitted, but the

74. WIPO, *Paris Convention for the Protection of Industrial Property*, available at: https://www.wipo.int/treaties/en/ip/paris/ (accessed on 26 Nov. 2023).
75. WIPO, *Summary of the Paris Convention for the Protection of Industrial Property*, available at: https://www.wipo.int/treaties/en/ip/paris/summary_paris.html (accessed on 22 Dec. 2019).
76. WIPO, *PCT – The International Patent System*, available at: https://www.wipo.int/pct/en/ (accessed on 26 Nov. 2023).
77. WIPO, *The PCT now has 153 Contracting States*, available at: https://www.wipo.int/pct/en/pct_contracting_states.html (accessed on 26 Nov. 2023).

national patent office does not have to grant a patent but might raise further arguments against the patentability.

Within a time limit of thirty months, for some Member States up to thirty-four months,[78] after the filing date and if the priority of an earlier application is claimed after the priority date, the applicant has to then convert the international patent application into a national/regional patent application. This process links to the entry into the national/regional phases, often making the translation of the international patent application into the national language necessary.

As the costs for the following national/regional examination/grant procedures are mainly the same as for direct filings in the respective countries/regions, it is often said that the PCT system provides some timely buffer aimed at reaching the final and cost-intensive decision when filing national patent applications. In other words, the applicant invests money to postpone the investment for the separate examination procedures at the plurality of national/regional patent offices to reach independent grants of a patent in the different countries/regions.

[4] Exclusion from Patentability

As mentioned before, patents are granted on subject matter that must fulfil a bunch of requirements. For example, European patents are granted according to Article 52(1) EPC for inventions 'provided that they are new, involve an inventive step and are susceptible of industrial application'.[79]

However, there is an important restriction to this Rule in the EPC that exists in other national European patent laws as well. According to Article 54(2) EPC, there is a list of subject matter that is not regarded as an invention. This list especially covers:

> (...)
>
> a) discoveries, scientific theories and mathematical methods;
> b) aesthetic creations;
> c) schemes, rules and methods for performing mental acts, playing games or doing business, and programs for computers;
> d) presentations of information.

The rationale for this restriction is that there is a general interest of the public that specific things do not become the subject matter of a monopoly right and that for some of the specific things, other protective rights exist, namely design rights and copyright.

Especially, the exclusions (a) and (c) are of increasing importance in relation to blockchain-related inventions. These blockchain inventions are predominantly based on mathematical methods and are mostly realized by programs for computers.

---

78. WIPO, *Time Limits for Entering National/Regional Phase under PCT Chapters I and II*, available at: https://www.wipo.int/pct/en/texts/time_limits.html (accessed on 26 Nov. 2023).
79. EPO, *Art. 52 EPC*, available at: https://www.epo.org/law-practice/legal-texts/html/epc/2016/e/ar52.html (accessed on 22 Dec. 2019).

Thus, on the first view, patent applications directed to the use of blockchain technologies as being at least partly realized as computer programs do not seem to be patentable by themselves. This is also the common opinion that software is not patentable.

This is, however, incorrect.

Article 52(2) EPC is restricted by Article 52(3) EPC, clarifying that Article 52(2) EPC 'shall exclude the patentability of the subject-matter or activities referred to therein only to the extent to which a European patent application or European patent relates to such subject-matter or activities as such'. However, the wording 'as such' should be interpreted strictly.

Thus, it is the common view that subject matter that goes beyond the program as such, for example, the source code is generally not excluded from the patentability. As outlined in the Guidelines for examination at the European Patent Office[80] under G-II-3.6,[81] 'the exclusion does not apply to computer programs having a technical character'. In other words, an abstract technical idea forming the basis for the invention might be patentable albeit being implemented in the computer. Such inventions are called computer-implemented inventions (CII).

To meet the criteria of showcasing a technical character, a computer program must produce a 'further technical effect' when running on a computer. That is a technical effect which goes beyond the 'normal' physical interactions between the program (software) and the computer (hardware) on which it is run. The normal physical effects of the execution of a program, e.g., the circulation of electrical currents in the computer, are not in themselves sufficient to confer technical character to a computer program.[82]

The principles developed for programs for the computer and CII are thus essential to assess the patentability of blockchain-related inventions as outlined in the Guidelines for Examination at the EPO F-IV-3.9.3.[83]

[5] Examples of Blockchain-Related EP Patents

To take these general principles of technical character and technical effect into account, the EPO has developed a two-step testing scheme for CII.

The first step is to check whether the claimed item is software in itself. In principle, this examination already leads to a positive result, meaning that no exclusion is given if the technical system 'computer' is included in the patent claim. For this purpose, the patent claim relates to a method executed by a computer, a data processing apparatus having means arranged to execute such a method, or a computer

80. EPO, *Guidelines for Examination in the European Patent Office* (March 2023), available at: https://www.epo.org/law-practice/legal-texts/html/guidelines/e/index.htm (accessed on 26 Nov. 2023).
81. EPO, Guidelines, G-II-3.6, available at: https://www.epo.org/law-practice/legal-texts/html/guidelines/e/g_ii_3_6.htm (accessed on 26 Nov. 2023).
82. *Ibid.*
83. EPO, Guidelines, F-IV-3.9.3, available at: https://www.epo.org/law-practice/legal-texts/html/guidelines/e/f_iv_3_9_3.htm (accessed on 26 Nov. 2023).

program (product) comprising instructions which, when the program is executed by a computer, causes the computer to execute the steps of the method. Examples for specific formulations are given in the Guidelines under F-IV-3.9–3.9.3.[84]

Like all other inventions, the claimed CII, in particular, blockchain application, must also be new and inventive.

A claimed object is new if there was no prior publication anywhere in the world showing all the features of the claimed object. Novelty, therefore, exists if the claimed application deviates from previously known applications by at least one peculiarity.

If this is the case, it must then be examined whether the application is inventive, i.e., whether it was not suggested to the skilled person on the basis of the previously known technical information.

The second step, including the assessment of the technical character of the testing scheme developed for CII, now takes effect in this test. Only technical features contributing to the technical character of an invention but features which do not contribute to the technical character of the invention cannot support the presence of an inventive step. This approach is called 'COMVIK approach'.

In Part G, Chapter II, 3.6., the Guidelines for Examination in the European Patent Office state as follows: 'for example, the control of a technical process or the control of the internal functioning of the computer itself or its interfaces as further technical effects'.[85]

The COMVIK approach is further outlined in Part G, Chapter VII, 5.4.[86] and has been confirmed and further specified in a decision of the Enlarged Board of Appeal G1/19.[87] To contribute to a technical effect, it is not sufficient that the claimed invention can theoretically use data or information of a technical system as input data. There has to be a clear link to a real technical system. The same applies to output data of the claimed invention. A theoretical influence on a technical system of the output data is not sufficient, but a concrete influence on a real technical system is necessary.

Practical examples of inventive and non-inventive CII are provided in Part G, Chapter VII, 5.4.2.[88] For example, for a method of facilitating to shop on a mobile device, it has been decided that besides the feature of using a distributed system comprising a mobile device connected to a server computer which has cache memory and is connected to a database, further features providing technical character are existing.

The claimed method also comprised the feature that an optimal shopping tour is determined by the server by accessing the cache memory in which optimal shopping tours determined for previous requests are stored, which has been novel in view of the state of the art known before. The EPO has determined this feature as to making a

84. EPO, Guidelines, F-IV-3.9 to 3.9.3., available at: https://www.epo.org/law-practice/legal-texts/html/guidelines/e/f_iv_3_9.htm (accessed on 26 Nov. 2023).
85. EPO, *supra* n. 77.
86. EPO, Guidelines, G-VII, 5.4, available at: https://www.epo.org/en/legal/guidelines-epc/2023/g_vii_5_4.html (accessed on 26 Nov. 2023).
87. https://www.epo.org/en/boards-of-appeal/decisions/g190001ex1.
88. EPO, Guidelines, G-VII, 5.4.2., available at: https://www.epo.org/law-practice/legal-texts/html/guidelines/e/g_vii_5_4_2.htm (accessed on 22 Nov. 2023).

technical contribution going beyond a business concept underlying the method. This is argued by stating that the feature does not only define the producing of an ordered list of shops to check out which one sells respective products. The additional technical contribution of this feature is seen in the technical implementation of the producing of a list. This implementation has the technical effect of enabling rapid determination of the optimal shopping tour by accessing previous requests which are stored in the cache memory.

A further example of a technical contribution, according to the stance taken by the EPO, is enlarging the user-friendliness by implementing a method of rearranging icons on a GUI.

The EPO's view of the future importance of blockchain applications and the relevance of patenting them is illustrated by the fact that the EPO devoted a full-day conference[89] exclusively to this topic.

In the recent past, the EPO has already granted patents related to Blockchain applications. For example, the following applications were considered patentable, i.e., new and inventive:

- The granted European Patent EP 3 257 191 B1[90] is directed to a procedure for controlling the visibility and/or performance of a contract. In the claimed method using an unspent output (UTXO) linked to the location of a repository where the contract is stored, it was considered inventive to use that UTXO to interpret whether the contract should be considered open or valid. The inventive step was justified by the fact that this step leads to a further technical effect: For the first time, it is possible to automatically check the conditions in the contract by means of a technical system and automatically trigger the contractual consequences of the fulfilment of the conditions.[91]
- For computer-implemented methods of verifying ownership of computer software for installation and after installation, respectively, and before running the computer software, the following, as claimed in EP 3 295 362 B1,[92] was considered inventive: The circumstance that in a licence enforcement a special use of a second public user key (PU2), a second public key (P2), a distributed hash table, and a peer-to-peer distributed ledger is provided in combination with the comparison of the keys using a transaction record stored in the ledger. From the EPO's point of view, the procedures using blockchain

89. EPO, *Event: Patenting Blockchain, Recordings*, available at: https://e-courses.epo.org/course/view.php?id=167(accessed on 26 Nov. 2023).
90. https://data.epo.org/publication-server/pdf-document?pn=3257191&ki=B1&cc=EP&pd=20180411 and https://register.epo.org/application?number=EP17708587 (accessed on 26 Nov. 2023).
91. https://register.epo.org/application?documentId=E0B6BTDK1654DSU&number=EP17708587&lng=en&npl=false (accessed on 26 Nov. 2023).
92. https://data.epo.org/publication-server/pdf-document?pn=3295362&ki=B1&cc=EP&pd=20180711 and https://register.epo.org/application?number=EP17724454 (accessed on 26 Nov. 2023).

principles should increase the security of the technical process of installing and starting the software as a further technical effect.[93]

- Inventive to a computer-implemented method for verifying the integrity of computer software, as claimed in EP 3 295 349 B1,[94] was considered to be the use of a third hash value, a fourth hash value, and metadata associated with a transaction record stored on a peer-to-peer distributed ledger. The third hash value is determined on the basis of the computer software, and the fourth hash value is determined from an entry in a distributed hash table. The verification of the integrity of the computer software is based on the comparison of the third hash value (H3) and the fourth hash value (H4). This is intended to improve the technical process of verifying the integrity of the software.[95]

Subject matter of the European Patent EP 3 095 044 B1[96] is a block mining method and a respective apparatus, wherein the method is used for mining a block in a blockchain, preferably Bitcoin. Obviously, the patent has been granted based on the following argument. By computing a plurality of mid-states, i.e., intermediate calculations leading to a final result starting from a respective unique mid-state, the technical effect is reached that an enhanced performance is provided. In particular, a reducing of computational resources, like computational time, energy consumption of the computer system and implementation efforts needed for mining a block in a blockchain is reached. The patent has been however revoked based on formal objections in the first instance decision in the course of opposition proceedings which has been appealed.

These examples show that the EPA is open to the protection of applications of blockchain principles in technical areas where these principles have not previously been used.

All the above granted patents are put under scrutiny with regard to patent EP 3 095 044 B1 which has not been challenged yet, i.e. no attacks against the legal validity through cancellation proceedings have been started.

[6] Opposition Procedure

Such opposition proceedings can be initiated according to Article 99 EPC[97] by any third party within nine months after the decision to grant a European patent is published. In this procedure, the legal validity of the patent can be challenged in front of an

93. https://register.epo.org/application?documentId=E0P1F1V73736DSU&number=EP17724454&lng=en&npl=false (accessed on 26 Dec. 2023).
94. https://data.epo.org/publication-server/pdf-document?pn=3295349&ki=B1&cc=EP&pd=20180711 and https://register.epo.org/application?number=EP17724453 (accessed on 26 Nov. 2023).
95. https://register.epo.org/application?documentId=E0P1FZPX9589DSU&number=EP17724453&lng=en&npl=false (accessed on 26 Nov. 2023).
96. https://register.epo.org/application?number=EP14864642 and https://data.epo.org/publication-server/pdf-document?pn=3095044&ki=B1&cc=EP&pd=20200923 (accessed on 26 Nov. 2023).
97. EPO, *Art. 99 EPC*, https://www.epo.org/en/legal/epc/2020/a99.html (accessed on 26 Nov. 2023).

opposition division at the EPO. The advantage of this procedure for the third party is that all validated national parts of the European patent can be attacked in only one procedure. The opposition can be based on the grounds given in Article 100 EPC,[98] namely that:

- the subject matter of the patent is not patentable as being excluded from patentability, being not novel, being not inventive or being not susceptible to industrial application;
- the European patent does not disclose the invention in a manner sufficiently clear and complete for it to be carried out by a person skilled in the art (so-called lack of sufficient disclosure/lack of enablement); and/or
- the subject matter of the European patent extends beyond the content of the application as filed (so-called inadmissible extension of disclosure).

The opposition procedure allows the general public to question the legal validity to avoid that patents which are obviously not legally valid are being upheld. Especially it allows the general public to provide the EPO with state-of-the-art information which the EPO is not aware of. This especially relates to prior public uses, publications of the claimed subject matter on fairs or by the oral description which cannot be researched by the EPO.

The decision of the opposition division to uphold the granted patent in amended form or to revoke the patent is, according to Article 106 EPC,[99] subject to legal remedy at the Board of appeal of the EPO. Such an appeal has to be filed within a time period of two months after the written decision of the opposition board has been forwarded according to Article 108 EPC.[100] Once the opposition procedure, including a possible appeal, has led to a confirmation of the EP at least in amended form, the national parts of the EP can only be attacked in national revocation procedures independent of each other.

[7] Enablement

The before mentioned ground of revocation of a sufficient disclosure/enablement is based on the requirement of Article 83 EPC[101] that 'the European patent application shall disclose the invention in a manner sufficiently clear and complete for it to be carried out by a person skilled in the art'.

98. EPO, *Art. 100 EPC,* https://www.epo.org/en/legal/epc/2020/a100.html(accessed 26 Nov. 2023).
99. EPO, *Art. 106 EPC,* available at: https://www.epo.org/en/legal/epc/2020/a106.html(accessed on 26 Nov. 2023).
100. EPO, *Art. 108 EPC,* available at: https://www.epo.org/en/legal/epc/2020/a108.html(accessed on 26 Nov. 2023).
101. EPO, *Art. 83 EPC,* available at: https://www.epo.org/en/legal/epc/2020/a83.html(accessed on 26 Nov. 2023).

To fulfil this requirement, it is necessary to provide a detailed description of at least one way of carrying out the invention according to the Guidelines.[102] In the jurisdiction of the EPO,[103] this requirement was further specified such that 'the application must contain, in addition to the examples, sufficient information to allow the person skilled in the art, using his common general knowledge, to perform the invention over the whole area claimed without undue burden and without needing inventive skill'.[104] In this regard, the interpretation of the features in the claim has to be carried out such that 'the skilled person, when considering a claim, should rule out interpretations which are illogical or which do not make technical sense. He should try, with synthetic propensity, i.e. building up rather than tearing down, to arrive at an interpretation of the claim which is technically sensible and takes into account the whole disclosure of the patent. The patent must be construed by a mind willing to understand, not a mind desirous of misunderstanding'.[105,106]

To fulfil these requirements is often problematic in the field of blockchain applications. It is necessary to avoid the description of black boxes for which it is only described – what is the input in the box and what is the output of the box. It is necessary to describe explicitly how the input is processed and in what way to arrive at the described output.

This might cause problems, on the one hand, with regard to the possibility to describe in a general technical description of the internal processes without unnecessarily restricting the claimed subject matter to specific embodiments. For CII, it is necessary to describe the elements used in the application not only in terms of structure but also in terms of function.

Describing such functions, however, must be done in such a way that the features in the claim lead to a scope of protection that is as broad as possible but, on the other hand, still allows the person skilled in the art to carry out the invention over the complete claimed range.

A further limiting aspect is that the patent application is published at a predefined time after the application or priority date. In general, a patent is an agreement between the general public and the inventor. The general public is interested in getting information on the invention to further develop the existing technology. However, the inventor is interested in getting a monopoly right to use the invention, i.e., that somebody else is not allowed to use or copy the claimed technology.

Both these interests have to be balanced with respect to each other. The legal solution is that the inventor gets a monopoly right in case it turns out that the invention is patentable, i.e., novel, inventive and susceptible to industrial application. However,

102. EPO, Guidelines, F-III-1, available at: https://www.epo.org/law-practice/legal-texts/html/guidelines/e/f_iii_1.htm (accessed on 26 Nov. 2023).
103. T727/95, available at: https://www.epo.org/law-practice/case-law-appeals/recent/t950727ex1.html (accessed on 26 Nov. 2023).
104. EPO, *supra* n. 95.
105. EPO, Case Law of the Boards of Appeal, II. A. 6.1., available at: https://www.epo.org/en/legal/case-law/2022/clr_ii_a_6_1.html(accessed on 26 Nov. 2023).
106. T190/99, available at: https://www.epo.org/law-practice/case-law-appeals/recent/t990190eu1.html (accessed on 26 Nov. 2023).

the interests of the public are addressed by the invention being published after a predefined time, in most jurisdictions, after eighteen months. This allows the general public to get knowledge of the invention and to use it as a basis for further developments and inventions. The delay in the publication is based on the idea of giving the inventor a timely advantage in comparison to the general public for further developments.

For some cases, it might be more advantageous for the inventor to not file the application and thus publish the invention to such an extent that it can be easily reproduced by third parties. Thus, it might be worthwhile to not file a patent application but to handle the invention and the internal functionality as a Trade Secret; *see* section §8.09 below.

A Trade Secret should especially be taken into consideration in case the invention:

- cannot be reversed engineered, i.e., it is not possible to easily extract from the marketed product/service the invention;
- is characterized by rapid development, i.e., the invention will be obsolete when the grant of the patent takes place;
- is such that the independent development is highly challenging; and/or
- cannot be described without extreme efforts.

A strategy might be to try to only include limited information in the application to fulfil the enablement requirement and to handle core features as Trade Secrets, aimed at not giving up a technical advantage compared to competitors.

[8] Invalidity Proceedings at National Courts/UPC for EP Patents and Double Patenting

After the expiration of the opposition term or after the completion of an opposition procedure wherein the opposed patent is at least partly upheld, it is possible to initiate invalidation procedures. Such invalidation procedures are possible not only during the lifetime of a patent but also after its expiration. The reason is that a patent owner can also claim damages for the past after the expiration of a patent as long as the claims are not time-barred. For the potential infringer, it has to be possible to defend against an infringement claim by bringing forward the argument of a lack of legal validity of a patent. To start such a invalidation procedure after the expiration of a patent, it is necessary to provide arguments for a legal interest, for example, ongoing infringement negotiations or pending infringement proceedings. Whether an invalidation procedure for a national part of a bundle EP patent can be initiated already during the opposition term or during the pendency of an opposition procedure at the respective patent office, for example, the European Patent Office depends on the national law of the respective country.

For example, in Germany, such a nullity action against a national part of a European Patent or a national German patent is only possible after the expiration of the opposition term at the EPO and the GPTO, respectively. Unlike Germany, in the United Kingdom, a parallel invalidation procedure is possible.

With the introduction of the patent with unitary effect, the situation has been extended by further options.

Already during the opposition term or a pending opposition an invalidation procedure against the patent with unitary effect can be initiated at the UPC. This also applies to European bundle patents that fall under the jurisdiction of the UPC where such an 'early' invalidation procedure with effect for all participating Member States is possible. Only in the case the bundle patent is opted out from the jurisdiction of the UPC the situation differs from the above scenario as a national German nullity action can only be initiated after the expiration of the opposition term or the closing of an opposition procedure.

The introduction of the European patent with unitary effect has a further impact on national regulations. For example, in Germany, it is not possible to have a national German patent and a German national part of European bundle having the same scope of protection. The German national patent loses its effect as long as it has the same scope of protection as the German national part of a parallel European bundle patent.

This does not apply to European patents with unitary effect. The European patent with unitary effect co-exists with a national German patent also for an overlapping scope of protection.

[E] Protection Requirements USPTO: Examples of Blockchain-Related US Patents

The general principles explained before for the patentability at the EPO are also applicable to other jurisdictions, however, with respective differences in procedural and substantive aspects.

In the following, the handling of blockchain-related inventions at the USPTO will be summarized shortly.

General differences between the European and US grant procedures are, for example, summarized in Annexe 8 of 'Das US-Patent'.[107] Since the implementation of the America Invents Act in 2011, also the US patent system knows a revocation procedure in the form of the Post Grant Review procedure having similarities to the European Opposition procedure. This procedure is now handled by the Patent Trial and Appeal Board (PTAB) of the USPTO. The PTAB also handles an invalidation procedure similar to the German nullification procedure and the planned nullification procedure at the UPC. This procedure is called Inter Partes Review procedure.

Under the US law (35 U.S.C. 101),[108] generally, 'whoever invents or discovers any new and useful process, machine, manufacture, or composition of matter, or any new and useful improvement thereof may obtain a patent therefor ...'.

107. Mayer, R., Butler, J., Molnia, D., *Das US-Patent: Erwirkung und Durchsetzung unter besonderer Berücksichtigung der Rechtsprechung*, Annex 8 (5th ed. 2017).

108. USPTO, *35 U.S.C. 101*, available at: https://www.uspto.gov/web/offices/pac/mpep/mpep-9015-appx-l.html#d0e302376 (accessed on 2 Dec. 2023).

Similar to the EPC, the US law provides exceptions from the patentability.

In the Manual of Patent Examining Procedure (MPEP),[109] the so-called judicial exceptions are as follows:

- abstract ideas;
- laws of nature; and
- natural phenomena (including products of nature).

These general terms have been specified by the USPTO in view of the recent case law:[110,111]

Like the EPO, the USPTO applies a two-step test. In the first step (step 1: statutory categories), it is analysed whether the claim is directed to a machine, manufacture, or composition of matter. If so, step 2 applies in which one has to assess, in a first part step (step 2A), whether the claim is directed to a judicial exception. If this is not the case, the eligibility test is finalized with a positive result so that the further patentability requirements are checked.

In case step 2A leads to the result that the claim is directed to a judicial exception, especially an abstract idea, in step 2B whether the claim recites additional elements that amount to significantly more than a judicial exception.

In 2019, it was clarified that step 2A had to be divided into two subsections. The first subsection still comprised the assessment of whether the claim recited an abstract idea, a law of nature or a natural phenomenon. In the added second subsection, one has to vet whether the judicial exception is integrated into a practical application. In case such a practical application can be identified in the claims and the specification, the claim is not directed to such a judicial exception per se.

Abstract ideas are seen in mathematical concepts (mathematical relationships, mathematical formulas or equations and mathematical calculations), mental processes (concepts performed in the human mind, including an observation, evaluation, judgment, opinion) and certain methods of organizing human activity like fundamental economic principles or practices including hedging, insurance, mitigating risk, commercial or legal interactions including agreements in the form of contracts; legal obligations; advertising, marketing or sales activities or behaviours, business relations or managing personal behaviour or relationships or interactions between people including social activities, teaching, and following rules or instructions. Further details

109. USPTO, *Manual of Patent Examining Procedure (MPEP)* (9th ed., revision July 2022, published February 2023), https://www.uspto.gov/web/offices/pac/mpep/index.html (accessed on 2 Dec. 2023).
110. Federal Register, *2019 Revised Patent Subject Matter Eligibility Guidance* (vol. 84, No. 4, 7 Jan. 2019), available at: https://www.govinfo.gov/content/pkg/FR-2019-01-07/pdf/2018-28282.pdf (accessed on 2 Dec. 2023).
111. USPTO, *2019 Revised Patent Subject Matter Eligibility Guidance – Advanced Module* (January 2019), available at: https://www.uspto.gov/sites/default/files/documents/2019peg_advanced_module_05mar2019.pptx (accessed on 2 Dec. 2023).

on these specific abstract ideas have been issued by the USPTO in the October 2019 Patent Eligibility Guidance Update.[112]

In the October 2019 Guidance update, it is outlined how to assess the integration into a practical application by improving the functioning of a computer:

> In short, first the specification should be evaluated to determine if the disclosure provides sufficient details such that one of ordinary skill in the art would recognize the claimed invention as providing an improvement. The specification need not explicitly set forth the improvement, but it must describe the invention such that the improvement would be apparent to one of ordinary skill in the art. ... Second, if the specification sets forth an improvement in technology, the claim must be evaluated to ensure that the claim itself reflects the disclosed improvement. That is, the claim includes the components or steps of the invention that provide the improvement described in the specification. The claim itself does not need to explicitly recite the improvement described in the specification ... [T]he 'improvements' analysis in Step 2A determines whether the claim pertains to an improvement to the functioning of a computer ... without reference to what is well understood, routine, conventional activity. That is, the claimed invention may integrate the judicial exception into a practical application by demonstrating that it improves the relevant existing technology although it may not be an improvement over well understood, routine, conventional activity.

In particular, in the area of autonomous vehicles, a plurality of use cases for blockchain applications other than financial applications and documentation applications like distribution chains exist.

An example of a practical application for the use of a blockchain for privatizing data to be used in the control of autonomous vehicles is US 10249194 B2. It claims a method, apparatus, and computer program product for assessing one or more features of drivers within a threshold distance of a self-driving vehicle which has sensors to monitor driving conditions on a travel route within the threshold distance, predicting the behaviour of one or more vehicles within the threshold distance based on the assessment of those features, and utilizing the predicted behaviour for the self-driving vehicle to drive on the travel route. It is proposed that the information regarding other drivers is stored, privatized and utilized using a blockchain system.

Other applications for which patent protection is applied are, for instance, automatically distributed electric power systems and computation systems for controlling such power systems. For example, in US 2018299852 A1, it is proposed to use blockchain technology in the peer-to-peer settlement for participation in energy and for energy consumption in distributed networks.

112. USPTO, *October 2019 Update: Subject Matter Eligibility*, available at: https://www.uspto.gov/sites/default/files/documents/peg_oct_2019_update.pdf (accessed on 2 Dec. 2023).

[F] Practical Hints Protection by Patents

[1] Strategic Considerations

In summary, patentability offers opportunities for innovative companies developing new applications for blockchain technologies to have another tool to distinguish from competitors. Thus, not only the protection of the special implementation of the application in the form of software is available to these companies. Rather, the abstract ideas on which these applications are based can also be protected with a much larger scope of protection.

That can strengthen the market position. Patents can especially be used to prohibit third parties to copy the claimed subject matter. But patents might fulfil much more functions.

An (additional) patent that does not cover the specific solution the applicant/patent proprietor is using but the patent covers that alternative solutions of the used technology might be filed and granted. Although the claimed subject matter of such a blocking patent is not used by the patent proprietor, it might on the first view be seen as 'dead capital'. But the blocking patent hinders competitors from using alternative solutions of the solution used by the applicant. Thus, neighbouring technological fields of the used solution are also blocked so that all these fields are reserved for the patent proprietor.

Especially such blocking patent can be used to, last but not least, generate licensing revenues by licensing the technology. In such licence agreements, it can then also be defined that further developments have to be filed together, allowing the licensor to also participate in such further developments.

For the drafting of patent applications, it is, however, important to make the link from the abstract blockchain-based algorithm or mathematical method to the technical applications to overcome the eligibility checks and inventiveness checks, especially at the USPTO and the EPO. It is important to show what effect the application of the algorithm to a technical system has to fulfil a technical purpose and to solve a technical problem. All these effects and advantages are preferably already included in the initially filed application documents to be used during the examination procedure to support the arguments for eligibility and inventiveness. However, this detailed description will also disclose significant know-how that will then become available for competitors.

Furthermore, the European Patent with unitary effect (UP) offers further strategic possibilities, in particular parallel protection by national patents and patent with unitary effect. As long as the possibility of an opt-out from the jurisdiction of the Unitary Patent Court (UPC) is given, at least until May 2030, possibly until May 2037, a parallel protection by a parent patent and a divisional patent is possible.

These two patents have to protect slightly different subject matter. The reason for this is that in most jurisdictions a double patenting is not allowed. That means that an applicant can only get one patent for the identical subject matter. However, according to the jurisdiction of the EPO, a slightly different wording is accepted to not see a double patenting although the patents overlap mostly.

This situation of two parallel patents can be used to establish the situation that one patent is litigated in front of the UPC in the form of a bundle patent that is not opted out from the jurisdiction of the UPS or a UP whereas the other patent is one under dispute at national courts. Thus cherry picking becomes possible. In particular, the national court would not be bound by the decision of the UPC and vice versa as two (slightly) different patents are disputed.

The protection by a UP has the further advantage that in most participating Member States a double patenting by a national patent in parallel to the UP is allowed, also in case the granted claims of the patents are identical in their wording. This provides the second option to have two (nearly) identical patents to be litigated both at the UPC and the national court, respectively.

Thus, important new developments can be protected twice in the participating Member States.

It is important to mention that the jurisdiction on the UP is with the UPC, both regarding infringement and invalidity, whereas the jurisdiction for national patents is with the national courts. Also, this allows to use the strengths and weaknesses of both court systems (UPC and national courts) for the own advantage. For example, the UPC and national courts apply different interpretations of the law for very important aspects. For example, often the questions are discussed in court, whether by an amendment made to the claims of a patent application during the examination procedure new technical information has been added. Thus, different interpretations for assessing whether a patent is inadmissibly extended, in particular what is seen as new technological information, might become decisive. For example, one court might see that the skilled person reads respective features between the lines, like some national courts, whereas the other court is of the opinion that the skilled person sticks to the literal meaning of a feature.

Another important aspect is whether a claimed subject matter is inventive. The courts apply a different standard, for example, whether a skilled person: (i) would take an alternative feature into consideration or (ii) would take a technical teaching in another technical area into consideration.

To that end, already a number of basic applications have already been registered or even protected, especially in Europe and the USA.

[2] Observation/Surveillance of Third-Party Rights

However, the area should also be closely monitored for patents applied for, patents expected to be granted and patents granted with the purpose of minimizing own risks by the infringement of protective rights of third parties. In Germany, for example, every business has an obligation to observe the market in this regard to determine whether the IP rights of third parties are infringed by its own activities. The excuse 'I knew nothing about this patent' does not matter.

Market players have to prepare themselves for not being trapped in the blockchain space, which some observers have already forecasted.[113][114] In such patent disputes, it has already proved to be very helpful in the past to be able to offer one's own IP rights as a give and take, for example, for cross-licensing issues.

In particular, US-based JPMorgan Chase & Co. was sued by Lighthouse Consulting Group, LLC at the Texas Eastern District Court for infringing of the patent FinTec patents US 8,590,940 and US 7,950,698[115] being directed to Image Capture Systems for Checks. The patent dispute has been pending since 2019. The Lighthouse Consulting Group, LLC is described as a so-called NPE (non-practising entity).[116]

The business model of such NPEs, also referred to as patent trolls, is to generate income by forcing third parties to license own, often only for this purpose acquired, patents necessary for the third party to continue its business.

Often the licence agreements are enforced by threat of legal actions or by actually enforcing the patents against the third party. NPEs mostly do not manufacture products or supply services based on the patents in question. In comparison to patent-holding companies that license their patented technologies on reasonable terms in advance, NPEs attempt to enforce patent rights against infringers far beyond the patent's actual value when the actual infringer is allegedly using the patented technology already for a longer time.[117]

Furthermore, the monitoring of patent documents offers the possibility to use the preparatory work of others. As mentioned before, patent applications are published after a certain time after their filing, in most jurisdictions, eighteen months. This means that existing developments do not have to be carried out again, and it is easier to carry out further developments and improvements based on existing developments as described in such patent application publications.

[3] Transfer of Rights

Furthermore, it is very important that the employer ensures that all rights on the invention are transferred/assigned to the employer from the inventors.

Generally, only the inventors are entitled to file a patent application. For the employer to be entitled to file a patent application in the own name and to hold the rights on the invention, it is necessary that an agreement with the inventors is found. Such an agreement is important for external inventors but also for employee inventors.

113. O'Neal, S., *Is Blockchain about to Become a Patent War Battleground?* (Cointelegraph, July 2018), available at: https://cointelegraph.com/news/is-blockchain-about-to-become-a-patent-war-battleground (accessed on 2 Dec. 2023).
114. Joseph B. Evans, J.D., 'Blockchain's Incumbent Patent War: a Rite of Passage' https://www.expertinstitute.com/resources/insights/blockchains-incumbent-patent-war-rite-passage/ (accessed on 2 Dec. 2023).
115. Case 2:19-cv-00283 – *Lighthouse Consulting Group, LLC et al. v. J.P. Morgan Chase & CO. et al.* (represented by Jones Day, Chicago); Texas Eastern District Court.
116. https://www.unifiedpatents.com/insights/2019/12/16/lighthouse-check-depositing-patent-challenged-as-likely-invalid (accessed on 11 Dec. 2023).
117. Patentlyo, *Chief Judge Rader: Improving Patent Litigation* (27 Sep. 2011), available at: https://patentlyo.com/patent/2011/09/rader-patent-litigation.html (accessed on 3 Dec. 2023).

In this regard, national regulations heavily differ from each other. In some countries, the employee inventor is obliged to transfer all rights to the employer for no or only marginal remuneration.

Such a transfer can be agreed upon in some jurisdictions already in the employment contract upfront to the invention. In other jurisdictions, very strict rules come into play. For each invention, a separate agreement between the employee inventor and the employer has to be reached.

[a] German Act on Employee Inventions

An example of comparable strict and formalistic regulations to handle the transfer of rights from employee inventors to employers is the German Act on Employee Inventions (Gesetz über Arbeitnehmererfindungen, ArbnErfG).[118]

This Act prescribes a defined way of transferring IP rights, defining a remuneration to be paid to the employee inventor on top of his salary.

The Act codifies that the employee inventor is obliged to disclose further development that might be protectable under patent or utility model law to the employer without delay (§2 and §5 ArbnErfG). This covers any potential invention that is made by the employee during the duration of the employment (service invention, §4(2) ArbnErfG), irrespective of whether the development is made during the work time, leisure time or holiday. Further, developments that are not connected to the work of the employee (free invention, §4(3) ArbnErfG) must be reported to the employer so that the employer can assess whether the development is related to the field of activity of the employer. The employee is obliged to treat the development confidentially provided it does not become free (§24(2) ArbnErfG). 'Becoming free' means that the technical teaching is given to the public by the employer so that it becomes freely usable for any third party.

Once the development has been disclosed to the employer, and the disclosure does include the necessary information, the employer has a four-month time limit to decide whether the invention is claimed or is given free to the employee (§6 ArbnErfG). In the last case, the employer might reserve a right to use the invention for an adequate royalty fee.

In case the invention is claimed, all rights are transferred to the employer, but the employer also has different duties, especially:

- a patent/utility model application has to be filed in case the invention will not be handled as a Trade Secret (*see* below) (§13(1) ArbnErfG);
- a remuneration in addition to the salary has to be paid (§9 ArbnErfG);

118. Federal German Ministry of Justice and Consumer Protection, Gesetz über Arbeitnehmererfindungen in der im Bundesgesetzblatt Teil III, Gliederungsnummer 422-1, veröffentlichten bereinigten Fassung, das zuletzt durch Artikel 7 des Gesetzes vom 31. Juli 2009 (BGBl. I S. 2521) geändert worden ist available at: https://www.gesetze-im-internet.de/arbnerfg/ArbnErfG.pdf (accessed on 3 Dec. 2023).

- in case the employer does not want to extend the application to foreign countries, such foreign filings have to be timely offered to the employee inventor (§14 ArbnErfG);
- in case the employer does not want to prosecute further the application or does not want to uphold a granted patent/registered utility model, it has to be offered to the employee (§16 ArbnErfG).

As the impacts of not fulfilling these obligations and in case one of the employer or employee does not comply with these obligations, the other party can claim damages, it is important to build up a disclosure system for employee inventions/developments within a company. For example, the publication of the development by the employee before it becomes free can hinder the protection of the development by a patent or utility model. Due to the missing monopoly right, the employer might face a severe economic disadvantage. Vice versa, the employee inventor might have marketed the development in other foreign countries in which the employer is not interested in and might have generated extensive licence revenues.

It is possible for the employer to pay the employee inventor a lump sum aimed at mitigating any risks as outlined before. It is highly recommended to do so to avoid claims, in particular.

Furthermore, the remuneration might be paid in the form of lump sum payments instead of payments based on a licence analogy, as suggested in the guidelines for the remuneration of employee inventions.[119] Such licence analogy payments lead to a high administrative effort, and furthermore, the books have to be opened for the employee to enable him to check the correctness of the payments.

All these payments and agreements should be made separately for each invention. A pre-arrangement of a transfer of the rights or the pre-determination of a remuneration amount in an employment agreement in advance is not allowed under the Act (§22 ArbnErfG).

Further, Trade Secrets as discussed later fall under the Act so that its regulations have to be adhered to with the purpose of ensuring that all rights are transferred to the employer and avoiding any claims raised by the inventor regarding the transfer of a patent or patent application as a right holder, and finally, avoiding any employee claims for remuneration.

[G] Utility Models

[1] Background

As the blockchain technology field has been developing rapidly over the recent years, in some cases, protection by patents might take too long to be effectively usable against competitors.

---

119. Richtlinien für die Vergütung von Arbeitnehmererfindungen im privaten Dienst vom 20. Juli 1959, Beilage zum Bundesanzeiger Nr. 156 vom 18. August 1959, geändert durch die Richtlinie vom 1. September 1983 (Bundesanzeiger Nr. 169, S. 9994), available at: https://www.dpma.de/docs/dpma/richtlinienfuerdieverguetungvonarbeitnehmererfindungen.pdf (accessed on 2 Dec. 2023).

According to the 'EPO Quality Report 2018',[120] it took the EPO, for example, in 2018 in the middle 4.4 months to establish a search report (*see* page 27 of the report) and another 22.3 months to finalize the examination procedure (*see* page 34 of the report). These timelines remained nearly unchanged, as in 2022 it has been 4.9 months for the establishment of the search report and additional 24.3 months to finalize the examination procedure.[121] Due to the timelines starting with requesting the examination (six months after the publication of the search report, that is, in most cases taking place with the publication of the application eighteen months after the filing of the application) and the timelines for responding to an intention to grant of the EPO by the applicant of four months and the time it takes until the grant of the patent is published (around four–six weeks), it might take three–four years from the filing date until the publication of the grant of the patent being necessary to enforce the patent.

According to the 'Data Visualization Center of the USPTO',[122] the timelines at the USPTO are about twenty-one months from the filing of the application until the issue of a first official action and about 25 months until the decision to grant or abandon as of December 2023. This time does not include, however, often mandatory requests for continued examinations (RCE) after the USPTO issues a final official action. With regard to the RCE procedure, the grant is delayed for an additional period of around three years until the USPTO comes to a conclusion.

To provide a way to obtain a protective right which is enforceable and which encompasses technical aspects of new development in some jurisdictions, the protection of abstract technical ideas is possible by way of a so-called utility model. A list of countries providing this protective right is available at the webpage of the WIPO.[123]

[2] Registration Procedure: Branching Off

The regulations on these utility models have not been harmonized between the countries so far. For instance, the grant procedure, the maximum duration and also the protectable subject matter differ from country to country, to name only some differences.

This means that in some countries, utility models are registered after passing only a formal examination, i.e., without an examination for novelty and inventiveness, such as in Germany, whereas in other countries, an examination for patentability is carried out, such as in China. The omission of the examination of a substance makes the

120. EPO, *EPO Quality Report 2018*, available at: http://documents.epo.org/projects/babylon/eponet.nsf/0/79B3608B5B4D3F71C125842D0040675A/$FILE/quality_report_2018_en.pdf (accessed on 11 Dec. 2023).
121. EPO, *EPO Quality Report 2022*, pages 39 and 47, respectively, available at: https://link.epo.org/web/general/annual-review-2022/en-quality-report-2022.pdf.
122. USPTO, *Data Visualisation Center*, available at: https://www.uspto.gov/dashboard/patents/ (accessed on 11 Dec. 2023).
123. WIPO, *Where can Utility Models be Acquired?*, available at: https://www.wipo.int/patents/en/topics/utility_models.html (accessed on 11 Dec. 2023).

registration process cheaper and also faster. For example, it is possible to reach a registration of a utility model within less than three weeks.[124]

This makes the utility model a very useful instrument for enforcing IP rights against infringers on fairs or the like or to protect intermediate development steps in fast-moving technical areas.

Especially, some jurisdictions allow to branch off utility models from pending patent applications. 'Branching off' means that the patent application is handled as an application for a utility model that has been filed at the same day. The applicant is thus put into the situation that he has two parallel applications, one for a patent and one for a utility model, although having initially only filed an application for a patent. The possibility of branching of a utility model is not restricted to the one-year priority term but can be made within ten years after the filing date of the patent application.

It has to be emphasized that the other way around, i.e., using a utility model application as the basis for a parallel patent application, is only possible within the one-year priority term.

The basis for a branched-off utility model does not have to be necessarily a national patent application for this country but could also be regional or international patent applications with potential impact on the respective country.

The German law on utility models (§ 5 Gebrauchsmustergesetz[125]) requires only an application with potential impact on Germany. Such a national application can be not only a national patent application filed with the German Patent and Trademark Office but also a European patent application designating Germany or an international patent application designating Germany directly or via a designation of the European Patent Office.

Such a branch-off might be helpful in the case a patent office has already affirmed the patentability of a subject matter during the examination procedure regarding a patent application, but due to different reasons, the related decision has not been issued yet and shall take longer to be issued. In such a case, a parallel utility model can be registered in a short term and can then be enforced against infringers that use the technology claimed in the patent application.

[3] Protection Requirements/Duration

The requirements for the legal validity of utility models differ. In all countries, the novelty of the claimed subject matter of the utility model has to be given, often combined with a grace period (unlike utility patents). This means that a publication that has been made by the applicant within a specific time, for example, six months in Germany, before the filing/priority date of the utility model is not taken into consideration when assessing the novelty and inventiveness. Also, in some jurisdictions, the

124. https://register.dpma.de/DPMAregister/pat/register?AKZ = 2020190059865&CURSOR = 14 (accessed on 11 Dec. 2023).
125. Article 5 GebrMG; Gebrauchsmustergesetz published on 28 Aug. 1986 (BGBl. I S. 1455), amended by Art. 3 on 10 Aug. 2021 (BGBl. I S. 3490), available at: https://www.gesetze-im-internet.de/gebrmg/__5.html (accessed on 11 Dec. 2023).

state of the art does not comprise all ways of publication; for example, prior public uses might not be factored in under specific circumstances. Further, in some jurisdictions, the requirements for being inventive are lower for a utility model than for a patent.

To that end, the 'maximum duration differs from country to country usually six to fifteen years'.[126] For example, the maximum duration is ten years in Germany according to §23(1) GebrMG,[127] six years in France (for a so-called Utility certificate) with an extension to also ten years since 11 January 2020, and seven years for a Greek utility model certificate.[128]

[4] Protectable Subject Matter

In Germany, a utility model can only be registered for devices as methods are excluded from the protection according to § 2 No. 3 GebrMG.[129] However, a coexistence between patents and utility models for the same claimed subject matter is possible, whereas, for example, in France also methods are protectable by a utility model and, unlike Germany, a coexistence between patents and utility models is not permissible. Moreover, in some countries, the protection as a utility model is restricted to specific technical fields or respective technical fields are excluded from the protection by a utility model.

[5] Summary of Pros and Cons of Utility Models

Thus, generally, utility models provide the advantages of:

- being less expensive than patents;
- being registered/granted and thus enforceable in most jurisdictions faster and in a less complex procedure;
- protection parallel to patents in some jurisdictions, especially during the examination procedure of a parallel patent application; and
- protection requirements that are less stringent in some countries.

However, utility models provide:

- less legal certainty in case of not being examined;
- shorter term of duration compared to patents;
- in some jurisdictions, protection only for restricted subject matter, like only devices, or only for specific technical fields.

126. WIPO, *Utility models*, available at: https://www.wipo.int/patents/en/topics/utility_models.html (accessed on 11 Dec. 2023).
127. Article 23 GebrMG, available at: https://www.gesetze-im-internet.de/gebrmg/__23.html (accessed on 11 Dec. 2023).
128. The Hellenic Industrial Property Organisation, *Patents and Utility Models*, available at: https://www.obi.gr/OBI/Default.aspx?tabid=266 (accessed on 11 Dec. 2023).
129. Article 2 GebrMG, available at: https://www.gesetze-im-internet.de/gebrmg/__2.html (accessed on 11 Dec. 2023).

However, the disadvantage for the applicant of legal uncertainty might, in turn, be an advantage against competitors. Especially where patent applications have not been published yet in parallel, the competitors cannot rely upon search and examination results of this patent application in comparison to the applicant of the utility model. Also, in case no (parallel) search has been carried out for the subject matter of the utility model, the third party has to invest time and efforts in the analysis of the legal validity of the utility model before having certainty on its (partial) legal invalidity before being sure to be allowed to use the claimed subject matter.

Thus, for each new development, it might be worthwhile to check for protection of the new development, especially in parallel to a patent application, by a utility model. This applies in particular to blockchain applications being related to fast-changing technical areas where you may capitalize on a fast-registered protective right. Especially, a competitor copying the protectable new development could be directly attacked, and a cease-and-desist order could be requested. In contrast, in case of a published but not yet granted patent application, only an adequate compensation could be reached retroactively, but the competitor can only be stopped by a cease-and-desist order after the grant of the patent.

A utility model allows for filing a utility model application while simultaneously requesting a search for a relevant state of the art. Then within six–eight months, the search report will provide more certainty on which aspects of the new development might be protectable, or in other words, which parts of the utility model might be legally valid. At this point in time, the utility might be already registered so that the legally valid parts might be enforced straight away. In comparison to a patent application, it would not be necessary to carry out the time-consuming patent grant procedure before enforcement becomes possible.

The registration of the utility model will also publish the new development. In some cases, this might not be wanted. For example, a publication before the marketing and put in practice, i.e., publication, of the new development might be negative as the applicant loses its time advantage to make further developments. In case the new development is published by the registration of the utility model, competitors could start with further developments before the marketing of the new development by the applicant. For these cases, the utility model law allows requesting a cost-free deferment of the registration by up to eighteen months after the filing of the utility model. Thus, the registration of the utility model might be coordinated with the publication of the new development and would offer the possibility to enforce the utility model from the time of the marketing of the new development.

§8.07 TRADE SECRET

[A] General Background

Under special circumstances, the protection of a new development by a patent or utility model might not be the best choice to secure one's own rights.

As mentioned, patent applications are published after a defined time period, in most jurisdictions after eighteen months. Thus, at this point in time, the competitors are informed about the new development and can use it for further developments and the like. The situation becomes problematic in case it turns out that the new development is not eligible for patent protection. For example, it might be problematic to disclose the invention in such a sufficient way that a person skilled in the art can carry it out. Also, it might turn out that the new invention is not considered to be inventive, especially the patent office might not be of the opinion that it has technical character in case of the EPO or might be of the opinion that the judicial exception has not been integrated into a practical application. In such a case, the applicant would not be awarded a monopoly right but would have disclosed the new development to the public by the automatic publication of the patent application eighteen months after the filing of the patent application.

For example, a respective algorithm used in a blockchain application cannot be reverse engineered from the blockchain application of the product as put on the market. That means a third party might not be able to gather all features of the algorithm from the marketed product, for example, by decoding the software by analysing the behaviour of the software depending on different inputs and comparing it to the respective outputs. Assuming the algorithm might provide the developer or the user of the algorithm with a significant, economical relevant advantage, the developer does not want to disclose the details of the algorithm to the public. In such cases, it might be worthwhile to handle the new development as Trade Secret.

[B] Legal Basis: Definition

A Trade Secret has been defined in the TRIPS Agreement. The TRIPS Agreement is an agreement between all Member States of the World Trade Organization (WTO). The WIPO describes[130] that this agreement 'establishes minimum standards of protection that each government has to give to the Intellectual Property of (...) WTO members (...)'.

In Article 39 TRIPS[131] it is defined that:

> natural and legal persons shall have the possibility of preventing information lawfully within their control from being disclosed to, acquired by, or used by others without their consent in a manner contrary to honest commercial practices so long as such information (a) is secret in the sense that it is not, as a body or in the precise configuration and assembly of its components, generally known among or readily accessible to persons within the circles that normally deal with the kind of information in question; (b) has commercial value because it is secret; and (c)

130. WIPO, *Advice on Flexibilities under the TRIPS Agreement*, available at: https://www.wipo.int/ip-development/en/policy_legislative_assistance/advice_trips.html (accessed on 11 Dec. 2023).

131. World Trade Organization (WTO), *Annex 1C of the Marrakesh Agreement Establishing the World Trade Organization* Art. 39 (signed in Marrakesh, Morocco on 15 Apr. 1994), available at: https://www.wto.org/english/docs_e/legal_e/27-trips_04d_e.htm (accessed on 11 Dec. 2023).

has been subject to reasonable steps under the circumstances, by the person lawfully in control of the information, to keep it secret.

These regulations were transposed into national laws. As per Germany, Trade Secrets are protected by special provisions in different laws, especially the law on unfair competition. In other European countries and in the United States, the TRIPS regulations have been implemented by special laws.

In June 2016, the European Parliament and European Counsel have issued Directive 2016/943[132] on the protection of undisclosed know-how and business information (Trade Secrets) against their unlawful acquisition, use and disclosure. To that end, national laws within Europe on Trade Secret protection have been harmonized in Europe.

In Germany, although the Directive had to be implemented into national law until 9 June 2018, it took until April 2019 to do so. This was accomplished by the 'law for the protection of Trade Secrets' (GeschGehG).[133] In this law, the definition of a Trade Secret of TRIPS has been adopted in Article 2.[134]

Article 7 of GeschGehG[135] (in line with Article 10 of Directive 2016/943) stipulates, among others, that the owner of the Trade Secret has a claim against an infringer for a recall of the infringing product, a permanent removal of infringing products from the distribution channels, destruction of the infringing products or withdrawal of the infringing products from the market provided that the protection of the Trade Secret is not affected by this. The Trade Secret owner has, in addition, a claim for information against the infringer, a claim for damages that have to be enforced at civil chambers of local district courts. The Trade Secret must be held confidentially during and after the court procedures, especially the participating parties are bound to confidentiality.

Thus, the holder of Trade Secrets has effective ways to secure and enforce the Trade Secret according to the Directive and the respective national laws.

In the United States, the protection of Trade Secret can be enforced, too. 'The Defend Trade Secrets Act of 2016'[136] came into effect. The USPTO summarizes the core aspects of the protection as Trade Secret under the US Act as follows:[137]

---

132. European Union, *Directive (EU) 2016/943 of 8 June 2016 on the protection of undisclosed know-how and business information (Trade Secrets) against their unlawful acquisition, use and disclosure*, available at: https://eur-lex.europa.eu/legal-content/EN/TXT/?uri=CELEX%3A32016L0943 (accessed on 11 Dec. 2023).
133. Gesetz zum Schutz von Geschäftsgeheimnissen vom 18. April 2019 (BGBl. I S. 466), available at: https://www.gesetze-im-internet.de/geschgehg/ (accessed on 11 Dec. 2023).
134. Article 2 GeschGhG, available at: https://www.gesetze-im-internet.de/geschgehg/__2.html (accessed on 11 Dec. 2023).
135. Article 7 GeschGhG, available at: https://www.gesetze-im-internet.de/geschgehg/__7.html (accessed on 11 Dec. 2023).
136. Defend Trade Secrets Act of 2016, Public Law 114–153, 11 May 2016, available at: https://www.congress.gov/114/plaws/publ153/PLAW-114publ153.pdf (accessed on 11 Dec. 2023).
137. USPTO, *Trade Secret Policy*, available at: https://www.uspto.gov/ip-policy/trade-secret-policy (accessed on 11 Dec. 2023).

> U.S. courts can protect Trade Secrets by (a) ordering that the misappropriation stop, (b) that the secret be protected from public exposure, and (c) in extraordinary circumstances, ordering the seizure of the misappropriated Trade Secret. At the conclusion of a Trade Secret case, courts can award damages, court costs, reasonable attorneys' fees and a permanent injunction, if warranted. Trade Secret.

[C] Practical Aspects

This protection is strictly limited because a Trade Secret holder is only protected from unauthorized disclosure and use which is referred to as misappropriation. If a Trade Secret holder fails to maintain secrecy or if the information is independently discovered, released or otherwise generally known, protection as a Trade Secret will be lost.

However, if the holder can ensure that the Trade Secret remains secret, the Trade Secret will not expire so the protection continues until discovery or loss.

Such a discovery might take place by independent development of the subject matter by third parties. Such third parties might also reach a grant/registration of a protective right for the subject matter by, for example, a patent or utility model. As the owner had not made public the subject matter of the Trade Secret, it would not form state of the art and could not be used to challenge the legal validity.

For example, the owner of the Trade Secret might be of the opinion that the final product is not identifiable and can also not be reconstructed by reverse engineering. A third party might independently develop the subject matter of the Trade Secret and successfully apply for an IP right. In the case the Trade Secret could be reversed engineered in end products, the third party being owner of the IP right might raise claims against the owner of the subject matter of the Trade Secret that is then not any more secret subject matter. The owner might then defend himself with a right of prior use that is subject to restrictions.

In a blockchain context, a blockchain relevant algorithm may have been developed and may be considered as a Trade Secret. The algorithm has been used in products/applications that have solely been marketed in a specific country/region. Here, region/country means the country/region in which a patent would be effective. The right of prior use would then only cover this specific country region. Furthermore, the right of prior use would only cover the specific products/applications in which the algorithm would be used and would not cover future further developments of the algorithm or the use of the algorithm in other blockchain products.

In addition, the right of prior use would only cover the individual user of the algorithm. With this having said, the right of prior use of the subsidiary generally does not give a right of prior use to the mother company or sister companies.

Thus, a Trade Secret might be used for subject matter giving an advantage relative to competitors when being kept secret. However, in view of the fluctuation of employees and secret holders, it might be problematic whether it is possible to maintain it under reasonable safeguards to protect its secrecy. Every disclosure will defeat the Trade Secret.

For planning the strategy with regard to the protection of a new development, the following questions should thus be taken into consideration:

(i) Is the new development a patentable subject matter?
(ii) Is it possible and if yes with what effort is it possible to reverse engineer the subject matter or to independently detect and/or develop the claimed subject matter?
(iii) Is there a risk that a third party will file a patent application directed to the subject matter?
(iv) What is the expected duration for the subject matter to be valuable?
(v) How likely is it that the subject matter can be maintained secret?

In case questions (i)–(iii) can be answered with yes, a clear indication is there that the subject matter should be protected by a registered protective right like a patent or utility model.

Depending on the answer to question (iv), the protection by a patent should be taken into consideration. If the answer to (iv) is more than five years, a patent application should be taken into consideration, especially accompanied by a parallel utility model application being registered already during the examination of the patent application in case patentability is likely to be given.

In case all questions (i)–(iii) are answered with no, the protection as a Trade Secret should be taken into consideration, especially in case question (iv) is answered with a duration of more than five years. Prerequisite is however that also question (v) can be answered with a predominant likelihood.

A combination of both a registered/granted IP right in combination with a Trade Secret should be seriously considered. It might be worthwhile to protect the core, preferably long-term valuable subject matter by a patent and to keep results of the further research and data sets secret in the form of a Trade Secret.

In any way respective measures should be taken before the filing of the IP right application that the subject matter is hold secret, if necessary by non-disclosure agreements, and internal measures for securing that fluctuations of the persons being involved in the development of the subject matter do not lead to a disclosure of the subject matter.

Confidentiality should furthermore be upheld as long as possible after the filing of the application, especially as long as the application is not published by the respective patent office.

In this way the forming of state of the art that might be taken into consideration for assessing any further developments for which additional patent protection will be aimed for later is avoided. In case the subject matter of the first application is disclosed before the publication of the patent application, the disclosure could be taken into consideration for assessing the inventiveness, whereas the content of the application itself in most jurisdictions can only be taken into consideration for assessing the novelty.

That means that any further feature of the further development not disclosed in the non-published application is sufficient to render the non-published application not relevant for assessing the patentability of the further development. Important exception to this rule is however the US.

Under the US patent act[138] also non pre-published applications form full state of the art and are taken into consideration also for assessing the inventiveness.

Second, when not publishing the subject matter of a not yet-published patent application, competitors are not familiar with the content of the application; otherwise, they could easily develop it and file own applications on such further developments.

With regard to NDAs, it is important to note that a violation of the non-disclosure agreement does not necessarily mean that the publication violating the NDA is not forming state of the art and is not taken into consideration for assessing the patentability of a subject matter claimed with a patent application filed after the violation of the NDA. Thus, the patent applicant might not be awarded with a patent grant due to a publication of the claimed subject matter by a third party representing a violation of the NDA. In this case, the applicant predominantly does only have claims against the party violating the NDA based on a breach of a contract in the form of the NDA. In such a situation, it is likely that the claims the applicant can raise against the infringer of the NDA are directed to a smaller amount compared to the profit the applicant might have taken advantage of in case a patent had been granted.

For the claim, the applicant would have to specify the suffered damages. This is only feasible for a hypothetical situation where the applicant would have been awarded with a patent, the applicant had been able to hinder competitors to use the claimed subject matter and he had reached an increased higher market share. As these circumstances are uncertain and also dependent on other factors, it is most likely that the awarded damages are below the actual damages.

Thus, the rule should be: 'first file the invention then talk about it', or better: 'first wait for the publication of the application, then talk about it'.

FURTHER READING

Monika Huppertz, Helge B. Cohausz, *Das Patentsekretariat: Die Bürofachkraft im gewerblichen Rechtsschutz* (8th ed., 2022).

James A. Cox, Mark W. Rasmussen, *Blockchain for Business Lawyers* (American Bar Association, 1st ed., 7 August 2019).

Helge B. Cohausz, *Gewerblicher Rechtsschutz und angrenzende Gebiete* (4th ed., 2023).

Claudia Schwarz, Sabine Kruspig, *Computerimplementierte Erfindungen – Patentschutz von Software?* (2nd ed., 1 October 2017).

European Patent Office, available at: https://www.epo.org/learning-events/materials/inventors-handbook.html.

138. 35 U.S.C. 102 (a) (2).

Adam Jolly, *Winning with IP – Managing Intellectual Property Today* (November 2023).

Daniel Closa, et al., *Patent Law for Computer Scientists: Steps to Protect Computer-Implemented Inventions* (2010).

Adam Jolly, *The Handbook of European Intellectual Property Management* (4th ed., 2015).

CHAPTER 9
Blockchain and Antitrust

Jay Modrall

§9.01 INTRODUCTION

Introduction of new technologies with the potential to disrupt competition across many markets inevitably raises questions about those technologies' antitrust implications. Indeed, blockchain technologies have attracted considerable interest from antitrust authorities and commentators for several years. In June 2018, the Organisation for Economic Co-operation and Development (OECD) held a roundtable on "Blockchain and competition policy."[1] One commentator asked, "Is Blockchain the Death of Antitrust Law?"[2] For better or worse, rumors of antitrust's death by blockchain are greatly exaggerated.

The application of blockchain technologies can indeed raise antitrust issues, but these issues are not different in kind from those raised by other business conduct. That said, companies implementing blockchain solutions must carefully consider their antitrust implications and take precautions to avoid inadvertently breaching antitrust law. In parallel, antitrust authorities are scrambling to understand blockchain and other new technologies and considering how their traditional approaches need to be updated. While most of the debate in antitrust circles has focused on the antitrust implications of the growth of large online platforms and their collection and use of "big data," the growing application of blockchain (and smart contract solutions) also raises interesting antitrust issues.

---

1. https://www.oecd.org/competition/blockchain-and-competition-policy.htm (accessed on Oct. 6, 2023).
2. Schrepel, T., *Is Blockchain the Death of Antitrust Law?* (The Blockchain Antitrust Paradox), available at: https://papers.ssrn.com/sol3/papers.cfm?abstract_id=3193576 (accessed on Oct. 6, 2023).

In this chapter, blockchain issues in three general contexts are discussed: (i) application of blockchain technologies by two or more undertakings in potentially anticompetitive agreements, decisions and concerted practices; (ii) application of blockchain technologies by a single undertaking holding a "dominant position"; and (iii) implications of the use of blockchain for the review of mergers and acquisitions involving companies using these technologies to store large volumes of data. In each section, the relevant antitrust concepts are introduced, and antitrust issues are covered that blockchain applications may be expected to raise.

This discussion is based primarily on European Union (EU) antitrust law. However, similar principles apply in many jurisdictions, and antitrust authorities around the globe can be expected to consider issues similar to the European Commission (EC). The issues raised in any particular business context are highly fact-specific, and this discussion will necessarily be general and not cover all business contexts in which blockchain will be used.

§9.02 ANTICOMPETITIVE AGREEMENTS, DECISIONS AND CONCERTED PRACTICES

[A] Introduction to Concepts

Article 101(1) of the Treaty on the Functioning of the European Union (TFEU) prohibits:

> all agreements between undertakings, decisions by associations of undertakings and concerted practices which may affect trade between Member States and which have as their object or effect the prevention, restriction or distortion of competition within the internal market, and in particular those which:
>
> (a) directly or indirectly fix purchase or selling prices or any other trading conditions;
> (b) limit or control production, markets, technical development, or investment;
> (c) share markets or sources of supply;
> (d) apply dissimilar conditions to equivalent transactions with other trading parties, thereby placing them at a competitive disadvantage;
> (e) make the conclusion of contracts subject to acceptance by the other parties of supplementary obligations which, by their nature or according to commercial usage, have no connection with the subject of such contracts.[3]

Agreements, decisions and concerted practices (collectively, agreements) that are caught by Article 101(1) TFEU are automatically void under Article 101(2) TFEU unless they yield competitive benefits recognized in Article 101(3) TFEU:

> [agreements which contribute] to improving the production or distribution of goods or to promoting technical or economic progress, while allowing consumers a fair share of the resulting benefit, and which [do] not:

3. OJ 115, 9/5/2008, pp. 88-89, available at https://eur-lex.europa.eu/legal-content/EN/TXT/HTML/?uri=CELEX:12008E101&from=EN (accessed on Oct. 6, 2023).

(a) impose on the undertakings concerned restrictions which are not indispensable to the attainment of these objectives;
(b) afford such undertakings the possibility of eliminating competition in respect of a substantial part of the products in question.

Thus, Article 101(1) TFEU applies only where there is (i) an "agreement," "decision" or "concerted practice" involving (ii) multiple "undertakings" or associations of undertakings and having (iii) an anticompetitive "object or effect" within the EU.

Each of these elements has been the subject of extensive discussion and enforcement action. For present purposes, it suffices to note that the terms agreement, decision and concerted practice (collectively, agreements) are interpreted broadly to include both formal and informal agreements. However, so-called tacit collusion, where competitors' behavior is influenced by one another's expectations as to how they will behave without any actual communication, is not caught by Article 101(1) TFEU. The line between parallel but independent actions and coordinated actions can be difficult to draw. In the coming years, the proliferation of smart contracts entered into by independent companies using the same or similar algorithms can be expected to test the boundaries between legal tacit collusion and illegal coordination.

The criterion of effect on competition in the EU's internal market may be met by any but the most localized conduct. If a blockchain solution otherwise raises antitrust issues, it is likely to meet this criterion except in the case of highly localized blockchain applications.

The term "undertaking" includes a wide variety of business organizations and even individuals, but for the sake of convenience, I use the more common terms "company" or "joint venture" instead of "undertaking." The distinction between violations "by object" and "by effect" relates to the standard of proof an antitrust authority must meet to show that a violation has occurred.

Another fundamental distinction is made between so-called horizontal agreements among head-to-head competitors and so-called vertical agreements among companies at different levels of a supply chain. As a general rule, horizontal agreements are viewed more negatively from an antitrust perspective, while vertical agreements are considered less likely to raise antitrust concerns. However, the application of blockchain technologies can raise antitrust issues in both horizontal and vertical agreements.

As mentioned, the EC has adopted so-called block exemption regulations exempting certain horizontal agreements among competitors (certain research and development agreements[4] and "specialization agreements," such as joint production agreements[5]) and vertical agreements among suppliers and customers[6] from the scope of EU competition law. In parallel, the EC published guidelines on the EU approach to

4. EC, Commission Regulation No. 2023/1066 on the application of Art. 101(3) of the TFEU to certain categories of research and development agreements, OJ L143, 2/6/2023, pp. 9-19.
5. EC, Commission Regulation No. 2023/1067 on the application of Art. 101(3) of the TFEU to certain categories of specialisation agreements, OJ L143, 2/6/2023, pp. 20-26.

assessing the legality of horizontal cooperation agreements[7] and vertical cooperation agreements.[8]

Although some blockchain-related agreements could be covered by the EC's block exemption regulations, the conditions set out in these regulations are quite technical and are unlikely to apply in most cases. Thus, there is no need to discuss them in this chapter in greater detail.

In the discussion below, emphasis has been put on the EC's Horizontal and Vertical Guidelines, which are the most comprehensive and authoritative analysis of the EU antitrust treatment of such agreements.

[B] Horizontal Agreements and Blockchain

Anticompetitive horizontal agreements include the most well-known examples of antitrust violations, price-fixing and market-sharing cartels. Such hardcore violations will not be discussed in this chapter, except to note that the use of blockchain or smart contract technology to implement such illegal agreements will not protect the parties from a finding of infringement and the imposition of significant fines and (in some jurisdictions) criminal penalties.[9]

Article 101(1) can also capture many cooperative agreements involving competitors that are not hardcore antitrust violations, including cooperative agreements involving blockchain.

As the EC notes in paragraphs 20-21 of the Horizontal Guidelines:[10]

> Horizontal cooperation agreements can lead to substantial economic benefits, including sustainability benefits, in particular where they combine complementary activities, skills or assets. Horizontal cooperation can be a means to share risk, save costs, increase investments, pool know-how, enhance product quality and variety and launch innovation faster. Similarly, horizontal cooperation can be a means to address shortages and disruptions in supply chains or reduce dependencies on particular products, services and technologies … . Horizontal cooperation agreements may, however, limit competition on the relevant market in several ways. Such agreements may, for instance, lead to collusion between the parties or to anti-competitive foreclosure.

6. EC, Commission Regulation No. 2022/720 on the application of Art. 101(3) of the Treaty on the Functioning of the European Union to categories of vertical agreements and concerted practices, OJ L134, 11/5/2022, pp. 4-13 (the "VBER").
7. EC, Communication from the Commission—Guidelines on the applicability of Art. 101 of the Treaty on the Functioning of the European Union to horizontal co-operation agreements, OJ C259, 21/7/2023, pp. 1-125 (the "Horizontal Guidelines").
8. EC, Commission Notice—Guidelines on Vertical Restraints, OJ C248, 30/6/2022, pp. 1-85 (the "Vertical Guidelines").
9. Cf. Decision of the UK Competition and Markets Authority, Online sales of posters and frames, Case 50223 of Aug. 12, 2016, available at: https://assets.publishing.service.gov.uk/media/57ee7c2740f0b606dc000018/case-50223-final-non-confidential-infringement-decision.pdf (accessed on Oct. 20, 2023).
10. *Supra* n. 7.

Blockchain technology can be used in a wide variety of horizontal cooperative agreements discussed in the Horizontal Guidelines, including research and development agreements, joint production agreements, purchasing agreements, and commercialization agreements. A discussion of all horizontal cooperative agreements in which blockchain may be used is outside the scope of this chapter. Instead, it is worthwhile to discuss two antitrust issues on the below that may be raised by blockchain applications in many types of agreement: information exchange and standardization.

[1] *Information Exchange*

At their heart, blockchains are a means of recording and sharing information. The EC recognizes in paragraph 373 of the Horizontal Guidelines that:

> Information exchange is a common feature of many competitive markets and may generate various types of efficiency gains. It may solve problems of information asymmetries, thereby making markets more efficient. In recent years, data sharing has gained in importance as a means to inform decision making, for instance through the use of big data analytics and machine learning techniques. Moreover, undertakings may be able to improve their internal efficiency by benchmarking against each other's best practices. Exchanging information may also help undertakings to save costs by, for example, reducing their inventories and enabling quicker delivery of perishable products to consumers. Information exchange may enable firms to develop new or better products or services or to train algorithms on a broader, more meaningful basis. Furthermore, exchanges of information may directly benefit consumers by reducing their search costs and improving choice (footnotes omitted).

In paragraphs 377-379, however, the Horizontal Guidelines outline three main ways in which the exchange of competitively sensitive information may restrict competition:

> By artificially increasing transparency between competitors in the market, the exchange of commercially sensitive information can facilitate coordination of undertakings' behaviour and result in restrictions of competition. First, information exchanges are likely to facilitate collusion if they allow an undertaking to signal to its competitors, through any means, the conduct that it would find desirable for those competitors to follow, or the conduct that the undertaking itself would adopt in reaction to the same competitors' conduct ...
>
> Second, the exchange of commercially sensitive information may in itself allow undertakings to reach a common understanding on the terms of coordination, which can lead to a collusive outcome on the market. The exchange can create mutually consistent expectations regarding the uncertainties present in the market. On that basis, undertakings can then reach a common understanding on their behaviour on the market, even without an explicit agreement on coordination ... .
>
> Third, the exchange of commercially sensitive information can be used as a means to increase the internal stability of an anti-competitive agreement or concerted practice. Information exchange can make the market sufficiently transparent to allow the colluding undertakings to monitor whether other undertakings are deviating from the collusive outcome and thus to know when to retaliate and

> against whom. Exchanges of both present and past data are capable of being used for such monitoring. This can either enable undertakings to achieve a collusive outcome on markets where they would otherwise not have been able to collude, or it can increase the stability of a collusive outcome already present on the market (footnotes omitted).

The term "information" covers all "types of data and information'," including "(i) raw, unorganised digital content that may need processing in order to make it useful (raw data); (ii) pre-processed data, that has already been prepared and validated; (iii) data that has been manipulated in order to produce meaningful information of any form, as well as (iv) any other type of information, including non-digital information."[11] Information exchanges include "direct and indirect forms of information exchange and information exchanges between intra- and inter-brand competitors," which may take place "directly between competitors (in the form of a unilateral disclosure or in a bi- or multilateral exchange), or indirectly, by or through a third party (such as a service provider, platform, online tool or algorithm), via a common agency (for example, a trade association), via a market research organisation, via suppliers or customers of the parties to the exchange, or via a website or press release."[12]

The extent to which blockchain applications raise information-sharing concerns is a function of the sensitivity of the information stored on the blockchain and the rules governing who can access that information. At one extreme, a company setting up a private blockchain to store information that will be accessible only within the corporate group will not raise any antitrust concerns, regardless of the sensitivity of the information stored on the blockchain.

At the other extreme, setting up a public blockchain on which public or otherwise non-competitively sensitive information will be accessible to all interested parties will also normally raise no antitrust issues. The Horizontal Guidelines note, however, that the "fact that an undertaking discloses commercially sensitive information through a public announcement (for example, through a post on a publicly accessible website, a statement at a public event or in a newspaper) does not in itself exclude the possibility that the announcement may constitute a concerted practice within the meaning of Article 101(1)."[13]

Antitrust issues are most likely to arise in situations between these two extremes, where a private blockchain is created by competitors to store proprietary information that will be accessible only to certain market participants. In these situations, stakeholders must take care of both the design and operation of the blockchain to avoid infringing antitrust rules. The Commission notes in the HORIZONTAL GUIDELINES that "[s]hared databases ... may ... have the effect of restricting competition depending on the economic conditions on the relevant market(s) and on the specific characteristics of the database concerned. These characteristics include the purpose of the database and the conditions of access to and participation in it, as well as the type of information exchanged (for example, whether it is public or confidential, aggregated or

11. *Ibid.*, para. 367.
12. *Ibid.*, para. 368.
13. *Ibid.*, para. 398.

detailed, historical, current or future information, the frequency with which the database is updated and the relevance of the information for setting prices, volumes or conditions of service). A database that covers a significant part of the relevant market and to which access is denied or delayed for other competitors may create an information asymmetry, placing those other competitors at a disadvantage compared to the undertakings that participate in the database. Fair, objective, transparent and non-discriminatory access criteria may alleviate competition concerns."[14]

As with any cooperation among competitors, the first step in the design of a private blockchain intended to store competitively sensitive information of competitors should be to determine whether there is a procompetitive rationale for the cooperation and whether the efficiencies to be generated by it outweigh the potential for competitive harm. This may be the case, for example, where a single operator is able to realize cost savings and offer capacity to competitors in a market as a sort of industry utility. In such a case, however, it will be important to ensure that the permissions built into the blockchain operating rules ensure that participants have access only to their own competitively sensitive information and not to that of competitors. Such "compliance by design" is critical to ensure that the creation of the blockchain does not infringe antitrust law.

Even assuming that a private blockchain storing competitively sensitive information for competitors has a procompetitive rationale and does not infringe antitrust law, care must be taken to ensure that antitrust laws are not infringed in the blockchain's day-to-day operation. For example, if the blockchain is structured as a joint venture in which competitors are equity holders, the joint venture's reports to equity holders and their representatives on the joint venture's board or other managing organs may not include competitively sensitive information. The joint venture and its personnel should adopt antitrust compliance policies and training procedures to mitigate the risk of inadvertent sharing of competitively sensitive information. Special procedures may be required if equity holder personnel are seconded to the joint venture.

What information is competitively sensitive must be determined on a case-by-case basis. The Horizontal Guidelines explain that "[i]nformation on pricing is generally considered commercially sensitive and Article 101(1) may apply even if the exchange does not have a direct effect on the prices paid by end users. Other categories of potentially commercially sensitive information include information on costs, capacity, production, quantities, market shares, customers, plans to enter or exit markets, or concerning other important elements of a firm's strategy that undertakings active in a genuinely competitive market would not have an incentive to reveal to each other. The fact that the information exchanged may be incorrect or misleading does not in itself eliminate the risk that it may influence the conduct of competitors on the market."[15]

As reflected in the detailed discussion of information-sharing issues in the Horizontal Guidelines, the information-sharing issues raised by blockchain applications are not new. These issues are familiar in a number of business contexts, such as

14. *Ibid.*, para. 383.
15. *Ibid.*, para. 385 (footnotes omitted).

trade associations and joint ventures. The permissioning arrangements to ensure that competitively sensitive information of one blockchain participant is not accessible to its competitors are analogous to the firewalls traditionally employed to avoid the sharing of competitively sensitive information among participants in a joint venture.

[2] Standardization

The creation of a blockchain on which competitors may store information for procompetitive purposes may require a level of standardization, for instance, as to the type and format of information to be stored. The Horizontal Guidelines address so-called standardization agreements, defined as agreements that "have as their primary objective the definition of technical or quality requirements with which current or future products, production processes, value chain due diligence processes, services or methods may comply."[16]

The guidelines recognize that "Standardisation agreements generally produce significant positive economic effects, for example by promoting economic interpenetration on the internal market and encouraging the development of new and improved products or markets and improved supply conditions. Standards thus generally increase competition and lower output and sales costs, benefiting economies as a whole. Standards may maintain and enhance product quality, safety, provide information and ensure interoperability and compatibility (thus increasing value for consumers)."[17]

"Standard development can, however, in specific circumstances where competitors are involved, also give rise to restrictive effects on competition by restricting price competition and limiting or controlling production, markets, innovation or technical development … . [T]his can occur in three main ways, namely (a) restriction of price competition, (b) foreclosure of innovative technologies and (c) exclusion of, or discrimination against, certain undertakings by preventing effective access to the standard."[18] Thus, in developing standards for information to be included in a blockchain, competitors must avoid "anti-competitive information exchanges [that] could reduce or eliminate price competition in the markets concerned, or limit or control production, thereby facilitating a collusive outcome on the market."[19]

Second, to the extent that the design of a blockchain may involve a choice of alternative standards for information to be included, competitors must consider whether the approach adopted could create barriers to entry for other competitors and potentially exclude them from a market or otherwise limit innovation. According to the Horizontal Guidelines, "If an undertaking is either completely prevented from obtaining access to the result of the standard, or is only granted access on prohibitive or discriminatory terms, there is a risk of an anti-competitive effect."[20]

16. *Ibid.*, para. 436 (footnote omitted).
17. *Ibid.*, para. 439 (footnotes omitted).
18. *Ibid.*, para. 441.
19. *Ibid.*, para. 442 (footnote omitted).
20. *Ibid.*, para. 444.

For example, if competitors representing a significant proportion of a relevant market agree on certain types and formats for information to be stored on a blockchain and that approach is expected to become an actual or de facto standard for customers in the market, a competitor following a different approach who was excluded from the process could suffer competitive harm.

Special considerations apply where the design of a blockchain among competitors involves intellectual property rights (IPRs), in particular, if those rights include so-called standard-essential patents (*see* section §9.06).

[C] Vertical Agreements and Blockchain

As mentioned above, so-called vertical agreements between companies active in different levels of a supply chain are less likely than horizontal agreements to raise antitrust issues. The EC has adopted the VBER, a block exemption regulation exempting certain vertical supply and distribution agreements[21] and published the Vertical Guidelines.[22] The VBER and Vertical Guidelines provide a framework for analyzing any restrictions on competition contained in vertical blockchain-related agreements, such as blockchain-related supply chain management platforms.

The VBER defines "vertical agreements" as "an agreement or concerted practice between two or more undertakings, each of which operates, for the purposes of the agreement or the concerted practice, at a different level of the production or distribution chain, and relating to the conditions under which the parties may purchase, sell or resell certain goods or services."[23] The VBER does not generally apply to agreements between competing companies.[24]

The VBER also does not apply to agreements between companies with market shares over 30% of the relevant upstream or downstream markets or to agreements containing so-called hardcore restrictions, namely restrictions on the buyer's ability to determine its sales price (known as "resale price maintenance", or RPM); restrictions on the territory into which, or of the customers to whom, the buyer may sell the contract goods or services (with exceptions for exclusive distribution networks, agreements with wholesalers, selective distribution agreements and component sales); restrictions on active or passive sales to end users by members of a selective distribution system (subject to exceptions); restrictions on cross-supplies between distributors within a selective distribution system; and restrictions on buyers of components that use the components to manufacture finished goods from reselling the components as spare parts.

21. *Supra* n. 6.
22. *Supra* n. 8.
23. VBER, Art. 1(1)(a), *supra* n. 6.
24. With the exception of non-reciprocal vertical agreements where (a) the supplier is a manufacturer and a distributor of goods, while the buyer is a distributor and not a competing undertaking at the manufacturing level; or (b) the supplier is a provider of services at several levels of trade, while the buyer provides its goods or services at the retail level and is not a competing undertaking at the level of trade where it purchases the contract services.

Even if the VBER applies to a particular agreement, it does not exempt certain so-called excluded restrictions that may be contained in otherwise-exempted agreements. These are non-compete obligations with a duration over five years (unless the buyer operates from premises owned or leased by the supplier); restrictions on the buyer's right to manufacture, purchase, sell or resell goods or services after the termination of the agreement (unless these are limited to one year, and other conditions are met); and restrictions on the ability of members of a selective distribution agreement to sell the brands of particular competing suppliers.

The Vertical Guidelines discuss the application of the VBER and the analysis under Article 101(1) TFEU of certain common categories of vertical agreements: single branding, exclusive distribution, exclusive customer allocation, selective distribution, franchising, exclusive supply, upfront access payments, category management agreements, tying and resale price restrictions. The Vertical Guidelines also explain that certain categories of vertical agreements—*de minimis* agreements, agency agreements and subcontracting agreements—will not normally infringe Article 101(1) TFEU whether or not the VBER would otherwise apply.

Blockchains are used increasingly for supply chain management in a wide variety of vertical agreements between suppliers and buyers. Many of these agreements are covered by the VBER, including in common categories of agreement, such as single branding, exclusive distribution, exclusive customer allocation, selective distribution, franchising and category management agreements. Importantly, the use of blockchains in such agreements does not impact the application (or not) of the VBER.

Given the variety of contexts in which blockchains may be used, a discussion of each such category is outside the scope of this chapter. For companies considering the use of blockchain in a vertical agreement or network of agreements, however, the VBER's list of "hardcore" and "excluded" restrictions provides a useful checklist of areas where companies need to be especially careful. Antitrust advice should be sought in particular if companies' proposed blockchain (or smart contract) structures could involve:

- RPM;
- restrictions on resales by members of exclusive or selective distribution systems;
- restrictions on effective use of the internet to sell contract goods or services; and
- restrictions on the resale of components as spare parts.

It should be noted that where a group of buyers or suppliers competing with one another at the upstream or downstream level set up a blockchain-based platform to manage the supply chains of multiple companies, the VBER will not apply. In such cases, the considerations above relating to horizontal agreements will apply.

[D] Appropriate Safeguards

Given the enormous variety of relationships, both horizontal and vertical, in which blockchain and smart contracts can be used, each situation must be assessed on a case-by-case basis. It goes without saying that hardcore antitrust violations, such as price-fixing and market partitioning, are illegal and subject to very significant sanctions, whether or not they involve blockchain or smart contracts.

Apart from avoiding such hardcore violations, particular care from an antitrust perspective is required whenever a blockchain application is developed in cooperation among competitors. In many cases, such cooperation will be procompetitive, allowing multiple stakeholders in a market to benefit from the efficiencies offered by blockchain. But in structuring such cooperation, the potential procompetitive effects must be balanced against any potential harms to competition. Where such potential harms are identified, possibilities to mitigate such harms should be considered. Even where proposed cooperation is considered procompetitive, care must be taken to ensure that competitors do not share competitively sensitive information without appropriate safeguards, both in the structuring and negotiation of the cooperation arrangements and through the blockchain application itself once operational.

Blockchain applications involving purely vertical relationships, such as supply chain management platforms, will normally raise fewer antitrust issues than applications involving cooperation among competitors. Indeed, many such arrangements will be exempted from EU competition law under the VBER. Nonetheless, proposed vertical blockchain applications must also be carefully reviewed from an antitrust perspective, in particular, if they are likely to involve potentially problematic features mentioned above.

§9.03 ABUSE OF DOMINANCE

[A] Introduction of Concepts

Article 102 TFEU provides that:

> Any abuse by one or more undertakings of a dominant position within the internal market or in a substantial part of it shall be prohibited as incompatible with the internal market in so far as it may affect trade between Member States.
>
> Such abuse may, in particular, consist in:
>
> (a) directly or indirectly imposing unfair purchase or selling prices or other unfair trading conditions;
> (b) limiting production, markets or technical development to the prejudice of consumers;
> (c) applying dissimilar conditions to equivalent transactions with other trading parties, thereby placing them at a competitive disadvantage;
> (d) making the conclusion of contracts subject to acceptance by the other parties of supplementary obligations which, by their nature or according to commercial usage, have no connection with the subject of such contracts.

Thus, Article 102 TFEU applies only where there is (i) an "abuse" of (ii) a "dominant position" in the EU or a substantial part of it by (iii) an "undertaking" and (iv) that abuse affects trade between the Member States. As with Article 101(1) TFEU, each of these elements has been the subject of extensive discussion and enforcement. The definition of "undertaking" is discussed above. As with Article 101(1) TFEU, any but the most localized blockchain applications in the EU are likely to affect more than one Member State. Thus, the critical elements of an Article 102 TFEU infringement for present purposes are the existence of a "dominant position" and the "abuse" by the dominant company.

To assess whether a company holds a dominant position, the EC defines the product market and the geographic market and then assesses the company's market power in that market. How a relevant market is defined for antitrust purposes is often critical to the EC's analysis of whether, and if so which, parties may have a dominant position. The EC's approach to the market definition is outlined in its notice on the definition of the relevant market for the purposes of Community competition law.[25] As this notice explains, "The main purpose of market definition is to identify in a systematic way the effective and immediate competitive constraints faced by the undertakings involved when they offer particular products in a particular area."[26]

Once a relevant antitrust market is defined, the next step in the analysis is normally to estimate stakeholders' shares in that market. The EC considers market shares as a useful first indication of the importance of each firm on the market in comparison to the others. The higher the market share, and the longer the period of time over which it is held, the more likely it is to be a preliminary indication of dominance. If a company has a market share of less than 40%, it is unlikely to be dominant. The EC also takes other factors into account in its assessment of dominance, including the ease with which other companies can enter the market—whether there are any barriers to this; the existence of countervailing buyer power; the overall size and strength of the company and its resources; and the extent to which it is present at several levels of the supply chain (vertical integration).[27]

Under EU law, holding a dominant position is not in itself illegal; dominant companies are entitled to compete on the merits like any other company. However, a dominant company may be found to abuse that position based on a number of different commercial behaviors. Examples of behavior that may amount to abuse include: requiring that buyers purchase all units of a particular product only from the dominant company (exclusive purchasing); setting prices at a loss-making level (predation); refusing to supply inputs indispensable for competition in an ancillary market; charging excessive prices.[28] The EC has published guidance on its enforcement priorities in relation to certain of these abusive behaviors known as "exclusionary"

25. EC Commission, Notice on the definition of the relevant market for the purposes of Union competition law, 8/2/2024, OJ C/2024/1645, 22/2/2024.
26. *Ibid.*, at para. 6 (footnotes omitted).
27. *See generally*, https://ec.europa.eu/competition/antitrust/procedures_102_en.html (accessed on Oct. 22, 2023).
28. *Ibid.*

abuses,[29] but in general, less guidance is available in relation to Article 102 TFEU than in relation to Article 101 TFEU.

As with anticompetitive agreements, the variety of markets in which blockchains and smart contracts may be used precludes a detailed discussion of EU precedents on individual types of conduct that may be found abusive. Given that blockchains can be used to store significant quantities of data and may be used by platforms accessible to multiple stakeholders, however, I briefly discuss two areas in which abuse of dominance issues may arise for companies using blockchain applications in their businesses: big data and online platforms.

Big data and online platforms have come under intense scrutiny in the EU and elsewhere, largely as a result of the growth of major business-to-consumer (B2C) platforms. However, the potential for enhanced enforcement is not limited to the B2C context. The discussion below draws to a significant extent on the 2019 report of three special advisors to the EC on "Competition Policy for the Digital Era" (the Digital Era Report or Report),[30] but a large number of official studies have been published in recent years. Other important studies include the 2019 "Furman Report" in the UK[31] and the joint Franco-German 2016 study on competition law and data (the Franco-German Study).[32] EU and other laws in this area can be expected to evolve in significant respects in the coming years. More recently, the EU has adopted an *ex ante* regulation known as the Digital Markets Act.[33] The Digital Markets Act is to a large extent inspired by the Article 102 TFEU concerns outlined below, but the Digital Markets Act and other EU regulations of the digital sector are outside the scope of this chapter.

[B] Big Data

Much of the debate around big data and its potential relevance for abuse of dominance cases revolves around two questions: (i) whether, and if so how, the accumulation of big data can contribute to the creation of a dominant position within the meaning of

29. EC, Communication from the Commission—Guidance on the Commission's enforcement priorities in applying Art. 82 of the EC Treaty to abusive exclusionary conduct by dominant undertakings, OJ C45, 24/2/2012, pp. 7-20, as amended by Communication from the Commission—Amendments to the Communication from the Commission—Guidance on the Commission's enforcement priorities in applying Art. 82 of the EC Treaty to abusive exclusionary conduct by dominant undertakings, OJ C116, 31/3/2023, pp. 1-5.
30. Crémer, J., de Montjoye, Y-.A. and Schweitzer, H., *Competition Policy for the Digital Era*, available at: https://ec.europa.eu/competition/publications/reports/kd0419345enn.pdf (accessed on Oct. 20, 2023).
31. Unlocking Digital Competition—Report of the Digital Competition Expert Panel, available at: https://assets.publishing.service.gov.uk/government/uploads/system/uploads/attachment_data/file/785547/unlocking_digital_competition_furman_review_web.pdf (accessed on Oct. 20, 2023).
32. Autorité de la Concurrence and Bundeskartellamt, *Competition Law and Data*, available at: https://www.bundeskartellamt.de/SharedDocs/Publikation/DE/Berichte/Big%20Data%20Papier.pdf?__blob=publicationFile&v=2 (accessed on Oct. 20, 2023).
33. Regulation (EU) 2022/1925 of the European Parliament and of the Council of Sep. 14, 2022 on contestable and fair markets in the digital sector and amending Directives (EU) 2019/1937 and (EU) 2020/1828, OJ L265, 12/10/2022, pp. 1-66.

Article 102 TFEU and (ii) under what conditions can dominant companies be required to share such data to remedy an abuse of a dominant position under Article 102 TFEU. Such debates tend to assume that these questions are linked in the sense that where the accumulation of big data gives rise to a dominant position, Article 102 TFEU may require the dominant company to give competitors access to that data.

In fact, the issues of dominance and remedy are independent. As noted above, the first step in an abuse of dominance case is to define the relevant antitrust market. Where data are themselves a product offered by a potentially dominant company, the accumulation of a large share of the relevant type of data may indeed be an indication of a dominant position. This has arguably been the situation in a number of Article 102 TFEU cases unrelated to blockchain.[34] Notably, the remedy sought in these cases has not typically been granting access to the underlying data but rather remedies to facilitate competitors marketing their own data-related services.

Much of the recent debate about big data, and the big data-related proposals in the Report, revolves around the alleged need for companies to gain direct access to competitors' data. The Report notes: "The significance of data and data access for competition will ... depend on an analysis of the specificities of a given market, the type of data, and data usage in a given case." In relation to proposals to require dominant companies to grant competitors access to data under Article 102 TFEU, the Report stressed the need for care. "It is necessary to distinguish between different forms of data, levels of data access, and data uses."

Much of the Report's big data discussion focuses on conditions in which antitrust law can be used as a tool to require companies to give competitors access to their data, but the Report also discusses new issues raised by companies voluntarily sharing and pooling data. Without discussing the issue in detail, the Report also notes the need for a new legal regime governing rights in data. The Report's approach to big data in these contexts is summarized below.

[1] Mandating Data Access

In a long and detailed analysis, the Report examines arguments for and against mandating data access in different contexts, depending on how the data are obtained (whether they are volunteered, observed, or inferred) and how data are used (use of

34. *See, e.g.*, Case COMP D3/38.044—NDC Health/IMS Health: Interim measures, OJ L59, 28/2/2002, pp. 18-49 (IMS considered dominant in a market for German regional pharmaceutical data. The EC proposed to adopt interim measures requiring IMS to license its "1 860 brick structure," which it considered to be a de facto industry standard for structuring such data. Although the European courts determined that the criteria for interim measures were not satisfied, IMS remains a seminal "big data" case); and CASE AT.39654—Reuters Instrument Codes, available at: https://ec.europa.eu/competition/antitrust/cases/dec_docs/39654/39654_2861_16.pdf (accessed on Oct. 20, 2023). Thomson Reuters found dominant in the worldwide market for consolidated real-time data feeds and to have abused that position by restricting the use of Reuters Instrument Codes in relation to data feeds of other providers; Thomson Reuters offered commitments to resolve the EC's concerns.

non-anonymous individual-level data, anonymous individual-level data, aggregated data, or contextual data).

The Report notes that the "debate is mostly framed as a debate on whether the criteria of the so-called essential facilities doctrine (EFD) are met." In the data access context, however, the Report argues against the application of the EFD and for the application of a broader interest-balancing test. In particular, the Report argues against application of the requirement that a claimant under the EFD shows that it requires access to the essential facility to develop a "new product." The goal of the "new product rule" is to preserve a dominant firm's investment incentives by ensuring a sufficient degree of appropriability of profits for the firm. But the Report argues that in some "access to data" cases, the danger that the firm will lose the incentive to invest in data collection and innovation is lower. Thus, rather than a formal "new product rule," authorities applying Article 102 TFEU to "access to data" cases should verify that an access mandate will not eliminate the appropriability of benefits resulting from successful investments. According to the Report, this consideration may be especially important outside the platform context.

As under the "standard" EFD, a precondition for data access remedies under Article 102 TFEU should be indispensability. To determine whether data access is indispensable for Article 102 TFEU purposes, it is important to distinguish access to a data set from access to the data in close to real-time where no substitutes exist. The non-substitutability of data may result from the richness ("number of columns") and size ("number of rows") of the dataset, in particular, where machine-learning algorithms play a role. The frequency of data generation also needs to be taken into account when discussing data access, both for providing a service to the person who generated the data and for aggregated applications.

The balancing of interests needs to take account of both the need to protect the dominant firm's investment incentives and the need to ensure that strongly entrenched positions of market power, protected by high barriers of entry, remain contestable. In some settings, such interest-balancing can result in a duty to grant access to data in a form that allows competitors to compete effectively in neighboring markets, which may include a duty to ensure data interoperability.

The Report outlines several data access "scenarios" to identify situations in which data access mandates would be more or less likely to be appropriate. Access mandates would more likely be appropriate where the data controller holds a gatekeeper position (i.e., access to its data is essential for competing on one or more neighboring markets) or data access requests are somewhat standardized. Access mandates would be less appropriate where a firm requests data for the purpose of training algorithms for uses unrelated to the fields of activity of the data controller, although even in such case an access mandate could be imposed "where the dominant firm is a large player in data markets and has an infrastructure for data access requests in place."

In the balancing-of-interest context, the Report discusses whether the threshold for granting access to data should be lowered as compared to cases involving access to infrastructure or IPRs, at least where data is produced as a by-product of another activity and incentives to generate such data will persist irrespective of a possible access mandate, for instance, in relation to machine-generated sensor data in the Internet of Things context. While the value of data to a dominant data controller may be taken into account at the original price (and therefore needs to be protected under competition law), competition law should not protect an aftermarket monopoly.

Indeed, the Report supports a more interventionist approach to data access—and possibly data interoperability—for use in complementary markets or aftermarkets, which are part of the broader "ecosystem" served by the data controller. The EC and EU courts have frequently had occasion to address the relevance of secondary markets and aftermarkets in the Article 102 TFEU context. But the Report argues that "some of the specificities of data could imply that the competition policy treatment of access to data should be different from that of standard aftermarkets ... but there is very little economic analysis of these issues, so [their] conclusions should be considered as very preliminary."

In the specific case of individual-level data, the Report discusses the implications of the data portability right under the EU's General Data Protection Regulation (GDPR)[35] but notes that data portability in the GDPR does not provide a right to continuous data access or interoperability, but simply a right to receive a copy of some accumulated past data. Thus, it may facilitate a data subject's switching between services but not facilitate multi-homing or the offering of complementary services, which frequently requires continuous and potentially real-time data access. Accordingly, "more demanding" data access regimes could be mandated under Article 102 TFEU for dominant firms, or through sector-specific regulation, in particular, to open up secondary markets. Tension with the GDPR may also arise where an access mandate involves personal data. The Report notes that the UK and French competition authorities have resolved this tension in past cases by ordering data access on an opt-out basis or permitting access to data only for specified purposes and specified acts of processing.

In summary, the Report concludes that Article 102 TFEU may be used in appropriate cases to give competitors access to data, but only from dominant firms and after a thorough analysis of whether such access is truly indispensable and after weighing the legitimate interests of both parties. Access to individual-level data to serve a user should only be granted if that user consents, irrespective of whether personal or non-personal data is at issue. Where the user can switch his/her service provider with sufficient ease without access to data, no mandated access is required. Where access to bundled individual-level data or aggregate data is requested, the indispensability criterion may be met if the data holder is a dominant platform whose dominance is strongly entrenched and exclusive data control may reinforce and extend such power.

35. Regulation (EU) 2016/679 of the European Parliament and of the Council of Apr. 27, 2016 on the protection of natural persons with regard to the processing of personal data and on the free movement of such data; and repealing Directive 95/46/EC (General Data Protection Regulation), OJ L119, 4/5/2016, pp. 1-88.

[2] Policing Data Sharing and Pooling

Although much of its discussion focuses on the potential imposition of data sharing requirements, the Report also discusses the antitrust treatment of voluntary data sharing and pooling. Data-sharing and data pooling arrangements will frequently be procompetitive, enabling firms to develop new or better products or services or to train algorithms on a broader, more meaningful basis. Such arrangements can be anticompetitive, however, for example, where some competitors are denied access or granted access only on less favorable terms; data sharing amounts to an anticompetitive information exchange including competitively sensitive information; data sharing or pooling discourages competitors from differentiating and improving their own data collection and analytics pipelines; or where the granting of access to data on terms that are not "fair, reasonable and non-discriminatory" (FRAND) results in an exploitative abuse. Where a dominant, vertically integrated platform provides privileged data access to its own subsidiaries, this can constitute a form of self-preferencing (*see* above). Where a data pool has market power and gives its members a significant advantage, the pool may be under a duty to give access to others, perhaps on FRAND or similar terms.

The Report references the treatment of data access issues under Article 102 TFEU and merger control, as well as established rules on research and development (R&D) agreements and patent pools, but notes that it may be more difficult to establish the market power of a data pool based on market shares, due to the multi-purpose use of data. Thus, an access regime may need to differ depending on the type of use, and the duty to give access should be proportional to the pool's market power. For example, a group of smaller players pooling their data to gain a competitive advantage should not be forced to give their pooled data to a much larger player. Where there is a FRAND or similar duty to provide data access, and the pool's data format standard is proprietary, the standard owner should not be able to raise its fees over time as the pool becomes more important in the market (by analogy to "patent ambushes"), and such duties should apply to both access to the data pool and the use of the data format standard.

The Report notes that the competition law treatment of data-sharing and pooling arrangements is relatively new and under-researched and recommends that the EC use guidance letters and "no infringement" decisions, as well as the next version of the EC's Guidelines on horizontal cooperation. Indeed, a separate block exemption regulation on data sharing and pooling may be called for.

[C] Online Platforms

As with big data, antitrust enforcement against online platforms is a major focus of the Digital Era Report and the EC's thinking about antitrust policy in the digital sphere. Depending on how a blockchain is structured, the evolving policy on online platforms may result in enhanced antitrust scrutiny. Indeed, the Report takes a relatively broad view of the definition of an online platform, rejecting arguments for limiting the discussion to two- or multi-sided platforms. The Report's definition of platforms includes networks and goes beyond online intermediation to include desktop, mobile operating systems and browsers, "offline" software, and app stores.

The Report notes that, especially in view of network effects, there might be room for only a limited number of "platforms," especially in the absence of multi-homing, protocol and data interoperability, or differentiation. The Report discusses ways to protect competition both "for the market" and "in the market," arguing that platforms play a form of regulatory role as they determine the rules according to which their users interact and, when they are dominant, have a responsibility to ensure that competition on their platforms is fair, unbiased, and pro-user. More specifically, the Report argues that dominant platforms have a responsibility to ensure that their rules ensure a level playing field. While non-dominant platforms also play a regulatory role, the Report argues, no far-reaching general rules would be needed for such platforms to the extent that they are disciplined by competition.

[1] *Most Favored Nations*

The Digital Era Report discusses several specific issues in the online platform context, including the so-called most favored nation (MFN) clauses, multi-homing, interoperability, transparency, leveraging and "self-preferencing."

The Report acknowledges the possible procompetitive benefits of MFNs but argues for strict scrutiny of such clauses because of their potential to protect platforms' incumbency advantages. In markets where there is a sufficiently vigorous competition between platforms, "wide MFNs" that prevent sellers on a platform from price differentiating between platforms should be prohibited, while "narrow MFNs" preventing sellers from offering lower prices on their own websites should be allowed. Where competition between platforms is weak, however, the Report argues that both forms of MFN should be prohibited.

[2] *Multi-homing*

The Digital Era Report also takes a nuanced approach to multi-homing. In general, the Report argues that any measure by which a dominant firm restricts multi-homing, including technical means and commercial practices such as fidelity rebates and bundling, should be suspect, and such firms should bear the burden of providing a solid efficiency defense. The effects of multi-homing can be different when the competition is "in the market" rather than "for the market," and multi-homing between large platforms could actually limit competition.

[3] *Interoperability*

The Digital Era Report distinguishes between three types of interoperability: protocol interoperability, data interoperability, and full protocol interoperability. Protocol interoperability, which allows for the development of complementary services and competition on the merits, may require the development of standards, but such standards could hinder innovation if defined too strictly or too early. Data interoperability allows for complementary services to be developed in a larger range of cases than protocol interoperability. Data interoperability can also limit incentives for new forms of data collection. Full protocol interoperability would involve the imposition of interoperability requirements to give direct competitors access to positive network effects stemming from the large user base of one platform extend to other platforms, but the need for strong standardization with full protocol interoperability could significantly dampen platforms' ability to innovate. The Report argues for imposing duties to grant protocol interoperability and (with the concerned users' consent) data interoperability upon dominant platforms but urges great caution in imposing a duty to grant full protocol interoperability.

[4] Transparency

The Report argues that transparency can be a competition policy issue because a lack of transparency presumably distorts competition. Platforms' actions to prevent research, from technical measures purposely designed to prevent transparency to legal measures such as making studies contractually inadmissible, should be viewed with great suspicion. The Report concludes that the impact of platforms on society requires more transparency vis-à-vis civil society and that public authorities should find ways to ensure a sufficient understanding of how platforms work, potentially including full access to data and algorithms in the context of competition law cases.

[5] Leveraging

The Report argues that large platforms possess strong competitive advantages over new entrants because of, *inter alia*, network externalities and privileged access to data that translate into advantages in related services. If bundling is efficient thanks to the shared use of data, data interoperability can help to level the playing field. Enforcement should be especially strict where dominant platforms try to use consumers' data to bundle services and products.

[6] Self-preferencing

According to case law, Article 102 TFEU may prohibit self-preferencing by the owner of an "essential facility," and even below this threshold where it is not justified by a procompetitive rationale and is likely to result in a leveraging of market power. In other words: self-preferencing is not abusive per se but should be subject to an effects test. In markets with particularly high barriers to entry and where the platform serves as an intermediation infrastructure of particular relevance, the Report proposes that platforms should bear the burden of proving that self-preferencing has no long-run exclusionary effects on product markets. Full platform unbundling should not be the general remedy to a finding of abusive self-preferencing; however, less restrictive ways to preclude self-preferencing may exist.

[D] Article 102 TFEU and Blockchain

Given the growing use of blockchain to store large volumes of data on platforms accessible to select groups of industry participants and antitrust authorities' growing focus on big data and online platforms, companies adopting blockchain applications may need to consider potential abuse of dominance risks. The potential for blockchain applications to contribute to the EC or other authority finding that a blockchain operator has a dominant position or that particular blockchain-related conduct may be found to abuse a dominant position must clearly be considered on a case-by-case basis. Given the wide range of blockchain applications, a complete review of ways in which abuse of dominance issues may arise is beyond the scope of this chapter. Instead, this section discusses aspects of blockchain applications that may give rise to particular concerns from this perspective and steps that participants can take to address them.

In blockchain applications, abuse of dominance issues may arise, in particular, where the format for information stored on the blockchain or the blockchain itself can be expected to become a de jure or de facto industry standard and/or where access to information stored on the blockchain may be considered essential to industry participants' ability to compete.[36]

Where the blockchain format may become an industry standard, competitors may seek access to IPRs needed to permit interoperability, such as an application program interface (API), rather than to the data stored on the blockchain as such. The Report suggests a number of changes to existing EU legal tests that would make it easier for the EC to find an abuse in such a situation and to order remedies to encourage interoperability.

Where the data stored on a blockchain are themselves critical to stakeholders' competitiveness, those stakeholders may seek access to the underlying data on the ground that a refusal to provide access may amount to an abuse of a dominant position under Article 102 TFEU. The legal tests for such a remedy are, and will likely remain, very strict, and such cases can be expected to be rare. The Report supports changes to the existing EFD criteria to facilitate access to data remedies, not necessarily to direct competitors of the blockchain owners but more likely to would-be competitors in related or downstream markets.

"Online platform" related concerns may arise, in particular, in applications where a private blockchain is operated by a company or group of companies that grant access to the blockchain to third parties for whom such access becomes important to their competitiveness. Although each situation will be highly fact-specific, issues may most likely arise where blockchain owner/operators adopt practices that have been

36. *See, e.g.*, Global Blockchain Business Council, GLOBAL STANDARDS MAPPING INITIATIVE 4.0, November 2023, available at https://gbbcouncil.org/wp-content/uploads/2023/11/GBBC-GSMI-4.0-Update-November-2023.pdf?mc_cid=4aad7d9f4f&mc_eid=55476ebd9d (accessed on Feb. 9, 2024).

singled out as potentially problematic, such as imposing MFNs on blockchain users; limiting third parties' freedom to use multiple blockchains; restricting interoperability to limit third parties' use of alternative blockchains; limiting transparency on the blockchain's operations, for instance, as regards the blockchain's data access rules and algorithms; leveraging the competitive significance of the blockchain by bundling other products or services with blockchain access; and introducing a measure to give preference to goods and services offered by the blockchain owner/operator over those offered by third parties.

[E] Appropriate Safeguards

As with horizontal and vertical agreements, the enormous variety of situations in which blockchain and smart contracts can be used means that the potential for blockchain applications to raise abuse of dominance concerns must be assessed on a case-by-case basis. Such concerns arise, in principle, only where a party holds a dominant position in a relevant antitrust market, which would normally be the antitrust market in which the blockchain is proposed to be used. Care should also be taken where a blockchain will be, or has the potential to become, an industry standard or otherwise become essential for competitors.

§9.04 MERGER CONTROL

[A] Introduction to Concepts

A variety of corporate transactions, including acquisitions of companies and joint ventures, may trigger merger filing requirements if relevant thresholds are met. The types of transaction that may be caught, as well as the applicable thresholds, vary considerably from jurisdiction to jurisdiction. At the EU level, the applicable requirements are set out in the EU Merger Regulation (EUMR),[37] but national measures at the Member State level may apply where a transaction is not caught by the EUMR.

Subject to exceptions, the EUMR applies to "concentrations" defined as "a change of control on a lasting basis [that] results from: (a) the merger of two or more previously independent undertakings or parts of undertakings, or (b) the acquisition, by one or more persons already controlling at least one undertaking, or by one or more undertakings, whether by purchase of securities or assets, by contract or by any other means, of direct or indirect control of the whole or parts of one or more other undertakings."

"Control" is in turn defined "the possibility of exercising decisive influence on an undertaking, in particular by: (a) ownership or the right to use all or part of the assets of an undertaking; (b) rights or contracts which confer decisive influence on the

37. Council Regulation (EC) No. 139/2004 of Jan. 20, 2004 on the control of concentrations between undertakings, OJ L24, 29/1/2004, pp. 1-22.

composition, voting or decisions of the organs of an undertaking." The EC's Consolidated Jurisdictional Notice (the CJN) under the EUMR[38] clarifies that the concept of "control" includes not only the positive power to determine a company's competitive policy, for instance, through ownership of a majority of the company's shares but also the power to block certain actions, for example, through veto rights of minority shareholders under a company's articles of incorporation or similar documents or applicable joint venture or shareholder agreements.

Creation of a joint venture qualifies as a "concentration" where the joint venture performs "on a lasting basis all the functions of an autonomous economic entity," i.e., "full-function" joint ventures.

Concentrations must be notified to the EC and approved prior to implementation if they meet the following thresholds: "(a) the combined aggregate worldwide turnover of all the undertakings concerned is more than EUR 2 500 million; (b) in each of at least three Member States, the combined aggregate turnover of all the undertakings concerned is more than EUR 100 million; (c) in each of at least three Member States included for the purpose of point (b), the aggregate turnover of each of at least two of the undertakings concerned is more than EUR 25 million; and (d) the aggregate Community-wide turnover of each of at least two of the undertakings concerned is more than EUR 100 million, unless each of the undertakings concerned achieves more than two-thirds of its aggregate Community-wide turnover within one and the same Member State."

Concentrations with a Community dimension must be notified to the EC and approved prior to their implementation. The EC must determine whether notified concentrations would "significantly impede effective competition" in the EU or in a substantial part of it, "in particular as a result of the creation or strengthening of a dominant position," in which case the EC must prohibit the transaction.

The interpretation and application of the EUMR have generated thousands of pages of commentary, and a full discussion of this topic is outside the scope of this chapter. I briefly discuss below three topics that are most likely to be of particular relevance to companies involved in blockchain applications: (i) the criteria for determining whether the formation of a new jointly owned blockchain will be considered "full-function" and thus potentially as a concentration requiring EUMR review if the thresholds are met; (ii) actions that may be considered illegal implementation, or "gun-jumping," if taken before approval is received under the EUMR; and (iii) the EC's evolving approach to assessing the competitive effects of combining big datasets, which may arise where two or more companies with existing blockchain applications merge.

38. Commission Consolidated Jurisdictional Notice under Council Regulation (EC) No. 139/2004 on the control of concentrations between undertakings, OJ C95, 16/4/2008, pp. 1-48.

[B] Full-Function Joint Ventures

The concept of full-functionality is discussed in Part IV of the CJN, paragraphs 91-109. The CJN clarifies that the formation of a full-function joint venture may constitute a notifiable concentration even where the joint venture is a "greenfield operation" or the parties contribute their own assets to the joint venture without the need for an acquisition of control over a company with pre-existing operations. The concept of full-functionality does not mean that the joint venture enjoys autonomy as regards the adoption of its strategic decisions. The issue is rather whether the joint venture is full-function in operational respects; i.e., it has sufficient resources to operate independently on the market; it performs activities beyond one specific function for the parents; it is not excessively dependent on sale/purchase relations with its parents beyond a start-up period; it is intended to operate on a lasting basis.

Where two or more companies cooperate in the establishment of a blockchain application, they will typically need to consider whether the blockchain (or a company formed to own and operate it) will give rise to a full-function joint venture. This may be the case, in particular, where a blockchain application is intended to provide services to third parties, not only to its parents, and will have sufficient resources (e.g., its own personnel) necessary to do so. This may be more likely in the case of a blockchain open to the public. If so, the EUMR thresholds can be met by the parents alone, even if the blockchain is created on a greenfield basis and has no turnover of its own. By contrast, a blockchain application that is owned and operated by one company, such as a supply chain management platform accessible to third-party suppliers, would normally not qualify as a full-function joint venture and would not be notifiable under the EUMR.

[C] Gun-Jumping

The term "gun-jumping" is not clearly defined in the EUMR. In practice, it is used to indicate two distinct, but closely related, violations: (i) violation of the obligation under Article 4(1) EUMR to notify concentrations with a Community dimension and (ii) violation of the obligation under Article 7(1) EUMR not to implement a notifiable concentration either before its notification or until it has been approved by the EC. Similar provisions exist in most national merger control regimes.

In addition, if the parties to the transaction are competitors, inappropriate pre-closing conduct may be caught by Article 101(1) TFEU (and its national equivalents), which prohibits restrictive agreements, decisions and concerted practices. Competition authorities are often unclear about which rules to apply in a given case: gun-jumping or general antitrust rules. A 2018 judgment clarified that pre-approval actions contributing to a lasting change of control over the target can be sanctioned as gun-jumping, while conduct that falls short of contributing to such a change of control but constitutes anticompetitive coordination between the merging parties may be challenged under Article 101(1) TFEU.[39]

The EC is demonstrating greater intolerance to breaches of procedural rules by merging parties, including, in particular, gun-jumping. The EC can impose fines up to 10% of companies' global group turnover for gun-jumping violations; in 2023, the EC imposed fines amounting to EUR 432 million on two U.S. companies, Illumina and GRAIL.[40]

The clearest case of gun-jumping occurs where the parties implement a notifiable transaction without making a required notification. Such an error can be surprisingly easy to make under EU law because some of the EUMR thresholds are relatively subjective or difficult to apply in practice, in particular in the case of minority investments in publicly listed companies and joint ventures, where it can be difficult to determine whether a transaction involves the acquisition of joint control or a creation of a full-function joint venture.

Another form of gun-jumping occurs where a transaction is duly notified, but some form of premature implementation takes place prior to obtaining clearance. While most companies are aware of this prohibition, the line between legitimate preparatory measures and partial implementation is often unclear. Merging companies, therefore, often face questions about the exact extent of the standstill obligation.

Gun-jumping questions may arise in the context of mergers and acquisitions involving companies that operate blockchains, but in such cases where the EUMR thresholds are met by the parties' turnover, those blockchain operations are less likely to be central to the gun-jumping issues. By contrast, gun-jumping issues may be critical where a blockchain, or company operating a blockchain, is being set up by two or more parents and the blockchain is likely to be full-function.

Merging companies and companies creating a new joint venture must carefully assess their pre-closing actions on a case-by-case basis, particularly in relation to exchanges of competitively sensitive information, integration planning, management changes, coordination of competitive behavior, and transfer of business risks associated with the target's business.

[D] Merger Control and Blockchain

The EC's substantive analysis of notified concentrations is, of course, highly fact-specific. It is not practical in this context to discuss all the substantive issues that typically arise in such review, such as the definition of the relevant markets, the assessment of the market positions of the parties and their competitors, and the assessment of the likely competitive effects of the combination of the parties' positions,

39. Case C-633/16, *Ernst & Young P/S v. Konkurrencerådet*, judgment of May 31, 2018, available at https://curia.europa.eu/juris/document/document.jsf?text=&docid=202404&doclang=EN (accessed on Oct. 20, 2023).
40. Case M.10483—Illumina/GRAIL, available at https://competition-cases.ec.europa.eu/cases/M.10483 (accessed on Oct. 20, 2023).

whether they are direct competitors (horizontal issues) or have a customer-supplier relationship (vertical issues).

[1] *Horizontal Assessment: Combining Datasets*

Given the role of blockchain in storing large quantities of data, one issue that has become increasingly important in recent years bears particular mention here: the EC's approach to analyzing the effects of mergers resulting in the combination of big datasets.

The EC has a long track record of assessing the effect of notified mergers on data-related markets. The EC has analyzed a wide range of data-related markets, from market research and marketing information services[41] to financial information,[42] to navigable digital map databases,[43] to online advertising.[44] In these cases, the EC's traditional tools for assessing the effects of a combination on horizontally and vertically affected markets can normally be applied in a straightforward way.

Recent debates on big data and antitrust, by contrast, focus on the antitrust implications of companies collecting and using big data that are not offered as a product on the market. The Franco/German Study opined that a combination of "data troves could raise competition concerns if the combination of data makes it impossible for competitors to replicate the information (…)"[45] possessed by the merged entity.

In several decisions, the EC has elaborated on its approach to big data issues in merger review. These decisions help to illustrate the EC's approach and its attempts to fit big data issues into its traditional analytical frameworks, as set out in its Guidelines (the Horizontal Guidelines) on the assessment of horizontal mergers under the EUMR, its Guidelines (the Non-Horizontal Guidelines) on the assessment of non-horizontal mergers under the EUMR[46] and its Notice (the Remedies Notice) on remedies acceptable under the EUMR.[47] These decisions go a long way toward formalizing the EC's approach to assessing data-related aspects of notified mergers where the data are not themselves being offered to third parties as part of a product or service. This emerging

---

41. *See, e.g.*, *VNU/AC Nielsen*, COMP/M.2291, dated Feb. 12, 2001 available at: http://ec.europa.eu/competition/mergers/cases/decisions/m2291_en.pdf (accessed on Oct. 20, 2023) and WPP/TMS, COMP/M.5232, dated Sep. 23, 2008, available at: http://ec.europa.eu/competition/mergers/cases/decisions/m5232_20080923_20212_en.pdf (accessed on Oct. 20, 2023).
42. *See, e.g.*, *Thomson Corporation/Reuters*, COMP/M.4726, dated Feb. 19, 2008, available at: http://ec.europa.eu/competition/mergers/cases/decisions/m4726_20080219_20600_en.pdf (accessed on Oct. 20, 2023).
43. For example, *TomTom/TeleAtlas*, Comp/M. 4854, dated May 14, 2008, available at: http://ec.europa.eu/competition/mergers/cases/decisions/m4854_20080514_20682_en.pdf (accessed on Oct. 20, 2023) and *Nokia/Navteq*, COMP/M 4942, dated Jul. 2, 2008, available at: http://ec.europa.eu/competition/mergers/cases/decisions/m4942_20080702_20682_en.pdf (accessed on Feb. 23, 2023).
44. *See, e.g.*, *Google/DoubleClick*, COMP/M.4731, dated Mar. 11, 2008, available at: http://ec.europa.eu/competition/mergers/cases/decisions/m4731_20080311_20682_en.pdf (accessed on Oct. 20, 2023).
45. Franco-German Study, *supra* n. 32 at p. 16.
46. OJ C 265/6, 18/10/2008.
47. OJ 267/1, 22/10/2008.

approach is discussed below, first in relation to horizontal issues and then in relation to vertical issues.

In one leading case, *Verizon/Yahoo*, the EC noted[48] that "[a]ssuming data combination is allowed under the applicable data protection legislation, there are two main ways in which a merger may raise horizontal issues as a result of the combination, under the ownership of the merged entity, of two datasets previously held by two independent firms. First, the combination of two datasets post-merger may increase the merged entity's market power in a hypothetical market for the supply of this data or increase barriers to entry/expansion in the market for actual or potential competitors, which may need this data to operate on this market. Competitors may be required to collect a larger dataset in order to compete effectively with the merged entity than absent the merger. Second, even if there is no intention or technical possibility to combine the two datasets, it may be that pre-merger the two companies were competing with each other on the basis of the data they controlled and this competition would be eliminated by the merger."

Concluding that the combination of the parties' data did not raise antitrust concerns, the EC noted the potential restrictions imposed by EU data protection rules and observed that the combination would not raise barriers to entry/expansion for other players since there would "continue to be a large amount of internet user data that are valuable for advertising purposes and that are not within the Parties' exclusive control". Indeed, the EC's market test confirmed that Yahoo's and Verizon's data were not "unique."

Since the EC has found no big data-related ground for concern as a result of the combination of big datasets, it has not been required to discuss potential theories of harm in detail.

[2] Vertical Concerns: The Role of Data in Foreclosure Assessment

Compared to horizontal concerns, the EC's analytical framework appears better suited to dealing with big data concerns in a vertical context. Input foreclosure concerns are addressed in the Non-Horizontal Guidelines, and potential remedies for such concerns are discussed in the Remedies Notice. The Franco/German Study also noted that a merger of companies holding "strong market positions in separate upstream or downstream markets can foreclose these markets for new competitors," for instance, where an online service provider acquires "producers of computers, smartphones or software in order to make sure to continue to access important amounts of data through users of these services."[49]

According to the EC's Non-Horizontal Guidelines, a "merger is said to result in foreclosure where actual or potential rivals' access to supplies or markets is hampered or eliminated as a result of the merger, thereby reducing these companies' ability and/or incentive to compete". According to the EC, input foreclosure may occur in

48. Paragraphs 81 et seq.
49. Franco-German Study, *supra* n. 32, at p. 16.

various forms. The merged entity may decide not to deal with its actual or potential downstream competitors, to restrict supplies, to raise prices to competitors and/or to otherwise make the conditions of supply less favorable (e.g., by degrading the quality of the input).

In assessing input foreclosure risks, the EC examines, first, whether the merged entity would have the ability to substantially foreclose access to inputs; second, whether it would have the incentive to do so; and third, whether a foreclosure strategy would have a significant detrimental effect on competition downstream. Concerns arise only if the input in question is important for the downstream product, for instance, because the input represents a significant cost factor or is important for other reasons.

According to the EC, a merged entity would only have the ability to foreclose if, by reducing access to its own upstream products or services, it could negatively affect the overall availability of inputs for the downstream market in terms of price or quality (e.g., because the remaining upstream suppliers are less efficient, offer less preferred alternatives, or lack the ability to expand output in response to the supply restriction) or due to the presence of exclusive contracts between the merged entity and independent input providers. Input foreclosure is only a concern where the merged firm has significant market power in the upstream market so that its conduct can be expected to significantly influence competition in the upstream market and thus, possibly, prices and supply conditions in the downstream market.

The incentive to foreclose depends on the degree to which foreclosure would be profitable. The merged entity faces a trade-off between the profit lost in the upstream market due to a reduction of input sales to (actual or potential) rivals and the profit gain, in the short or long term, from expanding sales downstream or, as the case may be, being able to raise prices to consumers. Other things being equal, a merged entity is more likely to have an incentive to foreclose where the upstream margins are low and the downstream margins are high. The merged firm's incentives also depend on the share of demand that may be diverted from downstream rivals to the merged entity.

In general, input foreclosure concerns may lead to a challenge when input foreclosure would lead to increased prices in the downstream market or raise barriers to entry to potential competitors, in particular, if input foreclosure would entail for such potential competitors the need to enter at both the downstream and the upstream level in order to compete effectively. Conversely, concerns may be rebutted if there are sufficient credible downstream competitors whose costs would likely not be raised, countervailing factors such as buyer power or the likelihood that entry upstream would maintain effective competition and efficiencies.

According to the Remedies Notice, concerns that competition may be significantly impeded by foreclosure can be addressed by "commitments granting non-discriminatory access to infrastructure or networks of the merging parties" or "information necessary for the interoperability of different equipment" where "the control of key technology or IP rights may lead to concerns of foreclosure of competitors which depend on the technology or IP rights as essential input for the activities in a downstream market."[50] Similarly, concerns that a merger may eliminate players' incentives to license patents may be eliminated by commitments to grant licenses on the same basis post-transaction to all third parties which depend on the IPRs or information for their activities.

In a number of cases, the EC has applied the analysis of input foreclosure effects to concerns about access to big data in the merger context. In *Microsoft/LinkedIn*, certain software solutions providers claimed that LinkedIn "full data" would, in future, constitute an important input for the provision of advanced functionalities of customer relationship management (CRM) software. One complainant, in particular, argued that Microsoft could restrict access to LinkedIn full data, thereby making it harder for other providers to compete and to bring innovation in the market. The EC noted that LinkedIn did not generally make available LinkedIn full data to third parties pre-transaction, and the complaint assumed that absent the transaction, LinkedIn would have started monetizing such data. The EC questioned that assumption but nonetheless analyzed whether Microsoft would have had the ability and incentive to reduce competition by restricting access to LinkedIn full data to downstream competitors. Microsoft argued that LinkedIn full data were not an important input and that alternative data were available from other vendors.

The EC considered that the transaction would not have given Microsoft the ability to foreclose competition since reducing access to LinkedIn full data would be unlikely to negatively affect the overall availability of data needed by downstream competitors, in part because LinkedIn did not appear to have a significant degree of market power in any potential relevant upstream market, which in this case would be a hypothetical market or segment for the provision of data.

In addition, the EC considered that LinkedIn full data could not be characterized as (and would not be likely to become in the next two to three years) an important input since all major CRM vendors had already started offering advanced functionalities or planned to do so in the next two to three years, without access to LinkedIn full data. Furthermore, even if LinkedIn full data were to be used for that purpose, it would constitute only one of the many types of data needed, and many other possible sources of data were already available.

Moreover, the EC considered that it was unclear whether Microsoft would have had the incentive to foreclose competing providers of CRM software solutions by restricting access to LinkedIn full data. The EC noted that the market investigation was inconclusive and that it was not clear to what extent any such foreclosing strategy would be profitable for Microsoft (since it was not possible to estimate what profits Microsoft would derive by licensing LinkedIn full data).

As regards the impact of a foreclosure strategy on the downstream market, the EC considered that the transaction was unlikely to have an overall negative impact on effective competition in the market for CRM software solutions, and any potential restriction of access to LinkedIn full data would be unlikely to lead to consumer harm since any impact would be felt in sub-segments representing less than 30% of the entire

50. *Supra* n. 47, paras 64-65.

CRM software solutions market, and LinkedIn was only one of multiple data sources required. Therefore, it was unlikely that competing CRM software providers would be hampered in their ability to compete and innovate or that the mere likelihood that Microsoft would carry out a foreclosure strategy would raise barriers to entry for potential competitors.

The analysis of big data-related input foreclosure concerns has tended to track the EC's traditional approach as set out in its Guidelines more closely than its analysis of horizontal issues. In *Microsoft/LinkedIn,* in particular, the EC closely tracked the Non-Horizontal Guidelines analysis of the merged entity's alleged incentive and ability to foreclose downstream competitors' access to data as an input, taking account of the parties' strength in upstream and downstream markets. The EC considered foreclosure effects in a "hypothetical" market since the concerns were based on an unproven assumption that without the transaction LinkedIn would have attempted to monetize its full data by selling it to downstream competitors. The EC itself noted the theoretical difficulties with this approach; it is hard to see how the EC could meet its burden to show that a notified transaction would create the incentive and ability to foreclose the supply of data to competitors where the data have not been supplied by either merging party in the past, there is no course of dealing to measure the profitability of such a strategy, and the data in question has by definition not previously been a key input for competitors.

Future decisions may clarify how the EC will apply its analytical framework for vertical issues to big data, where the data are not already available as an input to competitors. The EC should also consider potential anticompetitive effects in view of the characteristics of the data in question. Again, the cases in which these issues have arisen involve first-party data (often personal data) collected by companies on their customers for use (or potential use) in online advertising. As noted, such data are the type most commonly considered to be non-rivalrous and ubiquitous, as acknowledged by the EC in calling such data a "commodity." Such data is also more likely—depending on the use case—to suffer from diminishing returns and to decline rapidly in value. Where the value of particular data is likely to be short-lived, it may be more appropriate to consider the potential foreclosure impact of the merging parties' sources for generating new data, as opposed to the combination of existing datasets. By contrast, where merging companies' data may have longer-lasting value, such as for developing and improving a platform's own online advertising algorithms or other products (e.g., spell-check programs or voice recognition software), incremental data may have decreasing marginal value, which would likely limit the competitive impact of combining the merging parties' data. The EC would also need to take account of non-data alternatives to address relevant needs. For example, if competitors can license a suitable algorithm from a software developer, access to a particular dataset to develop its own software may be less relevant.

In conclusion, though the EC has been less vocal on big data issues than some national authorities, it has developed a significant track record in examining big data-related concerns in the merger context. Most of the older decisions concerned data-related markets, i.e., markets in which the data in question were themselves the product market. More recently, the EC has started to explicate its approach to big data concerns where the merging parties collect large amounts of data in their business but do not offer such data to third parties as a product. Given the EC's focus on big data, future cases may delve into these issues in more detail. Novel issues are most likely to arise in relation to combinations of first-party data (i.e., data collected or inferred by the merging parties themselves), in particular data on consumers.

[E] Appropriate Safeguards

Once again, the EU and other merger review implications of a proposed transaction must be assessed on a case-by-case basis. The EU and other antitrust authorities assess proposed mergers and acquisitions to estimate their likely impact on competition in relevant antitrust markets, i.e., the products and services offered by the parties. Whether and if so, how those parties use blockchains will often be irrelevant to the review of a proposed transaction. However, the EU and other authorities are increasingly concerned about the competitive significance of data. Where merging parties control (or have access to) blockchains with significant datasets, authorities are likely to consider whether and to what extent the parties' combination is likely to affect others' ability to compete. Together with their antitrust counsel, merging parties should consider the potential competitive significance of their data along with their review of the market overlaps of their products and services.

FURTHER READING

EC, Communication from the Commission—Guidance on the Commission's enforcement priorities in applying Article 82 of the EC Treaty to abusive exclusionary conduct by dominant undertakings, OJ C45, 24/2/2012, pp. 7-20, as amended by Communication from the Commission—Amendments to the Communication from the Commission—Guidance on the Commission's enforcement priorities in applying Article 82 of the EC Treaty to abusive exclusionary conduct by dominant undertakings, OJ C116, 31/3/2023, pp. 1-5.

Mateusz Blaszczyk, Trustless Trust and Antitrust: A Synthesis (August 13, 2023). Touro Law Review, Forthcoming, Available at SSRN: https://ssrn.com/abstract=4539525 or http://dx.doi.org/10.2139/ssrn.4539525.

Okan Yildiz and Rolf H. Weber, Market Definition and Market Power in the Era of Blockchain, in EUZ Zeitschrift für Europarecht 2/2023, available at https://eizpublishing.ch/artikel/euz/02-2023-euz/market-definition-and-market-power-in-the-era-of-blockchain/ (accessed on November 6, 2023).

Viktoria H.S.E. Robertson, *Antitrust Law and Digital Markets: A Guide to the European Competition Law Experience in the Digital Economy*, in Heinz D. Kurz, Marlies Schütz, Rita Strohmaier and Stella S. Zilian (eds.), The Routledge Handbook of Smart Technologies: An Economic and Social Perspective (Routledge, 2023).

Marc Wiggers, Robin Struijlaart, Joost Dibbits, *Digital Competition Law in Europe* (Kluwer Law International 2023).

Aurelien Portuese (ed.), Algorithmic Antitrust (Spring, 2022).

Thibault Schrepel, *Blockchain + Antitrust: The Decentralization Formula* (Edward Elgar Publishing, 2021).

Chris Pike and Antonio Capobianco, *Antitrust and the trust machine* (OECD 2020), available at http://www.oecd.org/daf/competition/antitrust-and-the-trust-machine-2020.pdf (accessed on November 6, 2023)

Jacques Crémer, Yves-Alexandre de Montjoye and Heike Schweitzer, *Competition Policy for the Digital Era*, available at: https://ec.europa.eu/competition/publications/reports/kd0419345enn.pdf (accessed on October 20, 2023)

Digital Competition Expert Panel, *Unlocking Digital Competition—Report of the Digital Competition Expert Panel*, available at: https://assets.publishing.service.gov.uk/government/uploads/system/uploads/attachment_data/file/785547/unlocking_digital_competition_furman_review_web.pdf (accessed on October 20, 2023)

Ariel Ezrachi and Maurice E. Stucke, *Virtual Competition—The Promise and Perils of the Algorithm-Driven Economy* (Harvard University Press, 2016).

Renato Nazzini, *The Blockchain (R)evolution and the Role of Antitrust* (King's College London Law School Research Paper No. 2019-20, September 28, 2018), available at: https://ssrn.com/abstract=3256728 or http://dx.doi.org/10.2139/ssrn.3256728 (accessed on October 20, 2023)

Maurice E. Stucke and Alan Grune, *Big Data and Competition Policy* (Oxford University Press, 2016)

Bibliography

Alkhalifah, A., et al.., A Taxonomy of Blockchain Threats and Vulnerabilities (2019), available at https://www.preprints.org/manuscript/201909.0117/v1/download

Aigner, Markus, Das international Privatrecht und die Blockchain – ein unloesbarer gordischer Knoten? (Zeitschrift für Europarecht, internationales Privatrecht und Rechtsvergleichung 2020, 211)

Anderl, Axel and Aigner, Markus, Blockchain in der Rechtspraxis (2020)

Anwar, H., *Smart Contracts: The Ultimate Guide for Beginners* (19 July 2018), available at: https://101blockchains.com/smart-contracts/#7

Aragon Network Jurisdiction Part 1: Decentralized Court, Aragon Network, 18 July 2017, available at: https://blog.aragon.org/aragon-network-jurisdiction-part-1-decentralized-court-c8ab2a675e 82/

Arning, Alexander and Rothkegel, Tobias Art. 4 DSGVO, in DSGVO, BDSG (Taeger/Gabel eds, 3rd. ed., R&W, 2019)

Article 29 Data Protection Working Party, Guidelines 04/2017 on Data Protection Impact Assessment (DPIA) and determining whether processing is "likely to result in a high risk" for the purposes of Regulation 2016/679 (WP 248, adopted on 04 April 2017)

Article 29 Data Protection Working Party, Opinion 03/2013 on purpose limitation (WP 203, adopted on 02 April 2013), available at https://ec.europa.eu/justice/article-29/documentation/opinion-recommendation/files/2013/wp203_en.pdf

Article 29 Data Protection Working Party, Opinion 05/2012 on Cloud Computing (WP 196, adopted on 01 July 2012), available at https://ec.europa.eu/justice/article-29/documentation/opinion-recommendation/files/2012/wp196_en.pdf

Article 29 Data Protection Working Party, Opinion 05/2014 on Anonymisation Techniques (WP 216, adopted on 10 April 2014), available at https://www.pdpjournals.com/docs/88197.pdf

Article 29 Data Protection Working Party, Opinion 06/2014 on the notion of legitimate interests of the data controller under Article 7 of the Directive 95/46/EC (WP 217, adopted on 14 November 2014)

Article 29 Data Protection Working Party, Opinion 1/2010 on the Concepts of "Controller" and "Processor" (WP 169, adopted on 16 February 2010), available at https://ec.europa.eu/justice/article-29/documentation/opinion-recommendation/files/2010/wp169en.pdf

Article 29 Data Protection Working Party, Opinion 03/2010 on the principle of accountability (WP 173 00062/10/EN, adopted on 13 July 2010), available at http://ec.europa.eu/justice/policies/privacy/docs/wpdocs/2010/wp173_en.pdf

Artzt, Matthias, Is Blockchain Compatible with the GDPR? (18 June 2019), available at https://platform.dataguidance.com/opinion/eu-blockchain-compatible-gdpr-part-1

Artzt, Matthias, Territorial scope of the GDPR from the US Perspective (26 June 2018), available at https://iapp.org/news/a/territorial-scope-of-the-gdpr-from-a-us-perspective/

Atzori, Marcella, Blockchain Technology and Decentralized Governance: Is the State Still Necessary? (University College of London, 2015), available at https://papers.ssrn.com/sol3/papers.cfm?abstract_id=2709713

Bacon et al., Blockchain Demystified: A Technical and Legal Introduction to Distributed and Centralised Ledgers (25 Richmond Journal of Law and Technology 1, 2018)

BaFin, Crypto tokens, (9 October 2023), https://www.bafin.de/EN/Aufsicht/FinTech/Geschaeftsmodelle/DLT_Blockchain_Krypto/Kryptotoken/Kryptotoken_node_en.html

BaFin, Initial Coin Offerings: Hinweisschreiben zur Einordnung als Finanzinstrumente 2018, WA 11-QB 4100-2017/0010

BaFin, Prospektpflicht – Rechtslage seit dem 21 July 2019, https://www.bafin.de/DE/Aufsicht/Prospekte/Wertpapiere/Prospektpflicht/prospektpflicht_node.html

BaFin, Tokenisation, (9 October 2023), https://www.bafin.de/SharedDocs/Veroeffentlichungen/EN/Fachartikel/2019/fa_bj_1904_Tokenisierung_en.html

BaFin, Zweites Hinweisschreiben zu Prospekt- und Erlaubnispflichten im Zusammenhang mit der Ausgabe sogenannter Krypto-Token dated 16 August 2019, https://www.bafin.de/SharedDocs/Downloads/DE/Merkblatt/WA/dl_wa_merkblatt_ICOs.html

Badr, Shaimaa, Gomaa, Ibrahim, Abd-Elrahman, Emad, Multi-tier Blockchain Framework for IoT-EHRs Systems (141 Procedia Computer Science 159-166, 2018), available at https://www.sciencedirect.com/science/article/pii/S187705091831812X

Balthazor, Andrew, The Bona Fide Acquisition Rule Applied to Cryptocurrency (Georgetown Law Technology Review, May 2019)

Bank of England, Cross-Authority Roadmap on innovation in payments, available at https://www.bankofengland.co.uk/paper/2023/cross-authority-roadmap-on-innovation-in-payments

Basel Committee on Banking Supervision, Consultative Document, Cryptoasset standard amendments (December 2023), available at https://www.bis.org/bcbs/publ/d567.pdf

Basel Committee on Banking Supervision, Discussion paper: Designing a prudential treatment for crypto-assets (December 2019), available at https://www.bis.org/bcbs/publ/d490.pdf

Basel Committee on Banking Supervision, Prudential treatment of cryptoasset exposures (December 2022), available at https://www.bis.org/bcbs/publ/d545.pdf

Beck, Roman, Müller-Bloch, Christoph and King, John Leslie, Governance in the Blockchain Economy: A Framework and Research Agenda (19(10) Journal of the Association for Information Systems Article 1 1021, 2018), available at: https://aisel.aisnet.org/cgi/viewcontent.cgi?article=1835&context=jais

Becker, Katrin, Blockchain Matters—Lex Cryptographia and the Displacement of Legal Symbolics and Imaginaries 118 (Law and Critique (2022) 33) available at https://doi.org/10.1007/s10978-021-09317-8

Behrens, Alexander and Schadtle, Kai, Erlaubnispflichten für Bank- und Finanzdienstleistungen im Zusammenhang mit Kryptowerten nach Umsetzung der Fuenften EU-Geldwaescherichtlinie (Zeitschrift für Wirtschafts- und Bankrecht 2019, 2099)

Bekeschenko, Edward, Determann, Lothar, Perevalov, Vadim and Wood, Inna, Keep Russian Data in Russia and Out of Clouds? (32(6) Computer & Internet Lawyer 1, 2015)

Berberich M. and Steiner M. Blockchain Technology and the GDPR – How to Reconcile Privacy and Distributed Ledgers? (European Data Protection Law Review 422, 2016)

Berg, Alastair, The Identity, Fungibility, and Anonymity of Money (10 July 2018), available at https://ssrn.com/abstract=3211011 or http://dx.doi.org/10.2139/ssrn.3211011

Bericht und Antrag der Regierung an den Landtag des Fürstentums Liechtenstein betreffend die Schaffung eines Gesetzes über Token und VT-Dienstleister (Token- und VT-Dienstleister-Gesetz; TVTG) und die Abänderung weiterer Gesetze, Nr. 54/2019, 55

Bermuda Digital Business Act 2018, Section 2, available at http://www.bermudalaws.bm/laws/Annual%20Laws/2018/Acts/Digital%20Asset%20Business%20Act%202018.pdf

Bertram, Ute, Smart Contracts – Praxisrelevante Fragen zu Vertragsabschluss, Leistungsstörungen und Auslegung 1416 (MDR 2018)

Bill to amend the Code of Virginia by adding a section numbered 8.01-390.4, relating to business records electronically registered on a blockchain self-authenticating, A, available at https://leg1.state.va.us/cgi-bin/legp504.exe?191+ful+HB2415&191+ful+HB2415

Blockchain Bundesverband, Blockchain, Data Protection, and the GDPR (Blockchain Bundesverband e.V., v. 1.0, 25 May 2018)

Blockchain Strategy of the Federal Government, We Set Out the Course for the Token Economy (18 September 2019) 4, available at https://www.bmwk.de/Redaktion/EN/Publikationen/Digitale-Welt/blockchain-strategy.pdf?__blob=publicationFile&v=3

Block.one, Order Instituting Cease-and-Desist Proceedings Pursuant to Section 8a of the Securities Act of 1933, Making Findings, and Imposing a Cease-and-Desist Order, Release No. 10714, at 2 (30 September 2019), available at https://www.sec.gov/litigation/admin/2019/33-10714.pdf

Bodó, Balázs, Gervais, D.† and Quintais, Joao Pedro, *Blockchain and smart contracts: the missing link in copyright licensing?* (25 September 2018), available at: https://academic.oup.com/ijlit/article/26/4/311/5106727

Bonomi, Andrea, Il nuovo diritto internazionale privato dei contratti: La convenzione di Roma del 19 giugno 1980 è entrata in vigore (Banca borsa e titoli di credito 1992, 48)

Bonomi, Andrea, Blockchain and Private International Law – Some general remarks, 153 (Yearbook of Private International Law, Volume 24)

Bont, Patrick, Kryptowährungen – und was machen die Regulatoren? (Handout to the speech held on 26 October 2017, Liechtenstein FMA, 2017), available at https://www.fma-li.li/files/fma/fma-digital-banking-liechtenstein.pdf

Boreiko, Dmitri, Ferrarini, Guido and Giudici, Paolo, Blockchain Startups and Prospectus Regulation (European Business Organization Law Review, 20(4), 665c694)

Botschaft zum Bundesgesetz zur Anpassung des Bundesrecht an Entwicklungen der Technik verteilter elektronischer Register (2019), 7 (1.1.3, III.), available at https://www.newsd.admin.ch/newsd/message/attachments/59301.pdf

Boyd, Thomas M., How a Rich Californian Hijacked the Legislature – Threatened with a Ballot Initiative, Lawmakers Pass a Ruinous Data-Privacy Law (The Wall Street Journal, 04/07/2018), available at www.wsj.com/articles/how-a-rich-californian-hijacked-the-legislature-1530723133

Bremann, Nils Lennart, Smart Contracts im Einsatz (DSRITB 2019, 299)

Bullmann, Dirk and Klemm, Jonas & Pinna, Andrea, In Search for Stability in Crypto-Assets: Are Stablecoins the Solution?, 230 Occasional Paper Series of the European Central Bank (August 2019), available at https://www.ecb.europa.eu/pub/pdf/scpops/ecb.op230 ~ d57946be3b.en.pdf

Bundesrat der Schweizerischen Eidgenossenschaft, *Rechtliche Grundlagen für Distributed Ledger – Technologie und Blockchain in der Schweiz – Eine Auslegeordnung mit Fokus auf dem Finanzsektor* (14 December 2018), available at: https://www.newsd.admin.ch/newsd/message/attachments/55150.pdf

Buocz et al., Bitcoin and the GDPR: Allocating Responsibility in Distributed Networks (Computer Law & Security Review 2019)

Byrne, Preston, New UK Rules, While Strict, Nonetheless Avoid America's Securitarian Trap (International Journal of Blockchain Law, Volume 7, October 2023), available at https://gbbcouncil.org/wp-content/uploads/2023/10/International-Journal-of-Blockchain-Law-Volume-VII.pdf

Canadian Securities Administrators, CSA Staff Notice (46-307 Cryptocurrency Offerings, 2017), available at https://www.osc.ca/en/securities-law/instruments-rules-policies/4/46-307/csa-staff-notice-46-307-cryptocurrency-offerings

CSA Staff Notice (46-308 Securities Law Implications for Offerings of Tokens, 2018), available at https://www.osc.ca/en/securities-law/instruments-rules-policies/4/46-308/csa-staff-notice-46-308-securities-law-implications-offerings-tokens

Cappiello, Benedetta and Carullo, Gherardo (eds.), Blockchain, Law and Governance (2021)

Carbonnier, Jean, Droit Civile, Tome 2 (2017)

Central Bank of Ireland, Crypto and how we can protect the consumer (5 May 2023), https://www.centralbank.ie/news-media/press-releases/blog-crypto-and-how-we-can-protect-the-consumer

Central Bank of Ireland, Investment Firms Questions and Answers, 5th Edition (8 October 2018), https://www.centralbank.ie/docs/default-source/regulation/industry-market-sectors/investment-firms/mifid-firms/regulatory-requirements-and-guidance/181008-investment-firms-qa-5th-edition.pdf?sfvrsn = 2

Central Bank of Ireland, Letter of response to the European Commission Consultation on the Market of Crypto Assets (30 April 2020), https://www.centralbank.ie/docs/default-source/regulation/innovation-hub/response-to-ec-consultation-on-the-market-of-crypto-assets.pdf?sfvrsn = 2

Central Bank of Ireland, Prospectus Regulatory Framework Questions and Answers, 1st Edition (4 August 2017), https://www.centralbank.ie/docs/default-source/regulation/industry-market-sectors/securities-markets/prospectus-regulation/regulatory-requirements-guidance/prospectus-reg-framework-qas-1st-ed-4-aug-2017.pdf?sfvrsn = 2

Central Bank of Ireland, Securities Markets Risk Outlook Report 2023 (March 2023), https://www.centralbank.ie/docs/default-source/regulation/industry-market-sectors/securities-markets/risk-outlook-reports/securities-markets-risk-outlook-report-2023.pdf?sfvrsn = dc0f991d_2

Chander, Anupam, How Law Made Silicon Valley (63 Emory Law Journal 639, 2014), available at https://ssrn.com/abstract = 2340197

Cheung, A., *Can You Write Your Will onto a Blockchain? Smart Contracts* (16 October 2023), available at: https://www.rocketlawyer.com/gb/en/blog/can-you-write-your-will-onto-a-blockchain-smart-contracts/

Chun Chang-Min, *Choice of Law Regarding Proprietary Aspects of Digital Asset Transactions*, Korea Private International Law Association, Private International Law Studies Vol. 29, No. 2 (December 2023)

Clayton, Jay, Statement regarding SEC Staff Views (13 September 2018), available at https://www.sec.gov/news/public-statement/statement-clayton-091318

Commission Nationale de l'Informatique et de Libertés (6 November 2018) Blockchain and the GDPR: Solutions for a Responsible use of the Blockchain in the Context of Personal Data, available at https://www.cnil.fr/en/blockchain-and-gdpr-solutions-responsible-use-blockchain-context-personal-data

Communication from the Commission, FinTech Action plan: For a more competitive and innovative European financial sector COM(2018)109 final (8 March 2018), available at https://www.europarl.europa.eu/doceo/document/TA-8-2018-0373_EN.html?redirect

Communiqué of the G20 Finance Ministers & Central Bank Governors Meeting 22-23 February 2020, Riyadh, Saudi Arabia, at 3, available at https://g20.org/en/g20/Documents/Communique%CC%81%20Final%2022-23%20February%202020.pdf

Copeland, Rory, FCA Final Guidance on Cryptoassets: Jettisoning Tech-neutrality?, Oxford Business Law Blog (23 September 2019), available at https://blogs.law.ox.ac.uk/business-law-blog/blog/2019/09/fca-final-guidance-cryptoassets-jettisoning-tech-neutrality

Crémer, Jacques, de Montjoye, Yves-Alexandre and Schweitzer, Heike, Competition Policy for the Digital Era (2019), available at https://ec.europa.eu/competition/publications/reports/kd0419345enn.pdf

Cusa, Emanuele, Le quote di s.r.l. possono essere valori mobiliari (Rivista delle societa, 4/2019, 675 - 694)

De Filippi, Primavera and Hassan, Samer, Blockchain Technology as a Regulatory Technology: From Code Is Law to Law is Code, 12 First Monday 21 (2016) 1, available at https://arxiv.org/ftp/arxiv/papers/1801/1801.02507.pdf

De Filippi, Primavera and Mannan, Morshed and Reijers, Wessel, The alegality of blockchain technology 358 (Policy and Society, Volume 41, Issue 3, September 2022) (16 February 2022) available at https://doi.org/10.1093/polsoc/puac006 (accessed 10 March 2024)

De Filippi, Primavera and Wright, Aaron, Blockchain and the Law – The Rule of Code (2018) 193

Deloitte, 2019 Global Blockchain Survey, available at https://www2.deloitte.com/content/dam/insights/us/articles/2019-global-blockchain-survey/DI_2019-global-blockchain-survey.pdf

Deloitte, Blockchain @ Media – A New Game Changer for the Media Industry?, available at https://www2.deloitte.com/de/de/pages/technology-media-and-telecommunications/articles/blockchain-at-media.html

Derouiche, Emir. The Relationship Between Voting Power Distribution and the Bug Resilience of an Ethereum Proof-of-Stake Blockchain. MS thesis. NTNU, 2023

Determann, Lothar and Gupta, Chetan, Indian Personal Data Protection Act of 2018: Draft Bill and Its History, Compared to GDPR and California Privacy Law (Berkeley Journal of International Law 481, 2019)

Determann, Lothar and Lorenz, Manuel, FinTech: Ground Rules and Checklist for Starting Up and Going Global (BNA's Banking Report, 27/11/2017)

Determann, Lothar and Lorenz, Manuel, Fintechs im Dschungel der Regulierungen (Börsenzeitung, 01/04/2017)

Determann, Lothar and Sprague, Robert, Intrusive Monitoring: Employee Privacy Expectations are Reasonable in Europe, Destroyed in the United States (26 Berkeley Technology Law Journal 979, 2011)

Determann, Lothar and Weigl, Michaela, Data Residency Requirements Creeping into German Law (Bloomberg BNA Privacy & Security Law Report, 15 PVLR 529 - 03/14/2016)

Determann, Lothar, Nebel, Michaela, and Michael Schmidl, EU-U.S. Data Privacy Framework: Practical Impact and Benefits for Companies in the EEA and USA Compared to Other International Data Transfer Mechanisms (6(2) Journal of Data Protection and Privacy 2023)

Determann, Lothar and zu Guttenberg, Karl-Theodor, On War and Peace in Cyberspace: Security, Privacy, Jurisdiction (41 Hastings Constitutional Law Quarterly, 1, 13, 2014)

Determann, Lothar, Adequacy of Data Protection in the USA: Myths and Facts (International Data Privacy Law 2016)

Determann, Lothar, Broad Data and Business Regulation, Applicable Worldwide (IAPP Advisor, 02/07/2018), available at https://iapp.org/news/a/analysis-the-california-consumer-privacy-act-of-2018/

Determann, Lothar, California Privacy Law, Practical Guide and Commentary – U.S. Federal and California Law (IAPP 5th ed. 2023)

Determann, Lothar, *Analysis: The* California *Consumer Privacy Act of 2018. Broad data and business regulation,* applicable *worldwide*, IAPP Advisor, 2 July 2018

Determann, Lothar, Data Residency Rules Cutting Into Clouds: Impact and Options for Global Businesses and IT Architectures (Bloomberg BNA Data Privacy & Security Law Report, 16 PVLR 496 - 04/03/2017)

Determann, Lothar, Datenschutz auf Kalifornisch (FAZ v. 11.7.2018)

Determann, Lothar, Determann's Field Guide to Data Privacy Law – International Corporate Compliance (Edward Elgar Publishing Ltd. 5th ed. 2022)

Determann, Lothar, Healthy Data Protection, 26 Michigan Technology Law Review (2020)

Determann, Lothar, New California Data Security and Breach Notification Requirement (Bloomberg BNA Privacy & Security Law Report, 15 PVLR 219, 02/01/2016)

Determann, Lothar, No One Owns Data (70 Hastings Law Journal 1, 2018)

Determann, Lothar, Privacy and Data Protection. **КОНФИДЕНЦИАЛЬНОСТЬ И ЗАЩИТА ПЕРСОНАЛЬНЫХ ДАННЫХ** (Moscow Journal of International Law 1, 2019)

Determann, Lothar, Social Media @ Work 2014 (BNA/Bloomberg Social Media Law & Policy Report, 2 SMLR 49, 12/17/2013)

Determann, Lothar, Social Media Privacy – A Dozen Myths and Facts (2012 Stanford Technology Law Review 7, 2012)

Determann, Lothar, US-Datenschutzrecht – Dichtung und Wahrheit (Neue Zeitschrift für Verwaltungsrecht 2016, 561)

Determann, Lothar, California Privacy Rights Ballot Initiative: Business, Watch this Space (The Recorder, 22 May 2020)

Determann, Lothar and Johnson, Teisha, Data Broker Regulation - Competition v. Privacy Considerations: Trade-offs, Competition Policy International, October 2023

Determann, Lothar and Tam, Jonathan, The California Privacy Rights Act of 2020: A broad and complex data processing regulation that applies to businesses worldwide, 11 World Data Protection Report #4 (2020)

Determann, Lothar, Reassessing EU Standard Contractual Clauses for Transfers of Personal Data to Processing Service Providers, 11 World Data Protection Report #4 (2011)

Dewey, Josias N., Blockchain & Cryptocurrency Regulation 2020 (Global Legal Insights, 23 October 2019)

Dubai Financial Services Authority, Consultation Paper No. 138, Regulation of Security Tokens, 29 March 2021, available at https://dfsaen.thomsonreuters.com/sites/default/files/net_file_store/CP138_Regulation_of_Security_Tokens.pdf

Digital Competition Expert Panel, Unlocking Digital Competition – Report of the Digital Competition Expert Panel (March 2019), available at https://assets.publishing.service.gov.uk/media/5c88150ee5274a230219c35f/unlocking_digital_competition_furman_review_web.pdf

DiMatteo, Larry A., Cannarsa, Michel and Poncibo, Christina, The Cambridge Handbook of Smart Contracts, Blockchain and Technology and Digital Platforms (Cambridge, 2019)

Distributed Ledger Technology and Governing Law: Issues of Legal Uncertainty, Financial Markets Law Committee, March 2018

Douglas, Laura, The Developing Regulatory Landscape for Cryptoassets in the EU and UK (International Journal of Blockchain Law, Volume V, March 2023), available at https://gbbcouncil.org/wp-content/uploads/2023/03/March-2023-IJBL-Volume-V-1.pdf

Eccher, Bernhard and Riss, Olaf, in Koziol, Helmut and Bydlinski, Peter and Bollenberger, Raimund, Allgemeines bürgerliches Gesetzbuch, EheG, KSchG, IPR-G, Rom I-, Rom II- und Rom III-VO (2020)

EFSA, Security Token, https://www.fi.ee/en/finantsinspektsioon/innovation-hub/security-token (accessed 21 November 2023)

Ekblaw, A. et al., A Case Study for Blockchain in Healthcare: "MedRec" Prototype for Electronic Health Records and Medical Research Data (IEEE Technology and Society Magazine, 2016)

EPO, Guidelines, G-VII, 5.4, available at: https://www.epo.org/en/legal/guidelines-epc/2023/g_vii_5_4.html

ERC-721 Non-Fungible Token Standard, (9 October 2023), https://ethereum.org/de/developers/docs/standards/tokens/erc-721/

ESMA, Advice on Initial Coin Offerings and Crypto-Assets (9 January 2019), https://www.esma.europa.eu/sites/default/files/library/esma50-157-1391_crypto_advice.pdf

ESMA, Final Report On ESMA's Opinion on the Trading Venue Perimeter (2 February 2023) ESMA70-156-6360, https://www.esma.europa.eu/sites/default/files/library/ESMA70-156-6383%20Final%20Report%20on%20ESMA%27s%20Opinion%20on%20the%20trading%20venue%20perimeter.pdf

Estonian Financial Supervisory Authority, Information for Entities Engaging with virtual Currencies and ICOs, available at https://www.fi.ee/en/finantsinspektsioon/financial-innovation/virtual-currencies-and-ico/information-entities-engaging-virtual-currencies-and-icos

Estonian Financial Supervisory Authority, The Legal Framework of Initial Coin Offering in Estonia, available at https://www.fi.ee/en/investment/aktuaalsed-teemad-investeerimises/virtuaalraha-ico/legal-framework-initial-coin-offering-estonia

European Commission, Questions and Answers on MiFID Directive 2004/39/EC (22 February 2007, https://finance.ec.europa.eu/system/files/2020-01/mifid-2004-0039-commission-questions-answers_en_0.pdf

European Banking Authority, Discussion paper on the EBA's approach to financial technology (FinTech), EBA/DP/2017/02 (4 August 2017) n. 8, available at https://eba.europa.eu/sites/default/files/documents/10180/1919160/7a1b9cda-10ad-4315-91ce-d798230ebd84/EBA%20Discussion%20Paper%20on%20Fintech%20%28EBA-DP-2017-02%29.pdf

European Central Bank, Opinion of 31 October 2023 on the digital euro (CON/2023/34); available at https://www.ecb.europa.eu/pub/pdf/legal/ecb.leg_con_2023_34.en.pdf?495c419f19a78fd8d5f40e7cffffb331

European Commission, Blockchain Now and Tomorrow – Assessing Multidimensional Impacts of Distributed Ledger Technologies (Joint Research Center of the European Commission, July 2019)

European Commission, Commission Consolidated Jurisdictional Notice under Council Regulation (EC) No 139/2004 on the Control of Concentrations Between Undertakings (OJ C95, 16/4/2008, pp. 1-48)

European Commission, Commission Notice – Guidelines on Vertical Restraints (SEC, 2010, 411), available at https://ec.europa.eu/competition/antitrust/legislation/guidelines_vertical_en.pdf

European Commission, Commission Regulation No 330/2010 on the application of Article 101(3) of the Treaty on the Functioning of the European Union to categories of vertical agreements and concerted practices (Official Journal L102, 23/4/2010, pp. 1-7)

European Commission, Communication from the Commission – Guidance on the Commission's Enforcement Priorities in Applying Article 82 of the EC Treaty to Abusive Exclusionary Conduct by Dominant Undertakings (OJ C45, 24/0/2/2012, pp. 7-20)

European Commission, Communication from the Commission — Guidelines on the Applicability of Article 101 of the Treaty on the Functioning of the European Union to Horizontal Co-operation Agreements (OJ 54, 14/1/2011, pp. 1-70)

European Commission, Notice on the definition of the relevant market for the purposes of Union competition law, 8/2/2024, OJ C/2024/1645, 22/2/2024

European Council, Council Regulation (EC) No 139/2004 of 20 January 2004 on the Control of Concentrations Between Undertakings (OJ L24, 29/1/2004, pp. 1-22)

European Data Protection Board, Draft Guidelines 2/2019 on the Processing of Personal Data under Art. 6(1)(b) of the GDPR (adopted on 9 April 2019)

European Data Protection Board, Guidelines 4/2019 on Article 25 Data Protection by Design and by Default (Plenary Meeting November 2019, adopted on 13 November 2019)

European Data Protection Supervisor and the Agencia espanola proteccion datos, Introduction to the Hash Function as a Personal Data Pseudonymisation Technique (October 2019), available at https://www.edps.europa.eu/data-protection/our-work/publications/papers/introduction-hash-function-personal-data_en

European Parliament, Resolution of 3 October 2018 on distributed ledger technologies and blockchains: building trust with disintermediation, (2017/2772(RSP), n. 65 and 68), available at https://www.europarl.europa.eu/doceo/document/TA-8-2018-0373_EN.html?redirect

European Parliamentary Research Service, Blockchain and the General Data Protection Regulation – Can Distributed Ledgers Be Squared with European Data Protection Law? (Scientific Foresight Unit, July 2019)

European Securities and Markets Regulator, Advice Initial Coin Offerings and Crypto-Assets (2019), available at https://www.esma.europa.eu/sites/default/files/library/esma50-157-1391_crypto_advice.pdf

European Securities and Markets Regulator, Guidelines on the Key Concepts of the AIFMD, available at https://www.esma.europa.eu/sites/default/files/library/2015/11/2013-611_guidelines_on_key_concepts_o

Evans, Joseph B., Blockchain's Incumbent Patent War: a Rite of Passage, available at https://www.expertinstitute.com/resources/insights/blockchains-incumbent-patent-war-rite-passage/

FATF Recommendations, available at https://www.fatf-gafi.org/en/

Faux, Z., Number Go Up: Inside Crypto's Wild Rise and Staggering Fall (Crown Currency, September 2023)

Federal Trade Commission, The Financial Privacy Requirements of the Gramm-Leach-Bliley Act, available at https://www.ftc.gov/system/files/documents/plain-language/bus53-brief-financial-privacy-requirements-gramm-leach-bliley-act.pdf

Felten, E., Does Hashing Make Data 'Anonymous' (22 April 2018), available at https://www.ftc.gov/news-events/blogs/techftc/2012/04/does-hashing-make-data-anonymous

Financial Conduct Authority, Cryptoassets: Feedback to CP19/3 and final guidance to firms, p. 13, (9 October 2023), https://www.fca.org.uk/publication/policy/ps19-22.pdf

Financial Conduct Authority, Guidance on Cryptoassets (Consultation Paper CP19/3 January 2019) para. 3.14, available at https://www.fca.org.uk/publication/consultation/cp19-03.pdf

Financial Conduct Authority, How we define cryptoassets, (9 October 2023), https://www.fca.org.uk/firms/cryptoassets (9 October 2023)

Finck, Michèle, Blockchain – Regulation and Governance in Europe (Cambridge University Press, 2018)

Finck, Michèle, Blockchains and Data Protection in the European Union (Max Planck Institute for Innovation & Competition Research Paper No. 18-01, 30 November 2017), available at https://edpl.lexxion.eu/data/article/12327/pdf/edpl_2018_01-007.pdf

Finck, Michèle, Moscon, Valentina, Copyright Law on Blockchains: Between New Forms of Rights Administration and Digital Rights Management 2.0, 2019), available at: https://www.ip.mpg.de/de/publikationen/details/copyright-law-on-blockchains-between-new-forms-of-rights-administration-and-digital-rights-management-20.html?pk_campaign = newsletter1

Finnish Financial Supervisory Authority, Fintech Counsel, Regulations and Guidelines 4/2019 – Virtual Currency Providers (14 June 2019, FIVA 12/01.00/2019)

Fischer, Michael J., Lynch, Nancy A., Paterson, Michael S., Impossibility of Distributed Consensus with One Faulty Process (J. ACM 32, 2, April 1985), 374-382, available at http://dx.doi.org/10.1145/3149.214121

Fotiou, Nikos and Polyzos, George C., Smart Contracts for the Internet of Things: Opportunities and Challenges (Department of Informatics, School of Information Sciences and Technology Athens, University of Economics and Business, 23 January 2019), available at https://arxiv.org/pdf/1901.10582.pdf

Freiwald, Susan, First Principles of Communications Privacy (Stanford Technology Law Review 3, 2007)

Fromherz, Thomas, Entmystifizierung digitaler Währungen (9 October 2023), available at https://www.der-bank-blog.de/entmystifizierung-digitaler-waehrungen/technologie/37685573/

FSR Energy Florence School of Regulation, Blockchain meets Energy, Digital Solutions for Decentralized and Decarbonized Sector (June 2019), available at https://fsr.eui.eu/wp-content/uploads/Blockchain_meets_Energy_-_ENG.pdf

Financial Services Regulatory Authority (FSRA) of Abu Dhabi Global Market (ADGM) Guidance – Regulation of Digital Securities Activities in the ADGM, 24 February 2020, available at https://www.adgm.com/documents/legal-framework/guidance-and-policy/fsra/guidance-on-regulation-of-digital-securities-activities-in-adgm.pdf?la = en&hash = EDCDD88518578D9E914BC2A27879755F

Fuchs, Andreas, Wertpapierhandelsgesetz (3rd ed., 2024)

Gatteschi, Valentina et al., Blockchain and Smart Contracts for Insurance: Is the Technology Mature Enough? (2018), available at https://www.the-digital-insurer.com/wp-content/uploads/2018/07/1243-futureinternet-10-00020-v2-1.pdf

Geis, George S., Traceable Shares and Corporate Law (Virginia Public Law and Legal Theory Research Paper No. 2018-13, 2-50), available at SSRN: https://papers.ssrn.com/sol3/papers.cfm?abstract_id = 3129042&download = yes

Geiser, Thomas and Wolf, Stephan (ed.), Basler Kommentar zum ZGB6

Gensler, Gary, Prepared Remarks Before the Aspen Security Forum (3 August 2021), *available at: https://www.sec.gov/news/public-statement/gensler-aspen-security-forum-2021-08-03*

Gerard, David, Attack of the 50-Foot Blockchain: Bitcoin, Blockchain, Ethereum & Smart Contracts (2017)

German Federal Financial Supervisory Authority, Initial Coin Offerings: Hinweisschreiben zur Einordnung als Finanzinstrumente (WA 11-QB 4100-2017/0010, 2017), available at https://www.bafin.de/SharedDocs/Downloads/DE/Merkblatt/WA/dl_hinweisschreiben_einordnung_ICOs

German Federal Financial Supervisory Authority, Merkblatt – Hinweise zu den Tatbeständen des Eigenhandels und des Eigengeschäfts (2019), available at https://www.bafin.de/SharedDocs/Veroeffentlichungen/DE/Merkblatt/mb_110322_eigenhandel_eigengeschaeft_neu.html

German Federal Financial Supervisory Authority, Prospektpflicht - Rechtslage seit dem 21 July 2019 (Verlautbarung, geändert am 5.8.2019), available at https://www.bafin.de/DE/Aufsicht/Prospekte/Wertpapiere/Prospektpflicht/prospektpflicht_node.html

German Federal Financial Supervisory Authority, Zweites Hinweisschreiben zu Prospekt- und Erlaubnispflichten im Zusammenhang mit der Ausgabe sogenannter Krypto-Token (2019), https://www.bafin.de/SharedDocs/Downloads/DE/Merkblatt/WA/dl_wa_merkblatt_ICOs.html

German Federal Ministry of Justice and Consumer Protection, Eckpunkte für die regulatorische Behandlung von elektronischen Wertpapieren und Krypto-Token (2019), available at https://www.bundesfinanzministerium.de/Content/DE/Gesetzestexte/Gesetze_Gesetzesvorhaben/Abteilungen/Abteilung_VII/19_Legislaturperiode/2019-03-07-Eckpunktepapier-Wertpapiere-Krypto-Token/0-Gesetz.html

German Government, Blockchain-Strategie der Bundesregierung (2019), available at https://www.bundesregierung.de/breg-de/service/publikationen/blockchain-strategie-der-bundesregierung-1672384

González-Meneses, Manuel, Entender Blockchain. Una introducción a la tecnología de registro distgribuido (Thomson Reuters Aranzadi, 2nd ed., 2019)

Government of Canada, Regulations Amending Certain Regulations Made under the Proceeds of Crime (Money Laundering) and Terrorist Financing Act, 2019 (SOR/2019-240, 2019), available at http://www.gazette.gc.ca/rp-pr/p2/2019/2019-07-10/html/sor-dors240-eng.html

Government of Germany, Gesetzesentwurf der Bundesregierung, Finanzmarkt-Richtlinie-Umsetzungsgesetz available at (Drucksache 16/4028 53, 2007)

Government of Germany, Regierungsentwurf eines Gesetzes zur Umsetzung der Änderungsrichtlinie zur Vierten EU-Geldwäscherichtlinie RL (EU) 2018/843 (2018), available at https://www.bundesfinanzministerium.de/Content/DE/Gesetzestexte/Gesetze_Gesetzesvorhaben/Abteilungen/Abteilung_VII/19_Legislaturperiode/2019-12-19-Gesetz-4-EU-Geldwaescherichtlinie/0-Gesetz.html

Government of Liechtenstein, Bericht und Antrag der Regierung an den Landtag des Fürstentums Liechtenstein betreffend die Schaffung eines Gesetzes über Token und VT-Dienstleister (Token- und VT-Dienstleistergesetz; TVTG) und die Abänderung weiterer Gesetze, Bericht und Antrag Nr. 54/2019 (2019)

Government of Liechtenstein, Stellungnahme der Regierung an den Landtag des Fürstentums Liechtenstein zu den anlässlich der ersten Lesung betreffend die Schaffung eines Gesetzes über Token und VT-Dienstleister (Token- und VT-Dienstleistergesetz; TVTG) und die Abänderung weiterer Gesetze aufgeworfenen Fragen, Bericht und Antrag Nr. 93/2019 (2019), available at https://www.llv.li/files/srk/bua_093_2019_stellungnahme-tvtg.pdf

Governor Lael Brainard from the U.S. Federal Reserve System on 'Update on Digital Currencies, Stablecoins, and the Challenges Ahead' (18 December 2019), available at https://www.federalreserve.gov/newsevents/speech/brainard20191218a.htm

Greenberg, Brad A., Rethinking Technology Neutrality (207 Minnesota Law Review, 1495 2016), available at https://www.minnesotalawreview.org/wp-content/uploads/2016/04/Greenberg_ONLINEPDF.pdf

Gresham, Josh, Is Encrypted Data Personal Data under the GDPR? (06 March 2019), available at https://iapp.org/news/a/is-encrypted-data-personal-data-under-the-gdpr/

Grinhaus, Aaron, A Practical Guide to Smart Contracts and Blockchain Law (LexisNexis Canada, 21 March 2019)

Grolimund, Pascal and Loacker, Leander D. and Schnyder Anton K. (ed.), Basler Kommentar Internationales Privatrecht (IPRG), Basel 2020, Art. 147 N 9

Guacccro, Andrea, Sandrelli, Giulio, in Bank Securities Exchange, Issue 6, 1 December 2022, p. 824 ff

Gyr, Eleonor, Blockchain und Smart Contracts – Die vertragsrechtlichen Implikationen einer neuen Technologie (Dissertation, Basel, 2019), available at https://biblio.unibe.ch/download/eldiss/19gyr_e.pdf

Habersack, Mathias, Münchener Kommentar zum Bürgerlichen Gesetzbuch (C.H. Beck, 6 A, 7th ed. 2017)

Harrington, L. *Sharing Economy 2.0: Can Blockchain Remove the Need for Single-Asset Ownership?* (9 January 2019), available at: https://www.iotforall.com/sharing-economy-can-blockchain-eliminate-single-asset-ownership/

Hayes, Adam, Investopedia, Stablecoins: Definition, How They Work, and Types (9 October 2023) https://www.investopedia.com/terms/s/stablecoin.asp

Heckelmann, Martin, Zulässigkeit und Handhabung von Smart Contracts (NJW 2018, 504)

Hileman Garrick and Rauchs, Michael, Global Blockchain Benchmarking Study (2017) 20, available at https://papers.ssrn.com/sol3/papers.cfm?abstract_id=3040224

Hinmann, Bill, Statement on 'Framework for 'Investment Contract' Analysis of Digital Assets (2019), available at https://www.sec.gov/news/public-statement/statement-framework-investment-contract-analysis-digital-assets

Hinmann, William, Digital Asset Transactions: When Howey Met Gary (Plastic), Remarks at the Yahoo Finance All Markets Summit: Crypto (2018), available at https://www.sec.gov/news/speech/speech-hinman-061418

Hirsch, R. and Deixler, H., Final HIPAA Omnibus Rule Brings Sweeping Changes to the Health Care Privacy Law: HIPAA Privacy and Security Obligations Extended to Business Associates and Subcontractors (BNA Privacy and Security Law Report, 12 PVLR 168, 2013)

HMT's policy paper, Update on Plans for the Regulation of Fiat-backed Stablecoins (October 2023), available at https://www.gov.uk/government/publications/update-on-plans-for-the-regulation-of-fiat-backed-stablecoins

Houben Robby and Snyers, Alexander, Cryptocurrencies and Blockchain, Legal Context and Implications for Financial Crime, Money Laundering and Tax Evasion, Study requested by the TAX3 committee (July 2018), 15, available at https://www.europarl.europa.eu/cmsdata/150761/TAX3%20Study%20on%20cryptocurrencies%20and%20blockchain.pdf

Ibáñez, L-D., O'Hara, K. and Simperl, E., On Blockchains and the General Data Protection Regulation, available at https://eprints.soton.ac.uk/422879/1/BLockchains_GDPR_4.pdf

Information Commissioner's Office, Deleting Personal Data (26 February 2014), available at https://ico.org.uk/media/fororganisations/documents/1475/deleting_personal_data.pdf

International Conference for the Unification of Laws on Bills of Exchange, Promissory Notes and Cheques, Geneva, 1930-1931, Convention for the settlement of certain conflicts of laws in connection with bills of exchange and promissory notes. London: H.M.S.O., 1930

International Swaps and Derivatives Association, Legal Guidelines for Smart Derivatives Contracts (January 2019), available at https://www.isda.org/a/MhgME/Legal-Guidelines-for-Smart-Derivatives-Contracts-Introduction.pdf

ISDA Linklaters, *Whitepaper Smart Contracts and Distributed Ledger – A Legal Perspective* (August 2017), available at: https://www.isda.org/a/6EKDE/smart-contracts-and-distributed-ledger-a-legal-perspective.pdf

Joint Canadian Securities Administrators/Investment Industry Regulatory Organization of Canada, Consultation Paper 21-402 – Proposed Framework for Crypto-Asset Trading Platforms (2019), available at https://www.osc.gov.on.ca/en/SecuritiesLaw_csa_20190314_21-402_crypto-asset-trading-platforms.htm

Jünemann, Michael and Wirtz, Johannes, ICO: Legal Classification of Tokens: Part 1 – Utility Token (2019), available at https://www.twobirds.com/en/insights/2019/global/ico-legal-classification-of-tokens

Jünemann, Michael and Wirtz, Johannes, ICO: Legal Classification of Tokens: Part 2 – Security Token (2019), available at https://www.twobirds.com/en/news/articles/2019/global/ico-legal-classification-of-tokens-2

Jünemann, Michael and Wirtz, Johannes, ICO: Legal Classification of Tokens: Part 3 – Currency Token (2019), available at https://www.twobirds.com/en/news/articles/2019/global/ico-legal-classification-of-tokens-3

Michael Juenemann & Johannes Wirtz, ICO: Legal Classification of Tokens: Part 4 – Utility Token, (9 October 2023), available at https://www.twobirds.com/en/insights/2019/global/ico-legal-classification-of-tokens-utility-token

Kaal, Wulf A., Blockchain-Based Corporate Governance (University of St. Thomas/Minnesota, Legal Studies Research Paper No. 19-10, 1-43), available at SSRN: https://papers.ssrn.com/sol3/papers.cfm?abstract_id=3441904

Kalss, Susanne, Oppitz, Martin and Zollner, Johannes, Kapitalmarktrecht (2nd ed., 2015)

Kaulartz, Markus and Heckmann, Jörn, Smart Contracts – Anwendungen der Blockchain-Technologie 618 (Computer Report 9/2016)

Kejriwal, Kunal, A Comprehensive Review of Blockchain in AI (14 September 2023), available at https://www.unite.ai/a-comprehensive-review-of-blockchain-in-ai

Kempster, K., *How Blockchain Might Transform Family Law*, available at: https://vardags.com/family-law/how-blockchain-might-transform-family-law

Kianieff, Muharem, Blockchain Technology and the Law, Opportunities and Risks (2019)

Kirli, D. et al, *Smart contracts in energy systems: A systematic review of fundamental approaches and implementations*, Renewable and Sustainable Energy Reviews, vol. 158 (April 2022), available at: https://doi.org/10.1016/j.rser.2021.112013

Koch, Philipp, Die Tokenisierung von Rechtspositionen als digitale Verbriefung 359 (ZBB 2018)

Koch, Rüdiger, Neue Regeln für Wertpapierprospekte (2019), available at https://www.bafin.de/SharedDocs/Veroeffentlichungen/DE/Fachartikel/2019/fa_bj_1906_Wertpapierprospekte.html

Kudzin, Alexander et al., Scaling Ethereum 2.0s Cross-shard transactions with refined data structures (2022), available at https://www.mdpi.com/2410-387X/6/4/57

Kumar, Satish and Lim, Weng Marc and Sivarajah, Uthayasankar and Kaur, Jaspreet, Artificial Intelligence and Blockchain Integration in Business: Trends from a Bibliometric-Content Analysis, 871 (Information Systems Frontiers 25, 2023), available at https://doi.org/10.1007/s10796-022-10279-0

Kumpan, Christoph, Kapitalmarktrecht (4th ed., 2010)

Lafarre, Anne and Van der Elst, Christoph, Blockchain Technology for Corporate Governance and Shareholder Activism (SSRN Electronic Journal, January 2018) 1-26, available at https://papers.ssrn.com/sol3/papers.cfm?abstract_id=3135209

Lambert, Thomas and Liebau, Daniel and Roosenboom, Peter, Security token offerings, Small Business Economics, 59(1), available at https://papers.ssrn.com/sol3/papers.cfm?abstract_id=3634626

Lautennschläger, Sabine, A Supervisory Perspective on 2019 and Beyond (Speech in Dublin, Ireland, 17 January 2019), available at https://www.ecb.europa.eu/press/key/date/2019/html/ecb.sp190117.en.html

Ledger Insights, *Eu Data Act requires smart contracts to have kill switch, not be permissionless* (14 March 2023), available at, https://www.ledgerinsights.com/eu-data-act-smart-contracts-immutability-permissionless/

Leppik, Kristen, Krüptovaradest, Õiguskeel 2020/2

Lesaege, C. and Ast, F., Kleros Short Paper v1.0.6, November 2018, available at: /https://kleros.io/assets/whitepaper.pdf/ (last accessed 3 April 2020)

Lessig, Lawrence, Code Version 2.0 124-25 (2006), available at http://codev2.cc/download+remix/Lessig-Codev2.pdf

Letter from Members of the House Committee on Financial Services to the SEC, Re: File No. S7-02-22, Reopening of Comment Period for Amendments to Exchange Act Rule 3b-16 Regarding the Definition of "Exchange", at 2, available at https://financialservices.house.gov/uploadedfiles/fsc_gop_letter_on_the_secs_proposed_definition_of_an_exchange_final.pdf

Levi, S. D. and Lipton, A., *An Introduction to Smart Contracts and Their Potential and Inherent Limitations* (26 May 2018), available at, https://corpgov.law.harvard.edu/2018/05/26/an-introduction-to-smart-contracts-and-their-potential-and-inherent-limitations/

Liechtenstein FMA, Faktenblatt 'Initial Coin Offering' (2019), available at https://www.fma-li.li/files/fma/fma-faktenblatt-ico.pdf

Liechtenstein FMA, FMA-Mitteilung 2019/2 – Pflichten für Emittenten von Wertpapieren und Security Token (2019), available at https://www.fma-li.li/files/list/fma-mittteilung-2019-2-emittenten-wp-st.pdf

Lightning Network White Paper, available at https://lightning.network/lightning-network-paper.pdf

Lopez, David, and Farooq, Bilal, A Multi-layered Blockchain Framework for Smart Mobility Data-Markets (arXiv preprint arXiv:1906.06435, 2019), available at https://arxiv.org/pdf/1906.06435.pdf

Lorente Howell, Jose Luis, Aprobado el Anteproyecto de Ley para la Transformación Digital del Sistema Financiero (Actualidad Jurídica Aranzadi, 2019)

Lorente Howell, Jose Luis, Una regulación flexible adaptada al entorno 'FinTech' (Actualidad Jurídica Aranzadi, 2018)

Low, Kelvin and Mik, Eliza, Unpicking a Fin(e)tech Mess: Can Old Doctrines Cope in the 21st Century? (2019), available at https://blogs.law.ox.ac.uk/business-law-blog/blog/2019/11/unpicking-finetech-mess-can-old-doctrines-cope-21st-century

Lupu, Ruxandra, Zulässigkeit, Handhabung und rechtliche Grenzen bei der Gestaltung von Smart Contracts 209 (DSRITB 2019)

Magnier, Véronique, Barban, Patrick, Blockchain et droit des sociétés (2019)

Malvagna, Ugo, Digital securities: first notes on the DLT Pilot implementation decree, in diritto (20 March 2023), available at https://www.dirittobancario.it/art/digital-securities-prime-note-sul-decreto-di-attuazione-del-dlt-pilot/

Mann, Maximilian, Die Decentralized Autonomous Organization – ein neuer Gesellschaftstyp?, 1024 (NZG 2017)

Martini/Weinzierl, Die Blockchain-Technologie und das Recht auf Vergessenwerden, 1251 (Neue Zeitschrift für Verwaltungsrecht 2017)

Marxer & Partner Rechtsanwaelte, Liechtensteinisches Wirtschaftsrecht (2021)

Maume, Philipp and Fromberger, Mathias, Regulation of Initial Coin Offerings: Reconciling U.S. and E.U. Securities Laws (19(2) Chicago Journal of International Law 2019)

Maume, Philipp and Maute, Lena, Rechtshandbuch Kryptowerte, 1st ed, 2020

Maume, Philipp, in Die Anwendung der Blockchain-Technologie im GmbH-Recht, NZG 2021, 1189

Maume, Philipp, Struktur, Definition und Anwendungsfaelle der Kryptoregulierung, NJW 2023, 1168

Mayer, R., Butler, J. and Molnia, D., Das US-Patent: Erwirkung und Durchsetzung unter besonderer Berücksichtigung der Rechtsprechung (Annex 8, 5th ed., 2017)

Mc Sweeney, T. and O'Dea, B., Data, Innovation, and Potential Competition in Digital Markets – Looking Beyond Short-Term Price Effects in Merger Analyst (CPI Antitrust Chronicle February 2018)

Mendelson, Michael, From Initial Coin Offerings to Security Tokens: A U.S. Federal Securities Law Analysis, Stanford Technology Law Review, vol. 22, no. 1, Winter 2019, pp. 66, available at https://law.stanford.edu/wp-content/uploads/2019/01/Mendelson_20180129.pdf

Malta Financial Services Authority, MFSA publishes its Feedback Statement following a Consultation Document on Security Token Offerings, 25 February 2020, available at https://www.mfsa.mt/news-item/mfsa-publishes-its-feedback-statement-following-a-consultation-document-on-security-token-offerings/

Miller, D. *The Sharing Economy and How is it Changing Industries* (19 September 2022) available at: https://www.thebalancesmb.com/the-sharing-economy-and-how-it-changes-industries-4172234

Miller, L. *Blockchain and the sharing economy – a match made in heaven? This startup plans to prove it* (13 April 2018), available at: https://thenextweb.com/cryptocurrency/2018/04/13/blockchain-and-the-sharing-economy-a-match-made-in-heaven-this-startup-plans-to-prove-it/

Mlynar, Theodore J., Fettman and Robert, M., Blockchain and Smart Contracts Will Change the Face of Insurance in the U.S. (23 May 2019), available at https://www.lexology.com/library/detail.aspx?g=b119f47b-764b-464c-9090-89b8e6e58219

Moeslein, Florian, Smart Contracts im Zivil- und Handelsrecht 254 (ZHR 2019)

Möslein, Florian, and Omlor, Sebastian, FinTech-Handbuch, 3rd ed. 2024

Momtaz, Paul P., Rennertseder Kathrin and Schröder, Henning, Token Offerings: A Revolution in Corporate Finance? (49 The Capco Institute Journal of Financial Transformation 2019) 32, 37 (2019)

Monaghan, Maura K., An Uncommon State of Confusion: The Common Enterprise Element of Investment Contract Analysis, 63 Fordham L. Rev. 2135 (1995), available at https://ir.lawnet.fordham.edu/cgi/viewcontent.cgi?article=3173&context=flr

Müller, Michael F. and Pieper, Christian, Gesetz über elektronische Wertpapiere (eWpG) Kommentar (2022)

Münchener Kommentar zum BGB, Rom I-VO, 2024

Myers, John, Ulloa, Jazmine, California Lawmakers Agree to New Consumer Privacy Rules That Would Avert Showdown on the November Ballot (Los Angeles Times, 21/06/2018), available at www.latimes.com/politics/la-pol-ca-privacy-initiative-legislature-agreement-20180621-story.html#

Naegele, Thomas, Die Rechtsnatur von Token nach dem liechtensteinischen TVTG (2021)

Naegele, Thomas, Bergt, Josef, Kryptowährungen und Blockchain-Technologie im liechtensteinischen Aufsichtsrecht (Liechtensteinische Juristenzeitung, Number 2, 2019)

Nakamato, Satoshi, Bitcoin: A Peer-to-Peer Electronic Cash System, available at https://bitcoin.org/bitcoin.pdf

Neu, Joachim, Ertem Nusret Tas, and David Tse. Two attacks on proof-of-stake GHOST/Ethereum, arXiv preprint arXiv:2203.01315 (2022)

Nisbet K, The False Allure of Hashing for Anonymization (30 April 2018), available at https://gravitational.com/blog/hashing-for-anonymization/

NIST, Blockchain Technology Overview (NISTIR 8202, 2018)

O'Hara, Claire, High-Net-Worth Investors Now Able to Hold Bitcoin Fund in Registered Accounts, The Globe and Mail (2018), available at https://www.theglobeandmail.com/investing/globe-wealth/article-high-net-worth-investors-now-able-to-hold-bitcoin-in-registered/

O'Toole, M., Kelly, C. and Hahn, D., *Smart Contracts Need Smart Corporate Lawyers* (7 February 2018), available at: https://www.law360.com/articles/1010335/smart-contracts-need-smart-corporate-lawyers

Olegario, Rowena, Credit-Reporting Agencies: Their Historical Roots, Current Status, and Role in Market Development, available at http://siteresources.worldbank.org/INTWDRS/Resources/477365-1257315064764/2429_olegario.pdf

Ontario Securities Commission, Decision in the Matter of the Securities Legislation of Ontario and in the Matter of the Process for Exemptive Relief Applications in Multiple Jurisdictions and in the Matter of Token Funder Inc. (2017), available at https://www.osc.gov.on.ca/en/SecuritiesLaw_ord_20171023_token.htm

Ontario Securities Commission (40(34) OSC Bulletin 2017), available at https://www.osc.gov.on.ca/documents/en/Securities-OSCB/20170824_oscb_4034_toc.pdf

Oppenheim, Robert and Romba, Eric, Initial Coin Offering (ICO) aus rechtlicher Sicht: Der Token als digitale Urkunde? (IT Finanzmagazin, 2018), available at https://www.it-finanzmagazin.de/initial-coin-offering-ico-rechtliche-sicht-token-digitale-urkunde-65569/

Orcutt, M., *Hate Lawyers? Can't Afford One? Blockchain Smart Contracts Are Here to Help?* (11 January 2019), available at: https://www.technologyreview.com/s/612748/hate-lawyers-cant-afford-one-blockchain-smart-contracts-are-here-to-help/

Paech, Philipp, Law and Autonomous Systems Series: What Is a Smart Contract? (University of Oxford, 9 July 2018), available at https://blogs.law.ox.ac.uk/business-law-blog/blog/2018/07/law-and-autonomous-systems-series-what-smart-contract/

Papadodimas, Georgios, Palaiokrasas, Georgios, Litke, Antonios and Vavarigou, Theodora, Implementation of Smart Contracts for Blockchain Based IoT Applications (Electrical and Computer Engineering Department, National Technical University of Athens, Greece, 2022), available at Implementation of smart contracts for blockchain based IoT applications | IEEE Conference Publication | IEEE Xplore

Paulmayer, Stefan, Die kapitalmarktrechtliche Einordnung von Token, in: Kirchmayr-Schliesselberger, Sabine et al. (ed.), Kryptowährungen 317 (Nomos 2019)

Paulus, Christoph and Matzke, Robin, Smart Contracts und Smart Meter – Versorgungsperre für Fernzugriff 1905 (NJW 2018)

Paulus, David and Matzke, Robin, Smart Contracts und das BGB – Viel Lärm um nichts? 431 (ZfPW 2018)

Pavloff, Ulysse, Yackolley Amoussou-Guenou, and Sara Tucci-Piergiovanni. Ethereum Proof-of-Stake under Scrutiny, Proceedings of the 38th ACM/SIGAPP Symposium on Applied Computing 2023

Payne, Bryan D. and Edwards, W. Keith, A Brief Introduction to Usable Security (Georgia Institute of Technology Published by the IEEE Computer Society, May/June 2008)

Pekler, Florian, Rirsch, Ralph, Ausgewählte kapitalmarktrechtliche Aspekte bei der Emission von Crypto-Assets, in: Kirchmayr-Schliesselberger, Sabine et al. (ed.), Kryptowährungen 333 (2019)

Pierce, Hester M., Commissioner of S.E.C., How We Howey (19 May 2019), available at https://www.sec.gov/news/speech/peirce-how-we-howey-050919

Piska, Christian and Voelkel, Oliver, Blockchain rules - Das FinTech-Handbuch (2024)

Poelzig, Doerte, and von Zehmen, Dominik, Kryptoaktien nachdem Referentenentwurf des Zukunftsfinanzierungsgesetz RDi 2023

Poldma, Jaak, Dragged to the U.S: Courts (Part 1): Jurisdiction and the Location of Blockchain Nodes, available at https://blogs.orrick.com/blockchain/dragged-to-the-u-s-courts-part-1-jurisdiction-and-the-location-of-blockchain-nodes/

Poli, T. N. MiCA, Pilot Regime and Fintech Decree: the regulation of the crypto phenomenon and the difficulties of framing it in the financial system, in dirittobancario.it, 13 December 2023

Popper, Nathaniel, Digital Gold: The Untold Story of Bitcoin (2016)

Prenafeta Rodríguez, Javier, Debe cumplir la emisión de criptomonedas y tokens la normativa de mercado de valores? (Colegio Universitario de Estudios Financieros, Trabaljo Fin de Grado, 2019), available at https://www.abogacia.es/publicaciones/blogs/blog-de-innovacion-legal/debe-cumplir-la-emision-de-criptomonedas-y-tokens-la-normativa-de-mercado-de-valores/

Pricewaterhouse Coopers, Initial Coin Offerings, A Strategic Perspective (2018), available at https://www.pwc.ch/en/publications/2018/20180628_PwC%20S&%20CVA%20ICO%20Report_EN.pdf

Prosser, William, Privacy (48 California Law Review 383, 1960)

Queen Mary University of London, Centre for Commercial Law Studies, Triggering Innovation How Smart Contracts Bring Policies to Life (2019), available at https://www.lloyds.com/~/media/files/news-and-insight/risk-insight/2019/triggering-innovation---how-smart-contracts-bring-policies-to-life.pdf

Ramos, Simona and Ellul, Joshua, Blockchain for Artificial Intelligence (AI): enhancing compliance with the EU AI Act through distributed ledger technology. A cybersecurity perspective, 1, (Int. Cybersecur. Law Rev. 5 2024), available at https://doi.org/10.1365/s43439-023-00107-9

Rappard, Matthew and Skeith, Zachary, Smart Contracts 101 – From a Technical to a Legal Understanding (2019)

Raskin, Max, Realm of the Coin: Bitcoin and Civil Procedure (20(4) Fordham Journal of Corporate and Financial Law 2015)

Raskin, Max, The Law and Legality of Smart Contracts (1 Georgetown Law Technology Review 304, 2017)

Reidenberg, Joel R., Lex Informatica: The Formulation of Information Policy Rules through Technology (76 Texas Law Review 553, 555, 1997-1998)

Report of the European Union Blockchain Observatory and Forum, Blockchain and the GDPR (16 October 2018), available at https://www.eublockchainforum.eu/reports

Report of the European Union Blockchain Observatory and Forum, Legal and Regulatory Framework of Blockchains and Smart Contracts (27 September 2019), available at https://www.eublockchainforum.eu/sites/default/files/reports/report_legal_v1.0.pdf

Reyes, Carla L., Conceptualizing Cryptolaw (96 Nebraska Law Review 384, 400 2017), available at https://digitalcommons.unl.edu/cgi/viewcontent.cgi?article = 3121 &context = nlr

Reyes, Carla L., Moving Beyond Bitcoin to an Endogenous Theory of Decentralized Ledger Technology Regulation: An Initial Proposal (61 Villanova Law Review 202-203, 2016)

Richter, Thomas, Blockchain – Rechtliche Aspekte aus Sicht der Finanzindustrie (DGRI Jahrbuch 2017, v. Briner, Robert G. and Funk, Axel (eds.) 2018) 165-178

Riehm, Thomas, Rechtshandbuch Smart Contracts (Tom Braegelmann and Markus Kaulartz, eds (2019)

Robinson, Jeffrey, BitCon: The Naked Truth about Bitcoin (Amazon Digital Services, 2014)

Rodrigues, Usha R., Law and Blockchain (104 Iowa Law Review 679, 682, 2019), available at https://ilr.law.uiowa.edu/sites/ilr.law.uiowa.edu/files/2023-02/Rodrigues.pdf

Rulli, Edoardo, Incorporazione senza res e dematerializzazione senza accentratore: appunti sui token, in Rivista Orizzonti del diritto commerciale (La Rivista, 2019), available at http://www.rivistaodc.eu/incorporazione-senza-res-dematerializzazione-token

Saad, M., Spaulding, J., Njilla, L., Kamhoua, C., Shetty, S., Nyang, D. and Mohaisen, A., Exploring the Attack Surface of Blockchain: A Systematic Overview (arXiv preprint arXiv:1904.03487, 2019), available at https://arxiv.org/pdf/1904.03487.pdf

Safran and Desai, Cybersecurity and the Human Element: We're All Fallible (Dark-Reading, 12 February 2019), available at https://www.darkreading.com/cybersecurity-careers/cybersecurity-and-the-human-element-we-re-all-fallible

Saive, David, Rückabwicklung von Blockchain-Transaktionen 371 (DSRITB 2018)

Salmon, John and Myers, Gordnon, Blockchain and Associated Legal Issues for Emerging Markets, 4 (Emerging Markets Compass Note 63, January 2019), available at https://hdl.handle.net/10986/31202

Saluste, Kadi, Tokenite kvalifitseerimine Eesti õiguse alusel ning kehtiva õiguse sobivus ICO-de reguleerimiseks (Juridica, June 2018), 390-399

Samuels, Benjamin, The Engineer's Guide to Blockchain Finality (23 August 2023), https://blog.trailofbits.com/2023/08/23/the-engineers-guide-to-blockchain-finality/

Samsung Newsroom, *A Relaxing Weekend with Samsung's AI-Enabled and Smart Appliances* (28 November 2019), available at: https://news.samsung.com/global/a-relaxing-weekend-with-samsungs-ai-enabled-and-smart-appliances

Savelyev, A., Contract Law 2.0: 'Smart' Contracts as the Beginning of the End of Classic Contract Law (Information & Communications Technology Law, 116, 2017)

Sayeed, Sarwar an Marco-Gisbert, Hector, Assessing Blockchain Consensus and Security Mechanisms Against the 51% Attack (9 Appl. Sci. 1788, 2019), https://doi.org/10.3390/app9091788

Schäfer, Sernetz, Kommentar zu Kreditwesengesetz, VO (EU) Nr. 575/2013 (CRR) und Ausführungsvorschriften (1 A, 5th ed., 2016)

Schawe, Nadine, Blockchain und Smart Contracts in der Kreativwirtschaft – mehr Probleme als Lösungen? 218 (MMR 2019)

Schiltz, Jean Louis, Blockchain: Chancen, Recht und Regulierung, MMR-Aktuell 2018 [news service], 400563

Schrepel, Thibaut, Is Blockchain the Death of Antitrust Law? The Blockchain Antitrust Paradox (3 Georgetown Law Technology Review 281, 2019), available at https://papers.ssrn.com/sol3/papers.cfm?abstract_id=3193576

Schrey, Joachim, Thalhofer, Thomas, Rechtliche Aspekte der Blockchain, 1431 (NJW 2017)

Schwartz, Paul, Preemption and Privacy (118 Yale Law Journal 902, 910 et seq., 2009)

Schwartz, Private International Law and Token Transactions, (9 October 2023), https://www.law.berkeley.edu/wp-content/uploads/2021/10/Private-International-Law-and-Token-Transactions.pdf

Schwarz-Schilling, Caspar, et al., Three attacks on proof-of-stake Ethereum, International Conference on Financial Cryptography and Data Security, Springer International Publishing, 2022

Serwin, Andrew B., Information Security and Privacy: A Guide to Federal and State Law and Compliance (2022-2023 ed.)

Serwin, Andrew B., The Federal Trade Commission and Privacy: Defining Enforcement And Encouraging Adoption of Best Practices (48 San Diego Law Review 809, 2011)

Sherborne, Andreas, Blockchain Smart Contracts and Lawyers (International Bar Association, December 2017)

Shikai, Yuriko Mary, Applying the California Translation Act to Consumer Agreements (Los Angeles Lawyer September 2012, 11-15)

Siibak, Kadri, Mõningad virtuaalrahaga seotud õiguslikud probleemid, Juridica (2015)

Sild, Judith, (ed.), Grundsatzfragen des liechtensteinischen TVTG (2021)

Skauradszun, Dominik, Das Internationale Privatrecht der Kryptowerte, elektronischen Wertpapiere und Kryptowertpapiere 56 (Zeitschrift für die gesamte Privatrechtswissenschaft 2022)

Solana White Paper, available at https://solana.com/solana-whitepaper.pdf

Solove, Dan and Schwartz, Paul, Privacy Law Fundamentals (IAPP, 2019)

Solove, Dan and Schwartz, Paul. Information Privacy Law (6th ed., Aspen Publishing Co., 2018)

Song, Alfred H., Oral History Interview (California State Archives State Government Oral History Program), available at http://archives.cdn.sos.ca.gov/oral-history/pdf/song.pdf

Spanish Central Bank and Spanish Stock Market Commission, Joint press statement by CNMV and Banco de España on 'cryptocurrencies' and 'initial coin offerings' (2018), available at http://www.cnmv.es/Portal/verDoc.axd?t={6f310cc7-6b39-4405-a8f7-70d2b1e682d1}

Spanish Ministry of Economy, Proyecto de Ley de medidas para la transformación digital del sistema financiero (2019)

Spindler, Gerald and Schuster, Fabian (eds), Recht der elektronischen Medien (München, 4th ed. 2019)

Spindler, Gerald, Initial Coin Offerings und Prospektpflicht und -haftung 2109 (Wertpapier Mitteilungen 2018)

Stanford, Erica. Crypto Wars: Faked Deaths, Missing Billions and Industry Disruption. Kogan Page Publishers (2021)

Stein, Matthew and Lisy, Christopher, Figuring Out if You Are 'Doing Business' in California Under the CCPA, Bloomberg Law News, 27 February 2020

Statista, Largest DeFI cryptocurrency exchanges or DEX in the world as of 29 March 2022, https://www.statista.com/statistics/1263110/biggest-dex-in-the-world/

Sultan, K., Ruhi, U., & Lakhani, R., *Conceptualizing Blockchains: Characteristics & Applications* (2018), available at: https://arxiv.org/ftp/arxiv/papers/1806/1806.03693.pdf

Swift, Ground-breaking Swift innovation paves way for global use of CBDCs and tokenised assets, (9 October 2023), https://www.swift.com/news-events/press-releases/swift-innovation-enables-global-use-of-cbdcs-and-tokenised-assets

Swiss Federal Council, Bericht des Bundesrates 'Rechtliche Grundlagen für Distributed Ledger Technologie und Blockchain in der Schweiz' (Federal Council report 'legal framework for distributed ledger technology and blockchain in Switzerland') (2018), https://www.newsd.admin.ch/newsd/message/attachments/55153.pdf

Swiss Federal Council, Botschaft zum Bundesgesetz zur Anpassung des Bundesrechts an Entwicklungen der Technik verteilter elektronischer Register (Report on the draft regarding amendments to Swiss federal law in connection with the developments with the distributed ledger technology) (2019), available at https://www.admin.ch/opc/de/federal-gazette/2020/233.pdf

Swiss Financial Market Supervisory Authority (FINMA), Circular 2018/1 'Organised trading facilities' (2018)

Swiss Financial Market Supervisory Authority (FINMA), Guidance 02/2019, 'Payments on the Blockchain' (2019), available at https://www.finma.ch/en/news/2019/08/20190826-mm-kryptogwg/

Swiss Financial Market Supervisory Authority (FINMA), Guidelines Regarding the Regulatory Framework for ICOs of 16 February (2018), available at https://www.finma.ch/en/news/2018/02/20180216-mm-ico-wegleitung/

Swiss Financial Market Supervisory Authority (FINMA), Supplement to the Guidelines for Enquiries Regarding the Regulatory Framework for Initial Coin Offerings (ICOs) (2019), https://www.finma.ch/en/news/2019/09/20190911-mm-stable-coins/

Szabo, N., *Formalizing and Securing Relationships on Public Networks*, firstmonday (9 January 1997), available at: http://firstmonday.org/ojs/index.php/fm/article/view/548/469

Szabo, N. *Smart Contracts: Building Blocks for Digital Markets* (1996), available at: http://www.fon.hum.uva.nl/rob/Courses/InformationInSpeech/CDROM/Literature/LOTwinterschool2006/szabo.best.vwh.net/smart_contracts_2.html

Szostek, Dariusz, Blockchain and the Law (2019)

Tai, Stefan, Jacob Eberhardt, Klems, Markus. Not ACID, not BASE, but SALT (Proceedings of the 7th International Conference on Cloud Computing and Services Science, SCITEPRESS-Science and Technology Publications, 2017), available at http://www.ise.tu-berlin.de/fileadmin/fg308/publications/2017/2017-tai-eberhardt-klems-SALT.pdf

Tendon, Steve and Ganado, Max, Legal Personality for Blockchains, DAOs and Smart Contracts (1 RTDF 1 2018) 1, see n. 5

Teubner, Gunther, Digitale Rechtssubjekte? Zum privatrechtlichen Status autonomer Softwareagenten, 218 AcP 155-205 (2018)

The Financial Action Task Force (FATF), FATF Recommendations (2019), available at http://www.fatf-gafi.org/publications/fatfrecommendations/?hf = 10&b = 0&s = desc(fatf_releasedate)

The Law Commission, *Smart legal contracts: advice to Government*, available at: Smart-legal-contracts-accessible.pdf (cloud-platform-e218f50a4812967ba1215eaecede923f.s3.amazonaws.com)

The Law Commission, *Electronic Signatures are valid say Government's legal experts*, available at: https://www.lawcom.gov.uk/electronic-signatures-are-valid-say-governments-legal-experts/

The Law Society, Society for Computers & Law and Tech London Advocates, Blockchain: Legal & Regulatory Guidance, 3rd ed., 2023, 276-282

The Monetary Authority of Singapore, Guide to Digital Token Offerings (2019), available at https://www.mas.gov.sg/regulation/explainers/a-guide-to-digital-token-offerings

The Monetary Authority of Singapore, Guidelines on the Regulation of Markets Guideline No. SFA02-G01 (2005)

The Monetary Authority of Singapore, Response to Feedback Received on the Proposed Payment Services Bill (2018)

The SEC's Manipulation of the Definition of Security (1999), College of Law, Faculty Publications 92, available at https://digitalcommons.unl.edu/lawfacpub/92

The Spanish Stock Market Commission, CNMV Considerations on Cryptocurrencies and ICOs Addressed to Market Professionals (2018), available at http://www.cnmv.es/Portal/verDoc.axd?t = {62395018-40eb-49bb-a71c-4afb5c966374}

The Spanish Stock Market Commission, Criteria in Relation to ICO (2018), available at http://cnmv.es/DocPortal/Fintech/CriteriosICOsEN.pdf

The Spanish Stock Market Commission, Portal FinTech / Portal de Innovación (2019), available at https://www.cnmv.es/portal/Fintech/Innovacion.aspx?lang = es

The Spanish Stock Market Commission, Questions and Answers Intended for FinTech Companies on Activities and Services That May Be Related to the CNMV, Sec. 6.4 (2019), available at https://www.cnmv.es/docportal/Legislacion/FAQ/QAsFinTech_EN.pdf

Thematic Report of the European Blockchain Observatory and Forum, Legal and Regulatory Framework of Blockchains and Smart Contracts, 7 (27 September 2019), available at https://www.eublockchainforum.eu/sites/default/files/reports/report_legal_v1.0.pdf

Timmons, John and Hickman, Tim, Blockchain and the GDPR: Co-existing in contradiction (Blockchain & Cryptocurrency Regulation, Global Legal Insights, 2nd ed., 2020)

Todd, Ross, Courthouse Steps Listening Devices Not Illegal (The Recorder, 25/07/2016)

Trail of Bits Blog, Ten Rules for the Secure Use of Cryptocurrency Hardware Wallets (27 November 2018), available at https://blog.trailofbits.com/2018/11/27/10-rules-for-the-secure-use-of-cryptocurrency-hardware-wallets/

Tulsidas, Tanash Utamchandani, Smart Contracts from a Legal Perspective (University of Alicante, Faculty of Law, 2018), available at https://pdfs.semanticscholar.org/370b/bc9f7af31fa01a8f61276d2a67591d22680e.pdf

UK Government Chief Scientist Adviser, Distributed Ledger Technology, beyond Blockchain (2016), available at https://www.gov.uk/government/publications/distributed-ledger-technology-blackett-review

UK ICO, Anonymisation: Managing Data Protection Risk Code of Practice, available at https://ico.org.uk/media/1061/anonymisation-code.pdf

UK Jurisdiction Taskforce, Legal Statement on Cryptoassets and Smart Contracts (The LawTech Delivery Panel, November 2019) available at: UKJT, *Legal Statement on Cryptoassets and Smart Contracts*, The LawTech Delivery Panel (November 2019), available at: https://www.blockchain4europe.eu/wp-content/uploads/2021/05/6.6056_JO_Cryptocurrencies_Statement_FINAL_WEB_111119-1.pdf

U.S. Securities and Exchange Commission, Chairman Gary Gensler's prepared Remarks Before the Aspen Security Forum (3 August 2021), available at: https://www.sec.gov/news/public-statement/gensler-aspen-security-forum-2021-08-03

Securities and Exchange Commission, Cryptocurrency/ICOs (9 October 2023) https://www.sec.gov/securities-topics/ICO

US Securities and Exchange Commission, Framework for 'Investment Contract' Analysis of Digital Assets (7 October 2023), https://www.sec.gov/corpfin/framework-investment-contract-analysis-digital-assets

U.S. Securities and Exchange Commission, Release No. 81207, 2017 Report of Investigation Pursuant to Section 21(a) of the Securities Exchange Act of 1934: The DAO (2017), available at https://www.sec.gov/litigation/investreport/34-81207.pdf

van der Laan, Jake, Smart Contracts and "Code is Law" – Some Additional Considerations, International Journal of Blockchain Law, Volume 4, December 2022, available at https://gbbcouncil.org/wp-content/uploads/202/12/Volume-IV-International-Journal-of-Blockchain-Law.pdf

van Valkenburgh, Peter, What Could 'Decentralization' Mean in the Context of the Law? (15 June 2018), available at https://coincenter.org/entry/what-could-decentralization-mean-in-the-context-of-the-law

Vannini, Marco, Detotto, Claudio and Mccannon, Bryan, Ransom Kidnapping (2015)

Varul, Paul, Anu, Avi and Triin, Kivisild, Restrictions on Active Legal Capacity, Juridica International IX (2004), available at https://www.juridicainternational.eu/public/pdf/ji_2004_1_99.pdf

Veil, Rüdiger, Token-Emissionen im europäischen Kapitalmarktrecht 183 (Zeitschrift für das gesamte Handels- und Wirtschaftsrecht 2019)

Veil, Winfried, The Emperor's New Clothes - On the Structural Shortcomings of Both the Old and the New Data Protection Law 686 (Neue Zeitschrift für Verwaltungsrecht 2018)

Vidal, Maria, Olivares, Jose Maria, Gutierrez Campiña, Sara, Ferrer, Jorge, FinTech. Chapter for Spain (Chambers Global Practice Guide, 2019)

Vinters, T., *Smart Contracts: A Boom or Bane for the Legal Profession?* (24 September 2018), available at: https://www.lexology.com/library/detail.aspx?g=f16551a7-e974-41d2-ba45-37e2dc7f6e41

Voelkel, Oliver, Initial Coin Offerings aus kapitalmarktrechtlicher Sicht 103 (ZTR 2017)

Vos Sir, Geoffrey, LawTech, Smart Contracts and Artificial Intelligence (Speech at the German Bundesministerium für Justiz und Verbraucherschutz at 02 May 2019), available at https://www.judiciary.uk/wp-content/uploads/2019/05/CHC-speech-LawTech-Smart-Contracts-and-Artificial-Intelligence.pdf

Vos Sir Geoffrey, *The economic value of English law in relation to DLT and digital assets* (25 July 2022), available at: https://www.judiciary.uk/speech-by-the-master-of-the-rolls-the-economic-value-of-english-law-in-relation-to-dlt-and-digital-assets

Wan, A., *Blockchain Smart Contracts: Weighing the Pros and Cons* (12 July 2018), available at: https://blocktribune.com/smart-contracts-weighing-the-pros-and-cons/

Wang, Gang, Zhijie Jerry Shi, Nixon, Mark and Song Han, SoK: Sharding on Blockchain (1st ACM Conference on Advances in Financial Technologies, 21-23 October 2019), available at https://doi.org/10.1145/3318041.3355457

Watters, Casey, When Criminals Abuse the Blockchain: Establishing Personal Jurisdiction in a Decentralised Environment, Laws 12: 33, (15 April 2023), available at https://doi.org/10.3390/laws12020033

Wehowsky, Ralf, Becksche Kurz Kommentar (Erbs/ Kohlhaas, ed., Strafrechtliche Nebengesetze, Band 1, 228th ed. 2020)

Weiß, Hagen, Tokenisation (BaFin Journal, 2019), available at https://www.bafin.de/dok/12477346

West, Katherine, Where Is Blockchain: Jurisdictional Issues That May Affect Distributed Ledgers, available at https://www.lexology.com/library/detail.aspx?g=35f40e2e-38d8-49d7-81ca-9872d8ab9532

Wilkens, Robert and Falk, Richard, Smart Contracts – Grundlagen, Anwendungsfelder und rechtliche Aspekte (Springer Gabler 2019)

Wilsch, Harald, Die Blockchain-Technologie aus der Sicht des deutschen Grundbuchrechts 761 (Deutsche Notarzeitung 2017)

Wilsch, Harald, The German 'Grundbuchordnung': History, Principles and Future about Land Registry in Germany 224 (Zeitschrift für Geodäsie, Geoinformation und Landmanagement, 2012)

Woebbeking, Maren K., The Impact of Smart Contracts on the Traditional Concepts of Contract Law (10, 2019, JIPITEC 105 paragraph 1), available at https://www.jipitec.eu/issues/jipitec-10-1-2019/4880

Young, A., *Take note: Emails can be legally binding* (6 July 2021), available at: http://www.contractflooringjournal.co.uk/blog/take-note-emails-can-be-legally-binding/

Zammit, Lara, The Evolution of Traditional Capital Markets Through Blockchain (2020)

Zekoll, Joachim and Wagner, Gerhard, Introduction to German Law, 3rd ed. (2019) available at https://www.jura.uni-hamburg.de/media/die-fakultaet/personen/wurmnest-wolfgang/wurmnest-contract-law-in-zekoll-wagner-introduction-to-german-law.pdf

Zepf, Tobias, Blockchain, Technologie, Innovationen und Anwendungen – oder eine Kette, die Ketten sprengt (Bachelor Thesis, 2016)

Zickgraf, Peter, Initial Coin Offerings – Ein Fall für das Kapitalmarktrecht? 293 (Die Aktiengesellschaft 2018), available at https://doi.org/10.9785/ag-2018-630903

Zimmerman, Evan Joseph, Machine Minds: Frontier in Legal Personhood (12 February 2015) 35-41, available at https://papers.ssrn.com/sol3/papers.cfm?abstract_id=2563965

Zogg, Samuel, Bitcoin als Rechtsobjekt – eine zivilrechtliche Einordnung 95 (recht, Zeitschrift für juristische Weiterbildung und Praxis 2019)

Zou, M., Cheng, G., and Heredia, M.-S., *In Code We Trust? Trustless and Smart Contracts* (31 March 2019) available at: https://www.scl.org/articles/10493-in-code-we-trust-trustlessness-and-smart-contracts

Table of Cases

British Virgin Island Case Law

English and Irish Case Law

European Case Law

European Commission

German Case Law

Singapore Case Law

US Case Law

Other Cases

Index

C

D

P

T

www.ingramcontent.com/pod-product-compliance
Lightning Source LLC
LaVergne TN
LVHW020003031026
849161LV00023B/868
* 9 7 8 9 4 0 3 5 4 1 5 7 0 *